The Spirit of the Game

Also by the author

Football
The World Cup: All You Need to Know
*Manchester DisUnited: Trouble and Takeover at the
World's Richest Football Club*
Manchester Unlimited: The Rise and Rise of the World's Premier Football Club
Behind Closed Doors: Dreams and Nightmares at Spurs

Cricket
The Magic of Indian Cricket
A Maidan View
A History of Indian Cricket
Cricket Voices
All in a Day: Great Moments in Cup Cricket
Keith Miller: A Cricketing Biography

General Sports
Sports Babylon
Sporting Colours: Sport and Politics in South Africa
The Sporting Alien

History and Biography
Bollywood – A History
Raj, Secrets, Revolution: A Life of Subhas Chandra Bose
The Memons
False Messiah: The Life and Times of Terry Venables
Michael Grade: Screening the Image
The Lost Hero
The Aga Khans

Business
How to Invest in a Bear Market
Fraud — the Growth Industry of the 1980s
The Crash: the 1987-88 World Market Slump
Crash! A New Money Crisis: a Children's Guide to Money
Insurance: Are You Covered?

THE SPIRIT OF THE GAME

Mihir Bose

Constable • London

Constable & Robinson Ltd
55–56 Russell Square
London WC1B 4HP
www.constablerobinson.com

First published in the UK by Constable,
an imprint of Constable & Robinson Ltd, 2011

A copy of the British Library Cataloguing in
Publication data is available from the British Library

ISBN: 978-1-84901-504-2

Printed and bound in the EU

1 3 5 7 9 10 8 6 4 2

To the memory of Ma, who did not live to see the book
completed but whose debt I cannot ever repay
and
Peter, who made me believe that there are good
men and women in this world

CONTENTS

Part 4 – The loss of innocence

Acknowledgements

This book could not have been written without the help and encouragement of many people from many parts of the world and many walks of life.

My first thanks are to my publisher, Leo Hollis. He helped me to flesh out my idea and realize the theme of how sport has developed, where it has arrived, and its impact on the modern world.

I am also indebted to the many friends and colleagues who helped me with the research. Richard Heller, whose reaction to dropping a catch off Peter Oborne's bowling got the Madras crowd going all those years ago, never dropped a ball as he helped me with vital research. Nigel Dudley, who often suffered on the cricket field because of my own catching, was, as ever, an island of sanity and good advice. His daughter Charlotte came in at very short notice to help. Hugh Pym kindly introduced me to Adam Baker whose research was also extremely useful.

My daughter Indira was very diligent in recruiting her friends and the research by Oliver Aiken and Tomo Takabatake in various archives unearthed some fascinating material. Daniel Walters was also helpful.

Douglas Eden, who combines his vast knowledge of history with a sharp appreciation of sport, was a very useful sounding board on American sport and Simon Blundell, the librarian of the Reform Club, was always ready to point me in the direction of a book or text I could not find. The staff at the London Library, the Public Record Office in Kew, and the British Museum have been extremely generous with time and space.

Sports writing has come a long way since the days, at the end of the 19th century, when the only events reported were those that took place on the field of play. Sport's broader impact on business and wider society is now much examined. This has been a theme of my journalism for almost thirty years. But I was intrigued that there was no book that drew all of this together and explained how sport changed from a recreational activity run by volunteers into a corporate entity, who the engineers of this change were and how it has affected the cherished concepts about the spirit of sport. In the course of my examinations I have used my own writing and also in the last two years interviewed many people ranging from politicians through administrators to sportsmen and women. Their thoughts and views have proved very helpful in shaping this book.

I have also relied on much available material and the bibliography lists many of the books, newspaper sources, websites and television programmes that have provided very useful source material. I would particularly like to highlight the work of authors like Tom Bower, Barbara Smit, Boria Majumdar, John Sugden, Alan Tomlinson, Richard Holt, Tony Collins and Xu Guoqi. They have in many ways been ground-breaking in this field. I cannot praise highly enough the diligent journalism of Jens Weinreich; his industry and unflagging energy are a model for us all. Sarah Sands, Doug Wills and Steve Cording have been great supporters and sounding boards. Duncan Mackay's excellent website has been a source of information and Andreas Herren has always been ready with useful material. Sarah Wooldridge was unfailingly helpful and, as ever, Edward Griffiths, despite being an Arsenal supporter, opened doors and shared his wise sporting perceptions with a man from the other side of the north London divide.

I have been fortunate in the support from my family and friends, many of whom are like family members. My sister

ACKNOWLEDGEMENTS

Panna, her husband Tapan and my niece Anjali were, as ever, extremely helpful. Susanna Majendie, who is like family, showed real family feeling in encouraging the book, despite having no interest in the subject. Andrew Cecil's help, letting me share his vast expertise on Formula One, was extremely valuable. And both my sisters-in-law: Rosalind, a fine equestrienne, and Jenny, with her keen sense for sport, have proved marvellously support-ive.This book could not have been written, or certainly in time, without the help of my wife Caroline and her entire office led by the amazing Nicky Swain. Nicky helped me in more ways than I can enumerate to make sure the typescript was fit for publica-tion. Caroline's love and affection is the rock on which my life is based. But her devotion to this book is the sort of faith that can move mountains.

Errors may still remain but for that I and I alone must take responsibility.

Mihir Bose, September 2011

AUTHOR'S PREFACE

On the Monday of the week that saw England and India start a Test series at Lord's, a dinner was held at the Hilton in London's Park Lane. Pre-Test dinners are part of English cricketing culture, but this one was different. It was advertising the new power of Indian cricket. It was appropriate that the hotel was within touching distance of the historic London home of the Duke of Wellington, the man who attributed victory at Waterloo to the playing fields of Eton and Harrow. Here were modern Indians trying to demonstrate that cricket was more than just a game.

Mahendra Singh Dhoni, the Indian captain, was launching his foundation. Rich Indians filled the hotel. Champagne flowed and the auction raised vast sums: £260,000 for a cricket painting, £100,000 for the bat Dhoni used to hit the winning six for the 2011 World Cup. The bidder had actually won the bat for £60,000 but, when he got to the stage to receive it from Dhoni, he was so overwhelmed that he offered to pay £100,000. For Dhoni, this was an occasion to use his position as India's most successful captain to meet some of the needs of the poor and deprived in society. Nothing could have better illustrated the power of sport to reach out beyond the playing fields. That sport has the capacity to move people has always been accepted ever since Henry Newbolt wrote his poem with the refrain *'Play up! play up! and play the game!'* But what we are witnessing now is sport's power to reach out across cultures and nations and the contrasting ways in which different countries use sport. The auction that night raised nearly half a million pounds when, normally, such cricket auctions in England generate less than one tenth of that sum as did one held two days later at the same venue. It demonstrated both the wealth of the Indians in England and how the Indians had taken to the English game of cricket and made it their own.

In China, during the 2008 Olympics, a different facet of sport's interaction with society was presented. When covering the Games for BBC News, I described them as China's great coming out party. Yet I was struck by how keen the Chinese were to convince the world that they could take the Olympics, a Western idea, and present the Games to the world in a way that the West could not match. The worldwide economic collapse following the Games means that, for its sheer opulence and expenditure of public money, Beijing 2008 will not be matched, let alone surpassed, for a long time. I was even more struck by this thought when visiting a museum in China, where I saw the Chinese pride in claiming that it was they who had originally invented football, not England.

These thoughts had come at a time when the Western media were full of articles about the decline of the West and how the Chinese, and possibly the Indians, would be taking over the world. But in sport there seemed to be a different story, a story of a Western invention that had so captivated mankind that the entire world claimed it as its own. It was not a story of decline but of non-Westerners taking to Western ideas, a story of the vibrancy and enduring power of Western concepts. I had further proof of this not long after the Games when I was in the metro in Kolkata, the city of my birth. Playing on the platform television monitors were endless repeats of English Premier League matches. The locals, many of whom had never been to England, also had their own favourite English teams.

My ideas were sharpened and focused by discussions with my editor Leo Hollis. That is when I embarked on my present odyssey to explain how modern sport originated, how it has changed and what these changes mean. This has been one of the themes of my journalism for the last thirty years: that sport is no longer just a case of men or women in shorts performing. That there is a wider story of men, and generally it is still men, in suits deciding how the men and women in shorts will perform. In the course of my journalism, I have often had to convince editors to give me space. This has not always been easy although in recent years, as politicians have jumped on to the bandwagon of sport, space has become more available. All this would have been unimaginable when I was a child and dreamt of scoring a hundred at Lords and a Cup final goal at Wembley. With this book I was keen to analyse not only how sport has become big business but also how this change has altered the original concept of sporting spirit and how sport resonates with society.

It was my wife Caroline who made me think again about how sport interacts with society. Her sports are equestrianism and tennis and, when I suggested she come to football matches with me, she said, 'You know I have always been intrigued why so many go to watch football matches every week. What is the communal element?' Then at our first match together, as she saw that the crowds became a family while they watched their team, she began to appreciate the effect that sport can have on society.

The most intriguing question was how the changes in sport have affected the spirit of the game. Can modern sport with its well-advertised failings still present itself as the great symbol of fair play? This has been the claim attributed to sport for more than a century and the idea pops up in the most unexpected places.

Back in 1899 Winston Churchill was in British India reporting on yet another war between the British and the tribes across the border in Afghanistan. In his book *The Story of the Malakand Field Force* he describes how British soldiers played polo in Malakand as they awaited an attack by the Mad Fakir. The locals watched them. Then, records Churchill, when the game was over 'a strange incident occurred':

As the syces were putting the rugs and clothing on the polo ponies, and loitering about the ground, after the game, the watching natives drew near and advised them to be off home at once, for there was going to be a fight. They knew, these Pathans, what was coming. The wave of fanaticism was sweeping down the valley. It would carry them away. Like one who feels a fit coming on, they waited. Nor did they care very much when the Mad Fakir arrived. They would fight and kill the infidels. In the meantime there was no necessity to deprive them of their ponies. And so with motives, partly callous, partly sportsmanlike, they warned the native grooms, and these taking the hint reached the camp in safety.

Within hours the Mad Fakir attacked and the great frontier war had begun. That Churchill, not noted for his love of sport, could identify with the spirit of sport in that inhospitable terrain shows how the idea had taken hold even then.

Much has changed since that time. Would a modern-day Churchill reporting from present-day Afghanistan be able to describe such a scene before a Taliban attack? Or have the changes been such that the spirit of sport has completely disappeared? Is the concept of the spirit of the game now mere words without any meaning? And, if it has been killed, who killed it and how can it be recreated?

PART ONE

ARNOLD'S CHILDREN

CHAPTER 1

THE CURIOUS SPORTING LEGACY
OF THOMAS ARNOLD

In the spring of 2011, the revolution many in the Middle East had hoped for suddenly began to take shape. Throughout the Arab world, millions rose to challenge and even change their despotic rulers, starting with Tunisia and rolling through Egypt into Libya and the Arab kingdoms of the Gulf. Then, suddenly in Bahrain, this desire for freedom came in conflict with modern sport. In the picturesque words of the *Daily Mail*'s Martin Samuel, the result of 'little brown people' wanting freedom meant 'the next thing you know is there is one less place for rich white guys to race cars'.

Formula One's first Grand Prix of the season was due to take place in Bahrain in March, just weeks after the kingdom had been engulfed by protestors demanding more freedom. This had seen highly publicized protests at the main Pearl Roundabout in the financial district of Manama with some 31 protestors killed. Armoured cars, containing Saudi forces and some from other countries, had rolled into the kingdom to restore order. So how could a sports event take place in such a climate? And where was the moral compass of sport in even thinking it could?

The race was the dream of the Crown Prince Sheikh Salman bin Hamad bin Isa Al Khalifa, who had made it clear that money was no object in bringing one of the most high-profile world events to his desert kingdom. The Bahrain government funded the race and the Sakhir circuit, where the race had been run since 2004, had cost some £92 million. The Formula One organizers had been paid

£24.6 million to allow Bahrain to organize the opening race of the 2010 season and this had risen by 60 per cent for the 2011 race. The protestors knew how dear the race was to the Crown Prince and that, if they wanted to wring political concessions from him, they had to hit at his beloved sport. As Hasan Dhani, a 23-year-old protestor at the Pearl Roundabout, put it: 'There is a big connection between it [the uprising] and Formula One. The race has been the prince's dream, since he was a child. He wants to negotiate so he can fulfil his dream and it makes me sad that his dream is more dear to him than the needs of his people.'

Another protestor, Mohammed Nimah, echoing the views of many, said, 'His precious Formula One is more important than the blood of his people which he spilt. We put pressure on the Formula One contract, the Crown Prince got scared and wants to negotiate.' However, the race organizers did not seem to understand or appreciate the moral questions involved. Neither the FIA, the governing body, nor Bernie Ecclestone — the Formula One rights holder — wanted to put their head above the parapet. Their reluctance, it was assumed, was due to the fear that if they cancelled the race they would stand to lose £37 million in rights fees.

Their silence in the face of the Bahrain revolt provoked anger in the wider world. Ecclestone, who had taken the sport to these new frontiers at the expense of more traditional racing circuits in Europe and South Africa, was denounced, but Martin Samuels saw it as a wider problem with modern sport:

> As for Ecclestone, watching him wrestle with the concept of the freedom movement in Bahrain has been a delight. First he declared it was all quiet, then he hoped it would blow over, as if the encampment on the Pearl Roundabout was no more than a few villagers campaigning about the by-pass near Chideock . . . Sport conspires with rulers from a different age, despots, theologians and hereditary Crown Princes. Administrators want to make modern millions, while exploiting systems of government from the Dark Ages, because that is also how they rule.

In the end the Crown Prince himself decided the race had to be put back, hoping it could be held later in the year. His wish appeared to have been granted when in May an inspection team from the FIA visited Bahrain and recommended that, 'there is no indication of any problems or reason why the Bahrain Grand Prix should not return to the 2011 calendar.' In June the FIA's World Council unanimously agreed that the Bahrain Grand Prix would now be held on 30 October. Ecclestone suggested the race might unite the people of Bahrain. Jean Todt, FIA President, told journalists, 'It is very peaceful in Bahrain. You should go there and have a look.'

The decision provoked outrage from human rights activists and race fans. Nor were the Formula One teams happy. The FIA's judgement was further called into question when details of the inspection report emerged. Over a two-day trip FIA men had met the Minister of Culture and Tourism, the Minister of Interior, had had lunch with the board that runs the Grand Prix, met circuit personnel and visited a shopping centre. But they had not met any of the dissidents. It was clear that the race could not go ahead. However, it was logistics not morality that was given as the reason for the cancellation. The new date meant Bahrain would get the date of India – the new Formula One commercial centre – and extend the calendar into December. The teams just could not cope with the pressures this would create.

The whole affair brought little credit to Formula One, least of all the highly paid drivers. Apart from Red Bull's Mark Webber, who acknowledged the moral question of sport taking part in the aftermath of a bloodbath, nearly all the other drivers avoided the moral issue. I could not even coax Britain's most successful Formula One driver, Nigel Mansell – who during his career chalked up 31 race wins and the 1992 world title — to take a stand on this issue. When I asked in the middle of the crisis whether it would be morally justified to stage this year's Bahrain Grand Prix, Mansell, who had been forthright on many issues, weighed his words very carefully: 'I try and be as professional but impartial as I can. One thing I do know and learnt over the years is that we don't have all the information, so to try and make any judgement is wrong. There are great people involved in Formula One who are in charge and it is up to them to speak to the power brokers of the country.'

The only one to raise the human rights issue was Max Mosley, the former head of the FIA. 'What the FIA should have done is sent a human rights lawyer to carry out the inspection. The Formula One world did not seem to appreciate that the government in Bahrain was about to use the Grand Prix in support of suppressing human rights.' Mosley's views carried little weight with Zayed Alzayani, the businessman appointed by the Crown Prince to run the Grand Prix. He was emphatic that the press, particularly the British press, had got the human rights situation in Bahrain dreadfully wrong. His country, he argued, was not to be compared with the rest of the Arab world. Indeed it was no different from most other countries. If Formula One could go to China why could it not go to Bahrain? 'They're going to the US next year,' he said. 'What about Guantanamo? Isn't that human rights violation?' As Bernie Ecclestone had told him, 'If human rights was the criterion for Formula One races, we would only have them in Belgium and Switzerland in the future.' Indeed by not going to Bahrain, he lamented, Formula One had missed out on a great chance of using the race to unite his country.

Now, sporting events being held against a background of state violence, often to make the outside world believe everything is normal in a repressive society, is hardly new. There have been many such examples. The 1936 Olympics remain the most blatant example of sport turning a blind eye to evil but since then there have been others. They include the rebel South African cricket tours of the apartheid regime, the 1968 Mexico Olympics, the Ali-Foreman fight in 1974 in a Zaire ruled by the brutal and corrupt despot Mobutu Sese Seko, and the 1978 World Cup in Argentina, organized by a junta which was, even then, embarking on a massive programme of killing people opposed to the regime.

But what made the Bahrain event exceptional is that sport, and sport organisers, were being subjected to greater scrutiny and there was much greater public disquiet that sport had failed its high moral principles. And the original row about Bahrain came just weeks after Queen Elizabeth had used her 2010 Christmas broadcast to talk about the exceptional power of modern sport to be a moral force that helps create wonderful, universal values:

> This sort of positive team spirit can benefit communities, companies and enterprises of all kinds. As the success of recent Paralympics bears witness, a love of sport also has the power to help rehabilitate. One only has to think of the injured men and women of the armed forces to see how an interest in games and sport can speed recovery and renew a sense of purpose, enjoyment and comradeship. Right around the world, people gather to compete under standard rules and, in most cases, in a spirit of friendly rivalry. Competitors know that, to succeed, they must respect their opponents; very often, they like each other too. Sportsmen and women often speak of the enormous pride they have in representing their country, a sense of belonging to a wider family.

The queen had even gone to the extraordinary length of linking sport with the celebrations to mark the 400th anniversary of the publication of the King James Bible. While some commentators were puzzled by this connection between sport and religion, the broadcast itself came when there was further evidence of sport's power for good and its quite remarkable capacity for reaching out beyond the playing fields and uniting people, even providing them solace in a time of great anxiety.

The winter of 2010 had seen England's cricket team achieve a rare win in Australia, England's first series victory in Australia for 24 years, and that by the convincing margin of 3–1. The news so dominated the media coverage that it overflowed from the sports pages on to the front, with some newspapers having special supplements to mark this momentous occasion. The time differ-ence meant it had made the English, following their team's success in Australia, a nation of night owls. As Valentine Low put it in a double-page spread in the main news section of *The Times*: 'It has not been about cricket, it has been about nationhood, about heroes and finding something to cheer about when all the news is about tax rises and job cuts and the terrible things the weather can do to us. Or as one Twitter poster put it more succinctly, 'I hate cricket but its [sic] a good day to be an Englishman.'

Even allowing for the fact that Formula One is very special-ized — some may argue it is not a sport at all — how could sport, within a few weeks, go from bringing such joy to a nation to being the instrument of another people's oppression? Have we got it wrong when we speak about the unique spirit of sport? Or does the fault lie in placing on sport a burden it was never meant to carry, whereby it is considered capable of contributing to human development and social cohesion? The answer lies in the curious way the idea of sport having univer-sal significance developed.

Just as modern sport was invented in Britain, with the laws of many games codified in this country, this over-arching sporting philosophy of fair play was also developed in these isles. The British overcame rival German and Swedish theories of how sport can help make a better man. However, unlike the northern Europeans, the development of this sporting idea came, as so often, through classic English muddle, rather than any grand plan. If the British acquired their empire in a fit of absent-mindedness, the philosophy of sport was an even more bizarre development. The result was a philosophy credited to an Englishman who had no interest in sport, and said nothing about it during his lifetime. He was a man of religion and there is little evidence that he even liked games.

The philosophy first emerged 15 years after his death — in the second half of the nineteenth century. It was to become such a powerful force because of the work of two of his disciples. One of them had known him as a young boy, but not very well. The other was born almost two decades after his death and spent much of his lifetime fruitlessly trying to find anything his master had said on sport. And what makes this story even more extraordinary is that, when the sporting philosophy first emerged, it was through a novel. It was as if Harry Potter had been credited with having invented a philosophy of witchcraft that had universal relevance, such was the impact of *Tom Brown's Schooldays*. In the novel, a fictional Thomas Arnold, our sporting guru, is presented as the man who first preached that sport was not mere recreation, but could reach out beyond playing fields into areas far beyond sport. Indeed, that sport could shape society for its greater good.

The author, Thomas Hughes, was an old pupil of the real Thomas Arnold, headmaster at the Midlands public school of Rugby. He felt so diffident about his book that he published it as 'An Old Boy'. The author's real name, as he confessed later, only emerged because 'it was such a hit that the publishers [Macmillan] soon betrayed the secret and I was famous'. The book immortalized the real life Thomas Arnold, the headmaster that Hughes had revered. In the first year, the book was reprinted five times, selling 11,000 copies, which may not be vast by modern standards, but was considerable for the time. By 1890 there had been fifty editions, and 29 of them were still in print in 1928. In a comment on 9 October 1857, *The Times* saw it as a book, 'every English father might well wish to see in the hands of his son'. In 1866 there was a German translation clearly meant to educate future rulers, part of the 'special duties', in the words of the translator, in 'the education of a young German prince'. In the foreword to the 1911 American edition, William Dean Howells, editor of the *Atlantic Monthly*, rhapsodized about the book.

Despite the fact that it was published by an Englishman at the height of the Victorian era, Howells said, 'the American father can trust the American boy with [Hughes'] book, and fear no hurt to his republicanism, still less to his democracy.' The sport-loving American President Teddy Roosevelt considered that it was one of two books that everyone should read (the other being Robert Aldrich's *Story of a Bad Boy*).

Hughes attributed to Arnold the belief that sport could build character and create discipline. Such was his success that Arnold's supposed philosophy took root not only in Britain, but across the world. And that philosophy continued to resonate down to modern times. In 1963, the West Indian Marxist C. L. R. James published *Beyond A Boundary* – to many, the greatest book on sport. James' thesis was that sport, and in particular cricket, could help us answer 'Tolstoy's exasperated and exasperating question: what is art?'

James went on to argue that cricket was art and his holy trinity was Arnold, Hughes and W. G. Grace, the first superstar sportsman and the man who established cricket as the national game. In addition, the creators of English sport, James argued, were motivated by ideas of universal brotherhood and fellow feeling for all mankind.

Arnold would have been astonished to have been converted into such a sporting icon. He was a prolific and often polemical writer, with forthright views on a great range of topics. He published a book or a pamphlet every year between 1829 and his death in 1842, at the age of 47. Yet in none of these, nor in his various sermons which were reprinted several times after his death, did he say a single word about sport. Not that he was averse to physical activity. His former pupil Arthur Stanley, the model for the character George Arthur in Hughes' novel, wrote:

> Arnold's bodily recreations were walking and bathing. It was a particular delight to him with two or three companions to make what he called a skirmish across the country; on these occasions we deserted the road, crossed fences and leaped ditches or fell into them ... Though delicate in appearance and not giving promise of great muscular strength, yet his form was light and he was capable of going long distances and bearing much fatigue.

At Rugby, Arnold's afternoon walk with his wife trotting along on her pony at four miles an hour, and sometimes accompanied by a sixth-form boy, became famous. Indeed, his one fear of taking the Rugby job was that he would not be able to exercise: 'the work I am not afraid of, if I can get proper exercise, but I want absolute play, like a boy'.

His son Thomas would write years later:

My father delighted in our games and sometimes joined in them. Stern though his look would be – and often had to be – there was a vein of drollery in him, a spirit of pure fun . . . He was not witty nor – though he could appreciate humour – was he humorous, but the comic and grotesque side of human life attracted him strongly. He gave to each of his children some nickname more or less absurd, and joked with us, while his eyes twinkled, on the droll situations and comparisons which the names suggested.

But he had no time for organized games. Indeed, on occasions he even banned certain sports at Rugby. The boys liked racing, running, shooting, hunting and fishing; at the confectioner's in the High Street they kept a pack of beagles and the necessary guns; they also organized point-to-point races. But when Arnold discovered this he sent for one of the riders and said, 'I shall expel everyone who rides and everyone who looks on.' And the confectioner's shop was put out of bounds. As a follower of Aristotle, he saw gymnastic training through organized sports as part of the brutal regime used by Sparta to bring up its youth. And as a result he never allocated organized games as the responsibility of any assistant master at Rugby.

But in order to make Arnold the centre of his sporting memoir, Hughes, like a modern spin doctor, completely ignored all these inconvenient facts. Hughes clearly struggled to give Arnold a sporting voice in his novel and the best he could manage was to convey an oblique, tacit approval. This is expressed at second hand, by Brooke, the captain of his house: 'If I saw him [Arnold] stopping football or cricket or bathing or sparring I'd be ready as any fellow to stand up about it. But he don't – he encourages them; didn't you see him out to-day for half an hour watching us?'

The novel's success came from presenting an alluring version of eternal boyhood. Written for Hughes' eight-year-old son Maurice, who died two years after its publication, it conveyed the wonder of a man who was still a schoolboy at heart. Hughes had been inspired by Arnold's weekly 20-minute sermons. Such religious enthusiasm was not universal among Rugby boys. Far from Arnold's gaze, prayer books often formed footballs which the boys kicked up and down the House corridors. One of his former pupils later wrote, 'if the devil had flown away with [the chapel] it would have been a matter of no concern to me'.

However, Hughes and many others were receptive to Arnold's oratory on Christian values and how boys could rediscover their true goodness through Christ. Arnold's depth of religious feeling often led him to cry when talking of the crucifixion and this clearly made a deep impression. The sermons proved so powerful that some of his pupils would rush back to their rooms and try to write them down. It was a time of intense religious debate and frequent controversy within English Christianity. Arnold, himself, failing to become an Archbishop, was keen to be appointed Regius Professor of Divinity at Oxford, but Lord Melbourne, the prime minister, felt that he was too 'indiscreet' in his views. Two headmasters who followed him at Rugby did become Archbishops of Canterbury. His pupil, Arthur Stanley, who did much to promote Arnold's image through a loving biography, became Dean of Westminster, appointed by Queen Victoria herself.

Hughes had clearly learnt much from Arnold's preaching. In a new preface to his novel (written for the sixth edition) he confessed, 'My whole object in writing at all was to get the chance of preaching . . . to preach to boys.' He had set out to explain to 'nervous and sensitive boys' how to adapt to English public school education. Like any preacher, he felt he had to set the record straight. He noted criticism that Arnold had turned 'boys into men before their time, a semi-political, semi-sacerdotal, fraternity giving the idea that they were a set of square-toes who wore long-fingered black gloves and talked with a snuffle.' Dismissing the criticism, Hughes argued that the mark of Rugby meant:

> genial and hearty freshness and youthfulness of character. They lose nothing of the boy that is worth keeping but build up the man upon it . . . But this boyishness in the highest sense is not incompatible with seriousness or earnestness if you like the word better . . . And what gave Rugby boys this character? . . . I say fearlessly Arnold's teaching and example . . . his unwearied zeal in creating moral thoughtfulness in every boy with whom he came into personal contact . . . He taught us that life is a whole, made up of actions and thoughts and longings, great and small, noble and ignoble; therefore the only true wisdom for boys or men is to bring the whole life into obedience to Him whose world we live in, and who has purchased us with His blood; and that whether we eat or drink, or whatsoever we do, we are to do all in His name and to His glory.

In making Arnold a sporting philosopher, Hughes was also well aware that sport, the central theme of his book, had a chequered reputation. For the previous two centuries, many sports had been outlawed, becoming a pawn in the battle between the monarch and Parliament. For the first 30 years of the Stuart period, sport was closer to the centre of the English political stage than it has ever been since.

Puritans had little time for games and made no secret of how much they hated sports, and Philip Stubbes in his 1583 *Anatomie of Abuses* described football as 'this murthering play'. Football as played then could be bloody, particularly the Shrovetide clashes between Chester and Derby, from which the term 'local derby' emanates. But even without such problems, the Puritans found any pleasure suspect. For them, life on earth was to seek salvation in the everlasting life and sport meant betting, swearing, drinking, dancing and men and women thrown together. As one Puritan put it, 'maidens and matrons are groped and handled with unchaste hands' with the result that 'many maidens have been unmaidened'.

The maypole, round which much dancing was done, was 'this stinking idol', all the more to be detested as it could be seen as a pagan symbol. John Dod saw the fact that people played cards and dice, or devised sports involving hounds and hawks, as a sure sign that there was 'some sick soul in the family'. William Hinde felt even a foot race was 'an exercise of profaneness'. With Sunday being the day of play, much of the argument centred on what could be permitted on the Sabbath.

Parliament's concern to impose restrictions on Sunday had become an issue during the closing years of the reign of Elizabeth I. But the queen successfully resisted the government. James I, who had less personal authority over his Parliaments, could not stop the Commons in 1606, 1614, 1621 and 1624 passing motions restricting Sunday sport. But he refused to make them law and played a crucial role in establishing sport in his kingdom.

The king saw himself as a Renaissance sportsman and he had brought golf and pall mall – a forerunner to croquet – to England from Scotland. The hunting lodge he established in Newmarket laid the foundation for the future home of British racing. On 24 May 1618 he issued the Declaration of Sports in Greenwich, more commonly known as the *Book of Sports*. This laid down, for the first time, which sports were, and were not, allowed.

He allowed May games, church ales, Morris dancing and maypoles and Sunday enjoyment 'such as dancing, men or women, archery for men, leaping, vaulting or any such harmless recreation'. Many sports remained on the banned list. These included bull-baiting, bear-baiting and bowling. And, in a statement that could be echoed by modern ministers, he asserted that playing sport was important as it kept people from drunkenness, idleness and discontent and made men 'fit and able'.

Like the King James Bible, the *Book of Sports* served a wider political purpose. It was meant to codify existing practices and was an assertion of the king's rights to lay down what his subjects could do. One reason James gave for it was to create more time on a Sunday to convert Catholics. Although the king called it a *Book of Sports*, the book did not preach any general philosophy of sport. That would have appeared outlandish in his time. The idea that sport had a wider social purpose beyond the actual physical effort involved was little accepted or even considered.

Sport continued to be distrusted by Parliament and James' son, Charles I, always short of money and seeking approval from MPs for funds, agreed to the Sunday Observance Act. This 1625 Act remained on the statute books until 1969 and shaped how and when sport was played in this country. Cromwell's Commonwealth brought further restrictions on sport. The 1644 Act banned all sports at any time on the Sabbath, maypoles were destroyed and the following year football and stoolball were outlawed. Cricket was not banned but indictments were issued to stop Sunday play and Cromwell ordered all cricket bats in Ireland to be destroyed, although this may have been done to prevent them being used as *shillelaghs* (cudgels).

The Restoration of 1660 provided a reprieve for sport. Cromwell's government had ploughed up the heath at Newmarket to prevent racing, but Charles II restored it, and Samuel Pepys was forced, to his annoyance, to go to the races at Newmarket to meet his sovereign. Nevertheless, sport still remained on the margins of society, occasionally subject to fierce denunciations, often suffering collateral damage as Parliament passed laws designed to institute a quieter Sabbath. By the eighteenth century, English society valued calm, moderation and reason while sport was turbulent, immoderate and passionate, encouraging the formation of large crowds, and the attendant problems of gambling, drink, crime, and threats to life and property. In the mid-century, three different football matches in eastern England saw enclosing fences pulled down, fen drainage stopped and mills demolished. Against this chequered background, Hughes sought not only to make sport acceptable, but to elevate it into a guiding philosophy for the British nation and the world. The book was only notionally fictional, a docu-drama, drawn from Hughes' own experience of the school and that of his fellow students. Tom Brown is clearly based on Hughes himself and many other characters were drawn from his contemporaries at Rugby.

Hughes makes it clear he sees sport as bringing society together: 'The true charm of cricket and hunting is that they are still more or less sociable and universal — there's a place for every man who will come and take his part.' When Tom Brown arrives at Rugby he starts preaching in earnest on the classic game of football between School-house and School, where the creed of sport is first enunciated by Brooke, the captain of School-house. Tom, playing his first match, has prevented a School try by falling on the ball. This secures victory for School-house and during the post-match celebrations Brooke, who is about to leave Rugby, lays out the higher value of sport.

'Well, but we beat them — [cheers]. Ay, but why did we beat 'em? Answer me that — [shouts of "your play"]. Nonsense! 'Twasn't the wind and kick-off either — that wouldn't do it. 'Twasn't because we've half a dozen of the best players in the school, as we have. I wouldn't change Warner and Hedge and Crab and the young un for any six on their side — [violent cheers]. But half a dozen fellows can't keep it up for two hours against two hundred. Why is it, then? I'll tell you what I think. It's because we've more reliance on one another, more of a house feeling, more fellowship than the School can have. Each of us knows and can depend on his next-hand man better — that's why we beat 'em to-day. We've union, they've division — there's the secret — [cheers]. But how's this to be kept up? How's it to be improved? That's the question. For, I take it, we're all in earnest about beating the School, whatever else we care about. I know I'd sooner win two School-house matches running than get the Balliol scholarship any day — [frantic cheers].

'Now, I'm as proud of the house as any one. I believe it's the best house in the school, out and out — [cheers]. But it's a long way from what I want to see it. First, there's a deal of bullying going on. I know it well. I don't pry about and interfere; that only makes it more underhand, and encourages the small boys to come to us with their fingers in their eyes telling tales, and so we should be worse off than ever. It's very little kindness for the sixth to meddle generally — you youngsters, mind that. You'll be all the better football players for learning to stand it, and to take your own parts and fight it through. But, depend on it, there's nothing breaks up a house like bullying. Bullies are cowards, and one coward makes many; so good-bye to the School-house match if bullying gets ahead here. [Loud applause from the small boys, who look meaningly at Flashman and other boys at the tables.] Then there's fuddling about in the public-houses and drinking bad spirits, and punch, and such rot-gut stuff. That won't make good drop-kicks or chargers of you, take my word for it. You get plenty of good beer here, and that's enough for you; and drinking isn't fine or manly, whatever some of you may think of it.'

For Hughes, this moment distils the essential message of the book. In Tom's second year, the young George Arthur arrives; delicate and the son of a clergyman who had died a year earlier, Arthur likes books and to kneel by his bed and pray. Tom becomes his mentor and, as they discuss a Biblical story, draws on Arnold's sermon to tell him that in life there is one righteous road that must be followed. 'I hate half measures and compromises . . . There's always the highest way and it's always the right one. How many times has the Doctor [Thomas Arnold] told us that in his sermons in the last year?'

Tom puts Arthur in a terrible dilemma when he fights Slogger Williams, from a rival house, in a boxing match. Williams is two inches taller, a year older and Arthur agonizes whether to tell the Doctor – the fear of Arnold intervening is ever-present during the boxing match. The under-porter warns that he is aware of the fight and then, as the fighters rest between rounds, the door of his library opens and the Doctor appears. The little boys that had surrounded the boxing ring melt away and the Doctor rebukes Brooke for allowing the fight. Brooke does his best to defend the staging of the fight, arguing that, given the strong feelings between the two houses, other more unregulated fights could have broken out. But the Doctor will have none of this and tells him, 'I expect you to stop all fights in future at once.' Brooke nods; he is soon concerned about Tom's bruises, invites him to his room for a tumbler of bottled beer, and then tells him to shake hands with Slogger the next day. They had fought but now they must show mutual respect.

The story makes clear that, whatever the wider meaning of Arnold's teaching, he did not approve of boxing. However, Hughes wanted to give 'a true picture' of school life and rebut the growing anti-boxing clamour. He was also anxious to rebut the contemporary attacks on the evil of boxing by Thackeray and *The Times*. 'Fighting with fists is the natural English way for English boys to settle their quarrels. What substitute for it is there, or ever was there, among any nation under the sun? What would you like to see take its place? Learn to box, then, as you learn to play cricket and football. Not one of you will be the worse, but very much the better for learning to box well.'

Two years later, Arthur has learnt much from Tom. Although 'still frail and delicate', he 'has learnt to swim and run and play cricket and has never hurt himself by too much reading'. However, Tom's missionary activity on behalf of sport is not complete as soon becomes evident when fever breaks out in the boarding house. The talk is that the boys may be sent home and they begin to celebrate getting five weeks extra holiday. Tom immediately says, 'I hope not, there'll be no Marylebone match, then at the end of the half.' The book ends with the match against the MCC and spells out the great moral of sport.

The two-day match is finely balanced. At one stage the school have five wickets in hand and require thirty-two to win. But stumps must be drawn at quarter past eight and, if the school does not make the runs, the MCC, who had a first innings lead, will win. Tom, Arthur and a young master, who would later become head at Marlborough, are watching the match. Tom, now nineteen and captain of the eleven, is in his cricket flannels, cradling his favourite bat on a bench. Arthur, who is in the team, is sitting at his feet, 'Turkish fashion with his bat across his knees'.

There then follows an extraordinary exchange between Tom, Arthur and the master:

'I don't understand cricket, so I don't enjoy those fine draws which you tell me are the best play, though when you or Raggles hit a ball hard away for six I am as delighted as any one. Don't you see the analogy?'

'Yes, sir,' answered Tom, looking up roguishly, 'I see; only the question remains whether I should have got most good by understanding Greek particles or cricket thoroughly. I'm such a thick, I never should have had time for both.'

'I see you are an incorrigible,' said the master, with a chuckle; 'but I refute you by an example. Arthur there has taken in Greek and cricket too.'

'Yes, but no thanks to him; Greek came natural to him. Why, when he first came I remember he used to read Herodotus for pleasure as I did *Don Quixote*, and couldn't have made a false concord if he'd tried ever so hard—and then I looked after his cricket.'

Then, as a boy is out, some other boys rush to Tom and one of them, Jack Raggles, asks him to change the batting order. Tom agrees, but then tells the master:

'I dare say now I've lost the match by this nonsense,' he says, as he sits down again; 'they'll be sure to get Jack's wicket in three or four minutes; however, you'll have the chance, sir, of seeing a hard hit or two,' adds he, smiling, and turning to the master.

'Come, none of your irony, Brown,' answers the master. 'I'm beginning to understand the game scientifically. What a noble game it is, too!'

'Isn't it? But it's more than a game. It's an institution,' said Tom.

'Yes,' said Arthur, 'the birthright of British boys, old and young, as *habeas corpus* and trial by jury are of British men.'

'The discipline and reliance on one another which it teaches is so valuable, I think,' went on the master, 'it ought to be such an unselfish game. It merges the individual in the eleven; he doesn't play that he may win, but that his side may.'

'That's very true,' said Tom, 'and that's why football and cricket, now one comes to think of it, are much better games than fives or hare-and-hounds, or any others where the object is to come in first or to win for one's self, and not that one's side may win.'

'And then the captain of the eleven!' said the master, 'what a post is his in our school-world! — almost as hard as the Doctor's; requiring skill and gentleness and firmness, and I know not what other rare qualities.'

The match finishes with the school failing to make the runs and the MCC winning because of their first innings lead. The MCC captain, Mr Aislabie, invites Tom to Lord's and offers him membership. However, the master, while now a fan of cricket, does say that, unlike Tom, Arnold would not have changed the batting order to please a boy and Tom has still much to learn about 'the art of ruling'. Arnold is so good at it that the master is certain, 'perhaps ours is the only little corner of the British Empire which is thoroughly wisely and strongly ruled just now. I am more and more thankful every day of my life that I came here to be under him.'

The Arnold way, as the master sees it, is not revolution, but judicious evolution so as not to provoke revolt, 'quietly and naturally, putting a good thing in the place of a bad, and letting the bad die out; no wavering and no hurry – the best thing that could be done for the time being, and patience for the rest.'

Tom confesses it had taken him time to appreciate how Arnold effected change, but he now fully subscribes to it. This is the over-arching philosophy of how society should be governed that Thomas Hughes preaches and for which he feels there is desper-ate need. That may seem surprising.

Tom Brown's Schooldays was published in 1857, six years after Prince Albert had organized the Great Exhibition of 1851 to adver-tise the wonders of the Victorian age. A book of this nature, written at the zenith of the Victorian era, might have been expected to exalt all that happened to make England great. If England was quite so wonderful, and its reach so extensive round the world, what need was there of any new philosophy? But, astonishingly, the book was not a celebration of the England that had created this Victorian wonderland, but a wail for the England lost with the coming of the railways and the modern inventions.

Early in the novel, Hughes agonizes about the England that has vanished:

O young England! Young England! You who were born into those racing railroad times when there's a Great Exhibition, or some monster sight, every year; and you can get over a couple of thousand miles of ground for three pounds ten in a five-weeks' holiday; why don't you know more of your own birthplaces?

The modern Englishman, sighed Hughes, may go to the top of the Swiss mountains, float down the Danube, speak French and German, eat sauerkraut, see the pictures in Dresden and the Louvre, but 'All I say is you don't know your own lanes and woods and fields. Though you may be chock-full of science not one in twenty of you knows where to find the wood-sorrel or bee-orchids which grow in the next wood or on the down three miles off, or what the bog-bean and wood-sage are good for.'

For good measure he accuses the boards of directors of rail-way companies, 'those gigantic jobbers and bribers', of paying doctors several millions to suggest to their patients that they should have a change of air every year necessitating a railway journey, even if they have to borrow money to pay for the ticket. 'If it be not for this, why is it that none of us can be well at home for a year together? The Browns did not go out of the country once in five years.'

Not that Hughes was against empire. Indeed, the Browns, the family of his hero Tom, are held up as just the sort of people who made Britain's empire possible. Unlike the noble families of England who had become noble by 'catching hold of, and holding on tight to, whatever good things happened to be going', the Browns were the salt of the earth. Today we might call them Middle England; for Hughes they represented the rising middle classes who had made England great and were now being forgotten:

> For centuries, in their quiet, dogged, homespun way they have been subduing the earth in most English counties, and leaving their mark in American forests and Australian uplands. Whenever the fleets and armed of England have won renown, there stalwart sons of the Browns have done yeoman's work. With the yew bow and cloth-yard shaft at Cressy and Agincourt — with the brown bill and pike under the brave Lord Willoughby — with culverin and demi-culverin against Spaniards and Dutchmen — with hand-grenade and sabre, and musket and bayonet, under Rodney and St. Vincent, Wolfe and Moore, Nelson and Wellington, they have carried their lives in their hands, getting hard knocks and hard work in plenty, which was on the whole what they looked for, and the best thing for them; and little praise or pudding, which indeed they and most of us are better without.

1857 was also the year of the Indian Revolt, when the British were horrified to discover how many Indians wanted to throw them out of India and did not appreciate the benefits of British rule for their heathen land. The result of the Indian Revolt was to bring India fully under the control of the British state. Previously, following Robert Clive's victory at Plassey in 1757, India had been ruled by the East India Company, who had gone to India to trade and then exploited the situation there to acquire an empire. The revolt of 1857 exposed the problems of company rule and the British Parliament now took direct control. In the aftermath, the empire made by traders and profiteers now needed a higher philosophy and Hughes' book was extremely well-timed to provide one.

At the end of the cricket match, Tom Brown and the master allude to India as they talk of the first friend Tom made at Rugby, Harry East. He has since left school and is now on his way there to join his regiment.

'He will make a capital officer', says the master. 'Aye, won't he!' Tom agrees. '[N]o fellow could handle boys better and I suppose soldiers are very like boys. And he'll never tell them to go where he won't go himself. No mistake about that — a braver fellow never walked.'

We are entering the world of muscular Christianity, one that Rugby embodied. The phrase that would be used to describe it was 'the Englishman going through the world with rifle in one hand and Bible in the other.' This was a world where young men were brought up as Christians but ready to fight for their beliefs, not turn the other cheek, as Christ had advocated. These were young men sent to rule an empire which was proud that it was built on high moral principles. They were expected to obey rules and enforce them because they knew they were on the side of right and goodness. Hughes never lost his faith in muscular Christianity. He was preaching this even a month before his death in 1895, converting King Alfred, whose victory over the Danes had much moved him, and Christ himself, into muscular Christians.

In all this Christian goodness, Hughes did his best to mitigate the stories of bullying and beating that went on in Rugby and other public schools in the days of Tom Brown. Hughes did refer to this in the book, but focused it through the villain, Flashman, who indulged in practices such as flinging little boys around in their blankets. Tom, in the end, gets the better of Flashman. But by making Flashman something of a caricature, so much so that in the twentieth century he inspired the Flashman novels, Hughes gave the impression Rugby had had problems, but was now reformed thanks to Arnold. Here Hughes performed a neat trick. He completely blotted out one facet of the real Doctor's school life: mercilessly flogging the boys. Indeed there was one notorious real-life Arnold episode of flogging which was much worse than anything the fictional Flashman ever did.

Arnold had flogged seven boys in his first year without comment, but in his third year his flogging created such a scandal that it might have finished his career. Arnold, having decided to examine the lower forms, asked a boy called March to construe a passage in Xenophon's *Anabasis*. He had checked that the boys had reached that part of the book before making the request. But March denied they had and when he persisted in this claim, Arnold got so furious that after calling him a liar several times, flogged him with a rod eighteen times. March then spent the next two days away from school in his boarding house recovering from the beating. Arnold saw this as malingering and gave him extra hours of work. Then it emerged that March had not been lying. March's parents were furious. The boy was delicate, having suffered a rupture at the age of three, and before his parents allowed him to continue at Rugby, Arnold had to submit an abject written apology.

The case also made the newspapers and commentators pointed out that his predecessor John Wool never gave more than twelve lashes and that for rebellion. If Arnold could be so cruel just for alleged lying, how many lashes for stealing, sexual offence or insurrection? The press reaction so upset Arnold that he even tried unsuccessfully to gag the *Northampton Bulletin*. Arnold survived, but there is no mention of this scandal in *Tom Brown's Schooldays*.

In fact, Arnold was surprised 'to see the wickedness of young boys' and became convinced that to make Christian men from

Christian boys required a continual battle against evil. As he wrote to a friend, just before taking over at Rugby, while he wanted to make it a place of Christian education, he felt that young boys, 'from the natural imperfect state of boyhood . . . are not susceptible of Christian principles in their full development upon their practice, and I suspect that a low standard of morality in many respects must be tolerated amongst them, as it was on a larger scale in what I consider the boyhood of the human race'.

Like the shrewd Victorian he was, Arnold saw money as the root of many problems. He had been made head in 1828 to tackle Rugby's decline, the school having a mere 123 boys when he arrived. The first thing Arnold did was increase fees; this not only brought more money but the numbers also increased and had risen to 349 in his last full year. Arnold himself did well out of the school and by the time of his death he was, probably, earning £4,000 a year – some estimates suggest as much as £6,000 – an income which put him in the top one per cent of the country.

Unlike Hughes, who became a Christian socialist and flirted with the newly formed Labour party, Arnold's radicalism was tempered. While he was in favour of the Reform Bill, which marked the start of the slow rise of mass democracy in Britain, he was far from being a true radical, let alone a revolutionary. He valued the English aristocracy as much as he valued the English Church. In contrast, Hughes in *Tom Brown's Schooldays* advised his young readers to be more egalitarian. They should, he said, invite to their homes and introduce to their wives and sisters not only lawyers, doctors and parsons, but also tailors, engineers, carpenters, engravers, 'give them good dinners and talk to them about what is really at the bottom of your heart, and box, and run and row with them [. . .] do all this honestly man to man'. That would be the way of creating a better society.

However, Hughes exactly matched Arnold in the way he saw British influence spreading round the world. Arnold had always been interested in the British populating remoter regions of the world. Days short of his twentieth birthday, while at Oriel

College, Oxford, Arnold won the English Prize for his essay on 'The Effects of Distant Colonisation on the Parent State'. The essay's theme was how people of the same race and stock would operate in different environments, a subject that always fascinated Arnold. It was read in the Sheldonian Theatre at Oxford, eleven days before Waterloo.

Arnold also saw populating the empire with British stock as part of the solution to poverty in Britain. Calling for the creation of 'home colonies' or emigration, he argued, 'this was the regular course pursued in ancient times [. . .] when a large population who had formerly been slaves or conquered in war, grew up to the condition of freeman and citizens, they were provided for by being settled on the unappropriated lands of the State or when none of these were to be found, they were sent out to be settled in a colony'.

Almost a century later, as rugby football spread from the home isles round the world, this was almost exactly the Arnoldian model it adopted. The game spread overseas almost exclusively in the white settler colonies initially of British stock to Australia, New Zealand, South Africa and North America, in a pattern that Arnold would have found fascinating, proof that in leaving their homelands the British had not lost their sense of Britishness, let alone their innate superiority to other races. Tom Willis, who organized the first football club in Melbourne, was educated at Rugby, and English-style public schools made the game popular in South Africa. In time, the game moved beyond the British settlers.

In the 1880s, the Afrikaners in Stellenbosch on the Cape had taken to it and it had also spread to North America via British stock settled in Canada. There, the students at McGill University in Montreal took the game across the border having been taught by British army garrisons in the town. There were variations, particularly in relation to the scrum, but as the American magazine *Outing* put it, 'there is very little in which the American has varied from English Rugby'. This was a sporting echo of a political plan long favoured by Hughes. He saw an alliance of Britain, the United States, Canada, the Cape, Australia and New Zealand that would bind the world 'round by a chain of free English-speaking nations which would have little trouble in making their will respected and keeping the world's peace for the rest of time or till Armageddon at any rate'. In that sense, Hughes pre-dated Winston Churchill, who sought to build such an alliance through much of his political career and through his *History of the English Speaking Peoples.*

By the time Hughes had used Tom Brown to spread the world of Arnold, other pupils of Arnold, in particular Arthur Stanley, had established his posthumous reputation as the great reformer of English public schools. This stressed his emphasis on the teaching of science and credited him with humanizing the barbaric ways of the pre-Arnold Rugby. Like Hughes, Stanley completely ignored the March flogging. Later, Lytton Strachey, who had suffered much at public schools, tried to debunk the Arnold myth in his essay on Arnold in *Eminent Victorians,* portraying him as an impostor and a clown. While the poisoned portrait may have been over the top, it is open to doubt how much of a reformer Arnold really was. One schoolboy, William Charles Lake, who had become a favourite of Arnold, went on to write that, 'it would be a mistake to support that [Arnold's] influence materially changed the character of school-life in the ordinary schoolboy'.

But by then, the myth was too entrenched to be demolished and had received the official seal of approval. The Clarendon Commission, established in 1861 to inquire into public school education in England, held up Rugby as 'a national institution, as being a place of education and a source of influence for the whole Kingdom [. . .] It instructs everywhere, is known everywhere and exercises an influence everywhere'. As for sport at Rugby, that, said the commission, 'distinguishes the strong, strengthens the studious and spares the weak'.

Hughes had also succeeded in creating a philosophy of sport that was inherently anti-intellectual and would leave a deep mark on British culture. This part of Hughes' philosophy did not travel to the United States where the British battle between hearties and arties is considered very alien. But Tom makes the role of sport very plain: 'I want to be A1 at cricket and football, and all the other games [. . .] I want to please the Doctor; and I want to carry away just as much Latin and Greek as will take me through Oxford respectably'. Sport even mattered more than political issues. Hughes may have become a prominent politician, but towards the end of the book he describes Tom tossing a paper aside, moaning it is full of the controversy about Corn Laws. Much more exciting is the match going on between Kent and England with Felix, the great cricketer, 56 not out and not having given a chance.

This belief that sport can overcome political problems would remain so much part of British society that nearly a century later it would provide Alfred Hitchcock some of his most memorable scenes in *The Lady Vanishes*. This 1938 film, set on a train rumbling through the continent towards England, was meant to convey a flavour of some of the nasty regimes coming to power in Europe and whose actions would soon horrify the world. An elderly lady passenger vanishes, other passengers pretend she was never on the train, a young British couple refuse to believe this fiction and she is found to be a prisoner in a sealed-off compartment, supposedly occupied by a seriously ill patient being transported to an operation.

The story ends happily; the woman returns to London where it emerges she is a British spy assigned to deliver some vital information to the Foreign Office. However, there are also on the train two characters, Caldicott and Charters, who could have been Tom Brown's contemporaries. Throughout the journey their concern is the 1938 Oval Test between England and Australia – at one stage they sit in the train's dining car using salt and pepper pots to work out the field set to contain Don Bradman. The moment they arrive in London they rush to buy a newspaper to find out the latest score. Fascism may have gripped Europe, the world may be sliding to war, but an Ashes Test between England and Australia is more important.

In many ways, the most curious thing about Tom Brown and his schooldays was that Hughes had spelt out the purpose of games long before most sports had drawn up their rules or codes of conduct. In effect, sport had acquired a philosophy before it had been properly organized and, to a great extent, the main problem of modern sport is this clash between its nineteenth-century philosophy and the subsequent development of many games as they have had to react to a very different, and constantly changing, world. No sport illustrates this better than the one Hughes had used to enunciate the philosophy of winning: rugby. Brooke ascribes School-house's victory to, 'We're union, they're division — there's the secret.'

The match has come down to us as the classic game of rugby, but as described in the book, it bears no relation to the modern game. It is not even clear how many players took part in the School-house versus School match. Hughes speaks of School-house having 'fifty or sixty boys in white trousers' facing 'that huge mass opposite' of School. In the School side, 'the goalkeepers are all in lumps, anyhow and nohow; you can't distinguish between the players-up and the boys in quarters'. Brooke, in his speech quoted earlier, spoke of facing 'two hundred'. It has the feel of something impromptu where rules are made up as you go along. A similar game must also have been witnessed by the Dowager Queen Adelaide when she visited Rugby after the death of King William IV, and unexpectedly expressed a desire to see football. The boys took off their coats and waistcoats and obliged.

The fact is, when Hughes wrote the book, the only sport that was properly organized was cricket. The first laws of the game had been in existence for more than a century, since 1744, and the MCC had been going for more than half a century, since 1787. All the other major changes, the legalizing of overhand bowling, the first county championship, the first issue of Wisden, came within a few years of the publication of Hughes' novel.

Nothing like this had happened in football. It was still organized on the random basis that had always marked the game and all its various codes were still to be properly regulated. It was several decades after the book was published that this took place. While in the middle years of the nineteenth century the Rugby version of the game was considered the most important, there were several other versions of football being played. In some, as with the Sheffield version, there was dribbling. In many other versions a player could carry a ball and even hack, take a kick at the shins of an opposing player. Indeed when, on the evening of Monday 26 October 1863, a dozen clubs met at the Freemason's Tavern in Lincoln's Inn Fields to form the Football Association, it was clear the rules favoured were those used in Rugby, including carrying the ball and hacking.

In a subsequent meeting, the FA considered whether to accept the rules of Cambridge University and decided that handling the ball was negotiable, but hacking was not. The FA required six meetings before non-handling and non-hacking rules were accepted, and even then, handling was allowed for some years. The Royal Engineers, for instance, who appeared in four of the first seven FA Cup finals, had their own set of rules, which allowed running with the ball. It was well into the 1870s, as the FA Cup became more popular, that the rules of the round ball version of the game began to be formalized.

This may explain why Hughes' book has no reference to the event that was supposed to have led to the birth of what we now call rugby football. The generally accepted myth is that in 1823 a boy called William Webb Ellis, playing football at Rugby School, suddenly decided to pick up the ball and run with it and the game of rugby was born. Given Hughes was at Rugby soon after, it is astonishing that this seminal event does not feature in the book. Many years later when Hughes spoke at the Old Rugbeian Society, he confessed that 'the Webb Ellis tradition had not survived to my day'. It had not because it was not true. It was one of sport's great fabrications. There was a William Webb Ellis who went to Rugby and ended his days as an Anglican clergyman, dying in 1872. But there is no evidence he ever played the game, let alone picked up the ball and ran with it.

The fabrication came four years after his death and was the work of another Rugby old boy, Matthew Bloxam. He named Ellis as the inventor of rugby but never provided any proof. In 1895 a committee was formed by the Old Rugbeian Society to ascertain if the story was true. No one came forward to justify it and there was no other evidence, oral or written. But the committee decided that it was probably true and five years later there was a plaque at the school to Ellis which honoured him as the boy who, 'with a fine disregard of the rules of football as played in his time, first took the ball in his arms and ran with it'. In 1987, when rugby finally got a World Cup, the last of the major team sports to do so, the trophy was inevitably named after Webb Ellis, the truth being more uncomfortable to deal with.

By then sport had changed so dramatically that Tom, Arthur, the young master and Brooke would not have recognized it. Indeed not long before his death Hughes began to fear that he might have helped create a monster. He deplored the excessive emphasis on games and felt it caused 'training and competitions [for] them to outrun all rational bounds'. It would, he feared, encourage professionalism where people would seek a living out of sport and would be attracted to sport for the money to be made, not the high moral values it would encourage. Games, he conceded, tested only skill and strength, and to hero worship athletes, who could be both brutes and cowards, led to obsequiousness and limited the development of idealism and an independent spirit. This, expressed in the last years of the nineteenth century, is language that could be echoed by many about the effect of modern sports in the twenty-first.

Some of this had come about because while Hughes never meant his ideas for anyone other than a British schoolboy, others had found the British sporting brand so alluring that they had taken to it and adapted it for their own purpose. The most prominent among them was a Frenchman. As a young man he had read *Tom Brown's Schooldays* and found it so irresistible that he decided to harness it for developing a truly worldwide movement that would go much beyond Rugby and Britain.

Thomas Hughes could not have predicted it, Thomas Arnold would not have recognized it, but the religion of sport was about to be exported from Britain. As with many religions (including Christianity and Buddhism) which were conceived in one country but flowered in another very unlikely setting, the export of the religion of sport led to dramatic transformations, not all of which appealed to its inventors. The English had provided a philosophy and begun to set down rules for various games, but the rise of a worldwide sport movement would require other nations and people far removed from the world of Arnold and Tom Brown.

CHAPTER 2

THE FRENCH DISCIPLE

One evening in 1886, as the light was beginning to fade, a 23-year-old Frenchman arrived at Rugby school. Small in stature, with a shrill voice, he had shown no aptitude in sport, nor had any training. In fact, he looked like a dandy. The most distinctive feature of his face was a carefully cultivated handlebar moustache. Richard Mandel, an Olympic historian, has tried to picture the man:

> His mustache was splendid. It was carefully pruned with sumptuous tendrils that swooped out to wisps at the end, beyond the width of his canted ears and broad, asymmetrical forehead. He looked like a whiskered cat destined for a long life [. . .] His heavy eyebrows and piercing eyes were always dark. In fact his eyes were so dark as to appear to be without pupils. They were a bit popped with Italian verve [. . .] dazzling and aggressive, they were the eyes of a man continually gauging the possibilities for action [. . .] this man with a peppy organ grinder's good looks.

He had been to Rugby before, had read *Tom Brown's Schooldays* and carried an English copy in his baggage. His head was full of word pictures from the book.

On a previous journey he had matched his images of Tom Brown with reality on the ground: there Tom had first met East and become friends; there, he had vanquished the bully Flashman; there, was the close behind the chapel where Tom had fought

Slogger Williams in the boxing match, suddenly interrupted by the Doctor arriving and rebuking Brooke for allowing fights. And, of course, Tom's last day at Rugby, the cricket match against the MCC with Tom, Arthur and the young master preaching a philosophy for the world through the game of cricket. The young Frenchman had actually stepped on the slope of the island, which looked to the cricket ground, where the three had pontificated about how the game was as important to an Englishman as *habeas corpus* and trial by jury.

He absorbed those images again, but on this visit the Frenchman was on the search for his Holy Grail. Walking through the quadrangle and into the close he headed for the chapel. There, having unlocked the door, he passed through the vestibule and glanced at the empty benches. As the rays of the evening light shone down on him from the painted windows, he stopped in front of the altar, underneath which Thomas Arnold was buried.

The Frenchman's journey was almost identical to Thomas Hughes' description of Tom Brown's in 1842. On hearing that Arnold had died, Tom, recently graduated from Oxford, had rushed back to Rugby from a holiday in Scotland to pay homage to his old master. But the Frenchman's real-life journey was to have more dramatic consequences. As he later wrote, 'in the twilight, alone in the great gothic chapel of Rugby, my eyes fixed on the funeral slab on which, without epitaph, the great name of Thomas Arnold was inscribed. I dreamed that I saw before me the cornerstone of the British Empire'.

Arnold would have been delighted by this adulation. He did not like France, or foreign countries in general, and after one of his trips to France he had written, 'we see here few whose looks and manners are what we should call those of a thorough gentleman . . . A thorough English gentleman – Christian, manly and enlightened – is . . . a finer specimen of human nature than any other country, I believe, could furnish.'

There was nothing strange about Charles Pierre Fredy de Coubertin visiting England to learn from the English. Many nineteenth-century Frenchmen were infatuated by English customs and ways: the novelist Stendhal had said, 'English government is the only one in Europe that appears to be worthy of being studied'. French visitors marvelled at the English elections and the English were praised for *'hardiesse à entreprendre, tenacité à conserver'*, bold in launching new things, tenacious in conserving old ones. This French visitor had read other books on England apart from *Tom Brown's Schooldays*, including the works of the French historian and philosopher Hippolyte Taine. After three visits to England in 1859, 1862 and 1871, which took in tours of various English public schools, Taine had expressed his fascination for the world Arnold had created. He thought it far superior to any French institution, as he made clear in his *Notes Sur L'Angleterre*:

> All the boys I saw in their class rooms in the fields and streets have a 'healthy and active' air. Obviously at least in my view they are both more childish and more manly than our own boys, more childish in that they are fonder of games and less disposed to overstep limits of their age: more manly in that they are more capable of decision and action and self government. Whereas the French schoolboy, especially the boarders in our colleges, is bored, soured, fined-down and precocious, far too precocious. He is in a cage and his imagination ferments. In all these respects, and what concerns the formation of character English education is better; it is a better preparation for the world and it turns out more wholesome spirits.

Taine had read *Tom Brown's Schooldays*, indeed he quoted from the book. But, while he felt English education 'turns out men capable of great moral and physical strivings, with all the advantages', he worried about too much emphasis on games at the cost of intellectual development:

> the rougher instincts are developed. 'Games take first place,' said an Eton master, 'books second.' The boys like Tom glory in being

35

fine athletes, and spend three, four, even five hours a day in noisy and violent physical exercise. When running (hares-and-hounds) they wallow for hours over ploughed fields and through sodden meadows, fall in the mud, lose their shoes, pick themselves up as best as they can [. . .] Almost all the games usually entail some cuts and bruises; the boys glory in not feeling them and, as a natural result, are no more reluctant to inflict than to suffer them. A boy thus becomes pugnacious, a boxer.

As the schoolmaster Mark Pattison had told Taine, 'These games are no longer amusements, they are organized as a system of serious activities.' He had described how the summer term was really given over to playing cricket – a hot breakfast between nine and ten, then the charabanc arrives and it is off to the cricket field.

But just as Hughes had blanked out Arnold's flogging of boys, Pierre Coubertin paid little attention to such criticisms of the effect of sport. He had decided that England, and its love of sport, could be a solution to the many problems of France. Coubertin should have been a very contended Frenchman. He could not have been more privileged, coming from a long line of distinguished French notables on both his parents' sides. On his father's side, Pierre Fredy dit Sieur de la Motte was ennobled by Louis XI in 1477 and served as his chamberlain. In 1821 his paternal grandfather, Julien-Bonaventure Fredy de Coubertin, was made a hereditary baron by Louis XVIII. Three months after that a similar honour was bestowed on Pierre's maternal grandfather, Etienne-Charles.

What troubled Coubertin was the upheaval the French revolution had caused. This had seen three monarchies, two empires and three republics in less than a century. Brought up by Jesuits, Pierre had been marked for priesthood, but then gone to St. Cyr, the French military academy, before deciding a life in the military was not for him. Seeking a solution for France's problems, he turned to sport, despite not having been a sportsman himself. What attracted him was the wider message of sport preached in

Tom Brown's Schooldays. As a boy of 12 he had read the book. Once he read Taine he decided he must journey to England to learn at first hand the English ways. Across the Channel was a new world, a world that worked and had exciting ideas that could benefit France. The 1886 visit to Arnold's tomb was not his first. He had come in 1883, probably the following year, then in 1886 and after that almost yearly.

Coubertin planned his journeys to England with care. His visits to an English public school followed a very strict pattern. He brought with him letters of introduction. The English offered him tea, both with masters and selected pupils. A tour of the school and its grounds would follow during which Coubertin would wander around and pay particular attention to the games that the boys were playing. He would follow the lessons they were taking and talk to them. Then he would join them for meals and, of course, visit the chapel.

Some years later, writing about his English experiences in *L'Education en Angleterre*, Coubertin described how the English treated him:

> You are a stranger in Cambridge?
> Not only in Cambridge, but in England.
> German perhaps?
> Frenchman.
> Frenchman, oh!'
> *Et, levant son chapeau avec un demi-sourire de courtoisie, il me dit*:
> 'Vive la république!'
> *Je réponds*:
> 'God save the Queen!'
> *Et nous nous séparons.*

By this time the English were getting used to French visitors. Taine's *Notes Sur L'Angleterre* had caused a stir, and here was a French baron, who spoke good English, not much older than the boys at the schools he was visiting. Every school, Rugby, Harrow,

Eton, and the universities of Oxford and Cambridge were happy to indulge Coubertin.

Coubertin took from Arnold only what he wanted to. Apart from ignoring his flogging and discipline, he also ignored the religious emphasis that was an essential part of the upbringing of children, emphasizing instead Arnold's moral development of a gentleman. 'The supreme goal of the English masters is to make men and to lead them. Character and good method, that is their aim.' In making such a restricted choice, the Frenchman was helped by Arnold's disciples. Not only Hughes, but others such as Stanley in his biography of Arnold, had presented a selective view of the man. Even then, Coubertin did feel at times like an explorer who had to teach the natives their own goodness. England, he moaned, could not see how great Arnold was, not interested in exploring what Coubertin called 'the interior mechanism':

> The English didn't help me at all to discover it: one could say that they themselves didn't perceive it. My worst disillusionment came from the fact that Thomas Arnold had nothing more to say about that than they did. I would have hoped, in the absence of the treatise on the matter, which no doubt the shortness of his life didn't leave him to write, to have found in his letters and sermons some precise information. But no. The subject, implied throughout, and one knows, a preoccupation haunting the brain of the great pedagogue, was nowhere explicitly approached.

For Coubertin had made the astonishing discovery that Arnold had left behind nothing on sport, let alone anything on the value of sport and its effect on society. This may have been a huge barrier for any other disciple trying to spread the words of his master, but the Frenchman was not to be dissuaded. Coubertin had he so chosen could have used other Englishmen to advance the case for sport: Edward Thring, headmaster at Uppingham until 1887, during the years Coubertin regularly visited England, told his biographer, 'mark me, cricket is a greatest bond of the English-speaking race, and is no mere game'. And while Arnold had said nothing about sport, his adversary on religion, Cardinal John Newman of the Oxford Movement, could have provided the moral argument for sport that Coubertin sought: 'There are bodily exercises which are liberal, and mental exercises which are not so [. . .] for instance [. . .] the Olympic Games, in which strength and dexterity of body as well as of mind gain the prize.'

Perhaps Coubertin did not know of Newman's views, or perhaps he felt it sacrilegious to choose Newman rather than Arnold as his Messiah of sport. Coubertin's solution was classic: preach the message of Arnold as if he had left behind voluminous writings on the subject of sport. In a sense this offered Coubertin an opportunity: there are constant disputes over what Christ or Muhammad, or other great religious leaders, said during their lifetimes. But since Arnold had said nothing about sport, nobody could challenge Coubertin about Arnold's real intentions. Nevertheless, the way he set about spreading the message of his English master was quite extraordinary. If Hughes was an artful spin doctor then Coubertin was to better him. No guru has had such a disciple; no faith has ever had such an evangelist.

Coubertin recognized that on his own he could not spread Arnold's faith. He needed powerful English support and aimed for the highest in the land. Gladstone was then prime minister and on his visit to England in 1888, Coubertin sought a meeting with the great man. It became apparent that Gladstone knew about Arnold. Although he had been at Eton long before the sport-as-salvation message attributed to Arnold had reached the public schools, he knew about Arnold as a man with very definite religious views, and had written about him approvingly to the queen. However, when Coubertin went to Downing Street, he talked to Gladstone about sport. Indeed, in his own account, he converted Gladstone into an unabashed sports fan, particularly the sport of rowing. Coubertin went on to describe Gladstone as a 'veteran boater' and quoted the prime minister as saying, 'I don't believe there's a single spot on the Thames where I couldn't tell you in calm water the power of the current and the depth of the water'. After that it was easy enough for Coubertin to picture Gladstone as approving Arnold's advocacy of sport and how this was central to the British Empire:

Arnold draws up [. . .] the fundamental rules of the pedagogy of sport. From Rugby, he affects the other public schools by the contagion of his example, without resounding phrases or indiscreet interference; and so the keystone of the British Empire is laid. I know that this point of view is not yet that of the historians nor of the British themselves, but I am content to have had it approved by one of the greatest survivors of the Arnoldian period – Gladstone. When I put the question to him, being afraid that I might be mistaken, he asked me for time to think the matter over, and having thought it over he said: 'You are right, that is how it happened.'

None of Gladstone's biographers refer to these observations. John MacAloon in his excellent biography of Coubertin has suggested he cobbled together 'scattered replies' to 'disjointed questions' to produce such an endorsement. Whether or not Coubertin told the truth, he had secured a great English name to advance the cause of Arnold. Armed with that, he returned to his homeland to spread the message of this English world of sport. In doing so he made sure to link it to a venerable past. The English were doing something radical, but it restored what humans had always had, but then had lost:

Sport is movement and the influence of movement on the organs is a thing well known through the ages. Strength and dexterity have always been admired, by savage as well as civilized peoples, and one obtains them by exercise in practice. The successful development of physical qualities generally produces a happy equilibrium in the moral domain. 'Mens sana in corpore sano' say the ancients.

He continued:

> All of whom I have questioned on the subject were unanimous
> in their answers: they have only to rejoice in the state of school
> morality, and they loudly declare that sport is the cause of it; that
> its role lies in pacifying the senses and calming imagination, stop-
> ping corruption by cutting it off at the root and preventing it from
> being shown off, and, finally, in arming nature for the struggle.

For good measure he quoted a line from *Tom Brown's Schooldays*:
'Fear God and make 100 kilometres in 100 hours'. The English, he
said, 'see an association of ideas in which sport is treated with
honour, where it is placed in the same rank as the fear of God'. But
he did point out that the English did not practise the great Christian
command of offering the left cheek when struck on the right.

Despite Gladstone's endorsement, Coubertin did not find it
easy to preach the British cult of sport to his fellow countrymen.
He realized that he required a Gladstone-like figure in France and
duly found France's Grand Old Man, Jules Simon, 74, a former
prime minister and senator and a long-time member of the
Académie française. While Coubertin had had to drag some
words on sport from Gladstone, Simon was all too ready to
provide an endorsement. In a critique of the French educational
system he had said:

> We give our society a ridiculous little mandarin who hasn't any
> muscles, who does not know how to leap a barrier, to elbow his
> way forward, to shoot a gun, or to mount a horse, who is afraid
> of everything, who, to make up for it, is crammed with all sorts of
> useless knowledge, who doesn't know the most necessary things,
> who can't give counsel to anyone, not even to himself, who needs
> to be directed in everything.

Simon wrote one passage which would have suited Coubertin
perfectly if it had come from the mouth of Arnold:

The right which I demand back for our children is the right to play. You understand well that I am the implacable enemy of games of chance; I entreat for active games, what the English call athletic games. I'm willing to have gymnastics, provided that you get rid of all your trapezes and your showman's apparatus; I accept military exercises which the boys like; but what I ask for, above all, are games, the development of physical strength in joy and liberty [. . .] I want races, wrestling, and ball games, in the open air, not in your pestilential halls, in the country air, if possible. I have no fear of a thump, given or received. If my boy so forgets himself as to whimper for a bruise or a black eye, I have my response all prepared: 'You are a man!'

Tom Brown could not have put it better.

Coubertin recruited Simon to write the foreword to *L'Education Anglaise en France,* his version of the Arnold method for the French. Obligingly, France's Grand Old Man set out the terms of the young nobleman's intended educational revolution through sport:

He [Coubertin] intends to remake the French race [. . .] He visited English universities and schools where cricket and rowing are institutions. He saw in the London parks the whole youth of both sexes on horseback. He knew that the German generals always had a profusion of good riders to pick from when they needed an aide-de-camp, whereas with us, no one, or practically no one rides. We barely have, here and there, a *jeu de paume* [. . .] What therefore is required? Quite simply to put athletic education in fashion.

Simon's remarks about the Germans addressed the issue at the heart of French society and also highlighted the huge barrier Coubertin faced in getting the French to accept Arnold and his English ways.

The Germans already had a gymnastic movement. This was founded by Frederich Ludwig Jahn, who was born 17 years before

Arnold, in 1778, and outlived him by 10 years. Known as the *Turnvater*, or father of gymnastics, his gymnastic movement involved physical training that included the use of rings, the pommel horse and parallel bars. It also had a very strong political undertone. Jahn's gymnastics were designed to promote not just physical fitness, but moral fibre, helping produce patriots who would liberate Germany from Napoleon and unite the Germans in a single state. The gymnastic movement played a prominent part in the German revolution in 1848.

Pictures of Jahn decorated German pubs, taverns, community centres and gyms. On either side of his picture were symbols: on one, his gymnastic cross formed by the first letters of the slogan, *'Frisch, fromm, froh und frei'*: fresh, god-fearing, happy and free; and on the other, the greeting *'Gut Heil'*, hail well. But unlike Arnold, Jahn was seen as a subversive and a demagogue. In 1819 he was arrested, his gymnastics field was closed down and he spent many years in jail. Nevertheless, the gymnastics movement grew and, in 1868, individual local gymnastics clubs were brought together under one umbrella of the *Deutsche Turnerschaft*. After Germany united, and the Kaiser became emperor in 1871, the gymnastic movement became more nationalistic, in support of the state and the imperial powers, working closely with the military leadership. The creation of the German state helped fashion a militaristic ideal and required, it was felt, real men who had physical skill, stamina and strength. The new German man had to be competitive, ready to make sacrifices, and German schools had begun to promote these qualities.

This was not the only way in which the German sporting system was different from the British. The Germans viewed with great distrust the English emphasis on sporting competitions and results, and the setting of records. Intent on physical fitness as part of a collective patriotic will, the Germans saw English-style sporting clubs as expressions of unhealthy egotism and individualism. English-style sporting clubs did develop in Germany nevertheless, and reached a membership of around 400,000 by the start of the First World War in 1914. However, the gymnastic movement had 1.2 million members.

There were many French admirers of the German system, an admiration increased by the Franco-Prussian War. The Prussians, led politically by Bismarck and militarily by Moltke, had crushed the French with spectacular victories in Metz and Sedan. They had occupied Paris and the Kaiser was crowned in Versailles as emperor of the new German state. The French pondered long and hard on their defeat and one of the factors they examined was the gymnastic system. Ironically Bismarck, the architect of the victory, had been taught the *Turnen* gymnastics system at his school and hated it. In his memoirs he complained, 'gymnastics were supposed to be recreation, but during this too the teachers struck us with iron rapiers'. But many Frenchmen admired the achievements of Germans and their system. As Eugene Weber has written, 'everyone knew that the Prussian schoolmaster had been the real winner of Sedan, and, somehow, Father Jahn's gymnastics seemed easier to imitate than the playing fields of Eton'.

But not for Coubertin. Like so many Frenchmen of his generation, he had grown up with the agony of Sedan and the idea of copying the methods of the conqueror of France was unthinkable. In his Olympic memoir he would deny he ever harboured any anti-German feeling, yet Germany always posed a problem for him. At the Congress in Paris, where the foundations of the Olympic movement were laid, Germany only sent an observer. And Germany very nearly did not attend the first modern Olympics of 1896 because of a Coubertin interview which was seen as anti-German. Coubertin had to work extremely hard, claiming the interview was a fabrication before the Germans were placated and sent a team. Coubertin always argued against gymnastics in his various statements over many years, not merely in France, but also on his visits to the United States where the influence of German ideas brought over by migrants threatened to undercut Arnold and the English model. It was on American soil that this Frenchman would emerge as the most brilliant evangelist for Arnold and his English creed.

Coubertin, while still trying to import Arnold into the French lycées, was sent to the United States by the Minister of Public Education in 1889 to examine how Americans and Canadians organized their physical education. Coubertin could not have timed his visit better, for Arnold was under severe attack in America. Coubertin arrived to find himself in the middle of an intense debate about whether the Americans should accept the English way of sport, Jahn's German gymnastics or a rival Swedish gymnastic system developed by Per Hendrick Ling, which laid more emphasis on individual physical capacity. Coubertin may have come to learn, but his first mission was to launch a valiant campaign to make sure the Americans took to his master. The opportunity came over two days in November of that year, at a conference in Boston.

There the cream of American educationalists met to discuss the right kind of physical training for the young. Before Coubertin could preach about Arnold he had to hear some of the most forthright criticism of the British system and praise for the Germans. Dr Hartwell of Johns Hopkins University made it very clear how inferior he thought the British were:

> Gymnastics have been the most popular and general among the most highly trained nations, such as the Greeks of old and the Germans of today. The most athletic and, at the same time, one of the most ill trained of modern nations is the British [. . .] An Englishman believes, and acts upon the belief that you come to do a thing right by doing it, and not by first learning to do it right and then doing it; whereas the Germans leave little or nothing to the rule of thumb, not even in bodily education.

Not that Hartwell had anything against athletics or games. His argument was that it was no mission of educational institutions to 'train up ball-players, carpenters, clerks, or professionals of any kind'. Games as 'pleasurable activity for the sake of recreation' were fine, but gymnastics 'are more comprehensive in their aims, more formal, elaborate, and systematic in their methods, and are more productive of solid results'.

German gymnastics were already established in America. Heinrich Metzner, Principal of the New York Turnverein, participated in the conference. The North American Turnerbund had 30,000 members, its property was valued at over $2 million and included a portfolio of 160 gymnasia and libraries, which housed 53,000 books. The German movement had produced 140 gymnastic teachers and the conference was told that 15,000 boys and 6,000 girls were studying in Turner schools in New York, Boston, Milwaukee, Chicago and St Louis. The Turners were more than just for gymnastics, for as in Germany these schools discussed political, social and ethical questions, taught German language and literature, ran theatres, singing groups, and provided domestic training. Some even had military cadet battalions.

Coubertin listened quietly to the German advocates, and also those in favour of the Swedish system. Then speaking in English – making a joke about a Frenchman speaking bad English – he went on to give his view on why Arnold was the best:

I was asked the other day what, in my opinion, American education was like. I answered in some respects it looked like a battlefield, where English and German ideas were fighting. While I fully acknowledge from the physical point of view, nothing can be said against the German system, I believe, on the other hand, that from the moral and social point of view, no system if so it can be called stands higher than the English athletic sports system, as understood and explained by the greatest of modern teachers, Thomas Arnold of Rugby. His principles are the ones on which was founded last year the French Educational Reform Association [. . .] It is no less than the general reform of secondary education.

Coubertin, as ever, was exaggerating. His French educational reforms had still not been accepted and many questioned that

Arnold should be the guiding light, but Coubertin was ready to take liberties, all the more readily in this new frontier of America.

At the time of this debate among the educationalists, spectator sports were booming in the country. Indeed, for many sports America had pioneered international competitions, many decades before Coubertin sailed there. The New York Yacht Club, set up in 1844, had sent the schooner *America* to Cowes in 1851 where it won a historic race against *Titania*. The victory gave the competition the name the America's Cup and the Americans retained the trophy for a century and a half, the longest winning sequence in any sport.

Cricket had also developed in America. Boston had a cricket club as early as 1809 and the New York Cricket Club won $500 in a match against Toronto in 1840. Four years later, in September 1844, St George's Cricket Club, Bloomingdale Park in New York was the venue for the first cricket international. This 'United States of America versus the British Empire's Canadian Province' match was watched by between 10,000 and 20,000 spectators, who placed around $120,000 worth of bets, with the Canadians winning by 22 runs. English cricket teams regularly visited America, including one led by W. G. Grace in 1872. Baseball was also developing and would soon overtake cricket as America's national pastime. The first Kentucky Derby had been held in 1875. The New York Athletic Club set up in 1876 had helped develop annual athletic competitions. Meanwhile, sports such as rackets, ice-skating, roller-skating, angling, shooting and cycling were all gaining adherents.

Helped by its popularity among college students, rowing had become a big sport in America. In 1869 the first international rowing contest took place when Harvard sent a team to battle Oxford – the Oxford victory on the Thames was witnessed by nearly 100,000 spectators. A few years later, in 1871, the Rowing Association of American Colleges was formed, yet another sign of the growing importance of college sport.

From the late 1860s, Americans had begun to adapt football, borrowing and tinkering with rules developed in England, and the game was growing in popularity. *The Spirit of the Times* had published rugby union rules in 1869. That same year had seen the first intercollegiate game between Princeton and Rutgers, conceived in part to decide who owned a war cannon dating from America's War of Independence. Four years later, Columbia, Yale, Rutgers and Harvard met to discuss the matter of rules and, a year later, a team from McGill in Canada came to Harvard to play. There were two matches, one played according to a mixture of American rules and known as the Boston game. The second was according to Rugby rules. Two years later, led by the Ivy League colleges, Harvard, Princeton, Yale, and joined by Columbia, the Intercollegiate Football Association was set up and adopted the Rugby rules. In the decade before Coubertin arrived, intercollegiate football of the type that the modern world would recognize had got going. By the time he went round the States, it was so well-established that it attracted vast crowds and had extensive coverage in the media. Matches were important social events.

Coubertin watched with interest how old boys kept up their college ties through sport: 'At the same hour, in New York, in Chicago, perhaps in San Francisco six or seven hundred Yankees sit around tables to celebrate gaily, to claim the alma mater, and to sing the old songs [. . .] Each college has its own and it serves to encourage its champions in the regattas, football matches and wherever honour is at stake.'

But Coubertin was also alarmed that the growth of college sport would mark the victory of Germany over his beloved England. John Hopkins University's Dr Hartwell had set up a 'department of athletics', and, aware of his contempt for Arnold and the English system, and love for the Germans, Coubertin railed against it and similar developments at colleges around America:

In the United States [. . .] the directors of gymnasiums [. . .] have a high hand [. . .] choosing among their pupils the strongest and most agile, to the training of whom they exclusively devote them-selves. As a result, during the fair season, the university teams go from competition to competition; crowds press in to see them struggle, enormous sums of money are wagered by their backers and, as soon as the champions give themselves over to this exaggerated athleticism, their comrades keep aloof so as not to interfere with their training [. . .] This is a warning to us not to let physical education take the scientific and authoritarian character that certain theorists [. . .] would like to give it.

This was almost a preview of the American college system that was to prosper and take such firm root in the country. All this suggested that Americans had taken old Brooke's words in *Tom Brown's Schooldays* – 'I'd sooner win two School-house matches running than get the Balliol scholarship'– to a different level. But although Coubertin's attacks on this system were largely futile, his American trip had given him another very important political contact: Teddy Roosevelt.

The feisty American politician had just been beaten in a New York mayoral race and had already begun to display all those virtues of muscular Christianity associated with Thomas Hughes. He had promoted boxing clubs in the poorer quarters of New York, and to make up for his sickly boyhood he had himself taken to manly sports and outdoor adventures. Coubertin would claim great friendship with Roosevelt and exchange correspondence. The letters have never emerged but Coubertin dedicated one of his books to him and in 1905 awarded him the first Olympic diploma. His closeness to the future president may have emboldened Coubertin on his return to France to be far more scathing about the German gymnastic system than he had been in America. Whereas athletic games of the Arnoldian variety provided freedom, he told the French, 'intolerance, on the contrary, is fundamental to German gymnastics, which knows nothing beyond ensemble movements, rigid discipline, perpetual regimentation'. He went on to reassure the French the Americans would never take to the German system because 'it is contrary to the genius of the country'.

Coubertin made other friends in America, in particular William Milligan Sloane, Professor of Philosophy and History at Princeton and son of a pastor and theologian of Scottish origin. Sloane was to be very useful to him in the future. It was not, however, until the Paris Exposition of 1889 that Courbertin first began to think about the Olympic movement. Exhibitions like the Exposition had become very popular ever since Prince Albert organized the Crystal Palace exhibition in 1851: they were essentially trade fairs, which aimed to project the power of the host states. A writer in the *Spectator* had seen the Crystal Palace exhibition as 'this Olympic game of industry, this tournament of commerce', while Horace Greeley called it 'the first-rate cosmopolitan Olympiad of industry'.

For the Exposition of 1889 Coubertin organized physical exercises, which had five sessions. They ranged from the art of horse riding and horsemanship through gymnastics, shooting, rowing, swimming, track and walking, with some sessions combining more than one sport. Although Coubertin had no part in it, a sort of early games was also organized at the Champ de Mars. The *Jeux Olympiques* was intended to be a sporting device bringing the various classes together. From the outset the social aspects of the games were paramount, but also important was the fact that just then Europe was rediscovering ancient Greece. In the 1760s Richard Chandler, fellow of Magdalen College, Oxford, and a member of the Royal Society of Antiquaries, had been to Greece. He went with a book by Pausanias, a second century AD Greek traveller, who had written about the monuments of ancient Greece. This spoke of wrestlers such as Milon of Croton, who had won at wrestling six times at Olympia. Chandler's voyage had helped rediscover the site of the ancient games. In the century that had followed the French had come to Olympia, but it was the Germans, led by Professor Ernst Curtius, who had really excavated the site and this had led to much interest in the ancient games.

Coubertin would later say that ever since his adolescence he had dreamt of Olympia and the games played there, and often thought of rebuilding them and seeing the silhouette rise again.

Here again there was a rivalry with Germany which he expressed quite openly:

> Germany had brought to light what remained of Olympia; why should not France succeed in rebuilding its splendours? It is not far from there to the less dazzling but more practical and fruitful project of reviving the Games, particularly since the hour had struck when international sport seemed destined once again to play its part in the world.

The idea of reviving the Olympic Games was not a new one. Pascal Grousset, an opponent of Coubertin (he felt 'sport was good but should be taken with a French sauce'), had called for the launch of the French Olympic Games. In many other countries, Olympic-style games had been revived. Indeed, the first version of the modern games emerged in Sweden in the 1830s. Professor Gustaf Johann Schartau, of the University of Lund, had, in July 1834, organized the pan-Scandinavian games at Ramlosa. Wrestling, high jump, pole vault, rope climbing, gymnastic exercises and long- and short-distance running featured. Two years later the second Scandinavian Olympic Games were also held in Ramlosa. But that is as far as it went.

Not long after this the English revived the games. In Shropshire, since 1849, an Olympic Games had been organized in Much Wenlock, the setting for A. E. Housman's poem *A Shropshire Lad*. The concept of Dr William Penny Brookes, who in addition to being a surgeon was also a magistrate, these were, probably, the most significant of such sporting events. At Much Wenlock the most important event, and the one Brookes undoubtedly cherished the most, was 'tilting at the rim'. This involved a mounted horseman charging down with his lance and spearing a narrow ring, which hung from a frame. The winner would then kneel down before a well-dressed young lady of Wenlock, and be crowned with a laurel. A picture exists of Brookes in top hat, his chest displaying a row of medals, looking on like a benevolent country squire.

Brookes even reached out to the Greeks, sending a silver decoration and a silver belt clasp to Queen Amalia of Greece. How much this consoled the queen, whose husband was about to lose his throne, is not clear. After King George ascended the Greek throne, he reciprocated by presenting a £10 silver cup as the prize for the Much Wenlock pentathlon. Coubertin visited Shropshire to see the 40-year-old Games in October 1890, and lavished praise on them: 'in Wenlock only something of the past has survived; it's safe to say that the Wenlock people alone have preserved and followed the true Olympian traditions'. In 1860 Brookes launched the Shropshire Olympic Games, held by rotation in Shropshire towns, but their appeal was strictly regional and they never attained a national, let alone international outlook.

The Greeks themselves had tried to revive the Games. Initiated by Evangelis Zappas, a Greek who made money in Romania in trade and financing Greek shipping, the 'Olympian Games' were held in Athens in 1859. This, the first such Olympics in Greece since ancient times, involved jumping over ditches and leather bags, races for 200 metres, 400 metres and 1,500 metres, as well as the discus, javelin and rope climbing. However, the one description of the event suggests it was very far from any modern idea of the Games:

> The 1859 games were held in a square – Place Louis – and in the streets of Athens, as no stadium was available. Confusion and chaos resulted. Although the King and Queen and many dignitaries attended, spectators were trampled on and injured by mounted police trying to keep the streets open for contestants, and athletes were arrested for acting like spectators. Boys and old men entered the competition and actually ran in some of the preliminary heats in order to get through police lines. A blind man presented himself to one of the officials for one of the events, using the opportunity to sing a song to the multitude, for which he was not recompensed. One of the runners dropped dead in a race.

However, Zappas must have been thrilled for, in the tradition of men who make money outside their homeland and want to leave a legacy for the country of their birth, he left his entire fortune to continue the Games. After his death they were held in 1870, 1875 and 1889, although there is some confusion as to whether that was indeed the last year.

It was another seven years before Coubertin was to launch the modern Olympics, and even if he did not originate the idea of an Olympic revival, he cannot be denied the credit for getting it going. The secret of Coubertin's success was his recognition that sport had to be internationalized. He acknowledged that he could not make sport popular in France without contacts between French athletes and those from other countries. As Coubertin put it in a speech in 1892:

> It is clear the telegraph, railways, the telephone, the passionate research in science, congresses and exhibitions have done more for peace than any treaty or diplomatic convention. Well, I hope that athletics will do even more [. . .] let us export runners and fencers; there is a free trade of the future, and on the day when it is introduced within the walls of old Europe the cause of peace would have received a new and mighty stay.

However, while 'everyone applauded' the idea, there was, he confessed later, 'absolute lack of comprehension' about what he wanted to do. So in order to get his way Coubertin decided to indulge in subterfuge. He invited people to a meeting at the Sorbonne where he pretended his first concern was not reviving the Olympics but something entirely different. The invitation to the first Olympic Congress in June 1894 clearly stated that its first aim was to define amateurism. In the invitation, sent on behalf of the French Union of Athletic Sports Clubs, USFSA, Coubertin made it clear that the amateur principle must be defended 'against the spirit of lucre and professionalism that threatens to invade their ranks'. Unless this was done it would 'transform the Olympic athlete into a circus gladiator'. This had become a major problem for many of the sports bodies and Coubertin knew it would attract delegates.

Years later, in his Olympic memoirs Coubertin confessed that he had never been concerned about amateurism. The first part of the invitation was 'a screen to convene the Congress designed to revive the Olympic Games'. Now that he was old and established he could come clean:

> I always showed the necessary enthusiasm, but it was an enthu-siasm without real conviction. My own conception of sport has always been very different from that of a large number – perhaps the majority – of sportsmen. To me, sport was a religion with its church, dogmas, service [. . .] above all a religious feeling, and it seemed to me as childish to make all this depend on whether an athlete received a five franc coin as automatically to consider the parish clergy an unbeliever, because he receives a salary for look-ing after the church.

The deception employed by Coubertin to revive the Olympics was to have a major impact on the movement, particularly in the way it handled amateurism. Half a century after Coubertin wrote those words, his successors found it easy to marry the Olympic Games to Mammon, and still insist that the principles of amateurism had remained intact. As the Games developed in the last decades of the twentieth century, no athlete could hope to obtain a five franc coin or any other coin for winning; their clothes could not carry spon-sors' names and the stadiums carried no advertisements. Yet the athletes knew that success in the Games was a passport to riches. And the Olympics were only possible because of the huge amounts of money brought in by companies keen to sell their products and television channels eager to cover the Games.

In the modern Olympics sponsors are allowed to display their wares, but they are kept well away from where the sporting events take place. They have their own village inside the venue and, outside the sporting arenas, there are several places where they can actively sell their products. So keen are the Olympics to make sure that their sponsors have all the freedom to sell that host cities must sign agreements to provide 'clean cities', meaning that rival companies cannot advertise. There is no 'ambush marketing' and use of anything remotely associated with the word Olympics or its symbols, sych as the five rings, is prohibited unless money has been paid to the organizers of the Games.

Sponsors pay good money to enjoy rights, as the London Games, like all recent Olympics, have demonstrated. So, to buy tickets, the only credit card a purchaser can use is Visa, a sponsor of the Games. On the Sunday of the week the tickets went on sale, the *Observer* ran a story in its business pages headlined 'a Visa card is a must for hopeful punters'. It then went on to explain how those who did not have Visa cards could acquire 'virtual Visa'. Visa's exclusive hold over the Olympics will be further emphasized when the Games begin as, within Olympic venues, it will be the only card accepted. Other sponsors enjoy similar privileges for their products.

Some modern observers consider this a Faustian pact, but one suspects that, had Coubertin been alive today, he would have applauded his successors for tying the knot with money so intricately. He could not have done it better.

It was in the second part of his invitation that he laid out his real aim: 'The revival of the Olympic Games [. . .] in conditions suited to the needs of modern life would bring the representatives of the nations of the world face-to-face every four years, and it may be thought that their peaceful and chivalrous contests would constitute the best of Internationalisms.' As with amateurism, Coubertin knew he had to tread carefully and in sending out this invitation he was quick to declare that he was not proposing a high and mighty role for himself or his organization:

In taking the initiative, which may have such far-reaching results, the Union is not trying to usurp a position of precedence which belongs to no country and to no club in the republic of muscles.

It merely thinks that the clarity of its principles and its attitude, together with the high friendships both in France and abroad upon which it prides itself, justify it in giving the signal for a reform movement the need for which is becoming daily more apparent. It does so in the general interest and without any hidden motive or unworthy ambition.

Coubertin had searched far and wide for people to support his Congress and as always concentrated on well-connected aristo-crats. The Congress was chaired by a French senator and former French ambassador in Berlin, Baron de Courcel. Among the royal patrons were the Prince of Wales, the Crown Prince of Sweden, Grand Duke Vladimir of Russia, Crown Prince Constantine of Greece and the Belgian king. Among the honorary members was Arthur Balfour, a future British prime minister (who coined the name 'lawn tennis'). Coubertin's list also included the director of the American School of Athens, Charles Waldstein, and Dr Brookes.

The 2,000 people that Coubertin attracted to Sorbonne included 78 delegates from 49 societies although they represented just 12 countries: Australia, Belgium, Bohemia, France, Great Britain, Greece, Italy, New Zealand, Russia, Spain, Sweden and the United States. Nearly all these countries were European and the non-Europeans were represented by people of European stock. The Greek representative was probably the most curious. He was Dimitrios Vikelas, who was living in Paris to attend to the mental problems of his wife. A well-known writer and an authority on Byzantine history, he was 62 years of age in 1894 and had shown no interest in sport whatsoever. He described a year later how he came to be associated with the Olympics: in the post one day he received a diploma as a member of the Panhellenic Gymnastic Association. He did not know who these people were but the next day the postman brought a letter from the Association begging him to become the Greek representative at the Congress. This story has a certain fictional quality about it and Vikelas may not have been that surprised or reluctant to be the Greek representative in Sorbonne. What is undeniable is that his presence was to prove very useful for Coubertin.

Coubertin was playing a very deep game here. Among the people gathered at the Sorbonne, many had thought that the first modern Olympic Games should be in London. After all, had Coubertin not sought to convince the French and the rest of the world of the wonders of Arnold and British sport? In his *Olympic Memoirs*, Coubertin says Athens was not part of his original plan for the first modern Olympics, and he only warmed to the idea after several discussions with Vikelas. But the historian David Young, after much research, has suggested it was Coubertin who blocked London. He may have been helped by the fact that Charles Herbert, secretary of the Amateur Athletic Association of Great Britain and the British Empire, who had been invited to the Congress, was not present. So keen was Coubertin to go to Greece, that he sent a telegram to King George, days before the issue was discussed. The Greek king replied, 'Very touched by Baron Coubertin's courteous request, I send him and the members of the Congress, with my sincere thanks, my best wishes for the revival of the Olympic Games. George.' Clearly Coubertin was inviting Greece to host the Games.

On the face of it the idea was absurd. A year before, the Greek prime minister, Harilaos Tricoupis, had declared Greece bankrupt. Vikelas had no mandate from anybody to propose that Athens host the 1896 games and, when he did, he saw it as no more than a talking point rather than a serious proposition. To his surprise, the Congress, marshalled by Coubertin, voted for Athens unanimously. The Congress also agreed that the 1900 Games would be held in Paris. Conditions were laid down as to what could take place in Athens in 1896. The Games would be open only to amateurs, apart from fencing, where professional fencing masters would be allowed to take part. In addition to fencing the sports on display would be track and field, rowing, sailing, swimming, football, tennis, skating, boxing, wrestling, equestrian sports, polo, shooting, gymnastics, cycling and pentathlon.

Coubertin knew that, in proposing the Olympics, he was trying to do something that most sportsmen of his generation abhorred:

One other source of misunderstanding existed among sportsmen themselves: their inability to collaborate between one sport and another. The present generation will never be able to understand how things were at that time. In fact, when you come to think about it, the lack of understanding between sports is hard to explain since all rest on the same foundation of physical well-being and preliminary physical training. Their psychological base is identical. But in the 19th century sportsmen were firmly convinced that the practice of one sport differed from that of another, the two were mutually harmful. A fencer would deteriorate if he were to box. An oarsman should beware of picking up the horizontal bar. As for the horseman of the day the mere idea of running or playing football would have been extremely distasteful to him. There was only tennis, still in its infancy, and swimming that did not arouse any mistrust: the first of the sports was only an elegant pastime, the second a useful accomplishment recommended for reasons of health and safety in the case of accident or lifesaving.

To bring these sports together in a four-yearly festival Coubertin needed an international set-up. This led to the creation of the International Olympic Committee, the first truly international sports body. Coubertin made Vikelas the first president, having introduced the rule that the president must come from the country hosting the Games. Real power lay in his hands as the secretary general.

In his *Olympic Memoirs* Coubertin was very frank about how he set up this most curious of sports bodies. His post of secretary general he described as 'a position of greater interest than most presidencies, for a Secretary General is the kingpin of an active administration'. Since childhood he may have disagreed with his parents about the need for the monarchy to return, being a man who believed in the French Revolution and the democratic republic. But when it came to the IOC he went back to English ideas. Thirty years later he wrote in his Olympic Memoirs: It was a "self recruiting body", like the organising body of the Henley Regatta is [. . .] a committee composed of three concentric circles: a small nucleus of dedicated active members; a "nursery" of willing members, capable of being educated along the right lines; and finally a facade of people, of varying degrees of usefulness, whose presence would serve to satisfy national credentials while lending prestige to the whole.'

Such a body, he said, would be 'permanent in its principle and stable in its composition'.

With the sports movement in its infancy, Coubertin was quick to state how it should develop (in 1909 only Hungary, Sweden, Germany, Bohemia and England had national committees). He argued that 'dictatorial' powers were necessary and decreed that the IOC members of a country could decide which national Olympic committee they would 'recognize'. Yes, he agreed, it was 'draconian', but in giving birth to such a unique movement such steps were necessary. No autocrat could have set out his objectives more clearly.

The IOC has changed over the years, acquiring an executive committee and various commissions, but essentially it remains the body that Coubertin invented in Paris in 1894. It still elects its own members, among which it counts a very large number of aristocrats. While its membership has grown from the original twelve, and now extends beyond its European heartland, it is still hard for a non-European to be elected president; there has been only one, the American Avery Brundage, who became president in 1952. It was conceived as a very select club, a sort of sporting House of Lords, and so it remains.

The Congress readily gave what Coubertin wanted, electing people such as C. Herbert, secretary of the British Amateur Athletics Association, and Lord Ampthill from England, a general from Russia, a colonel from Sweden and a priest, Fr Kemeny, from

Hungary. Many nominees were not even present in the Congress. In his memoirs Coubertin could hardly contain his glee:

> I was allowed a free hand in the choice of members [. . .] Nobody seemed to notice that I had chosen almost exclusively absentee members. As their names figured on the long list of honorary members of the Congress, people were accustomed to seeing their names and readily assumed they were staunch members always at their tasks. I needed elbow room at the start. For many conflicts were bound to rise. Some at any rate would want to seize the helm, either to benefit from the success of the venture or to modify the direction. Such is human nature.

Coubertin wanted to make sure that he alone directed the Olympic movement and many of the presidents who have succeeded him have ensured that this control is preserved. The Olympic Games were to be an expression of sporting democracy, but run by a body very far removed from any such idea.

But if Coubertin was, at best, a benevolent dictator he was an internationalist in the way that the British, despite their invention and codification of sporting rules, just could not be. Coubertin's thinking was in stark contrast to British thinking on international sport at that time.

At the same time as Coubertin's Olympic vision, the British had also begun to think of having a regular international sports event. Reverend John Astley Cooper had come up with the idea of a pan-Britannic festival to celebrate the power and achievements of the British race. Although Cooper did not specifically say that the British race was superior this was implied throughout. As he put it, Britons should be ready to undertake 'action for the benefit of mankind, which may make the name of England to be sung for all time as an example to races yet to come'. He saw athletic competition as a bond that could bind the Empire further together. For Cooper sport was the foundation of Anglo-Saxon greatness. 'Athletic exercises should have a place for, before we are a political or even a commercial and military people, we are a race of keen sportsmen.'

Cooper had always believed in the moral goodness of the British Empire. 'The real secret of the security of the British Empire is that we have acquired it not in the spirit of Hate, or the spirit of Conquest, or the spirit of Greed, but in the genial, good-natured spirit of sport, under which every man must play fair and in which every man gets his chance.' In a letter to *The Times* on 30 October 1891 Cooper made it clear that the games he had in mind were for the adult males of the so-called white dominions, Australia, New Zealand, Canada and South Africa, as well as those living in Great Britain. Cooper was no more of a racist than most of the people around him at that time. His insistence on race and the superiority of the British race was then commonplace. Unlike Coubertin, who could always disguise his real views to get his way, Cooper annoyed the British Amateur Athletic Association by suggesting competitions where the winners would get prize money of great value. He later modified this, offering symbolic trophies which could bring fame and honour to those receiving them. But by then the AAA, which had always seen him as an ideas man not an organizer, was thoroughly fed up with him. Without their support, the other colonial athletics bodies could not be persuaded to back Cooper's plans.

Even then Cooper could have staged his competition in 1893 had he been prepared to go beyond the British Empire. The Americans were holding Chicago's World Fair and offered to stage the first of Cooper's games as part of it. (Offered such an idea, Coubertin would have accepted it like a shot.) James Sullivan of the Amateur Athletic Union of the United States, in offering to stage the games, wrote to Cooper, promising to provide 'one grand carnival comprising all branches of athletics'. Yet Cooper rejected it and in his reply to Sullivan he wrote that his main aim was to have the games in England, 'the cradle of the English-speaking race'. And that could not be served by going to Chicago.

This whole episode illustrated that Cooper could not think out of the British box. Unlike Coubertin, he was imprisoned in his English island fortress.

As it happened Coubertin went to Chicago in the autumn of 1893 and was there for the fair, which also saw many of the world's religious leaders gathered together, including the Hindu monk Swami Vivekananda, who gatecrashed the assembly to speak on Hinduism. Vivekananda, now considered one of India's greatest men, his statue adorning the Gateway of India in Mumbai, would advise his fellow Indians, 'You will be nearer to heaven through football than through the study of the Gita [the Hindu holy book] [. . .] You will understand the Gita better with your biceps, your muscles, a little stronger. You will understand the mighty genius and the mighty strength of Krishna better with a little of strong blood in you.'

Coubertin used his American trip to further his own plans for an Olympic revival. He met William Rainey Harper, a noted American academic who had helped set up the University of Chicago, where he was president, and the meeting led to the award of the 1904 Olympic Games to the city. It demonstrated that one Frenchman's ability to reach out to people, in a way many in British sport just could not, was decisive for world sport.

Cooper was not the only Briton unable to think out of the box. This was true of most of his countrymen. So, in 1896 Great Britain should have been the leading sporting nation in the world, but in fact it had very poor representation. Indeed it came close to missing the first Olympic Games in Athens altogether and in the end only six Britons went, not as representatives of any club, but as pleasure seekers. In Athens they were joined by Australian Edwin Flack, who was a member of the London Athletic Club, and by Mr Bolland, an Oxford man living in the city. He entered the tennis competition, as did two servants who worked at the British Embassy, although certain Englishmen tried to prevent their entry on the grounds of their occupation.

Among the British competitors was G. A. Robertson, an

Oxford man who described himself as a competitor and prize winner. He won nothing in the discus competition but, to the delight of the Greeks at the closing ceremony, he recited in ancient Greek an ode he had composed. Robertson blamed the French organizers for the poor British presence – they sent the publicity material in French and used people without influence in England to promote the event. He did not mention that the British cause was not helped by the fact that its two IOC members, Herbert and Lord Ampthill, did not go to Athens. As a result, the first ever photograph of the IOC membership does not include either man.

But while there may be some merit in Robertson's complaint, what is more revealing is that he considered Coubertin's idea of a level playing field for universal sporting competition anathema:

> They seemed to suppose that the participation of all nations was of equal importance to the success of the game. They did not consider, or if they did, they gave no indication of having done so, that every nation except England and America is still in an absolutely prehistoric condition with regard to athletic sports. Unless England and America took a large share in the Olympic meeting, it was bound to be an athletic failure. In this matter, the committee pursued the suicidal policy of devoting the greater share of attention to Continental athletes. The original programme and book of rules was printed in French [. . .] no edition of the rules was ever issued in English till very shortly before the games when a private firm produced one.

Coubertin had also had to struggle against his fellow countryman who had initially supported him when he brought Arnold's ideas to France, but opposed his revival of the Olympics. Charles Maurras, who would become a royalist and a right-wing nationalist, went to Athens for the 1896 Olympic Games to cover them for *La Gazette de France*. He now denounced Coubertin as a 'zealot' and condemned international sport as an 'anachronism' that was the 'profaning of a glorious name'. Worse still he argued, it led to a tasteless 'mixture of races'.

Not that Coubertin was free of the prevalent assumptions of the racial inferiority of non-white people. Coubertin had been concerned with what was called the 'colonial question' or the 'conquest of Africa' and the January 1912 issue of *The Olympic Review* had discussed 'The role of sport in colonization'. In 1923, at the IOC session held in the main hall of the Capitol in Rome in the presence of the king and queen of Italy, Coubertin launched his thesis of taking sport to Africa:

> And perhaps it may appear premature to introduce the principle of sports competitions into a continent that is behind the times and among peoples still without elementary culture – and particularly presumptuous to expect this expansion to lead to speeding up of the march of civilisation in these countries. Let us think however, for a moment, of what is troubling the African soul. Untapped forces – individual laziness and a sort of collective need for action – a thousand resentments, and a thousand jealousies of the white man and yet, at the same time, the wish to imitate him and thus share his privileges – the conflict between wishing to submit to discipline and to escape from it – and, in the midst of an innocent gentleness that is not without its charm, the sudden outburst of ancestral violence [. . .] Sport has hardened them. It has given them a healthy taste for muscular relaxation and a little of that reasonable fatalism possessed by energetic beings, once their efforts have been accomplished.

In Rome all sorts of ideas were discussed, including an annual African games which Coubertin wanted 'reserved for natives alone'. By this he did not exclude European administration of the games but he did not want European participants. But nearly all of Africa was controlled by the European colonial powers – the Italian Minister of Colonies attended the IOC session – and the colonial delegates wanted European colonists who had lived in

Africa for at least two years also to have their own competitions. Coubertin announced that the first African games would be held in Algiers in 1925, but they were eventually moved back four years and relocated to Alexandria. A fine stadium was built and then, says Coubertin, 'an English political manoeuvre, in which France joined, rendered ineffective all the work done and King Fuad was left to inaugurate the fine stadium at Alexandria discreetly and on a purely local scale'.

Coubertin drew this lesson: 'There was the basic conflict, the struggle of the colonial spirit against the tendency to emancipate the natives, a tendency full of perils as far as the general staffs of the mother country were concerned.' He concluded by saying, 'In spite of everything sport will be organized throughout Africa but perhaps less well than if Europe had been clever enough to take over the running of the movement at the right moment.' His one consolation was that there was at least an 'African medal', one side of which showed 'a black throwing the javelin' and the other side the Latin inscription *Athletae proprium est se ipsum noscere, ducere et vincere*: to know, to govern and to master oneself – the eternal beauty of sport.

It would be unfair to blame Coubertin for failing to rise above the general racial views of that period. He deserves credit for skilfully manipulating the situation to his advantage in reviving the Olympics. Nothing that happened subsequently, including his wretched endorsement of the Nazi Olympics, should take that credit away from him. Finding the Greek government opposed to the Games, he shrewdly allied himself with Crown Prince Constantine. He was aware that the Greek state, which in 1896 was to celebrate its 75th birthday, had a monarchy imported from abroad – Germany. The royal family wanted to establish itself and, for the crown prince, the revival of the Olympics was a very useful tool.

Coubertin also knew how to play politics in Greece. Harilaos Tricoupis, the prime minister, did not want the Games, but his opponent Theodoros Deliyiannis was more sympathetic. 'I had thrown a football between the political teams,' Coubertin would boast later. A cartoon in a Greek paper showed the two politicians in oversized boxing gloves, slugging it out over the question of the Olympics. In the run up to the Games, Greece went to the polls, and Deliyiannis won. Although the Olympics was not the main issue, his victory helped Coubertin and even if there was no government money offered to the event, Greeks who had made money overseas, in particular George Averoff, were ready to help. Averoff funded the reconstruction of the old Panathenaic stadium. All this enabled the modern Olympics to get started, although there must have been moments when Coubertin wished he had not been involved. During and after the Games he was ignored by the Greeks, given no thanks and then they proposed to try to steal the Games from him by saying they should be based permanently in Greece.

In the face of such opposition Coubertin resisted, and demanded that the 1900 Games be in Paris and the 1904 in America. Both events, however, were little short of disasters. Coubertin tied the Paris Games to the Fifth Universal Exposition, but he could not overcome rivalries within French sport. Such was the lack of organization and lack of suitable officials that there were some of the most bizarre moments of the modern Olympics. The 1896 discus champion threw all his three throws into the crowd. Some of the competitors, even the winners, did not even know that they were at the Olympics.

The 1904 Games in St Louis were even worse. At the last minute, at the request of President Roosevelt, who was also president of the US Olympic Committee, the Games were moved from Chicago to St Louis. This was to make them part of the World's Fair being held to celebrate the centenary of the Louisiana Purchase. Very few people travelled to the Games; 85 per cent of the competitors were from the States and the US won 84 per cent of the medals. The marathon was won by Fred Lorz, who left the stadium first and returned first and then it was revealed that, for part of the way, he had a lift in a car.

The Games also had Anthropology Days during which competitions mimicking the Olympics were held for blacks, American

Indians, African pygmies, Patagonians, Ainus from Japan and even Turks and Syrians. The Paris Games had run from 20 May to 28 October; the St Louis Games stretched from 1 July to 23 November. Coubertin was glad he had not gone to America: 'The St Louis Games were completely lacking in attraction. Personally I had no wish to attend them.' He had not warmed to the town when he first went there and the Anthropology Days horrified him.

The Olympic Games in the years to come would produce other horrors and Coubertin's biographer, John J. MacAloon, describes his end, which came in September 1937 at the age of 74, in a Geneva park, his money gone, his personal life in disarray, 'marginal and alone'. Before his burial in Lausanne, at his request his heart was cut out and taken to be buried in Olympia, a symbol of Coubertin's intense desire to associate with the past he had brought back to life.

If all this sounds desolate, nothing can deny Coubertin the credit for taking an idea that he had read in a fictional book and using it to fashion an international movement that has not only survived, but adapted and prospered. This was something beyond his contemporaries who had neither the vision to conceive of such a project, nor the determination to implement it.

CHAPTER 3

THE TWO F'S THAT BRITAIN GAVE THE WORLD

In 1965, two years before the British left Aden, Sir Richard Turnbull, the penultimate governor, told Denis Healey, then Labour's defence secretary, that 'when the British Empire finally sank beneath the waves of history, it left behind it only two monuments. One was the game of association football, the other was the expression, "Fuck off".'

Turnbull was being unkind to the imperialists. They took more sports than football around the world, and took them to many places that were never coloured pink on the map. Indeed, they proved to be better sporting exporters than rival empires, including the empire that had a much longer head start and had controlled a far larger territory than the British.

The American historian Claudio Veliz explained in 1994, in his polemical book *The New World of the Gothic Fox*, why the English legacy in North America has been so much more powerful and productive than the Spanish legacy in South America:

The Spanish Empire was the richest, largest and most formidable since the Romans; it was ruled by monarchs, not renowned for diffidence who, in common with their subjects, seldom entertained doubts about the worth of their religion, manners, language, morals or domestic habits. It was also an empire remarkably well served by creative talents of a people who from the sixteenth century onwards, almost without pause, even in the darkest period of decline, astonished with the originality and excellence of their literary and artistic productions And yet, how difficult it is to discover cultural traits and artificats of Spanish origin that succeeded in gaining universal acceptance [. . .] there is a striking contrast with an English Industrial Revolution that from its very beginning exhibited a notable capacity to generate cultural forms that proved effortlessly acceptable virtually everywhere, even in places where no one had ever seen an English missionary or heard of the British Empire.

The question is all the more pertinent because in the sixteenth and seventeenth centuries Spain and its Indies were a global power, while English North America was little more than scattered settlements. But those scattered settlements turned into a modern superpower while Spanish Latin America was racked by misgovernment, neo-colonial dependency and serial economic collapse, from which it has only recently begun to emerge.

Borrowing Isaiah Berlin's analogy of foxes and hedgehogs, Claudio Veliz sees the British fox outwitting the Spanish hedgehogs, bringing a stubborn ability to thrive on diversity and change, forged by the Industrial Revolution and reflected in their muscular Gothic style. Sport plays a role in Veliz's thesis in which Arnold, Hughes and *Tom Brown's Schooldays* all figure, as does the myth of Webb Ellis and rugby. Veliz quotes the German writer Agnes Bain Stiven, who wrote in 1936 that English sporting terms had became 'the common possession of all nations in the same way as Italian technical terms in the field of music'. Veliz also observes shrewdly that the British popularization of games changed the way the world dressed

Sporting activities are probably the single most important influence in the determination of everyday contemporary sartorial usage. Before the Second World War, whether in the fabled Little Lord Fauntleroy attire or the ubiquitous sailor suit, little children would dress like adults; today we live in a world in which very large numbers of adults are happy to go about dressed like little children, and the explanatory linkage is invariably the popularity of a sporting activity. Even a cursory observation of a large assemblage of people in any Western country will show that many of the articles of clothing worn by most of these present owe their shape, colour and occasionally their very existence to one or another sport invented, modified or popularised by the English speaking peoples.

Veliz's book was not the first to recognize the power of British sport. J. A. Hobson, in his 1902 book *Imperialism*, a work which had a vital influence on Lenin, said, 'The leisured classes in Great Britain, having most of their energy liberated from the necessity of work, naturally specialise on "sport".' Lenin, evidently, took on board Hobson's view that sport like football was a 'sham' or 'artificial' substitute for the animal passion in humans for blood sports.

From the opposite side of the political spectrum, many other contemporary writers, including eminent sportsmen such as C. B. Fry, extolled sport as a projection of British power. In a much-quoted passage, J. E. C. Weldon, headmaster of Harrow school from 1881 to 1895, declared: 'Englishmen are not superior to Frenchmen or Germans in brains or industry or in the science or apparatus of war.' Instead, their dominance derived from 'the health and temper which games impart [. . .] the pluck, the energy, the perseverance, the good temper, the self-control, the discipline, the co-operation, the *esprit de corps*, which merit success in cricket and football [. . .] the very qualities which win the day in peace and war.'

For over a hundred years many other writers, not exclusively Marxist, have traced links between British sport and imperialism. The thesis has been that the British spread their sport around the world in a very deliberate fashion, using it as a leadership and character-building tool and also to assert and enhance British political, commercial and cultural power.

But it simply did not happen that way. The British at the height of their power would joke that their Indian empire was acquired in a fit of absentmindedness. The spread of sport was even less well thought out. British sports were transmitted overseas in a haphazard way and with no deliberate agenda. During the Victorian age, millions of British people moved overseas as colonists and settlers, as soldiers and sailors, as workers, managers and entrepreneurs. They wanted to go on playing the sports they enjoyed at home. At first they did this by kickabouts and pick-up matches, but expatriate Britons with money, power and time quickly established clubs where land could be permanently adapted to play the required sport – particularly cricket, the British sport which had greatest need of enclosed, dedicated outdoor space.

Some of these British sports fell both literally and figuratively on fertile soil overseas. They proved to be well adapted to various climates and terrains and popular with a significant number of local players, particularly those from elite classes who could make them fashionable. In many places, far from seeking to evangelize British sports among the natives, the British actually excluded them from their clubs and teams. This often made these sports even more fashionable to local elites, who formed their own organizations in order to play them.

The success of British sport overseas was more fashioned by the local response than by British policy. British rule induced some occupied peoples to revive traditional local sports, as in Ireland. But many other communities that rejected direct importation of British sports nonetheless borrowed from them, as in the United States, where the new local sport of American football was a descendant of rugby.

Other countries embraced British sports eagerly, as the Low Countries, Switzerland and Scandinavia took to soccer. Still others took up British sports specifically to surpass the British (New Zealand and rugby union, India and hockey). Australians adopted all three responses to football: they invented their own version, they out-performed the British at both forms of rugby, and turned their backs on soccer until modern times when non-British European immigrants gave it a new social base. Indeed, it is striking that soccer – the most successful British sporting global export – was least successful in the British Empire and the English-speaking world. The imperial agenda and bonds of culture and language were not strong enough to prevail over local preferences for other sports. It is also striking that so many of the early successful promoters of soccer were Swiss – representatives of the least imperial-minded advanced nation in the world.

The British style of promoting new sports overseas was also in contrast to that of the Americans. While the Americans were systematic, with strong commercial or religious and social motives, the British introduced sport in an unplanned, random way, and with no consistent motives except to find pleasant ways of passing the time. This explains why, despite the fact that they invented most modern sport (or perhaps because of it), the British were always reluctant to become involved in international sporting organizations and competitions. This pattern was established before the First World War and lingered for around forty years. Instead, British sport spread overseas through individuals with eclectic backgrounds and motives. Imperialism played a very little part; the pursuit of money was more important. George Parr, the cricket pioneer, was a wonderful example of this.

The first of the teams organized by George Parr, captain of the All-England cricket XI and Nottinghamshire in the 1850s, foreshadowed by a century the Australian Kerry Packer's circus of cricket mercenaries. They travelled England playing matches to make money, often against the odds. In the late 1850s their monopoly over England's finest players was challenged by several breakaway groups, and their receipts began to dwindle. By 1859, Parr was looking for new markets and this led him to organize England's first major sporting tour overseas, taking twelve of England's finest players to Canada and the United States aboard the SS *Nova Scotia*. They included John Wisden, who would become famous for his Almanack, and John Lillywhite, later to promote a more famous cricket tour and found a specialist sports goods store.

Parr did not go as an evangelist or an imperialist. He set up his tour to make money, because he thought there would be a paying public for matches against his team. He had good reason for this: cricket was well established in North America, and years ahead of England's first Test match in 1877 the United States and Canada had played cricket's first international, in Hoboken, New Jersey. Parr's team obtained substantial guarantees in advance: £750 from the Montreal Club, 75 per cent of receipts from Cincinnati Cricket Club, a special concession for Lillywhite to sell cricket cards, and two free trips to Niagara Falls. Parr's side played six matches (all against 22 players) in Montreal, Hoboken, Philadelphia, Hamilton, Ontario, and Rochester, New York, and three exhibition matches. They won them all handsomely and earnt over $5,000 from the tour, not including any winnings from betting.

Two years later, and for the same commercial motives, Parr took the first English touring party to Australia. He had a guarantee from the Café de Paris of Melbourne, a case of cricket taking over when a literary tour, by Charles Dickens, failed to materialize. This prompted Parr to offer a talented amateur cricketer guaranteed expenses of £500. The amateur player was E. M. Grace. On later tours his brother W. G. was able to extort even more.

At that stage it seemed that cricket would be the great British sporting export. Having begun in the forest of the Weald with a curved piece of wood as bat and a sheep-pen hurdle as wicket, it had fought off the claims of more popular village football, coming into prominence during Queen Anne's reign (1702–14). In late-Victorian England the great cricketer W. G. Grace became a national icon and cemented the hold of cricket over British society, which it mirrored in many ways.

Cricket was – and is – a finely structured game. The batsmen are the natural leaders, the bowlers the toiling middle classes, the fielders very much plebeian. Each has his own appointed place, each his own specific task, and yet players are also called on to perform outside their allotted roles. This is a fair image of traditional British society: hierarchical, but fluid enough to give people opportunity to change their station in life. The hierarchy of cricket was enshrined in the distinction made between gentlemen and players – a distinction long considered to be fundamental to the character of the game. The removal of this distinction in 1963 is even today resented by many in England, who claim that it led to a decline in quality. The professional was the man who played for money; his competence was unquestioned – he was often conceded to be more skilful than the amateur – but skill alone has never been the supreme criterion for cricket affection. The amateur represented virtues that were said to have made Britain great. He played not for money, but for the love he had for the game, the pleasures he derived, the enjoyment he gave, and his duty to serve others. This had the feel of the Arnoldian spirit.

The most remarkable feature of cricket is the system of appealing. In no other game is a decision by an official made only if one of the participants in the game appeals. A footballer can appeal for all his worth for a penalty, but it makes no difference to a referee's decision – indeed it could earn him a booking or, if he is particularly vociferous, a sending-off. But in cricket almost all decisions for the fielding side (except the very obvious as when a batsman is bowled) require a formal appeal to an umpire from bowler or fielders. Otherwise the umpire does not give a decision and a batsman who would have faced dismissal can continue batting. The appeal system assumes a certain shared set of values between the batting and bowling sides, especially fairness: the fielding side will not make false claims and the batsmen will not try to deceive or influence umpires. In football it is common to see players try to cheat, move the ball a few yards nearer the opposing goal when they win a throw or a free kick, claim a corner when it has come off their own boot, and congratulate their team mate who has won a penalty even if he has done so by pretending to be fouled in the penalty box.

Appealing has led to disagreements between English and Asian cricketers. The English often feel that Asians do not understand the delicate mechanism of this aspect of the game, and appeal needlessly, bringing rancour where there should be polite inquiry. But the appeal system itself remains a triumph of English values – demonstrated whenever Asians (whose mother tongue is rarely English) appeal in the universal English formula: 'Owzat?' Nothing could better illustrate that there is a certain underlying moral principle.

This was most dramatically demonstrated on the Sunday of the Trent Bridge Test between England and India in July 2011. It was as if the Indian team had *Tom Brown's Schooldays* by their bedside. Just before tea the Indians had successfully appealed for a run out against England's Ian Bell. The Indians were well within the laws to claim the decision. Bell did not dispute that, admitting he had made a mistake. Except that the poor Englishman had only sauntered out of his crease, thinking the game had come to an end for tea and was heading for a cuppa. After a plea by the England captain and coach, the Indians accepted that, while they were technically correct, they had violated cricket's moral code. They allowed Bell to resume. It was to prove a dramatic decision as England went on to thrash India. Such sporting gestures would not be unknown in golf, which also values honesty, but that is an individual not a team sport.

The cricket authorities were quick to hail the Indian decision as proof that, even in an age where sport is so corrupted, the cherished spirit of the game survives. So impressed were those who run international cricket that, at the end of the season awards ceremony, the Indians won the Spirt of Cricket Award. Not everyone in cricket, including many Indians, approved. While the older Indian cricketers, part of a generation that grew up in India immediately after independence, were in favour, the younger Indians felt the Indian captain, Mahendra Singh Dhoni, in acting as a cricketing equivalent of Mahatma Gandhi, showed weakness not strength. But the incident and the debate it generated also proved that, even at the highest level, in cricket there is still a premium on honesty.

Nevertheless in the 1890s, as a game, cricket was too complicated and its organizers not interested in popularizing it. Instead, association football carried the British sporting flag. Many football historians suggest the same basic factors behind its global success: simplicity of scoring, cheapness of equipment, the ability to play a basic form of the game instantly on all manner of terrain. They also point to economic and social factors which accelerated the game's development in favourable locations, notably the existence of an urban working class with the money, leisure time and transport facilities to provide a base of paying spectators. More than any other factor, this ensured that soccer broke out of its initial enclaves within an Anglophile elite and became a sport for the masses.

All of these factors applied in the British Empire and the English-speaking world, which also had more British soldiers, sailors and settlers actually playing the game than in countries not ruled by Britain. Yet the British Empire and the United States are the environments where soccer had its greatest failures and remains to this day a minority sport, while foreign countries, such as Brazil, Argentina and even Spain, now dominate the sport that the British first taught them.

This apparent paradox demonstrates the power of local conditions to shape the destiny of sport. Essentially, the United States and the nations of the British Empire took up sports that suited them better than association football, many of their own invention. American football was developed in the elite East Coast universities in the 1860s and 1870s. Soccer began as the favoured version, but Harvard held out for its own idiosyncratic mixture of soccer and rugby union, and the latter became popular when introduced by McGill University, from Montreal. But the Americans enjoyed their freedom to experiment, and went on changing the rules for about three decades. The leading figure on the rules committee, Walter Camp from Yale, exulted in the absence of British public schoolboys who knew how the game should be played: 'While the Englishman had a school where the traditions of what was allowed and what was forbidden in football were as fixed and unalterable as the laws of the Medes and Persians, the American player had nothing but the *lex scripta* to guide him, and no old player to whom to refer disputed points.'

The innovations by Camp and his colleagues – notably the system of 'downs' and the replacement of the scrum by the scrimmage – made the game more exciting and spectatorship grew eight-fold between 1876 and 1893, rising even more dramatically after 1906 when the forward pass was legalized. American football virtually drove out rugby union and pushed soccer to a marginal status, where it was further squeezed by the growth of baseball and basketball, and also by the ineptitude and factionalism of its professional organizers. Only recently has soccer been rescued from that status, largely by American mothers who prefer their sons to play a sport that costs less in terms of equipment and injury than American football.

Canada also invented a sport that suited them better than soccer: ice hockey, which thrived in frozen conditions instead of having to shut down. The Canadians also successfully adapted a sport from their indigenous populations: lacrosse. In Ireland, Britain's first colony and the most reluctant member of the British Empire, Gaelic football was seen as a nationalist symbol and promoted as a separatists' sport. However, not only was rugby played, but to this day the Irish rugby team unites the southern republic with its northern, British-aligned, neighbour in a remarkable case of a unified sporting team that has survived many years of violent intercommunal conflict. Indeed rugby players from the Irish Republic even tour abroad as the British Lions, as if all of Ireland was still part of a British nation.

New Zealand, which was settled later than most of the other 'white dominions', had the chance to examine the evolution of soccer and rugby union in Britain. They decided quickly that as a small country they would have no chance of beating the home country in a professional sport, but that training and technical innovation could give them a chance in amateur rugby union. This theory was triumphantly vindicated by the all-conquering All Black side in 1905, which established the paramountcy of rugby union. New Zealand soccer staggered on and teams competed for the Brown Shield (devised by a Glaswegian rugby merchant) from 1891, although it took over thirty years before anyone created an actual trophy to go with it.

In South Africa, soccer became popular with white working-class settlers, not only from Britain, but also from Greece and Portugal, and with urban Africans. This base of support ensured that it would fall victim to racial and national politics in South Africa. The Boers rejected soccer as a sport for foreigners (even though it was already popular in their mother country of the Netherlands), the English white elite felt that soccer was working-class and both groups were afraid of a sport that attracted black people. The English white elite turned to rugby union: as in New Zealand they were encouraged by a victorious tour of England, in 1912.

Australia had the distinction of inventing and codifying its own form of football several years before the English sat down to agree the rules of soccer. Remarkably, the leading figure in the invention of Australian Rules football was an old Rugbeian, Thomas Wentworth Mills, who had played the school's version of football with success. When he returned to Australia in 1857 he tried to persuade his friends in the Melbourne Cricket Club to take up a winter game to keep fit. But he rejected his old school's version: it created too much risk of injury on hard Australian grounds and it was 'unsuitable for grown men engaged in making a living'. This, of course, was the total antithesis of the English amateur spirit. Mills was thinking like an Australian. He and his committee studied all the other English school versions of football and Mills himself was almost certainly influenced by the Aboriginal game of Marn Grook.

The end-product of all their deliberations was Australian Rules football – a game specifically created for Australians to play and enjoy. They did a very good job: the rules were simple and easily understood, the play rapid and dramatic and well adapted to rough gum-tree fields. It spread with spectacular success through Victoria, South Australia and Tasmania and although other parts of Australia took to both forms of rugby, Australian Rules became a source of national identity. In 1906, only a few years after Australia became a federation, the Australasian Football Council chose to promote it under the slogan 'one flag, one destiny, one football game', with all matches to be played under an Australian flag and using only an Australian-made ball.

One reason why in some ways British sport often spread more extensively outside the British Empire was, curiously, because of the nature of British power and how it was exercised. Nothing illustrates this better than *Sporting Memories: My Life as a Gloucestershire County Cricketer, Rugby and Hockey Player and Member of the Indian Police Service,* by Major W. Troup. The book, exploring sport and society in India and Britain between the 1880s and the 1920s, is such a rare gem that when I came across it at the London Library I had to sign a special agreement to borrow the book, the main terms of which were that I should not put it in a bag with foodstuffs or leave it on the floor.

Published in 1924, as the title makes clear it recalls Troup's life in sport, playing county cricket for Gloucestershire with W. G. Grace, as a rugby reserve for England, and playing hockey and many other sports in India while serving in the Indian Police Service. He arrived in India in 1888 and worked there, with long breaks back in England when he played county cricket, until the opening decades of the twentieth century. There is little doubt he loved his time in India but had a very poor opinion of the 'natives'. As Troup put it, 'Bribery amongst them is an inherited vice, and try as hard as he can, the European police official will never entirely stamp it out – it can't be done.'

Troup played in some of the most important hockey tournaments in India, sometimes against Indian players, but he could not stomach the idea of having Indians as members of clubs. When in 1908 he was transferred to Agra there was the question of allowing Indians who held the King's Commission in the Indian Army to become members of the Agra club. The British objected and Troup agreed with his fellow Brits. 'However decent a native may be, his ways and ideas and manners are not ours, they never can and never will blend, and to quote a hackneyed phrase, but none the less appropriate expression, "Familiarity breeds contempt".'

The Arnoldian idea may have been that sport breaks down barriers but the limitation of using sport in India to do that was perfectly illustrated when Troup and a fellow Brit called Ropeland went to watch a police team play an Ajmer side in a hockey match:

> It was terrifically hot, and getting tired of standing, we wandered around to try and find a seat. All of those in our immediate vicinity were 'full up', and after a time we came across a native with a big form [bench] all to himself. Ropeland asked him to move up in Hindustani, whereupon the fellow insolently replied, 'When you speak to me in a language you understand – namely English – I will comply with your request.' The seat was vacated alright, in about half a second.'

Troup does not feel the need to describe how this was done; clearly the threat of force by these two Englishmen frightened the Indian, and it indicates how, even as the Indians took to British sport, it was made clear to them that there were barriers beyond which they could not go.

Some British rulers, like the Viceroy Lord Curzon, encouraged Indian princes to take to sport as a way of learning British values. In an address to the Indian college where Ranjitsinhji, the great cricketer, had been educated, Curzon said, 'learn the English language and become sufficiently familiar with English customs, literature, science, modes of thought, standards of truth and honour and [. . .] with manly sports and games.'

The spread of British sport often depended on individuals, such as the headmaster Reverend Cecil Tyndale-Briscoe. Faced with a revolt against soccer from his Kashmiri Brahmin pupils because of their strict religious rules about using a leather ball, he had them surrounded on the pitch by masters with sticks who beat them until they kicked the ball.

However, Curzon's agenda made no difference to India's newly trained sportsmen after school. The British continued to exclude Indians from their sporting clubs and they refused to yield any space for Indians to play sport. The unintended consequence of Curzon's policy was to create new classes of Indians who enjoyed playing British sports – or wanted to play them as a mark of education and acceptance – but had no opportunity to do so unless they formed their own clubs and organizations. Indian hockey players for example were accidental beneficiaries of exclusion from the crack British clubs. Forced to play on irregular baked mud surfaces instead of manicured fields, they learnt the stick techniques and ability to control the ball that gave India years of ascendancy in the sport.

Indian cricketers and footballers had to fight hard for space and recognition and their early years are marked by hugely symbolic battles and dramatic victories which fed self-esteem and nationalist feeling. India's Parsee community led the development of Indian cricket. An entrepreneurial, modern-minded community, they had fled to India from Persia in the seventh century when it fell to Islam. The local Indian ruler allowed them in provided they did not intermarry or propagate their religion and for the next millennium they hardly figured in Indian history. British rule was to see the Parsees emerge as a strong, vibrant community, seeing themselves as interlopers in India much as the British did. Their base was western India, centred on Bombay, and they were always proud to advertise their loyalty to the British Crown.

But with the British determined to maintain a form of apartheid against the Indians, even the Parsees, the locals were forced to fight for their right to play cricket. The Parsees led the protests in 1881 when the European-only Bombay Gymkhana tried to take over even more of the cramped space for Indian cricketers in order to exercise polo ponies. The Parsees, having endured years of condescending remarks from British critics, organized two ambitious tours of England, discovered the first great Indian cricketer, Mehellasha Pavri, and, most importantly, started beating English teams both in England and India. The biggest scalp was Lord Hawke's touring side of 1892–3 – all first-class players, including F. S. Jackson, a future Test match star and Governor of Bengal. The Parsee success inspired the Hindus and the Muslims to become involved in cricket. From then on, Indian cricket was essentially in Indian hands: the British could use patronage to reward their favourites, but not to alter the game's basic patterns.

One important consequence was that Indian cricket developed in a remarkable and almost unique way: religious teams competing against each other. The British had always stressed that India was not a nation, Winston Churchill famously saying the equator might as well be called a nation. To prove their assertion, they pointed to how the different religious groups, particularly the Hindus and Muslims, had fought each other. The Indian army set up by the British was organized along religious and caste lines. The British argued that this reflected Indian conditions, but it also served to emphasize that India was far too divided ever to be ruled by anyone other than a foreign power. However, now on Bombay's cricket fields, teams organized along religious, even race, lines played against each other in a tournament that helped Bombay become the centre of Indian cricket.

Starting in 1877 as a match between the Bombay Gymkhana, a club open only to Europeans, and the Parsees of the Zoroastrian Cricket Club, it developed over the years. The first Triangular tournament – Europeans, Parsees and Hindus took place in 1907. The tournament went through various name changes before assuming its final form, the Bombay Pentangular.

Observe that Parsees and Hindus represented different religions, the Europeans a distinct racial group. The British in India had always classified themselves as Europeans. So in their clubs and other places, notices barring Indians read not 'British only', but 'Europeans only'. In this way the British emphasized that they were a particular racial subgroup, all the more important as their rule was based on European supremacy over all other races. So, on the cricket fields of India they were called not British, but Europeans. They might have described themselves as Christians, but they were European Christians and they did not want to play in the tournament alongside the brown variety of Indian Christians. Eventually a non-British 'Rest' team was formed, in which Indian Christians and a few minority Jews joined the tournament.

A star of this assorted team was India's leading Christian cricketer, Vijay Samuel Hazare, who, long after this form of religious cricket was history, led India to her first ever Test victory against England in 1952. (In later years after the religious tournaments had ended few Indians knew Hazare was Christian as he was always known by his first name, Vijay, a Sanskrit word meaning victory.) In his memoir *A Long Innings* Hazare describes his pleasure at beating the European variety of Christians in the 1940s. 'My side, the Rest, clashed against the Europeans. As if to punish them for keeping us out of the tournament so long, we thrashed them, totalling over 400. I scored my first century in the carnival when I made 182 against them, and but for dropped catches we could have won by an innings.'

Since the Indians were not allowed in British clubs, they set up their own with the help of the local government. Two miles from the European-only Bombay Gymkhana, the government provided land along Bombay's water front, the Kennedy Sea Face, and here emerged gymkhanas catering for the different religious communities: Parsees, Hindus, Muslims, Catholics. These still exist, an amazing testimony to India's remarkable religious discovery of cricket.

Within this religious cricket battle there was also scope for significant social change. One of the Hindu cricketers was Palwankar Baloo, not only a great spinner, but from the so-called 'untouchable' class that higher-caste Hindus had, for centuries, treated as almost subhuman. Through cricket he could make a small dent in this caste-iron curtain. And after he retired from cricket he took to politics and came close to defeating B. R. Ambedkar, like him an untouchable. For many years the two men had formed a mutual admiration society: Baloo the cricketer breaking barriers, Ambedkar overcoming age-old prejudices to become a distinguished lawyer. But in 1937 they stood against each other for provincial elections held as part of a British plan to give Indians limited rights to rule themselves. Baloo lost. Ambedkar was to become the great leader of the community and after India secured its freedom in 1947 he helped to write the Indian constitution.

By 1912 Muslims had joined in the religious/racial cricket matches and neither the First World War nor Gandhi's campaign against the British stopped these games. The 1921 visit of the Prince of Wales to Bombay was marked by fierce protests by Indians opposed to British rule. But after the riots had ended, the match between Parsees and Europeans took place at the Bombay Gymkhana. The Prince attended and was cheered by the Europeans: he did not stay long enough to see the Parsees win.

The tournament also saw a cricketing innovation: the introduction of neutral umpires in the game for the first time. Initially, only Europeans umpired in the matches, as the British argued that Indians could not be trusted with such a delicate role. When in 2002 Bollywood finally made a film about cricket, *Lagaan,* a match between the English and Indians set in the nineteenth century, both umpires were English. The film uses cricket to show how Indians opposed the British – yet in the final scene the Indians' victory is made possible only because one of the English umpires gives a decision against the English team. The scene demonstrated how, even for modern Indians, the principle of fair play enshrined in cricket overrode any nationalist considerations.

The Bombay religious model was exported to other parts of India including Lahore, Nagpur and Karachi, boosting the growth of the game. Questions about the religious nature of such cricket and the damage it might be doing to the community, given the growing religious strife in the country, began to be raised in the 1940s, even though supporters said matches were played without any rancour Gandhi, who usually took little interest in sport, suddenly intervened and wanted such matches to be stopped.

Even before his call, however, others had sought the end of such matches, not so much because they were religious, but because other more lucrative forms of cricket were developing. However, such was the hold of the religious tournament that it lasted another six years. The final tournament was played in 1946, a year before India won its freedom and the country was partitioned and the Muslim state of Pakistan created. Yet, for many in Bombay, affection for this religious cricket remained undimmed. For them it was proof that, on the cricket field, a team from one religion, or even a racial group, could play another in perfect harmony. The idea may seem absurd today, but its supporters remained convinced that, in Indian cricket at that time, it worked and benefited the game. If this was a brilliant example of the lack of any central plan for the export of British sport, and the influence of local conditions, the contrast in the lives of the two great writers of the empire illustrates this even better.

C. L. R. James and Nirad Chaudhuri were born within years of each other, at other ends of the world, in small semi-rural areas. They would die within a few years of each other in England: James in a Brixton flat, Chaudhuri in Oxford. Their only common bond was that they were shaped by the British Empire. Chaudhuri, four years older, was born in 1897, the year Victoria celebrated her diamond jubilee, in Kishorganj, a small country town in east Bengal composed of tin and mud huts or sheds. James was born in 1901 more than 9,000 miles away in Tunapuna in Trinidad, a town of 3,000 people in the country's sugar-growing region.

In adulthood both left their unremarkable birthplaces for the nearest big city: Chaudhuri to Kolkata, James to Port of Spain. In time they would travel much further, James spending many years in the US before both settled down in England in a final homage to the empire that had made them and about which they wrote incessantly.

The conventional view is that James was the Marxist who fought the empire, Chaudhuri the apologist who mourned the departure of the British from India. Yet examine their writings in detail and a very different picture emerges, one that also tells us much about the way British values, including sport, spread and shaped colonial society. Chaudhuri, the so-called empire's poodle, was much the most trenchant critic of the British, being particularly severe on those who ran the empire. James, the Marxist, hardly had a harsh word to say about the British.

James's *Beyond A Boundary* describes how his love for cricket and English literature was very similar to that of boys in ancient Greece who combined poetry and games:

> If for them games and poetry were ennobled by their roots in religion, my sense of conduct and morals came from my two, or rather my twin, preoccupations, and I suspect that it was not too different with a Greek boy [. . .] The Greek lamp burns today as steadily as ever. They who laid the intellectual foundations of the Western world were the most fanatical players and organizers of games the world has ever known.

James notes that the ancient Greeks treated sports very seriously. For all the incessant fights between the Greek states, every four years a truce was called to stage the Olympics. James urged his readers to follow the ideals of the ancient Greeks, to take athletic activity seriously and honour athletes. It is sheer intellectual snobbery, he says, to disregard the achievements of men such as W. G. Grace, George Headley, one of the greatest West Indian batsmen, or Don Bradman. Their cricketing achievements were not mere sporting matters and extended beyond the cricket field.

James was highly taken by the idea of being the heir to Greek civilization. He even suggests that we will be able to answer

Tolstoy's question of what art is, 'only when we learn to integrate our vision of Walcott on the backfoot through the covers with the outstretched arm of the Olympic Apollo'.

As he burnished the myth of Greek sport James was keen to create another myth of an English sporting Eden where the whole world was welcome. Where did James get this view of English sports? His inspiration is clear. James refers to it again and again – the belief in the English public-school code. 'I learnt and obeyed and taught a code, the English public-school code, Britain and her colonies and the colonial peoples. What do the British people know of what they have done there? Precious little. The colonial peoples, particularly West Indians, scarcely know themselves as yet.'

Of course James was aware of the racial situation in the West Indies or what he calls the 'national question': the question of West Indian self-government and the formation of a West Indies Federation. But in school these things did not matter. James, in any case, was much taken by individual English men who may have been politically reactionary or even chauvinistic, but were personally kind and tolerant. All this made James think that they were following the right policy even if they could not at times help being partial to the white boy in the class in preference to him. And just as he saw the school as a bulwark against the world where he was to receive hard knocks, he saw the English world of sports as a bulwark against the reality of life.

Interestingly, the Nobel prize-winning writer V. S. Naipaul, in reviewing *Beyond a Boundary*, was one of the few to pick up James's references to the code of the English public school and commented, 'twenty years ago the colonial who wrote those words might have been judged to be angling for an MBE or OBE'.

Now contrast James with Chaudhuri. During his lifetime Chaudhuri was often virulently abused as an apologist for the British. Chaudhuri's image as an English poodle stemmed from the fact that he dedicated his autobiography to the memory of the British Empire, which had conferred subjecthood, but withheld citizenship. Yet Chaudhuri wrote 'all that was good and living within us was made, shaped, and quickened by the same British rule'.

However, between James and Chaudhuri there can be no doubt as to who is both more critical and perceptive about the British impact on their colonies. Chaudhuri is very severe on the British in India. At one stage he compares them to Nazis, and suggests that their personal behaviour towards Indians ruined the impact of British letters and British learning on the Indian mind. James, in contrast, has few harsh words about the English in the West Indies. In the 1950s, totally misunderstanding the situation in South Africa, he even opposed a boycott of sporting South Africa, and promoted a visit by a West Indian team because it would be the first such touring team to have a black captain – even though this team would play segregated non-white South African teams and tour under racist apartheid laws. It is therefore ironic that while Chaudhuri is reviled in India, James in the West Indies is seen as a great radical historian.

The contrast in the treatment of the two writers tells us much about how these two societies, India and the West Indies, viewed sport. In the Caribbean cricket has enjoyed an intellectual prestige it has never had in India. In the Caribbean a man of letters could also be a lover of cricket – that was rarely the case in India. For men like Chaudhuri the English learning they imbibed and revered was the culture of the eighteenth century long before sports entered the English cultural equation. James came to this culture when the nineteenth century sporting ethos had been formed.

So unlike James, Chaudhuri has little to say about cricket, except for one brief reference in his autobiography to the discovery of a picture depicting English cricket in a school text book. It made a profound impression, so much so that although he loved cricket and played it, he could not but compare the drab efforts of his team 'by the side of the cricket world revealed in that coloured picture. The game was transformed, it was cricket suffused with the colours of the rainbow.' This, it seemed to him, was how the game was played in England. After that he could not take the Indian efforts seriously. The glow cast by English cricket seemed to turn Chaudhuri away from the sport in India, instead of towards it as with James.

It probably did not help that while James met Englishmen from an early age Chaudhuri did not meet an Englishman until he was 55. Until then his exposure to England had been through books and art. But this, curiously, enabled Chaudhuri to make the more insightful observations on the contradictions of the English colonial experience. So while Chaudhuri is appreciative of the British influence in India, particularly Bengal, he is, unlike James, also aware of how the British did not follow through on what they had created.

The British in India opened the door to English education, but mocked Chaudhuri and his Bengali ancestors as 'babus' who would never be able to speak English properly. Chaudhuri blamed the English for destroying the benefits to India of British ideas and values, while James saw no contradiction in the ideals of the British and the way the British behaved abroad. This would be most evident in soccer where the British in India, having brought the game to the subcontinent, made little effort to use it to promote British values and left Indian soccer almost entirely to its own devices.

Indian soccer had its greatest support in Bengal and like cricket experienced significant struggle and triumph. After being introduced to cricket and football at elite schools, Bengali graduates began to form their own sports clubs in the 1880s. By 1892 one of these clubs, Sovabazar, was strong enough to win the only integrated football competition in Calcutta, beating the East Surrey Regiment 2–1 in the Trades Cup. The torch of Bengali soccer was taken up by the Mohun Bagan club, founded by intellectuals with an agenda of austerity and re-assertion of masculine Bengali values. To add to the novelty, Indian soccer players played in bare feet, a custom that carried on till the 1950s.

The club's matches became an outlet for nationalist feelings in 1905 when the British, for their own imperial purposes, partitioned Bengal. Mohun Bagan won a series of integrated competitions in Calcutta, but remained excluded from the leading tournament, the IFA Shield. At last admitted in 1909, the players endured derision from their rivals when beaten by the Gordon Highlanders. But in 1911 they battled through to the final against the East Yorkshire Regiment. In front of a huge crowd (some had journeyed from distant Assam) they came from behind to win 2–1. *Nayak*, the elite local newspaper, reported the mass celebrations and marked the symbolism of the victory: 'It fills every Indian with joy and pride to know that rice-eating, malaria-ridden, barefooted Bengalis have got the better of beef-eating, Herculean, booted John Bull in the peculiarly English sport.'

Mohun Bagan's victory was celebrated by nationalists throughout India and gave a huge lift to all the country's soccer players. Soccer could easily have become India's predominant sport, and there may be many different reasons why this did not happen. Climate and terrain and the shift in commercial and political power away from Bengal to Bombay may all have played a part. Some have suggested that cricket was better able to accommodate the Indian caste system (princes and higher castes could have runners and substitute fielders to avoid the indignity of exertion, whereas soccer required all outfield players to work and run). The cricket dress was more modest than that for soccer (Spain and Argentina are other countries that have fretted over the propriety of playing a game in shorts in public). Others have cited FIFA's ban on Indians playing barefoot (India wanted to play in bare feet as late as the 1950 World Cup), or traced the many blunders by administrators of Indian soccer.

All of these played a part in the prevalence of cricket over soccer in India. The significant thing is that all of these factors were 'made in India', and not determined by British imperialism. The Indians had taken a British brand and adapted it to their own circumstances. These changes became even more pronounced as British football spread outside the British Empire. Here the global conquest of soccer exhibited a consistent pattern.

Pioneers take a football and a set of rules to some outpost of

British commerce. Most of these pioneers are British, but some are foreigners educated in British schools and colleges. The pioneers have no agenda except keeping fit and enjoying themselves. Their efforts excite amusement and curiosity from local onlookers, but the new game is exciting and easy to play and other expatriate communities and more and more local people try to join in. Some of the pioneers are glad to have new players and welcome the locals; others try to keep the sport British-only, forcing the non-British to form their own sports clubs. In either case, the sport becomes particularly popular with local upper-class Anglophiles (especially those fighting for modern values against local traditionalists). However, it also proves irresistible to the urban working classes as soon as they have enough money and leisure time to enjoy it. From that point, soccer becomes a local phenomenon, its progress determined not by any British agenda, but by local social, economic and political forces.

This is, of course, a gigantic compression of soccer's history, but when one looks at the British pioneers in country after country one is struck by how little interest they have in any issue other than playing soccer. They are not evangelists for British society, and if local people choose to identify soccer with that society and a desirable way of life they do so of their own volition. Of all the British pioneers, only one could be said to have a wider agenda than soccer: Harry Charnock, a Blackburn Rovers supporter who founded a club in 1894 for the textile workers in his factory in Moscow. Part of his motive was to cut down their vodka drinking on their rest day.

Far from seeking to perpetuate British hegemony through sport, the British pioneers readily yielded control of soccer to local interests. Some stayed involved in local soccer as referees and patrons, and a second wave of Britons became very influential in many countries as professional managers and coaches, such as the much-travelled Jimmy Hogan, who played for five professional English clubs before coaching successfully in the Netherlands, Vienna and Budapest.

As soccer took hold in other countries, more and more British clubs, both professional and amateur, started touring during the summer. None of these second-wave Britons, any more than the pioneers, had any agenda outside of soccer. Compared to American sporting tourists, they made no effort to export culture or religious values. They did not even try to sell sporting goods. Like the pioneers, many were surprised at the enthusiasm for soccer overseas, but they treated this as a curiosity, preferring to patronize local soccer teams rather than seeing them as potential allies or challengers to British interests. In 1904 a British amateur team in Hungary congratulated their opponents for accepting defeat in good part and for being 'ready to take a few hints from a team with a far greater experience of the game'. It would be interesting to know if any of those amateurs survived to watch the Hungarians demolish England in the 1950s.

It is significant that the first countries to adopt soccer outside the British Isles were Denmark, the Netherlands and Switzerland, all strongly Anglophile countries, with well-developed commercial, educational and tourist links to Britain. They may have watched their first soccer being played by British sailors, workers and embassy staff, but they did not need Britons to pioneer the game in their own countries. Wealthy Danes, Dutch and Swiss (and later Swedes) discovered soccer in English schools or in commercial or tourist visits to England and quickly promoted it at home, where they founded their own sports clubs and schools in imitation of the British.

The Swiss then re-exported soccer outside their own country. They had no imperial or cultural pretensions and there were not enough Swiss expatriates anywhere to create viable Swiss-only sporting clubs even if that had been part of the Swiss mentality. Three pioneers of Swiss origin had as much influence on overseas soccer as any British enthusiast. Hans Kamper, from Zurich, was the founder and driving force of FC Barcelona, which began with his classified advertisement appealing for players in a local newspaper. Like many British soccer pioneers, Kamper happened to be in Barcelona for commercial reasons and he had no roots in the city nor any intention of remaining there until his soccer team took off. Far from seeking to bring foreign values to Barcelona, Kamper aligned himself and his team with Catalan nationalism and Catalanized his name to Joan Gamper. Henry Monnier, scion of a French Protestant banking family, had his commercial and soccer upbringing in Geneva before returning to France and founding the Sporting Club de Nîmes. Walther Bennsemann, son of a German Jewish doctor, went to a Swiss private school. His education there in soccer and other subjects enabled him to found Karlsruher SC at the precocious age of 15, before founding a string of other German clubs and creating Germany's leading soccer journal, *Kicker*.

Even in countries where Britons provided the initial impetus, education and organization of soccer, it is striking how quickly they lost their control over the sport. In Spain, the British first introduced football to the poor and backward province of Andalusia through an accident of commercial and political history. A bankrupt Spanish government had sold the rights to mine the province's rich copper deposits to a British company, Rio Tinto, at a knockdown price. A British garrison had been stationed there to protect the company during Spain's repeated Carlist civil wars. In 1889 Rio Tinto organized Spain's first club, Huelva, to play a match against the British-owned Seville Water Company. Huelva did not prosper, because Andalusia could not provide enough local people to support soccer as players, officials and spectators. Instead, Spanish football took root in the more advanced cities of Bilbao and Barcelona. Britain had strong commercial interests in both places, and British workers and managers were active and influential in all of their fledgling clubs, but so too were local people and the leading clubs were all intimately connected with local identity and local politics.

In both cities, people came to declare their political and social allegiances by their choice of football team. Liberals, progressives, trade unionists and separatists supported Athletic Bilbao and

FC Barcelona; conservatives, monarchists and adherents of the central Spanish state supported Real Sociedad and Espanyol. A similar pattern followed in other Spanish cities, including Madrid, where football teams became a focus for local identity. This was a Spanish development, which the British generally deplored. The Wittys, the British family who were co-founders of FC Barcelona, did not follow Hans Kamper in identifying with Catalan nationalism and progressively withdrew from the club as it became more politicized.

In Italy, British influence over soccer was shared from its earliest days with Swiss and Austrian expatriates – and with rich Italians. The first proper match in the country was organized in Turin in 1887 by an Italian businessman, Eduardo de Bosio – six years ahead of the Genoa Cricket and Athletic Club (later the Genoa Cricket and Football Club), founded by the British Consul, which first brought soccer to Genoa and then only for English and Scottish expatriates. This club was transformed in 1897 by the arrival of an evangelical all-round sportsman, Dr James Spensley. Although evangelical, he was far from being a conventional 'muscular Christian' or an imperialist. He had many other enthusiasms, including Sanskrit and Oriental philosophy – and it was he who insisted on opening the club's football team to other expatriates and to Italians.

In Turin, Bosio's two clubs enjoyed the patronage of Italian aristocrats and even royalty: perhaps in consequence they were too stuffy for a group of rich local young college students, who formed their own club, Juventus. In Milan Swiss businessmen joined the Briton Alfred Edwards in establishing the club that became AC Milan: the breakaway Internazionale was formed by discontented Swiss members and players. British pioneers, such as Spensley and Milan's eccentric Nottingham-born player Herbert Kilpin, continued to have important roles in their respective clubs, but by the First World War the British had long lost the power to set an agenda for Italian soccer.

The arrival of soccer in South America is a tribute to British commerce, whose power in this part of the world led to it being dubbed Britain's informal empire. The British dominated the commercial life of Argentina and Uruguay and had an important role in Brazil, Chile, Peru, Colombia and Paraguay. In the first two countries, there were enough British expatriates to support British high schools for their children in the capital cities. The result (in one writer's words) was that football was introduced to South America in the 1860s through 'the kit bags of British sailors, the leisure pursuits of British businessmen, and the peculiarities of British expatriates'.

In 1888, the British living in Buenos Aires and Montevideo held matches to mark Queen Victoria's birthday. In 1905, Sir Thomas Lipton, a businessman who loved sport, donated the challenge cup, which was contested by Argentina and Uruguay, joined later by Brazil and Chile. These were the seedbeds of soccer in Argentina and Uruguay. Two Scottish teachers, Alexander Watson Hutton and William Leslie Poole, were first local evangelists and organizers of competitive soccer, but, as in Italy and Spain, any early British soccer hegemony had to be shared.

Ten years after Hutton founded the first Argentine Football League, it had expanded to four divisions, to accommodate dozens of clubs with non-British players, including other migrant communities from France, Spain and Italy and urban Argentines of all classes. In Uruguay, soccer underwent a major expansion through all classes and communities when a long period of civil war was ended by a progressive liberal government. Nacional was founded by Hispanic students as an expression of Uruguayan nationalism. Its main rival, the British-dominated Central Uruguayan Railways Cricket Club, opened up its membership and symbolically changed its official language from English to Spanish and its name to Peñarol.

Brazil's great soccer pioneer Charles Miller was the scion of a wealthy Anglo-Brazilian family in São Paulo. Sent away for ten years of private education in Britain, he returned to his native city as an enthusiastic and skilful soccer player with two leather balls and an assortment of kit. At the British-only São Paulo Athletic Club, he persuaded some cricket chums to try football. Banished from the sacred turf of the club itself, they had to attempt their early kickabouts on land used to graze the mules that pulled the city trams. They eventually managed to organize a match against the British staff of the municipal gas company. Unlike Spensley in Genoa, Miller was either unwilling or unable to persuade his team to admit non-British people. As a result, German and American expatriates founded their own teams, as did the local Brazilian elite. Miller's team remained the best, however, and won the first São Paulo championship in 1902 at a glittering social occasion in which the match ball was toasted and bathed in champagne, but the British were already under significant challenge.

In Rio de Janeiro, the British were displaced as leaders of soccer by rich local families led by the Swiss-Brazilian Oscar Cox, founder of the playboy club Fluminense. It adopted some British mannerisms (the official cheer was 'Hip Hip Hurrah!'), but it was a Brazilian institution and it was quickly challenged by other local clubs with a more representative Brazilian membership. The advent of factory teams, from 1904 onwards, opened Brazilian soccer even further and created opportunities for black and mixed-race players.

Miller was no sort of evangelist for British sport, let alone for British values. Although he continued to serve Brazilian soccer as a referee when he retired from play, he was always surprised by the sport's expansion and popularity, as he reported to his old school magazine in 1904, when he refereed a 20-a-side schoolboy match in front of 1,500 people. 'No less than 2,000 footballs have been sold here within the last twelve months; nearly every village has a club now.' When Exeter City visited Rio ten years later, they were even more astonished by the street football. Miller himself summed up the attitude of British expatriates to soccer in Brazil: 'The general feeling at the time was, "What a great little sport, what a nice little game."' He never tried to make any more of it, either culturally or commercially. Interestingly, his post-soccer life was oriented to Brazil rather than Britain. He lived and worked in Brazil, married a leading Brazilian pianist (eventually losing her to a leading Brazilian poet), and raised a son named Carlos rather than Charles.

Given the way soccer had spread, it is not surprising that, when overseas patrons of football started forming international bodies, the British took no interest. As far as the British were concerned, the world of soccer already existed within the British Isles, and they saw no need to take any notice of Johnny Foreigner proposing international regulation, let alone world bodies to run the game. For the British an international was a match between England and Scotland (first played 1872) or Wales (first played 1879) or Ireland (1882), and for the four home nations these were all the international matches they cared for. In 1886, in keeping with the belief that the world of football only needed the British Isles, nothing more, the four home countries had formed the International Board. This was meant to decide any changes to the laws of the game and other matters affecting it. For the British this was all the international involvement they wanted.

In 1902 the English Football Association stonewalled a Dutch proposal for an international body. The following year the Frenchman Robert Guérin came to London to prod the FA. He complained that talking to the FA's president, Lord Kinnaird, was like 'slicing water with a knife'. Ultimately, Guérin went ahead without the British: FIFA came into being in 1904 with an initial membership of Belgium, Denmark, France, the Netherlands, Spain, Sweden and Switzerland (Spain were admitted even though they had not yet formed a national association).

England did join the next year, but with many reservations, and the next half century would be marked by a pattern of intermittent British participation and withdrawal from international football. England's attitude to all these foreign ideas had been made crystal clear a year before the FA joined. Then members of the FA went to an international conference in Berne and told the delegates it was joining so that 'the Football Association should use its influence to regulate football on the Continent as a pure sport and give all Continental associations the full benefit of the many years experience of the FA'. This British superior attitude was reinforced by the fact that the grateful foreigners were so eager to have the English that there was an English president of FIFA from 1906 until the end of the First World War. He was Daniel Woolfall, a civil servant from Blackburn.

Indeed, the same pattern of keeping the foreigner at bay was set in other sports: the British simply could not be bothered to control sports overseas, even those that they dominated. In 1910 a British veto killed off proposals for a European Hockey Federation. The British maintained that attitude in the 1920s, even though an international association was necessary for hockey to become an Olympic sport. As in soccer, the French and other European countries formed the Fédération Internationale de Hockey without them: this was recognized by the IOC as the world governing body for the sport even though its membership was dwarfed by that of the British Hockey Association. Before the First World War, the Amateur Athletic Association had an on-off involvement in the international Olympic movement, until the 1908 Games were shifted hurriedly from Rome to London. The Amateur Rowing Association (which maintained a ban on 'artisans') was embroiled in a dispute with the slightly more liberal National Amateur Rowing Association and was deeply suspicious of any foreign sports bodies, which were likely to be even more democratic.

No form of international regulation for cricket was established until 1909, and even then the English authorities had to be driven by chaos and crisis and by the money offered by a rich South African. It occurred to nobody that the chosen body – the Imperial Cricket Conference – fatally excluded the United States, although American cricket was still strong and had produced the world's best contemporary bowler, Bart King. This British attitude could not have been in starker contrast to that of the

Americans, who promoted their sports of basketball and base-ball overseas in a very different manner.

Although many domestic British soccer teams had religious origins, including Aston Villa, Birmingham City, Bolton Wanderers, Everton and Fulham, religious organizations played almost no part in spreading soccer overseas. By contrast, the chief promoter of American basketball, both at home and abroad, was the YMCA. And what is more, in the spread of sport by the Americans, commerce was a principal factor. When the Americans undertook a global tour to promote baseball in 1888–9, its major purpose was to sell the baseball equipment of its promoter, Albert Spalding. Many British teams went overseas in the expectation of making money (especially if W. G. Grace was among them), but none of them thought of selling sporting goods. Visiting British soccer teams were regularly surprised at the scale of local orders for soccer balls, but they never sought any relationship or alliance with their manufacturers.

Albert Spalding was also responsible for the myth that baseball was invented in Cooperstown, New York state, by a future American Civil War hero, Abner Doubleday. He did this primar-ily to make money: baseball was better served by a patriotic image than by its true origins in the English game of rounders. Of course, as we have seen, the British also invented a myth about the origins of one of their leading sports: William Webb Ellis at Rugby. But no one tried to exploit this commercially, not even Rugby school.

Indeed, it is significant that in spite of inventing and dominat-ing most of the world's most popular sports, the British never built a sporting goods business on anything like the scale of Spalding, let alone his modern counterparts. Two British contem-poraries of Spalding were Major Wingfield, the inventor of lawn tennis, and Lieutenant Chamberlain, the inventor of snooker. Chamberlain did not even bother to patent or copyright his new game, and gave the rules away to a stranger at a dinner given by the Maharaja of Cooch Behar. Major Wingfield, after a brief spurt of promotion, allowed the MCC to rewrite the rules of his new game and gave up his patent after just a few years. He made very little money from it: the pride of creation was enough. Ironically doing this in a rather muddled British way left a legacy that not only outlived them, but challenged and defeated more centrally directed operations.

But as the twentieth century descended into the two most ruinous wars in the history of mankind new rulers emerged who seized on the sports the British had created, moulding them for their own purposes and forcing the British, and the rest of the world, to react. The events that followed would have astonished Thomas Hughes and Pierre de Coubertin, let alone Thomas Arnold.

PART 2

SPORT IN THE AGE OF EXTREMES

CHAPTER 4

_____

GLOBAL WAR RESULTING IN THE
RISE OF GLOBAL SPORT

In June 1914 the International Olympic Committee, celebrating its twentieth birthday, held a congress in Paris. The celebrations included the presence of the President of France, and the Congress members were taken on rides through Paris. In the middle of all this little attention was paid to an event that occurred in Sarajevo on 28 June. Shots rang out and the heir to the Austro-Hungarian Empire, Archduke Franz Ferdinand, was killed by a Serbian gunman. Within a month Europe was gearing for war and by August it was at war.

Yet this event does not figure in Pierre de Coubertin's memoirs. He does devote a chapter to the four years of the First World War but this is shorter than the space given over to the Paris Congress and quite the most curious in the book. One of the great regrets in this chapter is that the war marked the end of the *Olympic Review*, the last issue of which had appeared in July 1914. Its cover graced the chapter and as he put it, 'The *Olympic Review* was one of the first victims of the cataclysm.' He may have been a visionary in recreating the Olympics but in this chapter he comes over like a man who has started a new kind of corner shop and is worried it might be taken over. This is despite the fact that he was writing in 1931, by which time he must have known the terrible consequences of the war. During the war he served in the propaganda arm of the French state, going round secondary schools in a military uniform – he was too old at 51 to serve. Given all this it is astonishing that he did not appreciate how different this war was nor the propaganda impact of his own re-creation of the Olympics, let alone how both the Olympics and sport in general would be shaped by this first truly global war.

Coubertin, of course, was not the only one who went into the First World War thinking it would have no wider impact. Indeed both at the start of the war and for many months afterwards, sport as a sort of recreational safety valve was much advertised. In Britain many sports carried on as if nothing had changed. County cricket continued for a time, in 1915 the FA Cup was staged and race meetings were held until public protests put a stop to them. Students at Marlborough likened the war to a 'glorified football match' and Christmas 1914 saw English and German troops actually playing football matches. One match saw the 133rd Saxons beat the Royal Army Medical Corps 3–2, after the Germans had sung 'God Save the King' and drunk a toast to the British monarch. The following month there was a report that a German soldier had told a British Lance Corporal, after they met in no man's land, that he had lived in Hornsey in London and watched Woolwich Arsenal play Tottenham.

The big question as the war started was whether the Germans, who were due to stage the 1916 Games in Berlin, should still have the right to do so. The Germans had no wish to give up the Olympics. They had been preparing for it since 1913; Kaiser Wilhelm had opened a stadium in Berlin, declaring it to be 'the greatest athletic exhibition Europe has ever witnessed', and just days before the war was declared Germany sent a team to the United States to tour American universities and military academies so they could bring the very best ideas to the 1916 Berlin Games. Given that as they marched into neutral Belgium the Germans had predicted a short war, there seemed no danger that Coubertin's four-yearly sports festival would not be held in Berlin. Until well into 1916 the Germans were convinced the Games would be held, and at one stage the Imperial Board even selected a team before events made the whole exercise redundant.

Coubertin acted as if the war precipitated by the shots at Sarajevo was no different from the wars between the ancient Greek states. This lay behind his insistence, long after the war had commenced, that the 1916 Berlin Olympics would go ahead. But he had also previously felt that, in awarding the Games to Berlin, war could be averted. In his memoirs he would say he was against taking the Games away from Berlin as he feared this would crack Olympic unity and during the war he publicly declared:

> The IOC has not the right to withdraw the celebration of the Olympic Games from the country to which the celebration has been given without consulting the country. The VIth Olympic Games will remain and will be credited to Berlin but it is possible they will not be held. In olden times it happened that it was not possible to celebrate the Games but they did not for this reason cease to exist.

Coubertin did, however, make sure that Berlin did not become the headquarters of the Olympics. Before then the headquarters had moved every four years along with the Games and he decided to make the permanent headquarters Lausanne. But this was done, he emphasized, to provide administrative stability given the uncertainties created by the war, not a response to Germany starting the war. He was genuinely horrified at any anti-German move. As soon as the war started, the British representative, Theodore Cook from the British Olympic Committee, demanded that Berlin be stripped of the Games. The British were also asking for international academic or scientific associations to expel their German members. For Coubertin this was British public opinion for the first time showing 'itself lacking in moderation and level-headedness'. He contrasted Britain unfavourably with Russia, Belgium and France and was relieved that the IOC had no German or Austrian members, otherwise it would have been 'embarrassing'. Cook, unhappy over Coubertin's rejection, resigned.

Coubertin can hardly be blamed for failing to understand the nature of the First World War or its dramatic consequences. Few, even the greatest of statesmen, understood how different it would be and almost nobody anticipated that this war to end all wars would end in the destruction of four empires – Turkey, Austro-Hungary, Germany and Russia – the rise of fascism and communism and the creation of new states. A year before the war Coubertin had taken great pride in devising the Olympic rings – five interlaced rings, signifying the unity of the five continents. But in creating the first global sports institution he just did not understand the nature of the genie that he had unleashed. This was the genie of sporting political nationalism and there was no way of putting it back into the bottle. The new states that emerged in the aftermath of the war were quick to seize the idea of international sport Coubertin had inspired and their arrival further spurred the growth of international competitions and encouraged nations and governments to place a new value on sporting success. This was expressed not only in performances by teams and athletes but also in the hosting of major sports events. The result was that the years post-1918 saw more national teams and more international sporting contests than ever before.

The 1912 Olympics in Stockholm had seen 28 nations competing but Australia-New Zealand competed as one nation, Australasia, and the Finns had to compete under the flag of Russia's Tsarist Empire. Hannes Kolehmainen, one of nine Finns who won gold (the Russians did not win any, just two silver and three bronze), said that he wished he had not won, so that he did not have to witness the raising of the hated flag of his country's occupier. But it was Kolehmainen's victory that was to inspire Paavo Nurmi, Finland's star of the 1924 Paris Games. As Nurmi said later, a few days after Hannes won he bought his first sneakers, an illustration of the power of sporting success.

By the 1928 Olympics in Amsterdam, Australia and New Zealand were also separate sports nations, and several new nations created as a result of the First World War even got on the medals table, including Poland, Yugoslavia and Czechoslovakia.

The total numbers participating had risen to 46. The number dipped to 37 in Los Angeles in 1932 because of the Depression, but rose again to 49 in 1936 in Berlin. While the total number of athletes in 1912 had been 2,407 (48 women), in 1928 it was 2,883 (277 women), and in 1936 it was 3,963 (331 women).

The interwar period also saw many new international athletic tournaments. Some were regional: the South American championships began in Montevideo in 1919 and were followed by the Central American and Caribbean Games (Mexico City 1926), the Balkan Games (Sofia 1931), and the European Championships (Turin 1934). Others made a statement about politics or gender, for example two versions of Workers' Olympics (one communist, one democratic socialist), the pro-Zionist Maccabiah Games, and the women-only Olympic Games organized by the independent Fédération Sportive Féminine Internationale as a protest against discrimination in the official ones. The British Empire Games came into being in the 1930s, as a result of a Canadian initiative. The Canadians had been much upset by the way the Americans behaved at the 1928 Olympics. As one of the Canadians put it, 'The United States gets or takes what it wants.' The Empire Games proved popular in Britain as an exhibition of British sportsmanship and because British athletes had more chance of winning something.

Interestingly, the Indians kept away from the competition, seeing it as promoting a white empire they wanted to break away from. Indian indifference was bolstered by the fact that, for the first Empire Games in Hamilton in 1930, the Canadians provided subsidy to the Australians and the New Zealanders, knowing their teams would be white, but not to the Indians.

Cricket, where India could take on England, was different. And here, in the late 1920s, the English, having shown little interest in introducing new Test nations, quite suddenly went on a remarkable expansion. The game, which had not seen a new Test-playing country since South Africa in 1889, acquired three more between 1928 and 1932: the West Indies, New Zealand and India. Their admission in itself says something about the relationship between sport and national identity and in particular the British management of it. Of the three, only New Zealand was an independent country; India was a dominion with a seat in the League of Nations, but that was largely to increase British influence in that new body. India, however, was not a self-governing dominion like New Zealand and the other white dominions of Australia, South Africa and Canada. Indeed in the early part of the century Congress, the Indian nationalist party, had campaigned not to sever links with the empire, but for the same self-governing dominion status enjoyed by the white dominions. It was only in 1930 after persistent British refusal that the Congress decided to demand complete independence.

British rule in India was a complex mix of direct colonial rule and princely states that had a large measure of autonomy in their territory, but accepted the overall power of the British state. They could have no external relations with any power. In 1917, piloting a measure through the war-time Cabinet promising India eventual self-government, Lord Curzon had estimated it would take Indians 500 years to learn to rule themselves. In the event India won its freedom fifteen years after it made its Test debut at Lord's in 1932. But, reflecting the curious way the British ruled its jewel in the Crown, the Indian cricket teams until 1947 were known as All-India, meaning they included players from British India and the princely domains.

The third Test-playing country, the West Indies, was even more curious. Its cricket team represented the idea of a nation, a West Indies Federation that, despite much effort over the following three decades, never saw the light of day. The West Indies was a collection of separate British colonies, and the term had no legal identity except through its cricket team. In the 1950s and 1960s, as the individual colonies got their freedom they all became members of the United Nations and participated as individual nations in the Olympics, FIFA and all the other major international sports. Cricket was the great exception; indeed, apart from cricket, there is no sporting team called the West Indies. It remains a marvellous example of sport giving birth to a national idea that is not backed by an independent nation.

The admission of these teams meant the number of Test matches virtually doubled. In the ten years before the First World War, 52 Test matches were played. In the first ten years of peacetime, the number was 51, but the next ten saw 96. In England before the war it was commonplace for a season to contain no Test matches: the last such season after the war was 1927.

In football, FIFA, which had 24 members in 1919, grew to 56 by 1939 although that number did not include any of the British home nations, which, as we shall see, were playing their usual dance with FIFA. In 1913, the last full year of peace, European nations played 26 internationals against each other (not including six UK 'home internationals'). In 1920 there were 40; in 1937 (before Austria disappeared) there were 86. England played only seven matches against continental sides in all the years before 1914: they played 19 in the 1920s and 28 in the 1930s.

By then England and the other home nations had once again withdrawn from FIFA. This came in 1920, because the other countries did not agree to British demands for cutting off football relations with Germany and the other so-called Central Powers defeated in the First World War. The FA rejoined FIFA in 1924, but withdrew only four years later over the vexed issue of whether amateur footballers could receive 'broken time' payments on representative duties. But the 1928 walk-out from the international body was not a complete severing of ties. This time a link with FIFA was maintained through the FA's International Board, which, in 1913, had finally admitted FIFA, having initially rejected advances from the then fledgling organization. If this meant Britain was acknowledging the rest of the football world, it was still keeping it in its place, with the home nations out-voting FIFA on the International Board. However, after 1928 the International Board provided a means of keeping the door open to FIFA until the home nations returned after the Second World War.

It was not Europe, but South America, the continent that had watched the war from afar, which led the development of international football, with nationalism playing a huge role in this. The first step in this direction was the formation in 1916 of the South American Confederation, CONMEBOL, the first such confederation. Untroubled by the faraway war, albeit greatly profiting from it economically, the South Americans set up an organization which not only held the high-quality CONMEBOL championship, but demonstrated the influence of politics on sport. Thus South America may have been a European creation, populated and controlled by millions of European stock, but the development of football reflected the fact that the South American nations were also the first non-European nations to break free from European political control.

In 1916, the centenary of Argentina's independence from Spain, to celebrate, the Argentine Football Association organized a tournament to which Uruguay, Chile and Brazil were invited. The event demonstrated the growing importance of sport, and how well a British-invented sport had been accepted by people with little or no links with Britain. Half a century earlier a country in a similar situation might have held a gigantic exhibition like the Crystal Palace one. Argentina did not manage to win the tournament: that honour went to Uruguay, marking the early ascendancy of this nation in South American and indeed, for a time, in world football.

The tournament also inspired a Uruguayan, Hector R. Gomez, to form the South American Football Confederation, which soon started holding regular football championships. South American football developed despite the fact that travel was not easy. In 1919 Rio held the South American football championships and while some Chilean fans managed to watch the event it took them two months to get there. To do that they had to use boat, train and mule.

Uruguay also took the lead in the next stage of football development, going where the English did not want to venture, and providing another demonstration of football as a tool of national-ism. Until the 1920s the winner of the Summer Olympic football event was considered the world's best team. In 1924 Uruguay won the Olympic football tournament at the Paris Olympics. This triumph was repeated four years later in Amsterdam, when Uruguay defeated Argentina. Such was the enthusiasm in the two countries that crowds in their respective capitals gathered to hear the news relayed by cable from Amsterdam.

By this time Jules Rimet, the Frenchman who had taken over from Woolfall as President of FIFA after the war and was some-thing like the Coubertin of football, was convinced that football needed its own tournament separate from the Olympics. While he believed football could bring people together he was also concerned that with increasing professionalism, Olympic football – confined to amateurs – was not adequate. His desire to create a world competition for professionals blended neatly with Uruguay's desire to advertise the fact that it had reached the top table of nations. Even as he was thinking of the World Cup he had been lobbied by Uruguayan diplomats to host such an event. Uruguay was celebrating the centenary of the adaptation of its constitution and what better way to mark the occasion than host the first football World Cup? In 1930 it all came together. Uruguay built a stadium for the competition in Montevideo and was will-ing to pay the fares and hotel costs of the players, not that this tempted many countries – certainly not many Europeans.

The first World Cup had just 13 entrants, of which only four were European: France, Belgium, Yugoslavia and Romania. Rimet had to work hard to persuade Belgium, and even France, to accept. The Romanians were sent only at the behest of their king and his mistress. There was no question of England, or any of the home countries, going. Both the amateur Football Association and the professional Football League were disdainful of international competition: the FA sent a one-sentence rejection of an invitation to play in the inaugural World Cup. Charles Sutcliffe of the Football League was even more scathing: 'I don't give a brass farthing about the improvement of the game in France, Belgium, Austria or Germany. The FIFA does not appeal to me. An organization where such football associations as those of Uruguay and Paraguay, Brazil and Egypt, Bohemia and Pan Russia, are co-equal with England, Scotland, Wales and Ireland seems to me to be a case of magnifying the midgets.' However, Britain could claim that the United States team had six members who were born in the British Isles: five Scots and one Englishman, although they had migrated to the USA and played football there. For good measure, Uruguay cemented its national pride and won the inaugural tournament.

Uruguay's initiative caught on and four years later the World Cup held in Italy had 32 entrants, requiring an elimination contest to bring the number down to 16. By then Europe was getting used to continental competitions, for in 1927, three years before the first World Cup, Hugo Meisl, the organizing genius of Austrian football, pulled together the Mitropa Cup – the first European club championship – for teams from Austria, Czechoslovakia, Hungary, Yugoslavia, Switzerland and Romania. It established the template for all such competitions, a home and away leg, and the games were the first to be broadcast on central European radio networks. They were extremely popular and established a brand of technically proficient football known as Calcio Danubio.

International competition raised standards of performance and interest in sport, but it also highlighted cultural differences. In the years that followed tension developed between Europe and South America, as the South Americans felt that their referees were neglected while Europeans looked askance at their football traditions. Many years later, one South American member of the FIFA referees committee told FIFA officials that, for World Cup qualifiers, it would be best to appoint referees at the very last minute, allowing fewer opportunities for teams to try to influence referees. As Dr Helmut Kaiser, then the FIFA general secretary noted, 'according to information received, it is customary in South America to make pilgrimages to the referees' countries'. It is not hard to imagine what these pilgrims were after.

The growth of international sport also saw a rise in violence by players and spectators (the Belgian referee in the first World Cup Final demanded non-stop personal protection and a fast getaway to the boat out of Montevideo), and both Slavia and Juventus were ejected from the Mitropa Cup in 1932 after brawls between the teams and spectator violence in both legs.

Such violence was not confined to football. Cricket, normally famous for its sedate atmosphere, provoked so much animosity during the infamous 'Bodyline' cricket tour of 1932 that it threatened the future of the British Empire. But this was a very exceptional cricket moment; for the British ruling classes the fear in the period between the wars was not crowd violence, but public disorder caused by working-class gambling, particularly in racing.

In contrast to Coubertin unleashing, albeit unwittingly, sporting nationalism, gambling had always been part of sport. In fact the lure of betting had led to the growth of many sports. But now governments, seeing another potential source of revenue, began to intervene. This was most prominent in racing, a sport with historic links with betting.

Racing, particularly in Britain, had always had a strong class bias. Very popular with the aristocratic classes, it was distrusted by many sections of the middle class, especially those with a nonconformist religious background. Reflecting this social base in its readership, until the 1970s the *Manchester Guardian* never published a full race card, limiting itself to a small table of good tips. Aristocrats had always been free to stake their entire estates on a single wager, and were admired for their 'bottom' when they lost without a murmur. But working-class gambling was seen as a threat to public morals and public order.

From the mid-nineteenth century, British governments made strenuous, although largely futile, efforts to control gambling. The 1853 Betting Houses Act simply drove off-course betting, which had begun to mushroom, underground and gave it a criminal association. It did nothing about on-course betting and credit betting used by the well-to-do. The shared interests of the aristocracy and on-course bookmakers also prevented the British from adopting *pari-mutuel* betting, invented in Paris in 1872 by a perfumier, Pierre Oller, whose customers had complained about the poor odds on offer from French on-course bookmakers. In this system, there were no bookmakers and all bets were pooled, the promoter taking a cut, and the remainder shared among the winners. It quickly became popular and was exported success-fully to the United States, Australia and New Zealand. Two New Zealand inventors made major contributions: Thomas Ekberg created a manual totalizator to sum all the bets and work out the winning payments, and George Julius created a much quicker electric version by converting his invention of a vote-counting machine to detect electoral fraud (which had failed to find a market among politicians).

The British, in contrast, continued to reinforce their class-biased system of on-course bookies and off-course credit betting for the aristocracy. The 1906 Street Betting Act drove off-course betting further underground and encouraged corruption. When sports clubs developed small-scale lotteries and a variety of short-lived competitions based on forecasting the results of a number of football matches, the well-organised on-course book-makers lobby (the National Sporting League) and the Football Association persuaded Lloyd George's post-war coalition government to crack down. The result was the Ready Money Betting Act 1920, whose message was that it was all right to bet if you were rich, not if you were poor.

In the early 1920s British working people therefore faced an invid-ious choice if they wanted to place a bet for cash. To do so legally entailed the expense and inconvenience of going to a racecourse, and then dealing with a privileged set of bookmakers in the ring, who disdained small bets and offered poor prices. Many were aggressive and frightening, particularly to women, and their activities often attracted violent crime as organized gangs tried to extort money from them or were employed to protect them. The problem of race-course violence persisted right through the interwar period: events at Lewes in 1936, which saw gangland fights, inspired Graham Greene to create the amoral Pinkie in his novel *Brighton Rock*.

Unsurprisingly, millions of working-class people preferred to bet illegally, placing anonymous bets on slips entrusted to runners such as window cleaners and milkmen. This system also ensured poor prices and left punters with little or no remedy against default. Nonetheless, informed estimates suggested that about 8 million illegal bets were placed each week during the interwar period, principally off-course, on horseracing. Ordinary Britons did eventually get a chance to gamble legally although this required the help of an American sporting import.

This was greyhound racing, introduced to Britain at Bellevue in Manchester in 1926. It caught on rapidly. The following year there were 18 tracks in Britain and by 1933 the number had risen to 233; including Wembley, they often shared their space with another successful American import, motorcycle speedway. In 1932, 9 million Londoners watched greyhound racing at clubs licensed by the National Greyhound Racing Club, and by 1938 there were 38 million paying spectators across the country – about the same as for football.

Greyhound racing offered on-course betting only, but still attracted millions of pounds in stake money, and by the end of the period it accounted for 10 per cent of all legal betting turnover. It was attractive to urban working people because the tracks were easy to get to and meetings were held in the evenings. The main promoter, Brigadier T. A. Critchley (whose popularity ensured him a brief spell as a Tory MP), was astute enough to introduce the newly popular Tote into greyhound tracks. Predictably, a book-maker claimed this was unlawful and took him to court. Critchley won on appeal and Tote betting on greyhounds took off. In 1934 the Betting and Lotteries Act tried to limit it to two meetings a week, but it was too popular and the limit proved unenforceable.

By this time racecourse bookmakers also had a competitor in the Tote. Its creation was prompted largely by the failure of Winston Churchill's betting tax of 1926 (levying 2 per cent on on-course bets, 3.5 per cent on off-course credit bets) to raise its predicted take of £6 million. Having rejected the Jockey Club's offer to run the French *pari-mutuel* betting system the Baldwin government set up a new bureaucracy, the Racecourse Betting Control Board. This ran the Tote machines at racecourses, and distributed the profits to horseracing.

The Tote proved popular with working-class people because it accepted small stakes of two shillings (ten pence) and, above all, because it always paid up. Women in particular were glad to avoid the aggressive on-course bookies. The Tote also entered the off-course credit market through a partnership with Guardian Pari-Mutuel Ltd, which created street outlets with commentaries on races, and moved into greyhound racing. Its only check came when Tote clubs, where people could get a drink while placing a bet, were ruled illegal.

But if the British could regulate in their own land they could do nothing about Ireland, and the Irish Hospitals Sweepstakes Derby, introduced in the Irish Republic in 1930, quite shook the system. Promoted with flair, it combined a charitable cause with classic British horseraces. Although technically illegal in Britain, hundreds of thousands of Britons purchased tickets in Dublin and the postal authorities found it impossible to stop them. As usual, moralists and vested interests demanded a ban: instead the government decided to legalize small-scale lotteries by British charities and sports clubs. These cut the income of the Irish Sweepstakes, but this still averaged £5 million annually in the run-up to the Second World War, mostly derived from Britain.

It was also an Irishman who was to mount the most successful challenge to the system – the football pools. John Moores was an Irish telegraph office clerk who with two partners began to distribute football pool coupons directly to Manchester United supporters in 1923, inviting them to forecast the results of a number of League football matches. In spite of their major innovation – offering credit betting through the coupon – their venture attracted few supporters, either at Manchester United or at Hull City, where it was also tried. They hid their identities behind the name of Littlewood (the unknown birth name of one of the partners). But while soon the other two left Moores to run the venture on his own, he successfully held on, sold more coupons, and was lucky enough to win a high-profile court case.

The football pools were formally legalized in 1928, after which several other companies followed Moores into the market, and they were astutely marketed. Moores dramatically exploited a week that produced a win of nearly £6,000 for a penny stake, and all of the companies were shrewd enough to use respectable language: punters were 'investors' and winnings were 'dividends'. The football pools all pretended to be exercises in skill and judgement and a vast subsidiary industry arose, principally in newspapers, but also through commercial European radio stations, of form analysis and forecasting of results. In practice, they were lotteries, and all the big payouts went to random punters rather than scientific 'investors'. In all other respects, the football pools were scrupulously honest and well-run and winners were always paid.

The pools promoters were strong enough in 1933 to lobby successfully against the introduction of casino gambling, and in 1936 they faced down a more serious challenge from the football authorities, who had always been hostile to them. When the prominent Methodist C. E. Sutcliffe became president of the Football League in 1935 he persuaded the League to try to strangle the pools companies by not publishing details of fixtures until two days before they happened.

It was a remarkably inept manoeuvre, which attracted outrage from punters and severely damaged gates. George Orwell complained that Hitler's recent march into the Rhineland had raised hardly a flutter of interest, but the League's move 'had flung all Yorkshire into a storm of fury'. The League backed down, its resistance softened by copyright payments for fixture lists from the pools promoters, although the high-minded football authorities refused to accept the tainted money. Two Parliamentary attempts to control football pools collapsed miserably in 1936 and 1938. The football pools were here to stay.

The interwar decade had proved the futility of trying to prevent Britain's working class from gambling and it was estimated that between 1920 and 1938 gambling expenditure rose from 1.3 per cent to 5 per cent of total consumer expenditure. Both figures are probably an under-estimate (spending on 'naughty' items has consistently been under-recorded in household surveys), but the growth rate is probably right. A reliable survey in the mid 1930s suggested that two football pools coupons were being distributed each week to every household in the city of York. By the end of the decade, about 10 million people across the country were sending in weekly coupons, and annual turnover had reached £50 million, enabling Littlewoods to diversify successfully into mail order.

Without knowing it, the British government, which had always feared working-class gambling, had created a major social pacifier. A contemporary social expert and popular broadcaster John Hilton analysed their appeal in his 1936 survey *Why I Go In For The Pools*: they were fair, they were a relief from boredom, and they offered working people who would never inherit a big legacy or make a killing on the stock exchange a chance to acquire overnight wealth. George Orwell grumbled that alongside fish-and-chips, art-silk stockings, tinned salmon, cut-price chocolate, the radio, the movies and strong tea, the football pools had saved Britain from revolution.

If in trying to cope with working-class gambling the British policy makers had had to worry about the Irish they also fretted about the example set by gambling in the United States.

In the so-called Progressive Era, before the First World War, gambling had been a major target of social reformers. In 1908 the Agnew-Hart Act had taken aim at on-course bookmakers. Many racetracks disappeared in consequence: Broughton was sold,

Saratoga closed down and other racetracks survived only by pretending to hold 'bet-free' meetings of pure, disinterested amateurs of horseflesh. In 1910 the *pari-mutuel* was legalized for the surviving racetracks, but as in England a great deal of betting was done illegally, almost openly in 'pool halls' in towns and cities, connected to the tracks by telegraph wires. Also, as in England, 'bookies' (the term was first coined in the United States in 1885) generally offered very poor prices. They also induced many punters to buy tipsheets, stud books, form books and even books on the interpretation of dreams in a desperate search for inside information – a practice satirized by Chico and Groucho Marx in *A Day At The Races*. Apart from the special books, American punters in the 1920s bought half a million racing editions of newspapers every day to get the 'morning line' of runners, jockeys, form, conditions and prices. This valuable market discouraged newspapers from exposing the many scandals in racing and betting.

Besides betting on horseracing, Americans could bet on their own version of the pools, which were especially popular in eastern cities. Punters could buy a 'pool card' from a bookie offering many options to bet on multiple baseball games ('parlays') for as little as ten cents at what appeared to be very long odds, stacked in favour of the bookie. Not even the Chicago 'Black Sox' World Series scandal in 1919 put punters off baseball pool cards, which were joined in the 1920s by cards for boxing, college football and college basketball. All of these sports were easy to fix for gambling interests, especially the last two because they offered spread betting on the margin of points between teams. A team confident of winning could throw a few points without risk to achieve a desired spread.

Unlike the honest and well-run British football pools, the American version was described by one contemporary expert as 'a stick-up, an absolute robbery, but you didn't know any better. The odds for a ten-team [parlay] were 100-1 and ties lost on every card. Now you can get 800-1 or 1000-1. You played for the danger of it. You played for a huge payoff if you would ever get lucky.'

American gambling was already causing serious social and public order problems – and then came Prohibition. Overnight, Prohibition created an enormous new source of criminal profit, with insufficient legitimate outlets to launder it. It was a natural process for this money to flow into gambling, which ceased to be a small-scale local activity and turned into highly organized businesses. Leaders of organized crime such as Meyer Lansky and Benjamin ('Bugsy') Siegel adapted the methods developed for bootlegging to create nationwide gambling empires, while Al Capone was proud that all of his enterprises were run on 'American business lines'.

The career of Moe Annenberg is instructive. He made two fortunes from illegal betting. The first was derived from the purchase of *Daily Racing Form*, a small special-interest sheet. The second and bigger fortune came from acquisition of the race wire service, which took the results to illegal bookies. In each case Annenberg used bribery, predatory pricing and violence to destroy competitors – even when he owned them. He collaborated with organized crime and enjoyed protection from Meyer Lansky. Annenberg considered himself a patriot and a friend of the working man. When reproached about making money from illegal betting, he described his race wire service as 'a source for social good. People who led humdrum lives of poverty or held grinding jobs that had them working five and a half or six days a week needed something to look forward to, a chance, no matter how slight, that good fortune could come their way.' Like his contemporary, the respectable bootlegger Joseph P. Kennedy, Annenberg was active in politics. He paid off Democratic politicians in Chicago for business reasons, but his sympathies were with the Republican party. His son Walter became President Nixon's ambassador to London, where, during a television documentary, he amused the queen and millions of viewers by complaining of 'elements of discomfiture associated with factors of refurbishing at the Residency'. In fairness, he also gave the National Gallery a much-loved picture, Henri Rousseau's *Tropical Storm With A Tiger*.

The Depression led to the repeal of Prohibition nationwide, and to the legalization of Tote betting at racetracks in nine states desperate for new sources of revenue. Nevada went even further and also legalized small-scale casino gambling. But these measures came too late to undo the fatal legacy of Prohibition. The 'noble experiment' had created a nexus between American sport, gambling and organized crime.

If gambling's impact on sport was often baleful, one of the major technological innovations of the period proved a godsend. Broadcasting brought giant new audiences to sport in many countries and radio transformed spectatorship in sport and the relationship of spectators with their sports. 'Listeners-in', including the blind and the housebound, could enjoy as vivid a sporting experience as those at the ground, and often be better informed. Radio created a new profession of 'commentator' (a long-dead seventeenth-century term revived for the purpose), whose work not only described events, but also interpreted them and often gave them a partisan agenda. Radio influenced the content and style of other media. In the United States particularly, radio in conjunction with movies and newspapers helped to commercialize sport and turn successful sportspeople into marketable celebrities. Above all, radio united national societies by giving them a common sporting experience.

In Britain and the United States, radio made a rapid advance from tentative beginnings. American consumer expenditure rose from $10.6 million in 1920 to $411.6 million in 1929; in Britain the number of radio licences grew from 36,000 in 1922, to 2 million in 1927 and to 9 million in 1939, covering nearly three quarters of all British households. Despite the Depression, radio grew dramatically in the 1930s after the introduction of mains-powered valve sets, which transformed the radio from a primitive 'cat's whisker' contraption to a luxurious piece of furniture (often combined with a gramophone) whose dials promised access to exotic places such as Hilversum, Lahti and Kalundborg.

In the United States radio grew as a free-for-all industry, with thousands of local stations relying on commercial advertising and sponsorship. Sport was vital to them in building audiences, and this continued even after the Depression led to the consolidation of American radio into major networks.

Britain was horrified at the 'anarchy of the airwaves' overseas, and had national newspapers which were far better able to protect their interests against the upstart medium. The result in 1922, was the BBC, the C first standing for Company, then for Corporation – free of advertising and sponsorship and with a high-minded agenda set by its founder, John Reith. The BBC was a monopoly service, although it was challenged, particularly on Sundays, by commercial continental stations such as Radios Paris, Normandie and Luxembourg.

Given their very different broadcasting models, it was not surprising that the two countries had different early experiences of broadcast sport. As early as 1921, American listeners heard dramatic coverage of the Dempsey–Carpentier heavyweight title fight, and of World Series baseball the same year. In 1924 the Chicago Cubs were the first major league team to allow local broadcasting of their games (most of their rivals were far more timid). By 1927 the radio coverage of the Dempsey–Tunney heavy-weight title fight (watched by 104,000 live spectators) had 50 million listeners. American newspapers failed to limit radio reporting of sports results or influence the content or style of commentary: on the contrary they themselves had to adapt by making their coverage more exciting.

In Britain the infant BBC was much more cautious in its sports coverage. From the outset the newspapers tried to prevent it reporting racing results and managed to persuade the official Sykes committee of inquiry to endorse this in 1923. There was a pointed contrast in 1925 between derby coverage in the two coun-tries. The Kentucky Derby had vivid, live radio commentary with an audience of millions. The BBC gave a terse 'sound picture' of the Epsom Derby with no live commentary. The following year, it did even worse: the announcer could only make a guess at the first three places before handing back to the studio.

In time the BBC came to broadcast sport with imagination and success. Recovering from its bad start in the derby, it used Meyrick Good to 'read the race' to listeners at major meetings as he did to King George V, while Quentin Gilbey (once disguised as a footman) conveyed the atmosphere and gave fashion notes. The unflappable Teddy Wakelam (he once carried on without missing a beat when his notes caught fire) was used for many sports, especially rugby and tennis. In association football he was joined by George 'By Jove' Allison and Raymond Glendenning. Cricket and rowing were conveyed reverentially by Howard Marshall and John Snagge. By the end of the 1930s, the BBC was also offering golf, clay pigeon shooting, darts, fencing, gliding, pigeon racing, racquets, speedway and table tennis.

The BBC's coverage always had a fundamentally different mindset from American radio. The emphasis was on accuracy and decency over entertainment. When former Harlequin Teddy Wakelam commentated on the England–Wales rugby match in 1927 he was accompanied by a blind man (to remind him to describe the match clearly) and a large sign saying 'Don't Swear!' To help listeners, the BBC also forced early commentators to refer to a grid of numbered squares to indicate the position of the ball or the players. In football, George 'By Jove' Allison studied American methods to put more verve and personality in his commentaries, but both he and the even more excitable Glendenning had to give a reliable account of the actual play. In 1931 Allison described his style in terms of 'conveying to the listener a mental photograph of what is taking place [. . .] keeping a steely grip on one's natural enthusiasm and reveal[ing] through the voice that excitement which is justified.'

No such inhibitions restrained American and other foreign commentators. In the United States, their purpose was to generate excitement and listeners, exemplified by the style of Graham McNamee, the first ball-by-ball baseball commentator. Red Barber was more objective, but still rewarded for building an audience. In smaller radio stations, which could not afford live coverage, commentators had to simulate the excitement of a game from tickertape reports and primitive sound effects such as tapping a pencil (this was also a feature of much early cricket coverage). One of Iowa's baseball commentators had this skill in high degree and built an interesting later career: he was Ronald 'Dutch' Reagan. Remarkably, major American sports teams often chose their radio commentators, a practice that lasted until the 1960s. Not surprisingly, their commentaries were very partisan.

Many other countries also produced commentators with a personal style and a mass following. Indian cricket reached thousands of listeners, often grouped in poor and rural areas around one collective radio, through the commentaries of All-India Radio's A. F. S. 'Bobby' Talyarkhan, voluble, anecdotal, opinionated – and determinedly solo. So determined was he that his was the only voice Indian cricket followers should hear that he resigned from All-India Radio when they asked him to share the commentary with others. Dutch football was narrated to listeners by the patriotic Henry Hollander, Italian football by the superpartisan, pro-Fascist and unreliable Niccolo Carosio. In Brazil the horseracing commentator Rebelo Junior switched to football and invented the extended chant of 'Gooooo-aalll!' imitated ever since. The polymathic Ary Barrosa, who was also a writer and composer of first rank, went one better in celebrating goals by his beloved Flamengo with a riff of harmonica music. More seriously, Barrosa was a pioneer of the post-match interview.

Popular commentators and their idiosyncrasies helped to create a shared sporting experience from radio in many different countries. In Argentina, radio brought remote areas in contact not only with urban football teams, but also with the best tango orchestras. Both there and in Brazil, many popular tunes were composed specifically about football. In Austria, commentators brought fans heavyweight intellectual analysis of football normally restricted to coffee houses. In Australia the simulated broadcast of the successful 1930 tour of England induced thousands of people to invite their neighbours to listen in the middle of the night. In this communal way, the broadcasts reached nearly one third of the Australian population, and were instrumental in turning Don Bradman into a national icon. In 1936, millions of Japanese listeners sat up until the small hours thrilled by the Olympic marathon victory of Son Kitei, as did listeners in his true country, occupied Korea. A Japanese commentator at the 1936 Berlin Olympic poolside could only cry 'Ganbare!' ('Come on') as Hideko Maehata led on the way to becoming Japan's first gold medal swimmer.

An eloquent testimony to the power of sport on radio came from the feminist intellectual and novelist Winifred Holtby. Writing in 1930 in the BBC's *Radio Times* about her first experience of soccer commentary, she said:

> I was excited. I had not, I have not to this day, the remotest notion of what they were all doing. But I know that I was excited. No one could listen with cold blood or sluggish pulses to the quickening crescendo of the roar preceding the final shout of 'Goal'. I wanted more goals [. . .] I wanted to feel my spine tickle, and my pulses beat, and my hair stir gently at the roots with suspense as that voice cried out from somewhere near our drawing-room curtains.

Radio was not the only new invention to affect sport and society: so too did newsreels. These had started before the First World War, but they really took off in the interwar period and created another new form of sports spectatorship. Although usually delayed by days or sometimes weeks, they brought spectators moving action of sportspeople or events they might never have otherwise seen. The advent of sound made the action still more convincing, although all too often it was mixed and added separately (with music) for entertainment rather than authenticity. The newsreel makers were well aware of the audience appeal of sport, which they mixed into a settled formula of current affairs, royal events, disasters, and light documentary features. One fifth of all surviving newsreel film consists of sport.

It was newsreel that made sporting organizations for the first time realize the commercial advantages of selling exclusive rights. Some sporting organizations made and marketed their own newsreels, including the FA for the 1936 and 1937 finals. The sale of exclusive rights provoked intense and often exotic efforts by excluded companies to secure coverage. In 1923 one of their employees used a giant hammer to smuggle a camera into the West Ham versus Bolton FA Cup Final in Wembley (setting for the legendary policeman's white horse which controlled the over-swelled crowd). In 1929 Pathé defended its Epsom Derby coverage with flares, smoke and balloons. At the Oval Test match in 1934, another balloon was used in Paramount's attempt to film from a tower outside the ground, a welcome distraction from England's heavy defeat on the pitch.

A single brilliant piece of play captured on newsreel could turn a sportsperson into an overnight star. One example was Prince Alexander Obolensky: newsreel film of his famous try against New Zealand is still shown regularly 65 years later. This is despite the fact that Obolensky received only seven caps in his entire career. Newsreels also brought spectators the first technical analysis through the use of slow-motion cameras (which revealed, for example, that Newcastle's controversial 1932 Cup Final goal should have been disallowed).

Newsreels also had an important role in globalizing international sport. Even before regular long-distance flying, British moviegoers could watch a major American horserace, the Belmont Stakes, in 1923. With the arrival of air mail and freight, overseas events were covered even more frequently, especially in boxing and golf. The actual sports covered tended to be those popular with the middle classes. Proletarian sports such as greyhound racing, speedway and walking races figured much less often, although all-in wrestling was used for entertainment.

As in radio, some of the voices in newsreel films became well-known, especially the remorselessly cheery Alan Howland of British Movietone News. The announcers gave little commentary or analysis of action, preferring a jolly, rapid-fire collection of weak puns and contorted links between items, which remain a gift to parodists. The tone was predictably nationalist. In the infamous Bodyline cricket series, a British newsreel reported the blow that nearly killed Australian wicket-keeper Bert Oldfield as 'Oldfield is hit, and Larwood is the unlucky bowler!'

In Britain, any sporting triumphs were celebrated exuberantly and the all-too-frequent losers (such as the yachtsman Sir Thomas Lipton) were praised equally extravagantly for their sportsmanship. British newsreels gave only 5 per cent of their sporting coverage to women's sports and the commentary was characteristically patronizing: 'Half a dozen of them show their pace – and a jolly good pace too – in the hundred yards. Come on, girls! [. . .] Away they go on the half mile. Miss Humphries takes it easy in third place here – but soon shakes out her permanent wave and shows a clean pair of heels to the others – winning comfortably by half a dozen yards. Now I suppose it's a visit to the hairdressers.'

The interwar years also put cinema on the world map and some sporting events and personalities, especially in the United States, were big enough to cross from newsreels to feature films. As far back as 1908 Jack Johnson and Tommy Burns fought in front of movie cameras for $30,000 and there were persistent rumours that Jackson held up the fight to provide better drama. The resulting movie of the proud black man's victory provoked riots and lynchings and was banned by Congress. The United States showed itself a little more tolerant after the war in 1921, when the film of the shock victory by Battling Siki, the Senegalese, over Georges Carpentier, the Orchid Man, generated large and appreciative audiences.

During the 1920s a number of American sports stars appeared in loosely plotted 'biopics' based on their sporting lives: the most successful, inevitably, was the all-conquering Babe Ruth. In 1931 the hugely popular football coach Knute Rockne died on his way to making a movie about himself for $50,000. The advent of sound in 1927, and colour in 1935, boosted movie opportunities for glamorous sports people. The young ice-skating prodigy Sonia Henie was showcased in *One In A Million,* a frothy confection with a disagreeably Nazi subtext. It was followed by nine similar movies, and its success led to movie careers for other skating stars. Decathletes Glenn Morris and Bob Mathias landed movie roles after the 1936 Olympics. Swimmers Buster Crabbe and Johnny Weissmuller (still the most remembered Tarzan) were followed into movies by Eleanor Holm, barred from the 1936 Olympics for drinking cocktails with journalists. Esther Williams was trapped into a series of spectacular, but physically exhausting, swimming musicals.

British sportspeople never made it that big in movies, although sport did become a popular subject for the so-called 'quota quickies' – cheap features made in response to a protectionist law to reserve 20 per cent of all films exhibited in British theatres for British productions. Veteran footballer Billy Meredith appeared in an American-style biopic. The popular jockey Steve Donoghue starred in two British features; so too did the popular British greyhound Mick the Miller. In 1929 Alfred Hitchcock made a fine film *The Ring,* set in the world of boxing. No other serious feature films were made about sport, although comedians Tommy Trinder, Will Fyffe, Max Miller and especially George Formby all exploited sport in their light comedies. Arsenal Football Club, which had a gift for self-promotion in the media, provided a setting for *The Great Game, Up For The Cup* and the successful thriller *The Arsenal Stadium Mystery.* Significantly, the latter's heroes were not Arsenal, but an amateur football team of ex-public schoolboys.

By the time *The Arsenal Stadium Mystery* was screened in 1939, television had become part of the sports scene. The Berlin Olympics were shown on closed circuit to around 150,000 viewers in and near the city. They required gigantic cameras and bright sunlight and four men were needed to change a lens. In the United States baseball was first shown on television in 1939, but viewers could not detect the ball. The first televised professional football match in the same year was shown on only 1,000 sets. The BBC had opened its television service in November 1936 and by the outbreak of war it had managed to broadcast two FA Cup Finals, Test cricket, two Wimbledon finals, international rugby and two Boat Races. A 1939 television set cost around £3,000 in today's purchasing power and delivered a poorly defined black-and-white image, which meant that only 25,000 were sold, all within 20 miles of the transmitter at Alexandra Palace. The Home Office hoped that television would reduce the problem of over-crowding at football matches: it was right, but it had to wait for several decades.

Not surprisingly the growth of this new medium alarmed newspapers. While sport sold newspapers and magazines, especially in the United States, they reacted vigorously to the threat from radio, newsreel and television. One of their first steps was to increase their photographic coverage – the biggest advantage over radio. In the 1930s the advent of faster films, longer lenses and bigger apertures allowed for more dramatic action pictures with 1/500th-second exposures. Greater use of photographs is one reason why sports coverage doubled in the interwar period, especially in the popular press. When the *Daily Mirror* was re-launched in Britain in 1933, it raised its sports coverage by a fifth to attract young working-class readers. By 1937 it was giving four times more coverage to sport than to 'serious' news. In both Britain and the United States sport sold hundreds of magazines, tip sheets and annuals throughout the interwar period. In Britain *Willing's Newspaper Press Directory* listed 117 sporting press periodicals in 1919, 197 in 1926, the same number in 1933 and a final figure of 135 in 1940, when wartime anxieties had already killed off several publications. Football was always the biggest single category.

Newspapers and magazines could offer fact and detail, analysis and results in a depth that was especially valuable to punters and which radio could not match, even in countries where it was free to broadcast results. In the United States, the morning line edition and in Britain the Saturday results edition were the financial lifeblood of many local papers. The greater part of sports coverage in all British newspapers before the war was simply list-ings or results.

Yet for all the emphasis on fact, the interwar period saw a trend away from purely factual coverage to writing with some kind of entertainment value. In both the United States and Britain, news-papers attracted sports writers for their literary quality rather than their ability to report. In the United States the peers were Grantland Rice, Heywood Broun and Damon Runyon, although the pre-war original, Ring Lardner, was so depressed by the Chicago Black Sox Scandal in 1919 that he gave up sports writing altogether. Leading American sports writers benefited from the lack of national newspapers, which meant that they were syndi-cated. Grantland Rice's heroic (occasionally racist) style attracted ten million readers and he also had his own regular newsreel.

But here the American and British sports writing traditions diverged.

America, unlike Britain, had never had an 'arties versus heart-ies' division, never assumed that just because you were interested in sport you could not possibly be interested in anything other than sport. Scott Fitzgerald did chastise Ring Lardner for wasting his time sitting beside the baseball diamond writing on the game when he should have been honing his life experiences. But Lardner did not think so and became one of America's finest short-story writers. In general American writers easily crossed the divide between sport and non-sport and do so to this day. Damon Runyon made baseball, American football and boxing central to his fiction. Normal Mailer's writing on boxing and his description of Muhammad Ali, arguably the greatest boxer in the history of the sport, as he fought George Foreman is Mailer at his majestic best. The late David Halberstam's non-fiction work ranged from a classic examination of the Kennedy and Johnson administration to baseball and Michael Jordan.

The contrast with the British sports-writing tradition could not be greater and is illustrated in the story of Neville Cardus. In 1919, recovering from a nervous breakdown, he was sent by the then editor of the *Manchester Guardian* to spend a few days in the sun watching Lancashire at Old Trafford. His writing about cricket was so successful that he created a new genre of sports writing in this country. He also became the paper's music correspondent and had the ideal existence of summers watching cricket, winters writing on music. But as a perceptive critic pointed out, while he often brought in musical analogies to describe cricket, he never introduced cricketing analogies when writing about music.

This was also the case with other British literary figures. Many of them played cricket: Lamb, Hazlitt and Leigh Hunt. Some, like J. M. Barrie, the creator of Peter Pan, were besotted with the game. Cricket, wrote Barrie, was a gift of the gods. He had his own cricket team, Allahakbarries, the name coming from the Arabic Allahakbar meaning Heaven help us, a reference to the fact that Barrie was not a good cricketer and the team did not play the game well. The list of literary giants who played for Barrie is impressive: Jerome K. Jerome, A. E. W. Mason, E. V. Lucas, Arthur Conan Doyle and Doyle's brother-in-law E. W. Hornung (who made his hero Raffles a fine cricketer). They were joined at times by Owen Seaman, a future editor of *Punch*, H. G. Wells, A. A. Milne and P. G. Wodehouse. But Barrie never made it central to his writing; nor did Milne.

On the other hand, Wodehouse is an interesting case. He followed the game religiously even after he went to live in America, and featured cricket heavily in his Mike and Psmith novels, but hardly mentioned it in his main fiction. Harold Pinter also loved cricket and wanted to become a professional cricketer. One of his plays has a reference to an Ashes series between England and Australia. But the reference is purely gratuitous, a curiosity to be debated by Pinter or cricket devotees. Remove it and it makes no difference to the appreciation of the play or Pinter's craft. There is nothing in English cricket literature that matches the treatment of baseball by Philip Roth, or by Bernard Malamud in *The Natural*, or by Don DeLillo in *Underworld*. Nor has there ever been an English film to compare with *Field of Dreams*, where constructing a baseball diamond is a means of exploring how the tarnished American dream could be rescued.

The arrival of radio in Britain did made newspapers seek big names as sports reporters. So *The Times* recruited Bernard Darwin, a descendant of Charles and a connexion of the high-powered Huxleys and Haldanes, to report on golf. Sent to cover the first Walker Cup he found himself playing in the British team (inspiring a similar fantasy in many later journalists). In America a former athlete, Paul Gallico, had invented a style of sports writing that others followed after the war – taking part in sports against famous athletes. He took a knockout from Jack Dempsey in his stride, but was mortified to be outrun by the glamorous female athlete Babe Didrikson.

As well as quality writers, newspapers made more and more use of ghost-written sports personalities. Their earnings were much higher in the United States, because they were free to endorse products on radio and because their crossover from sport to movies was much easier. Knute Rockne and Babe Ruth were the biggest earners, the latter pulling in $2 million in 1930 from all sources, even after the Wall Street crash. In England, sports organizations frowned on sportsmen writing for the media, but Jack Hobbs and Surrey's cricket captain Percy Fender wrote successful cricket columns (Fender's was all his own work). So did Lancashire's maverick spinner, Cecil Parkin, who ended his Test match career by criticizing the (inevitably amateur) captain, Arthur Gilligan. Arsenal's soccer star Charlie Buchan went so far as to found his own magazine, *Charles Buchan's Football Monthly*, after leaving the club. But that came in September 1951, after another war had devastated the world.

Apart from celebrity writers, popular newspapers resorted regularly to stunts, especially at major events. In 1927 the *Evening Standard* sent a fleet of Tiger Moths over London, scattering tips on classic horseraces. The *Star*, another London evening paper, also took to the air, using an autogyro over the 1927 Boat Race. In the 1930s, the revived *Daily Mirror* offered mass table tennis tournaments for 60,000 readers, including the service of the great Jack Hobbs.

More seriously, newspapers brought new sporting events into being. In England the *Daily Mirror*, the *News of the World* and *Sporting Life* combined most creditably in 1924 to organize the international Women's Olympics in London, because there were no track and field events for women in the official Paris Olympics. The *Daily Mail* promoted Amy Johnson's heroic flights (and her increasingly unhappy marriage to fellow-aviator Jim Mollison). In the United States, the *Chicago Tribune* invented the All-Star Football Game and joined with the *New York Times* to create the Golden Gloves boxing tournament, a breeding ground of future champions including Muhammad Ali. *Boxing Blade* not only invented a new category of light heavyweight, but invited readers to select its first champion.

One newspaper magnate who had always understood the value of sports was William Randolph Hearst, the real-life model for Orson Welles' movie *Citizen Kane*. Back in 1887 he had got one of his newspapers, the *San Francisco Examiner*, to have sports stories on the front page: baseball, boxing, horseracing and yachting. If there was any news of a scandal, like allegations of fraud in 1895 in the America's Cup, he made sure it was on the front page. But sport on radio really excited him as he saw the potential for using it to promote newspapers. His executives were not convinced by this new medium and in a letter in September 1927 he rebuked them and demonstrated his understanding of this new medium:

Howard [Roy Howard, the head of the Scripps-Howard newspaper chain] paid twenty five thousand dollars for exclusive rights to radio the Dempsey–Tunney fight. Every radio in the United States listened in and all heard as much about the Scripps-Howard papers as about the fight. This was the greatest advertisement I know of. It is astonishing how many people talked about it, even people who did not know much about newspapers. The effect on [. . .] advertisers must have been very great. I don't have to dilate on value to those who understand the universality of radio especially with the younger generation.

The universality of radio made sports on radio exciting, sports programmes were not expensive to make, and all of America might listen. Hearst advised, 'I would like to have all of our papers broadcast the World Series'.

Yet for all this activity to gain readers or listeners, the interwar media stuck constantly to one golden rule: giving no offence to the sports they were covering. This reticence was one of the most striking things about the interwar sports coverage. All the media, new and old, put themselves in a position of dependency to sports: for copy, for access, for personality, for sales and advertising. The result was an almost total absence of investigative reporting (except by crime reporters, when sport was swept into serious crime).

Media did not report matters that were open secrets in the sports world. No one knew from the media in 1924 how the Yorkshire cricketer Abe Waddington had generated a protest from Middlesex by his persistent appealing to the umpires – even though it happened on the field in front of spectators. The media did not reveal that Walter Hammond was a womanizer who lost a cricket season by contracting a sexually transmitted disease. No one knew from the media that Babe Ruth was a boor who was detested by his team mates. This censorship was serious enough to deny essential knowledge of what was happening. During the Bodyline cricket series, ex-Australian cricketer Alan Fairfax gave a 'commentary' for the many English listeners to Radio Paris, based on cabled information, on Jack Fingleton's courageous innings of 83 in the first Test match. The cables were censored, and no one could know from Fairfax's fluent description that Fingleton was repeatedly hit black-and-blue. Since most English morning newspapers lacked the means to send a correspondent to Australia and relied on the Reuters report, most of their readers simply did not know what Bodyline tactics meant.

Things were even worse at the Nazi Olympics in 1936. There few sports reporters investigated or reported the treatment of Germany's Jewish sportspeople. The overwhelming themes of coverage were about sporting successes and failures and the brilliant organization by the hosts. This, of course, was exactly what the Nazis wanted. Hitler, along with his fellow Fascist Mussolini, was the first leader to realize how useful sport could be for political purposes. The less the press explored what he and his henchmen were really up to the better.

CHAPTER 5

SPORT AS SHAPED BY THE BRUTES

The rise of totalitarian states transformed sport. No such regime could afford to leave sport alone, with its power to excite loyalty and passion and even violence and to offer people an outlet to express their personal identity. But those that emerged in this period, Fascist Italy, Nazi Germany and Communist Russia, all had their distinct ways of handling sport.

These three regimes very quickly established control over all sporting life in their countries. None of their citizens could play in any organized sporting competition, or support any organized team, except on terms dictated by the regime and through structures controlled by it. People considered undesirable, such as foreigners or Jews or Marxists or capitalists, were excluded from sport altogether. The primary motive for sports policies was to keep total control of their populations, and they sought to ensure that all the energy and pride released by sport belonged to the regime. All three also sought to use sport as a means of producing fit and motivated workers and soldiers.

Stalin was initially slow to see the potential of games and remained deeply suspicious of organized sport as a capitalist distraction for the masses. As a result the Russians remained conservative in their sporting policies compared to Fascist Italy and Nazi Germany. Throughout the period, Stalin's regime preferred physical training, typically in mass displays, to any form of organized sport. Soviet sports teams stayed out of major international competitions (largely for fear that its athletes would defect) and, even at the height of his 'Popular Front' policy, when he was seeking allies in the West against Nazi Germany and Japan, Stalin made very little use of sporting diplomacy. Stalin himself never cultivated sports personalities as he cultivated writers, musicians and artists nor had himself photographed in their company. However, Soviet sports, especially football and basketball, did receive patronage from Stalin's henchmen and the organs of the Soviet state under their control, especially the secret police. As with other such dependants, Soviet sports stars and their managers enjoyed periods of lavish privilege, filled with the constant terror of arrest and torture if they or their patrons fell out of favour.

Fascist Italy and Nazi Germany had more ambitious objectives in their control of organized sport. They used it for propaganda and image-building at home and abroad, to promote tourism and earn foreign exchange, to rehearse and reinforce diplomacy, and to underscore specific points about ideology, national identity and race. Mussolini in the long view was the least of the three dictators – some historians even consider him a buffoon. But he was the first of the three to come to power, in 1922, and the first dictator to demonstrate how a twentieth-century government could use sport for wider political purposes. He established a pattern for his successors, although Fascist sports theory and practice had some distinctly Italian features, especially its cooperation with leading Italian industrialists.

Mussolini inherited a virtually clean slate for reorganizing Italian sport: the Italian state itself was young and generally backward compared to other major European countries. In particular, it lacked the urban working-class base of support for organized sport that promoted its development elsewhere. Millions of Italians were simply too poor, too isolated and too busy earning enough for subsistence to take part in sport as players or spectators. Local and regional interests had militated against the formation of strong national organizations in sport as in other areas of Italian life. Moreover, Italy's liberal governments and its strongest institutions, the Catholic Church and the Socialist labour movement, had each neglected sport, for different reasons. The governments had been unwilling to spend money in training teachers to teach physical education. The Catholic Church was suspicious of Italy's most popular sports, football and cycling, as unwelcome products of Anglo-Saxon Protestantism, and the Socialist labour movement was generally wedded to Marxist theories of sport as a capitalist conspiracy to make the working classes forget the misery of their condition.

Against this background, Mussolini faced limited national resistance to his plans for sport, although he was forced to crack down strongly on local and regional interests, especially in football. He had little personal interest in sport – although he had flattering propaganda photographs taken of himself as an expert fencer or as a daring horseman – but his Fascist regime could not afford to leave Italian sport to itself, especially cycling and football, which had already acquired a strong following. Nevertheless, Fascist sports theory was always suspicious of cycling as an individual sport whose superstars, such as Alfredo Binda, attracted a personal cult, which the regime sought to reserve for the *Duce*. However, Fascism proved extremely adept at harnessing football for its propaganda.

The regime's first task was to take control of all of Italy's existing sports and social bodies. Socialist clubs and organizations were banned outright in 1923, but Mussolini planned to absorb and control Catholic ones rather than provoke a fight with the Church. The regime then built a new sports bureaucracy in stages, beginning in 1925 when Mussolini's handpicked Olympic Committee (CONI) took over all Italian sports federations. With the formal objectives of increasing Italian success at the Olympic Games and securing greater Italian representation on world sports organizations, CONI's chairman, Ferretti, imposed a Fascist ideology on all the federations, symbolized by forcing each to adopt the fasces in its badge.

The regime also took over sports clubs, which were brought under the control of local Fascist parties, and a new organization, the OND, formally took over all clubs and organizations providing after-hours recreation for workers, although some managed to retain a little independence. In 1928 Fascism's youth organization, the Balilla, took over responsibility for physical recreation for all children under eighteen. A large-scale building programme brought new gymnasia, swimming pools and sports stadiums to Italian towns, promoting a healthier and more productive labour force with less time to grumble. The regime pressured local employers to support this programme, and many recognized its benefits for themselves.

Apart from controlling the loyalties and leisure life of the Italian people, Fascist sports policy had the more ambitious aim of creating new model Italians. Celebrating ten years of Fascism, the *Popolo d'Italia* wrote in 1932: 'Making the Italian people idealistic and physically perfect was a task for sport in its many forms, as it demands discipline, order, rigour, sacrifice, and a spirit of dedication and healthy morals, while engendering in the individual a desire for the struggle for victory.' Sport was harnessed specifically to support public health campaigns and as Mussolini's foreign policy became more bellicose in the 1930s, the regime also sought to link sport to military readiness. Sport was used not only to create fit and disciplined cadres of young men, but to make them more ready to die in battle. This objective was promoted by a cult of Italian sports heroes killed in the Great War, but had a setback when three of Italy's leading footballers deserted during the Italo-Abyssinian war.

Mussolini also expected all Italian sportspeople to act as ambassadors for his regime overseas. His propagandists contrasted the shambolic Italian presence at the 1920 Antwerp Olympics with its brilliantly organized squad at Los Angeles in 1932. They were quick to exploit Primo Carnera, the gigantic Italian-born boxer, who won the World Heavyweight crown in 1933 and defended his title successfully against Paulino Uzcudun in front of Mussolini himself later that year.

Jack Sher, who got to know Carnera well, writing in *Sports Magazine* in February 1948, described how Mussolini took advantage of the boxer to promote his regime:

> In Rome, the Fascisti hailed the giant as they would a conquering hero returning from ancient wars [. . .] Mussolini stuck his jaw out an inch or so further, pounded his chest, dressed Carnera in military uniform, and sent pictures to the far corners of the earth showing Primo executing the Fascist salute. It is not to Carnera's credit that he played ball with the Fascist hoods. But he was politically unaware and, by this time, conditioned to take orders from anyone who held the whip-hand [. . .] Primo did disobey Mussolini once. It is not very well known, but the massive man had an inordinate love for automobile racing. He would cram his huge frame into a tiny racing car and, with utter fearlessness, give it the gun. The belligerent Benito forbade him to race, but Primo, on the sly, entered the annual 1,000-mile Italian auto race. He didn't have the moola for a car of his own, so he drove for the Alfa Romeo auto company and [was] placed third. 'When the boss heard about it,' Primo said, smiling, 'he called me to Rome to see him and he gave me hell.'

However, Mussolini was equally quick to dump him when he lost to Max Baer.

The Germans had a more complicated relationship with the boxer Max Schmeling. He was lionized by the Nazis when he knocked out Joe Louis and won the heavyweight crown in 1936. A delirious crowd welcomed him back to Berlin and Hitler met him at the Reich's chancellery. Goebbels ordered a documentary of the fight be made. The title: *Schmeling's Victory, A German Victory* indicated how the Nazi regime saw the fight. Schmeling was such a hero during the 1936 Berlin Olympics that one British journalist wrote, 'In rank and importance he did not seem to be much below Hitler and Goering.' Pictures taken at the time of the Games show him standing in an open top car while athletes mill round him trying to shake his hand.

Two years later the Nazis gave him a tremendous send off when he went back to America to fight Louis. But this time he lost in the very first round, hardly laying a glove on the American. He claimed Louis had won unfairly and then tried to retract the claim. The sensational victory stunned the Germans. Goebbels in his diary confessed to being depressed and blamed the press for over-egging the fight. A Frankfurt paper cancelled its planned extra edition but the reason it gave underlined the German confusion: 'The reports from New York were so contradictory that we, in the interests of accurate coverage, decided not to publish a special edition.' Hitler, himself, had got up in the middle of the night to ask about the fight and was reported to be both 'extremely depressed' and 'philosophical'. There was this time no welcome for the boxer. But the writer David Margolick, author of the book *Beyond Glory*, a study of Louis versus Schmeling, has concluded, 'Contrary to much that was written later, Schmeling and Ondra [his wife] remained in good official odour, even if he was understandably less lionized and conspicuous than before'. But Hitler made it clear Schmeling could not fight Louis again as the Fuhrer feared what another international defeat, and that at the hands of a black man, would do for German prestige.

Mussolini's greatest success was the exploitation of the winning Italian football side in the 1930s. Mussolini's takeover of Italian football used much the same technique as his takeover of the Italian state itself: Fascists caused chaos and were then installed in power to restore order. The chaos was triggered by the bitterly contested championship play-off in 1925 between Genoa and Bologna. After two drawn matches, Genoa were leading 2–1 in the third play-off. Bologna had a claim for an equalizing goal disallowed. The local Fascist leader, Arpinati, led a crowd invasion that panicked the referee, Mauro, into allowing the goal after all. Arpinati also intimidated Mauro into suppressing details of the crowd invasion in his report and the two teams were forced to play yet another match, behind closed doors. This time Arpinati's team managed to win (85 years later this 'robbery' still rankles with Genoa fans). This match precipitated a national referee strike, led by Mauro, due to pressures from club owners and crowds. This allowed the regime to set up a commission to resolve the crisis in Italian football. Its dominant figure was Arpinati – the leading hooligan, now appointed Mayor of Bologna.

The commission devised the Viareggio Charter, which imposed unity on Italian football on Fascist terms, although its major reforms were logical and overdue – the creation of a genuine national championship and the legalization of professionalism. Fascist influence was expressed in its other major reform, the banning of foreign players (many turned themselves into successful managers and coaches), but this reform was almost instantly circumvented by a redefinition of Italian-ness. Reflecting Mussolini's efforts to enlist Italians overseas to support the regime, Italian football clubs were allowed, even encouraged, to recruit the *oriundi*, players overseas who could claim any sort of Italian descent. This brought to Italian football a stream of highly talented players from Latin America.

In line with Fascist propaganda generally, the regime disguised the foreign origins of football and gave it a spurious Roman provenance. The sport was renamed Calcio, team positions and even cheers were given new Italian terms and clubs that had retained English names or spellings from their founders were compelled to Italianize them. The regime invested heavily in new stadiums, notably in Arpinati's Bologna, in a profusion of styles – some neo-classical, others hyper-modern, all intended as visual propaganda for Fascism.

Mussolini's was the first regime to influence the content of sports reporting. His controlled press regularly linked sporting success to his inspiration and spun defeats into near-victories, notably the Italian football team's comeback in the 3–2 defeat by

England at Highbury in 1933. In the bitter club match between Juventus and Slavia Prague in 1934 the Italian media orchestrated fury at the Czech players and fans and then obediently changed their tune when Mussolini wanted to calm things down. (In fairness, the media followed the same course in democratic Czechoslovakia.) On radio, Italian football was conveyed to the masses through the super-patriotic and ideologically correct commentary of Niccolò Carosio.

The most intriguing aspect of Fascist football was its cooperation with leading industrialists. Their involvement in football pre-dated the regime, but was intensified in the 1920s, in line with the regime's ideal of a corporate state where all economic interests became agents of a single national policy. The Pirelli rubber business ran AC Milan, Borletti, a leading consumer goods manufacturer, ran Inter Milan and, above all, Eduardo Agnelli of Fiat controlled Juventus. Through their clubs, the industrialists helped to cement workers' loyalty to their companies and to the regime.

Mussolini's investment in football paid off in the 1930s when he hosted the 1934 World Cup (almost no other country bid for it in the Depression) and turned it into a propaganda showpiece. He added a garish Coppa del Duce to the Jules Rimet Trophy and seized control from FIFA of the issue and design of its commemorative postage stamps. Like everything else in the tournament, the stamps featured the fasces symbol. The Fascist anthem 'Giovinezza' was sung at each match (foreshadowing the performance of the Nazi 'Horst-Wessel Lied' at the Berlin Olympics). Mussolini's own appearances at matches were greeted with mass hysteria (in a typical populist gesture he ostentatiously paid for his match tickets).

Expertly managed by Vittorio Pozzo, the Italian team won two successive World Cups, despite the occasional handicap of Mussolini's interference in team selection. In 1934, on home soil, it had some help from lenient refereeing when the talented Spaniards and Czechs were brutally fouled, but not in 1938 when it won in France. Mussolini gave the winners additional prizes and hospitality which amounted to an extended photo-opportunity. The team's star players, Meazza and Piola, both Italian-born rather than *oriundi*, were promoted as model Italians and products of the regime. Meazza was given the affectionate nickname of Balilla, after an historic young hero whose name had already been taken by Mussolini's paramilitary youth movement. (He was also used to sell toothpaste and brilliantine.)

The regime's exploitation of Italian football ensured that its national team was the first to attract protests for political rather than sporting reasons. Cardosio's chauvinistic commentary on the team's away match against Belgium in 1933 was interrupted when some exiled Italians snatched his microphone. Its 1938 World Cup match in Marseille against Norway brought demonstrations from some 10,000 Italian exiles and French anti-fascists. Both incidents were ignored in the Italian media, although the second provoked Mussolini to order the team to play their next match in black shirts.

The year 1938 was a golden year for Italian sport: besides the World Cup victory, the Italian Gino Bartali won the Tour de France and the Italian racehorse Nearco completed a string of classic victories. All these triumphs were linked by the media to Mussolini. Small wonder that the regime planned a special super-Olympic Games in 1942 to celebrate twenty years of Fascism. Its sporting policies were widely admired in other countries. In 1934 the Brazilians appointed a journalist to head their World Cup squad with no qualifications except admiration for the Duce, and after the Italian victory in 1938 a well-known French journalist, Maurice Pefferkorn, wrote that 'an Italian school is already talked of, to which one needs to aspire.' As the first ruler to attempt totalitarian control over his country's sport, Mussolini certainly gave lessons to many other contemporary regimes, including those of Spain, Portugal, Hungary, Brazil, Argentina – and, of course, Adolf Hitler's.

Hitler shared with Mussolini the ambition of controlling sport

144

as a social force. In *Mein Kampf* he had written: 'Give the nation six million impeccably trained bodies, all impregnated with fanatical patriotism and animated with the most fervent fighting spirit. In less than two years if need be, a nation state will turn them into an army.' His particular sporting interests were boxing, motor racing and handball, which was inserted at his behest in the 1936 Olympics. Of boxing, he said 'No other sport is its equal in building up aggressiveness, in demanding lightning-like decisions, and in tackling the body in steely agility.' But his treatment of sport was far more rigid and brutal than Mussolini's, partly because of the character of his regime and its racial agenda and partly because he inherited a different sporting tradition. His policy was also complicated by his inheritance of the Olympic Games from the Weimar Republic.

Hitler took office in January 1933, and almost immediately the Nazis began to remove Jews from German sport as from other walks of life. They also turned on communists, trade union leaders, homosexuals and immigrants. In April the regime seized thousands of Jewish bank accounts, sacked all non-Aryan officials in public administration and removed all Jewish teachers, including many sports coaches, from their posts. Schools, colleges and universities were limited to a maximum of 1.5 per cent non-Aryans among their students, which of course excluded thousands of Jews overnight from school or college sport.

The following month the Nazis banned all trade unions and sent many of their leaders to concentration camps. They also banned Jewish–Aryan marriages and set up a Race Council to define who was a true Aryan. They encouraged non-Jews to denounce Jews in any sort of authority, including honorary positions in sports and social clubs, to boycott their businesses and to exclude them generally from social life. In sport, Jews were specifically banned from tennis tournaments and rowing, boxing, gymnastic and ski clubs. Signs began to appear in public places, including parks and swimming pools: 'Jews Not Wanted'. They were formally banned from public recreational facilities in August 1935.

One of Hitler's earliest appointments was former army captain Hans von Tschammer und Osten, an early Nazi supporter, as director of all German sports and as president of the German Olympic Council. Tschammer und Osten was a sadist and a martinet and wholly ignorant of sport, although his aristocratic affectations impressed gullible foreigners. An English socialite, 'Bunny' Tattersall, who toured Europe in the 1930s in search of sport and leisure, described him as 'a man of outstanding ability, besides possessing extremely good looks'. The new sports director's brief was to create fit young Aryan Germans who were eager to serve their Fuhrer. He reported to Goebbels, the propaganda minister, who declared that 'German sport has only one task, to strengthen the character of the German people, imbuing it with the fighting spirit and steadfast camaraderie necessary in the struggle for its existence.'

Unlike Mussolini, Hitler had to deal with a vibrant and well-established sporting culture. German football had flourished under the Weimar Republic after the introduction of the eight-hour day and weekend breaks for working people and the abolition of the Imperial regime's restrictions on associations. Thousands of new town-based clubs were registered in the 1920s under the German Football Association (DFB). A Jewish journalist, Walter Bensemann, was a leading promoter of German football and many Jews were prominent as players and administrators. A stuffy conservative organization, the DFB, was alarmed by the working-class support for many of the new clubs, especially Schalke 04. It did its best to keep them out of the top flight and rigidly enforced a policy of amateurism, in spite of heavy defeats by the professional Austrians.

Predictably, the DFB offered little or no resistance to the Nazi takeover of football and accepted without protest a new subordinate status as the football and English sports section of the new Nazi Reichsbund; all its senior members joined the Nazi Party. In June 1933 the Nazi education minister, Rust, decreed the expulsion of Jews from all youth and sports organizations, but the DFB

was actually ahead of it, when in April it published an unequivo-
cal statement of its own policy: 'Members of the Jewish race and
individuals who are members of the Marxist movement are unacceptable in leading positions in regional organizations and clubs,
who are urged to initiate appropriate measures.' Almost all
German football clubs followed this instruction, with the honourable exception of Bayern Munich.

After the Jews, the Nazis turned on Christian churches and
trade unions that had long been active in football and sport
generally. Both had believed in offering their followers a
complete social life and had founded thousands of voluntary
sports clubs. Apart from recreation, these clubs aimed to promote
citizenship and solidarity, building on the tradition of gymnastic
patriotism developed by 'Father' Freidrich Jahn in the Napoleonic
period. The Nazis wanted Jahn to themselves, so in *Sport and
State*, an official handbook commissioned by Tschammer und
Osten and published in 1934, the Nazis linked Jahn's name to the
militaristic philosophy of the SA Nazi stormtroopers. The
manual was filled with images of young people in sports kit
posing alongside young people in uniforms. Although the SA
was suppressed violently in the Night of the Long Knives in July
1934, its philosophy survived in the Strength Through Joy (KDF)
movement, which enlisted millions of Germans and provided
them with 'sensible amusements'.

The regime compelled all sports and social clubs either to
dissolve themselves or accept the authority of the KDF or the
rapidly expanding Hitler Youth. Clubs that were explicitly
socialist or Communist were given no choice and were simply
closed down, as were many church-based clubs that had shown
too much independence. In May 1934 all remaining Protestant-
based clubs were put to the test when the Nazis reorganized
German Protestant churches into the pro-Nazi Protestant Reich
Church. This move was resisted by pastors led by Dietrich
Bonhoeffer and Martin Niemoller, who founded the independent
Confessing Church. To the Nazis' fury it made itself known at the

147

1936 Olympic Games, Just before the Olympics, a manifesto commenting critically on how the Nazis had made Hitler a God-like figure was smuggled out of the country and, during the Games, Bonhoeffer gave several anti-Nazi speeches which were well received.

Otherwise there was little resistance to the Nazification of sport. By the outbreak of war, virtually every German who took part in sport did so through an organization controlled by the Hitler Youth or the KDF. When in 1934 the Hitler Youth took over all responsibility for youth football from individual clubs, it meant that no boy could obtain coaching or develop his game without also being indoctrinated with Nazi ideology.

Like Mussolini, Hitler tried to use German sports stars as propagandists for his regime, but outside the Olympic Games he was less fortunate with his choices. He was only once persuaded to watch the German national football team: overawed by his presence it stumbled to a 2–0 defeat against the lowly Norwegians and he walked out after the second goal, five minutes before the finish. Hitler also made a special effort to enlist Gottfried von Cramm, the popular, handsome, 'Aryan-looking' tennis star. Cramm refused to cooperate and the Nazis tried and imprisoned him for having a homosexual affair with a Jewish actor.

Hitler was well aware of the power of sport and exercise to condition young people mentally as well as physically. In 1938 he declared:

> Boys and girls enter our organizations at ten years of age and often for the first time *get a little fresh air* [my italics]. After four years of the Young Folk they go on to the Hitler Youth, where we have them for another four years [. . .] And even if they are still not complete National Socialists, they go to Labour Service and are smoothed out there for another six, seven months.

The Nazis made athletic standards a condition of school entry and substituted them for academic achievements in the curriculum.

(One schoolboy's life was much influenced by this policy. When Bert Trautmann left school he was not qualified to achieve his childhood ambition of becoming a Luftwaffe pilot. Instead he tried to train as a wireless operator and joined a Luftwaffe regiment before becoming a paratrooper. He was captured and taken as a prisoner of war to England, where he went on to become a heroic goalkeeper for Manchester City.) Sport, including board games and toys, was used in the school curriculum to spread racial and political propaganda.

In 1936 it became compulsory for all boys and girls between 10 and 17 to be members of a Nazi youth group. For boys, the Young Folk and the Hitler Youth offered after-school activities and weekend and longer camps in which sports were blended seamlessly with military training and political indoctrination. The Nazis made shooting compulsory and also favoured hiking, climbing and swimming (sports especially useful for military preparedness) and boys were often required to perform highly dangerous tasks (such as climbing without ropes). For girls, the League of German Maidens concentrated on rhythmic gymnastics, which were thought more feminine and better training for motherhood. Although the Nazis celebrated the success of their female athletes at the Berlin Olympics, Nazi ideology preferred women to be mothers and housewives – a policy that persisted through the war, when millions of German women were encouraged to stay at home rather than join the armed forces or work in agriculture or factories.

From the outset, the Nazis were clear that the purpose of sport for boys was to prepare fit, brave soldiers who were ready for sacrifice. One observer in 1935 noted boys having sports training in special camps under banners proclaiming 'Our duty is to die for Germany'. Ivone Kirkpatrick, a far-seeing British diplomat at the Berlin embassy, wrote that 'The German schoolboy of today is being methodically educated, mentally and physically, to defend his country. He is being taught to die to protect his frontier. But I fear that [. . .] he will be found to be equally well fitted and ready to march or die on foreign soil.' In spite of the abundant evidence of Nazi militarism, many foreigners admired the Nazi approach to youth sport. Avery Brundage, the American millionaire who later became president of the IOC, declared that 'In 1930, German youth was undersized, anaemic and undernourished. They were of poor colour. Today, they are strong and vigorous, all because they are better athletes.'

At the onset of war, the Nazis intensified the nexus between youth sport and military training, and by the end of the war boys as young as twelve were being drafted directly into Hitler's version of the Home Guard, alongside men over sixty. In March 1945 thousands of them were summoned to the Olympic Stadium, where they were exhorted to 'show the Olympic spirit' by going into battle against the conquering Russians. The speaker was Hitler's Olympic organizer, Dr Carl Diem, and at least 2,000 of the boys were killed.

The award of the 1936 Olympic Games to Berlin was intended to symbolize the re-admission of a peaceful, democratic Germany to the family of nations. By a supreme irony, those Games have gone down in history as a triumph of Nazi propaganda. As the official *Olympic-Zeitung* proudly asked on 19 August 1936: 'Do we have to point out that the great victor at the Olympic Games is Adolf Hitler?' The 1936 Olympics have been well documented, but three themes remain compelling and relevant to our times. The first is the extraordinary mixture of opportunism, improvisation and thoroughness in the Nazi preparations for the Games. The second is the use of the Games for political and diplomatic goals, not only by the regime, but by its opponents. The third is the degree to which Hitler was assisted in his agenda by leaders of international sport who ought to have known better. They played into Hitler's hands by their willingness to believe dishonest public assurances by the regime and to accept gestures and symbols rather than look at reality.

Before he came to power, Hitler was hostile to the Olympic Games. He described them as 'an invention of Jews and

Freemasons' and a form of 'Judaistic theatre which cannot possibly be put on in a Reich ruled by National Socialists'. Alarmed that he might carry out this threat in power, the head of the German Olympic Organizing Committee, Theodor Lewald, appealed for help to Josef Goebbels, the propaganda minister. Goebbels changed Hitler's mind, and Lewald was able to secure an upbeat public statement of support for the Games from Hitler. Lewald had made a Faustian bargain. He had saved the Games only to turn them into a Nazi showcase. He himself was of Jewish descent and the Nazis preserved him only as a figure-head to impress foreigners. Effective power was transferred to his deputy, Carl Diem (who had a Jewish wife but was totally compliant with the Nazis), and Hitler's new sports director, Tschammer und Osten.

Within a few months, Hitler was a complete convert to the Olympic Games. Inspecting the proposed site in Berlin, he ordered it to be vastly expanded (at the expense of a leading Berlin race-course) to accommodate a giant amphitheatre. When the Games were over, Hitler summoned his favourite architect, Albert Speer, to plan a brand-new Olympic site. When Speer fretted that it would exceed the permitted dimensions, Hitler told him not to worry – after 1940 (when the Games had been awarded to his ally, Japan) the Olympic Games, and their rule-making body, were to be set permanently in Germany.

In January 1934 Goebbels formed and chaired a euphemistically named 'general publicity' committee to plan every detail of the use of the Games for propaganda, including the control of news and the preparation of works of art such as (important to Hitler the artist) the design of posters and medals. A casual suggestion at that meeting led to a spectacular combination of innovation and organization which proved to be the Nazis' great legacy to the Olympics: a torch-lit relay from Greece to Berlin. The idea perfectly suited the Nazis' love of pseudo-ancient ritual and dramatic lighting effects. After grasping the new idea, the Nazis planned every single step of its long route and the brilliant director Leni Riefenstahl was despatched to film the relay. Several of her sequences were invented, but there was nothing fictional about the last lap of the torch, entrusted to a young runner called Fritz Schilgen – selected less for running ability than for his perfect blond 'Aryan' good looks.

Many other incidents in the 1936 Olympic story show a similar combination of Nazi opportunism and thoroughness. Contrary to widespread myth, Hitler did not snub the great black American athlete Jesse Owens. Instead, he took advantage of an Olympic rule that only Olympic officials presented winners' medals. Hitler, of course, had been flouting the rules almost every day since he took power, but now they came to his aid – and they did not prevent him from greeting and entertaining favoured white 'Aryan' athletes so long as he did not bemedal them.

The Nazis took expert advantage of Coubertin. By then the founder of the modern Olympics was depressed and in poor financial straits: they gave him money and put him up for the Nobel Peace Prize (in the hope of forestalling its award to the German anti-Nazi journalist Carl von Ossietzky). They then had him in their pocket and he rewarded them with a long public statement defending their management of the Games: Coubertin actually suggested that there was no difference between the Nazis using the Games to promote their regime and Los Angeles four years earlier to promote tourism.

Before the Olympics the Nazis faced a selection problem over two German Jewish athletes of world class. They tackled each problem in opposite fashion, but with equal thoroughness. The flaxen-haired fencer, Helene Mayer, was induced by a mixture of threats and favours to take part, thus depriving protestors of a potential cause célèbre. Gretel Bergmann, the high jumper, was blackmailed, for similar reasons, into returning to Germany to train with the team, but the Nazis had a secret agenda of excluding her from final selection. To this end, they pitted against her a female impersonator, Hermann 'Dora' Ratzen, on the sexist assumption that any male jumper would be better than any female one. When this proved untrue, they simply sacked Bergmann with an unsigned letter.

Everything done at the Berlin Olympics showed obsessive attention to detail, driven by the same motive of impressing both Germans and visitors with the success of Nazism. The athletes were better housed and fed than in any previous Games, but were also the most carefully watched. The helpful guides assigned to each nation were handpicked from the German army; the eager young messengers and gophers were chosen from the Hitler Youth. Nothing at all was left to chance: to be certain of the right mood during the Games, the regime even decreed a National Laughter Week.

The 1936 Olympics were a test bed for Nazi diplomacy and political influence over other nations. The immediate priority was to meet the real threat of a boycott. The treatment of Jews had produced widespread pressure for a boycott in the United States, which would have been enough on its own to make any Games meaningless and would probably have been followed by other important nations, including Britain. Moreover, even the normally docile International Olympic Committee felt bound to warn the Germans that their anti-Jewish measures could forfeit them the Games.

The Nazis responded to this threat with methods that they would use successfully on more serious issues. They used respectable frontmen, such as Lewald, and blamed all criticisms on enemies of the regime, especially in the media. They made bland statements of good intentions (foreshadowing the piece of paper given to Chamberlain at Munich) and were indignant when anyone asked them to back them with formal guarantees. They made small concessions, especially on symbolic issues such as anti-Jewish signs. When they needed to, they told direct lies. And when all else failed, they wheeled out Hitler himself to impress foreign visitors as a man of sweet reasonableness.

Hitler bamboozled one important visitor, the American General Sherrill, an IOC member who went to Germany in August 1935 promising to confront the Nazis on the Jewish question. Instead he wrote a gushing letter to President Roosevelt about Hitler's face and figure which 'showed he is in perfect health [. . .] his eye is clear, his glance is frank, his replies prompt but limited.' He praised Hitler (the ranting monologist) for not speechifying, 'Especially, did I notice the clarity and neatness of his German – if all Germans spoke so, we poor foreigners would better understand them!' He even praised Hitler's physical fitness and suggested that his photographs 'give no hint of the engaging human being he can be when he wants to be'. As for the Jewish question, Sherrill was prepared to believe that Hitler was unaware of the anti-Jewish policies of his own Interior Ministry and was actually furious to be informed of them. Like many other Americans, Sherrill was defensive when the Nazis raised the issue of the colour bar in the United States. This tactic worked on many other Americans, and was unwittingly assisted by the young black athlete Benjamin Johnson, who declared that 'It is futile and hypocritical [to] attempt to clean up conditions in Germany before cleaning up similar conditions in America.'

To disarm the British, the Nazis used a new method: football diplomacy. The German national team visited England in 1935 to play an international. Of all the possible venues, the match was played at the ground of Tottenham Hotspur, a club with a high concentration of Jewish supporters. Both the team and the near 10,000 German supporters were under strict instructions to behave well, and both were gracious in a 3–0 defeat by England, even when they faced some hostile demonstrations. Among their fans was Tschammer und Osten, who later made a good impression as guest of honour at a dinner by the Anglo-German Fellowship (a gang of upper-crust Nazi admirers). All this meant that the Nazis deflected the threats from the IOC and from major sporting powers. Their only problem came from a few individual athletes, mostly Jewish, who boycotted the Games.

The only organized boycott came from the left-of-centre Popular Front government in Spain. At the very last minute it promoted an alternative festival called the Spanish Republic's People's Olympiad in Barcelona (the city which had lost the official Olympics to Berlin). The government's hasty preparations were impeded by its inability to find the address of the American Athletic Union, but eventually it managed to invite progressive athletes from all nations to a 'popular sports festival which does not hope for record feats, but intends to preserve the true Olympic spirit of peace and co-operation between nations'. Somewhat contradictorily, it added: 'In the struggle against Fascism, the broad masses of all countries must stand shoulder to shoulder, and Popular Sport is a valuable medium through which they may demonstrate their international solidarity.' Unfortunately, the chosen dates for the alternative Games, 19–26 July, coincided with the outbreak of the Spanish Civil War. Barcelona saw fierce fighting in which the Republicans suppressed the rebels. The worker athletes staged two parades in Barcelona in support of the Republic before being evacuated.

As in his more serious ventures, Hitler was lucky in his Olympic diplomacy in the calibre of the Western leaders he faced. Two in particular made his job much easier – the American athletic powerbroker Avery Brundage and the IOC's Belgian chairman Count Henri Baillet-Latour, through their determination that the Games must carry on (a belief that Brundage maintained with mystical fervour to the end of his career, even after the terrorist massacre of Israeli athletes at Munich). Brundage was also engaged in a bitter power struggle over American athletics against the pro-boycott faction led by former judge Jeremiah Mahoney. In this struggle he portrayed himself as protector of the rights of young American athletes to compete internationally, though later a less creditable motive emerged for Brundage's behaviour, when he touted for contracts to re-build the German embassy in Washington.

In his defence of the Berlin Olympics, Brundage consistently ignored and suppressed all evidence of Nazi wrongdoing, not only from newspaper reports, but also from the American

embassy. Brundage toured Germany in September 1934, supposedly to investigate conditions for Jewish athletes. He stayed for
just a few days, seeing only what the Nazis wanted him to see and
believing everything they told him. The following year he made a
speech on how much America could learn from Germany: his
notes say 'Hitler: a god [. . .] given back self-respect [. . .] a man of
the people'.

For all his failings Baillet-Latour did more to challenge Hitler
than most Western politicians before the war. In May 1933, on
behalf of the IOC, he warned the Germans that their 'measures
against certain athletes' (he could not bring himself to say Jews)
had created hostility in the sporting world and that if Hitler
attempted to take over the Games from the IOC they would be
removed from Berlin. But his determination to keep the IOC
together and safeguard the Games from political controversy
always made him reluctant to push the Nazis too far. In 1933 he
settled for a bland, weasel-worded statement from Lewald, which
left the Nazis free to pursue their agenda without outside interference. In 1936 Baillet-Latour actually confronted Hitler directly
over the anti-Jewish signs on the roads leading to the Winter
Olympics. Hitler began a monologue, but Baillet-Latour held his
ground and threatened to cancel both the Winter and the Summer
Olympics if they were not removed. Hitler shouted 'You will be
satisfied! The orders will be given' and stormed out of the room. It
was a victory and Baillet-Latour was vain about it, but a victory
over a relatively trivial issue, and his vanity made him more reluctant to confront the Nazis about more serious ones. (Again, this
foreshadowed Hitler's tactics at Munich, which gave Chamberlain
inordinate pride in winning trivial concessions.)

In their Olympic diplomacy, as on bigger issues, the Nazis
could count on many sympathizers in high places who were more
than willing to excuse their anti-Jewish policies and positively
admired their anti-communism and their restoration of discipline
to the German people after the decadence of the Weimar years.
The IOC's Swedish vice-president, Sigfrid Edstrøm, said nothing

exceptional in December 1933 when he wrote to Brundage to say, 'The day may come when you will have to stop the activities of the Jews. They are intelligent and unscrupulous. Many of my friends are Jews, so you must not think I am against them, but they must be kept within certain limits.'

There were also many in Britain who shared Ribbentrop's view that it was unfair of the Americans to bring black athletes to the Olympic Games because they were racially adapted to perform better than whites. Captain Webster, a leading British athletics journalist, endorsed that view when he described Jesse Owens as 'a black thunderbolt' who had 'a spontaneity of spring which is still the heritage of the native not yet too untrammelled by the filters of civilization'.

Both the Winter and the Summer Olympics attracted hordes of rich upper-class Nazi sympathizers, and the Nazis rewarded them with competing parties of ever-increasing opulence and vulgarity. Goering, festooned in decorations, presided over a state banquet, a lunch and a party with a funfair; Goebbels staged a party on a nature reserve and Ribbentrop held one at his giant villa (funded by his rich wife). The major embassies gave return parties of their own. Henry Channon, the rich Conservative MP who kept a splendidly indiscreet diary, was one of many who preferred the parties to the boring Olympic events, and the Nazis also welcomed the Lindberghs and the Mitford sisters Diana and Unity.

The parties provided opportunities for serious diplomacy as the Nazis took advantage of the visit of Sir Robert Vansittart, the staunchly anti-Nazi head of the British Foreign Office. On instructions from the Foreign Secretary, Anthony Eden, Vansittart tried to commit the Germans to join a new conference on the future of Europe: he was blanked by Ribbentrop and Hitler, but the British ambassador, Sir Eric Phipps (Vansittart's brother-in-law), judged the visit a success at a personal level and in helping reduce mutual suspicions. The parties were also a setting for internal German politics: Goering and the German foreign minister,

Neurath, plotted successfully to send Ribbentrop away as ambassador to London.

Apart from the rich and powerful, thousands of ordinary tourists visited the Nazi Olympics, attracted by a favourable exchange rate which made Germany a popular holiday destination until the outbreak of war. The regime made sure that ordinary tourists were looked after and it paid off in influence over British attitudes. In *The Long Weekend*, their popular social history of the interwar period, Robert Graves and Alan Hodge commented on Britain's apathetic response to the German re-occupation of the Rhineland in 1936: 'and anyhow, the Germans weren't such bad people really, although they did have a mania about the Jews – those Olympic Winter Sports at Garmisch had been marvellously organized, and everyone had been so hospitable and polite.'

Essentially, the Nazis got everything they wanted from the Olympic Games. They impressed foreigners, proved to Hitler that he could ignore international pressures, and bound Germans more closely to the regime. Goebbels, their sinister saviour in 1933, expressed in his diary his delight in the 'reawakening of national pride' and hailed the Games as 'a major breakthrough [. . .] helping us a lot in our cause'. Foreign correspondents confirmed Goebbels' view. In the *New York Times* Frederick Birchall (no Nazi sympathizer) wrote: 'Foreigners who know Germany only from what they have seen during this pleasant fortnight can carry home only one impression. It is that this is a nation happy and prosperous beyond belief; that Hitler is one of the greatest political leaders in the world today; and that Germans themselves are a much maligned, hospitable, wholly peaceful people who deserve the best the world can give them.' One Olympic competitor, who would play a major part in world sport in the decades to come, certainly returned to his homeland very impressed with the Germans. João Havelange was the son of Belgians who had emigrated to Brazil and was part of his country's swimming team. Even years later he could not hide his pleasure at being in Berlin in 1936. He waxed enthusiastically about the Nazi organization of the transport, the equipment and facilities for the 25,000 people at the Games. The Germans provided opportunities for the athletes to visit the Berlin Philharmonic and gave concessionary travel arrangements, as much as 75 per cent discount on tickets. As a result, Havelange, then twenty, managed to visit 25 different cities.

It would have been interesting if during all this travelling Havelange had met up with a man whose son was to have a tremendous impact both on Havelange and world sport. This was Adolf Dassler, a shoemaker from Herzogenaurach, a village near Nuremberg in northern Bavaria. His shoe company, which was later to be known as Adidas, had provided shoes for the German track team in the 1928 and 1932 Olympics. In Berlin he wanted more customers – especially Jesse Owens. Barbara Smit, historian of the Dassler family businesses writes:

> Equally awed by Jesse's unprecedented performances, Adi Dassler was desperate to get his shoes on the runner's feet. Joseph Waitzer [the German athletics coach] probably warned his friend that he would be well advised to keep a low profile. Surely, the Nazis would not be amused if they found out that the Bavarian shoemaker provided the spikes that helped a Negro to defeat their Aryan runners. But Dassler was undeterred. Regardless of the politics, Jesse Owens was a stupendous runner. There was no doubt that he would be the hero of the Berlin Olympics. Once he had found the American Dassler timidly pulled out his spikes, gesturing and mimicking until Jesse Owens agreed to try them out.

While wearing the Dassler shoes with two dark stripes of leather running down the sides Owen made history. Dassler was delighted. The Berlin Olympics generated annual sales of 200,000 pairs and was an important stepping stone on the eventual commercial domination of the sports business by Adidas. More than 40 years later, as we shall see, his son Horst used Adidas to create sporting alliances with Havelange, and others, which completely reshaped world sport.

There was another group of foreigners who went away with happy memories of Nazi Germany and in some ways this was the most curious team to take part in Hitler's sports show. Like Owens, the Indian Hockey team won great honour in their sport, but their interaction with the Nazis was very different from that of Owens. India had arrived on the Olympic scene in Amsterdam in 1928, winning gold at its first attempt, retained it at Los Angeles in 1932 and were now back again in Europe. But India, of course, was a British colony and its rise as the world's supreme field hockey power had resulted in an extraordinary decision by British hockey not to take part in the Olympics. Some Indians still see this as a racist reaction to India's dominance, not dissimilar to how the Nazis reacted to Owen. If there was racism involved here then there was also a sharp contrast between the British in Britain and those living in India.

Hockey, like all modern sports, had been taken to India by the British and become a popular sport in the Indian army much encouraged by the British officers in charge. Dyan Chand, the Bradman of hockey and its greatest-ever player, was introduced to the game while serving in the army and virtually ordered to tour with India on its ground-breaking visit to New Zealand in 1926 when India announced itself on the world stage. That tour saw India win 18 of the 21 matches, scoring 192 goals, ceding only 24. It helped New Zealand hockey make a profit of £300, after paying the Indians £500 in expenses, both considerable sums in 1926. Dyan Chan would later describe how he went on the tour: the British commanding officer summoned him and just said, 'Boy, you are to go to New Zealand.' In the army Dyan Chand served in the 'Other Ranks', a sepoy, an ordinary soldier, earning a few rupees (a few pence) a month. His clothes were basically his army uniform, but this tour made him, for a few weeks providing him a luxurious lifestyle which he had never experienced before and which, as he admitted later, changed his life.

Success in New Zealand also made the Indians venture into the Olympics, and in 1928 the Indians arrived in England on their way to the Amsterdam Games, where they met the England team at the Folkestone Easter festival and beat them 4–0. British hockey's response was to drop out of the Olympics altogether, despite the fact that it had dominated previous Olympics. It had won gold on the only two occasions field hockey had been part of the Games in 1908 and 1920 (there being no hockey in Paris in 1924). But from 1928 it refused to take part in the Olympics and stayed out for two decades. Dyan Chand says he heard Britain dropped out after the Folkestone game, fearing a beating by the Indians. He had long retired by the time Britain returned and as hockey's greatest player he always regretted not being given a chance to play in the Olympic arena against the country that had invented the game.

This British withdrawal, and more so the timing of its return to Olympic hockey in 1948, gave sustenance to the Indian belief that there was racism involved. As Balbir Singh senior put it, 'Britain never played an Indian XI as long as they remained our rulers. The 1948 Olympic hockey final was the first meeting between Britain and India.' The argument went that Britain could not contemplate losing to their brown colony. More so as this colony wanted freedom and saw sporting victories over their colonial masters as a sign of national glory. The 1948 Games were in London and it would have been unthinkable for the British not to have a hockey team there. However, by 1948 India was a free country and, while this was Britain versus India, it did not have a colonial/nationalist edge to it. For good measure, even without Dyan Chand, Indian hockey was so strong that in the final at Wembley India won 4–0.

Interestingly, British Olympic writers have not pursued the subject of why Britain suddenly dropped out of world hockey for 20 years between 1928 and 1948. Stan Greenberg in *Whitaker's Olympic Almanac* records how the Indian subcontinent was the superpower of the sport from 1928 to 1984, India winning eight

Olympics and Pakistan three. India did not lose an Olympic match until 1960. Then he adds, 'However, it should be noted that Great Britain, probably the world's strongest team at the time, did not participate in the 1932 and 1936 Olympics'. Not only does he miss out 1928, but the way he writes implies that India's dominance was due to the absence of the world power. He does not explain how Britain could be considered the world's strongest team when it refused to play India. Or why, if it was so strong, this world power sat out these two decades.

So how did the Indians cope with the even greater racist menace of the Nazis? The answer could not be more surprising. For a start the Indians were received in Berlin as if they were heroes. On Bombay pier as the champions left India (and this was the only world sport where India could claim such a status) hardly anyone had come to bid them goodbye. At Berlin rail station Diem was waiting for them personally. The anthem was British – 'God Save the King' – but Diem's speech at the station, full of praise, was relayed to a large crowd. Then they were driven to the city hall where the mayor spoke and gave presents, an album of the city and a medal to Dyan Chand, recognizing his superstar status. Dyan Chand was also much taken by the Olympic Village, so superior to Los Angeles in 1932. The cottage they were housed in had a telephone, fridge and two stewards for the team. One of them, Otto, an old sailor, had been to India and spoke English well. In the Village, Nazi top brass dropped in and the Indians rushed to get their autographs. Dyan Chand recorded, 'One day while we were in the dining hall, who should walk in but the burly Herman Goering, clad in his military attire! We were after him in a trice to get his autograph. Later some of us obtained Dr Goebbels's autograph.'

In perhaps the most curious moment of the Nazi Olympics there was an exhibition of traditional Indian games by a group of 24 specially chosen athletes. The Indian Olympic historians Boria Majumdar and Nalin Mehta observe: 'Interestingly the team was composed of Harijans, Brahmins and Mohammedans. Its organizers wanted to display an India that had overcome caste and religious divides and the participants from diverse social strata were chosen with deliberate care.' This display was a response to British charges that India could never rule itself because of its differences. For the Indians to make this point in the capital of a Reich that believed that humans would always be divided on race grounds illustrates the complexity of the Indian response to the Nazis. In 2008 when Majumdar and Mehta wrote their book *Olympics: the Indian Story* their subheading to the chapter on Hitler's Games was *Captain Dyan Chand and Indian nationalism in the Third Reich,* a choice of words that indicates how even modern-day Indians see this sporting episode.

The opening ceremony much impressed the Indians and one of them was so overwhelmed by this display of 'unity and solidarity' that it made him 'look with shame and regret at our poverty, destitution and discord'. But the Indians were one of the few teams (along with the other British dominions and the United States) who did not give the Nazi salute as they went past Hitler. Majumdar and Mehta argue that this was in line with Congress policy fashioned by Nehru, a fervent anti-fascist. Nehru had told that year's Congress session that 'capitalism in its difficulties took to Fascism' and 'Fascism and imperialism [. . .] stood out as the two faces of the now decaying capitalism'.

On the field the Germans were keen to prove that India's hockey powers were decaying and a German XI defeated India in a practice match just prior to the start of the Games. But once the real matches began India asserted her superiority. In the final India met Germany. Before the match, in the privacy of their dressing room, the flag of the Indian National Congress, the tricolour, which would become the flag of free India, was raised. In front of it the players pledged to fight for national honour. As if spurred by this on the field they beat Hitler's team 8–1. Dyan Chand, having discarded his spiked shoes and stockings and wearing rubber soles, scored six. This meant that in the Olympic tournament the Indians had scored 38 goals, conceding just one.

The German Consul General in Bombay praised the Indians. The head of the Deutsch Hockey Bund and the International Hockey Federation, Georg Evers, in a telegram to Dyan Chand, described the team as playing 'perfect hockey' and added, 'I hope you will return to India with good impressions and with the same feeling of friendship to the German hockey players as we feel towards you.' A 1992 biography of Dyan Chand describes a meeting between the Indian hockey legend and Hitler with Hitler offering the Indian a commission in the Wermacht if he would play for Germany, an offer Dyan Chand refused. However, this does not feature in contemporary accounts, or Dyan Chand's memoirs, and seems a bit of curious Indian myth-making.

A weird part of Nazi sports politics was the hunting diplomacy of Hermann Goering. Among his many titles was Chief Huntsman of the Reich. It gave him another excuse to wear lavish, self-designed costumes and an additional means of appealing to upper-class foreigners, especially the British. Although shocked by his ban on hunting foxes with hounds at the height of the Summer Olympics (he thought it unfair to animals), many Britons fell for Goering the huntsman. The socialite 'Bunny' Tattersall was one of them, penning a breathless tribute to the 'Mightiest Hunter' who 'deserves every sportsman's admiration'.

The zenith of Goering's private sporting diplomacy came in October 1937 with his patronage of the International Sporting Exhibition of game trophies, to which he invited Lord Halifax – as a British Master of Foxhounds who also happened to be a key minister in Neville Chamberlain's Cabinet. The exhibition greatly excited Phipps's replacement as British ambassador to Berlin, Sir Nevile Henderson, who was simultaneously a shot, a snob and a slavering appeaser. Henderson was appalled to discover that the British were not proposing to exhibit: he lobbied furiously and assembled a worthwhile collection of trophies, including some shot by the king and queen. He also pressed Halifax to accept Goering's invitation.

Halifax duly went to the exhibition and was gratified by his reception by German crowds. He was entertained at Goering's gigantic country estate and invited by Hitler to Berchtesgarden. Alighting from his car, the English aristocrat mistook the Fuhrer for a footman, and had to be prompted in the nick of time by Neurath, Hitler's foreign minister. It might have been better for the world if Halifax had persisted in his error. Instead of pressing Hitler on any question, as Anthony Eden had requested, Halifax praised Hitler's achievement in 'keeping Communism out of his country and [. . .] blocking its passage West'. Hitler was thoroughly unimpressed with Halifax (although he gave the former viceroy some advice on how to handle India: 'shoot Gandhi', and if that did not work, go on shooting leading members of the Congress Party until the Indians submitted). The entire episode confirmed Hitler's view that the British would do nothing if he moved against Austria and Czechoslovakia. It also confirmed Hitler's loathing of hunting and marked the end of Goering's private sporting diplomacy.

Hitler and Stalin shared many attributes, but on sport there was a huge divide between the two dictators. True, Soviet sport in the interwar period had many common features with sport in its totalitarian rivals, Italy and Germany. The regime controlled all the means for citizens to play their chosen sport or even watch it. Sport served as a showpiece for the regime and was harnessed to its political and ideological agenda. The Soviet Union had its own answer to Leni Riefenstahl in the photographer Andrei Rodchenko, who produced iconic images to order of Soviet athletes. However, Soviet sport had certain distinctive features which made it very different.

The most important reason for this was that it was far more isolated from mainstream international competition. The Soviet Union took no part in any of the official Olympics. It played no international football matches after two matches against Turkey in the early 1920s, although its club sides played occasional exhibition matches against foreigners. The great Soviet push for domination in ice hockey did not begin until after the Second

World War. In part this isolation was a legacy of the Civil War, which devastated the country and brought virtually all organized sport to a halt. The Soviet Union was a pariah state for many years after (the United States, for example, did not recognize the Communist government until 1933) and Lenin was personally hostile to organized sporting competition of any kind, which he regarded, in conventional Marxist terms, as a capitalist device to distract the masses.

However, for purely political reasons Lenin allowed the Comintern to attempt to wrest control of the international workers' sport movement from democratic socialist parties in the Socialist International. The workers' sport movement, founded in Germany as a Left counter to the conservative, nationalist German Gymnastics Society, was a pre-war success story, with federations in five industrialized European countries representing over a million workers. In 1913 the federations came together in Belgium to form the Physical Culture International. Interrupted by the war, the movement had started to regroup in 1920 with the formation of the Lucerne Sports International, part of the democratic Socialist International.

In 1921 the Comintern formed a breakaway Red Sports International, and the two bodies were bitter rivals until they belatedly united in 1936 to support the Spanish Republic's People's Olympiad in Barcelona. The Soviet Union sent a team to the (democratic socialist) unofficial Workers' Olympics in Prague in June 1921. Thereafter the Red Sports International promoted rival Workers' Games to the democratic socialist ones. Its most successful was the 1928 Workers' Spartakiad in Moscow, which drew 600 worker athletes from 14 countries. Its winter version had a novel feature: a skiing competition reserved for postal workers, peasants and border guards.

Stalin did begin to revive organized sport after 1925, but it was more closely linked to economic objectives than Fascist or Nazi sport. Stalin wanted sport to bolster productivity, especially in agriculture, and specifically to combat drunkenness and make workers fitter. Imitating Mussolini, he built stadiums and 'parks of culture and rest', but unlike Mussolini's their prime focus was on mass gymnastics, especially movements that mimicked work in factories or farms. This focus was intensified when Stalin harnessed sport to the Stakhanovite movement in the early 1930s. Workers everywhere were exhorted to imitate the heroic miner Stakhanov, who had allegedly cut 14 times more coal than normal in his shift. To help them, Stalin instituted a national daily keep-fit regime. The message was reinforced by regular mass displays of gymnastics, especially at the May Day parades.

In 1935 Stalin decreed the formation of Voluntary Sports Societies to offer recreation to workers and peasants. Initially the majority were based on factories and the state-controlled trade unions, but later in the decade, as Stalin grew more anxious about the prospects of war, a growing number of these societies were linked to the armed forces, especially the air force, which was the most glamorous and the most heavily exploited in Soviet propaganda.

Soviet sport, especially football, was also heavily influenced by the patronage of Stalin's henchmen and the state organs they controlled. Organized football had disappeared during the Russian Revolution, a victim of chaos and economic breakdown and Lenin's personal hostility. When Lenin was forced to allow a partial revival of Russian capitalism in the New Economic Policy, it allowed a little space to re-start organized football in the major towns and cities. Most of the impetus for this came from amateur sports clubs, but two professional clubs were founded by contrasting routes.

In 1919 the energetic and charismatic Starotsin brothers, both former stars of football and ice hockey, established Krasnia Presnia in the new capital of Moscow. They built a following for the club in the working-class suburbs and were able to finance it from ticket sales and tours of the wild, football-starved towns of central Asia and Siberia.

In 1923 Dinamo Moscow was founded on the direct orders of

Felix Dzerzhinsky, head of Lenin's secret police, the Cheka, later the NKVD. Like his master Lenin, Dzerzhinsky disliked football and would have preferred his new sports club to concentrate on organized gymnastics. Sheer pressure of demand, not least from his own secret police force, forced him to include football. In 1928 the Red Army decided that it too needed its own football team and created TsDKA Moscow.

By the early 1930s city-based football clubs and leagues were flourishing and the regime decided to bring them under control, decreeing that all clubs must belong to a public (i.e. Communist) institution. Nicolai Starotsin, who was an expert networker, moved quickly to exploit this decree by securing the patronage of both the Komsomol (the Communist youth movement) and the state organization that looked after small services. That enabled him to create a new club called Spartak, named for the revolutionary Roman slave whose name had already been appropriated by the German Communists. Other industry-based clubs emerged from the decree, including the railway team Locomotiv and the car factory team Torpedo, but the rivalry between Spartak, Dinamo and TsDKA dominated the thriving Soviet football league. The latter two teams represented privileged elites in the Soviet hierarchy, but Spartak remained proud of its working-class roots. Being a Spartak fan was a small, and officially tolerated, method of displaying individuality in the Soviet state.

In 1936 Spartak and Dinamo were set to play an exhibition match for Stalin in Red Square on Physical Culture Day. Knowing that Stalin had no interest in football, the conformist management of Dinamo decided to pull out, but Spartak decided to field two teams of its own and organized thousands of its fans to sew a gigantic green felt rug to cover the cobblestones of Red Square. Stalin watched for 40 minutes: it was his only appearance at any football match.

When Stalin's terror began in 1937 it claimed no fewer than five Soviet ministers of sport and thousands of sports administrators, coaches and ordinary players. The flamboyant Starotsin was a prime target. He was denounced for showing an obsessive attention to football and for behaving like 'the entrepreneur of a private sports club'. He was also accused of obtaining good players through cronyism and of currency speculation, correctly so since these were standard practices in Soviet football. Starotsin met the charges by securing the patronage of Stalin's terror chief, Yezhov, who regularly received over 1,000 free tickets to Spartak's big games. But when Stalin replaced Yezhov with Beria – an ex-footballer and a big Dinamo fan – Starotsin and Spartak acquired a vicious enemy. In 1939 Beria (for no valid reason) ordered a replay of Spartak's Cup semi-final against Dinamo Tbilisi. Spartak had won the first match 1–0 in spite of an ex-Dinamo referee, who was promptly imprisoned. Another referee (handpicked by the sports minister) failed to prevent Spartak winning the replay and a furious Beria stormed out of the stadium. He brandished an arrest warrant for Starotsin in front of the prime minister, Molotov, who had other things on his mind (including the imminent Nazi–Soviet pact) and refused to approve the arrest. Beria had to wait until wartime to secure Starotsin's arrest. Starotsin was then the victim of a bizarre series of kidnappings by Stalin's alcoholic son Vasily, who wanted him to manage his air force team, VVS. He ended up in a labour camp, the victim, like so many others, of the demented internal politics of the Stalinist state.

As with soccer and the Olympics, the Soviet Union shunned FIDE, the governing body of world chess, which was formed on French instigation in 1924. However, it was anxious to compete on the world stage, and, if possible, to find a challenger to the reigning World Champion, the anti-Soviet Russian émigré Alexander Alekhine. Chess was one of the legacies of the old regime that the Soviets sought to take over rather than abolish.

Tsarist Russia had a vibrant chess scene before the war. Three of the tsar's subjects, Chigorin, Alekhine and Rubinstein, were masters of international repute (although Rubinstein was Polish). Tsar Nicholas II (one of the dimmer members of his dynasty) was a patron of chess and supported three great international tournaments at his capital, St Petersburg, where he awarded the winners an Imperial porcelain vase and a new title of grandmaster, which survives to this day. On the eve of war, an All-Russian Union of Chess was formed, and although it made no headway it survived the war in opulent premises, with a liveried butler, in the renamed capital of Petrograd. This organization was soon liquidated by the Bolsheviks, who also turned on all the autonomous chess clubs run by the well-to-do middle classes. The Bolshevik onslaught was led by two men, Ilyin-Genevsky and Kyrilenko, both determined to make chess an instrument of class warfare and the new Soviet state. The first had been a chess player of international quality before the war. Kyrilenko, who supplanted him, was a mediocrity in every field except terrorism. As the first commander-in-chief of the Red Army, his first move was to abolish the officer corps. This ensured that the army was incapable of fighting either the Germans or the White Russians in the civil war that followed the Bolshevik coup. Lenin hastily transferred him to take charge of the justice system, which he promptly abolished. He replaced it with an apparatus of mass detention, torture and terror which added millions more to the casualties of war, influenza and starvation.

Kyrilenko took over chess from Ilyin-Genevsky in 1924, the year of Lenin's death, and accelerated his predecessor's policy of making chess a proletarian game. He kept his responsibilities for justice, and ran all of his empire on Stalinist lines. He was a regular prosecutor at 'show trials' of alleged traitors and economic saboteurs. In 1928, when Stalin launched the first Five-Year Plan, Kyrilenko, in slavish imitation, announced a Five-Year Plan to achieve dominance in world chess with shock brigades of chess players.

In spite of vicious purges of ideologically suspect players (which included, for unexplained reasons, composers of chess problems) Kyrilenko did preside over major growth in Soviet chess. By 1934 he could point to half a million registered chess players. Chess appealed to Soviet ideology because it was logical and scientific – as communism was supposed to be – and because it discouraged the workers from cards and vodka. It was especially favoured in the armed forces. A future defence minister, Marshal Malinovski, explained that chess 'disciplines a man, helps to increase strength of will and powers of endurance, develops memory and quick-wittedness and teaches logical thinking'. For ordinary people in Stalin's Russia, the appeal of chess was obvious and practical. Instead of mass exercise outdoors in a hostile climate with primitive equipment, chess involved long hours indoors. Success could bring economic privileges and a soft job. Above all, chess allowed people to think for themselves.

Kyrilenko discovered a player of world potential, Mikhail Botvinnik, groomed him and exploited him when he won the Soviet championship against generally undistinguished opposition. Botvinnik was allowed to compete at the great Nottingham International Tournament of 1937, and the regime was gratified when he beat the former world champion Capablanca. Kyrilenko sent a sycophantic telegram to Stalin in Botvinnik's name, thanking his 'Dear Teacher and Leader' for his inspiration. In a different way, it illustrated the same principle as Starotsin: all Soviet sports people and their fans, however famous, lived and played on sufferance from Stalin. Botvinnik received the astonishing reward of a private car and a supply of petrol.

Shortly after this success, Botvinnik lost his patron. Like so many, Kyrilenko fell victim to the terror of which he had once been a leader, having helped organize Stalin's show trials. One of the main charges against him was wasting time on chess. Botvinnik survived and acquired more powerful patrons: Molotov, the prime minister, and Zhdanov, Stalin's culture chief and heir apparent. He survived terror and war, and in 1948 he won the World Championship, vacated by Alekhine who had died in 1946, disgraced as a Nazi collaborator. By then the Soviets had begun to see sport and particularly its international usefulness in a very different way, indeed borrowing some of the ideas that the Nazis and Hitler had used.

Interestingly, the man who came to power in Spain with the help of his friends Hitler and Mussolini, Francisco Franco, had a very shrewd appreciation of what sport, particularly football, could do. But here the story is intimately bound up with Spain's own journey from democracy to dictatorship. Clubs, players and administrators were caught up in the regional, class and political conflicts that led to the Civil War, which left deep scars on Spanish football for many years afterwards.

The early twentieth century saw considerable growth in the Spanish economy (Spain profited from its neutrality in the First World War), and the development of an industrial urban working class in its major cities. This provided a fan base for football, but it also encouraged new political demands for trade union rights and local autonomy which Spain's weak post-war governments could not cope with. Political conflict intensified and the clubs in the major cities took sides.

In Madrid the leading club side took royal patronage, and became Real Madrid. Its ambitious and well-connected directors built a new stadium, the Chamartin, which opened with a 3–2 victory over Newcastle United. They bought up Spain's best players, the Basque forward Peña, and, to the fury of FC Barcelona supporters, the charismatic goalkeeper Zamora and the midfield schemer Samitier.

In Barcelona the rival clubs lined up on opposite sides of the political divide. Real Espanyol, as their name suggests, lined up with Spain, particularly the militant nationalist group Peña Ibérica, but FC Barcelona supported Catalan nationalism. In 1922 its directors joined a mass petition to the Madrid government for Catalan independence. Not surprisingly, local derbies between the Barcelona sides saw regular violence on and off the field, and foreign teams refused to visit the city.

In 1925, King Alfonso XIII supported a military coup, which installed a dictatorship under General Primo de Rivera. It was a mild dictatorship by the standards of the interwar period, but it repressed Catalan nationalism and, with it, FC Barcelona. The crackdown on the club in 1925 was provoked, unwittingly, by a visiting band of the British Royal Marines. Invited to play at a highly charged benefit match for a leading Catalan choral society, the band launched into the Spanish Royal and national anthem, which the FC Barcelona supporters booed and whistled. In surprise, the band hurriedly segued into 'God Save The King', which was cheered enthusiastically.

The new military government were outraged by what they chose to see as a public display of treason. They fined the club, shut down its fine stadium and forced its president into exile. Primo de Rivera also banned the club from using the Catalan language or flying the Catalan flag and, more sinisterly, ordered it to hand over its entire membership list to the police. He also forbade the fans from paying their annual pilgrimage to the shrine of the Virgin of Montserrat at the end of the Catalan championship. Instead, they were allowed to go there only for the Spanish championship, and not in any kind of procession.

In the same year, Barcelona was joined by Josep Sunyol, who was to become its president and guiding spirit. Only 27, Sunyol was a journalist with political ambitions. In his newspaper *La Rambla* he defended football from Marxist and elitist intellectual attack and identified it with Catalan aspirations. 'To speak of sport,' he wrote, 'is to speak of race, enthusiasm and the optimistic struggle of youth. To speak of citizenship is to speak of the Catalan civilization, liberalism, democracy and spiritual endeavour.'

In 1929 Spain was hit very hard by the world economic crash, especially Barcelona, a city that relied heavily on international trade and exports. Football crowds fell sharply as workers were laid off, and FC Barcelona nearly went under. The Primo de Rivera dictatorship could not cope with the economic crisis. He quit and King Alfonso looked for another general to replace him. Although the Spanish army was full of generals (there was no retirement and there was one full-pay general to every 1,000 men) he could not find one competent to rule the country, and in 1931 Alfonso left Spain in the wake of bad local election results (the only monarch in history to lose his throne for that reason). Spain became a republic and a democracy, and Sunyol was elected to its first Cortes as a deputy for a moderate socialist Catalan party.

Republican governments struggled for survival amid enduring economic depression and increasing political polarization between left and right, finally sliding into civil war in 1936 following a generals' uprising against the left of centre Popular Front government. These conflicts were mirrored in the boardrooms of the leading clubs. Sunyol had to fight against Catalan right wingers until he and his political faction managed to take over the club on the eve of the civil war. Meanwhile their Barcelona rival Espanyol (which had to drop the Real, as did Real Madrid) aligned itself more firmly with the anti-nationalist, anti-Catalan right. Many of their fans joined the Fascist Falange and fought for Franco. The street fighting in Barcelona at the outbreak of the civil war included many private wars between rival groups of fans.

Real-less Madrid FC managed to keep in with the Republican governments and was able to continue its policy of signing Spain's best players, adding the hardline defender Quincoces to its line-up in 1934. In 1936, on the eve of the civil war, its charismatic goalkeeper Zamora produced a save of the century to help win the League championship against his former club, FC Barcelona.

Spanish football took a heavy toll in the civil war, in which both sides used terror to suppress their enemies (Franco had more means and was more systematic than the Republic). All of the leading clubs and personalities were affected. Sunyol was executed in its early days by a Fascist militia – an incident that still generated intense bitterness and much official evasion and outright lying 60 years later.

FC Barcelona was saved from an anarchist takeover by its astute secretary, Calvet, who, with the help of its groundsman, Mur, turned it into a workers' cooperative. As already noted, Barcelona beat off the local general's attempted coup, and the club stayed loyal to the Republic until Franco conquered Barcelona in

January 1939. It sustained the Catalan championship and managed to make a successful tour of the United States and Mexico in 1938, which raised sympathy and funds for the Republic. In 1937 the Communists bloodily suppressed the Anarchist and Trotskyist organizations in Barcelona, and thereafter the club occasionally accommodated them by giving over their stadium to mass gymnastic displays.

Madrid also beat back the uprising and withstood a 30-month siege by Franco. FC Madrid fell into left-wing hands and purged any suspected rightists from its management and playing staff. Its future organizing genius Santiago Bernabeu, holed up in the French embassy, was denounced by the pro-Communist club secretary Alonso. He was saved from arrest and likely execution by the intervention of the Spanish Republican ambassador to France, who was a club supporter. Bernabeu was allowed to leave the city and ended the war a decorated veteran of Franco's forces. The two star players, Zamora and Samitier, also had lucky escapes from Republican and anarchist militiamen who suspected their loyalties. Zamora used his legendary charm against his captors and let them take penalties against him. Eventually both ended up playing for Nice, a good setting for their party-loving lifestyle. Meanwhile the club, like the Republic itself, fell under growing Communist domination: its president was a Communist colonel Vallejo and its stadium, like Barcelona's, staged regular mass gymnastic rallies.

During the civil war, Spanish football itself split into two, with rival football associations and leagues in each side's territory. One curious by-product of this was that both Madrid teams asked to be classified as Catalan because they were fighting on the same side. In 1937 FIFA recognized Franco's association as the representative of all Spain. Since the Republic was still in control of Spain's major cities and their clubs, and since it was still recognized by everyone except Hitler and Mussolini as the legal government of Spain, FIFA's decision was premature and smacked of appeasement.

Franco's victory led to the disappearance of all pro-Republican officials from Spanish football, and many players. Some went into exile, some (like Madrid's 1936 President Sanchez Guerra) served long terms of imprisonment, and a number (including Madrid's vice-president and its treasurer) were executed in prison. The Chamartin stadium was a ruin and the new regime used its wooden stands for firewood. FC Barcelona was systematically punished for its 'disloyalty' and once again forced to disown the Catalan language and flag. A pro-Franco board was installed and the club was allowed to function only under intense police supervision. Once again, its membership lists were thrown open to the police and an appearance on the list made it very difficult for many years to get a passport or an official job or state benefits.

The most notorious incident in the post-war treatment of FC Barcelona came with their Cup semi-final away leg against Madrid. Barcelona gained a 3–0 lead in the first leg, surviving violent tackling and biased refereeing, which provoked whistling and booing from the home crowd, even though it was heavily policed. A pro-Franco journalist wrote a wildly biased account of the crowd's behaviour, largely ignoring the match itself, and other pro-Franco journalists joined a campaign to induce the Madrid fans to take revenge. Before the match itself, the Barcelona players received a frightening personal visit from Spain's Himmler, Franco's secret police chief, Escriva de Romani. Already thoroughly unnerved, the Barcelona goalkeeper faced a barrage of coins and stones from the incited home crowd. He spent most of the match a long way from his goal-line, and made little or no attempt to stop the eleven goals that Madrid scored against him. This infamous match still stirs bitter memories.

In half-hearted emulation of Mussolini, Franco tried to use football for propaganda, staging a ludicrous fixture of Spain versus the Basques, which Spain won 9–1 in front of an apathetic crowd. The championship was renamed the Generalissimo's Cup. He put a prominent general, Moscardo, in charge of Spanish football, who compiled a lengthy 'Football Bible' for the new regime.

In practice, Franco had too many other problems (starvation, isolation, suppressing Republican guerrillas and keeping out of the Second World War) to worry much about football. Moscardo favoured 'loyal' Espanyol and a reconstituted Madrid FC, led by Bernabeu. Its Real title was restored in 1943: more importantly, Bernabeu's organizing genius and his connections with the new regime led to the building of a magnificent new stadium. He was astute enough to employ the same architect who built Franco's grandiose Monument to the Fallen. Moscardo and the Franco regime did their biggest service to Real Madrid when they bent the rules on foreign players to allow the club to sign the Argentine genius Alfredo di Stefano.

As Real Madrid began to triumph in the 1950s, Franco, like Mussolini, saw the advantages of associating himself with a winning team with a world following. He used its success to boost acceptance of his own regime. But this story belongs to another era, one shaped by the mighty new force of television and the eventual marriage of Mammon and sport.

By then few people outside Spain had much to say in praise of Franco's erstwhile benefactors, Hitler and Mussolini, the latter being painted as something of an idiot. This served to obscure the fact that almost until the outbreak of the war both Mussolini's and Hitler's policies were lauded. And Hitler's sport policies evoked great admiration as late as 1938. Then the Bishop of London praised the 'marvellous results' and 'perfectly astounding physical perfection' that the Germans had achieved 'by a system of outdoor camps, of compulsory exercises, and the successful inculcation of the belief that love of country comes first, before any personal enjoyment, and that patriotism comes first and "having a good time" comes last'.

Two years earlier the Fuhrer had made an even more important sporting conquest: Britain's then chancellor, Neville Chamberlain. As prime minister, Chamberlain would make his infamous journey to Munich to appease Hitler. Now in 1936, introducing a National Fitness Campaign, he cited 'the splendid condition of the German youth', and added 'although our methods are different from theirs, in accordance with our national character and traditions, I see no reason why we should not be equally successful in our results'.

It was an indication of how the democracies were struggling to respond to the dictators and their use of sport.

CHAPTER 6

THE MUDDLED DEMOCRATIC RESPONSE

Totalitarian sport evoked a variety of responses from the rest of the world. Some ignored it; some admired its successes and tried to replicate them; others, notably the United Kingdom, muddled somewhere between, comforting themselves with faith in the superiority of their own sporting systems and values, but occasionally acknowledging that they needed to catch up. However, the ultra-nationalism of totalitarian sport did encourage all countries to use sport as a means of establishing national identity. This was especially true of newly emerged nations and those trying to break free of colonial rule or neo-colonial patronage.

For most of the interwar period France had a very casual attitude to sport. This changed dramatically with the election of the left-of-centre Popular Front government in 1936. It rapidly negotiated with striking trade unions an ambitious package of social reforms, including big wage increases, an eight-hour day and paid holidays. French industry, which then was not as advanced as the British, struggled to cope with the cost of these reforms, but they created almost overnight a new working-class fan base for sports, with spare money and leisure time. To meet their new demands for recreation, the government appointed Leo Lagrange, a young, energetic socialist politician as France's first-ever minister for sport. He declared: 'Our simple and human goal is to allow the masses of French youths to find in the practice of sport, joy and health and to build an organization of

179

leisure activities so that the workers can find relaxation and a reward for their hard labour.'

Lagrange was genuinely impressed by the results of the sports policies of the totalitarian countries, especially the gains in public health and public morale. Like them, he shared the hope that sport could reduce alcoholism and absenteeism at work. However, he was anxious to show that democracy could equal or out-match the achievements of fascism. Like Mussolini and Hitler, he channelled large-scale investment into local sports facilities, especially swimming pools, and new football stadiums. The pick of these was the Parc Lescure in Bordeaux, intended to be a democratic riposte to the fascist stadiums of Mussolini. Lagrange and his government also placed high hopes on the 1937 International Exposition in Paris as a showcase for democracy. He organized an exhibition match between 'democratic' Chelsea and 'fascist' Bologna, but unfortunately the wrong side won.

Lagrange was in office for less than two years, in a series of short-lived governments with little money to spare for sport. (He was killed in the war, although, as a deputy, he could have avoided military service.) But he made a difference and his interventionist approach was continued by the right-wing Vichy regime's minister of sport, the tennis star Jean Borotra.

American sport in the interwar years reflected American political life. Woodrow Wilson's failure to persuade the Senate to support membership of the League of Nations, an idea he had inspired, signalled a return to pre-war isolationism. Similarly, American sport took almost no account of the outside world. Its two main team sports, baseball and American football, played domestic matches only. Although baseball was popular in Latin America, the 'World Series' was for US Major League teams only and these never thought of touring overseas or importing any overseas players. (The separate Negro Leagues did both: their teams made regular 'barnstorming' tours of the Dominican Republic and took several black stars from Cuban baseball.) American teams competed at the Olympics, and individual athletes competed overseas, but these activities had almost no influence on the development of American sport, largely because the Americans usually won. Their successes confirmed the success of the American way – a model in which sport was driven by a combination of voluntary effort and commercial exploitation.

The American government had almost no involvement in American sport, and nobody wanted it to. In stark contrast to Hitler's Olympics and Mussolini's World Cup, the Los Angeles Olympics of 1932 were run as a private business venture. There were no calls in this period for any official sports policy or even for government support or concessions for sport. American politicians courted votes by pretending to be sports fans, and each president continued the dutiful ritual of throwing the first pitch of the season (incongruously inaugurated in 1910 by William Howard Taft, who weighed over 300 pounds). Otherwise, sport and politics hardly mixed at all in the United States until the second half of the 1930s, when it was used to make gestures against Fascism and Nazism. These gestures did not extend to racial segregation in American sport, which was virtually unchallenged in the interwar period.

It was not surprising that American sport was isolated from the rest of the world, since the United States had everything it needed to grow sport on its own. It had emerged from the First World War as the greatest economic power in the world. The long boom of the 1920s created an urban working class with substantial income and shorter working hours. By 1925, 40 per cent of American workers were earning at least $2,000 a year, enough to feed and house a family of four in tolerable conditions and leave a reasonable surplus for leisure activities. In 1928 the economist Stuart Chase estimated that nearly a quarter of America's national income was spent on 'play and recreation broadly interpreted'.

As in the totalitarian countries, the United States in the 1920s saw a proliferation of new sports stadiums, but all of these were built simply to accommodate spectators, without any underlying political agenda. New stadiums for college football in the 1920s included Washington (46,000 capacity), Stanford (86,000) and Michigan (over 100,000). In baseball, the exploits of Babe Ruth enabled the New York Yankees to build a stadium in the Bronx for 62,000 spectators. For boxing fans, a new Madison Square Garden opened in 1925 with 18,000 seats at a cost of $6 million. Even tennis, a minority sport, had its first purpose-built facility in Forest Hills in 1923, with seating for 14,000. Alongside these giant spectator stadiums there was a nationwide boom in new private clubs for leisure activities, principally golf, but also offering tennis, swimming and athletics: these too had no political motivation; they were there to make money from people enjoying themselves.

Big businesses and individual entrepreneurs invested in stadiums and franchises for Major League teams – and in individual athletes, whom they turned, with media help, into celebrities who could draw audiences outside sport and sell non-sporting products as well as sporting ones. Commercial interests also promoted changes in rules and equipment, which made many sports more exciting. However, there was also a strong survival of the amateur tradition in American sport, especially in American football, which commercial interests valued highly. The Depression led to a revival of non-professional sport in the 1930s, for simple economic reasons. Millions of newly poor and unemployed people could no longer afford to pay for sporting entertainment.

American isolation from the rest of world sport was emphasized by the country's love for baseball. There is a long-held American belief that in the 1850s baseball was a gentleman's sport and teams rode in decorated carriages singing their team songs. This may or may not have been the case, but what is certain is that by the turn of the twentieth century, baseball was a working-class game popular among Irish and German immigrants. Its reputation was as a rowdy, drunken sport linked to gambling. Indeed, gambling had been associated with baseball as early as 1877 when players in the Louisville team were expelled for 'crookedness' in conspiring with gamblers to throw games. However, by the turn of the century baseball had begun to be presented as a game that occupied a special place in the hearts of Americans – the national pastime. Intrinsically connected to the rural beginnings of America, it conjured images of green pastures amid the metropolitan jungle of an increasingly urbanized country.

Reality often did not match this image, with teams being owned by a cabal of wealthy, distrustful, misanthropic white men; player strikes, lockouts, gambling and racism marred the twentieth century. Baseball was also slow to take advantage of the technological advances, from playing night games to broadcasting on radio or television, and franchises were happily moved, often from one coast to another, by owners with little regard to fans, and despite the protestations of home markets.

But those who ran baseball were always keen to cultivate the myth and one owner went as far as saying:

> Baseball is the greatest sport in the world. It is the cleanest [. . .] Formerly sport was not regarded as a proper calling for young men. It is beginning to assume its rightful place in society. To me baseball is as honourable as any other business [. . .] It has to be or could not last a season out. Crookedness and baseball do not mix.

That owner was Charles Comiskey, the owner of the Chicago White Sox team, speaking in 1919, a year before the greatest scandal in the history of the game. Then it emerged that eight players of the team had thrown games in the 1919 World Series against the Cincinnati Reds in return for money from bookies. Their motives were partly financial (inducements from bookies) and partly industrial (a dispute over wages, meals and laundry). The team got a new nickname – Black Sox – and this is also how baseball history describes the affair. But no players were convicted, in no small part because Comiskey engineered the disappearance of the player confessions from the prosecutors' office. However, the newly appointed baseball commissioner, a first for a sport, the fearsome Judge Keneshaw Mountain Landis, intervened.

Landis looked like God, with a severe, jutting jaw, high fore-head, shaggy white hair and stern countenance. He banished all eight players of the White Sox and subsequently banned 11 other players for gambling and even went after Babe Ruth. He was incredibly conservative and hostile to anything new. He was preoccupied with moral struggle at the expense of the business. He was the perfect custodian of the game while it was trying to regain the image of being wholesome and honest. His efforts also turned out to be very beneficial to owners of the Major League clubs. In effect what Landis was doing was laying the foundation for recognizing that the sport was also a busi-ness, one of the first sports to move in that direction. This process was also helped by some very curious decisions by the highest courts in America.

In an early court case, the Lajoie case, baseball was recognized as 'peculiar in nature and circumstances', which allowed the courts to ignore established contract law principles. Far more significant was the Federal Baseball case. It concerned a rival league, the Federal League, which was set up in competition with the Major League. The Federal League had more generous conces-sions to players, namely increased salaries, the team would pay for uniforms and players would be released from their clubs after 10 years' service. This was much more liberal than the Major League baseball's 'reserve clause' (like English football's retain-and-transfer system), which tied players to clubs for life even when their contracts expired.

The leagues settled their dispute, but a disgruntled former Federal League club sued the Major League, claiming they could not attract players because of its restrictive and anti-competitive practices. It was alleged that Major League baseball was involved in interstate commerce, and that it monopolized a portion of that commerce through the reserve clause and the blacklisting of contract violators, which had the effect of depriving a rival league of skilled players. In 1922 the Supreme Court of the US ruled that Major League baseball was not involved in interstate commerce and as such was beyond the purview of the federal Sherman Act, the major US anti-trust legislation.

The conclusion was patently ridiculous – teams from different states played one another both home and away and the express purpose of the reserve clause and blacklisting was to monopolize the buyers' market for players to keep salaries down and retain talent. What the case proved was that baseball was indeed peculiar, but no one seemed to be able to offer a principled and academically rigorous reason why. Perhaps the best explanation was, inevitably, from Comiskey: 'Baseball is too much of a business to be a sport, but too much of a sport to be a business.' America accepted that, and in the following years the Court and Congress would have many opportunities to correct this aberration, but they chose not to. Armed with this helpful decision from the highest court in the land, the club owners went on a long building spree in the 1920s, constructing new steel ballparks. They were not only more modern, safer, sturdier and more uplifting than the wooden predecessors, but they also became the centrepiece of cities and created a sense of community. They encouraged more moral and civilized behaviour, attracting essentially more middle class, more prosperous, family-oriented spectators to ball games.

The stadiums also demonstrated that baseball had made it as a potentially lucrative business – after all, if you could not make any money in baseball, why would you go to the time and expense of building great new ballparks?

The spectators were also attracted by the revival of big hitting. For the first two decades of the twentieth century, baseball had been a low-scoring game whose stars were nearly all pitchers. This changed in the 1920s, due partly to the introduction of a bouncier ball and the outlawing of the spitball (where a ball was altered by the application of saliva, petroleum jelly or other substances), and even more to the genius of Babe Ruth, who set 56 separate records. With the help of an expert agent (a new profession which grew in the interwar period), Ruth built his basic salary from $20,000 in

1920 to $52,000 in 1922. This topped the salary of President Harding, but as Ruth accurately explained: 'I had a better season than him.' By 1930 Ruth was pulling in $2 million a year, mostly from off-field earnings in ghosted newspaper articles, radio and vaudeville appearances, and endorsements for cars and cigarettes. As we have seen, his celebrity status owed much to the reticence of the media and would not have survived present-day scrutiny.

Although baseball was a professional and commercial enterprise, the other great American spectator sport was resolutely amateur, at least officially. Until as late as the 1960s, American college football was more popular than professional football, and was able to set tough rules to protect its status. Two leading clubs were created through industry sponsorship immediately after the First World War – the Green Bay Packers and the Chicago Bears, who became founder members of the American Professional Football Conference in 1920 (soon to become the American Football League). Drawing lessons from earlier, failed professional leagues, the new Conference tried to cap wages and block 'poaching' of star players by the richest clubs. Above all, recognizing the popularity of college football on Saturdays, the clubs agreed to play only on Sundays.

However, these rules largely failed in their objectives. The bigger clubs were able to recruit and showcase star players, such as the disqualified Native American Olympic champion Jim Thorpe, and Red Grange, the 'galloping ghost', and the college football authorities continued to resist professional football, even though they were supplying it with nearly all its players and coaches. In 1921, the college Football Coaches Association resolved unanimously that all its members should 'lend their influence to discourage the professional game'. In 1925, Chicago's signing of Red Grange while still at college led to such an outcry that the NFL was forced to agree not to sign any more students until they had graduated.

None of these rules prevented college football from earning a great deal of money. The most successful personality was Notre

Dame's coach Knute Rockne, another star guided by an expert agent. Backed by his team's legendary 'four horsemen', he was earning $2,000 for a speech, $15,000 a year from sports camps, and even more from ghosted articles and product endorsements. He also built Notre Dame's football profit from $234 in 1918 to half a million in 1930. His untimely death in 1931 cut short his projected movie career – a route followed by many other American sports personalities in the 1930s.

The 1920s saw rich pickings for American sports promoters and agents. In boxing, the promoter Tex Richard made so much money in 1921 from the Dempsey–Carpentier heavyweight fight, that he was able to take over and rebuild Madison Square Garden. In golf, the wisecracking, flamboyant Walter Hagen turned himself into a millionaire with the help of two astute agents who also enriched the Professional Golfers Association. Some promoters grew rich on eccentric events, such as C. C. Pyle and his 'Bunion Derby', a cross-country race across the United States. More conventionally, but less successfully, he also signed up tennis stars, including Suzanne Lenglen and Bill Tilden. The 1920s also saw short-lived crazes for pogo sticks and pole-sitting, as well as lasting new inventions such as greyhound racing, all-in wrestling and motorcycle speedway, all exported successfully to the United Kingdom and other countries. All of these were eclipsed by America's greatest export, contract bridge (if it counts as a sport), promoted as a commercial venture by the celebrity Culbertsons.

But if this period marked the marriage of sport and Mammon, not even American sport could ride out the Depression following the 1929 Wall Street crash. Mass unemployment and poverty destroyed much of its market and the collapse of share prices wiped out many of its investors. The 1920s building boom in stadiums and private clubs ground to a halt. In partial replacement, the Works Public Administration, part of President Roosevelt's New Deal, built thousands of new Art Deco swimming pools in small towns and invested in other leisure facilities, including a travelling circus.

The Depression hit professional sport, baseball in particular, especially hard. Attendances and salaries fell dramatically. Commissioner Landis took a $10,000 pay cut and the highest-paid Major League player, Lou Gehrig, had to bump along on $40,000 a year, compared to Babe Ruth's peak earnings of $80,000. Like many other Depression-hit businesses, baseball club owners preferred to cut costs rather than risk innovation. Two more modest innovations – the All-Star game of 1935 and the creation of the Hall of Fame the following year – did little to revive attendances. The owners were, curiously, reluctant to introduce night games (although they had been popular for years in the Negro Leagues). The first one was an exhibition game held by the Cincinnati Reds in 1909, but it was not until the mid-1940s that most teams hosted night games, and, extraordinarily, it was 1988 when the Chicago Cubs held their first. The resistance was initially because night games were apparently contrary to the romantic and natural traditions of the game. It was also difficult for newspapers to cover the game with deadlines and the conclusion of the game coming very close together. Modern baseball could not be more removed from that, with night games now ubiquitous and some teams playing few, if any, day games. Even further removed from the rural evocations, some fields have artificial turf and the stadiums are completely covered.

The clubs also cold-shouldered radio, with clubs taking almost a quarter of a century to make it commonplace. This was partly for fear of alienating established print media and partly because of a traditional belief that sport should be watched in the open air. The first national broadcast was in 1921, the first World Series broadcast was in 1923, and as late as 1939 New York clubs did not broadcast any of their games. The baseball print media were initially hostile to radio because there was a feeling that the game was to be seen rather than heard. There was a degree of snobbery associated with radio coverage as well, although those advancing the anti-radio argument could say they were the true heirs to the Arnoldian spirit of the game.

Their view of why baseball should not be on radio can be encapsulated as such: going to a ballpark was exercise; it was good, clean and honest. If fans could hear the game on the radio then they would become too lazy to go to the game. Men should be outside getting oxygen; games were meant to provide them with mental awakening instead of their being sluggishly engaged at home with their minds getting duller and duller. There was also the idea that radio commentary debased the sport of the nation. Baseball was not traceable through an ear trumpet; instead it was something to see – red-blooded men giving an exhibition of grace, strength and mental alertness. Ideas which could have come straight out of *Tom Brown's Schooldays*.

The one club to buck the trend and embrace radio was the Brooklyn Dodgers, who astonished their rivals by selling their broadcast rights for $70,000 a year. Both night games and radio broadcasting were curious examples of how money-conscious owners acted against their best commercial interests for the sake of loyalty to the pastoral and rural associations of the game.

The United States' entry into the Second World War had a further devastating effect on baseball and two Major League baseball teams almost closed down. It required President Roosevelt to dissuade the owners, on grounds of national morale. With most of the best players absent on military duty, attendances remained poor even though the war economy had put Americans back to work. This prompted P. K. Wrigley, the chewing-gum king and owner of the Chicago Cubs, to set up the All-American Girls Baseball League, with some success in the Mid-West.

For American football, the Depression had the effect of wiping out emerging competitors to the NFL, but monopoly status did not help the professional clubs to overcome falling attendances. Small-town teams were hit especially hard and owners rushed to relocate clubs in big cities in pursuit of spectators. The biggest example was the Redskins, pulled out of Boston by their owner, G. P. Marshall, and presented to a gratified Washington DC. Marshall tried to woo fans with season tickets, half-time shows and even away travel packages, then extremely unusual. However, his more significant move was to establish a formal colour bar in professional American football in 1933.

The Depression made college football even more attractive to spectators, since it was skilful, exciting, local and free. The surviving professional clubs tried even harder to cultivate it. In 1935 they formalized their relationship through the 'farm' system, in which colleges were used as nurseries for clubs, and the college draft system, which gave weaker clubs an automatic share of the best new college leavers. The professional clubs also encouraged a style of spectatorship that mimicked college football, with cheerleaders, marching bands and 'tailgating' parties in cars.

One major sport benefited substantially from the Depression. Like college football, basketball was skilful and free (it became faster and more appealing with the abolition of the centre jump after each score), but it was even more local and convenient. It thrived in small-town high schools. By the end of the 1930s, as many as 95 per cent of American high schools were sponsoring a varsity basketball team. Basketball continued to benefit from religious support, as it had done since its invention. Protestant, Catholic and Jewish organizations promoted basketball for their members, and challenged each other annually. Overseas, the YMCA continued to evangelize for basketball. Their converts included Nazi Germany, which ignored its origins and incorporated the game into its plans to produce athletic soldiers. Thanks to the Nazis, it became an Olympic sport for the first time in 1936.

In total contrast to the Berlin Olympics, the Los Angeles Games of 1932 were a commercial rather than political enterprise. The American President did not even show up, and the organizers, led by William Garland, probably did not even want to be associated with the now thoroughly unpopular Herbert Hoover. With the Depression at its height and a global phenomenon, there were widespread suggestions that the Olympics should be cancelled, especially when not a single overseas country had accepted an invitation with only six months to go. Garland and his team persuaded Californians to vote them $1 million in a public refer-endum, with promises to use the Games as a showcase for tourism and investment.

They also took a series of commercial decisions with lasting impact. One was to cut out a range of unpopular sports, includ-ing soccer, and reduce the length of the Games from 78 days to 16. Another was to offer male athletes free food and board at the first specially created Olympic Village. The women competitors were parked in a downtown hotel, but otherwise they received far more encouragement than at the 1920s Games in Antwerp, Paris and Amsterdam, which had provoked a series of break-away 'Women's Olympic Games'. This American shift of policy on women also had a simple commercial motive: female athletes had become big box office. In winter sports, the young teenage skater Sonja Henie had acquired a world following, and in the Summer Games, Los Angeles hoped to exploit the supposedly teenage prodigy Mildred Didrikson, who had astutely knocked three years off her age, and even more wisely acquired the nick-name of Babe.

The transformation of sports stars into celebrities and enter-tainers, with the help of agents, continued a trend from the 1920s. So did the pursuit of speed records on land and water, daring flights by lone aviators, and the invention of bizarre sports and stunts such as dance marathons. Almost matching the success of contract bridge in the 1920s, the United States exported Monopoly – not only a board game, but a reaffirmation of faith in capitalism.

But if the interwar years, generally, saw dramatic innovation in American sport, one innovation remained totally off the table: the ending of segregation in sport. Either formally or informally, or through lack of means, black Americans were excluded from the upper reaches of American sport, with the limited exceptions of athletics and boxing, where black athletes could rise through supreme talent under conditions dictated by white men.

This state of affairs was scarcely challenged, either in sport or in the political system. Indeed, most American sports administrators and commentators thought it natural and even praiseworthy. In 1923 the *Sporting News* declared that:

> In a democratic, catholic, real American game like baseball, there has been no distinction raised, except tacit understanding that a player of Ethiopian descent is ineligible [. . .] No player of any other 'race' has been barred [. . .] The Mick, the Sheeny, the Wop, the Dutch and the Chink, the Cuban, the Indian, the Jap or the so-called Anglo-Saxon – his nationality is never a matter of moment if he can pitch, hit or field.

A similar 'tacit understanding' excluded blacks from leading basketball clubs. Unlike American football, these sports never formalized their colour bar, but it was real.

The black response was not only to form their own leagues but to be innovative in the way they marketed the games. The Negro National Baseball League, formed in 1920, combined organized championship play with traditional 'barnstorming' – one-night stands in unfavoured locations which offered entertainment as much as sport – in addition to night games and tours of Latin America. The Negro League was far less lucrative than the Major League, and conditions were often degrading. Its clubs sometimes had to field 'Comedy Teams' in grass skirts. However, the Negro League had a high standard of play. Its best player, pitcher Leroy 'Satchel' Paige was at least equal to any Major League star, but no club signed him until after the war – as a 42-year-old 'rookie'. He was good enough to continue pitching in the majors until he was 59.

In basketball, the leading black club was the Harlem Renaissance Five, formed in 1922. Dependent on barnstorming engagements, they evolved a fast, fluid, dramatic style which was years ahead of its time. In athletics and boxing, certain black athletes were simply too good to ignore. But unlike successful white athletes, their performances did not allow them to break out of the terms set by a white-dominated society, still less turn themselves into rich celebrities. Jesse Owens received no reward in the United States for his exploits in Berlin. He was snubbed by President Roosevelt as thoroughly as he was snubbed by Hitler. Simply for showing interest in some lucrative offers he was stripped of his amateur status by Avery Brundage. The offers came to nothing and he was forced into dire stunts, including exhibition races against horses.

In boxing, Joe Louis had to force his way into title contention by knocking out all his opponents, so as to give no opportunity for biased referees. Even after 22 knockouts in 26 fights, he secured a title shot only by promising a portion of his future earnings to the beaten champion, James J. Braddock. His manager kept him on a tight leash: he could never go to a nightclub alone or be seen in public with a white woman, this no doubt to prevent him meeting the fate of the last black heavyweight champion, Jack Johnson, convicted on trumped-up charges of immorality. The shadow of Johnson, who had outraged white America in the early years of the century by beating white men, and then consorting with white women, hung over Louis. His manager was even afraid of association with Johnson, and snubbed him when he offered his services in preparing Louis for his first fight with Max Schmeling. Johnson helped Schmeling instead – an act of multiple ironies as the first black boxing icon advised an unwilling Nazi poster boy how to defeat the second black boxing icon.

By the time of his re-match against Schmeling, Louis had a white working-class following and had also been adopted by progressives as an icon of democratic values against Fascism and Nazism. Even President Roosevelt caught the mood and asked him to 'win for America'. But his spectacular victory did not prompt any of his progressive supporters to change the conditions he and other black athletes suffered from. The only political party that campaigned for integrated sport was the American Communist Party (not the most useful advocate). As a result, during the 1930s black athletes heard more about sporting segregation from the

Nazis, cynically defending the Berlin Olympics from threats of an American boycott, than they did from American progressives.

If American sport went its own way in the interwar years, British sport muddled through in two minds – clinging to the belief that Britain was best at sport while uneasily aware that it might have to modify its methods and values to meet the challenge of foreigners. Britain also discovered that dominions and colonies would no longer accept British sporting leadership as a matter of course. British sport also had to cope with domestic pressures that threatened the control of its traditional aristocratic leadership: class conflict, the growth of commercial interests including the media, and the rise of organized betting, some of it criminal. The result was an unprecedented level of government intervention in sport in the interwar period: by the end of the 1930s the government was even contemplating the outlandish and continental appointment of a minister of sport.

To outward appearance, British sports were run in the same way (and often by the same people) as they were before the war. The MCC, a private members' club with a committee of Establishment figures, continued to regulate cricket, not only in England and in the British colonies, but in independent dominions. Both forms of football continued to be run by well-connected amateurs determined to resist the influence of organized professional leagues. Rugby union had its own problems with international competition. Matches against France were ended in 1931 over allegations of hidden professionalism and excessive violence by French clubs. *The Times* commented loftily: 'the French must get away from championship methods and follow British ideas.'

In rowing, the Amateur Rowing Association (which maintained a formal ban on manual workers) faced a serious challenge from the National Amateur Rowing Association, which was only slightly less stuffy, although it nerved itself to admit as amateurs 'metropolitan policemen who had to use motor boats in the course of their duty'. The Jockey Club maintained aristocratic, autocratic rule over racing and set its face against rich interlopers such as the Aga Khan.

Golf was still controlled by another private members' club, the Royal and Ancient, in the interests of amateurs. While the club hierarchy was determined to resist professionalism it was not against innovation and the officials accepted the technological advance of the steel-shafted club. In athletics, the Amateur Athletics Association was admired by foreigners for its openness to any club or group that wanted to join: however, its main focus was on resisting professionalism (including specialized training) as well as the recruitment of Oxbridge men to athletics. Lawn tennis was in the hands of the All-England Club (which also ran croquet), whose secretary Commander Hillyard in 1924 deplored 'the taint of pot-hunting'.

Hillyard's complaint was prompted by the inability of British men to win any pots. It was a typical response to British lack of success on the sporting field. In 1925, the golf journalist Mrs J. E. McNair reacted to a string of defeats by declaring it far more important 'to maintain our reputation for being a nation of sportsmen and sportswomen [. . .] who play their games in the right spirit'. A year later, the same phrase appeared in *Wisden Rugby Union Almanack*'s criticism of the brilliant New Zealanders: 'they did not always play the game in the right spirit'. The comforting myth of British sportsmanship was extended to British spectators. The MCC complained as much about Australian barracking in the 'Bodyline' series of 1932–3 as the Australian authorities complained about Bodyline itself. At the end of the series, the MCC commented that 'barracking unfortunately has always been indulged in by spectators in Australia to a degree unknown in this country', and added that unless controlled, it would threaten the future of representative matches. There were also press complaints against Italian and German football supporters.

This habit of using British sportsmanship as an excuse for failure began to be questioned only after the Berlin Olympics. The *Daily Express*, then Britain's largest-selling newspaper, described Britain's performance at Berlin as 'lamentable, not because our luck was out, but because the majority of our representatives were not good enough [. . .]. The Americans and the Germans and the Japs and the Finns, licked us hollow. What was worse, they made us look ridiculous.' In 1936, a shock report was published on the state of public health by the eminent scientist Sir John Boyd-Orr. In *Food, Health and Income* he found that half the nation were ill-fed, and that the poorest 10 per cent of the population (which included 20 per cent of all British children) were very badly fed indeed. The response to both Berlin and Boyd-Orr was a new departure – a government policy on sport and physical recreation.

For many centuries, British governments had interfered with British sport, but always for reasons that were tangential to sport itself. So, in 1930, when the Labour government built 'Lansbury's Lido' on the Serpentine in London's Hyde Park – with its creator spending much time defending mixed bathing against self-appointed guardians of public morals – its main purpose was to create employment rather than recreation. Generally for much of the early part of the twentieth century governments saw sport as a public order issue with home secretaries particularly alert to this danger. In 1911, Winston Churchill had banned the entry of the provocative black boxing champion Jack Johnson. In 1919 his successor Edward Shortt banned Battling Siki, the black Senegalese world light-heavyweight champion, because 'the colour issue might awaken grave partisan passions and animosities among the spectators' (Shortt expected Siki would beat his British opponent). In 1924 the first Labour home secretary, Arthur Henderson, asked the elite Metropolitan Police Flying Squad to investigate violence at race meetings, and a Parliamentary Committee asked all sports organizers to consult the local police before staging events. A later Labour home secretary, J. R. Clynes, banned a visit in 1930 by a Soviet miners' football team as a Communist sports organization that would be used in strikes, pickets and 'the military training of working-class youth'. The same J. R. Clynes banned Trotsky from coming to Britain.

The one politician who was different, and did play a major role in sport, was Lord Birkenhead. Considered to be one of the great British politicians of the early twentieth century and the finest legal brain he occupied several high posts, including lord chancellor and secretary of state for India. An active player of sport, he regularly played tennis, with such stars as Bunny Austin and Jean Borotra, and golf. He fully subscribed to the Hughes–Coubertin vision of sport helping to develop a healthy body, which was so vital to a healthy mind. He acted as chairman for the Appeals committee to raise money to send the British Olympic team to Paris in 1924, raising £27,000 and sending a team of 450. He was also chairman for the 1928 Games, although this time raising only £18,000 and a much smaller team went to Amsterdam, but he was not present at the Paris Games. In the film *Chariots of Fire*, Birkenhead was portrayed as also travelling as team manager to Paris and trying to persuade Eric Liddell, the Scot, to run in the 100 metres on a Sunday (he would not on religious grounds). However, this was fictional licence.

And unlike the dictators, Birkenhead would never have dreamt of setting sports policy. For him sport was useful, often a distraction. So as secretary of state for India in his regular letters to the viceroy, he would often amuse himself by writing about cricket, in particular England–Australia Tests and events at Wimbledon. And he offered Sir John Simon, a Liberal politician, the chairmanship of the commission to report into whether Indians were capable of governing themselves on the golf course.

The commission Simon took to India only had white members and provoked such fury that Gandhi launched another campaign against the British. Birkenhead was not bothered as he was convinced that Indians would never be capable of managing their affairs. Towards the end of his life he wrote a book called *The World in 2030*, which predicted many things such as the automation of industry, mass air travel, synthetic food and the atom bomb, but he was sure India would still be ruled by the British. Birkenhead, of course, also fully subscribed to the Raj's view of the master race theory that underpinned the Raj. Essential to this was to make sure that Indians were always kept at arm's length from the white women. In 1926 there had been some reports about some of the Nizam of Hyderabad's retainers at a London theatre 'leering at inadequately dressed dancing girls'. Birkenhead wrote immediately to the viceroy that 'few things are more damaging to our prestige as a people than the exposure of the bodies of white women before Indians'.

The only exception in the 1930s to British ministers staying aloof from sport was the Bodyline affair. But then the very unity of the empire was at stake. In general it was the Nazis who showed Whitehall how to use sport, particularly the Olympics, as a diplomatic weapon. This led to somewhat comical results. In January 1936 the foreign secretary, Anthony Eden, encouraged support for Tokyo's bid for the 1940 Olympics in the hope that it might contribute to peace in the Far East. (Japan had then been fighting a brutal war of conquest in China for over four years.) Eden added: 'I could even run in the mile myself!' He was embarrassed to discover a few weeks later that Britain had put in a counter-bid with the support of the Lord Mayor of London. But he and Cabinet colleagues leaned on the British Olympic Committee to withdraw it, an action unimaginable today. The Foreign Office also promoted soccer diplomacy, persuading the FA to send England teams to Italy and Germany in what turned out to be the last year of peace, and arranging for them to give the appropriate, later infamous, Nazi salutes.

What Germany and Italy had done to sport was clearly a spur, for the British government was now beginning to formulate a policy for sport in which the National Fitness Campaign was to be very significant. In this they had lagged behind the royal family. To celebrate his Silver Jubilee in 1935 King George V had created a trust whose object was the provision of playing fields for children and young people. His son, the Duke of York (who had competed at tennis at Wimbledon), went further by creating summer camps for young people. He and his family visited the camps and he was filmed performing a popular novelty number 'Under the Spreading Chestnut Tree' – he continued his camp visits even after he was crowned king. Less successfully, but equally earnestly, the royal family became patrons of a new Central Council of Recreation and Physical Training.

In January 1937 the government followed the royal lead with a Physical Training and Recreation Bill. It proposed to spend £2 million over three years to help local authorities and voluntary bodies provide sports facilities and to train fitness teachers. It also established a National Fitness Council under the well-respected sporting peer Lord Aberdare, to give out the grants. The new council was careful to do this in small sums (the largest grant was £50,000; many were for £50 or less) and without strings, but it was widely seen as a government bid for control over British sports policy. It was even rumoured that one of its leading members, the former Olympian the Marquess of Exeter, would be appointed as Britain's first sports minister. But this never came to pass. And by then the MCC was ready to welcome another visit by the Australian cricket team, having overcome the gravest cricket crisis it had faced and one which, at one stage, had threatened to fatally undermine the British Empire.

The crisis created by what was later known as the 'Bodyline' cricket tour was, arguably, the greatest sporting/political crisis that Britain faced until apartheid sport became an issue 40 years later. It so unnerved the British government of the day that they actually procured the dismissal of one of England's most success-ful cricket captains, and her best fast bowler – both of them with a huge following among fans and the media. It is inconceivable that any modern government could take such a course of action, even if they could guarantee the same secrecy. Even today this secrecy cannot be penetrated since key official papers have simply disap-peared, as have the records of the MCC. More books have been written about Bodyline than almost any other sporting event, with some excellent writing on this subject. Here let us briefly summarize the story to discuss how it impacted on society and why British politicians, otherwise so reluctant to be dragged into sport, were drawn in.

Bodyline was the name coined by an Australian journalist to describe a system of bowling applied by the touring English cricket captain Douglas Jardine during the 1932–3 Australian tour. He relied on two aggressive fast bowlers, Bill Voce and the even faster Harold Larwood, to direct short-pitched balls at the bodies of Australian batsmen, with almost every fielder placed behind them in the hope of taking a catch from the (often involuntary) strokes they used to defend themselves. In cricket terms it was successful: England won the series 4–1 and regained the Ashes. In terms of public relations, it was a disaster: several Australian batsmen were injured, Australian officials protested, Australian media were bitterly critical, spectators came close to rioting and Anglo-Australian relations went into deep crisis.

Jardine's plan was targeted at the phenomenal young Australian batsman Don Bradman, who had pulverized England's bowlers (including Larwood) using normal methods on Australia's tour of England in 1930. Great players change their sport and Bradman had already made an impact. That summer at Lord's, England batted first and, helped by a 173 in only 235 minutes by Ranji's nephew, Duleepsinghji, scored 425 early on the second morning. In any previous Test the score, and the speed with which the runs were scored, would have made it a match-winning score. But Bradman made 254, then the highest score in a Test in England, at one stage adding 231 in two and a half hours. He gave Australia a big lead with time for her bowlers to dismiss England quite cheaply in the second innings. By the third evening, England had effectively lost. In Sydney, thousands gathered outside the offices of the *Sydney Morning Herald* for the scores to be posted on a board.

This was one of many innings Bradman played to make him a legend. His achievements lend weight to the theory that he was one of the best – if not the best – sportsmen who ever lived: statistically no other sportsperson has so out-performed everyone else in the history of his or her sport. Bradman swiftly became an

Australian national icon, and for a country without much sense of history, sporting heroes fulfilled a powerful longing for national identity and pride. Walter Lindrum, the billiards player, and Phar Lap the racehorse were part of the pantheon (indeed, Bradman was once described as the 'Phar Lap of cricket'), but Bradman's dominance over England put him in a special category. His return to Australia after the 1930 tour became a triumphal coast to coast procession with adoring crowds at every stop.

Bradman's iconic status was all the more important against a background of deep economic and social crisis and a growing collapse of confidence by Australians in their relationship with Britain. Belief in British leadership had been severely shaken during the First World War by British generalship of Australian forces, especially at Gallipoli. The Australian official history was written first and established a narrative of Australian courage sacrificed by British incompetence. When the official British historian sought to challenge this, a leaked draft of his conclusions provoked a furious response in Australia and was withdrawn before publication. During the Versailles Peace Conference, the dyspeptic Australian prime minister Billy Hughes clashed angrily with the British prime minister David Lloyd George, over Australia's claims in the Pacific, and briefed against him to a sympathetic Australian press man – Keith Murdoch (father of the media tycoon Rupert). He and all his successors criticized Britain for ignoring the challenge of Japan.

Anglo-Australian tensions grew much sharper when the Australian economy went into Depression in the late 1920s. It was widely blamed on the City of London, from whom Australia had borrowed freely in the boom years of the decade. When the Depression hit both countries, the City called in its loans and refused new ones. The Bank of England sent its financial wizard Sir Otto Niemeyer (a sinister figure to Australians) to preach deflation and balanced budgets at Australia's baffled Labour federal government, and state governments. The federal government gave way to a budget-cutting coalition, but Jack Lang, the charismatic Labour premier of New South Wales, refused to take the medicine and defaulted on his state's debts, on the grounds that his voters 'needed the money more than those bowler-hatted bastards in Britain'. He was sacked by the British governor-general and replaced by an opposition coalition. Although this won the subsequent election, the episode created lasting bitterness against Britain amongst Labour supporters.

While these political and financial dramas were being played out, thousands of Australians were plunged into poverty. Extremist groups flourished in these conditions, including a proto-Fascist New Guard, which disrupted the opening of the new Sydney Harbour Bridge. Many Australians feared an uprising, and the states formed militias to maintain public order. (Private Don Bradman was one of their recruits.) All in all, it was not a good time for the MCC to send to Australia a team led by an aloof captain who hated Australians, with the set intention of intimidating the host's national icon.

The MCC were disposed to ignore the Australian outcry against Bodyline, and were infuriated when the Australian Board of Control used the term 'unsportsmanlike'. Nearly all the British media and public agreed with the MCC. But the outcry caused serious alarm to the government, especially the dominions secretary, Jimmy Thomas. He was a vulnerable minister: a boozy, glad-handing lightweight who had followed his leader Ramsay MacDonald out of the Labour party into the National coalition. He had therefore lost his party and trade union base and held office only on sufferance from a huge Conservative majority in the House of Commons. Thomas had been given the Dominions Office under the Labour government only to mask his failure to overcome unemployment. As a centrepiece of its programme, the new National Government had recently signed the Ottawa agreement to promote trade within the British Empire.

For all of these reasons, Thomas could not afford a rupture with Australia on his watch.

The British governor of South Australia, Sir Alexander

Gore-Ruthven, happened to be on leave in England at the height of the Bodyline crisis during the Adelaide Test match. Unlike most other Britons, he was well aware of the strength of Australian feeling and he briefed Thomas accordingly. He was shrewd enough to include a warning that Australians were ready to boycott British goods. Thomas responded by summoning leading members of the MCC for an 'informal meeting' at which he urged them to remember their duties to the empire. As luck would have it, the president of the MCC was his Cabinet colleague Lord Hailsham, the secretary for war. Putting the army minister in charge of the governing body of a national sport would have been a commonplace appointment in totalitarian countries. In England, it was purely a social issue: Hailsham was a suitably titled amateur (as regards both cricket and defence).

Together, Thomas and Hailsham nudged the MCC into a settlement with the Australians, which was negotiated painstakingly over a series of expensive cables. The Australians would withdraw the terrible word 'unsportsmanlike'. There would be no Bodyline tactics when they came to England in 1934 – and neither Larwood nor Jardine would be in the England team. Thomas and Hailsham got their wish when Jardine resigned, although he led England on their first tour of India in the winter of 1933. There being no Bradman present, the authorities knew he could not cause any trouble in the British Raj. With Larwood, matters were not so simple. He refused to make a humiliating apology for his bowling. To make matters worse he put his name to an ill-advised, but accurate, press article blaming his exclusion from the England team on political pressures. This was denied by Thomas, although he hinted archly at the truth at several well-lubricated social functions. Apart from Larwood and Jardine, the England selectors in 1934 also excluded Bill Voce, and as a result Australia won back the Ashes rather easily (Bradman scored 758 runs including a triple century), but the empire was saved.

Australia was not alone in using sport to establish a sense of national identity. Austria – a shell of a country created by the collapse of an empire – rallied behind its admired footballers, the Wunderteam, far more enthusiastically than behind its political institutions. In 1938 the country was extinguished in the Anschluss with Nazi Germany. This was endorsed by 99 per cent of Austrian voters – some out of fear, but most of them genuine. But three weeks later, the Vienna crowd staged an emotional farewell to their national team when it beat the Germans 2–0, and the secret police reported 'anti-German chants, fights, stone-throwing and fanatical support for the home side'. When Austrian players were incorporated into the German side, on Hitler's orders, they refused to integrate. The star player, Sindelar, refused to play for Germany and died in mysterious circumstances a few months later.

Czechoslovakia was another new European state under pressure that rallied around its footballers. Its fans and media had a simmering feud with Italy after ugly matches between Juventus and Slavia Prague, inflamed even more in the 1934 World Cup when the Italians fouled the star Czech player Puch in the final.

In the Irish Free State, another post-war creation, the Gaelic Athletic Association promoted traditional Irish sports as an instrument of national identity and unity. It banned its members outright from four 'English' sports: rugby, soccer, hockey and cricket. One prominent player was suspended for six months just for watching a soccer match.

As we have seen, football created a new dimension of nationhood in Latin America, especially in Uruguay, Argentina and Brazil. This was further reinforced by resentment when the Italians poached their best players. For Uruguayans, hosting the first World Cup and winning it in 1930 showed the world that their small country was not only a football power, but a successful, democratic nation with an advanced welfare state. In the words of a Uruguayan writer, Eduardo Galeano, 'the sky-blue shirt was proof of the existence of the nation: Uruguay was not a mistake. Football pulled this little country out of the shadows of universal anonymity.' Memories of the triumph sustained national spirit during the Depression, when, like most other Latin American countries, it fell under military rule.

Argentine football in the 1930s acquired a mass following (thanks largely to the spread of radio) and served as a unifying force in a country governed by equally incompetent civilians and military men. When Perón took over in 1944, he quickly harnessed football loyalty to his populist regime: Eva Perón was photographed at charity matches in aid of her Justicialist foundation, kicking off elegantly in high heels.

In Brazil, another populist military dictator, Getulio Vargas, used carnivals and big football matches to deliver important announcements. He followed Mussolini in setting up a corporate state and, at ground level, investing in stadiums and sports facilities. However, the Vargas regime was also the first to celebrate Brazil's African heritage, and this was prompted by its successful racially integrated football side. The star players in its third-place finish in the 1938 World Cup were both black: Leonidas and Domingos de Guia. A leading intellectual, Gilberto Freyre, claimed for Brazilian football 'a set of characteristics such as surprise, craftiness, shrewdness, readiness and I shall even say individual brilliance and spontaneity, all of which express our "mulattoism"'. The concept of mulattoism, to describe not only social organization, but a uniquely Brazilian state of mind, was developed further by another intellectual, Mario Filho, who was also the country's leading sports journalist.

Sport was an especially important national force in countries struggling for independence. In Palestine, ruled under an uneasy British mandate, a Jewish football enthusiast, Josef Yekutieli lobbied FIFA to admit its federation on the promise that it would include Arabs and Christians. He was successful, but when the national team played it added LD to their shirts – the initials of the Hebrew name for Palestine. More importantly, the Maccabiah Games, first held in Tel Aviv in 1932, and repeated in 1935, were an outlet for Zionist feeling, especially in 1935 when German Jewish athletes defied a Nazi ban on attending. Athletes at those

Games protested not only against the Nazis, but against the British, who had severely restricted Jewish immigration.

In India, sport, especially cricket, attracted the attention of nationalist politicians. The Congress Party campaigned to free Indian cricket both from princely patronage and from communal divisions, although as we have seen the religious matches between Hindus, Muslims, Parsees, Christians and Europeans remained the most popular with the public. In 1936 the Socialist mayor of Bombay was quick to make a political point when celebrating the return of the Olympic gold medal Indian hockey team. 'The secret of its success was that it consisted of the best men of India. If it had been selected on communal representation and reservation of seats on the lines of the [British-devised] Government of India Act of 1935, it would have been doomed to failure [laughter].' Their success contrasted with the abject under-performance in the same year of the Indian cricket team – mismanaged by a princeling, Vizzy. He was not remotely qualified to be a first-class cricketer, let alone a Test cricketer, and proved a willing stooge of the hard-line viceroy Lord Willingdon – which generated scathing criticism. Apart from defeats on the field of play, it saw India's best cricketer and the first man to score a Test hundred against Jardine's side, Lala Amarnath, sent home for using rude language to the British manager of the tour.

Nevertheless, the British allowed the Indians to have their own teams. Japan, whose rule over Korea was much grimmer and has still not been forgiven by the Koreans, did not even allow its colony that modicum of comfort. Here the sporting story of the 1936 Olympics was more poignant. Sohn Kee-Chung, the record-breaking marathon winner in the Berlin Olympics, was a Korean compelled to compete under the banner of the occupier of his country, Japan, and under the Japanese name of Kitei Son. For him the victory meant a great deal. The Japanese had silenced many Koreans – the musicians, the singers, the speakers – but they could not stop him running. He also managed a discreet gesture of defiance in the march past Hitler at the opening ceremony by writing his name in Korean when he signed in for the ceremony. After his victory he bowed his head in protest at the medal ceremony and planned to lobby Hitler in support of Korean independence. (But while he met Hitler, he did not raise the issue and it would have made no difference: Hitler was about to sign the Anti-Comintern Pact with Japan.) His victory was hailed as a triumph for Japan (where indeed it was greeted rapturously) and the Japanese authorities ordered it to be reported that way in Korea. One newspaper defied them and printed a picture of Sohn without the little Japanese flag on his tracksuit. The staff were arrested, and Sohn never again ran competitively.

CHAPTER 7

THE WORST OF WARS AND
THE BEST OF SPORTS

On the website of the German club FC Schalke 04, the history section has a very interesting date: 22 June 1941. This is what it says happened on that day: 'Schalke suffer a curious defeat in the championship final as Rapid Vienna beat them 4–3 to become champions of Germany – despite Schalke having taken a 3–0 lead with goals by Hinz (2) and Hermann Eppenhoff.'

The really curious thing about this is the one event which took place that day that the website does not mention, an event of such historic significance that it went far beyond a football match, even a championship final. In the early hours of 22 June 1941, when the football players would have been fast asleep, Hitler's 3 million strong army – including not only Germans, but Croats, Finns, Romanians, Hungarians, Italians and even Spaniards – backed by 3,600 tanks and 2,500 aircraft, launched the biggest invasion in history. This was Operation Barbarossa, Hitler's plan to conquer the Soviet Union. That day, the Second World War changed and Winston Churchill, whose hatred of communism could not be doubted, famously said, 'If Hitler invaded hell I would make at least a favourable reference to the devil in the House of Commons.' Churchill knew the invasion meant eventual victory for the Allies. Hitler's move against Russia made sure this would be the most devastating war in history, taking nearly 50 million lives, four times as many as the First World War. But in Berlin that day, 90,000 fans gathered to watch Schalke 04 and Rapid Vienna as if nothing in the world had changed.

We can understand the historian who asked in genuine disbelief: what were the Germans who gathered to watch the match thinking? But the event also illustrates the role of sport in the Second World War. If the staging of the match showed the special wartime use of sport by the Nazis, the Allies also realised how useful sport could be. This was not quite what either of Arnold's disciples, Hughes and Coubertin, had in mind when they began their missionary zeal to spread the gospel of sport. But by the 1940s, after nearly a hundred years of proselytizing, the value of how useful sport could be for political purposes was widely accepted.

Ironically, it was more accepted in Nazi Germany than in Britain, where for a time after war started, sport became very much a secondary activity, necessary only to provide some relief from the war. Even after the British realized this was self-defeating and sport, even in war, could be useful, the idea of 100,000 gathering in Wembley for an FA Cup Final on D-day, in June 1944, as the Allies invaded Europe, would have been unthinkable. In contrast, Nazi Germany, from the beginning, used sport not only to convince their people that their lives had not been affected by war, but as a symbol of their hegemony over Europe, particularly through football and chess.

In occupied countries, the Nazis hoped that sport would secure the loyalty, or at least acquiescence, of the population – a policy that had very mixed success. In the United States, professional sport languished because so many top players were inducted into the forces, but the wartime economy opened up new opportunities, especially for black people and women, and created full employment and restored prosperity for working people: this had a lasting impact on post-war sport.

British sport began the war in September 1939 with an immediate shutdown and what remained of the county cricket season was abandoned. The touring West Indian cricket team sailed home with seven matches unplayed. The FA announced the suspension of all football matches under its jurisdiction: it was followed instantly by the associations in Scotland and Wales, but not Northern Ireland. Soon after, rugby union and rugby league both followed suit. In part, this was in response to what happened in the Great War, when many British sportsmen were fiercely criticized for carrying on with sport instead of joining the colours (the cricketers were shamed in an open letter to the *Sportsman* from W. G. Grace). In part, it reflected official fears that the war would open with a devastating air attack on Britain, with hundreds of thousands of civilian casualties. Baldwin had warned 'the bomber will always get through', and this was universally believed.

But nothing happened. The 'phoney war' set in and the only British casualties were road accident victims of the over-zealous blackout. The Home Office and sporting authorities both realized that a ban had been an over-reaction. Football was hurriedly re-started, but on the basis of regional leagues and friendly matches, with a limit on crowds of only 8,000. The restriction was largely unnecessary. Many people had to work on Saturday, and in any case, few were attracted to meaningless matches, often between pick-up sides with little relationship to the clubs playing under their peacetime names. In one such match, Norwich City played a Brighton and Hove Albion side with two Norwich reserves and five soldiers recruited on the ground. Norwich won 18–0: regular goal feasts were a consolation of wartime soccer. The football pools patriotically combined in the Unity Pools, but their takings from forecasts of wartime matches fell dramatically.

Rugby league also re-started on a regional basis, with relaxed rules over registrations of servicemen and munitions workers. Rugby union matches were restored and the RFU even relaxed its ban on amateurs playing alongside professionals in the forces. Racing struggled on, despite the loss of several important racecourses, and boxing remained popular.

During the early months of the war, there were significant findings from an early survey by Mass Observation (one of the world's first social survey organizations, which was launched in Britain in the late 1930s). 'Only 9 per cent of [pre-war football fans] continue to attend regularly', but general interest in sport remained very high. No fewer than 49 per cent of respondents paid more attention to sports news than war news, and only 30 per cent were more interested in war news than sports news. Mass Observation concluded: 'Sports like football have an absolute major effect on the morale of the people.' That view was confirmed by a report on the impact of the fall of France by the *Daily Mail's* racing correspondent: 'The people were stunned by the news just after the first race at Wolverhampton yesterday, but, of course, carried on and presumably the meeting today will go through if only as a gesture of stoutness.'

In the same period, with a shattered British Expeditionary Force returning from Dunkirk and a German invasion expected imminently, an observer on the road from London to Guildford noticed that 'all along the line young men in flannels were playing cricket in the sunshine on beautiful tended fields shaded by stalwart oaks and poplar trees.' Not all the beautiful tended fields survived. Many famous sports facilities were taken over for military use. Twickenham, the home of rugby, was given over to allotments and Civil Defence; Wimbledon became a drilling ground for the Home Guard; Epsom racecourse was taken over by the army, while Arsenal's new showpiece stadium at Highbury became a fortified HQ for Civil Defence and the club had to accept the bitter pill of sharing with Tottenham Hotspur. The Oval cricket ground was used as a prisoner-of-war camp (many of the German POWs helped restore it after the war). Lord's had to give up its nursery ground to the RAF and even its holy-of-holies, the Pavilion. However, the MCC's guiding light, Sir Pelham Warner, was able to prevent a complete takeover by arguing that 'if Goebbels had been able to broadcast that the war had stopped cricket at Lord's it would have been valuable propaganda for the Germans'.

There were persistent calls to ban horseracing as a drain on resources (backed by Britain's wartime economic supremo Sir Stafford Cripps), but it was simply too popular, and the Jockey

Club was able to restart classic races in Ripon and Thirsk, two courses in rural Yorkshire that were remote from possible air-raids. They attracted good crowds and heavy betting. The government had no success in curtailing dog-racing and boxing, and was attacked in the media for trying to reduce the entertainment available for troops and war-workers.

Racing did try to help the war effort by making sure that if owners sold horses then the money was not taken away from the country. This led to a fascinating duel with the Aga Khan, the pre-eminent racehorse owner before the war. The Aga, or to give his full title, Sir Sultan Muhammad Shah Aga Khan III, was the spiritual leader of the Ismailis, a Shia Muslim sect. Born in Karachi in 1877, he was of Persian stock and worked closely with high Raj officials to make sure Indian nationalists' efforts to dislodge the British from the subcontinent were defeated. His grandfather, the first Aga, had fled to Afghanistan after a failed revolt against the Shah and taken shelter with the invading British forces. The British let the first Aga settle in Bombay and, giving into his pleading, offered him a pension, although he was never satisfied with the amount and always complained. But in 1866 a British judge in Bombay, Justice Sir Joseph Arnold, came to his rescue after some of his followers filed a case against him in the Bombay High Court. Justice Arnold ruled in favour of the Aga and in his memoirs, *World Enough and Time*, Aga III referred several times to the judgement, saying, 'My grandfather had been confirmed in his rights and titles by a judgement of the Bombay High Court in 1866.'

It was also Aga III who made the family famous. He ventured west, cultivated prominent leaders like Lloyd George, Beaverbrook, who was also his financial adviser, and Churchill, often presenting them with mangoes from India. He eventually divorced his first Indian Muslim wife for a succession of Western wives. While his political prominence was marked before the First World War, he was still a figure of note in the interwar period. In 1937, with British help, he became president of the League of Nations, representing the British Indian Empire. During this period he met

Hitler and, reflecting the British circles he moved in, was an admirer of the Fuhrer.

By this time the Aga was also a huge figure in British racing, having taken it up properly in 1921. His golden years were 1935 and 1936. In 1935 his horse Bahram became the first horse since Rock Sand, 32 years earlier, to win the Triple Crown: the 2,000 Guineas, the Derby and the St Leger. In 1936 Mahmoud won the Derby. Epsom rang to shouts of 'good old Aga', proving how popular a figure he was, a fact already known to users of London buses where a popular advertisement of the time ran: 'Chocolates as rich and dark as the Aga'. But his relations with the racing establishment were not always cordial.

As the Aga's Turkhan, ridden by Gordon Richards, won the St Leger in 1940, the race having been transferred from Doncaster to Thirsk because of the war, it emerged that he had sold three of his Derby winners, the 1930 winner Blenheim and also Bahrain and Mahmoud, to an American syndicate for around £60,000. The reaction in the media was swift. 'Tattenham' in the *Sunday Express* on 6 October 1940 wrote, 'The dollar voice of the tempter is heard in the homeland. The sons and daughters of our true-blooded Derby winners may [. . .] come back to us as half-breeds.' As Sir Derek Birley noted in *Playing The Game,* the Aga's action 'was viewed not only as an abuse of hospitality and an evident vote of no confidence in British survival, but as a defilement'. In British racing, to help American racing and make money was almost treasonable. More serious charges of treason were to be considered by the British as a result of the Aga's alleged wartime activities.

The Aga spent the war in Switzerland, having found himself there as he was trying to go to Germany. In July 1939 he had arranged to meet Hitler with the help of Walter Hewel, a favourite of the Fuhrer and a top Nazi official in Ribbentrop's Foreign Office. The Aga had got to know him well. But, as he arrived in Switzerland from Deauville, he developed a bad earache and had to postpone his visit to Germany. His belief that he could do something to prevent war remained strong. However, as the Aga nursed his ear in Switzerland, Hitler marched into Poland. The result was that the war found him in neutral Switzerland and he remained there until February 1945.

But he needed money. With the British imposing strict foreign exchange controls, he was always petitioning the India Office to try to unfreeze his funds, often from the sale of his horses in the United States. This would lead to comical moments. In November 1940 he wanted £6,000 out of the £60,000 he had raised in the United States, with the rest remaining in dollars to help Britain buy arms. The Aga had pleaded, 'We are not here for pleasure but had to come as refugees.' But the telegram he sent to the India Office added an extra zero – it came over as £60,000 – and British officials were not best pleased. In the end, the figure was clarified and he was sent £6,000, along with £500 proceeds from another horse sale. The Aga by this time was worried about the Germans taking over his considerable properties in France. Indeed, the Germans soon sequestered all his French studs. This made him ask the India office in December 1940 for Iranian protection. 'This procedure,' he wrote, 'might prevent useful substantial assets being acquired by Germany.' The India Office was almost apoplectic that such a prominent British citizen, who had the title 'first class chief of the Bombay Presidency' and title of High Highness, with a salute of eleven guns, should now seek the protection of a country his grandfather had fled. But one official noted, 'There may be grounds for winking at the Aga Khan's methods of protecting his property of which the department is not aware.'

Later in the war, according to German documents, there were allegations of more substantial contact with the Aga promising to help the Germans. After the war British officials discussed whether this was possibly treasonable but in the end they concluded that there was no way of knowing whether the Germans were telling the truth. An official concluded, 'there is nothing in this business which can really be held to be the discredit of the Aga Khan'. By then, with the war over, the Aga was again a prominent Muslim worth cultivating in the crucial years as the British settled the fate of their Indian empire. His horses were also back racing in Britain and proving to be winners.

Boxing flourished in the war, particularly in the services: among civilians, bicycling, athletics, lawn tennis and squash all gained popularity, and more people played cricket, football and hockey as opposed to watching them. The number of women participants in all sports rose dramatically, encouraged by the provision of service and workplace facilities and by their improved economic and social status as war workers.

Sport played an essential role of occupying both servicepeople and civilians, and keeping them fit in a war with protracted periods of waiting. Fitness was a major concern of the government throughout the war, and it poured out exhortations on diet and exercise. The BBC took up the call with a determinedly cheerful programme, 'Up In The Morning', later caricatured by George Orwell in *1984*. From the outset of the war, it sought to enlist famous sportsmen to teach physical fitness and many served in the forces on that basis, including Len Hutton, Denis Compton, Raich Carter and Stanley Matthews (Don Bradman did the same in Australia). So many footballers went to Blackpool and Aldershot as instructors or advisers that they became major popular centres of the game for the first time.

As the war continued, the authorities realized that these sportsmen could do more for morale than they could as trainers, and allowed them to spend long periods playing their chosen sport at a high level. Denis Compton recalled, 'Cup finals, League South matches and army representative games followed one on top of each other in a seemingly endless stream.' Compton was also able to enjoy playing first-class cricket in India during the war, including an epic innings when recruited into the Indian side of Holkar (then a princely state). India saw little actual fighting and that was limited to the north east bordering Burma when the Japanese launched an invasion in 1944. The war years did ravage the country, however, and an estimated 4 million died during the Bengal famine, more than the number of Indians killed in the two World

Wars, or the events that followed the partition of the country in 1947. The famine, the worst in twentieth century Indian history, was a dreadful blot on the British Raj, a story of British incompetence and negligence aided by Churchill's refusal to divert war shipping to provide food for the Bengalis. His adviser, Lord Cherwell, who had contempt for all non-whites, felt the Bengalis deserved to die.

After 1942, Gandhi launched the last of his great non-violent campaigns to free the country; such was the scale of the revolt that a British officer called it an 'occupied hostile land', with the British using large-scale force, including bombings from the air, to hold on to India. But despite this, cricket flourished, producing some of the most remarkable batting feats in Indian cricket history. Interestingly, it was the only time Compton, one of England's greatest batsmen, played in India, as he never toured India with England. Compton's wartime memories were echoed by Joe Mercer, who told an interviewer:

> For seven years, I probably played twice, sometimes three times a week [. . .] It was a funny kind of thing in the war [. . .] Sometimes I didn't know who I was playing for, the army, the command, the unit, England or the club. I knew once the CO said when I wanted a pass to play, 'Mercer, I don't know whether you want a pass to come into the camp or to stay out!'

As the war progressed, and particularly when it became certain that Britain would not lose, crowds returned to sporting fixtures with celebrity players. Visiting forces boosted the crowds. The Australian Air Force team gave the British their first sight of Keith Miller, one of the most exciting cricketers of the post-war era. Crowds even showed up at baseball games played by American GIs: the 'Plymouth Yankees' managed to fill a greyhound stadium, using a broadcast running commentary to tell the British what was happening.

But football drew the biggest audience, reflecting the pent-up longing detected by Mass Observation at the start of the war.

Wartime England–Scotland soccer internationals were watched by 60,000 people: in 1944 the English won 8–0 (thanks largely to the preparation from all those matches enjoyed by Mercer and Compton). Other 'ersatz' internationals against sides made up from exiles were also well attended, to the surprise of the FA, which recorded in May 1943, 'It is a fact of no little interest that war time has seen an increase rather than, as might have been expected, a decrease in the number of matches on an international basis.' On Boxing Day 1942, nearly a third of a million people saw the opening matches of the War Cup, and the four quarter-finals in the next spring drew more than 100,000 spectators.

In the middle of the war, Stanley Rous wrote a paper in which he praised the FA's War Emergency Committee for helping increase the international profile of the game. This had been done by building contacts with government departments, other influential people and by working together with the armed forces. In March 1942, a writer in the popular magazine *Reveille* commented that, 'Soccer football, like cricket, is a shining example of providing entertainment for war workers, except that some of the Service players might be quizzed on how much actual military duty they do in the course of a week.'

Not all sportsmen had the same kind of war as Compton or Mercer. At least 80 Football League professionals were killed in the war, many more in accidents than in battle. Other prominent casualties included Test cricketers Kenneth Farnes and Hedley Verity, and Prince Alexander Obolensky, scorer of a legendary try for England against the All Blacks. Compton's post-war comrade Bill Edrich had a highly dangerous war as a squadron leader of daylight bombing raids. He left a vivid memory of playing cricket for his squadron against a local village, which contrasts the normality of the match with the toll of a raid in the North Sea:

At times it seemed like a strange dream [. . .] Both cricket teams played well, and it was a hard and exciting game. Every now and then would come the old, accustomed cry 'HOWZAT?', and then one's mind would flicker off to the briefing, and to joking with a pal whose broken body was now washing in the long, cold tides, and one saw again his machine cart-wheeling down, flaming from nose to tail; and then a ball would roll fast along the green English turf and in the distance the village clock would strike and the mellow echoes would ring through the lazy air of that perfect summer afternoon.

It is a curious fact that Nazi Germany imposed far less wartime sacrifice on its civilians than democratic Britain. Hitler was aware that the war was unpopular, especially in Berlin, and he did not want to remind the German people of it. Until the last years of the war, when Speer took control of German industry, he operated a largely peacetime economy, geared only for short-term conquests. Through slave labour by Jews and foreigners, and looting occupied countries, he sought to improve living standards for Germans and suppress resentment of the war.

The Nazis were therefore even more determined than the British to use sport as a sign of normality and continuity with peacetime life. German football paused for two months at the outbreak of war and then resumed almost without interruption or restriction until the autumn of 1944. The official match programme for the German War Final in 1940 boasted about the number of football matches played in Germany and about the 80,000 attendance. It added: 'At the same hour the men and women of the British Isles fearfully await the German general attack, where the pitches of English football clubs have been ploughed and torn up, in the hope that this panic measure might be of some use at the decisive hour.' The following year, as we have seen, 90,000 turned up for a final played on 22 June 1941.

In 1943 the Nazis abandoned international matches, but the relevant decree stated also that 'sporting competitions of a local character are to be carried through in order to sustain the work ethic.' The local restriction had to be abandoned under popular pressure to allow a form of national championship to continue in football. By 1944, heavy Allied air raids were regularly devastating German cities, so that kick-off times were often kept secret as long as possible, and yet the national championship final was played, just after the D-Day landings, before 70,000 spectators. It was won by Dresdner FC: a few months later the city was incinerated. On 22 April 1945, with Allied troops at the gates of the city and unconditional surrender barely two weeks away, the two big Munich clubs played a friendly match in front of thousands.

From the outbreak of war to the end of 1942, the Nazis staged 35 international football matches against neutral, satellite and occupied countries, as well as ice hockey internationals. (The early conquest of Poland allowed them to add the country's best football player, Ernst Willimowski, to the national side, just as they had previously incorporated Austrian players and added Czech tennis stars to their Davis Cup team.) The matches were the brainchild of Ribbentrop, the foreign minister, if such an asinine man can be said to have inspired anything. He 'placed the highest value on German teams appearing abroad and foreign teams coming to Germany'. It was part of the policy of showing the German people that life was normal and reflected Nazi ambitions to control international sport, also exposed by Hitler's plans for a permanent Olympic stadium in Berlin.

The Nazis had a clear field to take over European football. FIFA lay dormant during the war at its headquarters in Zurich: Jules Rimet remained president, but was eased out of his other job in charge of the French Football Federation by a hostile Vichy regime and lay low for the rest of the war. In the early years of the war, Ribbentrop's international matches were popular, both at home and away. In Switzerland in 1942, the Swiss spectators handed out five-franc pieces to the German players, whether in fear or admiration is not clear. Results did not always go the way the Nazis decreed: the worst setback was a 2–1 defeat by Switzerland in 1941 on Hitler's birthday. Goebbels reacted: 'definitely no sporting exchanges when the result is the least bit unpredictable'. To prevent such accidents in future, he allowed Germany's great coach, Sepp Herberger, to pluck players out of the forces and keep them together in training camps for three weeks.

As Germany's war fortunes worsened, these matches grew more and more unpopular. In 1942, not long after Germany's defeat at El Alamein, and with a German army involved in desperate fighting at Stalingrad, the German football team lost 3–2 at home to neutral Sweden. Ribbentrop's deputy, Martin Luther, wrote: '100,000 have left the stadium depressed, and because victory in this football match is closer to people's hearts than the capture of a city in the East, such an event must be prohibited for the sake of the national mood.' In their last international against the satellite state of Slovakia, the German team had to endure protracted booing and whistling. More important, the team was becoming unpopular at home, especially with German mothers (an important constituency to the Nazis). They saw the footballers as a privileged elite, escaping the Eastern Front where their sons were fighting and dying. Goebbels ended the internationals. Reversing his previous policy, he decreed that 'soldiers are no longer available and people doing labour service will not be granted leave of absence'.

The Nazis also tried to assert themselves by taking control of European chess. They were helped when the reigning World Champion, the White Russian Alexander Alekhine, fell into their hands, along with his Jewish wife. They induced him (whether easily or forcibly is still disputed) to write six pro-Nazi articles on 'Jewish and Aryan chess'. These accused Jews of playing 'defensive, cowardly chess' in contrast to the Aryans' attacking chess, which was aggressive and brave. The Nazis also forced him to play in seven tournaments organized by their chess controller, Ehrhardt Post, including a so-called European Championship in September 1942, which was briefly visited by Hitler. Alekhine won, under the flag of Vichy France, ahead of Paul Keres, from German-conquered Estonia, and a high-quality field of players under the Nazi flag, or from allies, satellites and neutrals. The field included a Nazi poster boy, the teenage genius Klaus Junge, a fanatical admirer of Hitler: he was killed fighting in the last weeks of war. The one exception was the Dutch former World Champion Max Euwe, who was so affronted by Alekhine's articles he courageously refused to play.

The Nazis, keen to promote the idea that life under Nazi rule was normal, encouraged sport in every country that they occupied. Generally they gave it a surprisingly high degree of autonomy. The Reich sports minister, von Tschammer und Osten, was nervous about allowing matches 'that are suited to raising the temperature of large local spectator masses such that the limit of political demonstrations is reached'. This ruled out international matches against occupied countries such as the Netherlands, where the Nazis were nervous of their team's reception. But they were happy to allow domestic sport to continue. The Nazi ruler of the occupied Netherlands, Seyss-Inquart (previously Hitler's agent in Austria), explained his policy: 'he who plays sport does not sin'.

In France, football clubs actually found conditions easier in the occupied zone than under the unoccupied Vichy regime. In pursuit of its reactionary and anti-Semitic ideology, the Vichy regime set its face against professionalism in football, which it linked to decadence and Jewish influence in the defeated Third Republic. Its sports minister was the tennis star Jean Borotra, who before the war had been a frequenter of Lord Birkenhead's country house in Charlton. Borotra began by insisting that every club under his jurisdiction should contain at least four genuine amateurs. It was not enough for Vichy and the following year Borotra outlawed professional footballers altogether. Instead, he made all clubs government offices and their players civil servants. Borotra also copied the policy of his socialist predecessor Leo Lagrange in investing in sports facilities in small towns. Meanwhile, the French football cup was still contested on a national basis, and in 1942 a record-breaking crowd of 45,000 watched F. C. Sète go down 2–0 to Red Star Olympique Audonien (a provocative name which survived the war).

221

Much has been made of the Dutch resistance to the Nazis, yet in sport, the Dutch carried on as if nothing had changed. Dutch sport flourished during the war years – essentially because it helped Dutch people to pretend that nothing had happened. Until the last year of the war, when the country came close to starvation, the Dutch occupation was boring rather than oppressive. In 1944 the editor of Feyenoord's journal summed up the mood: 'Oh well, what more does a person have to entertain himself with at the moment than the sport on the green field? For all of us in the club, the league will be a good interruption of the daily grind and pressure which these war years have brought us. In a time like this, we need a stimulant.' Only days after the country was over-run, a Dutch sports magazine wrote a cheerful leader: 'The May sun is shining over the Low Countries; the sports fields and the water call.' Indeed, in the first year of the occupation, the Dutch, with a population of around 12 million, bought 4 million sports tickets, and in 1943 this had doubled to 8 million. Sports clubs could not cope with the flood of new applications for membership.

Except in one vital respect, the Nazis left Dutch sport to itself during the occupation. Sports clubs were ordered to remove any references to the exiled Dutch royal family, and the cricketers were compelled to find Dutch equivalents for cricket terms such as leg before wicket. The separate Dutch football federations were merged into one. Otherwise, Dutch sports clubs were free to run themselves – *if* they were prepared to exclude their Jewish members and pay no attention when they were stigmatized, incarcerated, deported and exterminated.

Almost all of them complied. There were Dutch people who took great risks to save Jews, but not many came from the ranks of Dutch sport, even though Jewish clubs and personalities had been very prominent before the war. An honourable exception was the minority sport of korfball, whose association declined to play matches under Nazi terms. Another was Ajax Football Club, where Gentile members made real efforts to shelter their Jewish colleagues, although several prominent ex-players collaborated. (One earned good money from valuing stolen Jewish property for the Nazis.) Among the Jewish victims of the war were the popular Ajax winger Eddy Hamel and the even more popular radio commentator Henry Hollander, who had misguided faith in his fan letter from Hitler. The disappearance of Jews from Dutch sport caused a serious shortage of referees, and a sports magazine urged Dutch Gentiles to come forward and replace them, for fear that the Dutch league might stagnate. It produced a furious, sarcastic response from the illegal newspaper *Het Parool*, but the magazine's appeal was successful and the league did not stagnate.

Denmark took a very different course. The country was conquered even more quickly than the Netherlands and it did not even have time to form a government in exile. The Danish government and parliament were allowed to function by the Nazis, who treated Denmark as the 'Model Protectorate'. Germany played two international football matches at home against the Danes, and allowed them to host fixtures at home themselves against Sweden. The hosting of such matches showed that the Nazis had no evident fear of Danish crowds. The Danes not only protected their Jews, but confronted their German occupiers when they demanded punitive measures against them. The elderly King Christian X threatened to wear the Jewish star on his daily rides through his capital. Their attitude influenced the occupation forces, even the special SS units, who resisted orders from Berlin. In October 1943, when the Nazis sent special units to round up the Danish Jews, virtually all of them were hidden and smuggled successfully to neutral Sweden.

In Norway, sport was a major focus of national resistance. As part of the collaborationist government led by Vidkun Quisling (whose name became part of the English language) the Nazis appointed a sports fuhrer to run every sports club in the country. The Norwegians responded by a total boycott of all officially organized sports events, whether as players, officials or spectators. Their skiing champion Ruud Birger threatened to burn his skis rather than compete in Nazi-sponsored events. Official teams had to depend on press-ganged members of the Quisling administration for players and spectators. In 1942 a cup semi-final was played in the big stadium at Bergen in front of just 27 people. Instead, the Norwegian people went to illegal sporting events deep in the countryside, which quickly provided networks of organized resistance. By 1943 sport had made the security situation so bad as to provoke a rare visit from Himmler. He ordered a mass round-up of Norwegian sportspeople who had joined the boycott. One victim, tortured in a concentration camp, was the national football coach Asbjorn Halversen, whose team had beaten Germany in the only match Hitler ever watched.

Like other leaders, Roosevelt recognized the value of organized sport in maintaining wartime morale. He resisted calls for the ending of Major League baseball and gave it a 'green light' to continue, so long as none of its players evaded the draft. The administration also encouraged American football and basketball to continue. In practice, so many top sportsmen did join the forces that all professional sport was hit hard, while 200 colleges abandoned their football teams. By 1945, over 500 Major League baseball players had been inducted, along with 4,000 boxers, including five world champions. Joe Louis joined an army that was still segregated, and made propaganda films and morale-boosting appearances, although he refused to appear before segregated audiences. American GIs overseas introduced American sports to new populations, especially basketball, which required so little equipment and space.

The absence of stars, and patterns of shift-working in factories, depressed attendances at all major sports events, and many teams struggled to play matches at all. Two prominent American football sides, the Steelers and the Eagles, were forced to merge into the Steagles. The shortage of skilled players also led coaches to prepare separate squads for offence and defence – a change that proved to be lasting. But the most important wartime influence on US sport happened off the field, rather than on it.

The war restored full employment to the American economy. In 1940, despite the New Deal, official unemployment stood at 14.6 per cent of the labour force. By 1944 it had fallen to 1.2 per cent of a labour force which had been swollen by many groups that had not even tried to seek work in the Depression. Quite simply, the war had restored a prosperous working-class base of support for American sport. Of special importance for the future, the war had brought millions of women and black people into employment. By the end of the war, almost 19 million women were working outside their homes, mostly in clerical and service jobs, but including a million in aerospace, and another million in other war industries. These were celebrated in the cult figure of Rosie the Riveter.

In June 1941, President Roosevelt made an executive order outlawing racial discrimination in the employment of workers in defence industries or in government (although this did not extend to the armed forces themselves). He reinforced this order in 1943 with a general ban on discrimination in all government-operated facilities. The effect of these measures was generally confined to the north, and they helped to secure a new wave of large-scale black migration from southern farms to northern cities. By the end of the war about 8 per cent of all American war workers were black – not far short of the black percentage of the total adult population.

After the war, black employment fell back, but many remained in work in northern cities and their economic power underpinned the ending of segregation in post-war American major sports. Women's employment also fell back after the war, as women vacated jobs for their returning men, but also by choice, as they became housewives and homemakers. In these roles they had far more disposable income than their mothers, and far more say in family decisions. During the 1950s they were to spend a great deal on sports and leisure for themselves – and even more propelling and equipping their offspring in organized junior sports. A generation of reluctant Little Leaguers can blame the war for their unhappy weekends.

What the war did not change was the American belief that its sport was different. This was in marked contrast to the wider political sphere where the war dramatically changed America. Having played a crucial role in defeating the Axis powers, the new world riding to rescue of the old, as Churchill put it, America could not, and did not want to, retreat into its old isolationism as it had done after the First World War. But in sport it remained in its bunker. It was only as the other great power to emerge from the Second World War, the Soviets, began to show how much they had learned from the Nazis about the political use of sport, that the Americans slowly, almost reluctantly, shed their sporting isolationism.

PART 3

———

A DIFFERENT KIND OF SPORTING WAR

CHAPTER 8

COPING WITH THE RUSSIANS

The Second World War led to an iron curtain descending on Europe, as Winston Churchill famously put it, but in sport there was the exact opposite. Here, the return of peace marked the lifting of the Soviet sports iron curtain and the end of nearly 30 years of largely self-imposed isolation from world sport. In the first 20 years of its life, the Soviet regime was generally hostile to international competitive sport and preferred instead to exert its influence through various forms of international workers' sporting contests or carefully controlled exhibitions by Soviet soccer teams and gymnasts. Soviet sport did have to adjust itself to the violent shift in Stalin's foreign policy of the Nazi–Soviet Pact of 1939. One little-known by-product of the Pact was that Nazi sports experts went to Russia to advise their Soviet counterparts, and throughout 1940, the two regimes staged a series of friendly international competitions, with both teams on best behaviour and swearing eternal friendship.

The defeat of Nazi Germany in 1945, however, made the Soviets fundamentally rethink their sports policy. It was as if, having discovered the political use of sport, they were determined to make up for lost years and outdo the Nazis, and they were to do it with a vengeance. Sport became an extension of Cold War propaganda, to win influence in neutral and newly independent states and to reinforce control over the Soviet satellites in Eastern Europe. Internally, Soviet sport was used to cement and channel loyalty to the regime, to create an elaborate reward and punishment system under the regime's control and to fashion an ideal Soviet man (and woman), combining brilliance with discipline.

An early sight of Soviet sports diplomacy came only a few months after VE day in May 1945, when the Moscow Dinamo football team made a short tour of Britain. Significantly, Dinamo was a fiefdom of Stalin's henchman Beria, head of his huge security and internal terror apparatus, the MVD. Although vicious and amoral, Beria was also the most competent of Stalin's cronies, a modernizer and a realist and the source of much of the impetus behind Soviet sports policy. Aware that the Soviet Union could never compete with the economic achievements of the West, he and his circle saw sport as an area where the regime might achieve parity or even dominance.

Moscow Dinamo's tour set conditions which were later followed by other touring Soviet sports teams – strict supervision, no socializing within the host country and all meals and accommodation in the Soviet Embassy or consulates. That probably ensured that the team ate better than their rationed hosts. At a time when Britain was still regarded as the world leader in football, Dinamo surprised everyone by being unbeaten. They drew 3–3 with Chelsea and 2–2 with Glasgow Rangers, beat Arsenal 4–3 and thumped Cardiff City 10–1. Although instructed to be on their best behaviour (the team presented bouquets of flowers to their embarrassed opponents), their on-field aggression drew an angry response from the crowds.

The main result of the tour, suggested George Orwell in an ironically titled essay *The Sporting Spirit*, 'will have been to create fresh animosity on both sides'. Orwell suggested that this was inevitable: 'Even if one didn't know from concrete examples [. . .] that international sporting contests lead to orgies of hatred, one could deduce it from general principles.' In large towns, it was an outlet for people's physical strength or sadistic impulses, and at the highest level, sport was 'frankly mimic warfare'. Orwell's essay provoked a spirited reply from E. S. Fayers of Harrow, Middlesex:

George Orwell is always interesting, but he does write some bilge
[. . .] I suggest that George is in danger of falling into the error
of intellectual contempt for the "mob". These football crowds, if
only he got among them, he would find are not great ignorant
mobs of sadistic morons. They are a pretty good mixture of just
ordinary men. A little puzzled, a little anxious, steady, sceptical,
humorous, knowledgeable, having a little fun, hoping for a bit of
excitement and definitely getting quite a lot of enjoyment out of
that glorious king of games – football.

With great accuracy, Fayers concluded, 'I'm sorry for George. He's
missed a lot of fun in life.'

Fayers' view was confirmed when Britain played the Rest of
Europe at Hampden Park in May 1947. The match had been hyped
up in the newspapers, especially in the still mass-circulation *Daily
Express*, where Frank Butler declared that national prestige was at
stake and that even a draw would 'leave us the laughing stock of
Europe'. He and other writers singled out the threat of the sinister
and 'sallow-skinned' Italian stopper centre-half, Parola, as much
for his ultra-short shorts as for his tackling. Butler and company
need not have worried. A good-humoured crowd of 135,000
watched the British side stroll through a 6–1 victory and prove
themselves the 'bosses of Europe'. Significantly, there were no
Hungarian players in the Rest team, although the significance of
this only emerged later.

The match had come about because FIFA was broke and
needed money. On holiday in Switzerland, Stanley Rous, then
establishing himself as the power in British football, was told by
the president of the Swiss Football Federation about 'FIFA's
desperate financial problems'. The gate money of £30,000 proved
very handy for a cash-strapped FIFA. It also saw the British
home nations return to FIFA and they negotiated special rights
which, more than 65 years later, remain the envy of the rest of
the world of football. These rights mean the four home nations
have a British vice-president on the FIFA executive. In contrast,

all the remaining FIFA members, 204, have to hold elections to get on the 24-man executive. It can mean that at any one time, one or more of the major powers of football may miss out being on the body that runs the world game, but not the British. Each of the four home nations were also allowed to have their own teams. In effect, FIFA recognized that, in footballing terms, Britain was four nations, not one. This again was a privilege shared by no other place in the world that is not a sovereign state. The British made one concession. They gave FIFA equal status on the International Board: FIFA's four matching the British four. With the board deciding rule changes for the game this further emphasized the power of the four British nations. British sport could not have felt more on top of the world. It was not to last long, but felt wonderful while it did.

The arrival of peace made sport even more attractive – people turned to it to help them get over the ravages of war. In 1949, British soccer attendances reached an all-time high of 41 million – 95,000 people watched the FA Amateur Cup at Wembley. Cricket and both codes of rugby also reached their highest-ever attendances, as did greyhound racing and speedway, which were promptly hit with a new 'entertainment tax'; but, as some ironists noted, this was not applied to cricket. This was a brief era when British sports belonged to their paying spectators and before they generally became inextricably bound up with power politics and global commerce.

Attendances boomed not merely in Britain, but across the world as post-war economies recovered and gave people jobs, income and leisure, especially in cities. But while sports in other countries welcomed and even initiated major change, Britain was fooled into thinking that everything was back to the halcyon pre-war days. British sport, football and cricket in particular, resisted innovation and improvement. The need for change was also masked by the make-do-and-mend London Olympics in 1948, which proved a great triumph of British sporting values. Accidental it may have been, but the Games were in the best traditions of the British, the last that could justifiably claim to be a pure sporting festival, and certainly the last to pass without a hint of controversy or scandal. The drug of choice among its athletes was Horlicks, a milky drink used to promote sleep rather than performance.

London held the Olympic Games in 1948 only because Helsinki, the original choice, had been too damaged by the war. London was hardly in better shape. The country was virtually bankrupt and rationed even more severely than during the war (bread had been rationed for a period in 1946 to help avert famine in India). Avery Brundage, who had become vice-president of the IOC, had no confidence in London's ability to host the Games and the London *Evening Standard* agreed with him in a leader in September 1947: 'The average range of British enthusiasm for the Games stretches from lukewarm to dislike. It is not too late for invitations to be politely withdrawn.' A long, freezing winter cooled the public mood even more. The hard-pressed Attlee government was persuaded to keep the Games going only with the promise of major tourist income – a promise since offered to many other governments and cities.

One welcome result was that the government had a hands-off attitude to the Games. There was no special Olympic minister, and the highly efficient organizing committee was left to run things without government interference, although it had to cope with the bureaucracy of post-war Britain in which labour, materials and building were controlled as well as food, clothing and petrol. In keeping with a patched-up Britain, the committee made a series of improvisations, some inspired, some desperate.

Sir William Elvin, managing director of the company that owned Wembley Stadium, secured its conversion from greyhound track to international stadium by its original engineer Sir Owen Williams at the very low price of £750,000 without calling for public money. He also had the Empire Pool restored and had a railway link built by German prisoners-of-war. Canada and Finland were asked to supply building materials and all visiting athletes were asked to bring food with them. The Olympic Village for men was a converted barracks in Uxbridge. The javelin event at the decathlon had to be lit by car headlamps. For all the expedients, the Games saw two important innovations: starting blocks became standard on the running track, and a photo-electric 'magic eye' was used to give winning times and sort out close finishes.

Apart from saving money, the Games were kept low-key as a deliberate reaction to the hyper-nationalism of the Nazi Olympics. One organizer, Harold Abrahams, made famous as the Jewish sprinter in *Chariots of Fire*, sought a return to the amateur tradition:

> [T]he Berlin Games were such a spectacle that something very vital was missing. I came away having watched a wonderfully organized, but rather mechanical and inhuman exhibition. How to combine world-record achievements with the spirit of amateurism is a problem which becomes more and more acute each year. We have a grand opportunity to make the first post-war Olympic meeting the starting point for something really worthwhile.

In contrast to Leni Riefenstahl's flamboyant celebration of Nazi rituals at the Berlin Olympics, the official British Olympic film in 1948 was a stodgy and reverential tribute: *The Glory of Sport*. Bizarrely, the director used slow motion for the end of the marathon.

Harold Abrahams' vision of an amateur sporting festival was assisted by the fact that almost all controversial countries were excluded for one reason or another. Defeated, partitioned Germany was not invited, nor was Japan, still technically at war with the Allies (the peace Treaty was not signed till 1951). King George VI opened the Games in uniform. The Soviet Union, confronting the Western powers in the Berlin blockade, maintained its pre-war policy of boycotting the Olympics. Official party journals added a bizarre twist to this policy by describing the Games as an American conspiracy to promote the sales of canned Spam. The Soviet Embassy demanded tickets to the open-ing ceremony and enjoyed it so much that it announced that they would send a team after all, which had to be headed off by the Foreign Office. The newly formed state of Israel was excluded on a technicality (it had not formed an Olympic Committee), thus averting an Arab boycott. China, approaching the end of a long civil war, made extensive use of expatriates. Bermuda sent its first multi-racial team even though racial segregation there remained official policy for over a decade longer. The South Africans, who had just elected an overtly racist Nationalist government, sent an all-white team. Foreshadowing the D'Oliveira affair, the black South African weightlifter Ron Eland competed with the British team. Apart from a row with the Irish Republic over the qualifica-tion of Northern Irish athletes and the description of their team as 'Eire', the London Games managed to escape political contro-versy, although all of these issues were to haunt international sport for the next 40 years.

The 1948 Olympics were the first in which television and commercial sponsorship played a significant role. The organizers, especially Elvin, showed far more awareness of the power of tele-vision to win new audiences, and they were rewarded by exciting and technically proficient coverage from the BBC. This helped to double the number of television sets in use to over 90,000 and it was watched at some point by an estimated 500,000 people – all denied television coverage of the year's main sporting attraction, Don Bradman's 'Invincible' Australian cricket team. Whether in gratitude or by accident, the Olympic organizers returned the BBC's cheque for £1,000. Besides Horlicks, the energetic pursuit of sponsors yielded Nescafé, Guinness and Craven A cigarettes, while many English children got their first taste of Coca-Cola at the Games. The Olympic symbol itself was franchised to any company that would pay £250. Each British male athlete received a free pair of Y-front underpants.

Although these developments anticipated major changes in the future, in other respects the 1948 Olympics represented the end of an era. They were the last to fulfil de Coubertin's ideal of awarding medals to artists, writers and composers. Thousands paid to see the exhibits at the Victoria and Albert Museum, although the BBC complained that the musical entries were too mediocre to broadcast. Athletes and observers from all over the world commented on the friendly atmosphere and the absence of disputes. In one of many incidents which seem unimaginable today, the chief American swimming coach allowed a young British swimmer to join one of his training sessions and interrupted his routine to give him pointers on technique. Coverage of the stars emphasized their ordinariness, not their exceptional qualities, still less their nationality. The multiple record-breaker Fanny Blankers-Koen, from The Netherlands, was depicted as a home-loving housewife; the best British female athlete, Dorothy Tyler, was photographed training by leaping over her baby's nappies on her washing line. The great Czech long distance runner Emil Zátopek was praised for allegedly training with his fiancée (herself a star athlete) on his shoulders.

It was Zátopek himself who best summed up the mood of the Games: 'After all those dark days, the bombing, the killing, the starvation, the revival of the Olympics was as if the sun had come out. Suddenly there were no frontiers, no more barriers, just the people meeting together.' The official poet, A. P. Herbert, expressed it even more simply in the words of his closing anthem: Let Us Be Glad. No future Games were ever so focused on sport alone, and so free of politics, ideology, commerce and scandal.

If the 1948 Olympics summed up what many saw as the spirit of the game, then so did the visit of the 1948 Australians. This tour was to see one of the finest cricket teams of all times crush England. The tour will always be remembered as Bradman's last visit to England and for his famous duck in his final innings at the Oval. This meant he just missed out on a career average of 100. But despite the fierce rivalry between the teams, the summer was also remembered for the sporting spirit that marked the tour, in particular that displayed by Keith Miller. His attitude to sport seemed to have been taken directly from *Tom Brown's Schooldays*. During the tour, when Australia played Essex, they scored 721 on the first day, the highest ever score in a day's play. Bradman made 187 and all the other Australians feasted on the hapless Essex bowling. However, Miller, going out to bat at 362 for 2, let a straight ball from Trevor Bailey hit his wicket and walked away relieved he had no part in what he saw as senseless slaughter. Bradman told Bailey, 'He'll learn', but for Miller this was just not cricket. The debonair Aussie had been a fighter pilot during the war, and did not make the mistake of confusing danger on cricket field with danger in real life. His attitude chimed with the English public. They knew all about war and took to him. It was a period when, probably for the last time, sport did not lead to bad behaviour among players or spectators but actually often brought out the best in them. And when it did not, it caused surprise and anguish.

In January 1952, the *Barnsley Chronicle* was shocked when the home crowd pelted the referee with orange peel and cigarette cartons after a disappointing draw with West Ham: 'They were placed under extreme provocation, but to hurl missiles was carrying things a little too far.' Fans were not segregated and standing spectators were free to change ends at half time. Unaccompanied children attended matches with no fears of crowd trouble or 'stranger danger'. The novelist B. S. Johnson remembered childhood outings to Chelsea: 'These were usually sober, orderly crowds carrying little or no threat of physical violence.' A social survey of the crowds at Derby in 1953 suggested that over a quarter of football-watchers were middle class, and this proportion was confirmed by major research in the early 1960s.

Football's administrators saw no incentive for change. As in the inter-war period, they managed to resist every innovation that was transforming sport overseas. Other countries introduced new tactics and dramatically improved kit and tactical skills. They built new stadiums, reorganized their domestic and international seasons and created new relationships between football, media, commerce and the state. British football remained in the 1930s; major club stadiums, including Wembley and all those used for the 1966 World Cup, were pre-war and any improvements were done on the cheap. In 1946, the worn-out stadium at Bolton Wanderers could not cope with the huge crowd for an FA Cup tie with Stoke. While police attention was diverted to guarding a stock of rationed foodstuffs under the stands, panic-stricken fans were crushed against walls and barriers: 33 were killed and 400 injured. A Home Office investigation recommended controls on numbers and local authority inspections. Club boardrooms resisted and the over-burdened Labour government did nothing to challenge them.

Nor did the government challenge the feudal relationship between players and clubs. The 'retain and transfer' system, which locked a player into his club even when he was out of contract, stayed in place. So did the maximum wage, although the Professional Footballers' Association did make use of the government's new industrial tribunals to get this raised to £12 a week and secure better minimum pay for juniors. English clubs operated as a very effective cartel against their players, officially justified by concern for poorer clubs, although the richer ones, including Chelsea, Leyton Orient and Sunderland, found ways to make illicit payments to top players. Thanks to a FIFA ruling against poaching, they were able to maintain the cartel internationally, although some talented players 'escaped', first to a new and unrecognized league in Colombia and later to the rich Italian clubs backed by major industrial firms. One effect of the clubs' control over players was that even major stars had a lifestyle that was little different from the fans who watched them. England captain Billy Wright – married to one of the chart-topping Beverley Sisters – went to work at Molineux by bus.

The football authorities even resisted floodlighting. They limited television to the FA Cup Final and radio was restricted to one match a week, which could not be announced in advance lest it affect attendances. They made no attempt to deal with commercial television companies when in 1956 they emerged as competitors to the BBC. British football pools had revived dramatically after the war (when they had been merged into a single patriotic coupon). In 1949–50 about 10 million people filled in a coupon each week, staking an average of 2s 6d (12½ p): average male earnings were then £7 a week. Filling in the coupon and listening in silence to the results were a ritual of life in urban working-class families in the post-war era. Unlike Italy and even hardline Communist Hungary, where the pools provided a major stream of income for football, in Britain the football authorities still had moral objections to such forms of gambling and kept the pools industry at bay until the late 1950s.

Buoyed by the post-war victory against the Rest of Europe the British maintained their pre-war assumptions of natural football superiority. Foreigners were either sinister or comic: I once heard a 1950s newsreel describe England's Italian opponents as 'tricky little ball players from Spaghetti Land'. The FA, vaguely aware of the successful methods of Continental and Latin American national sides, got as far as appointing Walter Winterbottom as the first England national coach in 1946. They did not let him pick the team, which was still left to a committee, and they also expected him to overhaul coaching at all levels in the whole of England. Winterbottom, an ex-professional and a qualified physical education instructor, struggled to impose some tactics and system on the England team, with little success.

At the fourth time of asking, England entered the 1950 World Cup. Significantly, the FA made almost no advance preparations and sent the team off to a faraway tropical country (Brazil) without a doctor. They also sacked England's best centre half, Neil Franklin, for trying his luck in the Colombian league. In a generally shambolic tournament, England were defeated not only by Spain, but by the part-timers of the United States. The press were muted about England's disaster (the BBC had declined to report the World Cup at all), but there was no hiding place when England were humiliated, at home and away, by the Hungarians in 1953.

The loss at Wembley was England's first defeat by a foreign team at home and therefore could not be blamed on foreign conditions or crowds. The Hungarians used modern, lightweight kit and boots and were not in the least handicapped by the sodden leather English football, which they controlled at will with a single touch using every lawful part of their bodies. They contented themselves with six goals, one after 45 seconds, and graciously allowed their hosts to reply with three.

This defeat caused much anguish in the media, expressed most elegantly by Alan Ross in the *Observer*: 'It showed the difference between artists and artisans, between strategists with a flair for improvisation and stumbling recruits bound by an obsolete book of rules.' However, it did not provoke any practical response from the FA. Winterbottom was still not allowed to pick the team, nor work with chosen players. As a result, England fared little better in the World Cups of 1954 and 1958.

The FA, under Stanley Rous, did encourage the formation of UEFA, the body that now controls European football, in 1954 although it declined to enter the first European Nations Cup in 1958. Two years earlier, the Football League had leaned on Chelsea not to enter the new European Champion Clubs Cup, an idea inspired by French journalists. The reason given was that it would cause fixture congestion, but there were also fears that English clubs would be exposed to the corruption and cheating associated with Continental football. At the same time, however, Manchester United defied the League ban for two years running and in 1958, returning from a quarter-final in Belgrade, the club was devastated by the Munich air tragedy, which killed seven players, three coaches and eight accompanying journalists. In sympathy, UEFA offered them a free place in the next year's tournament; the League objected because it might interfere with the new domestic League Cup.

British football was not alone in refusing to innovate after the war. Cricket, buoyed by the false euphoria of post-war crowds, clung to the formula of three-day first-class cricket played by counties, which generated less and less loyalty. As the crowds dwindled, the authorities exhorted the counties to play 'brighter cricket' and tinkered regularly with the scoring system, but set their faces against a real innovation – one-day cricket – until the 1960s. They also clung to the distinction between amateurs and professionals, although in reality many talented amateurs such as Trevor Bailey were paid to play for their counties.

For years, nearly all counties had an amateur captain, although few were worth their place in the side. In 1949, Surrey had the embarrassment of appointing the wrong Nigel Bennett as their amateur captain. He accepted with gratitude and proved a total no-hoper. In 1951, one county, Warwickshire, boldly appointed a professional, Tom Dollery, and promptly won the championship. Warwickshire also showed enterprise in signing overseas players and deriving new income from a football pools scheme organized by a supporters association. It took a lot of doing, fretting about whether it was within the law, but by 1972, nearly twenty years after its inception, it had raised £2 million. A million was used to refurbish the ground at Edgbaston with money going to other counties including a loan to Essex to buy their headquarters at Chelmsford. Other counties relied on dwindling traditional sources of income: gate receipts, memberships and raffles.

The administration of the game, both domestic and international, remained in the hands of the MCC, a private members' club dominated by traditional Establishment figures. In 1952, the MCC appointed England's best professional batsman, Len Hutton, as England's captain, but only because no amateur was good enough for the role. However, as soon as a plausible amateur, David Sheppard of Cambridge University, Sussex and the Church of England, became available, a powerful lobby sought to depose Hutton in his favour. And Hutton never led his beloved Yorkshire, where he continued to play under an amateur captain. The idea that the amateur was somehow worthy of greater respect was still prevalent on the 1958–9 tour of Australia. Then the professional fast bowler Frank Tyson was rebuked by his amateur manager, Freddie Brown, for addressing his amateur captain as 'Peter'. instead of Mr May.

Cricket, at last, abandoned the amateur/professional distinction in 1963 (one day after the death of the supreme amateur, Sir Pelham Warner), but the idea that you play for the fun of it and not for money remained a principle of rugby union, tennis and athletics. This was despite all the evidence which showed that most amateurs were 'sham amateurs' and were often given money by various firms eager to market their products. For the rugby union authorities, which had always been wary of the professional game, their way of demonstrating they were part of the modern world was to let France return to the Five Nations in 1951 and they promptly beat England. Rugby also embraced air travel, which markedly increased the number of overseas tours to the southern hemisphere. But going professional was a bridge too far. So, while rugby league followed football in setting up a world cup in 1954, and cricket followed two decades later, it was 1987 before rugby union got its first world cup and 1995 before the game finally accepted that it could no longer remain an amateur sport.

By the end of the 1950s it was widely realized that British sport was failing to produce spectators, participants – or winners. The British failure was all the more glaring given the success of Soviet sport, which by the 1950s was having a marked impact on international competitions. The British government carefully monitored the Soviet plans with the conclusions set out in a secret 1955 Foreign Office report. For the government to take such interest in the sporting plans of a foreign government showed how much of a menace the Soviets were seen as, not only to British sport, but to the British way of life. Soviet sport had come a long way from the post-war tour of Moscow Dinamo.

For a time after that visit, and despite the success of Moscow Dinamo, Soviet sports policy returned to its former pre-war course. But as Stalin's health and powers declined, it took a new direction under his lieutenants Beria and Zhdanov (the cultural supremo and boss of the Cominform, the successor to the Comintern). Sport was harnessed to Soviet foreign policy objectives. It served to strengthen its control over the new satellite regimes in Eastern Europe and suppress the appeal of independence on the model of Tito's Yugoslavia. It was used specifically to boost the legitimacy of the East German state.

As the Cold War intensified, sport was used more and more for propaganda, first among potential Soviet sympathizers in the West, and later in newly independent non-aligned states. For this purpose, sport served to demonstrate the supposedly peaceful intentions of the Soviet Union and the ultimate superiority of its economic system and ideology. Their aims were set out in the lucid report by the British Foreign Office in September 1955. It cited a contemporary Soviet handbook on football: 'Every new record and every fresh success by our sportsmen in international matches – all are victories above all for socialist culture.'

The Soviet Union and its admirers claimed that it had created a new sports system. Its basic aim was to create elite athletes with the individual proficiency to beat the rest of the world, but still imbued with collective loyalty to the Communist state. Essentially, it offered these athletes a bargain: the opportunity to achieve excellence in their chosen sport and a privileged lifestyle in exchange for complete subordination to the regime. Its key features were replicated, with some variations, in all the satellite countries. These entailed the identification of promising athletes at a very young age, intensive specialist training, often in state boarding schools and always with the priority of the state over the wishes of the children and their parents, and the opportunity to progress to higher and higher standards of coaching and preparation. As they progressed, the trainers took more and more control over their lives – with set athletic and academic targets and rigid rewards and penalties. (One heartrending reward for children in East Germany was the right to have a teddy bear.) And as two East German defectors, Dr Alois Muller and Renate Neufeld,

243

revealed in the 1970s, young athletes were also compelled to accept any drugs their trainers gave them.

Drugs have been a feature of sport almost from the beginning. Even the ancient Greek Olympics had drug cheats, but the Soviets went further than any other nation. Drugs became a feature of Soviet sport as soon as it entered the international arena, and the regime did very little to hide them. At the 1952 Winter Olympics, their competitors left behind a large number of syringes and ampoules to be removed by the cleaners. At the 1954 Weightlifting Championships, the secret police minders of the Soviet team ana-lysed the chewing gum left behind by the Americans. They assumed that all nations used drugs and did not want to be left behind. In 1959, the Soviet sports minister was informed that the cycling team could not win without psychotropic amphetamines: he promised to deal with the matter officially and the team received a supply in time for the Rome Olympics in 1960.

During the 1950s, the Soviets also started to make use of steroids. They were far from alone, and world sport has since undergone an almost unbroken period of international competi-tion in the use and concealment of new steroid drugs. The crazed doctor 'Montana Jack' Ziegler was their apostle and promoter in the United States and Western countries, but the all-time steroid champions of the world were the East Germans in the 1970s, who pumped women athletes full of steroids developed for use with chemotherapy patients. The East German steroid programme was given the evasive name of 'State Planning Theme 14.25'. Although it was exposed extensively in the media after the collapse of Communism, the records gained through the programme were allowed to stand and athletes who had trained under it competed successfully for a united Germany in 1996.

In the Soviet Union, sporting organization had long been dominated by the armed forces and the secret police (under vari-ous names), with a minor role for regional and local parties, youth and trade union organizations. This model was applied to the satellite countries, especially in football. Pre-war clubs with a traditional following were taken over and merged into new clubs controlled by the regime, and the best players were forcibly transferred. The great Hungarian team of the 1950s was built around MTK, a long-established club controlled by the secret police, and the artificially created Honved, run by the army. Honved's greatest player, Ferenc Puskas, was nominally a major (he was outranked by the great Soviet goalkeeper Lev Yashin, a KGB colonel).

Star athletes in Communist countries could count on privileged treatment in housing, holiday homes, foreign travel and shopping, cars and other luxury goods – not that they had much time to enjoy them. Their biggest privilege – and their biggest burden – was being full-time athletes with sinecure jobs to allow the pretence that they were amateurs. They had to accept long hours of training and conditioning as well as regular tests in party ideology. Those who did not quite make it to the highest level could hope for an equally privileged life as a Master of Sport, teaching young athletes, as, of course, could politically loyal champions in retirement.

The privileged status of Communist sport was conditional on victory. Lowest and highest were punished for defeats. When the Soviet speed skaters were unexpectedly defeated in the European championships in 1948, the sports minister, Nikolai Romanov, was instantly sacked. Characteristically, he was replaced by the deputy head of state security, Appolonov. The top Soviet footballers were demoted after losing the 1952 Olympics to, of all people, the Yugoslavs, who had defied Stalin and quit the Soviet bloc. After defeat in the 1954 World Cup final, Groscis, the Hungarian goalkeeper, was arrested, jailed and abused for 15 months. On eventual release, he was forcibly transferred to a tiny provincial club for miners. Exile to the provinces, and a dreary, low-paid job or a miserable and often unpaid pension, were common fates for lesser athletes after defeat or decline.

The Communist sports regime was directed at the production of victorious elite professional athletes. The Foreign Office report in 1955 dwelt on the long and intense training camps used by Communist countries to select their athletes for international competition, and emphasized that all those attending were guaranteed full pay from their nominal employers by state law. Of course this professionalism could never be acknowledged and, for internal and external propaganda, the Soviet Union and satellite regimes claimed to be bringing sport to the masses. The Foreign Office report was scathing about the reality. It pointed out that even on official figures, the Soviet Union and Hungary had a smaller proportion of young men playing football than Britain (where there was widespread alarm about the supposed apathy and unfitness of the younger generation). The FO also pointed out that many sports participants in the Soviet official figures were reluctant or even invented, that facilities and equipment were desperately short even in major cities, and that funds intended for sport for workers were regularly diverted to secure the purchase and loyalty of stars.

Significantly, the Soviet system made no provision at all for sport for disabled people. This reflected a general judgement by the regime. For although war veterans were admired, naturally disabled people were hidden away in institutions, lest they detract from the image of successful Soviet society and exposed the failings of Soviet medicine. In fairness, this attitude was commonplace in Western societies, although without such an overt ideological motive. At the opening ceremony of the London Olympics, the young disabled cox Jack Dearlove was excluded from the British team in the march past the king.

The Soviet Union captured 22 gold medals at the Helsinki Olympics in 1952 and almost equalled the American medal tally. This success apparently came from nowhere, and the aura of the Soviet team was reinforced by their seclusion in separate, heavily guarded quarters away from the Olympic Village. The Soviet tally disappointed Stalin, who had been promised that the team would 'win' the Games and the athletes received no honours on their return to the Motherland. But they achieved their prime propaganda aim – making people believe in the success of the Soviet system. Few noticed that most of the medals were won for weightlifting – a sport where the strength gained from intensive training and drugs had most impact.

The dramatic Soviet entry into international competition pitched world sport into power politics. Athletics in particular witnessed long-running political disputes over the status of Germany, China, Korea and Israel, and the Soviet bloc opportunistically exploited African and Asian nations' hostility to apartheid South Africa and the breakaway white settler regime in Rhodesia. It turned individual sporting contests into a battle of ideologies, in which Western athletes were as eager to assert the superiority of their values as those of the Eastern bloc. The American Bob Mathias, who successfully defended his decathlon title at Helsinki in 1952, declared that 'there were many more pressures on American athletes because of the Russians [. . .] They were in a sense the real enemy. You just loved to beat 'em. You just had to beat 'em [. . .] This feeling was strong down through the entire team.'

The mighty Hungarian football team of the early 1950s was encouraged to think along the same lines by the coach, Gusztáv Sebes, who was also a long-time Communist and deputy minister of sport in Hungary's hard-line government. His goalkeeper, Groscis, later recalled that, 'Sebes was deeply committed to socialist ideology and you could feel it in everything he said. He made a political issue of every important match or competition; he often said that the fierce struggle between capitalism and socialism took place as much on the football field as anywhere else.' Ironically, Sebes' team, the greatest showpiece of Communist sport, owed little to Communist values. The players had learned their basic game before Communism in a state with a strong football tradition: Sebes encouraged them to experiment and innovate and express their individuality.

Nonetheless, they fought their World Cup final against West Germany in 1954 as champions of the socialist system and their unexpected defeat (attributed variously to poor team selection, bad English refereeing and being kept awake at night by a Swiss military band) had profound political consequences. On the way home the West Germans' team train was greeted by two million people, celebrating the arrival of the state as an independent power. *Der Spiegel* declared that 'after 2,000 years of taking the wrong path Germans have now discovered the true destiny of their national existence.'

For the Hungarians, whose wonder team had to slink back into Budapest under armed guard, the defeat destroyed belief that the country could achieve under socialism. It signalled a long period of political turbulence, leading eventually to the doomed uprising against Soviet occupation in November 1956. A month before, the Hungarian team had restored national feeling by beating the Soviet Union 1–0 in Moscow. Anticipating the worst, the reform government of Nagy arranged for the best players to be out of the country when the Soviets invaded. They finished their careers in other countries, and Hungarian football never again became a showcase for any political system.

The crushing of the Hungarian uprising reminded Westerners of the ruthlessness of the Soviet Union and masked its weakness. Few Westerners visited the country, and those that did usually saw only the show-pieces of its great cities, under close supervision. The Soviet Union appeared to be a superpower and Communism was considered a serious challenge to Western economics and political values. This feeling was reinforced in November 1957 when the Soviet Union beat the Americans in launching an artificial satellite. In 1960, Jack Kennedy was able to attack the Republican Party for allowing a 'missile gap' to develop between the United States and the Soviet Union. The 'gap' was wholly illusory, but it helped to secure his narrow victory over Richard Nixon, and only a few months later Kennedy's message was strengthened when the Soviets were the first to send a man into space. Within this context, the visible successes of Communist sport ceased to be a curiosity. Years after the execution of Beria, who had lost out in the power struggle following Stalin's death, sporting success began to fulfil the role he had given it in propaganda – showing that the Soviet Union was overtaking the West. The democracies had to react, but their response was far from uniform.

For the British, the organization and professionalism of Soviet sport looked like an existential threat to the cherished amateurism and voluntary governance of British sport. They became seriously alarmed that their sportspeople could never win anything in international competition without the degree of training and preparation on offer to Communist athletes. Britain's established sporting structures could not remotely offer this in the 1950s, and Britain lacked the entrepreneurship to turn sport into a successful commercial business on American lines. British sport faced the terrible prospect of soliciting organized support from government.

Many sports lovers resisted any relationship with government. They preferred traditional British sporting values to latter-day British sporting success. The Duke of Edinburgh, who became a powerhouse in British sport during the 1950s, expressed their attitude cogently and consistently after the 1956 Olympics. In a clear reference to the Soviet system, he rejected the idea of government grants or loans to athletes and deplored the idea that Britain should send 'temporary civil servants to the Games'. He maintained that view in 1979, telling a London meeting that he had 'no patience' with people seeking more government support and control of sport. For him, sport was not about international prestige, but a means of enjoyment. Although a fierce competitor he also believed that, if necessary, sport must also teach how to lose gracefully. Others pressed for official support for British athletes forced to train for international competition in impossibly straitened circumstances. The British walker Don Thompson was much cited: he had trained for his medal-winning performance at Rome on a treadmill in his stifling bathroom during the exceptionally hot summer of 1959.

In the 1950s Britain also had a long-running anxiety about

teenage gangs of 'Teddy boys' idling and misbehaving in city centres. The Teddy boys were mild by the standards of later delinquents, but older Britons were unused to British teenagers with autonomy and economic power. With the end of National Service in sight, many hoped that sport might absorb teenagers' surplus energies and give them more discipline.

The British responded to their sporting dilemma in the traditional way: they set up a committee to examine the issues. Characteristically, it was not initiated by the government, but by a voluntary organization, the Central Council for Physical Recreation, and headed by a high-profile chairman, Sir John Wolfenden. A former athlete and public school headmaster, he was already famous as an inquiry chairman for recommending the decriminalization of consenting homosexual acts in private. The other members of the inquiry team also had a strong background in sport, education or public administration; they included Sir Arthur Porritt, a power in the Olympic movement and one of the chief organizers of the 1948 Games.

Aware of the touchiness of Britain's amateur sports administrators, Wolfenden and his team were painstaking in soliciting evidence from them and sat for no fewer than 58 days. Their final report, *Sport and the Community*, was an exceptionally well-written and comprehensive document, whose 57 recommendations continue to influence British sports policy to this day. Many were focused on 'the gap', a term the inquiry invented to describe the lack of facilities for young people to continue to take part in sports they had enjoyed at school or to experience non-sporting outdoor activities. They recommended enhanced awareness of the role of sport and recreation in the youth service, greater access to existing sporting and outdoor facilities and coordinated investment in new facilities, especially swimming pools, principally by local authorities.

More realistic than most sports administrators, the committee recommended cooperation between sports and the media, particularly television and radio. They emphasized the need for accurate and unbiased reporting, and made a futile plea for newspapers to stop using ghostwritten columns by sports personalities. Although pushing for more coaching and training, Wolfenden's committee was anxious not to imitate the degree of state support in other countries for the preparation of athletes. In a passage that might have pleased the Duke of Edinburgh, the report said:

> we are not prepared to admit that the comparison with other countries is wholly unfavourable to ours. In many important directions our record is [...] a good one; for instance in the public provision of games and sport through our schools and other educational institutions, the extent of personal participation among those who have left school, the degree of voluntary and devoted service given to sport in so many ways, and perhaps above all, the place that ideals of sportsmanship occupy in our national habits of thought and behaviour.

The committee saw no public desire for a single large organization to coordinate all sport, but they did recommend an advisory Sports Development Council with an annual budget of £5 million to support additional expenditure by existing English sporting and recreational bodies. This cautious compromise preserved the cherished independence of English sport, but it still unnerved a Conservative government with strong links to the sporting Establishment, especially through the MCC. After long deliberation, the government appointed Britain's first sports minister, but characteristically made the role only part-time by giving it to Lord Hailsham, who was already responsible for science, regional policy and employment. (Intriguingly, he was the son of the Lord Hailsham who had brokered the peace deal with Australia after the Bodyline cricket tour.) A full-time sports minister had to await the appointment of Dennis Howell by Harold Wilson in 1964, and it was he who established the Advisory Sports Council in 1965. Hesitant as this was, it marked the first step the British had taken towards government support for British sport and a national sports policy.

The American response to the Soviets' sports challenge could not have provided a greater contrast to the British. Where the British hesitated and stumbled, reluctant to abandon their amateur and voluntary traditions, torn between the goals of elitism and participation, and generally distrustful of any systematic policy for sport, the Americans were confident and willing to harness all the resources of a dynamic capitalist economy. The Americans, by now, had a well-established system of sporting scholarships, and links between college and professional sport continued to guarantee a steady supply of well-trained, world-ranking athletes. The major American sports were driven, successfully, by commerce, which led them to embrace television, sponsorship, franchising and (when air travel became easy and commonplace in the late 1950s) the relocation of major clubs to capture new spectator markets.

The threat of Communism did, however, produce an outpouring of patriotism in American sport. Like Bob Mathias in Helsinki, many sportspeople had expressed their patriotism in military service, the most famous being Ted Williams, the mighty hitter of the Boston Red Sox. Although he had already served in the Second World War, he re-enlisted for Korea and gave up another three years of his career at his peak. Nor did Williams get a soft job coaching baseball: he served as a fighter pilot.

The battle with the Soviets was seen in America as a fight for freedom, which gave a little extra impulse to the desegregation of American sport. This became the dominant development of the post-war period, particularly when the Soviet Union started to court the newly independent states of Asia and Africa. It would be a mistake to exaggerate this effect, however – desegregation arrived in US sport incrementally in the 1950s, and primarily for economic and commercial reasons, rather than political. Non-white people had too much talent for professional teams to ignore them as performers, and too much spending power to be ignored as live or television spectators. In baseball, this saw Jackie Robinson become the first black player in the Major League in

1947. In the wider world it was the year India got its freedom and Pakistan came into being; the following year the Jewish state was created. While this sporting event does not compare with such momentous developments, it still required a great deal of effort by Branch Rickey, the man who ran the Brooklyn Dodgers. To help break the colour bar he read books on race and slavery, consulted academics, addressed black meetings to warn them not to make Robinson a hero and overcame opposition from players of his own team.

The authorities were well aware of how the Soviets could exploit the racism prevalent in American society, and during the Cold War the US was determined to enlist non-white sports stars to testify to the strengths of the American system. Althea Gibson, the first non-white Wimbledon tennis champion, made regular tennis trips for the State Department; Jesse Owens promoted the US Olympic Committee while the boxer Sugar Ray Robinson offered patriotic testimony to Congress against the dissident Communist Paul Robeson.

The Americans, with reason, will always claim that their sports system was not government controlled like the Soviets'. However, the treatment of Muhammad Ali in the late 1960s, taking away his world heavyweight boxing title and exiling him from the sport, showed that in certain circumstances the US, too, could play politics with sport and play it with a ruthlessness that matched the Soviets.

The whole affair revolved around Ali's refusal to serve in the US Army. Back in April 1960, when Ali was still Cassius Clay – the name he had been given at birth (and under which he had won Olympic gold in Rome that year) – Ali had been registered for the military draft. But he failed aptitude tests, getting an army IQ score of 78. This, as his biographer Thomas Hauser says, placed him in the 'sixteenth percentile, well below the passing grade of thirty.' Ali felt humiliated by his failure and his response always was, 'I said I was the greatest, not the smartest.' But this failure was seen as somehow politically motivated and led to much public debate as to whether such a prominent sports personality was being let off. The question was, how much intelligence was required to drive an army truck or help in the army kitchen? The secretary of the army even had to write to the chairman of the House of Representatives Armed Services committee to explain why Ali had been so classified. But then, in 1966, with America now heavily involved in Vietnam, the passing marks for the aptitude tests were lowered and Ali was drafted. That is when, questioned by the press, he exploded and made the infamous comment that would haunt him, 'Man, I ain't got no quarrel with them Vietcong.'

By now, much had changed with Ali. He had become a Muslim and a member of the controversial Nation of Islam, given up what he called his 'slave' name and called himself Muhammad Ali. All this proved too potent and heady a mix for much of white America, more so against the 1960s background at a time when the nation seemed to be tearing itself apart over Vietnam, race and other social issues. In 1963, President Kennedy had been assassinated, the late 1960s were to see riots in American cities and in 1968, Bobby Kennedy and Martin Luther King fell victim to gunmen.

In April 1967, when Ali appeared before the US Armed Forces Examining and Entrance Station in Houston, he was first called by his former name, Cassius Clay, and then by Ali, but refused to respond on both occasions. He had already told *Sports Illustrated*, 'Why should they ask me to put on a uniform and go ten thousand miles from home and drop bombs and bullets on brown people in Vietnam while so-called Negro people in Louisville are treated like dogs?' He had no fear of going to prison, saying, 'I have nothing to lose by standing up and following my beliefs. We've been in jail for four hundred years.' Politicians called for his fights to be boycotted, while papers contrasted his behaviour with that of Joe Louis, who was seen to be the model sportsman, cherishing the principles of Arnold. Ali made favourable comments about Jack Johnson, and like Johnson, the US government put him under surveillance. Hauser, whose biography of Ali was written with the boxer's cooperation, describes what happened when Ali refused to fight for his country:

> Nineteen sixty-seven was the year that Muhammad Ali confronted the nation with his principles, and those in power struck back with a vengeance. One hour after Ali refused induction – before he'd been charged with any crime, let alone convicted – the New York State Athletic Commission suspended his boxing license and withdrew recognition of him as champion. Soon all other jurisdictions in the United States had followed suit, and the title Ali had worked for throughout his life was gone.

Ali was sentenced to five years in prison and the maximum possible fine – $10,000. The Supreme Court found in his favour in June 1971, but by then he had not been able to fight for three and a half years, with one estimate suggesting it cost him $10 million in purses and endorsements. He did not regain his heavyweight title until 1974 when he beat George Foreman in Kinshasa, Zaire. Ali's return to boxing in 1971, when he fought Joe Frazier, came when Nixon was in the White House and was closely followed by the president, who took a keen interest in sport and often tried to harness its power for his political ends. Bob Haldeman, his chief of staff, noted in his diary, 'The fascinating thing that P raised was the observation of enormous uplifting effect of the Cassius Clay–Frazier fight. It had the chemistry and drive that really lifted public spirits. The P feels that people need to be caught up in a great event and taken out of their humdrum existence.' Interestingly, Haldeman refused to accept Ali had changed his name. It is hard to avoid the conclusion that the whole Ali affair demonstrated that, for all the talk, American political figures did get involved in sports when it suited their needs.

The Soviet sports challenge, arguably, made more difference to American children than to any other group. Recurrent images of healthy, sporting Soviet children prompted worry about the new generation of American children – flabby, asocial, and perpetually slumped in front of a television. In 1956, President Eisenhower (a golf addict who practised putting wearing his spiked shoes on the priceless parquet floors of the White House) set up a Council on Youth Fitness to recondition them. Its main remedy was organized sport, and a generation of American children were pressed into Little League Baseball, Pop Warner Football or Biddy Basketball. These activities were of little use in promoting general fitness as they largely excluded girls (who were expected to get their exercise cheerleading) and tended to benefit boys who were already active and well-motivated while the fat slackers stayed on the bench. However, organized children's sport thrived on its promise of 'developing character', based on the Corinthian spirit of sport that Thomas Hughes had formulated. It also promoted local identity and, not least, provided opportunities for commercial sponsorship by local businesses.

In what proved to be one of the most remarkable stories of the Cold War, chess played a major part in US–Soviet struggle. In keeping with the many ironies of this tale, it was an extraordinary American maverick who challenged and routed a Soviet domination of the sport that had lasted for over 40 years. Botvinnik, having become champion in 1948, held on to the World Championship for the next fifteen years, with two short interruptions. He became the Soviet Union's best-known sportsman. When he went to the ballet or opera at home, the entire audience stood for him. Botvinnik was both an individual genius (apart from chess he was an electrical engineer of international standing) and a total Soviet loyalist. In 1954, he even offered the regime a plan for peaceful world domination: he was rudely told to stick to chess. Sadly, his identification with the regime tarnished his record as champion, with persistent allegations that his most dangerous rivals, Paul Keres and David Bronstein, were intimidated into throwing key matches against him.

Like other sports personalities, chess stars certainly had good reason to fear punishment or disgrace for the wrong result. The terror of losing that could grip Soviet players would later prove an asset to Bobby Fischer, the American who finally succeeded in taking on the Soviets. One of his conquests, Mark Taimanov, collapsed completely after early defeats and lost his series against Fischer 6–0. He was subsequently humiliated by the Soviet Sports Committee, stripped of all his privileges in the chess world, and even forbidden to continue his second career as a concert pianist.

Botvinnik created the 'Soviet school of chess' – an intense grooming and training regime for all levels of play. Its inspiration was Stakhanov, the iconic, but probably mythical, Soviet miner of the 1930s, who achieved unheard-of output from hard work. The regime required rigorous study both of theory and of specific likely opponents, and long training sessions with a trusted partner, combined with physical conditioning. Above all, it treated chess as a collective enterprise on behalf of the Soviet state. Soviet players were not only expected to train and second each other, but also accept the regime's choice of winners. Although Botvinnik himself never encouraged this, the regime certainly expected them to collude on results at key tournaments, especially against foreigners. The system certainly succeeded in manufacturing a great number of players. In 1929, there were 150,000 registered players in the Soviet Union; by 1970 this number had risen to 5 million, and 20 new masters were being created each year. Soviet satellites replicated this growth: East Germany had over 30,000 registered players in 1968 – more than three times the number in the United States.

This system was defeated by a lone, obsessive American genius. The great Fischer–Spassky battle of 1972 in Reykjavik is often depicted as a proxy war between West and East and a triumph of American values over Soviet ones. The participants were certainly encouraged to see themselves in that light: with Fischer proving very difficult, and making all sorts of demands on the organizers, there was a danger he might forfeit the match. It required phone calls from Henry Kissinger, then Nixon's national security adviser, to pacify him. In one of the calls Kissinger is believed to have said, 'This is the worst player in the world calling the best player in the world,' before appealing to his patriotism. This had a key role in changing his mind. But the great match was not a clash of countries or systems; instead, it restored chess to its true role as a battle of individual minds and personalities. Boris Spassky was no advertisement for the Soviet system. He came from a priestly family and was a pleasure-loving intellectual who despised the Communist party. He did not train like Botvinnik, but relied on his instinct and genius.

As for Fischer, he never in his life represented anyone but himself. In chess, he was an auto-didact, another one-off genius in the tradition of Morphy, Pillsbury and Marshall. There was no 'American system' to train him, because until his triumph, American chess was a minority pastime that relied on the fitful benevolence of rich patrons. This was severely hit by the Depression, and the best American players of the thirties could not make a living from the game. Reuben Fine gave up the game altogether to become a psychoanalyst; Sammy Reshevsky (who was a serious contender for the world title won by Botvinnik in 1948) became an accountant. Even in the prosperous fifties, American chess never attracted serious money or popular support.

Fischer had no interest in the Cold War and the battle of ideologies – except to validate his own personal drama of being cheated by the Soviets. This began very early in his career, and was dramatically expressed in an article in *Sports Illustrated* magazine in 1962 entitled 'The Russians Have Fixed World Chess'. It set out an *idée fixe* that governed Fischer's behaviour for a decade: with the connivance of FIDE, the international body, the Russians had fixed major tournaments, including the World Championship, through arranged draws so that no one but a Russian could win. Fischer was then only 19, and he had not yet performed well enough in any international tournament to claim that the Russians had cheated him out of anything.

This is not the place to narrate the long record of alternating brilliance and tantrums that preceded Fischer's triumph. But it is worth emphasizing again how far Fischer was his own man, and how often he exasperated fellow Americans, including his few personal friends, as much as Soviet opponents. His views on issues other than chess were ugly and weird (especially his anti-Semitism). They put him into the lunatic fringes of American life and eventually turned him into an exile and a fugitive from justice. However, it was Fischer's very weirdness that made his victory a triumph for American values. In the Soviet system, he would have been ordered to conform and faced punishment in a gulag or an asylum when he refused. The American system let him play chess on his own terms and become champion of the world.

But just as Fischer was finally humbling a Communist state-sponsored sport, across the world in China, a man who had once seen Stalin as his older brother was using sport to seek rapprochement with the Americans. Fischer's victory over Spassky had no impact on world politics. This Communist's use of sport did reshape world politics.

CHAPTER 9

HOW THE CHINESE REINVENTED ARNOLD'S SPORTS BATON

On 1 April 1917, an article appeared in the Chinese magazine *Xin Qingian* (New Youth). The article, entitled '*Tiyu zhi yanjin*' ('On Physical Culture'), stated, 'Among today's civilized powers, Germany really stands out; fencing is widespread there, while in Japan, the samurai spirit was very influential [. . .] it is absolutely right to say that one must build a strong body if s/he wants to cultivate inner strength.' The author went on to say, 'physical education or exercise [. . .] should be the number one priority'.

This was the young author's first published work. His choice of topic, sports and physical training, was significant; still more impressive, the young author would become known as Mao Zedong. During his years of power, Mao did more than any other leader, even Hitler or Stalin, to make sport an instrument of state policy. When, in 1971, Mao decided to restore his country's relationship with the United States after over 20 years of frozen hostility, his chosen medium was sport – ping-pong diplomacy. The United States–China rapprochement might have happened without the ping-pong players, but their interaction greatly smoothed the path and helped both Mao and Nixon get past formidable obstacles.

Of course, the Chinese had had their own sports and games since ancient times, including a form of football which FIFA now recognizes as the ancestor of the world game. China's adoption of modern Western games began in the closing days of the Qing (sometimes called Manchu) Empire, as part of an attempt to learn from the Western powers who had repeatedly humiliated them and wrested territory and economic concessions. The Qing court in 1903 had copied some of the educational models that Japan had introduced under Western influence, and required all schools to have physical education classes and teach shangwu, fighting spirit, through military-style exercises. But the major player in introducing sport in China was a Western organization, the Young Men's Christian Association (YMCA). Such was the YMCA's determination to spread sport in China and the Far East that one historian has called this period from 1895 to 1928 'the YMCA era', when most of the major sports came to China.

The YMCA, founded in England in the 1840s by George Williams, a 22-year-old drapery merchant, was designed to improve the then desperate working conditions of young boys and girls. It acquired its missionary sporting zeal after it arrived in America in 1851. There it saw itself as a movement to promote Christian character through fostering speech, sportsmanship and scholastic achievement, reaching out to youth of all ages. It remains proud of the fact that YMCA instructors helped create both basketball and volleyball. In that sense the institution was very much in the Arnold mould, combining fervent Christian religious belief with high moral values and a belief that sport could further them both. And the arrival of the American David Willard Lyon as the YMCA representative in China in 1895 played a major part in fostering Western sport in that country.

That year the Chinese suffered a humiliating defeat by the Japanese, which had followed a series of capitulations to the Western powers. It gave China an image of weakness and decay. Many Chinese patriots began to think of physical activity as the only means of removing that image and renewing the empire.

The YMCA soon realized it was working a fertile field, and organized the first Chinese National Games in 1910. English was the language of the Games and most of the officials and referees were non-Chinese. The YMCA was spreading 'Western morality and masculinity among the weaker Oriental people'. The writer Fan Hong has described how the high-jumper Sun Baoqing decided that to perform well he had to discard traditional Chinese ways. Like most Chinese men he had a long pigtail. But this kept knocking off the bars and ruining his performance. His response was to cut off his pigtail and the next day he was the high-jump champion. Fan Hong sees Sun's action as 'more than a symbolic gesture: for men, the body became an icon of modernity, reconstruction and rehabilitation'. By that time, cutting off the pigtail was a rejection of the obsolete Qing Empire. The identification of this gesture with sporting success could not have been more dramatic. The first Far Eastern Games, also organized by the YMCA took place in 1913. Three years after Mao had emphasized the need for physical activity, J. H. Gray, director of the YMCA's physical education department, who had recently arrived in Shanghai, was encouraged by the way the Chinese were taking to Western sports. 'A good start,' he observed, 'was made in the beginning, which showed that China was in the early stages of great physical Renaissance in which the old ideas of the body and of living were being rapidly changed for new and different ones.'

By this time the YMCA had begun to play a major role in the development of sport, not just in China and Asia, but also in Latin America. Initially, the YMCA's involvement in sport had greatly worried Coubertin. Always keen to make sure that nobody stole his Olympic concepts, he was concerned that the hosting of regional games could make them a rival to the Olympics. In spring 1919, General Pershing, Commander of the American forces in Europe, organized the inter-Allied games to keep troops busy after the Armistice (and forestall growing indiscipline over the slow pace of demobilization). Coubertin was initially very opposed to this until Elwood S. Brown, International Director of the YMCA, wrote to him saying that the military Olympics were not 'a rival of the Olympic games in any sense'.

This led to an alliance between Coubertin and the YMCA.

Brown suggested to him that the YMCA could be used to spread the Olympic message: 'A most unusual opportunity now exists to give a great impulse to physical training throughout the world, to develop backward areas along the lines of Olympic ideas and ideals, and to contribute definitely to the extension of your Committee's influence.'

Coubertin, much flattered, agreed and Brown made a presentation to the IOC session in Antwerp in August 1920. Two years later, the Latin American Games took place with Brown very much in charge. The Games produced what historian Cesar Torres has called the Latin American Olympic explosion. Asia did not explode in quite the same way, although this was not for lack of effort by the YMCA. Asia had far less in common with Latin America; many countries were ruled or dominated by the Western powers, and few athletes or associations had the money or independence to travel the huge distances required. So the Far Eastern Games, known from 1915 as the Far Eastern Championship Games, basically meant three countries: Japan, China and the Philippines.

They were a curious mix: Japan was assertive and seeking to emulate Western powers, menacing both China and the Philippines, an American dependency. India was invited in 1921 – the year Gandhi launched the first of his civil disobedience campaigns against British rule – but could not raise the money to travel to Shanghai, and this was also the reason Thailand, Java and Malaya did not attend. In 1930 India did take part, but that was the only occasion, and the Dutch East Indies entered in 1934.

The Indians tried to have their own version of the Games, the Western Asiatic Games, but after one edition held in Delhi in 1934, where only four countries took part – India, Afghanistan, Ceylon and Palestine – they were never held again. The 1938 version, due in Palestine, fell victim to the events that were to lead to the Second World War. The YMCA's involvement gave the Far Eastern Championship Games a longer history, with ten Games between 1913 and 1934, but none of them was ever held outside East Asia:

Manila held the Games four times and Shanghai and Japan three times each.

As the YMCA spread the message of Western sports, it provoked an intense debate in China about the Olympics; when would the country have winning teams in the Olympics and when would China host the Games? Indeed, had the First World War not prevented the 1916 Games, due in Berlin, China might well have participated. By 1922 there was a Chinese member of the IOC, Wang Zhengting. He was the second member from Asia, joining Dorabji Tata from India. He had become a member a year earlier through his efforts to ensure that India took part in the Antwerp Games of 1920.

China and India had very different approaches to sport and sporting politics. In China, even before Mao came to power, sport was seen as a very strong political tool. In India that was never the case. China was nominally a free country, but one virtually without a government, dominated by foreigners and in fear of further threats, plagued by civil war, bankruptcy, famine, disease and natural disasters. India was a British colony, with no external enemies. It enjoyed a stable currency and an efficient, if increasingly resented, administration. Its people were growing more and more confident of their ability to govern themselves and create a successful modern economy and society. Compared to China, India did not need to use Western sport as a spur to reform and independence.

As we have seen, modern sport had been brought to India by the British, but there was no central British direction for its development. It was up to individual Englishmen to encourage it, and its growth depended on the response of the Indians. Indian princes, who ruled a third of the country, played a part in this, as did businessmen like the Tatas. India's first IOC representative, Dorabji Tata, was the man who would fulfil the dream of his father and prove that Indians could manufacture steel. The British had mocked this dream: one even said that if India ever produced steel he would eat it.

In China, sport was always more centrally directed, as exemplified by the 1932 Olympics in Los Angeles. By then, India had taken part in three Olympics – Los Angeles was its fourth – and the Indian hockey team was on its way to becoming a great sporting team, having won gold at their first Olympics in Amsterdam in 1928. Los Angeles marked China's Olympics debut and, as the historian Xu Guoqi has rightly observed, it was more of a political gesture than a sporting one. The Chinese had not planned to take part. In May 1932, two months before the Games were due to start, the official sports body of the country decided it did not have the money to go to America. All it could afford was to send an observer.

Then early in June, it emerged that the Japanese, who had occupied Manchuria and created a puppet state called Manchukuo, intended to send two athletes from the occupied territory to represent it: Liu Changchun and Yu Xiwei. This resulted in a huge campaign in China to send one of the athletes, Liu Changchun, who by then was living in Beijing, to Los Angeles – as a *Chinese* representative. True, there was no government money, but many Chinese contributed, including a Chinese warlord ejected from Manchuria. The Japanese interned Yu to make sure he could not join Liu. Chinese officials made it clear that Liu was going to try to present the true face of China and denounce Japanese aggression. Liu spoke of strengthening China's international status, and one observer wrote of the pride of seeing the Chinese national flag flying along with those of other nations. Liu did little in the two events he competed in, the 100 and 200 metres, but he did succeed in putting China on the map, receiving much favourable publicity in America. The official Olympic report called him 'the lone representative of four hundred million people'.

In contrast, the Indian hockey team dominated their sport, winning gold again and beating the United States in the final 24–1. However, when the Indians went up to collect the gold, the anthem played was, of course, the British anthem, emphasizing that India was not a free nation.

In the preparation for the Games, when Gandhi was asked for money to help the team, he had famously enquired, 'Hockey? What is hockey?' Gandhi's Alfred High School in Rajkot made cricket and gymnastics compulsory, no doubt because the headmaster was a Parsee, the first sect amongst the Indians to take to cricket. But in his autobiography, written at the age of 56, Gandhi confessed:

I disliked them both. I never took part in any exercise, cricket or football, before they were made compulsory. My shyness was one of the reasons for this aloofness, which I now see was wrong. I then had the false notion that gymnastics had nothing to do with education. Today, I know that physical training should have as much place in the curriculum as mental training.

One of Gandhi's reasons for disliking gymnastics was that, rather than practise physical routine, he wanted to hurry home to nurse his sick father. Interestingly, Gandhi had a touch of Thomas Arnold about him when it came to taking exercise:

I may mention, however, that I was none the worse for a training exercise. That was because I had read in books about the benefits of long walks in the open air and, having liked the advice, had formed a habit of taking walks, which has still remained with me. These walks gave me a fairly hardy constitution.

Observer, that Gandhi, like a true follower of Arnold, said nothing about the higher values of sport. Mao, in contrast, instinctively accepted the theories of Arnold's disciples, Hughes and Coubertin, that sport could be used for much wider purposes.

The contrasting attitudes to sport of Mao and Gandhi were to be reflected in their political actions. In 1930, when Gandhi launched his second and greatest campaign against British rule in India, he walked 240 miles to the sea to make salt. The British taxed salt heavily, imposing a great burden on the Indian poor.

Gandhi was going to break the law by making salt from sea water. This he argued would avoid paying tax, reduce the burden on the poor and illustrate the iniquities of colonial rule. During the walk he was accompanied by a select group of followers and Gandhi saw his journey through the villages of western India as an exercise in reawakening his fallen country. It was one of the most dramatic moments in modern history, closely followed by the media, and it illustrated Gandhi's ability to use simple images to illuminate a greater truth and reach out to millions.

More than three decades later Mao, too, conjured up a physical image at the start of his Cultural Revolution. On 16 July 1966, Mao swam in the Yangtze River at Wuhan the day before he travelled to Beijing to lead what he called the Great Proletarian Cultural Revolution. That picture of Mao was flashed round the world and was meant to demonstrate strength, resolve, character and determination to launch this revolution. Mao, who had grown up in Hunan province, had always liked swimming. Indeed, at times of high political tension, he often advertised his swimming prowess. In September 1959, Mao had a swim in the hills near Beijing. One of his biographers, Han Suyin, has said he did so to strengthen his resolve because he was then in a minority in China and threatened by external danger. 'All this spelled danger to the Revolution. Mao swam in the ice cold water for forty minutes and came out smiling, his mind made up.' In the summer of 1962, as he was about to clash with Liu Shao-chi, also from Hunan and long considered his successor, both men swam in the reservoirs of the Ming tombs. Mao emerged and proudly displayed his body to admiring young Chinese as he dried himself. Liu, who probably suspected his old comrade was about to turn on him, said nothing.

Gandhi was not alone among Indian leaders in shunning sport. So did other prominent Indians – Subhas Bose, for instance, felt his youthful dislike of sports had probably made him more introverted. Unlike the Chinese, very few Indians, with the exception of Vivekananda, saw the decline of their country, and its subjugation by foreigners, as due to lack of physical education. Mao was not unique among Chinese leaders in seeing sport as vital to reviving China. So did the enemy he overthrew, Chiang Kai-shek, the Nationalist leader.

The two leaders, and many others, shared the belief of the organizers of Chinese sport that the Chinese needed physical education and to play games for the country to recover from being 'the sick man of East Asia'. Chinese leaders were made all the more aware of the need to demonstrate the country's strength on the world stage as Japan used the Far Eastern Championship Games to assert its superiority. The 1923 Games, held in Japan, were particularly galling. The Chinese team was led by Gray, demonstrating the YMCA involvement in China. But dreadful defeats at the hands of the Japanese made the Chinese realize how weak and helpless they had become. As one Chinese official moaned:

> The Republic of China, with three thousand years civilization [...] was defeated, sent away crying, by a small nation of three islands! This is not only a shame – it is pathetic [...] If we still have hot blood [...] Wake up, healthy athletes of the Republic [...] Use your blood and freshness and move forward to take back your position on the international sports stage.

Zhang Boling, President of Nankai University, who is known as the man who brought the Olympics to China and exercised great power in Chinese sports, came back from the ninth Far Eastern Championships admiring how well the Japanese were doing. He proposed two solutions – one long term, the other short term:

> In the long term, we need to have a mandatory physical education from elementary school on and must encourage the whole nation to develop a lifelong habit of physical fitness. The short-term fix is to organize many games and competitions between Chinese and foreign teams. This type of direct competition may

help the Chinese learn not to fear competing. If we carry out both these suggestions, with effective and quality training, we may achieve very good results down the road.

In 1933, Chiang's government organized the National Games and issued guidelines to government officials: 'Since the Great War every European nation has made efforts to advocate sports because their citizens' physical condition is clearly related to their national rise and fall.' Chiang himself made many speeches about why the people needed to be physically strong if China was to recover as a nation. In one speech to Chinese youth leaders, he asked, 'Why do foreign aggressors dare to look down on China? Because the Chinese are weak physically and inferior to them. The decay and weakness of our citizens' physical condition has been our nation's greatest shame. From now on, we have to work hard to make our country strong, if we don't want to be despised by other nations, and our foremost task is to emphasize physical education and work on it.' The speeches were backed by much effort to promote sport, despite the fact that for much of the 1930s and 1940s China was resisting Japanese aggression, and Chiang's government was also fighting a civil war against the Communists. Between 1910 and 1948, seven National Games were held and China took part in both the 1936 and 1948 Olympics.

But it was Mao and the Communists who took sport to a very different level, linking it with politics and the nation in a way that had never been done before in China, or, for that matter, in the rest of the world. Not all of the cadres of the party may have cared for sports, or even understood them, as party officials conceded. But Mao and the leadership did. The first head of its national sports commission was a military man and the party tightly controlled sport. Mao listened to sports broadcasts and Zhou Enlai, the Chinese prime minister, often instructed broadcasters on how they should do their work. Chinese players were encouraged to see sporting activity as a metaphor for nationhood. When a Chinese player took part in the 26th World Table

Tennis Championship, every time he directed a shot at the Japanese player, he saw this as revenge for all the humiliation Japan had inflicted on China since the defeat in 1895.

The political use of sport by Mao and the Communists was best expressed in the saying, 'friendship first, competition second'. This was most rigorously enforced when the Chinese played the North Koreans, although it did not always work out in the way the Chinese wanted. Indeed, it embarrassed the Chinese during the 31st World Table Tennis Championships held in Nagoya, Japan in April 1971, an event that would play such a decisive role in Sino–US relations. The North Koreans were worried about performing badly in front of many Koreans who lived in Japan and did not want to participate. The Chinese reassured them that they would help. Before the Chinese team set out for Japan, they were told that they should lose some games to the Koreans and also the Japanese. But the Chinese players, then probably the best in the world, could not quite manage that. They beat the North Koreans 3–0, and thrashed the Japanese in a friendly encounter 8–0. On their return to China they found themselves treated, not as heroes, but as near criminals. Zhou Enlai not only criticized the team, but got its leader to write a self-criticism report and even sent him with a delegation to North Korea to apologize.

This led to one of the most amazing moments in the intertwined history of sport and politics. As the Chinese delegation apologized, Kim II Sung, the then North Korean dictator, said, 'It is common sense that everyone wants to win in a game. Even father and son do not give the other special treatment when they're playing chess. In a world championship game no country wants to intentionally lose to the other country's team. It does not sound right.' This propaganda showed an unexpected side of the demented Korean dictator as a good sport, but he would later express delight that Mao and Zhou Enlai had made such attempts to strengthen Chinese–Korean friendship. However the real, historic significance of the World Championships in Japan lies in the way Mao used them to open the door to the United States.

The Chinese had not been to these championships since 1966 and the start of the Cultural Revolution. That Mao-inspired lunacy had taken a toll on sport, as it had on many other walks of Chinese life, and even led to the death of some table tennis players. After much debate, and only because Mao insisted, the Chinese team went. At the championships there were two problems: the Americans and the Cambodians.

Prince Norodom Sihanouk had been ousted from power in Cambodia by the pro-American Lon Nol and had taken refuge in Beijing. Just before the championships started, he discovered the Lon Nol clique, as he called it, was sending a team. He did not want China to go as it would mean facing this Cambodian team. China's sop to the deposed prince was to instruct Zhuang Zedong, its best player and three-time World Champion, not to play a Cambodian.

America presented different problems. The Chinese team were given very precise guidance as to what they should do when they met the Americans. They should not initiate contact, and those little courtesies that mark sports between nations, like exchange of flags, should not take place. But the Chinese could shake hands.

The Japanese organizers made sure the Chinese were in a separate hotel and their travel arrangements were distinct, which meant contact with Americans was very limited. However, the American team, aware of how good the Chinese were at table tennis, were eager to contact the Chinese players and even visit China on their way back from Japan. In the years since then, there has been much debate and discussion as to whether the Americans sought such an invitation. One of the leaders of the American team, J. Rutherford Harrison, would later say that they did not. But the Americans did approach the Chinese, once during a coffee break, when one American found himself next to a Chinese. All this may not have amounted to anything but for a dramatic gesture by an American player.

That player was Glenn Cowan. One day suddenly he jumped on to the Chinese bus. The American had been practising for 15 minutes with the Chinese player Liang Geliang, when a Japanese official closed the training area. The practice session meant that Cowan had missed the American bus and, as he wondered how he could get back to his hotel, a Chinese player waved to him to get on the Chinese team bus. Cowan had long hair in the style favoured in 1971 and looked like a hippie, and initially, the Chinese did not know what to do with him. But then Zhuang Zedong, sitting at the back of the bus, got up, greeted Cowan and said through an interpreter that, despite the hostility of the American government, the people were friends.

Many years later, in a television interview, Zhuang Zedong would describe what happened: 'The trip on the bus took fifteen minutes, and I hesitated for ten minutes. I grew up with the slogan "Down with the American imperialism!" And during the Cultural Revolution, the string of class struggle was tightened unprecedentedly, and I was asking myself, "Is it okay to have anything to do with your Number One enemy?"' Then Zhuang recalled that Mao had met the American writer Edgar Snow on the Rostrum of Tiananmen on the National Day in 1970 and said that China should now place its hope on the American people. Zhuang wanted to give Cowan a gift. However, he felt the pins, badges with Mao's head, silk handkerchiefs and fans were not appropriate and settled on a silk-screen portrait of Huangshan Mountains, a famous product from Hangzhou. Cowan wanted to give something back, but all he had was a comb. The American confessed to the Chinese, 'I can't give you a comb.' But he was determined to give a present and bought a T-shirt with a red, white and blue peace emblem flag and the great words from the Beatle song 'Let It Be'. The next day, Cowan gave Zhuang the T-shirt and said he hoped he would be able to visit China.

There is a photograph of this historic meeting. It shows the two shaking hands just outside the Chinese team bus. In the background the Japanese bus driver can be seen looking bemused that a meeting between two table tennis players outside a team bus should be of such significance. He could not have imagined what a breakthrough this was, for later, many people in table tennis would say they had urged the Chinese to use the sport to re-establish contact with the world. H. Roy Evans, the Welshman who was then president of the International Table Tennis Federation, claimed that he advocated this course of action on a visit to China before the 31st World Table Tennis Championship. But whether such advice had an impact is not known. What is clear is that the Cowan–Zedong meeting had created a new momentum.

The question now was whether the Chinese would allow the American team to visit the mainland after the Championships. The Colombians and the Jamaicans also wanted to visit China. But their visits would be routine as China sought to use sport to increase its political influence in that part of the world. Only Mao could authorize an American visit.

America had had no relationship with China since the Communist takeover in 1949. Indeed, the Communist victory was seen as a great loss by the Americans. 'Who lost China?' became a burning issue in the 1950s in America, used by the Republicans to berate the Democrats, in particular Dean Acheson, President Truman's secretary of state. The slogan revealed a commonplace attitude that China was once an American property. Instead the US pretended that the man they had supported and financed, Chiang Kai-shek, still ruled China, even though he had fled to Taiwan and the Nationalist government he had set up there depended on American military support.

America made sure that Chiang Kai-shek's Nationalist government retained China's seat in the United Nations and with it the veto in the Security Council. Despite the total absurdity of this position, many countries took their lead from the United States and refused to accept that the Communists ruled the Chinese mainland. Richard Pound, a veteran of the Olympic movement, noted the surreal nature of Taiwan's belief that it still controlled mainland China. He wrote: 'I remember once, during a visit to Taiwan, reading in a local newspaper of the criticism launched in the national assembly at the minister responsible for mines for his failure to prevent some disaster in a mine on the mainland.'

Any action against Taiwan, even the most reasonable, provoked American wrath. This was vividly demonstrated in 1959 at the IOC Munich session. Prompted by the Soviet Union Taiwan was asked, not unreasonably, to change its name since the country could no longer claim to supervise sport on mainland China. Taiwan called it a 'betrayal' and nearly all of America seemed to agree. The reaction in America was so extraordinary that even the anti-Communist Avery Brundage felt his countrymen were 'going off on an emotional binge in unprecedented proportion'. The State Department termed it 'a clear act of political discrimination'. The *New York Times* saw it as a move to expel the Taiwanese. The House of Representatives unanimously voted to withhold the $400,000 earmarked for the 1960 Winter Games in California, arguing that a free nation was being prevented from taking part. F. E. Dorn, a Congressman from New York, said that 'the United States must not allow a friend of many years to be pushed aside by Communist blackmail.' He also demanded US withdrawal from the Olympic Games, and President Eisenhower condemned the IOC.

Richard Nixon, elected to the Presidency in 1968, and a dedicated anti-Communist, could hardly have been expected to alter such long-held American views. But from the moment he got to the White House he began to think of opening the door to mainland China. Working with his foreign policy adviser, Henry Kissinger, he used various intermediaries to find the key to this long-locked door. This included a Dutch minister in Beijing, Yahya Khan, the military ruler of Pakistan, who would later be better known as the butcher of Dacca, and even another Communist dictator, Nicolae Ceaușescu of Romania. Nixon even went public on his China quest, telling *Time* magazine in October 1970, 'If there is something I want to do before I die, it is to go to China.'

Mao, too, wanted a rapprochement, especially after falling out with the Russians, once regarded as China's older Marxist brother.

The Chinese no longer looked up to the Soviets, or sought their advice. They were even reviving claims to ancient Chinese territories lost to the tsars. Now, suddenly Mao realized that a bunch of table tennis players might provide the long-lost key to relations with the United States.

Initially, after receiving the American table tennis players' request to visit China, Mao had said no. That was considered the end of the matter with the next day being the last day of the World Table Tennis Championships. But around midnight Mao, having taken his sleeping dose and quite drowsy, suddenly asked his personal assistant, Wu Xujun, to ring the Chinese Foreign Ministry and say he had decided the Americans could come. However, Mao had also decreed that when he said something after taking sleeping pills, he should be disregarded. Wu did not know quite what to do. Then Mao reminded her of what he wanted and the deed was done. The next day in Japan, a Chinese official went to the American hotel and phrased the invitation very delicately: 'How would you react to an invitation for your team and officials to visit China?'

The Chinese were clearly playing a very intricate game. If the Americans had said no, they would not have extended an invitation, and nothing would have been lost. If they said yes, then the question could be said to be an invitation, implied, if nothing else. The Americans needed no second invitation. They accepted and were even more delighted to find that the Chinese would pay for them to travel to China. So, on 10 April 1971, 15 members of the US table tennis team became the first official group of Americans to arrive in China since 1949 when Mao's Red Army marched into Beijing.

Zhou Enlai, the Chinese premier, managed the visit to the last detail. He demonstrated China's confidence by making sure that the Americans were taken to a performance of *Taking Tiger Mountain by Strategy*, which contained strong anti-American, as well as anti-Chiang, propaganda. The Chinese prime minister also instructed the Chinese audience to applaud the American players. He approved the broadcasts for the matches and laid down the procedure for the two teams as they went to the table to play a match. They were to shake hands and then walk to the table holding hands. Although the Americans could not have been expected to win a game against the Chinese, the Chinese made sure they did. One Chinese competitor, Zheng Minzhi, recalled, 'I knew their significance and my responsibilities. I knew I was not only there to play, but more important, to achieve what cannot be achieved through proper diplomatic channels.' Although Mao did not meet the table tennis players, Zhou did and made it clear that he saw this visit as resuming the old ties China had had with America: 'with your visit, the door to our friendship has been opened.'

The Americans, even the State Department, took some time to understand what the Chinese were playing at. But Henry Kissinger realized that the Chinese had played a brilliant game and established a new relationship between the two countries:

> Like all Chinese moves, it had so many layers of meaning that the brilliantly painted surface was the least significant part. At its most obvious, the invitation to the young Americans symbolized China's commitment to improved relations with the United States; on a deeper level it reassured – more than any diplomatic communication through any channel – that the emissary who would now surely be invited would step on friendly soil. It was a signal to the White House, but our initiatives had been noted. The fact that the players could not possibly represent a particular political tendency added to the attractiveness of the manoeuvre from the Chinese perspective. China would be able to make its point without any possibility of a jarring American commentary.

Xu Guoqi, who expertly analysed the story in *Olympic Dreams, China and Sport 1895–2008*, put it succinctly: 'the successful matchmaker that Mao and Nixon had worked so hard to find turned out to be the small white ping-pong ball.' Within a couple of months,

Henry Kissinger was in Beijing, and in less than a year, Nixon himself had arrived. It was then that he met Mao and heard the great helmsman's version of the ping-pong diplomacy:

> The situation between our two countries is strange, because during the past twenty-two years our ideas have never met in talks, now the time is less than 10 months since we began playing table tennis; if one counts the time since you put forward your suggestion at Warsaw, it is less than two years. Our side also is bureaucratic in dealing with matters. For example, you wanted some exchange of persons on a personal level, things like that, but rather than deciding that we stuck with our stand that without settling major issues there is nothing to do with small issues. I myself persisted in that position. Later on I saw you were right, and we played table tennis.

Fifteen years later, the Chinese would use tennis to engage with the South Koreans. The occasion was a Davis Cup tie held in Kunming in southern China, the first visit to China by South Korean sportsmen. By then Mao was long dead, and Nixon had had to resign from the Presidency in disgrace. Yet their ping-pong diplomacy had changed the world and it is hard to quarrel with Xu Guoqi's conclusion:

> Ping-pong diplomacy was a major achievement for Mao and Nixon, who both struggled with domestic scandals during their time in power. But the game of ping-pong not only saved the political legacies of these leaders; more importantly, it brought the two countries together during the 1970s, a critical time of uncertainty and conflict worldwide. The small ping-pong ball, worth only about twenty-five cents, played a unique and significant role not only in accelerating China's internationalization, but also in transforming Sino-US relations and shaping world politics in the last part of the twentieth century.

Although the ping-pong players had helped the US and China finally to come to terms with political realities, China in the early 1970s was still on the edges of world sport. In 1971 the People's Republic of China was admitted to the United Nations, ending the fiction that the government in Taiwan represented the mainland, but as far as the IOC was concerned, Taiwan still spoke for all of China. China had used sport to further its political objectives, but it was yet to learn how to play the politics of sport and use sport to brand China's re-emergence as a great power. It had taken to sport to cope with Western power and live down its image of the 'sick man', but it was yet to realize how useful sport could be as a nation's calling card. By the time Beijing staged the Olympics in 2008, it had worked that out very well. I described them as China's giant coming-out party. However, the party took a long time to prepare.

It is arguable that the Chinese could have held the Olympics earlier, or played its sporting cards better, but to be fair to China's Communist rulers, they were dealt a bad hand when they first came to power, and had no one who could explain how sport worked in the West. The Communists had long appreciated the power of Western sport and its influence on issues outside sport, but they did not understand its curious structure. Their incomprehension was demonstrated almost immediately after their takeover of mainland China. At the time of the Communist takeover in October 1949, China had three members of the IOC, although one of them, Kong Xiangxi, a member since 1939, had never attended an IOC meeting. After the Communist takeover he left Hong Kong to reside in the United States while his colleague Wang Zhenting continued to live in Hong Kong. The third member, Dong Shouyi, carried on living in the mainland. But it seems that the Communists were not aware that China had been part of the Olympic movement since 1922, let alone that they had an IOC member living in Beijing.

The Nationalists, in contrast, knew all about the power of the Olympics and were determined to keep their Olympic position. In

1948, even as the Nationalists were struggling to hold on to the mainland, they sent a team of 30 athletes to the London Olympics. It was not easy to field a football team and Chiang declared that any person of Chinese origin would do. So China had players from Saigon, Manila and Singapore, then a British colony. But, despite all their problems at home, the Chinese brought gifts to rationed Britain: oiled bamboo shoots, preserved eggs, dried shrimps and green tea.

The Communist ignorance and IOC incompetence was further exploited by the Nationalists, even after they had to abandon the mainland. In 1951, the Nationalists wrote to the IOC saying that China's Olympic Committee address had changed from Beijing to 147 West Gate Street, Hsin Chu, Taiwan. In any properly run organization such a letter should have set alarm bells ringing. There had been a change of regime in China. Now the deposed regime, which had moved from the mainland to an island, was claiming to represent the Olympic movement on the mainland. How could this be possible? But when this letter arrived in the IOC offices in Lausanne, the officials merely recorded it as if it was a very routine address change. As Avery Brundage would later put it, they did it without 'any thought of the political significance'. This administrative decision would haunt the IOC for almost two decades.

It was against this background that Communist China first tried to take part in the Olympics and the opportunity came in 1952 at Helsinki. The Games had not been on their radar and it was only the Soviet participation (after years of spurning the Olympics) that induced the Chinese to take an interest. However, this raised the question of who could claim to represent China – what would become known as the two-China question. By this time Beijing, having accepted Russian advice to go to the Games, had also finally discovered that IOC member Dong Shouyi lived in Beijing. They began to work out how useful he could be to help China take part in the Olympics. He was sent to take part in the IOC session that preceded the Games. Dong's arrival must have surprised some of his fellow members, for Taiwan had put out a story that Dong was dead. But after the IOC members recovered from this shock they had another shock coming. The Dong who arrived in Helsinki pretended he could not speak English and was accompanied by an interpreter who insisted that Dong only knew Chinese. This enraged the IOC president Sigfrid Edström. He had met Dong in 1948, during the London Olympics, and spoken to him in English. 'You're lying,' he said, tapping his cane on the table, and told the translator, 'Leave the room immediately.' Under IOC rules, members could not attend sessions with translators. The translator left, but he took Dong with him.

By this time, Beijing's team was in Leningrad waiting for word as to whether they could participate in the Games. In the end, the IOC session decided, by 29 votes to 22, that both Taiwan and mainland China would take part. Had both participated it might have raised interesting issues as to which of them could claim to represent China. In the event, the Taiwanese decided not to come. If they had been clever in getting the IOC to change the address from Beijing to Taiwan through a simple letter, they were less than smart in deciding not to take part in the Helsinki Olympics. They had stayed away fearing this would mean a confrontation with the Soviet Union.

In Beijing, Mao, Zhou and Liu Shaoqi, the Communist 'big three', had decided Beijing would take part. But they waited until Taiwan said it would not be there before making this public. Zhou said, 'It is a victory for the PRC when its flag is flying at the Olympic Games.' Not that there was much time for the flag to fly or the team to do anything as the Games had already started. The Chinese arrived a day before the closing ceremony. No Chinese athlete took part in the competitions, apart from a swimmer in a preliminary competition who failed to go through to the next round. However, the Chinese acrobatic troupe performed in Helsinki's cultural programmes and was hailed by Zhou as the country's national treasure, bringing glory to the Motherland.

The next two decades would be dominated by the two-China question. Beijing was keen to take part in the 1956 games. But when the Chinese team got to Melbourne they found that Taiwan, claiming to represent China, was already there in the village, its flag proudly fluttering along with other nations. The Communists could not accept that and withdrew. Two years later, in August 1958, Dong resigned from the IOC and his letter to Brundage, who by then had taken over as president, makes it very clear that his Communist rulers were speaking through him. After accusing Brundage of being 'a faithful menial of the US imperialists bent on serving their plot of creating "two Chinas"', Dong continued: 'I feel pain that the IOC is today controlled by an imperialist like you and consequently the Olympic spirit has been grossly trampled upon. To uphold the Olympic spirit and tradition, I thereby declare that I will no longer cooperate with you or have any connection with the IOC while it is under your domination.' The same day, China withdrew from the IOC saying, it 'ceases to recognize the IOC'.

Nineteen fifty-eight was to be the great year of no for China's sport for it also walked out of FIFA over the Taiwan issue. But the Chinese Communists were not content just to withdraw from Western-controlled sport. They began to work on plans to organize their own Games in competition with the West. In this, ironically, the Chinese were following an example set by the Japanese before the Second World War. Then, after the Japanese invasion of Manchuria in 1931 and the installation of a puppet regime, Japan had tried to secure a place for its puppet at the 1934 Far Eastern Championship Games. But so successfully did China protest that the Games died. Four years later Japan tried to revive the competition under the title of the Oriental Championship Games to be held in Tokyo and featuring its puppet state and the Philippines, then an American colony. But with the Second World War on the horizon the event never took place. In contrast the Chinese did hold their rival Games in the 1960s. It was against a very different background and the Chinese allowed another country to take the lead. The Chinese frontman was Indonesian President Dr Sukarno. He was an ally of China and for the Chinese his plans for a rival Games presented an opportunity to damage their main Asian rival, India.

This was an important consideration for, until then, India had been in the lead in Asia, both politically and in sport.

India had staged the first Asian Games in Delhi in 1951. The idea had emerged from a political conference held just before Indian independence. Although the Asian Games Federation was born at the Mount Royal Hotel in the middle of the London Olympics, India had a big role in creating the Games. The name Asian Games was given by India's first prime minister Jawaharlal Nehru and he also coined the Asian Games slogan, 'Play the Game in the spirit of the Game'.

Not all of Asia made it to Delhi: only 11 countries, no Pakistan, no Vietnam, Syria, Iraq, China nor Korea, where a civil war was raging. Moreover, the Games featured just six sports: athletics, aquatics, basketball, football, cycling and weightlifting. But the Indians had reason to be pleased with their efforts given the Games were staged four years after the chaos and killings that had accompanied independence.

In his inaugural speech at the Games, with Edwina Mountbatten (who was his lover although this remained a secret for decades) standing next to him, Nehru said that the Games 'bring together the youth of many countries and thus help, to some extent, in promoting international friendship and cooperation. In these days when dark clouds of conflict hover over us, we must seize the opportunity to promote understanding and cooperation among nations.'

The Games played a big part in building India's new image. Proud of the way it had won its freedom through Gandhi's non-violent methods and feeling morally superior, India saw itself as 'the big brother of Asia'. One of the tasks it set itself was to guide the renaissance of this long-suppressed continent. As Nehru later put it, 'there was a certain looking in the direction of India', which he felt could 'possibly play a fairly important part in bringing Asian countries together'.

Four years later, in April 1955, Nehru was playing the big brother to China at an international conference in Bandung in Indonesia.

The idea for the conference was Indonesian, bringing the newly independent countries of Asia and Africa together, but it was Nehru who was the star. Rejecting the advice of the United States and the United Kingdom, Nehru insisted China must be present in Bandung. According to his official biographer, Nehru used Bandung to set the stage for Prime Minister Zhou En Lai to present the new China to the world. Nehru was then riding the crest of a wave with his former adversary (and fellow Harrovian) Winston Churchill calling him the 'Light of Asia'.

For a time all this seemed to bring India and China close together and a popular Indian slogan was 'Hindi-Chini bhai-bhai' – India and China are brothers. However, by the time the Asian Games were staged in Jakarta in August 1962, that brotherly love had turned to hate and the two countries were locked in a bitter dispute about borders. India claimed China was occupying its territory on the north-east frontiers of India. China countered by saying that the land had always belonged to the Middle Kingdom. The duplicitous British had taken it away and the Indians were using British-imposed borders to rob China. The Indian decision to give sanctuary to the Dalai Lama, who escaped from Chinese-controlled Tibet in 1959, had also infuriated the Chinese. It was China's turn to dim Nehru's and India's lights.

At Jakarta China was taking part in its first Asian Games and both Zhou En Lai and the foreign minister Chen Yi made it clear to the Indonesians that they could not allow Taiwan to participate. Indonesia duly obliged and used extraordinary tricks to keep out Taiwan and Israel (the latter to keep the Arabs happy). They sent athletes from both countries identity cards, but when the athletes opened their packages they found that they were blank cards. A plane carrying a Taiwanese official did try to land at Jakarta airport but was refused permission.

The Indian member of the IOC, G. D. Sondhi, urged the Asian Games Federation to declare that the Jakarta Games were not an Asiad (as the Asian Games are officially known) as two accredited nations, Taiwan and Israel, had been denied entry. The Indonesians saw this as an insult to their President Sukarno. Such was their fury that it resulted in mob violence and the storming of the Indian embassy in Jakarta. Another mob went to the hotel where Sondhi was staying. Luckily for him, he had just left and that evening managed to escape from the city.

Amidst all this, the Jakarta Games were actually going very well for the Indians on the field of play. Their football team won gold but such was the anti-Indian feeling that, as they went to collect their medals, the crowd's booing drowned out the Indian national anthem and continued during the closing ceremony.

For the Indonesians the Indians had behaved treacherously and, after a meeting at the Merdeka Palace with ministers present, Sukarno declared that he wanted nothing more to do with the Asian Games. He was creating the Games of the New Emerging Forces (GANEFO). According to one Chinese author the idea was given to him by a painter at the palace. Sukarno now declared India to be a traitor to the spirit of Bandung:

> If it is the view and attitude of the majority of the AGF, which is the representative of the 13 nations that signed the convention of Asia–Africa Bandung Conference, that the Asian Games does not truly reflect the true spirit of Bandung, then we must stage a new Asian Games, which does truly present the spirit of Bandung. Right now, we stage a new Games among the New Emerging Forces at once, as soon as possible, yes, in 1963.

Sukarno may never have read *Tom Brown's Schooldays*, or been aware of Coubertin, but he was clearly determined to use sport for a wider political purpose. Sukarno, like Mao, had always considered sport to be a particularly important political tool. After wresting control of the country from Dutch colonial rule, he had abolished sports such as korfball and kasti, because they were considered part of the Dutch inheritance, and instead revived old Indonesian sports such as the martial art pencak silat. For Sukarno this was crucial as sport meant a country could sum up 'many revolutions in one generation'. His decision to host the Asian Games against a dire economic situation, inflation running at 600 per cent per annum and government debt reaching $1.1 billion, had shown the value he put on hosting a big sporting event.

Sukarno was also in the middle of a wider political game. He was keen to secure West Irian, which was still under Dutch control, and was confronting Malaysia. For the Indonesians, these new Games were an essential part of completing their revolution. In the words of Sr Soebandrio, Sukarno's state minister: 'Indonesia is now struggling to finish its revolution [. . .] GANEFO aims to finish mankind's revolution to achieve a New World order which will be full of fairness, prosperity, safety and peace, and free from exploitation and suppression.'

The formation of GANEFO was, of course, a challenge to the IOC and, led by Sondhi, the Olympic movement decided to act against Indonesia. As Sondhi put it in a letter to Avery Brundage:

It is clear that the government of Indonesia – under strong pressure from the local Chinese and the Communist Government of China – was determined not to invite the Taiwanese teams. Pressure from Arab states was likewise responsible for non-issuance of Identity cards to Israel [. . .] All show of welcoming Taiwan and Israel representatives, prior to the Games, was an elaborate hoax. The government of Indonesia were determined not to invite these countries.

On 7 February 1963, for the first time in its history, the IOC indefinitely suspended a member country. It is interesting that at this stage the IOC had gone further against Indonesia than against South Africa. The expulsion of that country would not come until many years later and after much tortuous vacillating. The Indonesian sports minister responded by calling the Olympic Games 'an imperial tool' and Sukarno started to prepare for his own rival Olympics.

The Chinese were quick to see great advantage in supporting

Sukarno's ideas for an alternative games. In October 1962, within weeks of the end of the Jakarta Games, China unleashed a short, sharp border war against India resulting in a humiliating Indian defeat and a devastating blow for Nehru from which he never recovered. Eighteen months later he died, a broken man. It became clear that China not India was the big brother of Asia. Sukarno's sporting plans provided China with another opportunity to reinforce its new status and, from the first moment, China was prepared to bankroll Sukarno and the Indonesians.

China provided the Indonesians with $18 million to organize the first GANEFO Games in 1963, and it offered to pay the expenses of any 'newly emerging nation' that could not afford to send a team. This may explain why the first Games held in Jakarta in November 1963 saw 42 countries take part, although not all of them sent official teams, worried that the IOC might expel them from the Olympics. The Chinese were still in their friendship first, sports second mode, and the foreign minister, Chen Yi, told the Chinese badminton players that they should not take all the gold medals, even if they were better. 'Be considerate of the feeling of the host country and let Indonesia win a few gold medals in badminton, and when you return I'll treat you.' Vice premier, He Long, who went with the team, was not happy about these orders but accepted them.

He Long had a weak heart and could only watch the badminton match on his hotel television. He was considerably upset to find the Chinese so far ahead of the Indonesian in one match that there could be only one possible result. He told the Chinese player in no uncertain terms that he had to lose. This was to produce one of the most farcical moments seen in sport. In order to lose from this position, the Chinese either hit the ball low or out of bounds. The Indonesian broadcaster could not understand how the Chinese, so commanding moments before, had now apparently forgotten how to play badminton. He wondered if the Chinese player was possessed. But the end result, a defeat of the Chinese player, pleased the Chinese rulers. The official Chinese biographer of He Zhenlian, the current IOC member for China who played a major role in Beijing getting the 2008 Games, wrote approvingly, 'From this it can be seen that although He Long had a character that loved to win, he still dealt with issues from a high-minded political vantage point. The Indonesians had a tacit understanding of this match and were very grateful to China.' Some time later, when the Indonesian sports team visited Beijing, Zhou, welcoming them, admitted the standard of sports was not of the highest level, but that the future of GANEFO was secure.

Three years later there followed a second GANEFO, albeit a miniature one, held in Cambodia with 37 countries taking part. China was again the banker and Cambodia got a brand-new stadium. China's use of sport to build its diplomatic and political power had also meant Congo-Brazzaville got $20 million for sporting activity. Avery Brundage noted all this with alarm, and indeed the warnings the Chinese leadership uttered every time they spoke at a GANEFO occasion.

At the second council meeting of the GANEFO Federation in Beijing in 1965, He Long, the man who fixed the badminton match, gave a speech. He Long had always believed that sport was an important political tool. This was the theme of his speech back in 1955 when Beijing held the first Workers' Games. Now almost a decade later, as head of the sports commission, he was ready to use this political tool to challenge the traditional sporting powers:

No matter what may happen in the world, the Chinese people will never shirk their international duty of aiding and supporting peoples of the world in their revolutionary struggle against imperialism. We are determined to unite with all anti-imperialist people and carry forward to the end our revolutionary struggle against the imperialists headed by the United States and their lackeys. However desperately and frantically it may struggle, US imperialism can never save itself from doom. Just as Mao Zedong has said, the days of imperialism are numbered. The prospects for us newly emerging forces are infinitely bright.

But the prospects for Sukarno were not very bright. A year later, he was ousted from power in a bloody coup. The new regime of General Suharto was much more pro-American and had no interest in using sport like Sukarno. Although there was due to be another GANEFO Games in 1966 in Cairo, with neither China nor Indonesia involved, there was no future for these Games. The GANEFO Games had marked the high point of China's attempt to create a worldwide sports movement that was distinct and different from the one Coubertin had set up. Mao was about to launch the Cultural Revolution, which impacted on sport as devastatingly as it did on all other aspects of Chinese life. The revolutionaries declared that winning medals in sports was the wrong policy; sport was put under military control and athletes put under such pressure that a famous table tennis player, Rong Guotuan, committed suicide. It would take China years to recover from the turmoil of the Cultural Revolution, although it would be a catalyst for a new China to emerge with a very new attitude to sport. But even while still in the grip of it, the Chinese finally dealt with the two-China sports problems and succeeded in marginalizing Taiwan.

The catalyst for this was Pierre Trudeau and his Canadian government, the occasion being the Montreal games of 1976. For Olympic opponents, Montreal has always been cited as a demonstration that the Games can cost huge sums of money that take years to be repaid and produce little benefit. For China they demonstrated, finally, that the People's Republic represented the whole of China in world sport. There was, of course, no question of the People's Republic taking part in these Games, since it was not a member of the International Olympic Committee, Taiwan was. It still claimed to represent China and this gave the Canadian government a very stark choice. In winning the right to stage the Games, the Canadian government had promised the IOC that all the national Olympic committees and international sports federations recognized by the IOC would be free to enter Canada. However, the letter had a qualifying phrase, which was to cause a lot of confusion. The phrase was that this guarantee was 'pursuant to the normal regulations'.

Montreal had won the right to host the Games on 12 May 1970. On 13 October 1970, Canada finally broke away from the US-inspired fiction that the Communists did not control the main-land and recognized the People's Republic of China as representing the country. This also entailed accepting that Taiwan was legally part of China. As the Games neared, the question for the Canadians was: how could Taiwan be allowed into the country for the Games if it called itself the Republic of China?

For Trudeau's government there was no economic merit in up-setting the Communist regime in Beijing. Trade between the two countries was booming, and in 1975 Canada had sold wheat worth $307 million to the People's Republic. In an editorial en-titled 'The Tarnished Olympic Games' the *Wall Street Journal* commented, 'last year Canada posted a $144 million trade deficit with Taiwan and a $320 million trade surplus with Peking. Had the situation been reversed it is likely Taiwan would still be partici-pating in the Olympic Games as the Republic of China.'

For a year the Canadian authorities tried to work with the IOC and the Beijing government to achieve a compromise. But on the eve of the Games no solution was in sight. Documents of these discussions have since become available and provide much work for historians. They also reveal moments of unexpected humour. For example, what did the Canadians mean when they said, 'pursuant to the normal regulations'? Lord Killanin, then presi-dent of the IOC, had the impression that this meant excluding people who might be suffering from cholera. Arthur Andrew, a senior official in Canada's External Affairs Ministry, commented delphically, 'At its most obvious, it meant that we reserve the right to exclude persons with cholera, but that any decision on a less obvious issue would only be taken at the ministerial level as a matter of national policy. No official could commit the govern-ment on how this would be applied in advance.' In other words, no one would know whether they would be allowed into the Games before they arrived.

With the Games about to begin, the Canadian government

made it clear to the IOC that Taiwan could participate only if it did not claim to represent China. In a modified replay of what the Indonesians had done with the Taiwanese in Jakarta in 1962, the Canadian government also made it clear that the Olympic identification cards, which under the rules of the international Olympic Committee served as a visa for the Games, were no longer valid. The IOC was furious, but it knew that at this late stage it could not take the Games away from Montreal. At its session just before the start of the Games, the IOC said that Taiwan could take part, but under the Olympic flag, playing the Olympic anthem, and using either a board showing the Olympic rings, a blank board or no board at all. During the 1960 Olympics, Taiwan had been forced to call itself Taiwan in order to participate. Its athletes had marched into the Olympic Stadium in Rome behind a banner which read 'Under Protest'. At one stage, the Canadians had appeared to favour the Rome option, but in the end settled for the so-called 'neutral option'. The Taiwanese rejected it.

The Canadian–IOC struggle impacted on America, which in 1976 was celebrating its bicentennial. American public opinion was very hostile towards the Canadians and the White House spokesman criticized the Canadian action. The president he served, Gerald Ford, was about to seek re-election and keen to take on the Canadians. But Ford was restrained by his secretary of state, Kissinger, who told him, 'I think you should stay out of it. If Peking thinks we are trying to force Taiwan in, we could end up in a confrontation with Peking.' Ford complied, but told Kissinger and Donald Rumsfeld, his defence secretary, 'that Trudeau is being a real bastard'.

The final result was that Taiwan did not attend the 1976 games. Four years later, when the Winter Games were held in Lake Placid, it was made clear to the Taiwanese that they were not welcome in the United States either, even though the American bid for those Games had been accompanied by a promise from President Ford: 'I pledged that every team recognized by the International Olympic Committee will be welcomed at Lake Placid 1980. I repeat that pledge to you.' Ford had made the pledge to demonstrate (in his words) that 'attempts to use the Olympic games for international power politics will ultimately backfire'.

But that was in 1976. By 1980, America had already recognized the People's Republic of China, and while Taiwan challenged the decision to exclude them from the Games in a US court, it failed. Mao had been dead for four years, and a new China was emerging from the ruins of his Cultural Revolution, led by Deng Xiaoping. He, like Mao, had always been a sports devotee. He had been in charge of sports before the Cultural Revolution and had developed a love of football, first discovered during his years in exile in France.

The historian Xu Guoqi has argued that Deng Xiaoping used the Olympics to formulate his one country, two systems idea:

> As China's new leader, Deng Xiaoping wanted this country to quickly re-establish international relationships, including those with the Olympic movement. He became deeply involved in negotiations with the IOC and personally made all the crucial decisions on Beijing to return to the Olympic movement, including those concerning Taiwan's use of the Chinese anthem and flag [. . .] Significantly, the final solution of the two-China issue in the IOC and in other international sports federations reflected Deng Xiaoping's idea of 'one country, two systems'. Many people know that Deng used this idea to deal with Hong Kong's return from British colonial control, but few realize that the idea was first applied in solving the Olympic dispute over Taiwan.

The new China that Deng was creating meant the end of 'friendship first, competition second'. In 1979, China's National Sports Commission put forward an Olympic model whose aim was to win at the Games. The following year the commission came up with a new slogan: 'Break out of Asia, advance into the world'. China would now seek to win glory on the sporting fields to demonstrate its growing power.

Nineteen eighty was also the year China returned to world football, an event that made João Havelange very proud as he felt he had played a major part in it. In 1975, a year after he was elected, the Brazilian FIFA president presided over a FIFA executive meeting in Senegal. There, he told his fellow committee members that, as the new president, he had a diplomatic status 'so to speak' and would try to bring China back. In May 1975 he made a trip to Beijing – the first of many, but quite the most dramatic. It lasted seven hours and Havelange would later tell the football historians John Sugden and Alan Tomlinson:

> Every time the conversation came back to a political aspect. Mao Zedong was still in power, and negotiations were very, very difficult. I put forward six ideas during this meeting, and they rejected all of them. Halfway through this meeting, when they were rejecting everything I said, 'Excuse me, I would like to go and make a telephone call.' And they said, 'To whom?' I said, 'I want to call my Brazilian ambassador here' and they said 'What for?' I said, 'Well, as you don't seem to want to talk about football, you only want to talk about politics, it's better that the ambassador is here and not me – I've got nothing to do with this conversation.' So they immediately changed their attitude and said, 'Now wait a minute, I'm sure we can find a solution.'

A solution was found, although it took three more visits by Havelange over the next four years, and a visit to Taiwan. There he met the military commander General Chung, who was also president of its Football Federation. The Chinese had agreed they would come back to FIFA as the China Football Association, but Taiwan would have to drop its claim to represent China, and would not be allowed to fly its flag or play its anthem in the competitions. The general was in no mood to agree to drop the name of China. Then Havelange went to his briefcase and brought out a product whose label said 'Made in Taiwan'. The general immediately surrendered. At FIFA's Zurich Congress in 1980, China came back and Taiwan was accepted under its own name.

The success of China's marriage of sport and politics would take some years to become evident – not until the 2008 Beijing Olympics. But in many ways, the 1984 Los Angeles Games marked the first publicly significant moment on that long road. China had returned to the Olympic arena with the Lake Placid Winter Games, but that created little impression. Los Angeles was different. China had followed the American lead and boycotted the 1980 Moscow Olympics following the Soviet invasion of Afghanistan. The Soviets were now boycotting the Los Angeles Games and for the Americans it was vital that China took part.

In the run-up to the Games there had been problems. In July 1982, Hu Na, a Chinese tennis player, had defected while playing a Federation Cup tournament in Santa Clara, California. Things worsened when in April 1983 she was granted political asylum despite a warning by Deng. This led to the Chinese cancelling all official cultural and athletic exchanges, including participation in pre-Olympic test events being held in Los Angeles. But the Games were different. Boycotting them would not have fitted in with Deng's policy of the new China. And the Americans could not have been more grateful for the Chinese presence.

So, on 14 July 1984, Zou Zhenxian had the honour of being the first athlete to enter the Olympic Village. Peter Uberroth, the organizer of the Games, wrote in his memoirs, 'When the team from the People's Republic of China entered the stadium, the audience erupted in cheers. The entire crowd of 92,665 stood and applauded. It was a grand welcome.'

There was enormous symbolic significance in China's return to the Summer Games, to the same city where, back in 1932, a single athlete had marked China's debut on the world stage. The 1984 Los Angeles Olympics also had a wider significance for the way sport was organized and marked the beginning of major changes in sport's relationship with the world of commerce.

These changes went far beyond the Olympics and affected all

of sport. They would raise the question as to whether the religion of sport, as preached by Hughes and Coubertin, creating an almost mythical spirit, could survive.

But even as sport and society were forging a new relationship, in another part of the world the spirit of sport was suddenly blossoming. This could not have been in a more unlikely setting. There, for almost a century, far from being used to bring people together, sport had been a deadly weapon to keep them apart. Now that country was about to discover how sport could reach out to people and bring races and nations together in a way that nothing else could.

CHAPTER 10

SUNDAY MORNING COFFEE WITH MANDELA

It was early Sunday morning in Johannesburg, 30 June 1991. We were on our way to Nelson Mandela's home in Soweto and the roads were eerily quiet. It was as if Johannesburg had a hangover and could not quite believe what it had witnessed the previous day. Certainly South African sport, particularly its cricket world, had never before seen such a night of celebration.

The Saturday morning had seen the birth of a unified cricket board for South Africa. For the first time since South Africa made its Test debut in 1889, it had a cricket body that could truly claim to represent all the races of the country.

In the 1970s the world had woken up to white South Africa's racist sports system and ejected it from international competition. During that time the white administrators had pulled any number of PR stunts to fool the world that white South Africa had changed. But the latest changes were the real thing, and final proof came on the Saturday night as the newly formed body had a celebratory black-tie dinner in the ballroom of the Sandton Sun. In this symbol of white South African prosperity, where not long ago the only blacks would have been servants, blacks were honoured guests, wearing elegant tuxedos as they mingled with whites. In some ways, the more striking sign of change was the presence of guests of all hues from round the world, including some from India.

India then had no relations with the white South African government. Indeed, in New Delhi, the Indian government treated the

African National Congress as if it was the government of South Africa, having granted its mission diplomatic status. There were no direct flights between the two countries and it was hard for them even to talk on the telephone. But here were Indians at the dinner, wearing their national costume of the buttoned Nehru jacket, next to South Africans of Indian descent, two distant cousins long cut off by apartheid, rediscovering each other.

The presence of one particular guest was the most powerful sign of real change. He had travelled only a few miles down the road, but from a world totally removed from Sandton: Soweto. He was Walter Max Ulyate Sisulu. Just over 18 months previously, he had been a prisoner in Robben Island with Nelson Mandela, and had been released just a few months before Mandela after 26 years in jail. Now he was in his best dinner jacket accompanied by his wife, Albertina. Richie Benaud, the former Australian captain, now a prominent cricket commentator, who had specially flown in from London, even made a joke at her expense. South Africa was changing so quickly, said Benaud, he could see Albertina leading a South African women's cricket eleven at Lord's later in the summer.

But even as the entire Sandton ballroom rocked with laughter, it was difficult to shake off the feeling that the evening in this smart hotel was somewhat surreal. This was, after all, a cricket occasion.

How could a game, bringing together the races in such a social setting, lead to real change in South Africa, a country which was built on the basis of races never mixing? In Pretoria the whites still held power. Many of the laws of the apartheid regime were still on the statute books and the different political groups could not even agree how to begin the talks designed to convert white South Africa into a rainbow nation that would give Mandela, and all the other non-whites, a vote. Surely, when the different groups all sat down to talk, if they ever did, the prophets of doom would be proved right and the country would collapse into violence and bloodshed?

And then, on that Sunday morning, quite unexpectedly, Nelson Mandela summoned Sunil Gavaskar, one of the guests who had flown in from India, to his Soweto home. A group of cricket journalists accompanied Gavaskar and, at the Mandela residence that morning, we got a glimpse of how the great man saw sport playing a role in creating his new rainbow nation.

I was in Sunil's party, having played a small part in bringing him to Johannesburg with a group of Indian journalists. It had made me aware that the new South African transracial amity was very recent and very fragile. My involvement had come about because in the previous 18 months I had got to know Ali Bacher, the managing director of white South African cricket, and the man now heading the unified cricket body.

Cricket had been good for Bacher. The son of a Lithuanian father and a Polish mother, both of whom had fled European anti-Semitism to seek refuge in white South Africa, he was the Jew who had become the great white South African hero, using the success of his cricket team to attract Afrikaners to an English game. The Boers did not take to cricket until the 1960s. The first Afrikaans book on cricket, *Amper Krieket Kamnpioene* (Almost Champion Cricketers) by Werner Barnard, was published only in 1955. Until then Afrikaners had seen it as an alien, imperial sport. Afrikaners warmed to the game in the late 1960s, when white South African teams started winning consistently under the captaincy of Peter Van der Merwe. Although not, in fact, an Afrikaner, his name sounded Afrikaans. Bacher advanced this process when he became captain of the 1970 South African team that demolished Australia, South Africa's most feared cricketing opponent.

Bacher's dark, swarthy looks, and a nickname of Ali – his real name is Aron – could have created a problem. Many took him for an Indian. Back in 1961 he had played a rare match against the non-whites. Ayob Hossain, an Indian-born South African who later worked for him and was in the crowd that day, wondered, 'What is the Indian boy doing playing for the whites?' Even the

Economist once described him as an Indian. In 1965 when he played in England for the first time, the Yorkshire wicket-keeper suggested he should settle here: 'We have a lot of Indians living here.' Interestingly, his white South African team-mates had never had any problems recognizing him as a fully fledged white and after the comment by the Yorkshire wicket-keeper they jokingly addressed him as a Nawab.

Five years later, in 1970, Bacher was poised to return to England with probably the best-ever white South African cricket team, which had just beaten Australia 4–0 in South Africa. But pressure from Peter Hain, who had played a pioneering role protesting against apartheid sport, and the anti-apartheid movement had forced the British Labour government to stop the tour. Bacher's mother, Rose, drew horns on a photograph of Hain and pasted it in the scrapbooks she kept of her son's achievements. When Bacher met John Vorster, the South African prime minister, Vorster shouted: 'As long as the Nationalists are in power no black man will play against a white man.'

Little did Bacher realize that that would be the start of South Africa's long cricket and sporting isolation. At 28, he thought that another tour would soon round and he went along with the attempts by the South African cricket authorities to get back into world cricket. By the time I met Bacher in 1989, he had repudiated all these efforts. 'In the seventies I did believe there was merit selection. But that was nonsense. We were not 100 per cent committed to black cricket. We were heavily involved in trying to get back into world cricket.'

Bacher himself had gone into cricket administration in the 1980s, and was involved in attempts to lure international cricketers to break the sporting boycott by bringing rebel West Indian, Sri Lankan and Australian tourists to the country. The Australian tour took two years of planning and finally came together when Bacher suddenly flew into Singapore, took over the hotel room that Jimmy Connors had just vacated, and signed up the Australian team as they were returning from India. They were going to stop in Singapore for only a day but that was enough. After that, Bacher was ready, at 24 hours' notice, to fly to any corner of the world to get cricketers to play in South Africa. It meant he met some of the world's leading cricketers in the unlikeliest of places: Larry Gomes in New York, Desmond Haynes in Bacher's sister's home in Gateshead, Gordon Greenidge in a cafe in Portsmouth, Phil De Freitas in a buffet bar at Manchester railway station and Ian Botham at his home.

The last two meetings took place in the summer of 1989 when Bacher signed 16 English cricketers led by Mike Gatting to play in South Africa from January 1990. In 1982, when a similar band of English mercenaries went to South Africa, Botham had disapproved. He couldn't have gone, he said, and looked Viv Richards, his then Somerset colleague, in the eye. When they met in the summer of 1989, Bacher reminded him of that. Botham replied, 'I have spoken to Viv. It is all right, now.' Then he asked for £600,000 to play in South Africa. Bacher said, 'I couldn't justify that sort of money. If it got out what would the people in the township say?'

The anti-apartheid movement alleged that these tours were official government propaganda, funded by the government. In 1994, when I wrote my book *Sporting Colours, Sport and Politics in South Africa*, I came to the conclusion that, 'The rebel tours were in fact government-funded operations which brought aid and comfort to the apartheid regime and the whites.' The white cricket authorities always denied this, arguing that they needed the rebel tours to keep their cricket alive. But in 2004, long after apartheid was history, Rodney Hartman, in his official biography of Bacher, revealed that money for the tours came from the South African taxpayer. The sponsors who funded the tours could always set their expenses against their income, but for projects classified as 'international projects', and the rebel tours came under that category, they could claim an additional 'double tax allowance'.

'These tax rebates,' wrote Hartman, 'amounted to anything up to 90 per cent, so in effect, the taxpayer was footing most of the bill; and the sponsors were getting enormous commercial value for minimum net cost.' Indeed, the double tax allowance came about as a result of Bacher organizing a rebel tour by a West Indian team, the first time a black team had played cricket against whites in South Africa. 'The amendment,' said Hartman, 'came about, in fact, because of the heavy financial demands of the West Indies XI tour. To the normal tax rebate claimable by the sponsors was added a special one: together they constituted the double tax allowance that became very palatable to would-be sponsors'. That tour also saw the then foreign minister Pik Botha offer to pay 4 million rand from the foreign affairs budget for the tour, although in the end the cricket authorities did not need the money. The double tax allowance was so attractive that they could get enough money from sponsorship to cover all the costs of the tour.

It was Bacher's decision to organize the Gatting tour that had first brought me in contact with him and South Africa. When we met in the summer of 1989, Bacher was keen to emphasize that his rebel tours were not just to keep white cricket alive, but raised money to fund his township programme of introducing cricket to blacks. Bacher encouraged me to visit South Africa before Gatting and his men arrived, to see how his pioneering township programme was using sport as an instrument of social engineering. He offered unrestricted access and dismissed suggestions that my colour would mean I would have to be classified as an 'honorary white', as the Japanese were. Within hours of my arrival I was introduced to two young cricketers whose stories could not be more contrasting: Roger Wentzel, a 13-year-old white boy, and Paul Masilo, a 14-year-old black boy.

It took a 20-minute drive to go from Roger's home to Paul's, but they might as well have been living on different sides of the Moon, such was the gulf between Roger's all-white suburb of Linden and Paul's township of Soweto. Roger's home, by white South African standards, was very middle class – which meant it had a swimming pool, but no tennis courts or maid. Roger's mother, Mich, had thought of having a maid but it would cost 25 rand a day (then about £6) and Mich would have needed to go out to work. Unlike many white homes in the Johannesburg suburbs you could see the Wentzel home from the road. 'We didn't want to live in a jail,' said Mich. In neighbouring suburbs, most of the houses were hidden behind high walls, some topped with barbed wire with a chilling sign nailed to the outer wall: Armed Response. This meant that, within three minutes of hearing the alarm, security guards would deal with any intruder. The only people walking on the road in these white suburbs were the black servants – the maid or the gardener. The only sound was the growl of the Dobermann pinscher.

Roger's father Ray had said to him that, 'If they [meaning blacks] were sitting at one table and we were sitting at the same table then we would eat together. There is nothing wrong with that.' Occasionally Roger had asked Ray, 'Why do they live in Soweto? Why can't they live next door?' Ray had explained, 'Next door costs 300,000 rand [then about £50,000]. I don't mind if a black man could afford that, then he can live there. As long as he doesn't mess me up.' A neighbour had a coloured man living with her and Linden wives gossiped about whether he was a lover or just a gardener. He had once helped Mich with the garden. 'He's horrible-looking,' Mich told me with evident distaste. Roger had hardly ever stepped out of his all-white world. His government school was only for whites – and Japanese, who qualified under apartheid as 'honorary' whites. He had never had to take a bus ride, never been to Soweto. Ten years earlier, Mich had been on the official guided tour of Soweto – the ultimate voyeuristic experience for white visitors to Johannesburg. When she learned we were going to visit Paul, she was excited. 'Can I come? Will I be allowed?'

She arrived early at our hotel, expectant but fearful. The mother of one of Roger's schoolmates had been alarmed that Mich should go to Soweto. 'Do you know how dangerous it is? You could get hurt.' Sure enough, within minutes of her arrival in Soweto, Mich was hurt. By Paul. A cricket ball bowled by him had escaped the protective net and hit her painfully just below the knee. It was just as well Mich was not seriously hurt for the Johannesburg ambulance service ran along racial lines. Before they sent out the ambulance they asked the colour of the person. A white woman asking for an ambulance to a Soweto address might have caused tremendous confusion. So, gingerly rubbing the swelling, Mich ventured into Paul's world.

Paul was an orphan. Nobody knew his father; his mother was lost somewhere in Soweto, drunk, a vagabond. Paul had not heard from her for three years. Although 14 years old, at school he was in a class with nine-year-olds. He lived with an uncle, his mother's brother, in a room behind the Good Hope Fish and Chip shop. The lettering had faded and the shop had long since stopped serving fish and chips, becoming instead the area's general store. Only ten minutes from the centre of Johannesburg, the store had the feel of a place in the outback: there were grilles protecting the store's goods and customers were served through holes in the grille.

Paul's room, in the courtyard at the back, had a tin roof; the bottom of the door had a tin panel, the curtains were torn and in the middle of a bright, sunny day it was pitch dark. There was little natural light and no electricity. The only light was from a candle placed on a broken chair next to the bed. The chair and the bed were the only furniture in the room: there would have been no space for anything else. At the bottom of the bed was Paul's wardrobe: a cardboard box. It contained a cricket T-shirt and two pairs of shorts. These and the grey trousers he was wearing constituted all his worldly goods.

The only book in the room, next to the window, was a cricket book. If he got bored with that he could always read the newspapers stuck on the discoloured walls. Next door was a dumping room that housed empty bottles, discarded furniture, clothes, some buckets, a wash basin and a tin bath hanging from a hook on the wall. That was where Paul had his bath. By the time we had looked round Paul's home Mich's knee had swollen up and she was applying ice provided by Paul's aunt. But more than the physical hurt, she was tortured by what she had seen of Paul's home. It was a revelation, and as we left she said, 'It is sick. Roger would ask a lot of questions.'

That was just what Bacher wanted. Yes, he was disrupting world cricket through his rebel tours but his township cricket was also making Roger and other white children like him start asking awkward questions, part of a strategy of using cricket to change political and social thinking. 'The biggest problem in this country is communication. South Africa is an abnormal society. Cricket could help make it normal,' Bacher kept telling me.

By 1989 he had been managing director of the South African Cricket Union for three years. When he had taken over the townships were in flames, whites feared that the blacks would march to the white areas and the whole country seemed on the verge of collapse. One weekend, Bacher himself thought of fleeing, but then on an impulse ('I am a very impulsive man') he thought: why not take cricket to the townships? It meant challenging the conventional white South African wisdom that the blacks did not play cricket because they preferred football – and it meant confronting white fears about going into the townships.

So on 20 October 1986, 'we first went into Soweto'. This sounds like a military operation, and in a way it was. Bacher's home in the luxurious white neighbourhood was not far from the township of Alexandria, but that day's journey to Soweto was more like going into Beirut in the middle of the civil war: the army was still there, and the children had been confined to the township for three years. 'We went in two cars, Volkswagens,' recalled Bacher. 'We were all whites and we got lost. We ended up in the middle of Soweto and I was frightened.'

But although Bacher was impulsive, he was also meticulous. He had prepared for this foray by organizing coaches, both white and black, and made radio and television appeals to get black children to come to a cricket clinic. The response was electric. One thousand turned up. Three years on, Bacher had built up an impressive cricket network in the townships. Cricket coaches of all colours could now be seen in Soweto and the other townships. Bacher had developed a new cricket form: mini cricket played with a soft ball, and a new kind of cricket coach. He quickly discovered that the great majority of the teachers in the black schools were female, so in a remarkable cricket revolution, he encouraged these teachers to learn cricket. One of the teachers he recruited had always thought cricket was an insect – now she was part of the group of middle-aged black ladies teaching young black kids the game.

But this still left the problem of getting Paul on to the same cricket field as Roger in the trials to select the Transvaal Under-13 side. They were held in a private school in a white suburb and for Roger it was an easy car journey. It was made even easier by Ray taking a week off work to make sure Roger had the best possible help and support. On the day the selection was announced, the school was packed with Ray, Mich and the parents of the other white kids. The car park provided evidence of the affluence of white South Africa: Rolls-Royces, Mercedeses, Porsches and Audis filled the car park. The school hall was like a fashion parade of designer clothes. The only blacks there were Paul and the black coaches from Bacher's cricket union. But Paul nearly did not make it. Even if Paul had had parents it would have been impossible for black parents to drive to a white suburb to see their children play cricket. They would not have had the time, the money, nor, perhaps, the courage. So every time a black team played a white school, invariably on the white school's ground, bussing arrangements had to be made for the black children.

In Soweto, Bacher employed a black coach, Laurence Mvumvu, who every Friday morning went round Soweto 'knocking up' the children and getting them ready for cricket. And when the children played in the white suburbs Mvumvu arranged for transport, usually one of those little Japanese vans, a combi, the vehicle of transport for blacks in South Africa, and large enough to pack in a cricket team. In Paul's case, the arrangements Mvumvu made worked on the first day of the trial, but on the second day they broke down and Paul arrived an hour late. Did this, perhaps, cost him a place in the Transvaal Under-13 side? Roger was selected, but Paul, much to Bacher's fury, had to be content with selection for the lesser Invitation XI. Bacher was pensive as he heard the selections. Just before that he had told me he was convinced Paul would be selected for the Under-13 side. 'Paul is a natural bowler. He will have the same opportunities as my son David.'

After the selection, as the white parents, some of them in tears of joy at their sons' success, drove their children away, Bacher comforted Paul. The selection for the Invitation XI would mean that he would still go to Port Elizabeth where Roger and the other boys were going. He would have to travel in a plane. Had he travelled in a plane before? When Bacher asked Paul this he nodded, but the blank eyes gave it away. Bacher turned to me and said, in a stage whisper, 'He has never travelled in a plane before. For him to come to Johannesburg is a big thing. He will probably have a heart attack when he sees the plane.' Then he turned to Paul and reassured him that someone from the cricket union would accompany him on this important trip.

If all this suggests that Bacher had became a surrogate father to Paul and the other black boys, then that was, perhaps, inevitable. Paul was able to play cricket only because Bacher's cricket union paid 150–200 rand (then £40-£45) a month for Paul's education and living expenses. The story of Paul's rescue from a life of crime, Bacher told me, was a classic case of the redemptive power of sport. The previous March, at a cricket match, Paul had seen a white boy's cricket bag: it had a camera and money. He stole them both. Then, fearful of what might happen, he vanished. After three months, and a lot of searching, Mvumvu found him and brought him to Bacher. 'I told him what my university professor had said: "Everyone can make one mistake." Paul appears to have learned the lesson and now concentrates on hurling a cricket ball as fast as he can.'

Paul was not Bacher's only weapon against apartheid. Through Bacher's efforts some of the most promising black players had become members of the prestigious Wanderers club where once the only black man would have been the *kaffir*, rolling the wicket for the *baas* (boss) to play. The club still had that starchy colonial feel and very few non-white members, but on its various cricket fields Bacher's young boys were making an impact. The weekend that I spent with him involved speeding from one sumptuous Johannesburg club to another to watch these players. We arrived at one club to find a team was a player short. Bacher immediately drafted one of his black players into the team. As we watched he had eyes only for his black players. As one of them played well he said with pride, 'Look at that, just natural.'

Bacher's use of cricket as a form of social engineering was emphasized when, in one school match, a black batsman asked a white fielder to help him with his boot laces. It is the sort of natural thing that happens in millions of cricket matches every day, but in apartheid South Africa the moment was hugely symbolic. As the white boy bent down in front of the black boy to tie up his laces, Bacher turned to me and said, 'They'll grow up thinking that is natural.'

Bacher knew how great the gulf was between white and black. At that stage, Nelson Mandela was still in Robben Island and most white South Africans did not even know what he looked like. No photograph of him had been permitted in the South African media since he was imprisoned in 1963. Even Bacher's wife Shira had never seen a picture of Mandela. Bacher's trick was to make this abnormal society look normal.

His two principal coaches were an Indian and an Afrikaner: Hossain Ayob and François Weidemau. Hossain, a fast-medium bowler, who might have played for South Africa but for apartheid, lived in a white area courtesy of François. The house he lived in was owned by a company where François controlled 51 per cent of the shares. This got round the Group Areas Act where different races could only own property in their own racially defined areas. This meant Hossain could live in a white area as the house belonged to a white and this did not violate the Group

Areas Act. South Africa's apartheid laws had created many such absurdities. Hossain said, 'I have to keep on the right side of François; he could always throw me out of the house.' But even as he said it he burst out laughing, aware that the mild-mannered François was the complete antithesis of the stereotypical *kaffir*-hating Boer. The thought of turfing out the burly Hossain would not enter his head.

The interaction of whites and blacks could be awkward. Professor Masilo Mkhatlas, the chairman of the Thembisa Townships Sports Council, was a fan of Bacher's township programme, but opposed to the Gatting tour. We were having tea just behind the splendid Long Room of the Wanderers stadium and the professor had shown me the cage where a few years ago non-whites were herded in to watch the match. Now black and white children were seated there as part of Intuba, a day of opportunity, to raise funds to promote sports in the townships. Bacher had run two miles in support, carrying aloft a torch, and as he entered the stadium, he had grabbed the hand of a black kid and together they had raised the torch of Intuba. It was a symbolic act and the sort of PR Bacher was adept at. The event had touched the 'Prof' and he had just told me about his love for Ali Bacher. 'He has opened an avenue which we never knew existed. He has gone beyond cricket. Through cricket we have met white teachers, our schools are exchanging visits, our families are going across the colour line. He has succeeded where the white local authorities have failed. That is why we love him.' Then, as he finished his tea, he spilled some on to the saucer and slurped the tea from the saucer. Most of the whites round us turned to look at him in dismay. The 'Prof' hardly noticed them.

In some ways, the most interesting social engineering was being displayed by Imtiaz Patel, a South African of Indian origin who coached Paul. He had the sort of good looks, a bit like Imran Khan, that turned heads. Imtiaz had brought his girlfriend, Juliet Glover, to the trials to see if Paul would be selected. Bacher introduced him and with a mischievous smile referred to Juliet as 'Mrs Imtiaz'.

Juliet and Imtiaz smiled, but for them it was not really a laughing matter. The Immorality Act, prohibiting sexual relations between whites and non-whites, had gone and their relationship was not illegal. But the other restrictions of apartheid made it very difficult. Imtiaz lived in an Indian area, Juliet in a white suburb. Juliet taught at an Afrikaans school where the boys had told her it was disgusting for races to mix. 'I could never take him to the matric [school leaving] dance or any social function,' Juliet confessed to me. Imtiaz shuddered at the thought of taking Juliet back to Schweijer Reneke, the small Afrikaans town where his parents lived. Forty years ago, the Afrikaans just threw the Indians out of the centre of the town and while some of them had been allowed back, the idea of going back with Juliet made Imtiaz close his eyes in dread.

Imtiaz had tried hard to 'integrate'. He played for a white club, but when he took Juliet to one of the weekend games she preferred to sit in the car: she couldn't stand the scrutiny of the other white players. Imtiaz felt he was like an ambassador of the non-whites to a distant, ignorant, sometimes hostile white world, constantly having to explain. He had thought of going back to the old segregated system, but was drawn by Bacher's township programme and was reluctant to give up. They both conceded the relationship was doomed. Juliet said, 'It is what we call the half an hour of happiness.' By the time I returned to South Africa in 1991 for the unification celebrations that half-hour of happiness could no longer be sustained and the couple had parted.

Our visit to Mandela had been organized by Imtiaz. Mandela had seen Gary Sobers, who had also been invited to celebrate the new South African Cricket Union. Bacher had taken both Sobers and Gavaskar to the township and, at my suggestion, got Gary to bowl to Sunil. The picture made the headlines in the South African media the next day. Imtiaz felt that after Sobers had met Mandela, Gavaskar should not miss out. For Imtiaz, a South African proud of his Indian origins, it was a point of principle that Mandela should receive a great Indian cricketer as well as a great West

Indian. So it was that we, a whole host of cricket journalists, all of Indian origin and all, barring me, from India, were tagging along with Gavaskar to Mandela's home.

I had played a small part in helping Gavaskar and the Indian journalists get to Johannesburg. When Bacher drew up the list of those to be invited he had no problems with cricketers from England, Australia or even Gary Sobers. While South Africa had never played the West Indies, West Indian cricketers were known and Bacher knew Sobers. But he knew nobody from India and turned to me for help.

My visit to South Africa had made me aware of how little white South Africans knew of Indian cricket. India may have been a Test-playing country since 1932, but white South Africa had not only never played them, but never taken any interest in their cricket. Growing up in India in the 1960s, I had, like many cricket-mad Indians, followed South African cricket. Indian newspapers regularly reported South African Tests against England, Australia and New Zealand. We knew India would never play South Africa, but names of players such as McGlew, Tayfield, Heine and Adcock were familiar to us. But for white South Africa, Indian cricket just did not exist. Indeed, soon after I got to South Africa it amused me to ask white South African cricket followers which cricketer had the second highest first-class batting average, after Don Bradman's 95. When I said it was Vijay Merchant, one of India's cricketing greats, the look on their faces told me everything. Apartheid had also cut any surviving historic links between South African Indians and India. I was therefore not surprised to receive a call in my London home from Bacher asking for the names of Indians to invite to the black tie event in Sandton. I suggested Gavaskar, who was not only my old schoolmate from St Xavier's in Bombay, but the cricketer who had helped take Indian cricket to a new level in the 1970s, helping fashion Indian wins in the West Indies and England for the first time. He had recently retired from the game and then held the record for most Test runs. He had also, for good measure, just written a foreword to my *History of Indian Cricket*.

Back in 1983, after India had won the World Cup, the white South Africans had approached the Indians, hoping to entice them into a rebel tour. As Gavaskar later told me, 'The proposition was put to us after we won the World Cup, but to the great credit of the players they turned it down without another thought. It was just out of the question.' But this visit was different: it was to see South African cricket at last come together. I also suggested to Bacher names of some prominent Indian cricket journalists. So here we were, on our last day in Johannesburg, being driven to see Mandela.

We left Sandton that Sunday morning for Nelson Mandela's home. For several miles there were no cars on the highway except our convoy. Then, just as we turned off the main highway to Soweto and neared his home, suddenly a Ford Cortina zoomed ahead of us as if it had been waiting. It now escorted us to the great man's home. 'That is Mandela's security car,' said the man who was driving us. 'They watch every car that approaches his house.' Sure enough, as we turned into the driveway of Mandela's home, the car so positioned itself that we had to stop. The electric gates opened to let the Cortina in, two men got out, our credentials were checked, then the gates opened to let us in to the palatial home that Winnie Mandela had built while Nelson Mandela was in prison. It would have looked impressive anywhere. In Soweto it looked incongruous – hidden behind high walls, it looked like a house from the white suburbs of Johannesburg transplanted to the township.

But then, everything about this meeting with Mandela was strange. This was one of the most momentous weeks in his life. The ban on the ANC had been lifted and it was about to hold its first open session in South Africa for thirty years. That session was to confirm Mandela as president, with Sisulu becoming vice-president. The previous week, the media had reported that Mandela had his hands full trying to cope with the bitter divisions between the old guard, so long in exile, and the young activists who had been carrying on the struggle against apartheid within the country. When some of us had asked whether we might see Mandela at the cricket celebrations, we were told he was far too busy preparing for the historic Congress to see anybody, certainly not a cricketer accompanied by some cricket journalists.

But Imtiaz, through his contacts, had opened the door and now we were led up a small flight of stairs to a room dominated by a huge oil painting of Robert Mugabe on one wall. In the middle was a long V-shaped table filled with the presents and gifts Mandela had acquired from his various foreign travels since his release. It looked like the office of a company chief executive, although when Mandela arrived, dressed in a tie and a jumper, it became more of a throne room. His associates, who had been milling round in the room, withdrew to a distance whispering softly, 'Madiba', father, the term invariably used to refer to him. As he began talking it became obvious that he quite liked using the royal we, reflecting his own royal roots.

We had been told before the meeting that Mandela would not talk about politics and that we should not ask him political questions. But once the pleasantries were over and coffee was served, it was clear Mandela was more than happy to talk about sporting politics and how politicians could use sport. Without much prompting he said, 'De Klerk has made it clear in our conversations, "Look, if you would make it possible for the All Blacks to come here, then we can smash the system."' Mandela was all too aware of the part sport had played in the boycott of South Africa and saw the ANC successfully using sports to its own advantage. In the 1970s, the ANC had pioneered the boycott of South African sports to spotlight apartheid, but now, with the cricket bodies united, Mandela made it clear he wanted the world to start re-admitting integrated sports bodies back into the international sports community. While he continued to insist that the economic sanctions should continue, he was full of praise for Bacher's township programme. 'We have never been against cricketers coming to South Africa to coach our children. What we object to is anything that has interrelationship with the regime. We want to use it to isolate the regime.'

Mandela himself had never played cricket – boxing being his sport – but he told the story of watching the Australians playing a Test match in Durban in 1950. 'Yes, we watched it from the segregated stands and, of course, we cheered the Australians. The South Africans had made a big score. We were cheering [Neil] Harvey who was playing very well for the Australians but we were both nervous and excited. As he took Australia to the South African score we were very scared. What if he gets bowled out? Then Harvey came to our segregated stand and spoke to us. But I didn't speak to him. They would have kicked us out if we had tried to approach him.'

Since his release, cricket had figured in his travels. Bob Hawke, the Australian premier, mentioned it in Australia, and when he stopped over in London to meet John Major, one of the first issues the then British prime minister raised was cricket. Major had asked Mandela whether he would allow South Africans back into cricket. 'You know,' said Mandela, 'Mr Major seemed more interested in cricket than the issues.' As he recounted the story he was overcome with laughter. 'I have instructed Steve Tshwete to visit London and meet Major.' Tshwete was the ANC executive member in charge of sports and had played a crucial role in helping the cricket bodies to unite. This movement on sport was taking place, said Mandela, despite the fact that the government had not

> kept its promises. If mutual confidence had been built, we would have been advanced now as far as removing the various forms of boycott. But, unfortunately, the government has acted vey shabbily in building mutual confidence. We have had solemn agreements and they have subsequently emerged and put a different interpretation. The government destroyed that spade work we had built with regard to mutual confidence. So now we are insisting on the removal of all racial laws and let's build non-racial coordinating bodies before we make any move.

Mandela also knew that he could not move too far ahead of the young radicals in the ANC on the sporting front. 'On our side we have people who are extremists who want not only that sport must be normalized. They argue that there can be no normal sport in a racial society. That is true. But at the same time sport is sport and quite different from politics. If sportsmen of this country take steps to remove the colour bar then we must take that into account.'

None of us wanted our conversation with Mandela to end, but we had been told he had very little time. He had chatted much longer than his minders wanted. However, as we were being ushered out Gavaskar suddenly piped up, 'Sir, can I have a memento of this visit?' Most of the journalists there reeled back in shock, fearing Gavaskar had committed a dreadful faux pas. But Mandela just nodded, went out of the room and, leaning on the stairs, called out to Winnie to give him a key. He re-emerged with a key and went to a locked door behind the huge conference table. 'That,' whispered one of his associates, 'is where he keeps all the presents he has received on his travels.' He quickly returned, saying, 'I thought I might give you the belt Joe Frazier has given me. But I would like to keep it.' Mandela, a keen boxer in his youth, could clearly not part with such a gift. But he did present Gavaskar with a book to which he added a gracious inscription. Then the electric gates opened and we were back in the heat and dust of Soweto.

The conversation with Mandela lasted no more than half an hour but it revealed how the man who was to lead his nation out of apartheid saw sport. At that stage Mandela was much like Gandhi had been in the British Raj: a man of enormous prestige, whose power over the masses inspired respect and fear from his country's rulers, but also a man with no official position. Mandela did not even have a vote. As we drove away from Soweto that day it was unimaginable that in little over three years Mandela would be president of South Africa after the first one-man-one-vote elections. The thought that the house where we had coffee would in time become a museum dedicated to Mandela seemed even more fantastic.

When Mandela spoke to us, the National Peace Accord, crucial to the talks, was another three months away. The Convention for a Democratic South Africa (CODESA), under the chairmanship of three judges, did not begin until 20 December 1991. This collapsed and there was a second CODESA, which also collapsed, leading to bilateral negotiations between the ANC and the National Party, followed by a Record of Understanding between the two. It was only on 1 April 1993 that the Multiparty Negotiating Forum (MPNF) gathered for the first time. An interim constitution was not agreed until 18 November 1993, with elections held only on 27 April 1994.

As all this was going on, the violence in the townships continued. Some of the killings, as was later revealed, were orchestrated by the so-called 'Third Force', which the South African Truth and Reconciliation Commission called 'a network of security and ex-security force operatives, frequently acting in conjunction with right-wing elements and/or sectors of the IFP [. . .] fomenting violence and which resulted in gross human rights violations, including random and target killings'.

There were also huge problems with the demands of the Inkatha Freedom Party and its leader Mangosuthu Buthelezi. In Natal, this had led to black-on-black killings, violence that would later spread to the townships round the Rand. Mandela had to make public appeals for weapons to be thrown away. But even as many despaired that apartheid would ever end and one-man-one-vote arrive, the new rainbow nation of South Africa was being forged and accepted by the world of sport.

In November 1991, a month before the first CODESA, Bacher and a South African cricket team made their first journey to India. The pilot flying the plane had often flown De Klerk, but no South African plane had ever flown to India and he had to carefully check the flight plan to make sure he was heading in the right direction. The Indian government still did not recognize the Pretoria regime – the ANC office in Delhi continued to act as the South African Embassy – yet it was encouragement by Indian politicians that had made the tour possible. A crucial role in this was played by Jyoti Basu, then the chief minister of the state of West Bengal, heading a hard-line Marxist government – the local Bengalis having for decades voted the Communists to power. Indeed, the plane's first stop was Kolkata, the capital of the state.

Months earlier, helped by the Indians, South Africa had been readmitted to the International Cricket Conference. There had been a few hiccups, but the Indians had cleared it with the ANC and pushed it through, despite serious doubts from the West Indies that Mandela's release had really changed things in South Africa. Once, as doubts were raised, Steve Tshwete shouted angrily, 'We are the best doctors in South Africa.' The result was that while the Indians proposed South Africa's return, the West Indians abstained on the re-admission vote. The West Indian doubts were shared by Colin Cowdrey, who had been captain of England during the D'Oliveira affair, and was now head of the ICC, the international body. Despite their being admitted back, he ruled out South Africa's participation in the 1992 World Cup due to be played in Australia. But then Mandela intervened and everything changed.

In August 1991, Clive Lloyd, captain of the greatest-ever West Indian side and one of the best in cricket history, visited South Africa to see the township programme. Bacher took him to see Mandela, where he was meeting a Swedish delegation. This gave the international media a chance to ask about the World Cup. Mandela's response was immediate: 'The World Cup? Yes, South Africa should be in the World Cup, why not?'

Suddenly politicians round the world were following his lead. The Sri Lanka minister Tryoon Fernandes proposed a special ICC meeting in Sharjah in October. At the meeting there were many doubters who felt that events were moving too fast, but in the end even the West Indies agreed that South Africa should take part. For Mandela, admission to the cricket World Cup was an important card to play as he sought to persuade the South African whites to consider sharing power for the first time.

As the cricketers played back home in South Africa there was a 'whites only' referendum on the reforms and negotiations. De Klerk made much of the fact that if they approved, one of the benefits would be more of the sort of international sport South Africans had once again begun to enjoy since Mandela was released. One of the advertisements used during the campaign showed a deserted and overgrown cricket field with broken wickets, contrasted with a picture of South African cricketers celebrating their victory over Australia at the start of the competition. The advertisement read: 'Without reforms South Africa hasn't got a sporting chance. Vote yes on March 17 and keep South Africa in the sporting game.' It worked like a dream and 68 per cent of the whites voted for a continuation of the reforms.

By the time the ICC welcomed back South African cricket, everyone seemed to want to welcome back South Africa. In October 1991, the week before the ICC met at Sharjah, the Commonwealth Prime Ministers Conference met at Harare and had agreed that the sports boycott should be lifted on a sport-by-sport basis. On 6 November, as the cricketers prepared to leave for India, the National Sports and Olympic Congress (NSOC) announced that it had decided to accept the IOC invitation to participate in the 1992 Olympic Games.

It was not an easy decision. There was not merely the question of the sports boycott, although that was tricky enough. South Africa not only had a white minority government, but it also displayed the hated symbols of apartheid, and the Olympic Games were an occasion for flag waving. So what flag should South African athletes carry in Barcelona? What anthem would be sung if they won a gold medal? The NSOC could hardly accept the present flag of the white government, whose rejection of non-whites was so painfully evident. *Die Stem*, the national anthem, was also very much an Afrikaner anthem. It was decided that the flag would be a specially designed one of blue, red and green with a grey diamond-shaped background representing the country's wealth and the other colours representing sea, the land and the crops. Should South Africa win a gold medal, then Beethoven's 'Ode to Joy', the last movement of the choral symphony, which was also the Olympic hymn, would be played. Of course, there could be no place for the springbok emblem, which successive apartheid governments had reserved for white sportspeople only. The decision provoked a storm of protest from the government, including a furious De Klerk. Another IOC delegation had to visit South Africa to complete negotiations for the country's participation in Barcelona.

It was still a largely white South Africa that went to Barcelona, a team of 85 whites and only 12 non-whites — a 7 to 1 ratio in a country where non-whites outnumbered whites 4 to 1. But Mandela and the ANC knew this was a symbolic act, especially in the choice of the South African flag bearer. He was 32-year-old Jan Tau, a marathoner, black, and born in 1960, the year the old white South Africa had last taken part in the Olympics. The athletes themselves seemed to understand they had a mission beyond sport. As Bruce Savage of South Africa's yachting team put it, 'We're athletes first of all, but let's not kid ourselves. We have a very strong message to deliver. We need to prove to people that we can get along.'

Six weeks prior to this, Mandela and his ANC colleagues had considered calling for South Africa to withdraw from the Olympics. This followed the 17 June 1992 massacre of more than 40 people in the black township of Boipatong, an atrocity in which the ANC suspected De Klerk's government might be involved. All talks between De Klerk and Mandela came to an end, and while they soon resumed, they again illustrated the hostility between the political leaders.

But now, hours before South Africa took part in the opening ceremonies, Mandela was himself in Barcelona, talking to South African athletes and officials. He gave them the message he had given us some months earlier in his Soweto home:

All I want to say is that our presence here is of great significance to our country, a significance which goes beyond the boundaries of sport. Our country has been isolated for many years, not only in sports but in other fields as well. We are saying now, 'Let's forget the past. Let bygones be bygones.' I want to tell you that we respect you, we are proud of all of you and, above all, we love you.

Edward Griffiths, then sports editor of the *South African National Sunday Times*, wrote from Barcelona, 'On a balmy evening beside the Mediterranean, the [. . .] world, in its most visible and emotional form, had welcomed South Africa back to the fold [. . .] We will never stray again.'

Mandela knew it was easy enough to stray. The same year, 1992, also saw South African rugby back in Twickenham after an absence of 23 years. Just before that, in August 1992, there was an arguably more symbolic moment for white rugby when an official All Blacks team visited Ellis Park in Johannesburg. But that night, whites at a rugby match, as opposed to those in cricket or the Olympics, made it clear they could not understand why old South Africa should change. They just could not accept the rejection of the apartheid flag or the anthem. That evening, the old flag was much in display at Ellis Park and *Die Stem*, with its evocation of Afrikaners creating this land and humiliating the blacks, sung with gusto. It showed that, for all the talk of the new South Africa the old one was not that easily eradicated. Mandela understood rugby's special problems, which would only be fully tackled after he was installed in the president's office in Pretoria's Union buildings.

If some of the whites could not understand, let alone accept, what Mandela and the ANC were doing, in the world at large there was just as great a confusion. Through the 1970s and 1980s, the world had struggled to evolve a policy to combat white sporting South Africa. This had resulted not only in 'rebel' tours of sportspeople, but also in third-party damage to countries caught in the political crossfire.

The most damaging example came in the 1976 Montreal Olympics. An All Black rugby tour of South Africa led Jean-Claude Ganga of the Supreme Council of Sport in Africa to demand New

Zealand be banned, even though rugby then was not an Olympic sport and the New Zealand Olympic Committee had no power over the All Blacks. Ganga (who was later disgraced and expelled from the IOC during the Salt Lake City corruption crisis) over-played his hand and the IOC leadership did not handle things well. When the IOC refused to ban New Zealand, the African teams boycotted the Games. Many African athletes, including the star runner Fibert Bayi from Tanzania, were already in the Village and left Montreal in tears.

This led to the famous Commonwealth Prime Ministers' agree-ment at Gleneagles the following year. The signatories

> accepted it as the urgent duty of each of their Governments vigorously to combat the evil of apartheid by withholding any form of support for, and by taking every practical step to discourage, contact or competition by their nationals with sporting organisations, teams or sportsmen from South Africa or from any other country where sports are organised on the basis of race, colour or ethnic origin [. . .] Heads of Government specially welcomed the belief, unanimously expressed at their Meeting, that in the light of their consultations and accord there were unlikely to be future sporting contacts of any significance between Commonwealth countries or their nationals and South Africa while that country continues to pursue the detestable policy of apartheid.

The agreement did not mean a uniform boycott policy – South Africa still managed to evade it – but over time, although never specifically stated, everybody agreed how this should end. The sporting boycott of South Africa could only end when one-man-one-vote was ushered in and Nelson Mandela became president.

The strength of this understanding can be judged from the reaction of the media to the announcement in August 1990 that Sam Ramsamy, who from his exile in London had run SANROC, the South African Non Racial Olympic Committee, would return to South Africa for the first time in nearly two decades, to examine whether South Africa could be re-admitted to the Olympics. *The Times,* in an editorial entitled 'Sport in the Bearpit', said:

> By appointing him, the arbiters of participation in the Olympic Games are signalling that they have no intention of re-admitting South Africa until black majority rule is established. The Gleneagles accord remains in force. There is little prospect of cricket authorities – terrified of losing lucrative tours to non-white countries – lifting their boycott. South Africa retains a seat on rugby's ruling body, but only in the sense that Banquo had a seat at Macbeth's table.

It would take many months before the world understood that this sports policy had, in fact, been abandoned by the ANC itself. It had been making moves in that direction even before Mandela was released. Three years before Mandela walked free, at a meeting in Lusaka the ANC had effectively abandoned its blanket boycott of apartheid sport. South Africa now had a non-racial alternative and this was to be encouraged. In the early years of the sports boycott, the ANC had not taken much interest in sport. The boycott had come about because of the determined efforts of individuals like Dennis Brutus, a man who had played a key role in making the world aware of apartheid in sport, Peter Hain and Sam Ramsamy, helped by their friends in the wider world. Now the ANC was looking hard at using sport, but in a very different way. Mandela sought to hold out sporting incentives for whites to grant political concessions. In that sense, sport was creating a rainbow nation even before the politicians could agree on what spectrum it would take. To an astonishing degree, it was an almost exact reversal of what white South Africa had done for decades – using sport to push its own, particular, racist agenda.

The conversation with Mandela showed his understanding of the use of sport for wider political and social purposes. Mandela, without quite using those terms, had bought into the entire

Arnoldian view: both the idea that sport could reach beyond the playing fields, and that it could be a link between nations. In many ways, the sports boycott inspired by the anti-apartheid movement was a development of the Coubertin idea as he had put it in his 1892 speech. Then, he had seen sport as doing more than 'the telegraph, railways, the telephone, the passionate research in science, congresses and exhibitions' in reaching out to nations. 'Well, I hope that athletics will do even more [. . .] let us export runners and fencers; there is a free trade of the future.' What the sports boycott had done was turn the tables on the white regime.

For almost a century the whites had used sport to reach out to other white people round the world. The sports boycott had made much of the world realize how unfair this sporting trade was, how it was not really a free trade in the sense Coubertin imagined it, and why it ought to be resisted. This marvellous modification of the Coubertin sporting weapon had worked wonderfully well on the international sporting front. Mandela now had to concentrate on his homeland.

He knew that sport in general, and rugby in particular, had an extraordinary hold on the white nation. Now that the apartheid regime was at last willing to talk to the ANC, the need for international boycott was less pressing, indeed hardly necessary. What was necessary was to use sport to reach out to the whites and convince them that they could give power to the blacks and live in peace with them. Mandela knew how well the whites had played the sports game in the previous century. He was ready to play the same game, use the same weapon, not merely to undermine apartheid, but bring about a normal society. Sport, he had decided, could reach out where nothing else could.

White South Africans had, in many ways, pioneered the use of sports for a wider social and political purpose, long before Hitler had emerged, and decades before the Soviets started doing the same thing. Indeed, their political use of sports was, in many ways, more far-reaching than anything managed by Hitler or the Soviets. For almost a century, white South Africans not only determined which nations they would play – only other white nations, of course – but also dictated who their opponents could choose. They simply refused to play against any team which dared to select a non-white. They did this in England in 1929 when England was forced to drop Duleepsinghji, nephew of the great Ranji and then the best batsman in England. He played in the first Test, but then the South Africans objected and he was dropped. This was despite the fact that, such were his performances that season, he was selected as one of Wisden's Five Cricketers of the Year, one of the most treasured awards in the game.

The South Africans were even more ruthless in imposing their will on the All Blacks. They consistently did this for decades, leading to many a promising Maori rugby union career being destroyed. The presence of Maoris in the All Black team was seen as an affront by the white South Africans. In the 1920s, New Zealand had a wonderful Maori player called George Nepia. South Africans objected to his presence in the team, New Zealand gave in and he drifted away into rugby league. So craven were the Kiwis that before the 1949 tour of South Africa by the All Blacks, the New Zealand Rugby Union announced that 'much as it regretted, players to be selected to tour South Africa cannot be other than wholly European'. For the white South Africans, this was a seminal tour, coming a year after the Nationalists, campaigning on the slogan of apartheid, had won power. To further appease the white South Africans, the All Blacks also did not perform their famous Haka during the tour. As their manager Jim Parker explained, 'The war cry is a creation of the Maoris and as we have no Maoris with us we are not giving the war cry.'

It was only in 1960 that New Zealanders themselves began to voice some protest about the exclusion of Maoris, particularly after the Sharpeville massacres. But that year, the All Blacks again toured South Africa and New Zealand again caved into South African demands to exclude Maoris. Nash, the prime minister, felt it would be cruel to send Maoris to a country where they would be discriminated against and so New Zealand sent a whites-only team. The All Blacks were given a state reception as they left for South Africa. On their return they were hailed for 'the great work you have done in the cause of Commonwealth trust and friendship'. Such was the power and influence of South Africa within international sport that it was able to play this role of superselector until well into the 1970s.

It is fascinating to observe that, in many ways, the white South Africans accepted the Arnoldian idea that sport can reach out beyond the mere physical activity involved. It was just that they feared that playing non-whites in sport would take them to a place they did not want to reach, forcing social intercourse with them. This was the clear message of the Afrikaans newspaper *Die Transvaler* when, in reference to the ban on Maoris, it applauded the South African authorities for not allowing foreign teams to field their non-white players against South Africa: 'In South Africa the races do not mix on the sports field. If they mix first on the sports field, then the road to other forms of social mixing is wide open [. . .] With an eye to upholding the white race and its civilisation not one single compromise can be entered into – not even when it comes to a visiting Rugby team.'

What made it easy for the whites to propagate this message, and for the outside world to accept it was that in South Africa non-whites had never been part of the consciousness of the whites and this state of mind long predated apartheid. The whites lived surrounded by them, were served by them, and depended on their labour for their prosperity, but non-whites simply did not count as normal human beings for white South Africans. This is best illustrated by two contrasting views on South African sport, separated by nearly 30 years. The first was written in 1939:

> The sports field of South Africa knows neither politics nor ritualism; and there is no ghetto, nor will there ever be as long as sanity reigns. When politics clash with sport, the high ideals of sportsmanship are lost. And as long as there is no segregation in South African sport, there will be understanding. The Jewish

sportsman will go out and mix with his fellow human beings, and between them and him the bonds of fellowship will be woven.

The writer, Joseph Brauer, was Jewish and he was writing just as Nazi Germany was preparing the final solution for Jews in Europe. It is clear that his sporting world only meant whites, both Jews and non-Jews – other races just did not come into this picture.

In 1969 John Morgan covered the Lions tour and found nothing had changed:

> Of all the curious experiences in observing South African rugby and talking to its followers none was more astonishing than that none of them raised a question of African or Coloured players. The matter did not appear to exist in their minds. The African and Coloured Rugby Federation might have been in another physical continent, not merely a separate continent of the spirit. Old Springbok players would talk earnestly, even with passion, about the virtues of rugby in uniting the races – but for them, the races were Afrikaner and English, the religions Dutch Reform and Anglican. The blankness with which they responded to the idea that rugby might bring together other races with whites, revealed the hopeless naivety of those who insisted that 'tours build bridges.'

In the rewriting of South African history that followed apartheid, it became an established view that it was the Nationalists who were racists and had introduced race barriers into South African life. This rewriting was encouraged by the white opponents of the Nationalists. It was very far from the truth. Apartheid, essentially, further institutionalized the racism that had long ensured that non-whites had few rights in South Africa. Segregation had been the norm of South African life going back almost to the moment the first whites landed. When the Nationalists assumed office in 1948, they found a host of existing laws on which to base their infamous 'separate but equal' development ideas. One of the most notorious laws of the apartheid regime was the 1950 Act which prohibited sexual intercourse between whites and non-whites. However, the actual title of the Act was the Immorality Amendment Act, because it amended previous legislation dating back to 1927, which had made it illegal for whites and Africans to have sex. Now, whites could have lawful sex only with other whites. With this, and other laws they passed, the Nationalists added their own particular twist to the racist laws that already governed South African life.

What the white South Africans also very cleverly did was turn any argument about their white-only sport policy into a political question, accusing their enemies of introducing politics into sport. Even the young Donald Woods, who would later befriend Steve Biko and whose anti-apartheid activities forced him to flee South Africa dressed as a priest, upbraided protestors outside Lord's in 1960 for criticizing the visit of the South African cricket team. 'They are sportsmen not politicians', argued Woods. By his own admission, at that stage of his life Woods was a racist. In his student days he had argued that blacks should be kept segregated. Later, he was mortified when he heard that Jackie McGlew, the South African cricketer, had joined the Nationalists and even stood for Parliament for them. 'That,' he wrote, 'was the start of my disillusion with the doctrine of "keeping politics separate from sport" – a lunatic view in retrospect, since sport is a part of life, and all life is connected to politics.'

It helped white South Africans that their two most loved sports were rugby and cricket. Their proficiency in these was to prove crucial. Cricket and rugby were two classic British games whose reach beyond the British Commonwealth had always been very limited. Until the 1980s, there were only seven countries that played Test cricket – even now there are only ten. And until a decade ago, the major rugby countries numbered no more than about eight, four of which came from the British Isles and Ireland. Both sports were run in the traditional English style of management, by a club with a certain kind of English administrator in charge: old school, middle class, invariably white, with sporting and other ties with white South Africa. They were naturally prepared to excuse South Africa's uniquely white set-up – and even sympathize with it. What is more, English rugby saw the white South African version as a game played in the best traditions of sportsmanship.

The 1906 South African tourists were, for many in England, a wonderful illustration of the Coubertin principle that sporting contests can bring nations and races together. Of course, this did not mean whites and blacks, but the different white communities: English-speaking whites and the Afrikaners. This was of particular importance as the tour had come four years after the end of the Boer war, which had brought such misery on the Afrikaners and split the British. The *Manchester Guardian*, contrasting them favourably with the New Zealanders said, 'They have no system of tricks for execution when the referee was close at hand, and penalties against them for infringing the rules have been surprisingly few in number.' George Hartnett, manager of the Anglo-Welsh tour Down Under two years later, was to say the RFU 'should keep in touch with the South African players, who besides being amateur to the core, are genuine sportsmen who pay clean and honestly'.

Such a special affection developed that, even at the height of the sporting boycott of South Africa, rugby never cut its links. The Lions toured South Africa in 1974, four years after English cricket had ended official contacts, and again in 1980. It was during this Lions tour that, in their cell in Robben Island, Mandela, Steve Tshwete and others crowded round their radio sets listening to the commentary and, despite the anger of their Afrikaner guards, cheered the Lions on. There can be little doubt, as the sports historian Tony Collins has argued, that these tours added 'sporting and moral sustenance to the South Africa regime'. When, in 1992, South Africa returned to Twickenham, Mick Cleary in the *Observer* felt it was 'almost an apologia for the old South Africa'.

Not that cricket was that far behind in trying to make white

South Africa feel at home. This was best expressed by Jack Bailey, the long-serving secretary of the MCC, which at that time ran both the English and the international game. In his memoir, *Cricket Conflicts*, he describes how the MCC saw the moral position of playing cricket with white South Africa, in words that Formula One racing drivers and Bernie Ecclestone could have borrowed in relation to the Bahrain crisis:

> Moral issues were for individuals and these beliefs should be respected; but in those days retaining contact through the game, linked with an old-fashioned notion of not letting down those in South Africa who had contributed so much to the game internationally, were principles to which the majority adhered. It was understood that those who nourished cricket in South Africa were in the grip of a government whose laws were anathema to most who thought about it at all, and that included those who played and administered cricket there. They had fought side by side with England during the war. Now they needed our help and support. We should lend it to them.

Not that South Africa, despite being a founder-member of the Imperial Cricket Conference in 1909 along with England and Australia, did much to spread the game. In 1929 this produced one of the most extraordinary moments in international cricket: two MCC sides travelled out from England to the opposite ends of the globe playing Tests a day apart. On 10 January 1929, an MCC team led by Arthur Gilligan introduced Test cricket to New Zealand. A day later, on 11 January, another MCC team, led by the Hon. Freddie Calthorpe, played at the Kensington Oval, Barbados, bringing Test cricket to the Caribbean for the first time. The arrival of the West Indies as a Test nation, followed three years later by India, made the South Africans divide the cricket world by race. There was a white world where South Africa only played against England, Australia and New Zealand, and another world where all the nations barring South Africa played each other. Those who administered international cricket saw no problems with such a racial divide.

It is fascinating to contrast how white South Africa played the game of sports politics with the position Australia took. Australia's policy towards its darker races could be said to have been even crueller: it had just exterminated most of its original native inhabitants. And from the 1890s until well into the 1970s, it vigorously followed its White Australia policy. Not only were Asians kept out, but after the Second World War a £10 Pom policy meant white British people could emigrate by paying just £10. This white-only policy also built sporting bridges. Harold Larwood may have been the scourge of Australia during the Bodyline series and nearly caused a major rift in the empire, but in 1950 he took advantage of the policy to escape post-war poverty in Britain and re-settle in Australia. And in Australia he was welcomed with all the old hurt forgotten.

However, unlike South Africa, Australia recognized that sport could occasionally reach out beyond entrenched racial ideas. So it was prepared to make concessions to accommodate non-white cricketers. In 1897–8 when Ranji, Duleep's uncle, toured with A. E. Stoddart's England team, New South Wales waived the tax it levied on any coloured person entering the state to enable him to play. And Australia played the West Indies and India. Indeed, from the 1950s Australia would get its cricket teams to stop off in India on the way back from an England tour. This meant that, barring Bradman, the Indians saw almost all the great post-war Australian cricketers. In contrast, England sent B teams to India until 1976. In 1951, England created a dubious record of sending a side to India under Nigel Howard, who had never played a Test match. His first Test as captain also marked his debut as a Test player, and he played only four Tests for England, all as captain against India. For good measure he won one of the four Tests, did not lose any and this remains a remarkable record for a man with his lack of Test experience.

This resulted in an entire generation of Indians growing up

resenting England while much admiring Australian cricket. Their love for Australian cricket was further nourished in the 1950s and 1960s by oddities of the Indian broadcasting policy. In those days All India Radio, reflecting a certain puritanical zeal among the Indian leaders, did not broadcast Bollywood film songs. This gap was brilliantly exploited by Radio Ceylon, a sort of Indian sub-continental Radio Caroline. But in addition to songs, Radio Ceylon relayed cricket commentaries from the Australian Broadcasting Commission. Most Indian cricket followers were completely ignorant of Australia's treatment of the aborigines, or even its White Australia policy. What mattered was that, through Australian cricket, Indians felt part of a greater cricket world. It was an amazing illustration of the Coubertin idea of sport creating a bond between countries which, in every other way, could not have been more different.

In 1960, South Africa's decision to leave the Commonwealth should have led to its exclusion from cricket and rugby. But rugby's International Board responded by saying it took 'great pleasure to convey to South Africa the view shared by all member countries that the change would not make any difference whatever in regard to South Africa's position in Rugby'. At that stage, all member countries of the International Board were, of course, white and they saw no reason to pay any attention to political changes.

Cricket had non-white member countries – India, Pakistan, the West Indies – and their voices could not be silenced. The relevant ICC rule also stated: 'Test matches are matches played between sides duly selected by recognised Governing Bodies of cricket representing countries within the Commonwealth.' So South Africa should have lost its Test status. But when the ICC met on 20 July 1961, the issue was too late to be included on the agenda, although there was a long discussion between the members, who divided along racial lines. England, Australia and New Zealand were in favour of the proposal to change the ICC rule and let South Africa continue, but India, Pakistan and the West Indies, countries that South Africa had always shunned, were not surprisingly against. The issue was deferred for the next meeting. Wisden, the game's bible, interpreted this as:

> As the next meeting was not due to take place for a year this meant that the Test matches between South Africa and New Zealand in 1961–62 would be unofficial, though the three-day matches played would rank as first-class. MCC made it known that whatever happened they intended to continue playing South Africa both in South Africa and in England. It was also intimated that the tour of South Africa to Australia in 1963–64 would take place.

In the years that followed nothing changed. England, Australia and New Zealand behaved as if South Africa were still a member of the ICC. They argued they were 'building bridges'. It was to lead to Derek Wyatt, who played rugby for England, to ask, 'How long is this bridge?' In time, even New Zealand's Tests against South Africa, which had started off by being unofficial, became official. As Wisden put it, 'Later at the Imperial Cricket Conference at Lord's in July 1962 it was agreed that there was nothing to prevent matches played by South Africa being called Tests, though these were not recognised as official by the Conference.'

The close relationship between white cricket administrators both in England and South Africa was demonstrated during the D'Oliveira affair. The whole saga has generated much literature, including contributions from Basil D'Oliveira himself. I told the story in my book *Sporting Colours*. The best analysis, by Peter Oborne in *Basil D'Oliveira – Cricket and Conspiracy: the Untold Story*, lays bare the sporting and political machinations that preceded England's proposed tour of South Africa in the winter of 1968. These were conducted at the highest political level and involved South African Prime Minister Vorster and Sir Alec Douglas Home. Home, the only British prime minister to have played first-class cricket, was in 1968 the Conservative shadow foreign secretary and a major power in the cricket establishment. Besides Vorster and Home, cricket administrators in both countries, diplomats, businessmen, and a host of official and unofficial emissaries, conducted lengthy secret negotiations to preserve the tour from the terrible threat posed by the possible selection of Basil D'Oliveira for the England party. D'Oliveira was not only a nonwhite, but a South African non-white.

Classified under apartheid as a Cape Coloured, he had been denied the cricket opportunities that his brilliance as an all-rounder deserved. He had migrated to England, achieved great things in League and the first-class game, and earned a place in the England team. For months preceding the tour the D'Oliveira question much exercised minds: letters flew back and forth, Home met Vorster and South African cricket administrators journeyed to London to make sure D'Oliveira was not selected. This included spying on the English selectors to find out what was happening. The game they played was intricate. Vorster and the South Africans clearly did not want D'Oliveira to tour, but could not risk saying so. Instead, they wanted the MCC not to select him. English cricket officials wanted to maintain their cricket links and pretend that all that was happening was solely for cricket reasons. They were desperate not to give any hint that they were appeasing a foreign government's racial politics.

In the Ashes summer of 1968, D'Oliveira played in the first Test and was dropped. He was recalled for the last Test at the Oval with England still 1–0 down in the series. During this period the South Africans and the MCC had been conspiring about how they could keep him out of the tour. Oborne describes two initiatives which he calls attempts at 'bribery' by Vorster. D'Oliveira was offered huge sums to coach in South Africa and make himself unavailable for England's tour. At the Oval D'Oliveira scored 158 and, in a dramatic finish, took a vital wicket to help England win and thus draw the series. During his innings Tienne Oosthuizen – one of the men involved in the 'bribery' plan – telephoned the Oval saying he was speaking from Vorster's office. It was made clear that if D'Oliveira was picked, the tour was off.

After long deliberations the selectors decided D'Oliveira was just not good enough. But he was in the reserves. The decision astonished cricket lovers across the world and generated intense protest and media criticism, in which the selectors and the MCC were publicly accused of having political motives. Three weeks later, the all-rounder Tom Cartwright dropped out (ostensibly because of injury, but Cartwright was a man of principle and an anti-Establishment figure). D'Oliveira was chosen in his place and an outraged Vorster called the tour off.

'We are not prepared to accept a team thrust upon us by people whose interests are not the game but to gain certain political objectives which they do not even attempt to hide. The team as constituted now is not the team of the MCC but the team of the anti-apartheid movement, the team of SANROC and of Bishop Reeves [a prominent anti apartheid campaigner].' Vorster, having tried to conceal his motives, had now come out and done what he had always planned to do if D'Oliveira was selected. As Oborne says, 'the English cricket establishment had cheated and connived with South African apartheid'. The white South African cricket body, for all its protests that it had nothing to do with government, acted as the foreign sports arm of the Pretoria regime.

The crisis had an impact on English cricket, but this was largely structural. The MCC lost power and, as in other countries, a cricket board emerged – now called the England and Wales Cricket Board – to run the game. But English cricket did not ask itself this question: if sport had a higher moral purpose, as both Hughes and Coubertin had argued, how could this be squared with maintaining cricket links with white South Africa? Two years later, as if nothing had changed, the new authorities running English cricket planned to entertain South Africa's whites-only team in the English summer of 1970. It required intervention by the British Labour government to stop it. But during a Commons debate on sport, itself a remarkable event, the speeches of Conservative politicians such as Tory deputy leader Reginald Maudling made it evident that many felt any move to ban cricket with South Africa was unlawful. They trotted out the traditional bridge-building argument: show the whites in South Africa how we do it in this country and they will learn. The implication of Maudling's argument was that white South Africa was a legitimate, elected government and a cricket tour by the country a very lawful pursuit. Maudling (and other 'bridge-builders') never once considered how non-white South Africans viewed the white ruling regime. To them, it had no legitimacy at all: it was no better than the Nazis (who had also been elected). As for the higher moral values of sport, this just did not figure. There was, of course, great irony here. The organizers of cricket and rugby, the games that Tom Brown and his friends had argued so eloquently help make us better human beings, could not see the moral problem of playing with white South Africa. However, the sport organizations Coubertin had created or influenced, both the IOC and FIFA, took a very different position on South Africa's participation in international sport.

Football was the first to act. The game in Africa exemplified the Coubertin idea of sport providing a free trade between nations. One feature of colonial rule was to tell the colonized that they were not capable of ruling themselves. The British were masters at this and did it both in India and in Africa. The Indian and African way of dealing with this was very different, the Africans used sport, the Indians did not. The Indian response was to go back to their mythology and history. So Bal Gangadhar Tilak, who in a famous statement said 'freedom is my birthright' and was jailed by the British as a dangerous rebel, used the festival of the Hindu god Ganesh to get the masses behind his freedom campaign. Gandhi, in his campaign to rouse the Indians, spoke of recreating Ram Rajya, the perfect, mythical, reign of the Hindu god Rama.

But in Africa, Europeans had created nations that had never existed, binding tribes together to suit their purpose. In such a situation, to find common historical threads was difficult and football provided a ready medium to bring together those opposed to European colonial rule. These anti-colonial activists realized they were using a European sport, but it served their purpose. It helped them demonstrate that they were capable of organizing themselves and had the right to rule themselves.

An important instrument of this was the Confédération Africaine de Football (CAF) which was established in Khartoum in 1957 with four members: Egypt, Ethiopia, Sudan and South Africa. Although three of the four founding CAF members were former British colonies or, like Egypt, under British control, the CAF, as its name implied, was French-inspired, and was soon under the control of the former French colonies in Africa such as Cameroon. As more African countries became independent, they joined the CAF almost simultaneously with joining political organizations such as the Organization of African Unity and the United Nations. Many African rulers were soon taking an active interest in football, and this shaped the game on the continent. As independence led not to good governance, but often brutal, one-party, even one-man rule, the role of football became all the more important. One historian of African football has noted:

In Africa, where the activities of military dictators and self-imposed iron fist life presidents have stifled open political debate, the ordinary man's ideal self-expression emanates from the terraces [. . .] such is the power of football that, the world over, aspiring and actual rulers whether constitutionally elected, military dictators or civilian autocrats, have tended to exploit the game's influence on the populace in order to buy time for their moribund administrations. Governments tend to look upon the game as the public relations wing of the ruling class. Administrators are often appointed without the interests of the game at heart, but according to how sycophantic they are and to the extent that they can use the popularity of the game to further the interests of their rulers.

However, simply watching football could also provide a safety valve:

In the soccer crowd there was a refuge for political and nationalist leaders constantly in fear of government spies or arrest. Soccer, popular among both the labouring classes and the African elite, became an ideal tool with which to win mass support from the majority of the population. African political leaders were not slow to exploit soccer in this way.

South Africa did not remain a member of CAF for long, after refusing to send a mixed-race team to the first African Cup of Nations that the Sudanese proposed to host in their capital. And while Africa struggled to get even one place in the 1966 World Cup, leading the continent to boycott the competition, it did manage to keep South Africa out of FIFA.

South Africa had originally been suspended in January 1963. However, FIFA decided to send a commission to look at the situation on the ground. Before it arrived the white football body successfully created a new Indian Football Federation and a new Coloured Association, both of which sought affiliation with the white organization. By the time the two-man FIFA inquiry team had arrived, led by its president Sir Stanley Rous, the non-racial body was virtually defunct: it had lost grounds, supporters, and its secretary, George Singh, was a banned person. The Rous inquiry was ten days of hard feasting and cocktail parties during which the white body told Rous that the non-racial body was made up of 'political agitators' who could not decide what was best for South African football and that, as for non-Europeans, 'the very large majority [. . .] are uneducated and not fit to assume positions of authority in any sphere of life'.

Rous had had no problems in accepting the Coubertin idea that international sport furthered understanding between nations. Indeed the formation of CAF was made possible with his encouragement and, interestingly, in the teeth of opposition from the South Americans. They had used football to advertise their nationalism but now advised the Africans against this. But when it came to white South Africa he, like the people who ran rugby and cricket, felt they were ideal representatives of the true Corinthian spirit of sport.

Rous and his colleague McGuire were so impressed by what

the white sports administrators showed them that they 'unreservedly' recommended suspension be lifted and went on to condemn the non-racial body as destructive: 'We found that they desired to hinder and to act contrary to government policy which clearly indicates their inability to propagate the game of soccer in that country.' Vivian Granger, the manager of the white-sponsored National Football League, who had declared 'total war' on the non-racial soccer clubs, hailed this as a 'defeat for communism'. South Africans, he said, 'were obliged to practise apartheid in sport because it is the policy of the government and traditional, but we must ensure in future that it is Christian apartheid'.

The FIFA executive accepted Rous's judgement by 13 votes to five, with Rous denouncing the five as left wingers who were motivated by politics. But in Tokyo in 1964, the FIFA Congress overruled the executive. It did not help South Africa that FIFA had long had 'one nation, one vote', which prompted Dave Marais, president of the white soccer body to moan: 'The tragedy is that most of the important countries are sympathetic. But there is such a large block of African countries when it comes to one man, one vote, we don't have a chance of reversing the decision. I think there should be a qualifying vote. It is absurd for each little country to have the same voting power as countries like England or Italy.' He could almost have been reading the script Rous had written in the UEFA bulletin (Number 16 April 1961):

> Many people are convinced that it is unrealistic for example that a country like England, where the game started and was first organized, or that countries like Italy or France who have been pillars of FIFA and influential in its problems and world football affairs for so many years, should have no more than equal voting rights with many of the newly created countries of Africa or Asia.

Rous's views had been echoed by many in Europe. Historians of football have debated whether Rous was a racist. John Sugden and Alan Tomlinson call him 'naive'. This must be considered a very charitable view. Rous, an Englishman who liked taking cold baths in the morning, was, at best, a paternalist. Yet it is hard to see how he cannot, by any of the terms we now accept, be seen as a racist. He had grown up in an age when the supremacy of the white man was never questioned and could not see the world in any other light.

When Africans asked Rous if he would help keep South Africa out of FIFA his reply was, 'I can't promise you because I follow my country, the United Kingdom.' Rous felt he was expressing a politically neutral stance. But this was as political a statement as any: the expression 'follow my country' must mean following the political wishes of one's country. The UK's political establishment had always argued that South Africa had to be engaged, not isolated, and reinforced this view in the 1960s. Rous was clearly being political without wanting to acknowledge it. Indeed, many of Rous's statements on South Africa revealed this clearly.

In January 1968, when the CAF met in Addis Ababa, Rous told delegates: 'I have noted that you attach undue importance to the SANROC (South African Non Racial Olympic Committee). In fact, you should take no notice of their letter [. . .] I know these peoples. I've been in South Africa to meet them [. . .] this group was more interested in Communist politics than in football.' This prompted the Kenyan delegate to make the following response:

In his declaration we saw the manifestation of old and dying colonialism. It is of no avail of him to say that the Football Association of South Africa has committed no crime because it is the government which is responsible of [sic] the apartheid policy. It is the government which controls the affairs of the FASA. We in Kenya wish to see that all means possible are used to bring about change in South Africa so that our brothers there may enjoy the freedom of sports we have.

As late as 1973 Rous was trying to bring South Africa back into world football and proposed a controversial postal ballot for a

South African multi-racial sports festival. This was condemned as a dubious vote by SANROC. The Soviet Union was against and so was the African federation. His attempt proved a failure. Rous would later claim he was misled and argued that, 'this gesture was made as an experiment to overcome apartheid in sport'.

Rous either did not understand or did not wish to understand how the white South Africans were using sport as a political and social tool. In order to keep on playing world football, the white body had proposed to enter a black-only team for the 1966 World Cup in England, but a white-only team for the 1970 tournament in Mexico. This black–white alternation was to carry on every four years. However, even more bizarre were white South Africa's proposals for Olympic sports. Here, in the organization shaped by Coubertin, the country had been under constant pressure since the 1960s.

South Africa had taken part in the 1960 Olympics, but after that its future in the movement was under considerable scrutiny, even though Africa, as such, had little clout at the IOC. It had only two IOC members, both of them white and both called Reg. Reg Honey was from South Africa and Reg Alexander from Kenya. The problem for both Reges was that the Olympic charter outlawed racial discrimination. Interestingly, there was no such provision in the International Amateur Athletics Federation. When asked about South Africa, the IAAF chief, the British running legend Harold Abrahams, said, 'I do not believe South Africa is in danger of being expelled. What would such a move achieve? The Olympic body forbids the practice of segregation, the IAAF does not.' (This episode did not figure in the heroic film portrayal of Abrahams in *Chariots Of Fire*.) In 1966, when the IAAF met in Budapest, it rejected banning South Africa, the vote heavily influenced by the voting structure. The 37 white member associations had 244 votes and the 99 non-white ones only 195. A similar system in the International Tennis Federation also helped South Africa.

The IOC could not ignore the nature of South African sport. White South Africa had enough friends in the Olympic movement who were always pleading for it be given just one more chance to change. But IOC pressure did make the South African sports bodies put forward proposals that they thought were ground-breaking, but actually became more and more ridiculous. For white South African sport officials, merit selections were a night-mare. This may be the essence of sport, but it meant racial mixing. In 1962 the white Amateur Athletic Union had sent what was described as a team selected on merit to compete in Mozambique. The team, however, did not include black runners, although two black athletes had run their heats faster than their white competi-tors. When Matt Mare, head of the white athletics union, was asked why Henry Khosi, whose time was 0.1 second faster than the white man selected, was not chosen he uttered the immortal line, '0.1 second does not really count.'

About this time, merit selection for South African sportsmen wanting to compete in the 1964 Olympic Games, necessary to avoid the IOC's threatened ban on South Africa, produced an even more bizarre response from the white administrators. The white South African Olympic Games Association proposed that blacks of merit would be selected for their Olympic team but not in direct competition with whites, as such competition would go against government policy. But what if separate trials produced the same results? The white body had a wonderful answer for this: tests would be carried out in medical laboratories to deter-mine which athlete was better.

> By the use of objective tests of physiological and psychological capacity we hope to help with the final assessment of material available for selection in 1964 [. . .] Thus should a situation arise in which two sportsmen of like ability vie for the final place avail-able in our athletics or cycling team, this laboratory will be able to recommend which of the two performers should be selected.

In 1963, so-called multi-racial teams did leave South Africa to compete abroad. One was an amateur boxing team. Five whites and three non-whites were chosen. However the whites left on one aeroplane, the non-whites on another. The South African press was not allowed to photograph them together and since government ministers had said often enough that non-whites could not qualify for the Springbok colours, none of the boxers was awarded them. Once they left South Africa, however, they did live together.

All this ensured that for all the sympathy white South Africa had within the IOC, it could not be allowed to continue in the movement. South Africa was not invited to the 1964 Tokyo Olympics, the first it had missed since it started participating in 1908. Like FIFA, the IOC had struck a major blow against white South Africa. But the decision was reached tortuously after several meetings and innumerable last chances. It demonstrated how tenaciously South Africa could fight to maintain its international sporting position and the sympathy it still commanded. But while South African athletes did not participate in an Olympics until after Nelson Mandela was released, Reg Honey remained an IOC member. The absurdity of this has been well portrayed by Dick Pound in his Olympic memoirs:

He was not expelled at the time South Africa was, based on the philosophy that IOC members were not delegates of their country to the IOC, but rather, were representatives of the IOC to the country. He was constantly urging the IOC to take another look at South Africa. I remember, at the 1980 IOC session in Moscow some ten years after the expulsion of South Africa, he was trying to attract the attention of Lord Killanin [the IOC president], who made every effort not to notice him and was about to close the meeting. I was clearly in Killanin's line of vision and raised my hand. 'Mr Pound,' he said. 'Mr President,' I said, 'I think Mr Honey is trying to attract your attention.' He was then stuck and had to give the floor to Honey, who made his request once again to no avail.

Back in 1961, as non-white South Africa began to organize against apartheid sport, Honey had gone to a meeting in Johannesburg and proposed what he saw as a great concession. The non-white bodies would be accepted as part of the then white-only National Olympic Committee if they allowed a white man to represent them. 'I say, you must accept. It will at least give your candidates an opportunity [. . .] the non-European should give in even if he only has a foot in the door.' For whites to compete against non-whites on the sporting field was, he argued, 'an ideal state of affairs'. It happened in the US but was the 'perfect state of affairs', impossible in South Africa.

By 1980, the argument of the whites had changed and as international pressure grew, white sports administrators, proclaiming their opposition to apartheid, would blame it all on the Nationalist government. The government, in turn, would say as it often did – taking expensive advertisements in Western papers for this purpose – that there were no laws relating to sport, that sports bodies were autonomous and that they liked to organize along separate lines as per the traditions and customs of South Africa. The hypocrisy involved was transparent but the doublespeak was useful at times in fooling gullible outsiders.

The only sport where whites did not have to work hard to fool the world was rugby. They knew the great rugby world supported them as demonstrated by the views of John Reason, the legendary rugby correspondent of the *Daily Telegraph*. Writing in *Rugby News* in December 1985, he had said that, 'any study of the world shows that not only is nationalism (i.e. racialism) here to stay, but anyone who is Not [sic] racialist is a pervert [. . .] I am not a pervert [. . .] When it comes to Us versus Them, South Africa are Us.'

The sport, as Serge Saulnier, the coach of the first French rugby team to tour South Africa in 1958, described it, was for Afrikaners a 'religion with temples, high priests and the faithful'. The Afrikaner love for rugby had echoes of the language Tom Brown had used to convince Arthur of the values of cricket. As the historians Robert Archer and Antoine Bouillon put it:

Rugby is a collective sport of combat, which values physical endurance, strength and rapidity [. . .] these qualities lent themselves
peculiarly well to appropriation by a social elite with aristocratic
ideals, who were able, in the 19th century, to transform rugby
(like boxing) into a school of moral discipline for future leaders
[. . .] It is a sport ideally suited to 'ideological investment' and
people conquering barbarism recognised an image of their own
ideology in its symbols.

For the Afrikaners there was something mystical about the sport
as John Morgan discovered on the 1969 Lions tour when he went
to see Northern Transvaal, probably the most conservative area of
white South Africa, play the Lions:

I had travelled to the match with a crowd of farmers from a small
town called Brits, few of them able to speak English, all of them
convinced they were kind to their workers [. . .] all believing their
workers loved them [. . .] And until ten minutes from the end
of the match this astonishingly kindly false view of themselves
endured. At which point the British Lions team took the lead. In
thirty years of watching rugby I have never known any experience
comparable to the chilling transformation of spirit amongst that
multitude. The silence was that of a people witnessing a tragedy
rather than the normal disappointment of a home crowd. When
the game was lost and over, the crowd did not cheer or groan.
Without a word or a sound of any kind, they shuffled out into
the dusk and away back to the farm lands and their enchanted
dreams and unspoken fears.

Mandela may not have played rugby, but Steve Tshwete had.
Indeed, he had organized rugby on Robben Island. Unlike many
of his supporters, Mandela instinctively understood that if he
wanted to reach out to Afrikaners, he could not confront them on
rugby and its past, even present, sins, but had to cater to the Boer
love of the game. So, unlike cricket, where the unified body

abandoned the name Springbok and became the Proteas, rugby was allowed to keep the springbok symbol, despite its racist origins and the fact that it was seen as a hateful symbol by most non-whites. And even as Mandela struggled to create his rainbow nation, he always made sure he and his supporters paid due homage to this unique Afrikaner religion.

So in January 1993, Walter Sisulu, leading an ANC delegation, met members of the International Rugby Board and said the ANC was 'elated' to support the IRB's decision to award the 1995 World Cup to South Africa. This is despite the fact that it was by no means clear the rainbow nation would be born. Indeed, four months after Sisulu had expressed his joy about the World Cup coming to the country, Chris Hani, after Mandela the most charismatic ANC leader and seen as his successor, was assassinated by a Polish immigrant and member of the far right Afrikaner Weerstandsbeweging (AWB). This provoked immediate fears of a race war. Many were convinced this could not be prevented by the ANC's rugby 'charm offensive'.

Yet within a year, Mandela was being sworn in as president after the first one-man-one-vote election in the country's history. During this process he and Steve Tshwete argued against many of their ANC colleagues and continued to use rugby to entice the Afrikaners into supporting the new settlement in South Africa. As John Carlin puts it in *Playing the Enemy*, 'Mandela understood that rugby was the opium of apartheid, the drug that dulled white South Africa to what their politicians were doing. It might well be useful to have on hand a drug that could anaesthetize white South African minds to the pain of losing their power and privilege.'

Mandela continued to use the rugby drug even after he had won power and with brilliant effect during the 1995 World Cup. Just before the competition started he met the South African captain François Pienaar, visited the South Africa team before their first match against the reigning champions Australia, and told the players, 'You now have the opportunity of serving South

Africa and uniting the people [. . .] Just remember, all of us, black and white, are behind you.'

He had Pienar's mobile number and he would often ring him to show that the first black president was very interested in this special religion of the Afrikaners. On the day of the final he famously wore the green Springbok jersey with Pienaar's number 9 on it and a green Springbok cap. Thus attired, he took the field to meet the players before the final. The largely white and Afrikaner crowd erupted, shouting Mandela's name. It showed how well Mandela understood the importance of the sporting symbols.

Carlin writes:

> The symbolism at play was mind-boggling. For decades Mandela had stood for everything white South Africa most feared; the Springbok jersey had been the symbol, for even longer, for everything black South Africa most hated. Now suddenly before the eyes of the whole of South Africa, and much of the world, the two negative symbols had merged to create a new one that was positive, constructive, and good. Mandela had wrought transformation, becoming the embodiment not of hate and fear, but of generosity and love.

For Brendan Venter, a member of the team, this made Mandela a special person. As he told me: 'Why Mandela is special is because of his ability to forgive. In jail for twenty-seven years he could not have had a worse life but he is not bitter. That is something I can admire.' The Afrikaner joy was complete when at the end of the match, with South Africa the victors, Mandela presented the trophy to Pienaar, still wearing his Springbok colours.

Kobie Coetsee, the Nationalist minister of justice, who years earlier had initiated the talks with Mandela in jail that opened the door to the ending of apartheid, watched the match in a bar in Cape Town. As he saw Mandela and Pienaar together he wept, telling Carlin: 'It went beyond everything else that had been accomplished. It was the moment my people, his adversaries, embraced Mandela. It was a moment comparable I felt then to the creation of the American nation. It was Mandela's greatest achievement.'

Perhaps Coetsee went a bit over the top. Certainly, *Invictus*, the subsequent movie made about this World Cup, invented scenes that just did not take place. It showed Pienaar throwing a bottle of beer in the dressing room after an early South African defeat, the sort of thing Pienaar would never do, as Venter, his teammate, confirmed to me. The whole thing had come together more by chance and it was not quite as planned and orchestrated as the movie depicted. However, it did demonstrate accurately how Mandela appreciated the importance of sport to white South Africans and used it to build a new nation, which many had thought impossible. That new nation would require more than sport. But sport, Mandela knew, could go a long way.

And in so doing Mandela was taking the ideas Hughes and Coubertin had first advanced in the closing years of the nineteenth century and putting a twentieth century spin on them. Both men would have understood what he was attempting. They would have found it much more difficult to comprehend many others who, over the same period, were putting an entirely new construction on their sports. So much so that many of them did not even acknowledge that there was such a thing as the spirit of sport.

PART 4

THE LOSS OF INNOCENCE

CHAPTER 11

THE CHEFS WHO CHANGED
THE SPORTING MENU

In September 2009, as Max Mosley was preparing to leave the Presidency of the Fédération Internationale de l'Automobile, the Paris-based organization that runs motor sport, he likened Formula One to a restaurant. 'It may have been very run down. We got this very good chef in. He is now making money and doing very well.'

The chef he was talking about was Bernie Ecclestone. The image makes him seem warm and cosy, especially since Mosley was his close associate – the maitre d' who helped him run the restaurant. Many reject the image as flattering and false. A month later, just after Mosley had stepped down amidst much controversy about his private life and management of Formula One, Richard Williams, a seasoned observer of the sport, wrote that Mosley and Ecclestone 'will leave behind a sport stripped of its integrity, its old values replaced by superficial prosperity that can no longer conceal a putrescent core'.

But however Ecclestone and Mosley are finally judged, Mosley's words resonate beyond Formula One. During the late 1960s and 1970s many sports acquired some of the most unlikely chefs, whose new concoctions radically changed sport and our perception of it. These chefs operated in sports as diverse as snooker, golf, tennis and cricket, and ranged from a Yale law graduate who also had a degree in French to a British chartered accountant and Australia's richest man. Their skills were just as diverse and had to take into account how the different sports were organized. But by the time they had served up their dishes, their sporting restaurants had indeed been transformed.

Bernie Ecclestone was the most remarkable chef of them all. He was the great pioneer of making a business out of a sport, but unlike most of his contemporaries who came into sports with the same motives, he paid no homage whatsoever to the higher ethics of sport as enunciated by Thomas Hughes. He made it clear he saw sport purely as a way of making money, not as an inspiration for morality. In the process he also reversed the long-established pattern of the British creating sport and then letting the foreigners take over. In Formula One, he took over a sport which had been much more the creation of the Continent, French and Italians in particular, and moved its centre decisively to Britain. In recent years, many of Formula One's most decisive meetings have been held at the Excelsior Hotel in Heathrow as foreigners fly in from round the world to consult the British master chef. It helped that Formula One, as a sport, came into being only in the 1950s and was a poorly organized weekend recreation, regulated in a shambolic way. However, Ecclestone, in taking over the sport, showed what a determined individual could do, and the money he made easily dwarfs anything any of the other sporting chefs managed.

Ecclestone came to motor sport as a fan. Born to a fisherman in Suffolk in 1930 – his family moved to Dartford, near London, a year before war came – he not only grew up in the Depression, but had to overcome the fact that he was virtually blind in his right eye, as his mother discovered after a medical examination soon after his second birthday. As he grew older he realized he would also always remain short, although this gave him a Napoleonic outlook on life, as he declared: 'Short people have to fight a lot. Small people have to fight to survive. I learned to fight the battles I had a good chance of winning, or I'd run.' Encouraged by his father, Sidney, he began to tinker with cars, engines and bikes from a very early age and took to heart Sidney's advice: 'Never waste, but always buy the best you can afford.' In his youth, his highest ambition lay in motorbikes and as a 17-year-old he even sold a 2500cc Excelsior Manxman to Jack Surtees, the pre-war British motorbike champion. It was through bikes that he moved into the second hand car business, first persuading a car dealer in Bexleyheath to let him trade his bikes on his forecourt, then taking over his car business. At this time, motor sport was developing, although it was far from the menu of Formula One that Bernie created years later.

Cars racing each other was not new; they started from almost the first invention of the automobile. France led the way with the first race, if it can be called that – a two-kilometre ride from Neuilly Bridge to the Bois de Boulogne. Held on 28 April 1887, it was won by Georges Bouton of the De Dion–Bouton Company on a stream quadricycle. It helped that he was the only one competing. The second race, in 1894, was a more substantial affair and is generally regarded as the world's first motor car race, a 79-mile reliability run from Paris to Rouen. Such was the demand for this race that there was an elimination where 69 cars participated in a 31-mile race. After that, 25 were chosen for the main race.

An international competition, between nations rather than individuals, began with the Gordon Bennett Cup in auto racing. From the beginning the sport was seen as a useful marketing tool, and these early races were promoted by newspapers, the two-kilometre run from Neuilly Bridge to the Bois de Boulogne by the chief editor of the Paris cycling publication *Le Vélocipède*, Monsieur Fossier. The Paris to Rouen race was the idea of *Le Petit Journal*, which offered £200 in prize money, and the Gordon Bennett race was originated by the *New York Herald*. Such car racing extended far and wide. In 1905, there was even the Delhi to Bombay race, authorized by the then viceroy Lord Curzon. The year 1908 saw the longest automobile race in history: New York to Paris, 22,000 miles in 169 days, won by the American Thomas Flyer driven by George Schuster. The route went from New York to Seattle, north to Alaska, across the frozen Bering Straits to Russia, to Vladivostok and Moscow, and to Berlin and Paris.

As we have seen, the 1930s saw sport both grow and diversify almost despite the Depression. In motor sport high-priced road cars turned into pure racers, as Delage, Auto Union, Mercedes-Benz, Delahaye, and Bugatti constructed streamlined vehicles with engines producing up to 450 kW (612 hp), aided by multiple-stage supercharging.

By then, cars imitating horses and racing round a circuit had begun and provided the first glimmer of what has become modern motor racing. Appropriately, the first motor car track in the world was a converted horserace track, the Milwaukee Mile, which had started sometime in 1876, before becoming a car race circuit in 1903. Four years later, Britain had its first race track, Brooklands in Surrey, with high-speed banked corners. The First World War helped racing, as Vickers set up a factory and aerodrome there, but the Second World War saw the racing circuit closed, and war-time damage meant it never reopened.

But that war did provide collateral benefit for racing, as the Goodwood example illustrates. The immediate post-war years were to see motor racing at a place more famous for horseracing. The grandfather of the present Lord March was a keen driver, fond of all things mechanical and, in the eyes of the aficionado, the motor racing that he revived after the war was racing at its most glamorous and dangerous. The revival came about because of a quite accidental legacy from the war. The Ministry of Defence had requisitioned some of the land at Goodwood estates for a Battle of Britain aerodrome, and built a perimeter track around it. After the war, according to the present Lord March, his grand-father 'realized it would make a great race track. In 1948, it was the first motor racing track to open after the war. Stirling Moss had his very first race here in 1948, which he won, and his very last race in 1962 here, when he had his huge accident and never raced again.' The track closed in 1966 because, says Lord March, 'My grandfather went off it. He didn't like wings on Formula One cars, saw quite a lot of his friends hurt and felt he'd done it for long enough.'

The current Lord March, who came back to live in Goodwood in 1992, decided to bring his grandfather's race track out of mothballs, reviving motor racing as a piece of theatre. March persuaded the owners of cars to come and 'show the car off', promising them 'a great environment. The first thing is people want to look at the cars, they want to get up close, they want to talk to drivers and they want to see this wonderful stuff. We promise them a great party, a fabulous time, a great weekend where everybody, hopefully, goes away happy.'

Lord March accepts that his revival of motor racing was motivated by a desire for the estate to generate cash, part of a varied sporting business that extends through motor sport and horseracing to golf, and brings him an income of £50 million a year. However, he also sees his revival of motor racing 'in the whole amateur country house sport tradition, people doing it because they love doing it. Cricket, horseracing, motor racing too, were all started in this fashion by amateur members of the family. They had a house party at Goodwood so they all played cricket, or they raced.'

March's ancestors encouraged the growth of horseracing, getting horses to race on top of the Downs with other members of the Sussex Militia or with the king's horses. This led to the Goodwood flat racing festival. And in 1702, Goodwood hosted its first cricket match, which in 1727 led to the earliest written rules of the game (which made it clear that they did not apply to Goodwood's owner, the Duke of Richmond). Many of these activities were gambling-related, a feature in the development of sport at that time.

The introduction of post-war motor racing was in the same Goodwood tradition. As described by the present Lord March,

Motor racing was run by teams who loved motor racing for their own pleasure. And they were racers. They didn't really mind how it was presented to the public or what it looked like on television. They just wanted to win. In the old days, when Stirling was driving here, he would have driven six races in an afternoon, been paid £25 and gone out for the evening with some girls and thought life was brilliant. Now they drive once every two weeks, they get paid a million quid every time they step in the car and it is very different.

The difference Lord March is talking about is not only the pursuit of money by the drivers, but the pretty naked pursuit of money by the organizers of the sport. Given that this was the one sport which, even at birth, was hardly touched by the philosophy attributed to Thomas Arnold, this may seem a harsh view. What really transformed the sport was the staggering weight of money which started to come into it. It was Ecclestone who made the difference, although it took him almost 20 years before he graduated from an enthusiast to Mosley's supreme motor racing chef, without whose culinary skills there could be no Formula One restaurant chain. During this long journey, which mainly involved complicated manoeuvres and business deals that outfoxed his opponents, he had the odd success on the track. In April 1951, Ecclestone won the junior Brands Hatch championship in a Cooper MK 5/JAP driving at 62.3 miles an hour. But he was turned off the sport, for a time at least, after the 1958 Moroccan Grand Prix in Casablanca, in which his friend Stuart Lewis-Evans, for whom he also acted as manager, died of burns.

By then, Ecclestone was already the biggest car dealer in Bexleyheath, and had acquired a reputation as a man not to be crossed. As his biographer Bower records, when a buyer discovered the car he had bought did not have a heater and complained, Ecclestone said, 'Are you calling me a liar? You want to be careful, boy. I've had fingers cut off.' His business methods attracted judicial censure. After he had been pursued by the Inland Revenue over tax arrears, a judge ruled that he had broken company law, although Ecclestone insisted that he had always acted on legal advice and been unfairly treated. The judgement came at a crucial time for Ecclestone. The events the judge was hearing had taken place a decade earlier, but the judgement in 1971 came the year Ecclestone really entered Formula One by buying Brabham, a team created in 1960 by two Australians, the driver Jack Brabham and the designer Ron Tauranac. The previous year, Ecclestone had become manager of the German driver Jochen Rindt, who also became a great friend. As he negotiated to buy Brabham, Rindt was killed at Monza driving a Brabham car. Ecclestone mourned his friend, but in making the deal showed his sharpness as a businessman. He bought a company which had been valued at £130,000 by Tauranac for £10,000.

Ecclestone quickly realized that this was a sport ready to be taken over. Unlike many other sports, such as cricket, Olympics, football and rugby, motor racing did not come with an encrusted layer of high-sounding principles or talk of being a pathway to a superior way of life. The only pathway that mattered was money and he went about making it for the sport, and for himself, in an extraordinary manner. By this time, despite the fact that an F1 World Championship had been going for 20 years, the sport had no real organization to run it. Indeed, in a sense there was no proper championship that all teams entered.

Until the mid 1970s, Formula One specification cars were by no means confined to the races that formed part of the F1 World Championship. There were often as many as eight non-championship races. Many of the top teams and drivers would enter a variety of non-championship F1 races such as the popular Race of Champions at Brands Hatch. The likes of James Hunt, Gilles Villeneuve and Keke Rosberg all won this race, the last of which was held in 1983. This was also the last time there was a non-championship F1 race.

The requirement to attend all championship races came in 1981, a decade after Ecclestone had entered Formula One. By then, much had changed, not least the TV revenue that teams began to receive. This ensured that the benefit of attending championship races far outweighed that of attending non-championship races. The costs of competing were also rising, which meant the cost of entering a non-championship made it unattractive.

By the time Ecclestone became an owner, British individual teams still dominated the sport as they had done through the 1960s. In 1970, for example, just four of the regularly entered cars were not made in Britain. However, there was a big divide between Britain and the Continent, a case of Continental car manufacturers backing motor sport as opposed to British individualism. British motor racing was still dominated by motor enthusiasts or mechanics, men Enzo Ferrari had dubbed 'garagistes'. Ranged against them were European teams like Ferrari, owned by Fiat.

At the time, each team negotiated with the organizers of races independently over how much starting money they would receive, as they had done since well before the formation of the F1 World Championship in 1950. Starting money was one of three main sources of income for most teams, the other two being money from suppliers for promoting their parts, and prize money. But this was never more than $10,000 in total.

Teams were under so much pressure from the circuits that they were required to negotiate their terms in secret and could not compare notes with other teams. This meant that smaller and newer teams lost out, receiving far less starting money than established teams such as Ferrari. While this created problems for private teams without the backing of a car manufacturer, race organizers justified it on the grounds that they were following the market. Larger teams like Ferrari attracted more paying members of the public to the circuits, generating greater revenue for the race organisers. Individual negotiations often led to disputes and Ferrari even missed the first F1 World Championship race at Silverstone in 1950 over just such a dispute. The Ferrari team believed they were worth more than the organizers of the race were willing to offer. Such was the power of the circuits that in the early 1970s, teams were getting $10,000 per race, when circuits were earning more than 10 times that.

There had been some attempt at organizing the Formula One

teams. In 1963, the Formula One Constructors' Association (F1CA) had been formed by Colin Chapman, to enable British teams to transport their cars jointly to the races. But it was Bernie's arrival that transformed the situation. Soon after buying Brabham, Ecclestone made the first of his radical proposals. At a meeting in Heathrow's Excelsior Hotel he suggested to F1CA that they negotiate collectively with the eleven circuits: eight in Europe and the rest in South Africa and America. Gathered round were Max Mosley, owner of the newly created March racing team, Frank Williams, Ken Tyrell, Colin Chapman and Teddy Mayer. They did not require much convincing. Their value together was far more. If none of them was to turn up for a race, the organizers would be left with fewer than 10 cars to take part, hardly an attractive proposition to sell to the race punters. Ecclestone's proposal was quickly agreed, although there was dispute about how much of a commission he wanted for this service. The recollection varies from 2 per cent, according to Colin Chapman, to 7 per cent according to Ecclestone's auditor, and there was even talk of 10 per cent. If this was the first of such disputes over an Ecclestone deal, it was also his first step to becoming the master chef of Formula One.

Before the end of 1971, Ecclestone was demonstrating his worth, getting improved terms and making sure the Argentinian Grand Prix, where the junta ruled, went ahead. The next year he organized a race in Rio de Janeiro, although it was not approved by the world body. By 1973, all 15 race circuits had signed agreements with F1CA. Argentina, South Africa and Brazil were paying $110,000 each, European circuits $56,000. Circuits round the world were soon reeling from the power Ecclestone wielded. For the 1974 season, he demanded $350,000 from circuits in the United States and Canada. Formula One was a big part of the Canadian sporting calendar, but the Canadians did not want to meet his demand. Ecclestone cancelled the race and although the Canadians agreed to pay, he would not relent. As a result, the 1975 Montreal race was not held, but after Ecclestone got his way and demonstrated his power it returned in 1976.

By this time, he had decided that motor sport and Formula One were his passport to riches and he could give up being a car dealer. There was less money to be made from the trade and the arrival of Value Added Tax had complicated matters. He announced he was retiring, declaring, 'I don't want to be a tax collector for the government. I'm going to travel around the world with Brabham cars.' If all this demonstrated Ecclestone's shrewdness, what lifted him on to an entirely different plane in the mid-1970s was his understanding of the power and economic value of television, long before most other people in sport. At that stage, Formula One was not regularly televised. Before 1978, the BBC had only covered the most important F1 races in the season, such as Monaco and the British Grand Prix. But one year, at Silverstone, when John Surtees's car displayed a Durex advertisement, the BBC cancelled the screening.

The idea of using television was not an Ecclestone original, but borrowed from Mark McCormack, the man who had originated the concept of the sports agent and who had arrived on the sporting scene a decade before Ecclestone. McCormack was born the same year, 1930, but he could not have been more different from Eccelstone and he epitomizes the very different nature of the American sporting landscape.

The American, who grew up in Chicago, was a distant relative of David Hume, the Scottish philosopher and historian, hence his middle name, Hume. A Yale law graduate, he also had a degree in French. Ecclestone thrived on things being hazy so he could manipulate the situation to his advantage. As he once told Mosley, 'Your problem is, you always want things absolutely clear, and sometimes it is better if things are not clear.' In contrast, the lawyer McCormack was a glutton for precise details. He noted things down on yellow legal pads. So, for instance, he was able to tell the journalist Stephen Aris that in one year he had slept for 2,621 hours, and that running on the spot his left foot hit the floor 147,001 times. By the time he met Ecclestone he could also claim to have changed the nature of sport, moving it far away from any lingering influence of Thomas Hughes.

He had achieved this in Atlanta in November 1958. Arnold Palmer was playing in the Carling Golf Tournament. McCormack had taken to golf because he had injured his hand in a car accident when nine years old and the doctor advised that golf would be better for him than American football, which was his first love. McCormack had met Palmer before and now he persuaded him to sign up with the sports management business that he had set up alongside his law practice. He promised Palmer between $350 and $500 for exhibition matches. Palmer, impressed, suggested McCormack become his manager and the two men shook hands in what is often described as the most celebrated sports handshake, leading to the birth of a new industry: modern professional sports business management.

Compared to what sportsmen had earned before, golfers, at least in America, were doing quite well. By 1958, total prize money in America had gone over $1 million and Palmer was earning $59,000. Palmer's earnings were not out of line with Babe Ruth's earnings of over a million dollars between 1915 and 1935. But in that period the player whose name could be exploited as a commodity for money had not yet been discovered. Ruth, for instance, earned nothing from a candy bar named after him.

Before McCormack, Palmer earned relatively little from off-course activities. He had a contract with the Wilson sports goods company, for which he was paid $6,500, and he could charge for exhibition matches, the fees for which never exceeded $1,000. But he did get free shoes and slacks and his wife got free underwear. McCormack's first task was to get around the Wilson contract, which had not changed since it was first signed in November 1954, and Palmer's other contracts. As a result, within two years Palmer was earning half a million dollars. Jack Nicklaus and Gary Player were also signed up. McCormack would later confess that when Nicklaus, then an amateur, asked him how much he would earn if he went professional, McCormack estimated he would make $69,000 plus prize money. In Nicklaus's first year as a pro he actually made $200,000.

In 1970, Nicklaus left to set up his own outfit, the Golden Bear organization, called after his affectionate nickname. His golf business grew, reflecting both Nicklaus's rise as the game's greatest player and the growing worldwide appeal of the game. By 2008, Nicklaus Design, as the enterprise was now known, had taken golf into new dimensions with Nicklaus designing golf courses for Vladimir Putin and Roman Abramovich, and in Thailand and China. The empire, now run by his children, was worth $300 million and, in addition to offering Nicklaus's golf expertise, it sold golf equipment, clothing and operated golf academies.

While all this was in the future, by the early 1980s McCormack had reason to be happy with how Arnold Palmer Enterprises had developed. Some time in that period, McCormack had estimated that Palmer's off-course earnings were between $7 million and $10 million. By then, this wholly private company, jointly owned by Palmer and McCormack, had hotels and other properties in several American states, aviation charters, was leasing businesses, ran a big car dealership in the United States and also had dry cleaning and insurance businesses.

By then, McCormack had also moved into another sport. It was very like golf in that individual players pitted their skills against each other, and its central organization was almost non-existent. That sport was tennis. McCormack had timed his arrival in tennis just right, as it was evolving to its present status where it is run through a loose alliance between the players, tournaments and the International Tennis Federation. This is perhaps the most remarkable structure of any world game, although it did not come about without a lot of strife and pain. In essence, tennis had evolved to a point where the players were the effective masters, with the ATP and the WTA, the men's and women's circuit, running most of the tournaments apart from the Grand Slams. The four Grand Slams are so much their own masters that although there is a Grand Slam committee, this has no powers. It is more of a sounding board where those who run the four Grand Slams meet, exchange ideas and, in a sense, act as an insurance against too many demands by players, agents or the media. The main purpose of the committee is to stop players or their agents playing one Grand Slam off against another.

In 1968, when McCormack came on the scene, no one could have predicted how tennis would change, given the curious world it inhabited. It was still wedded to its 'no professionalism please, we only play for the love of the game' stance and watched helplessly as every year it lost its best male players to a professional circuit. This was the era of the Jack Kramer circus of top-flight exhibition matches. Kramer, the son of a Las Vegas railway worker, had won Wimbledon just after the war. Then he turned promoter and every year poached the Wimbledon champion. The moment a player won, there was Kramer luring him away. Lew Hoad, the great Australian, won Wimbledon in 1956 and 1957, and joined Kramer after his second triumph. In 1957, as an amateur, he barely got £50 for winning a tournament. Tournament play did not mean staying in luxury hotels. Hoad and other players were often put up with a family, although manufacturers keen to advertise their products might offer the odd bit of money, generally under the counter. Kramer offered Hoad $100,000 to sign, plus a bonus of $25,000 every time he won a tournament.

Turning professional ensured that the entire tennis world shunned Hoad and he was thrown out of every club in Australia as well as Wimbledon. The sport's failure to accept commercial reality meant that almost an entire generation of the most gifted tennis players in history never really fulfilled their promise, because they could no longer go on playing in the major tournaments of the world. Such was the animosity Kramer generated that four years after the open era had started, and players like Hoad had returned to Wimbledon, the past could not be forgotten. Donald Dell tells the story of an incident in London's Westbury hotel where he was staying with Kramer. It was 1973 and, due to a dispute, the top players were boycotting Wimbledon. Dell was approached by an old lady who asked him if he was Jack Kramer.

When he replied no and pointed out Kramer, the lady started hitting Kramer over the shoulder with her umbrella, saying, 'How could you do this to Wimbledon?'

Unlike golf, which had no proper international structure, tennis had an international structure that was almost as old as that of football or cricket, but its powers were very limited. Set up on 1 March 1913 by Charles Barde, Honorary Secretary of the Swiss Tennis Association, and Henri Wallet of the French Tennis Federation (the third man involved, Duane Williams, died on board the Titanic before he could realize his idea), the International Lawn Tennis Federation carried a strong French flavour. The official language was French and the Federation was run from Paris – the headquarters were moved to London during the Second World War. Its control over the sport was minimal. Until 1979 it did not even control the Davis Cup, which since its start in 1900 had been run by a Committee of Davis Cup Nations.

The birth of the Davis Cup demonstrated how fragmented international tennis was and how it had basically just grown through the enterprise of individuals. The Davis Cup came about in 1899, when four members of the Harvard University tennis team sought a match between the USA and Great Britain. Dwight Davis, one of the four, designed the tournament format and even bought a trophy with his own money. While the first tournament in 1900 was called the International Lawn Tennis Challenge, it was soon renamed the Davis Cup. Over the years it attracted other nations but it was only in 1972 that the Challenge Round was abolished. Until then the reigning champion got a bye directly into the final.

All this left tennis a game ripe for McCormack to exploit and in 1968, as he started working for Wimbledon, he wasted little time in imposing his personality on the sport. But unlike Ecclestone, who had to barge into Formula One, McCormack was introduced to Wimbledon in the classic way. Buzzer Hadingham, who chaired Wimbledon through much of the 1980s, but was at the time chairman of Slazenger, was very influential and pushed McCormack's name forward. There was some suspicion among committee members about McCormack's ruthlessness and possible conflicts of interest. The American already controlled a great many tennis players and was involved in advising a number of tournaments. Wimbledon already used an agent, Bagenal Harvey – the man who, back in the 1950s, had identified the cricketer Denis Compton with Brylcreem and they tried to encourage a certain amount of tension between McCormack and Harvey, but in the end, McCormack emerged as the only commercial player at Wimbledon. Having started with negotiating television rights, he was soon negotiating everything.

Television paid peanuts. In 1957, the BBC paid Wimbledon £5,000 a year. In 1960, Eurovision, representing the whole of Europe, paid £1,500. In his 26 years at the helm at Wimbledon, Chris Gorringe, who retired as chief executive in 2009, saw Wimbledon's income grow 'exponentially'. In 1973, when Gorringe joined Wimbledon, five years after McCormack had begun to work for the club, the surplus was £58,000; in 2010 the surplus was £31 million. Gorringe is convinced that McCormack:

> played a fundamental role in that growth and we owe him a great deal. He seemed to know all the right people and was a wonderful networker, whether with the heads of multi-million-pound companies, or sports stars [. . .] The connections that he had were very important and useful to us and he was a great negotiator. We were always very glad to have him on our team rather than on the other side of the fence. I remember going to a Eurovision meeting in Paris where he really tore strips off one person because they were offering what he thought was a derisory amount. It was not particularly nice to watch, but it was interesting to see him at work when confronting the other side in a negotiation. His face would puff up and he would snarl across the table 'How can you offer such a paltry amount for Wimbledon when you're paying this for a vastly inferior event? Get real.' Whether he had actually lost his temper or deliberately

worked himself up to that state, I do not know, but he seemed to take it as a personal affront.

This was a traditional sport learning how to make money and enjoying the thrill of it.

Over the years, McCormack would reshape Wimbledon and in 1982 Sunday play was introduced. Gorringe admits they had been reluctant, worried what the local community or the churches might feel. McCormack persuaded them by pointing out that this would earn an additional £400,000 from television. It was a McCormack initiative getting Wimbledon to market its products in Japan, which also forced the All England Club to change the title of the man who ran its organization. Gorringe found that on travelling to Japan and presenting his card, which described him as secretary, the image-conscious Japanese were puzzled. Wimbledon decided to change his title to chief executive, which the Japanese instantly understood.

Wimbledon did not always accept everything that McCormack suggested. He proposed Wimbledon stage Viennese horseriding, concerts, boxing matches and bicycle racing on Centre Court. There was the odd Barbra Streisand concert, but the other ideas were discarded as the committee felt the grass needed to be protected. Wimbledon's great claim is that it went down the commercialism road without discarding too many traditions apart from changes to the way it organized drinks parties. When Gorringe first started at Wimbledon, as McCormack was settling in as the commercial overlord, the first Monday would see a 12:15 p.m. cocktail party in the large garden adjacent to the old Number One Court. He recalls:

Umpires and officials were plied with G&Ts and sherry before going out to officiate over matches that afternoon . . . the tradition came to a halt some time after Mrs Dorothy Cavis-Brown fell asleep while acting as linesperson on one of the tramlines on Court 3. Abe Segal, playing at the time, could not understand why she had not called to signal the ball was out until he looked around and found that she had nodded off on the job. So soundly was she asleep that the South African Segal was forced to go over and tap her on the shoulder to waken her.

After that, the umpire's cocktails were shifted to an evening slot.

By 1975, McCormack had stamped his personality on both golf and tennis and was looking for other sports to exploit. He met Ecclestone during that year's Brazilian Grand Prix. It is not clear if this was the occasion when McCormack had asked for a meeting with João Havelange and been turned down by the Brazilian. Having missed out on the leader of world football, the American described to Ecclestone how he had organized the sale of tennis rights to broadcasters and combined that with making tennis a place where corporate bodies could organize hospitality. McCormack also acted for Jackie Stewart and Graham Hill and was keen to forge a partnership with Ecclestone. The Englishman declined the offer, but listened carefully to his ideas, particularly those for exploiting television and making more of the commercial potential of Formula One. However, while McCormack acted as an agent and took a fee of anything up to 30 per cent, Ecclestone would be different. He would not market other people's rights, but become the owner of the rights himself.

To do that, Ecclestone inserted clauses in contracts with the circuit owners whereby they gave their television rights to FOCA, as F1CA was then called. The circuit owners clearly did not understand the value of these rights. They were more concerned with the demands being made for the race fees on behalf of the teams. By 1976 this had gone up to $300,000 per race. Ecclestone had cleverly turned the negotiations with the circuit owners on their head. In the past, they had always insisted on negotiating separately with each car manufacturer. Ecclestone made sure the manufacturers presented a united front, but met each track owner individually. They could not combine and in the end he settled for $275,000 per circuit. Television was something else again.

Ecclestone could not have imagined the growth of television, although in the mid-1970s he was not alone in beginning to realize the importance of the medium for sport and the money to be made from it. In 1975, a year before Ecclestone inserted a television clause in these contracts, the Australian Kerry Packer's Channel Nine television network had worked out that televising sport was one sure way of getting audiences and selling advertising. In 1975, the marketing analysis carried out by Packer's network had concluded that to attract viewers it needed exclusive sports coverage. Packer would successfully bid for rugby league, Wimbledon, French and US Open tennis, and even had a go at getting the 1980 Moscow Olympics. He failed, which was just as well since Australia did not participate. But cricket was his great love and Packer wrote to the Australian Cricket Board for the exclusive rights to the 1975–76 West Indies tour of Australia. The board's response was to sell non-exclusive rights to the Australian Broadcasting Corporation, their long-standing partner.

Cricket Australia had always distrusted television. Back in 1956, when the Australians were about to tour England, the board turned down an MCC request that the Australians practising at Lord's be filmed. The Australian board's reason was that this would stop people coming to matches. When Sir William Beecher, head of the Associated-Rediffusion commercial television company, wrote to the Australian board asking for rights to film and televise the 1958–9 England tour of Australia, he was told, 'nothing could be done at the present time'.

In September 1956, the Australian board had a presentation from Channel 9 about televising Sheffield Shield cricket. The channel had begun to televise the Davis Cup and thought they could do a very good job with cricket. Not only was this rejected, but so alarmed was the board that it lobbied the Australian Postmaster General to have a new clause written into the broadcasting and television bill, then being debated in the Australian Parliament. This clause read:

The Australian Broadcasting Commission, or the holder of a license for a commercial television station, shall not televise, either directly, or by means of any recording, film, or other material device or otherwise, the whole or a part of a sporting event or other entertainment held in Australia, after the commencement of this section, in a place to which a charge is made for admission, if the images of the sporting event or other entertainment originate from the use of equipment outside that place.

As a historian of Australian cricket, Chris Harte, has pointed out, 'the clause gave the board total power of the televising, or not, of cricket in Australia. Their incompetence and misuse of this act twenty years hence would prove catastrophic.'

Packer kept courting the board and 20 years later, just as Ecclestone was inserting the television clauses in the track contracts, he came back with an offer of $2.5 million to televise cricket exclusively for the next five years, including half a million dollars for the 1976–7 series against Pakistan and Sheffield Shield cricket. The board again turned him down, sticking with ABC and still with a non-exclusive contract. Packer left the room saying, 'Well. Damn, I don't know why we don't put on our own cricket Tests.'

He did, in the end, organize his World Series cricket, but in the process he had to go against the cricket establishment. The boards took him to court and while they could not stop his World Series, the Packer wars split cricket. At one stage even General Zia, then martial law administrator of Pakistan, got involved. In Pakistan, the head of state is also the patron of the Cricket Board but he does not normally play selector. However, one consequence of the Packer wars was that in the winter of 1977, Zia very nearly became the chief Test selector, deciding, in the middle of a home Test series with England, whether Pakistani players who had signed with Packer could play for their country. The Packer players had flown in to play. However, it soon became clear that if they did the England players might strike. In the end the Packer rebels were kept out.

The whole Packer saga would leave a mark on cricket, leading to dramatic changes and considerably shaping its future. A game where players in white played with a red ball became, as critics labelled it, the pyjama game, where cricketers in all sorts of coloured uniforms played with a white ball. Night cricket came in and the game, based on five-day Test cricket, acquired a more instant form of limited over cricket. But unlike Ecclestone, who reshaped Formula One even more dramatically, Packer in acting as cricket's new chef had to set up his own restaurant and take the rebel route.

One reason for this was that as a team game cricket employed players under contract. For cricketers to play for someone else meant breaking employment contracts. In the mid-1970s, cricket was ruled by England and Australia and Packer could do nothing to divide them. Indeed, when Packer signed the then England captain, the South African-born Tony Greig, England immediately sacked him as captain, the English press treated him as a pariah and the English authorities took Packer to court, albeit unsuccessfully. Cricket, a game that had also always cherished its high moral principles, saw Packer as someone who was essentially immoral. So, when Tony Greig was asked to justify what he was doing, he uttered the immortal lines that his actions were meant to help the living standards of the cricketer. This became known as bettering the conditions of the Glamorgan No. 10, Glamorgan then being the least successful of English counties. Greig, sounding like a politician on the stump, said,

> The plight of modern cricketers is not the best in the world and I am talking about lots of cricketers. There are lots of cricketers living on the breadline with mortgages and having to travel 12,000 miles for a coaching job in the winter, and some have to leave families behind to do this. A young man coming into sport today would be a bit silly to choose cricket.

He then uttered the sentence that would have made no sense to young Tom Brown, or his friend Arthur. 'Those prepared to give up their lives for the game should be rewarded accordingly and something may well arise from this situation and will ultimately benefit all cricketers.' But just to underline how well he too could aspire to a higher morality, and that he understood the political game he was now playing, Greig went on to say that, to better the lot of his fellow downtrodden cricketers, he was willing to sacrifice his England captaincy. Surely no sacrifice could be greater?

There was another interesting morality play also at work here. One of the players Packer was keen on was Michael Holding, who had just emerged and was to prove one of the game's great fast bowlers. However, the Jamaican Holding would not sign until it was approved by his prime minister, Michael Manley. Jamaica was keen on the sporting boycott of South Africa and, when Greig approached him, Holding told him that he would not play with white South Africans. In the end, there was an interesting, messy compromise, showing how well sporting morality could stretch. Some South Africans already played in English county cricket alongside West Indians. These players were accepted as colleagues by Holding in Packer's World Series Cricket, but not players such as the South Africa Graeme Pollock who did not play in the English game.

Greig became so much of a pariah that in July 1978, almost a year later, he found his daughter Samantha was not invited to children's birthday parties because of who her father was. Some commentators did recognize that cricket had become 'just a job'. But others, like the lyricist and cricket fanatic Tim Rice, felt that Greig was being 'clandestine' just for money and offered to find him a role in his musical *Jesus Christ Superstar* to augment his wages. For many in the game Greig's position as captain meant he had to aspire to a higher morality, one that Arthur would recognize. As Jim Swanton, the doyen of the old school of commentators, declared, Greig had a position that carried responsibility. He could not sacrifice that for filthy lucre.

Ecclestone, in contrast, had no such scruples, moral or other-wise, to worry about. He was heading a group of entrepreneurs whose business was racing cars. They could always threaten to take their trade elsewhere. There was, however, one similarity between cricket and Formula One. If England and Australia were central to cricket, Ferrari had always been at the centre of Formula One. Indeed, it has been said that without Ferrari there could be no Formula One. Ecclestone realized this and made sure he was on the right side of Ferrari. So, on 16 February 1977, coincidentally just as in another part of the world Packer was making his plans to sign a whole host of rebel cricketers, Ecclestone flew to Maranello to meet Enzo Ferrari for the very first time.

Despite the language problems – Ecclestone had no Italian, Ferrari no English – the two men understood the power of Formula One and the power of money. Ferrari chided Ecclestone for talking too much about money. Max Mosley, who was there, later recalled the advice; Ferrari told Ecclestone, 'after all, if you're going to run a brothel, you wouldn't put up a sign saying Brothel. You would put up a sign saying Hotel and run a brothel in the basement.' It is worth noting that Enzo Ferrari was not making a moral point as Packer's opponents had made. Ferrari's point was a presentational one.

Having made his bond with Ferrari, Ecclestone turned to the body that claimed to control motor sport. In strict terms, the sup-posedly regulatory body for Formula One was a subcommittee of the FIA, FISA (Fédération Internationale du Sport Automobile). The British had always believed the French organization was biased against British teams and grumbled about it, although its control was minimal. From the early days of international motor sport, the organizers of an event would typically be of the nation-ality of the country where the event was being held. It was quite common for the organizers to be far more favourable to local rather than foreign teams and drivers. The complexity of even quite simple motor sport regulations made it quite easy to use the interpretation of rules to favour teams and drivers without actually going against the letter of the law. Jim Clark, F1 World Champion in 1963 and 1965, noted in reference to his attempted entry into the Le Mans 24-hour race in 1962, 'As someone discovers every year, the organizers at Le Mans have rules of their own and stick to them. If they don't want a car, which has been officially entered, to start in their race, they make jolly sure it doesn't.' Colin Chapman, the boss of Lotus, vowed never to enter the Le Mans 24-hour race again when, one year, his Lotus team modified the car to suit the scrutinizers, and was told that something else was now not acceptable.

It did not take long for Ecclestone to realize that motor sport had nothing like a formal regulatory structure with a central body as cricket or many other sports had. Its regulatory body was porous and he was dealing with men of straw he could easily overcome. This gave Ecclestone the sort of freedom Packer could never even have imagined. His first meeting in 1975 with the authorities running motor sport illustrated this. With Pierre Ugueux, a retired Belgian civil servant, representing the French organization, the meeting was held on the Englishman's turf, at the Excelsior Hotel. Ecclestone was soon in his element – with Britain then in the middle of the IRA bombing campaign, a fire alarm made the participants fear an IRA device. With 'characteristic sangfroid', says his biographer Tom Bower, Ecclestone persuaded everyone to go to the rear not the front, as he felt the bomb was more likely to go off in the front of the hotel.

There was a second meeting in Brussels in November 1975, and that is where Ecclestone showed the sort of power that Packer could never wield. Packer, with his money, could take established players away from the game. In June 1976, when he met the men of the Australian board, a frustrated Packer could say, 'Come on now, we are all harlots. I know you haven't signed your contracts [with ABC]. What's your price?' But Packer could not stop the established game, whereas Ecclestone could stop his entire sport on a whim. As he told the Belgian at this meeting, 'Where's your cash? We won't race, and then you'll have no Formula One.' Those words, in essence, summed up Ecclestone's power and he ruthlessly used it. At one stage during a meeting, Ecclestone even turned off the lights and proudly declared that he was not afraid of the dark. The meeting ended with a victory for him, the first of many.

Ecclestone's most celebrated battles with the French regulatory body involved the Frenchman Jean-Marie Balestre. Balestre was first the president of FISA from 1978, and then in 1985 took over the presidency of the FIA, getting elected on the promise that he would curb Ecclestone's power if not squash it. He was to be so thoroughly outwitted by the Englishman that in the end he even lost the presidency to Ecclestone's nominee, Mosley.

The war was essentially a battle over whether Ecclestone or Balestre controlled Formula One races. It had many dramatic moments, including the one in June 1980 at the Jarama race circuit in Spain. FIA officials were confronted by local police armed with guns and removed from the circuit with Ecclestone claiming FOCA, not the FIA, had the right to sanction the race there. At a tumultuous meeting with Balestre, Ecclestone got Mosley to upset the table, which sent Balestre's papers crashing to the floor. Ecclestone pocketed a copy of a list of 12 countries supporting the French president, which proved very useful information.

In February 1981, during the South African race in Kyalami, which the FIA had not sanctioned, Ecclestone and Mosley had an extraordinary phone call with Balestre. Ecclestone pretended to be the South African operator and Mosley was Nelson Mandela ringing from his prison cell. In this phony call, Mosley as Mandela invited Balestre to visit when in South Africa. The Frenchman was flummoxed and could not work out how he could visit Mandela, then held in Robben Island under very strict rules. Ecclestone was clearly playing a practical joke, part of the war he had designed to rattle his adversary.

The war continued for over a year before it was finally settled on 11 March 1981, with what came to be known as the Concorde agreement, over breakfast at the Hotel de Crillon on the Place de la Concorde. The agreement confirmed Ecclestone's position in Formula One. The regulatory body could not sanction a Grand Prix unless it was on the terms that Ecclestone had negotiated with the circuits. For this he received 8 per cent of the gross fee. Balestre's organization retained the right to make and enforce technical rules. But what really mattered to Ecclestone was that FOCA had all of Formula One's television rights for four years.

The following year Ecclestone set up FOCA TV and a two-year deal was negotiated with the European Broadcasting Union, which spoke for 92 television broadcasters, including the BBC. His next move was to make sure that Max Mosley moved into the FIA. Balestre was persuaded to take Mosley on. This English partnership was to prove crucial to Ecclestone becoming the master chef of the sport. Back in 1980, when Mosley introduced Ecclestone to his aunt Deborah (the Duchess of Devonshire), his mother Diana had asked, 'Did Max produce Bernie out of a pouch?' It caused much amusement in the Mosley family and was one illustration of how very different these two Englishmen were.

Mosley was the son of Britain's Fascist leader Oswald Mosley. A flamboyant womanizer who had started with the Tories, then moved to Labour before forming his own Fascist party, Oswald was fond of saying, 'Vote Labour, sleep Tory', on the grounds that Tories had the better-looking women. For Max, who qualified as a barrister and had harboured his own political ambitions, his life-long struggle was this: can the son of the wartime British Fascist leader ever be detached from his father's name? Mosley was to be all the more convinced he could not escape his father's shadow when, in March 2008, the *News of the World* filmed revelations about sado-masochistic sessions he had with prostitutes. For the tabloid paper this was news and it devoted seven pages to it, alleging the hookers were dressed in Nazi uniforms and had mocked Holocaust victims. Mosley successfully sued the paper, winning £60,000 in damages for breach of his privacy.

Eighteen months later, when I met him in his house in London, Mosley was convinced that it was because he was his father's son that the *News of the World* characterized his sex sessions as having a Nazi element.

> It was a gift to them. It was probably not family viewing, but there wasn't any Nazism there. It was just nonsense [. . .] Again and again, you have this feeling, it's an awful thing to say, but that you are being discriminated against. You see it is a little bit like the situation 50 years ago for the black man. When he does not get something he should have done, he does not know for sure whether it is because he is black. There is always this feeling that it is actually that, but you have to be careful not to get paranoid about it. Nowadays it is not acceptable to discriminate against anybody because of their religion, their race, their ethnicity, because they are handicapped in some way. But it is perfectly permissible to discriminate because of what their father did.

Then, looking across over his gardens, he said quietly, 'I just accept that.' In contrast, he was to find that, in motor sports, the name Mosley more often meant the coach builder Alf Mosley, rather than Oswald. 'Formula One is a separate world, nothing to do with my father. You are judged on your merits.'

The burden he carried in Britain was also a reason why he would eventually decide to live in France, where he felt more comfortable. 'In France they had the real thing. They had the Wehrmacht. And so they have got to understand these things and put it behind them, otherwise the country would be divided for ever. Whereas in England it is much more theoretical; people can afford the luxury.'

The bond between Mosley and Ecclestone was to be emphasized in the summer of 2009. In, of all places, Biggin Hill, a Battle of Britain landmark, Ecclestone showed off the Lancia Asturia open-topped stretch limousine, which drove Hitler and Mussolini through Rome in 1938 as they signed their infamous 'Pact of Steel'.

Propped up against a car were photographs commemorating the two dictators' agreement. Then, in an interview with *The Times*, Ecclestone named Hitler as his favourite dictator saying, 'He was, in the way that he could command a lot of people, able to get things done.' But while many felt this was outrageous, Mosley was ready to forgive and forget. He only saw a politically naive person who had made comments he did not understand.

But Mosley and Ecclestone were far from naive in understanding how to take charge of the FIA, and Mosley soon persuaded Balestre to appoint Ecclestone head of promotions for all of motor sport. The title meant little to Ecclestone, since he was only interested in promoting Formula One and taking it to places where it had never been before. There was talk of having a race in Moscow, but in the end it was Hungary, in 1986, that became the first communist country to host Formula One. Ecclestone's power to reach out to politicians had been demonstrated the year before when he moved the Australian Grand Prix from Melbourne to Adelaide. This followed a meeting with the premier of South Australia, John Bannon, over lunch at the Star club in Chessington. The event proved a spectacular success.

In 1987 there was a second Concorde agreement which gave the FIA 30 per cent of all the EBU payment, while Ecclestone and the teams received the remainder. In reality this meant that the FIA's actual income was no more than $1 million. The break-up of the 70 per cent spoils between Ecclestone and the rest of the teams gave Ecclestone 23 per cent and the teams 47 per cent. But, as his biographer Tom Bower has chronicled, things changed decisively when Ecclestone proposed another amendment to the contract. He suggested that the teams transfer the management of their commercial rights from the Formula One Constructors' Association, the loose group that had no legal basis and dated back to the days of Colin Chapman, to a properly set up legal entity: Formula One Promotions Administration. More significantly, FOPA was a company that Ecclestone owned. Broadcasters still signed with FOCA, but there were back to back contracts with

Ecclestone's company. All the teams agreed with the exception of Frank Williams, Ron Dennis and Ken Tyrrell. In the end, even they gave in.

None of the teams was privy to the television contracts, leading to much debate about how much Ecclestone earned. One estimate was that between 1992 and 1995 he made $341 million from television. In contrast, the FIA received $37 million. Bower says, 'In reality, after 1992, Ecclestone was taking 73 per cent of the television income and the 12 teams divided the remaining 27 per cent. McLaren received 2 per cent.' Ecclestone's argument for taking the lion's share was that he was taking the risk; the teams were not.

A further Concorde agreement was signed in 1990, commencing in 1992, and was even more favourable to Ecclestone. The FIA was believed to have lost $65 million as a result of this deal from television rights. With the deal secured, Ecclestone was ready to challenge Balestre directly by making Mosley his candidate for the Presidency of the FIA. Mosley might have given up hope of becoming a politician like his father, but he had inherited sharp political skills and, on 9 October 1991, after a shrewd campaign, he secured the election with 43 votes against 29. That year also saw Flavio Briatore come into Formula One, taking charge of the Benetton team with much help from Ecclestone. The two would become great friends, and 16 years later they even jointly owned a football club, Queen's Park Rangers. But Mosley was always less enamoured with Briatore. This would have consequences for the sport later.

Formula One had now become an industry, not quite as dominant as the car industry, but still significant. Adam Parr, the Oxfordshire-based Williams F1 chairman, has estimated that the motor sport industry is worth more than £500 million to the county's economy and is responsible for approximately 4,000 engineering jobs. These assets are clustered in central England, dubbed 'Motor sport Valley'. Bower quotes estimates ever higher: 2,000 companies employing 20,000 people and generating revenues of $6 billion, most of them located in the south in an arc from Southampton to Norfolk. The difference between the two figures, while considerable, turns on how the industry is defined. But however it is defined, what cannot be denied is that, thanks to Ecclestone, the sport was no longer a bit of weekend fun for car enthusiasts.

Ecclestone could point to the fact that he had made the drivers multi-millionaires, a sharp contrast to the early days of the sport. In the 1950s and earlier, the drivers had not earned much, with only the very top drivers paid at all. And even then, those driving for the major motor manufacturers were the ones who were handsomely paid. In 1956, for instance, Stirling Moss was paid £500 (£10,000 in today's money) per F1 championship race and £300 (£6,000) for each non-championship F1 race, along with 60 per cent of prize money, giving a total for the year of at least £6,500 (£130,000) from F1 races alone. By the late 1970s, drivers' salaries had gone up considerably. In 1979 Jody Scheckter was paid $600,000 ($2.7 million) to drive for Ferrari.

The next decade saw a further rise. In 1993, the year before he died, Ayrton Senna was paid $1 million ($1.6 million) per race for the first six races and a further figure of between $5 and $15 million ($8–24 million) for the remaining 10 races. Michael Schumacher was rumoured to have been paid at least $20 million per year from 1996 at Ferrari. But it was Kimi Räikkönen who was widely seen as the highest paid F1 driver, with rumoured earnings as much as $60 million per year.

Such lavish income was, of course, confined to the top of the sport. Those nearer the back end of the grid have always earned much less and in many cases paid for their drives. And before earning any money in Formula One most drivers have to fund expensive entries into other racing series. The most prominent, just below Formula One on the motor sport ladder, is GP2, where drivers often have to find £1 million to pay for a single season. Drivers find the money from sponsors, family businesses and the lucky ones get on to driver development programmes. Formula One teams fund these programmes in the hope of grooming successful stars of the future. The sport has long accepted this money divide between drivers, with those who fund themselves being called 'pay drivers'. The term is often associated with drivers who are not as talented but some pay drivers have gone on to have great success. The classic case is Niki Lauda, who started his career in Formula One with the March team in 1971 as a pay driver. Despite failing to score a point in his one appearance in 1971, or the complete season in 1972, he went on to win the World Championship three times with Ferrari and McLaren. By 1980 he was in such demand that Ecclestone's Brabham tried and failed to lure him with an offer of $2 million ($9 million) for one year.

The increased money for drivers recognized the power of the sport and its growing popularity not just with race goers, but also politicians. In 1993, Ron Walker, an Australian businessman and treasurer of the country's most conservative party, persuaded Ecclestone to return to Melbourne. The local Victoria government backed the move and Walker saw this as part of his dream to make Melbourne the sports capital of the world. Despite local misgivings, when Formula One returned in 1995, the race attracted over 300,000 spectators who spent an estimated US $150 million. Walker became a great Ecclestone fan and proposed to John Major that he be knighted. He also worked hard to make him leader of London's bid for the 2012 Olympics. He succeeded in neither mission, but maintained an unshaken faith in Ecclestone as a man who could understand the business power of sport and take it where it had never been.

Ecclestone, as ever, chased the money and, a few months after the season had drawn to a close in Melbourne, he moved the British television deal from BBC to ITV. The BBC were paying £7 million; ITV had offered a five-year deal from 1997 worth £65 million. Formula One was not the only sport making money from television, for many other sports about this time had also discovered the medium and begun to milk it. The major difference was the role of Ecclestone. Unlike McCormack and others he was not an agent for his chosen sport but claimed to be its owner. This set Formula One apart from all other sports. It did not have to mouth the high-flown rhetoric that other sports indulged in. However, the way it had developed meant that, for Ecclestone's friend Max, now running the regulatory body, it posed a problem. Mosley says:

> The question was who owns it? Was it Bernie or was it us at the FIA? I always said Formula One is like a restaurant. It may have been very run down. We got this very good chef in. He is now making a lot of money and doing very well. Bernie for twenty years had built up the business. The restaurant belongs to us. Bernie said, 'No, I am the big chef, I can go down the road and open a restaurant in another place. All the customers would come to me.' In other sports like football, cricket and rugby they developed the rights themselves and there was no dispute as to who owned them. We actually went to leading counsel, a very senior commercial silk, to discuss the ownership of Formula One.

The advice Mosley got was that a legal battle with Ecclestone would prove futile and that the FIA might not have been able to claim ownership of Formula One.

Mosley thought that one way out for the FIA, which could give it a hold on the ownership, was to offer Ecclestone the television rights for 15 years. For this, the FIA would receive $9 million a year. Ecclestone could continue to negotiate his own television deals.

> Bernie was less than happy because he still says we sold him his own business. It was, he argued, never our business. The business from Bernie's point of view belongs entirely to him. So how could we charge him for the television rights? The arguable case from our point of view was he couldn't have done it without us. But without him there wouldn't be anything to do.

Mosley's justification for the 1995 deal with Bernie was that it finally gave the FIA a contract with Ecclestone. 'Till then we in the FIA had no contract with Bernie. We had a contract with teams and the teams had a contract with Bernie. We had no authority over Bernie at all. He was within the FIA, but representing the teams. In our 1995 deal with Bernie we said, "You can continue to do what you are doing and pay us a very modest amount, 7 million euros, but at the end of 15 years, that is in 2010, all the rights come back to us." After 15 years we will then be rich. It was a very sensible deal.'

Not everyone agreed and there was much muttering that, in 1996, Ecclestone earned $103 million from television while the FIA had traded a 30 per cent share, which would have been worth $67 million, to get just $9 million. Frank Williams, Ron Dennis and Ken Tyrrell all voiced their concerns, but in the end they toed the line. As Williams acknowledged, the sport had sold its basic control over its own television rights to Ecclestone back in the 1970s and it was too late now. (Ecclestone clearly felt he could make even more from television and in 1996 launched F1 Digital+, a pay-per-view service to allow viewers to see all practice sessions, qualifying and races. The take-up of this service was below expectations, and although a large initial investment had been made to support the editing capabilities required, the service was cancelled at the end of 2002.)

If the 1995 deal was wonderful for Ecclestone, five years later he got an even better one. It was negotiated at a time when the sport appeared to be destabilized. Ecclestone himself played no small part in the turbulence of the sport with talk of floating his company and then making rapid changes to its structure. The intervention of the European Commission also played a part in creating uncertainty. This 'mother of all deals', signed in May 2000, saw Ecclestone's family trust fund, Bambino Holdings, get a 100-year leasehold on television rights by paying $360 million. This gave Ecclestone's company, Formula One Management (FOM), the sole right to negotiate television deals with broadcasters. Three years earlier, in 1997, Sky had done a four-year deal with the Premier League worth £743 million, £185 million a year. The Formula One deal cost Ecclestone just $3.6 million each year.

Mosley, again, had no problems arguing that this was also a very good deal for the sport.

> We found ourselves in 1998/99 with Bernie saying 'Can I have another ten years and I will pay you a lot of money? I can do an IPO.' Then the European Commission got involved and said the existing deal of 15 years is already far too long. Another ten years is out of the question. That is when we had the idea of doing a deal for 99 years, analogous to what the Duke of Westminster had done. Once upon a time he owned many fields. He said, 'Build a house on my fields and I shall charge you peppercorn rent. After 99 years the house belongs to me.' That is the basis of the Westminster fortune. We could have sold our interest lock, stock and barrel, then we would have lost control. We told the commission it is virtually the same as selling the freehold; how about that? To the astonishment of the Brussels lawyers they said 'Yes' and that's how the hundred years came about.

Mosley, understandably, is compressing history and also underplaying his own role in getting the European Commission to change its mind. It showed how curiously politics and sports business worked. In 1998 Ecclestone had cancelled the Belgian Grand Prix in Spa-Francorchamps following a ban on tobacco sponsorship of Formula One by the Belgian government. It would only return, he said, if the ban was lifted. The Belgians, with great reluctance, agreed.

Karel van Miert, a Flemish Belgian politician, who was vice chairman of the European Commission and in charge of competition policy, was evidently furious. He launched an investigation into Formula One. Even if van Miert's motive was no more than resentment against what Ecclestone had done, the commission's lawyers put forward what seemed a formidable case. Formula One Holdings, Ecclestone's company, they argued, was 'abusing its dominant position to favour Formula One' and the 15 year agreement was 'excessive' as the commission felt any agreement over five years constituted 'a serious infringement of EU competition rules'. The commission's lawyers were certain Ecclestone could not float his company and would have to change the way he operated.

However, by the time Mosley came up with the 100-year deal, things had changed dramatically. In March 1999, van Miert and all the commissioners had to resign following allegations of financial wrongdoing. Van Miert's successor, Mario Monti, was a fan of Formula One, having watched his first race at Monza as a nine-year-old. Mosley worked on him and did a deal with him in January 2000 which saw the commission leave Ecclestone and Formula One alone. Mosley was so happy with the new deal that he says,

> If we could have done the same with World Rally Championship Sports Cars we would. But we could not because there was no Bernie building it up. Maybe we should have stayed with our 1995 deal and we would get the rights back in 2010. But nobody knew in 2000, when we did the deal, whether Formula One would still be a success in 2010. And in 2010 there would have been nothing to stop Bernie walking down the road and starting his own Formula One restaurant chain. Bernie could have done it very effectively. There was nothing we could have done to stop him. Here we had a bird in the hand, $300 million, which was paid as a lump sum. And on top of that we got a few million a year. We were able to set up a foundation. Bernie was not happy. He still says it was his business and his view was supported by legal counsel.

Whether Ecclestone would have gone down the road and set up his own Formula One chain is hard to say, but between 1996 and 2000 he made an almost bewildering series of changes to his business. As we have seen, when the Concorde Agreement ended in 1987, Ecclestone ceased to own a team and set up FOPA to manage TV rights for the teams. FOPA would later become known as Formula One Management (FOM).

In 1996, Ecclestone transferred his ownership of Formula One businesses to his then wife, Slavica, to prevent her having to pay inheritance taxes on his death (due to her Croatian nationality). However, to further guarantee his inheritance SLEC Holdings was created as the holding company of the Formula One companies with the idea of floating it on the stock market some time in 1997. The profits from the flotation would go into a family trust free from government interference. This idea received a blow, partly because it was leaked in the press.. In March 1997, when the *Sunday Times* reported that Ecclestone was floating his company at a valuation of £2.5 billion, the figure, as much as the idea of the flotation, shocked the sport. It fuelled jealousy about the money Ecclestone was making. The leak came at the worst possible time and, with growing anxiety about who actually owned Formula One, Ecclestone abandoned plans to go to the market. Instead, he began to look for buyers.

In a few months between the end of October 1999 and early 2000, there were a series of rapid changes. In October 1999, Morgan Grenfell Private Equity (MGPE) acquired 12.5 per cent of SLEC for £234 million. In February 2000 Hellman and Friedman purchased a 37.5 per cent share of SLEC for £625 million and combined its share with that of MGPE to form Speed Investments, which thus had a combined holding of 50 per cent of SLEC. On 22 March 2000 the German media company EM.TV & Merchandising purchased Speed Investments, providing Ecclestone around £2 billion.

But this proved far from a clever move by EM.TV. When it announced that its 2000 earnings would be below expectations and it was struggling with its debts, the share price dropped 90 per cent. This opened the door for the Kirch Group, which agreed to rescue EM.TV, taking a stake in the company and control of Speed Investments. In late March 2001 Kirch was required to purchase another 25 per cent of SLEC for approximately £600 million as a result of an agreement made between EM.TV and Ecclestone before EM.TV's difficulties began. To do that Kirch borrowed €1.6 billion from three banks: €1 billion from Bayerische Landesbank, the rest from Lehman Brothers and J P Morgan Chase. But just as EM.TV had taken on more than it could manage, so too had Kirch. Its financial troubles meant receivership in 2002. The banks broke up the group, but Bayerische Landesbank, J P Morgan Chase and Lehman Brothers retained Kirch's share of SLEC through Speed Investments.

Initially, relations between the banks and Ecclestone were far from cordial. Through a series of board changes Ecclestone had put Bambino Holdings in control of his companies. In mid-November 2004, the three banks sued Ecclestone for more control over the sport. On 6 December 2004, Justice Andrew Park ruled that 'In [his] judgement it is clear that Speed's contentions are correct and [he] should therefore make the declarations which it requests.' Ecclestone refused to accept that this meant he had lost control and said he would appeal. Not long afterwards Gerhard Gribkowsky, a board member of Bayerische Landesbank, for whom he was also the chief risk officer, and the chairman of SLEC, stated that the banks had no intention of removing Ecclestone from his position of control.

Between November 2005 and March 2006 CVC Capital Partners purchased the shares in SLEC owned by Bambino Holdings and the banks, Bayerische Landesbank, JP Morgan and Lehman Brothers. As a result, the Formula One Group was now owned ultimately by a new Jersey-based company, Delta Topco. CVC Capital Partners' Funds owned approximately 70 per cent of this new company, JP Morgan approximately 20 per cent, and Bernie Ecclestone's family trust had the remainder apart from a small number of shares held by financial advisers and Ecclestone himself.

Ecclestone had sold his business, but, as the chief executive, was still the master chef running the restaurant for CVC Partners. It meant an annual salary of £2.5 million plus £1 million bonus and expenses, including fuel for his Falcon jet. Although these deals were complicated, there was no suggestion of any skulduggery.

However, on 5 January 2011 Gribkowsky was taken into custody for allegedly receiving kickbacks for organizing the sale of his bank's holdings to CVC. The prosecutors alleged that he had not had a 'proper valuation' of the shares. Gribkowsky's November 2005 deal was for $835 million, but only $770 million was shown in the accounts. Part of the difference was alleged to have made up the $61 million Ecclestone and his family trust Bambino Holdings received as consultancy fee for negotiating the sale to CVC.

The Munich state prosecutor, Hildegard Baumer-Hosel, declared in a statement, 'According to current findings the suspect, in turn, received $50 million in payments disguised via two consultancy agreements.' The payments were said to have gone to an Austrian trust whose German name translates as 'sunshine' via two shell companies in Mauritius and the Virgin Islands. The investigations had been triggered when Bayerische Landesbank had been notified that Gribkowsky had deposited $50 million five years earlier and the bank could not account for this money.

While the prosecutors did not say who had made the payments, German newspapers published a letter which suggested payments may have come from Ecclestone's office in London. Ecclestone indignantly denied he had bribed Gribkowsky and threatened to sue the German publications. Ecclestone later confirmed that he was helping the Munich prosecutor and had been to her offices to answer questions. CVC Partners also denied it had any know-ledge of wrongdoing, but set up its own investigation, instructing both auditors Ernst and Young and lawyers Freshfields for this purpose. This in-house investigation fuelled further speculation that this was an attempt at spring cleaning prior to another sale of the business. The allegations brought another touch of drama in a sport never short of it.

By this time, Ecclestone's long-term partner Mosley had gone, having arranged for Jean Todt to succeed him. Ecclestone had also lost his friend Briatore, despite his best efforts to defend him, in what many saw as the worst case of cheating in the sport. This involved events in the 2008 Singapore Grand Prix where Briatore, team principal of the Renault F1 Team, and Pat Symonds, his engineering director, conspired with driver Nelson Piquet Jr to crash on purpose in order to bring out a well-timed safety car. This was crucial for the victory of the team's other driver Fernando Alonso.

The bosses at Formula One had known about 'Crashgate' for almost a year before it became public. As Mosley recounts it,

> Nelson Piquet Senior told Charles Whiting (head of Formula One races) at the Brazilian Grand Prix three or four weeks after Singapore in strictest confidence. I was told early in February 2009. Both Charles and I said we could do nothing until we had concrete evidence. If we had moved in earlier Nelson Junior would have been under enormous pressure to deny it; there could have been a cover-up. We decided to wait. Sooner or later somebody would come forward.

That somebody was again Piquet's father, who called Mosley from the 2009 Hungarian race (by then his son had fallen out with Renault) and came to see Mosley in Monaco in the last week of July. Mosley refused to meet Piquet Junior, his neighbour in Monaco, but asked him to provide a sworn statement to the FIA's lawyers in Paris. Even then Mosley kept it absolutely secret. 'Nobody was told. We decided that at the next Grand Prix we would take the team by surprise.' That happened in Spa, during the Belgian Grand Prix.

'We set up everything in Belgium and as the team arrived we asked them one by one. It took them completely by surprise.'

The key questioning was that of Fernando Alonso. As Piquet's fake crash had given him victory in Singapore, was he then part of the conspiracy? 'According to people very expert in interrogation', says Mosley, 'they were quite satisfied he was telling the truth.' The man Alonso convinced was a former police officer, part of the team under Lord Stevens, the former head of the London Metropolitan Police, who runs Quest, a company Mosley had also used in his privacy case against the *News of the World*.

But it was Renault's response when given the Formula One investigation that really impressed Mosley. 'When we sent them the dossier of evidence, says Mosley, 'they made no attempt to cover up. They immediately instituted an internal investigation headed by a top lawyer.' That inquiry, conducted by Ali Malek, a leading English barrister, unmasked witness X who confirmed Briatore's role. 'And when that investigation was complete, says Mosley, 'they told us they would not contest the report that we had sent them. Impossible for a company to behave better than that. What they did was impeccable.'

When the World Motor Sport council met in Paris in September 2009 20 of the 26 members were present (proxies were cast by the absentees). Mosley has never disclosed the voting figures, merely that there was a 'substantial majority' in favour of banning Briatore for life, Symonds for five years and suspending Renault from the sport for two years. However, Ecclestone was not part of this majority and did not vote for the life ban on his friend Briatore. Instead, Briatore and Symonds took the FIA to court, arguing that the FIA over-reached its powers in imposing bans on them as individuals, because the FIA can grant licences only to drivers and teams rather than individuals. The pair won their case and reached a settlement with the FIA. As a result, the FIA made plans to introduce licences for the management of F1 teams in the future.

The FIA's decision not to ban Renault raised many questions about their impartiality. Two years earlier, in 2007, during the 'Spygate' affair, the World Motor Sport Council had fined McLaren $100 million and stripped it of its constructor's points for the season (the fine was moderated to the extent that it was to be paid after taking off the income lost as a result of the points deduction). Yet Renault was not held collectively guilty over Crashgate. The suspicion was that McLaren had been treated more harshly because its boss Ron Dennis had often been a thorn in both Ecclestone and Mosley's side. Mosley, however, has never had any doubts that the two scandals were fundamentally different. Crashgate, unlike Spygate, was a limited conspiracy between three people. The rest of Renault's executives and its 700 or so employees had not been involved.

Spygate had emerged when an employee of the copy shop near McLaren's Woking headquarters became suspicious that confidential data from Ferrari were being copied, and alerted Ferrari. He discovered Trudy Coughlan, wife of McLaren's chief designer Mike Coughlan, duplicating a 780-page document containing confidential technical data about Ferrari's F1 car. Ferrari suspected Nigel Stepney, the team's performance director and a friend and former colleague of Coughlan (the pair had worked together at Lotus in the late 1980s). Ferrari sacked Stepney and initiated court proceedings against him in Modena, Italy. McLaren sacked Coughlan claiming that Spygate was his work.

In its first hearing, the FIA accepted that McLaren did not know what had happened. But then the FIA received emails between McLaren test driver Pedro de la Rosa and the then reigning World Champion, Fernando Alonso. It emerged that the conspiracy went much deeper. For Mosley, the difference was that McLaren had lied whereas Renault came clean.

> What became clear was that even in September they were still lying to us. This is after we imposed a fine. McLaren got off very lightly. We were on the point of excluding them from 2008, but in the end they finally issued a detailed apology and admitted everything, and were prepared to make management changes so that it would never happen again. What they did was really annoying because they should have come and admitted the entire story in the July meeting instead of telling lies to the World Council. There would have been a penalty, but it would have been more modest. As it was they got off very lightly. It is very important for us that when something like this happens we are not confronted by a big organization doing its utmost to conceal the truth. Another reason for treating Renault as we did – the company was open and honest and truthful about who was responsible. In that case they have every prospect of being treated leniently.

THE CHEFS WHO CHANGED THE SPORTING MENU

All of these affairs have suggested to many that there is still something rotten in Formula One. Whether or not this is true, they have certainly taken it a long way from the ideals inspired by Thomas Arnold and his disciples. They also suggest that Ecclestone is constantly experimenting with new concoctions in his sporting menu. However, it is also worth stressing that for all the media focus on chef Bernie's restaurant, Formula One is a very limited activity, as Mosley reminded me. 'One must not confuse Formula One with motor sport. We have 30,000 competition licence holders; there are only 20 Formula One drivers, 20 cars. Formula One is a tiny part of the world of motor sport.'

This explains why, as he left office after nearly two decades, his great regret was:

> not having a Michael Schumacher in China or in India. If we had organized karting for young people, talent would have emerged. Lewis Hamilton started that way; Ayrton Senna was karting at six. Motor sport is a middle-class sport, not one for impoverished Third World countries, but there is a growing middle class in China or India and we could have done more.

In recent years there has been a growing middle-class appetite for the sport in China and India, but it is far removed from finding an audience there in the sense Mosley is talking about. Bernie, as the master chef, may have developed the business, but to develop a worldwide interest in sport is something else.

By contrast with Formula One, snooker illustrates what can happen to a sport where the business model works, but then interest drops off. Snooker and Formula One, of course, could not be more different, as even serious sports books describe snooker as a pub game. Nonetheless, there is much in common between Ecclestone and Barry Hearn, who in his own way has also been a master chef of snooker, among other sports. Hearn is from a different generation, being 30 years younger than Ecclestone, but

389

shares a working-class background. Hearn was brought up in London's East End and Ecclestone in nearby Dartford. Like Ecclestone, Hearn rose to affluence through his own efforts and his ability to make the most of his opportunities. Moreover, as in Formula One, Hearn was able to reshape two sports, first darts and then snooker, because they had virtually no proper regulatory bodies. They left Hearn free to create imaginative dishes to replace a traditional stodgy menu.

But while Ecclestone made Formula One a sport the rich and famous yearned for, Hearn, equally working class, makes no bones that he only promotes sports that his working-class audience likes, and is confident that he knows his market. 'I am appealing to mainstream white working class, absolutely.' Etched in Hearn's memory is his home in the London suburb of Dagenham immediately after the war. The house had an outside lavatory, and he shared a bedroom with his sister until he was 18. 'There was a cupboard in the middle of the room and a curtain to separate me from my sister, who was two years younger.' Hearn wanted to be an accountant from the age of 12, but when he qualified as one, he encountered the pervasive influences of class in Britain. His accountancy firm told him he could never be a partner because he had not been to university and did not have a posh enough accent.

Now, in marketing a sport, he asked a simple question: 'What would be my ideal night out? I would watch a fight, have a couple of pints and curry with the lads, or go and enjoy the darts or watch the snooker.' This led him to promote nine sports – darts, poker, prize boxing, ten-pin bowling, bowls, coarse fishing, golf, pool and snooker – which now provide 40,000 hours of televised sport a year. Seven per cent of all sport broadcast by Sky has been developed by Matchroom, his family-owned company. In this, Hearn has shown that he can successfully marry sport to business, make money for himself and give fans what they want. When he first proposed coarse fishing to Sky Television they told him he was mad. He reminded them that more people 'go fishing of an afternoon than watch football'. Coarse fishing has been on Sky for 19 years.

In the last decade, Hearn has made poker a television sport and, in the last five years, his Premier League darts has transformed the game's profile. Once only for the over-40 market, it now attracts many in their twenties. The 2010 season's starter at the O2 centre in London attracted 10,000. By the time it finished at Wembley some 83,000 had watched live darts. The secret, he explains, is simple: 'Make the experience more enjoyable at a competitive price.'

Hearn's discovery of snooker, which started him off in sports business in the mid 1970s, was a case of finding himself at the right time and right place. The sport was, in many ways, a gift of the British Raj, developed in 1875 as a variation from the more established billiards by the Devonshire Regiment stationed in Jubalpur in central India. The name was given by Neville Chamberlain, a subaltern, who shouted out when a fellow soldier missed an easy pot, 'Why, you're a real snooker!' The term had originated at the Royal Military Academy at Woolwich to mean the lowest of the low, and as Chamberlain later explained, this became the perfect name for the game. The game spread among the British in India and was adopted by sundry Maharajas before reaching England. However, a century later the sport was still to catch on there.

In 1969, in order to promote the advent of colour television, BBC2, a recently launched new channel, had started the programme *Pot Black*, which gave the game prominence. However, six years later, it was still to become a truly national game. In 1975, as Ecclestone was inserting TV clauses in track contracts, Hearn was finance director of a fashion design company, looking to diversify the business. His first foray into property and garment-manufacturing ventures failed miserably. But Hearn had also bought a chain of snooker halls. Unlike Ecclestone, who dreamed of being a racing driver, Hearn had no interest in snooker, had never played it and did not know the snooker business. For him it was just 'a good property deal in attractive town centres'. Quite by chance, that very year the BBC got more involved in snooker by televising the World Championships. 'I don't know why,' says Hearn. 'I think they were trying to promote colour television, but suddenly all these places I had bought for next to nothing were full up. Everyone said I was a genius; I knew I was lucky.'

If lightning strikes twice, that was confirmed by Hearn's discovery of Steve Davis, the first great star of snooker and its first millionaire. Like Hearn, Davis was a working-class boy, brought up in a council flat in Plumstead in south-east London. He took to the game because he could go with his father to the local working men's club. There he was allowed to play, despite being under age. At that time the idea of making money from snooker seemed extraordinary and the game had not made it on TV, but, with Hearn keen to promote his clubs, Davis was an ideal vehicle. Hearn may not have understood the sport, or realized how good Davis was, but when Davis played at his clubs he could see that he created a thrill and attracted people. Encouraged by Hearn, Davis turned professional in 1978 at the age of 21. Six months after that, Terry Griffiths won the 1979 World Championship. That year, the entire World Championships were televised by the BBC, the first time they had ever shown two weeks of the contest, creating for snooker the equivalent of the Wimbledon tennis fortnight. Davis recalls, 'The viewing figures went through the roof. They thought, "We've got a monster on our hands – we never realized it."'

The following year, 1980, Davis beat Terry Griffiths in the first round and became the young kid on the block who had beaten the World Champion. He was soon World Champion. He recalled:

Snooker had gone massive and I went massive at the right time, right place. I'd sit and watch Barry on the phone selling me as a commodity. The figures went up every time. I was doing exhibitions for thousands of pounds whereas before it was like 300 quid. And I was watching him and he would basically be making numbers up. One day I said, 'How are you working out what you should charge for me?' He said, 'Well I think of a number and treble it.' And, of course, the thing is when you've got something that people want you're in a good position. From being basically a snooker player who was very good I became an overnight, well-known snooker personality who was then on the road every day.

In 1982, Hearn sold his 16 snooker clubs to set up Matchroom and walked away with a profit of £3.5 million.

Three years later, snooker's magical moment arrived on the Bank Holiday weekend in May 1985, as 18.5 million stayed up until 12 a.m. to watch Dennis Taylor pot the last black on the deciding frame to beat Davis for the World Championship at the Crucible at Sheffield. When Taylor went back to Ireland, the police told him that whilst that final frame was happening, the crime rate went down to zero. The burglars didn't want to take the television out of the wall because they were watching the snooker. It is believed that the national grid nearly went down with the number of kettles that were boiled in between the frames. This would have been Davis's third successive World Championships, but with Taylor the underdog, all of Britain wanted the Ulsterman to win. Davis says that, had he been a bystander, he would have wanted Taylor to win. That was snooker's golden era, much in demand on television and with stars worthy of display.

'Snooker in the eighties,' says Hearn, 'had Coronation Street characters: Jimmy White, Alex Higgins, Cliff Thorburn, Terry Griffiths, the list goes on.' It was also an era before multi-channel television; choice was limited and the sport seemed glamorous. But that 1985 May night, as Hearn says, 'has been the albatross round snooker's neck ever since. What do you do to beat it?' Those glory years also carried the seeds of snooker's subsequent fall, not least because of incompetent management of the game which has seen a '10-year spiral of decline' with much needed to overcome the heavy burden of past glory. Hearn admits he was one of the vested interests that helped bring the game to its present dismal state.

> When I managed eight players – Steve Davis, Cliff White, Dennis Taylor, Terry Griffiths, Tony Meo, Cliff Thorburn, Steve Foulds and Willie Thorn – I also sat on the board of World Snooker. Did I do what was best for snooker? Or did I do it for my players? Hands up – I worked for them and not for the game as a whole. Snooker has never had anyone strong enough to say, 'I am running the game'.

In 2009 Hearn, the poacher, turned gamekeeper. In December 2009 the players voted out the chairman of the World Professional Billiards and Snooker Association (WPBSA), Sir Rodney Walker. Before that the players had approached Hearn to stand against Sir Rodney. Hearn's response, in effect, prompted Walker's removal. 'I told them I am not going to stand for election. I don't do democracy. For years players have whinged but done nothing. So I said come to me after you have [got rid of Walker]. I never believed the players would ever do anything. Lo and behold they got off their backside and did it.'

There followed radical changes to the game's structure, with the players agreeing to a break-up of WPBSA into two bodies. This gave Hearn control of the money while the players worried about the rules. Hearn's justification for it was very simple: 'I took World Snooker Ltd, the commercial arm, away from the players. They are not qualified to run the commercial arm. I have majority control; I don't run any business I don't control. The players are my junior partners.'

The commercial arm pays a licence fee to the governing body and, with the deal done, Hearn and the players have set out to try to make money. In many ways it is similar to the way Ecclestone runs Formula One, but unlike that sport, this was all agreed smoothly and is a classic illustration of how Hearn, the sporting chef, operates. Unlike many who feel snooker's time has gone,

Hearn sees the present recession, like the one in 1975 when he first got involved, as an ideal opportunity to re-launch the game. 'The present recession is not bad for snooker. Working-class people – where are they going to go? They are out of work, either queuing up to play snooker or gambling on the fruit machine. Ninety per cent of my events are sponsored by gambling companies. They are doing well out of the recession.'

Hearn's big problem is to find players the public can identify with. 'The stars of the eighties were replaced by technically very good players, but without the personality or the charisma.' He recently went into the players' room at a tournament and asked someone, 'Whose son are you?' He turned out to be the world number 11. As he waits for new stars to emerge, Hearn is looking at 'new formats, new tournaments, quick-fire, bish-bosh-bang snooker, maybe a single shoot-out frame to decide matches.' Hearn's innovations have included players taking to the stage jigging like Fred Astaire to music. For Hearn this is a search for 'younger markets that need a lot more entertainment, a lot more value to the paying spectator. We cannot go on living on Taylor versus Davis circa 1985.'

However, for snooker to survive it has to be exported, or rather re-exported back to India and other far-off places including China, since it is widely acknowledged that the game will never again be prominent in Britain. As Davis puts it:

> What we've got is two different things happening. We've got the UK public that have been exposed to snooker for 30 years who have either moved on, or given up. We've seen it for so long that we don't realize how good it is. Once upon a time, back in the eighties, you had one television in the house, the kids watching what the parents were watching, no internet, no computers, no YouTube. Now the kids are not watching what their parents are watching.

If Davis blames the internet for the eclipse of snooker as a family entertainment in Britain, he has a different view of its global impact on the game.

Worldwide we're seeing another thing happening; we're seeing more interest in snooker. Europe, Asia. Brazil has taken an interest. A tournament in Brazil; one in Australia; India has always liked the game. A lot of the ex-Iron Curtain countries are starting to love snooker. Now because of the internet they've got access to it. The community for snooker now worldwide is massive. I reckon in 20 years' time you might find that snooker is big in a lot of other countries and smaller in the UK. Actually the amount of people watching the World Championship at the Crucible year upon year gets bigger and, whilst people in this country think the game's dead, that's actually not what's happening. There has been a lot of press saying the game's dead now. A lot of sport writers don't really like it; they would rather it wasn't on their sports pages. We were quite concerned about that at one stage, thinking this is not doing snooker any good. Now I think it doesn't matter because the UK is not going to be anywhere as important in the grand scheme of snooker as it was back, say, ten years ago. The sport has now broken free of the UK.

During this period the sport, like Formula One, has had to contend with allegations that it is bent. John Higgins, its great champion, was exposed in a sting operation by the *News of the World*. This alleged that Higgins and his then manager, Pat Mooney, had agreed to lose frames for money. Higgins was not charged with match-fixing, but was found guilty of failing to report an improper approach, suspended for six months and fined £75,000. Higgins later admitted,

It was a difficult six months. I did not pick up a cue. It was in the cupboard and I just helped out being a dad, taking my kids to school, things which are normally left to my wife to do when I am away at tournaments. I never thought I would be put in such a position when I first picked up a snooker cue. It was a big learning curve for me. I was worried when I returned that I might be booed or barracked. Nobody has waved fivers at me. I am touched by the reception since I have come back.

On his return from suspension, he was convinced that the whole episode had not damaged the sport.

It is hard for me to say but it could have been the best thing that has happened to the sport. It has brought things to the fore. Somebody like Barry Hearn has come in and brought a new integrity to the game. This tournament and every tournament now have very, very strict conditions for the players. In the years gone, they were very slack on a few things.

Indeed, at the end of the year celebrations at the Dorchester, as Hearn narrated how the sport had attracted sponsors and money, Higgins was hailed back as a champion. There was the odd boo, but mostly it was wonder that despite the six-month absence he could win so many honours. It was as if the past was just a minor inconvenience. Higgins had erred, paid his dues, and moved on.

The celebrations at the Dorchester were proof of the game's revival and was used to raise money for a cancer Charity. This aspect was particularly pleasing to snooker's great players like Steve Davis, who had always felt that snooker and snooker players were considered socially inferior. Now they could not be seen just as men who played a pub sport and cared only for money. However, there was no attempt to link this fundraising to the higher moral values of sport. It was more like a modern business showing it had a caring side and a social conscience.

In the midst of the developments in these specialized sports, a shoemaker had emerged to concoct deals that would completely reshape the world's most popular sport: football. His deals would take the game invented by the British away from their control for ever. But, more than that, his activities would raise fundamental questions about whether, in getting into bed with Mammon, football had completely lost any sense of the moral purpose that was supposed to be the bedrock of the game. Football had found money but had it lost its soul in the process? Remember, this is the sport Tom Brown and his schoolfriends had held up as providing a pathway by which human beings could live. The search for riches meant the sport now faced some of the most serious corruption allegations. Football's response to the allegations suggested that, for all its rhetoric of reaching out to the world, it had completely lost the sporting spirit that had inspired its birth. All this because a shoemaker wanted to find a sport that could help him sell more shoes.

CHAPTER 12

THE SHOEMAKER'S DEADLY LEGACY

In April 1987 three of the most important men in sport journeyed to Herzogenaurach, a village near Nuremberg in northern Bavaria, to attend the funeral of a 51-year-old shoemaker who had died quite suddenly from cancer.

There is a photograph showing the three at the funeral. At the front of the funeral cortege, as it walks through the tree-lined cemetery, is the priest, then comes the widow and the two children, Adi and Susanne, and behind them the three men who made modern sports: Sepp Blatter, then general secretary of FIFA; to his left João Havelange, president of FIFA; and to his left Juan Antonio Samaranch, president of the IOC. Blatter in dark glasses adds an element of mystery, but even without the dark glasses this is a fascinating photograph. Study the picture and it seems that the men are courtiers paying homage to a dead king.

For this was no ordinary shoemaker. He was buried wearing a watch the Romanian tennis star Ilie Nastase had given him, engraved lovingly to a man he called his friend. And the three men present were also not only equally dear friends of the shoemaker but their presence that spring day indicated that they acknowledged how he had shaped all their lives, helped make them powerful and, in the process, recast international sport.

The shoemaker they were honouring was Horst Dassler. Presented in fiction Dassler's story would have been dismissed as fantastic; in real life it was even more extraordinary. As the

German magazine *Der Spiegel* wrote about him, just as the 1986 World Cup was to start in Mexico, he was not somebody who captivated a crowd with his brilliant conversation; he listened rather than talked. In ill-fitting, ready-made suits he could 'easily be taken for the head of a suburban shoe store'. But, by the time of his death, such was his power that he could make or break sport and those who ran it.

Horst was the only son of Adolf Dassler, who had been so astute at the Berlin Olympics in 1936 in getting Jesse Owens to wear his running shoes and help humiliate his own country and embarrass Hitler. As we have also seen, Havelange had taken part in that Olympics, but he did not know of Adi, as Adolf was called all his life. Much had happened in the 50 years since, although for a long time nothing had suggested that Adi's son Horst would help João and play such a huge part in reshaping football.

For a start it was by no means certain that Adi and his brother Rudolph would be able to return to their shoe business after the war. Rudolph had voted for the Nazis in 1932 and three months after Hitler came to power Rudolph, Adi and Fritz, the eldest brother, were registered party members, and Adi joined the Hitler Youth in 1935. Relations between Adi and Rudolph were never the best and the war and what followed helped deepen the split. Rudolph was always much more devoted to the Hitler cause and a post-war American investigation showed he had joined the Wehrmacht. Its conclusion was that he had worked for the Gestapo and the Abwehr. In response to the allegation, Rudolph was convinced that Adi had had a hand in stirring up the Americans and the division between the two brothers was formalized in April 1948, when they formed two rival shoe companies, Addas and Ruda, with the Aurach River as a convenient physical barrier between the two factories. A complaint by another German shoe company forced Adi to change the name to Adidas, and Rudolph changed Ruda to Puma.

Adi's pursuit of Owens during the 1936 Olympics had shown his skills in marketing, and as peace saw the world again playing sports, Adi was quick to grasp the opportunities. His first big moment came in the 1952 Helsinki Olympics, although he was faced with a ticklish problem. While many athletes wore shoes marked by three stripes, these were not Adidas's three stripes, but those marketed by Finland's shoe manufacturer Karhu. This company, carrying on from its pre-war Olympic success, dominated the Games with 14 gold medals. The Finnish shoe manufacturer's ascendancy was marked as soon as the Olympics began: Paavo Nurmi, who had won such honour in the 1920s in the company's shoes, advertised the make again as he entered the stadium with the Olympic torch.

The event did show the Dassler business touch. He met the people from Karhu and, according to Adidas historian Barbara Smit, 'for a relatively small sum and two bottles of schnapps' they agreed to stop using the three stripes. It would have been even better if the runner who made his mark at the Olympics, Emil Zatopek, could have openly advertised Adidas's three stripes, but he specifically requested shoes with only two stripes. He did not want to wear something that reeked of capitalism, lest it upset Czechoslovakia's Communist regime.

However, it was another communist versus capitalist sporting battle that gave Adi Dassler worldwide prominence. This was the 1954 World Cup when the Germans, despite going a goal down, unexpectedly beat the Hungarians 3–2 in the final at Berne. With the match played on the fourth of July, the Germans celebrated their own kind of freedom. The Germans, who had always appreciated how sport could be a metaphor for conveying a broader message, hailed this as the 'miracle of Berne'. For Germany, this triumph proclaimed it was recovering from the war. 'Germany is somebody again,' rang out the phrase.

For Adi this meant business. The German team manager, Sepp Herberger, was ready to acknowledge the part played by the shoes of Adi Dassler. These were not the heavy boots that the English had made popular. They were shoes whose studs could be adjusted to fit the circumstances – short studs if the surface was dry, longer studs on wet surfaces. Dassler was hailed as the shoe-maker of the nation, and one English newspaper ran a piece on him with the headline, 'What a Dassler'. The light boots were not exactly a German innovation. The Brazilians had used them in 1950, long before Dassler, and Stanley Matthews had brought a pair back after the 1950 World Cup in Brazil. The Co-operative Wholesale Society also started manufacturing the boots for him, with Matthews earning sixpence a pair as his price for the endorse-ment. But the Brazilians and the British had failed to market these on an international scale – that was the work of Adi Dassler.

But for all these marketing triumphs, Adi was essentially a shoemaker. He loved nothing better than to design new shoes or make refinements to existing ones. It was Horst who was the first to realize that modern sporting events were essentially trade fairs. Much was made of the principles that the victors did not get money and that what mattered was not winning but merely taking part, but these high principles required thousands of athletes to be summoned to one place for weeks. There could not be a better marketing opportunity to sell them sports goods. Horst was determined to use such occasions to take sports marketing to an entirely different level.

His first opportunity came two years after the 1954 World Cup when he was sent by his mother Kathe to the 1956 Melbourne Olympics. Horst had the amazing idea of not getting athletes to buy Adidas shoes, but giving them away free. Olympic rules about using sponsored equipment were very strict. But shoes could be considered technical equipment necessary for running. He was certain that the publicity from pictures of athletes wearing Adidas would be money well spent. At the end of the Games, Horst could claim that more than 70 medals had been won by athletes wearing Adidas shoes.

If Melbourne had been a first run for Horst, the football World Cup in England in 1966 proved what a marketing genius he was. It is a measure of how different those times were that the English FA hoped that their normal supplier might give them a discount on shirts and boots, particularly in the opening ceremony of the World Cup with the Queen present. Adidas's English partner, Umbro, offered to supply them for free. By the time the final rolled on, Horst had been told that three-quarters of players competing in the tournament were wearing Adidas shoes. The one prominent exception was Eusebio of Portugal, the most dazzling player of the tournament. He wore Puma, but England beat Portugal in the semi-finals and set up Horst's dream final against West Germany, which, as ever, was faithful to Adidas.

Both Puma and Adidas offered players money. Some players were annoyed – such as Jack Charlton, who threatened to wear one Adidas shoe, and one Puma shoe – but most were happy to take Adidas money. Geoff Hurst, who made history by scoring a hatrick in the final, was paid £300 by Adidas every time he wore the company's shoes when playing for England. Given that Hurst was put on £140 a week wages by West Ham after the final this shows how lavish Horst was.

Years later, Alan Ball would describe what took place in the England team hotel on the morning of the final. His words show where sport was in 1966, the very limited expectation of making money that even the world's leading players had, and also where the marriage of sport and money was headed:

Imagine that I was just 21, playing for England and carrying £2,000 upstairs for wearing Adidas boots. I would have brought my own but this was different. I walked in the room and Nobby [Stiles] was still lying in his bed as I tossed all the notes so that they came down all over the place like confetti. The World Cup final against West Germany was only hours away. We laughed like kids.

It was Dassler who laughed all the way to the bank. England won, but it was Adidas shoes that dominated the match. All except two players in the final, Ray Wilson and Gordon Banks who wore Puma, advertised the three stripes of Adidas.

Indeed, the fight between Adidas and Puma awakened the sports star as a business mercenary. During the 1968 Mexico Olympics, *Sports Illustrated* had a cover story by their investigative reporter, John Underwood, called 'No Goody Two-Shoes'. This detailed what it called the 'The $100,000 payoff' and included stories about how an athlete had earned $10,000 by hawking his services to both Adidas and Puma. A gold medallist had won $6,000 switching to Puma and justified it by saying, 'Why should I sit around like a hermit when everybody is making money out of these people?' Even athletes, keen to use sports for wider political purposes did not forget the marketing potential for events such as the Olympics.

The Mexico Olympics of 1968 will always be remembered for the moment when, on 16 October 1968, two American black athletes used the Olympics to protest about racial segregation in their homeland. Tommie Smith and John Carlos, first and third in the 200 metres final, stood on the podium in black socks, with black scarves round their necks, and as the American anthem was played they lowered their heads as if in shame while raising their right arm to the sky, their clenched fist displaying a black glove. It signified Black Power protest.

But that is not all that Smith and Carlos carried on the podium. The protest was made to make the world aware of the wretched nature of American society. There could be no higher purpose. But as athletes, they were also part of the commercial world. Both were Puma men (as Horst had noted, Puma's brush shoe was popular with black athletes). They each carried a single Puma shoe with them and before they made their gesture they placed the Pumas on the podium, as if to say that, amidst all their concern for human rights, they had not forgotten the sponsors.

There were some sportsmen whose every word was a command. In December 1970, when Muhammad Ali was getting ready to fight Oscar Bonavena in New York, he refused to wear shoes that Adi Dassler had made for him for years. He insisted his new found religion of Islam meant he had to wear all black boots.

Dassler agreed to design whatever boots he wanted. Ali demanded boots with tassels. This was hurriedly arranged. At the weigh-in, Ali talked about his 'secret weapon', telling reporters that a man would come from Germany to provide this weapon to him. If the weapon had any special power this was not evident for 14 rounds, during which Ali was mediocre, before winning with a knockout in the 15th round.

There was one player both Adidas and Puma had agreed not to bid for: Pele, the acknowledged 'king' of world football. The result was that while other Brazilian players benefited, Pele lost out. Eventually, at the instigation of a German journalist infiltrated by Puma into the Brazilian camp, Pele got a contract of $25,000 for the 1970 Mexico World Cup, $100,000 for the next four years and royalties of 10 per cent for every Pele shoe Puma sold. Pele was so pleased that he came up with a wheeze to make even more for his sponsors. Before one of the matches, he had a chat with the referee and asked him not to start the match just then. He then bent down and tied his shoe laces, providing wonderful images of Puma on the television screens.

In his biography, written in 2006, Pele does not refer to this incident or even mention Puma. He acknowledges how he knew from the late 1960s about his increasing value as a worldwide brand. As his Santos team played abroad he made sure half the money came to him. But he is very keen to emphasize that advertising products was not just about making money. So, he says, his principle was never to endorse a product he did not believe in.

He describes how when a cigarette manufacturer tried to lure him to advertise the product he turned him down. Long after retirement he endorsed Viagra but did so, he says, in order to teach young people how to use it correctly. Pfizer, the manufacturer, had convinced him that too many young people round the world were using it incorrectly, mixing it with alcohol, which caused heart problems and even death. The message was that Pele, the greatest footballer in the world, would not just take money; he would make money and help the world.

For Horst, all this talk of business and morality never came into his calculations. He was none too pleased when his uncle and cousins at Puma had signed the greatest player. He would also in time have to suffer as they nabbed another great player. This was Johan Cruyff, then a young Dutch player on his way to becoming an all-time legend. The agreement, in January 1967, for the 20-year-old, signed by Cruyff's mother, provided him with 1,500 guilders for each game and training session that he wore Puma shoes. Puma also sold shoes called Puma Cruyffie, that being the player's nickname.

Cruyff proved a more difficult customer than the compliant Pele. He complained about the Puma shoes, started wearing Adidas shoes and was successfully sued by Puma in 1968. The judge, finding in Puma's favour, summed it up well. 'The truth of the matter is that [Cruyff] wants more money.' It did result in a better contract – 25,000 guilders for the next three years. There were more problems, more approaches from Horst and Adidas before Cruyff, in 1972, finally signed another deal with Puma which meant he could earn at least 150,000 guilders a year. This covered not only shoes but also clothes, a field sports marketers had been entering for some time.

However, Adidas had done a deal with the Dutch federation which required all their players to wear Adidas, and this raised a delicate issue. With the Dutch heading for Germany and the 1974 World Cup, would Cruyff play in an Adidas shirt? Holland were then playing some of the best football in the world, branded as total football, and the thought of the Dutch playing without Cruyff was unthinkable. Eventually, a compromise was reached where Cruyff did not have to wear the traditional Adidas three stripes, but only two stripes. However, when the team photograph was taken, Adidas's man in Holland made sure that Cruyff was not only in the photograph, but also used his Adidas bag to cover his Puma shoes.

The 1974 World Cup Final was a rematch of Adidas versus Adidas. The two stripes on Cruyff apart, both the German and

Dutch teams were wearing traditional Adidas. Germany in anything but Adidas was unthinkable, given all that had happened in 1954 and the more so as this was the first ever World Cup on German soil. However, this time, the German players had a voice and they wanted money. No one was willing to accept only what his football federation offered him. The players wanted cash from the marketers themselves. Franz Beckenbauer, acting as agent, said that each player wanted 100,000 Deutsche Marks. Agreement was reached at 75,000 Deutsche Marks. After that, Adidas decided it was not worth doing a deal with the federation. Now they would deal with players directly.

It could be argued that the commercial war was also having a social impact. Back in 1968, Kareem Abdul-Jabbar, the black American basketball player, had preferred not to go to the Mexico Olympics. As he recalls:

> The year I was supposed to go to the Olympics, there was a lot of political activity. I was aware that America was practising a lot of hypocrisy. I had the opportunity to try out for the team. I didn't feel comfortable representing my country. My own personal agenda was more important than flying the flag. It was very difficult because, in a lot of ways, I love America. But also I remember just five years earlier, in 1963, when the girls in Birmingham were killed by an explosion, the cowards putting a bomb in the church. America tolerated too much of that. So something had to be done about that. Had I gone, would I have given the Black Power salute? I don't know. I'm glad they did. They needed to make a statement.

Yet in February 1976, he was signed by Adidas for $25,000 a year, the first basketball player and the first black player to be signed by Adidas, demonstrating that, just as segregation between amateurs and professionals was breaking down, so that between blacks and whites in America was also slowly dissolving. It would take another two decades and the arrival of Michael Jordan before this was taken to another, more universal level.

Tennis was to take Dassler to a new, very different field and the way he exploited it throws an interesting light on how sports business was expanding in the 1970s. If football and athletics were sports where an entrepreneur like Dassler had to indulge in subterfuges to make money, then tennis provided plenty of opportunities to do so quite openly. But in tennis, Dassler had help from an American, Donald Dell, who had quickly worked out that modern sport provided greater opportunities for business than his own chosen profession.

Dell shared many characteristics with McCormack. Like him, he had studied law at Yale and then become a partner in a law firm in Washington DC. But, unlike McCormack and most others in American sport, he was not a diehard Republican, but a rare Democrat. He worked for John Kennedy's brother-in-law, Sargent Shriver, was close to Robert Kennedy, and could have had a career in politics. And while McCormack was, at best, a good amateur golfer, Dell came into sports management with a proven track record in tennis, having played for America in the Davis Cup, and been the non-playing captain of the team in the early 1960s. His thoughts turned to tennis again as he realized the restrictions of his law practice.

> We were a group of lawyers at the time but in the sixties and early seventies you couldn't advertise, you couldn't solicit, you couldn't do a lot of things as lawyers. So we switched to a business vehicle which allowed us to be a law firm on one side but compete as a business on the other. My first two clients were Arthur Ashe and Stan Smith. I was very proud of that because they were such extraordinary people who happened to be good athletes. I was really the first person to ever represent a tennis player professionally.

Dell's activities would enrage his fellow tennis players: the Romanian player-turned-agent Ion Tiriac once told Dell, 'You only want to make more and more money for yourself and your group of players. But you're clever, so very dangerous.' Not that Tiriac, acting for Boris Becker, needed much tutoring in making money for his sports clients. The deal he signed with Puma for Becker, just before the 17-year-old won Wimbledon in 1985, was for a reputed $24 million. It led to Puma's racket sales going up from 15,000 to 300,000 in two years and shoe sales of 3 million pairs in one year alone.

However, Dell saw himself, probably because of his Democratic political connections, as more than just a money man. He laid claim to being an innovator, not merely in marketing, but in the wider social sphere. His deal for Arthur Ashe suggests there is some merit in the claim. Ashe was more than just a client; he was also a friend and Dell is convinced would have gone on to play a major role in American politics had he not died of Aids in 1993. Ashe was the first black man to win the US Open and the first, and still the only, black male tennis player to win Wimbledon. In 1975, he outfoxed and out-thought Jimmy Connors at a time when Connors looked absolutely unbeatable. In working with Ashe, Dell not only engineered some lucrative deals, but also broke through the racial barriers which then continued to suffocate American sport.

In his memoir, *Never Make The First Offer (Except When you Should)*, Dell describes how he persuaded the chairman of a US company to agree to a handsome deal for Ashe. Howard Head, the ski designer, had designed a metal racket for Ashe. He had also agreed a very good deal for Ashe: 5 per cent on all racket sales and this covered six or seven models. However, when the contract came up for renewal, AMF, the company that now owned HEAD Ski, refused to authorize a new deal. Dell just could not get the chief executive to agree.

We were at a complete impasse until that door swung open and the chairman of AMF came storming in. He was so angry I could see the veins popping on his neck. 'God dammit,' he screamed, 'we're not paying Ashe any more royalties. This is outrageous. He's making 10 times what I'm making and I'm the chairman of this company' [. . .] there were eight or nine people in the room, and they were all looking at me to see how I was going to respond. There was a dead silence, and you could feel the tension. After thinking for a moment I said, 'But Pierre, Arthur has a much better service than you do.' Everyone laughed and the tension in the room was immediately broken.

The new agreement meant Ashe not only got his royalties, but an endorsement contract for life. The way Dell did the deal emphasized not Ashe's colour, but his tennis ability and in that sense helped make Ashe more universal, not just a brilliant black tennis player.

By this time Dell had already dealt with Dassler, having negotiated his very first shoe deal. The deal was for Stan Smith, who had won Wimbledon in 1972. Dell knew how keen the German was to break into the American market and demanded a 5 per cent royalty on all Stan Smith's shoes. 'Horst went ballistic, but I knew what his goals were: Stan was his ticket into America. So after a lot of back-and-forth he eventually agreed. Neither of us knew at the time how big Adidas would become in this country, so it was sort of like dealing with play money.'

The deal was to prove so valuable that it continues to keep on rolling. Speaking in 2010 Dell said, 'It's by far the largest selling shoe in tennis, in the history of the sport. Last year they sold over 600 million pairs of shoes and the Smith has eight models, men and women, boys and girls. It's a phenomenal deal.'

Dassler was soon signing up the man Stan Smith had beaten at Wimbledon, the artistic but temperamental Romanian Ilie Nastase. He had first emerged in the West a few years earlier at the French Open in Roland Garros in completely inappropriate shoes made by the Chinese. In 1972 Nike had tempted him with a $5,000 contract with the heels of the shoes broadcasting his nickname, 'Nasty'. A year later Dassler, despite the misgivings of his

410

staff, signed him on a four-year contract of $50,000 a year. He was not only wearing shoes but socks, shirts and the entire gear.

By this time, Adidas dealt in all sorts of sporting gear. In 1972 the Olympics returned to Germany, this time to Munich, and Horst was determined not to miss out. He set up his own store at the Olympics, getting round official restrictions on marketing products. The store was not only for the men and women of sports, but the great and good of the world including VIPs like Princess Grace of Monaco. Horst's most celebrated coup in Munich, of course, was to target Mark Spitz, the American swimmer who created a record by winning seven gold medals.

But how could a swimmer, even a genius like Spitz, display shoes? The Dassler solution was classic: go on to the victory podium carrying a pair. This is what Spitz did after his win in the 200 metres freestyle. He carried a pair of Adidas Gazelle to the victory stand and after the anthem had been played and he had collected his medals, he waved to the crowd making sure the shoes were prominent. Horst may have got away with the Adidas store, but the IOC investigated this matter; in the end Spitz was exonerated.

All this was a prelude to Horst's major move. While his father, uncle and others had tried to contact individual athletes and get them to promote their products, Horst realized that to make a real mark in sports marketing you needed to build up contacts with the men in suits, the men who ran the sports organizations. By getting their endorsement you got not one athlete but an entire sport. In the process, Horst Dassler brought a new interpretation to the old Chinese proverb that if you sit by the river bank long enough you can see the head of your enemy float by.

In cities where important sporting events were taking place, like in London during Wimbledon, he targeted the main hotels where prominent officials were staying. This could mean sitting in the lobby just opposite the lift in the hope of meeting someone. John Boulter, who was in charge of international promotions at Adidas, told Barbara Smit the story of going for a jog round Hyde

Park, leaving Dassler sitting in the hotel lobby. He returned to find him still sitting there. 'I'm fine, John,' said Dassler. 'I'm sitting here in case someone important walks by.'

As Barbara Smit has observed, 'Wherever he was, Horst Dassler seized every opportunity to reinforce his friendships among sport officials, or to seal the new ones. While others regarded schmoozing as a tiresome obligation, Horst went about it with almost fanatical zeal. This was perfectly in line with one of Horst Dassler's adages that, "everything is a matter of relationships". He had the right skills to make friends all over the world: he was fluent in five languages, displaying an affable manner, never asked any awkward questions, and he was amazingly considerate.'

The world had, until then, mostly ignored these sports officials. They were volunteers; some were even retired. Now they were being courted by a man who ran one of the most important sports goods companies in the world. He understood they had the power to make deals for their federations and the various national teams that formed part of the federation – deals that offered tremendous, often worldwide media exposure, for the products of his company.

The location of Dassler's Adidas factory in Alsace also helped. Three years after the Melbourne Olympics, Dassler's family bought a struggling shoe plant in Dettwiller in Alsace, the province just across the German border and long a German–French battleground. Horst was settled there. The intention may have been to make sure he was away from the main family firm and did not disrupt it – the Dasslers did not find it easy to get on – but it had another dramatic effect. What his parents had done was give him a platform and he was to make the most of it. He soon moved into nearby Landersheim.

This was a village time had forgotten. Horst was to make its name resonate around the world. Here he built his headquarters, acquiring Auberge du Kochersberg, a former hunting lodge. This was to prove ideal for him to hunt the sports officials he targeted with such relentless fervour. Round the villa he built offices. The villa he converted into a five-star hotel with a choice cellar; there were chefs to prepare gourmet meals, the Michelin Guide gave it one star, and there were luxurious suites and chauffeur-driven cars to ferry the guests. There were presents galore for guests with important visitors even given a bottle of vintage wine from the year of their birth. He also cultivated guests through a relentless series of dinner parties, where three lots of guests dined in three separate rooms. During the course of the evening, Dassler made sure he had some part of the meal in each of the three rooms. The impression created was a man of business who was always busy, but always had time to spare for his special friends.

Such cultivation of sports officials meant that, leading up to the 1968 Mexico Olympics, he got the Puma brush shoe (which had steel needles not the usual metal spikes) disqualified on the grounds that it had more than six spikes, despite Puma's protests that these much smaller needles were not like the nail-like metal spikes. At the same time, he cultivated the International Weightlifting Federation, and made sure that a special shoe was developed for weightlifters. The federation then passed regulations that meant all shoes from other manufacturers were banned.

Dassler then targeted Eastern Europe, despite the fact that it cost a lot of money to get on the right side of the Soviet officials. The officials were entertained at the company's French head-quarters and also at a hotel in Paris. Soviet officials made it clear that on such trips they expected Adidas to finance their shopping fancies and Dassler was happy to oblige. Michael Payne, who worked for him, says, 'He courted world leaders and was probably better known in Moscow and the Kremlin than many heads of state.' Perhaps the most intriguing deal was with the East German dictator Erich Honecker. The East Germans had their own sports shoe brand called Zeha, which had two stripes. Now their athletes were required to wear the three stripes of Adidas. This did not mean sales, since East Germany was a closed economy where Western products did not enter easily. But it meant influence and power.

Dassler, it seems, even got an East German sports official, Karl-Heinz Wehr, appointed general secretary of the International Boxing Federation. Dassler could not have known that Wehr was also a Stasi spy, codenamed 'informant Seagull'. Inevitably, the East German secret service developed files on Dassler himself. Seagull told his bosses that what Dassler was running was a 'sports political department' which he was convinced was 'the most important unit of sport espionage in the capitalist foreign world'. In another report he told his spymasters, 'We are faced with the fact that in the current sports world, nothing happens without this company – and that, in my eyes, many things happen under the influence of this group.'

Dassler collected sports officials as other people might collect stamps or book tokens. These included the former Yugoslav goal-keeper, who subsequently became the coach of the Moroccan football team, Blagoje Vidinić. The Tunisian Mohammed Mzali was another Dassler client. He could not have been more important. At various times he headed the country's football federation, Tunisia's Olympic Committee, was a member of the IOC and even Tunisia's prime minister. Dassler funded the magazine *Champion d'Afrique*, where African sports officials like Mzali, as well as Adidas, were eulogized. There were several German newscasters and broadcasters who were said to have been on his payroll. It has been suggested that Dassler also financed *Sport Intern*, the magazine edited by Karl-Heinz Huba. While no proof ever emerged, the magazine had uncanny details of what went on in federations and always promoted the Dassler cause. Adidas also supplied footballs to Thomas Sankara, president of Burkina Faso. Some years later, after he was murdered, the cellar of his presidential palace was found to contain 3,000 Adidas balls.

Dassler's most important African conquest was, probably, Jean-Claude Ganga, the IOC member from Congo. He was a leading light in the African sports world, and an important member of the IOC until the truth emerged in 1999 as a result of the Salt Lake City corruption crisis. Then it was found that he had received

$200,000 for invented travel expenses, medical costs and other gifts, and was one of the members expelled by the IOC in the wake of the crisis.

David Yallop has described, in *How They Stole the Game*, how Horst's decisive moment in cultivating men in suits had come in Frankfurt in June 1974, just before the World Cup football matches started. As we have seen, that World Cup demonstrated player power. Now, just days before the tournament began, Horst Dassler, having eagerly courted the men-in-suits around the world, began to acquire decisive influence on the choice of the man-in-suit to run the world's most popular game.

Stanley Rous was being challenged by João Havelange for the presidency of FIFA. Dassler had given conflicting messages, telling some of his aides to look after Havelange but also confident that his friend Rous would win. In Frankfurt there were Dassler men working with both Rous and Havelange. The night before the vote, he had a drink with Blagoje Vidinić. Now coach of Zaire, ruled by the dictator Mobutu, Vidinić had guided Zaire to the World Cup finals. As the Yugoslav and the German drank in the bar at the Frankfurt hotel, Vidinić told Dassler that during the African Nations Cup Havelange had won the support of the African Confederation – and that he would win. He gave Dassler Havelange's room number and told him to go and see him. Dassler did. This meeting sealed the alliance between the German and the Brazilian, with Dassler abandoning his old friend Rous.

The next day, when the vote took place, Rous did indeed lose. It required two rounds of voting and the margin was small, 68 to 52, but it was a decisive moment in world sport. It meant that control of the world's most popular game had moved from England and the Anglo-Saxon world to the Latin world, with a German sports goods manufacturer calling all the shots. But was the conversation in the bar the one that made Dassler switch to Havelange? Or had he changed his allegiance earlier and was part of a much deeper plot?

Some years later Lord Howell, the former British sports

minister, headed a committee investigating sponsorship in sport and asked some questions of Dassler. In particular, Howell explored his relationship with FIFA. This is how Howell summarized what happened, to football historians John Sudgen and Alan Tomlinson:

> I started by asking questions such as 'Can you give me any justification as to why a football boot manufacturer should wish to decide who should become the president of FIFA and control world football?' And his reply was that he had in his office a tremendous computer and records department which had every periodical and newsletter issued by every sports body round the world and these were all tabulated. Therefore, it is very natural that if anyone wanted to pursue a career like Havelange [. . .] they would come to him to get the names and addresses of all the contacts. This is what he supplied and the same facilities, he said, were available to Sir Stanley Rous, except Sir Stanley Rous didn't ask for them.

This suggests that Havelange had long-established ties with Dassler, while Rous, playing the perfect English gentleman, missed a trick. As Payne has observed, 'For those seeking success in any sports industry election – whether for the Presidency of FIFA or the selection of an Olympic host city – his support was critical.' There were also suggestions that the election was not above board. The *Sunday Times* reporter Keith Botsford (a friend of the novelist Saul Bellow, and later to become Professor Emeritus of Boston University) wrote of 'small brown envelopes going into large black hands'.

Whether the election was bought or not has never been proven and these examples may have been no more than tales, but what was undoubtedly true was that, in contrast to Rous, Havelange treated the election as if it was a political campaign. He travelled the world courting voters for years beforehand. He realized that while Europe was the centre of world football and would remain so, if he secured enough non-European votes from round the world he could beat Rous.

He made the most of the fact that FIFA provided opportunities unlike any other sports body by giving all associations an equal vote. This contrasted especially with cricket and rugby. At that time the governing bodies of these sports still allowed veto powers to countries such as England which had first organized them. Such privileges are hardly unusual. All countries may be equal at the United Nations General Assembly, but this body has very limited powers compared to the Security Council, which has authority to take executive decisions affecting crucial issues of war and peace. Here the five victorious allies of the Second World War, the US, Britain, France, Russia and China, have veto powers. Unless all five are agreed, the UN can do nothing. Similarly, the International Monetary Fund has a weighted voting system which has ensured that since its birth, its managing director has always been a European. This balances the World Bank where the United States dominates. But at FIFA, a state like Fiji's vote counts as much as England or Italy, and Havelange was quick to realize what this meant.

The English played into Havelange's hands after Rous was defeated. They went into a sulk and did not bother with this British seat. As the most important of the four home nations, they could have secured it and exerted pressure on Havelange. Instead, it was occupied for the next 30 years by Harry Cavan, a trade union official from Northern Ireland. Havelange showered him with honours, constantly presenting him as proof that the British supported him, and Cavan, effectively, became a crony of Havelange. This demonstrated how well Havelange understood the political game. Indeed he was the first of the sports politicians to emerge on the world's stage. Like a consummate politician, he knew what his electorate wanted and was ready to court them. His eight-point election programme included the promise that there would be 24 teams in the World Cup from 1982, a 50 per cent increase from the 16 teams that had contested every final competition since 1954. There would also be an Under-20 world championship and a new FIFA headquarters, appropriate for the coming twenty-first century. In addition, underdeveloped associations would receive support, both materials and money, to construct and improve stadiums. There would be courses for sports professionals, technical and medical teaching and an intercontinental club championship.

For critics of Havelange like Artemio Franchi, the former UEFA president, what Havelange was doing was 'South American ostentation'. The veteran football writer Brian Glanville was convinced that Havelange ruined the World Cup by selling the game, 'down the river to the Afro-Asians and their ilk'. As Havelange expanded the world game by adding new tournaments, Glanville dismissed them as part of an ultimate Havelange plot to organize 'a World Cup Tournament for embryos'. It should be emphasized that Glanville had a deep understanding of the hunger for Western sport in the non-Western world. However, he felt that Havelange was meeting this hunger in the wrong way.

Havelange's supporters say that he arrived at the right time and that he reflected the world in which he found himself. It was not a case of Havelange working any magic, let alone practising black arts, as his critics allege, but it was what needed to be done. Football was about to explode, television was coming and it was bringing money. But the way Havelange seized the moment ensured that he converted what had been a sports club into football's first political organization and a unique one at that. He, and even more so his successor, Sepp Blatter, proved to be adept politicians who used the money football now attracted to build up a worldwide vote bank. The largesse they could distribute translated into votes and they distributed their gifts in the manner of politicians bringing benefits to their constituents. This was what American politicians call 'pork barrel politics', using federal money to help their districts to ensure support during elections. FIFA, created to serve world football, was not meant to be a political organization. But that is what it became as a result of the money that Dassler helped attract to FIFA. The change in the nature of FIFA was to have enormous consequences for football.

In 1974, when Havelange took over, football was a game where most of the football world was a spectator at the highest level. On the face of it, the World Cup looked like a competition to which all nations were invited equally – but as in George Orwell's *Animal Farm*, some animals were more equal than others. For the 1974 World Cup, 98 countries started the qualification process to select 14 teams that would join West Germany, the hosts and Brazil, the holders in the finals. However, not all 98 teams had an equal chance of getting to Germany.

The biggest continent in the world, Asia, had only one place in the final and even this had to be earned by competing against the winner from Oceania. As a result, Australia qualified for the finals for the first time and in Germany it represented not only Oceania, but also Asia. In contrast, the European nations had eight places, in addition to West Germany. This meant that even East Germany had a chance to participate. South America's nine football countries competed for three places and, with Brazil guaranteed a place, the smallest of the continents had four teams at the 1974 finals.

It could be said this was a very fair representation of football power as Europe and South America had the best teams and only a European or South American team could have won the competition. Even today, no nation from another continent has even got to the final match, nor the semi-finals (ignoring the very special case of the USA coming third in the first competition), let alone won it. But it also meant that the 'haves' started with a huge advantage. The 'have-nots' had to play very much better than most of the 'haves' to have any chance of reaching the top table. Nor had the great football competitions travelled much outside Europe. Nineteen seventy-four was the tenth World Cup; six of them had been held in Europe and four in South and Central America.

Havelange held out the hope that under his leadership he would cater to this great, disenfranchised mass of the world.

These nations were like children pressing their noses at the window of a sweet shop where they were never allowed in. Now, said Havelange, they would be given the chance to savour the best of the football sweets. If they could not get inside the famous football sweet shop of the World Cup, he would open new football sweet shops for them. In this he was enormously helped by the fact that his arrival on football's world stage coincided with another region of the world discovering sport: the Middle East.

Today, this region is an Aladdin's cave for the sports fan. The world's greatest players, the most glamorous sponsors, the best of the A-list celebrities, have all been attracted by region's superb first-class sports and leisure facilities and five-star hotels. And it has become a second home to many stars who have bought homes there. If football has always been the most popular sport in the region, with Qatar winning the right to host the 2022 World Cup (the jewel in the region's sporting crown), other sports have long since embraced the region as part of their global tours. It is now barely possible to pass a week between early September and mid-April when there is not some world event taking place in the Middle East. The tennis tour wends its way through a series of international tournaments; cricket matches take place across the region, even in Saudi Arabia. Rugby Sevens championships attract the best players; snooker tournaments abound in settings that provide a stark contrast to the bleak Norbrick Castle Hotel in Blackpool. Golf tournaments are graced by the game's best players and it is difficult to find a more dramatic marriage between money, glamour and sport than the Middle East hosting Formula One races. And the most valuable horserace in the world takes place in Dubai. The Gulf States have even made an impact in athletics, both when Qatar hosted the 2006 Asian Games, and when Arab governments found that athletes would transfer nationality at a price in much the same way as footballers changed clubs.

The transformation in what the Gulf has to offer in sport would have been beyond the belief of visitors in the late 1970s, who wandered through a region barely coming to terms with a telephone network. Then, it had such a shortage of hotel rooms that hoteliers did not even blush with embarrassment when they charged guests $50 a night (in 1978!) for the privilege of sleeping in the lobby. There was not even much television in the region, let alone sport on television. ARAMCO TV (provided by the eponymous Saudi oil company) served up a diet of cowboy shows made deeply confusing by the removal of any public display of affection to appease the Saudi censors. The only sport the region could boast was camel racing. Sharjah did have a nine-hole golf course, but it lacked grass and players took green mats with them for the fairway shots – not a setting to attract even the most journeyman professional.

The early sporting steps of the region provoked much derision. In the 1970s, as it began to use the first oil boom to change its sporting landscape, it attracted entrepreneurial souls like the amiable Englishman Dicky Hickman. He floated the idea – which was adopted relatively rapidly – for a racecourse in Bahrain. Hickman's credibility was slightly undermined by his readiness to suggest that, if Bahrain did not want a racecourse, he was able to build prisons. The Western media laughed at Hickman and also at the Shah of Iran, who was not only attracted by the idea of building a racecourse, but also had grandiose dreams of hosting the World Cup and the Olympic Games. Indeed, Tehran bid for the 1984 Olympics, but Ayatollah Khomeini's Islamic coup in 1979, which ended the Shah's reign, meant that the world never got to discover whether the Shah was a visionary or just delusional.

The ideas of Hickman and the Shah emphasized that the rise of sport in the Middle East had nothing to do with the sporting vision of Thomas Arnold and his disciples, but was always driven by a sharp business sense. Although the oil wealth drove the sporting expansion, the prospect of the oil running out provided the first impetus for sporting projects in the region. In the late 1970s, the ruler of Dubai, Sheikh Rashid Al-Maktoum, was concerned that Dubai had limited oil reserves. Indeed today, despite improvements in production technology, the emirate has only 20 years of reserves left. The ruler concluded that it would be necessary to diversify Dubai's economy if it was to keep up with its neighbours. Sheikh Rashid and then his son Sheikh Mohammed decided that the solution would be for the emirate to become the Gulf's business and transport hub as well as an international tourism and sporting destination. There was more than enough money to build first-class facilities and create the conditions to attract private investors and bank funding.

Dubai's plans were controversial in the region. One of the seven emirates which make up the United Arab Emirates (UAE), Dubai, with its other UAE colleagues, was also part of the Gulf Cooperation Council (GCC), along with Saudi Arabia, Kuwait, Oman, Qatar and Bahrain. The GCC had been set up to ensure that the states developed complementary rather than competitive policies. Sheikh Rashid unashamedly ignored the conventions and set up institutions and services designed to take business away from other Gulf States. To make matters worse, Dubai marketed itself with scarcely a mention of the UAE, which irritated its wealthier fellow UAE member Abu Dhabi.

Nonetheless, the strategy worked. Throughout the 1980s an infrastructure was put in place – hotels were built, roads turned from two to eight lanes, the airport redeveloped with excellent facilities and the most hyped duty-free store in the world was opened. In 1985, the high-profile Emirates Airline was launched. Significantly, all these state-owned organizations became the initial sponsors of all the sporting tournaments – fulfilling the double role of promoting Dubai and underpinning events until private sponsors could bear some of the costs.

The sports targeted were those that could be broadcast for long hours during the day. When Sheikh Mohammed was asked once why golf was the first sport chosen for investment, he replied that it kept Dubai's name on the television for eight hours a day and was watched on TV by the sort of people the emirate wanted to attract. A comparable targeted advertising campaign would have cost many times as much as the sponsorship. The effect of showing attractive pictures of a part of the world that most people, only 15 years ago, regarded as nothing but desert, was considered incalculable.

Football, of course, was the sport the region had always coveted and, by the 1970s, it had begun to target Western managers who could take the Middle Eastern countries to the ultimate glory of World Cup qualification. So in 1977, Don Revie suddenly abandoned his job as England manager in favour of the United Arab Emirates football team, a deal said to be worth £340,000 over four years. He would later manage club sides in the region. The outrage his sudden departure caused led to the FA banning him and reflected a sense of disbelief that a region like that could tempt away a serving England manager. But this marked the start of the region looking for experienced Western football experts. While Revie was still in the Middle East there was also talk of Sir Alf Ramsey becoming the Kuwait manager. There was some symmetry here. Revie had been appointed Ramsey's full-time successor after Sir Alf had been sacked for failing to get England to the very World Cup that saw Havelange rise to supreme power. Nothing came of the talk of Ramsey managing Kuwait but the journalist Nigel Dudley remembers seeing him in the lobby of a hotel in Kuwait, 'with an expression on his face that showed Sir Alf was more of a footballer than an Arabist'.

By the early 1980s, Arab specialists, particularly those in the British Foreign Office, were also seeing sport, particularly football, as a vehicle for their political/business agenda. This was, perhaps, most clearly illustrated in the 1980s by Saudi Arabia and the involvement of British Aerospace (BAE). For BAE sport – specifically football – was a perfect vehicle. In the 1980s the company was in tough competition for military aircraft contracts with the Americans and the French and saw a unique opportunity to generate a good image with the young Saudis who would be the next generation's decision makers. It would also create business for Ballast Needam, their construction company, which had some success building stadiums. This led a memorandum of understanding between the two governments which encouraged sporting connections between the two countries. The plan was put into action by a middle-ranking BAE executive, sitting in a Portakabin at the company's head office in Preston, England. Several stadium contracts were awarded to Ballast Needam and BAE continues to this day to win lucrative arms contracts in the kingdom. The most public manifestation of this relationship came in 1988 when England and Saudi Arabia played two friendly internationals, one in each country.

In that year, English football reporters were bewildered and indignant when the England team climbed on to Concorde, were greeted by the smiling face of the BAE chief executive and were whisked off to the desert for a game which appeared to serve little football purpose The reporters did not realize that they were seeing the willing collusion of the English football authorities in the arms trade.

Havelange could not have anticipated these changes but his very first tournament, and the first new FIFA tournament since the 1930 World Cup, clearly spelled out his intentions: the 1977 Under-20 World Cup, staged in Tunis, targeting both Africa and Arabs at the same time. The competition has since gone to various parts of the Arab world, having been held in three other Arab countries. This special concern for the new Middle East market was emphasized when Riyadh hosted the first three editions of the Confederations Cup, starting in 1992. The competition now provides a dry run for the country hosting the World Cup. The Saudis followed this up by hosting the Under-20 World Cup in 1989. Havelange, having opened up China, was also keen on that country and in 1985 it staged the first Under-17 World Cup.

The Middle East, not surprisingly, has not seen any of the four new tournaments for women: a Women's World Cup, Under-20 and Under-17 World Cups and a Women's Olympic football tournament. But it has seen some Blatter initiatives which include Club World Football and also the Beach Soccer World Cup. One by-product was the banning of the Iran women's team for wearing over-modest clothing.

Havelange was always very proud of his business skills and proud of the links he made between football, business and world politics. He would always deny that he had any personal reasons for fashioning such an alliance, for he claimed he had no reason to make money from football. As he told *Sport*, the Swiss magazine, in July 1986 in the midst of that year's World Cup:

> I'm a businessman, and I have too much money to make even more from soccer. In my transport company, 3,000 buses carry 240 million people a year. I'm a member of several supervisory boards, President of an insurance company, own a finance company, a factory for chemical products, have shares in a stock broking company, but not in Brazil, nor anywhere else in the TV network.

Although Havelange always said he had no reason to benefit personally from the activities of Dassler – a claim he made several times when Yallop and others interviewed him – by his own admission, FIFA had great need for money when he was elected. Havelange dramatically declared that when he succeeded Rous there were hardly 20 dollars in FIFA's kitty. This may be an exaggeration but FIFA certainly did not have the money to open the doors of the sweet shop to the children pressing their noses against the window. This is where Dassler came in and his first task was to help Havelange make a deal with Coca-Cola, a deal done in London in 1975 with Al Killeen, then president of the company. It was to prove the bedrock of Havelange's expansion plans. Havelange would later claim that football opened many doors for Coke. But Coca-Cola was a company that had always been aware of the power of sport and even before Havelange emerged had been knocking on all sorts of doors.

Coke had been prominent in the 1936 Olympics, providing drinks to the athletes and building up relations with Nazi officials. Herman Goring was photographed drinking Coke at the Dusseldorf Fair and it was said Hitler, the movie buff, had a sip or two as he watched *Gone with the Wind* in his private theatre. As the Cold War closed doors, Coke kept using the Olympics to open them. At the Helsinki Olympics it donated a cooler to the Russian compound, taking pictures of Russian athletes with the drink. In Melbourne, four years later, Coke calculated that Russian and Czech athletes drank 10,776 bottles of the capitalist drink. Coke got into the Soviet Union in 1978 on the back of Spartakiadas, the Eastern Bloc sports festival.

Wider political events also helped Coke. A year after Dassler did the deal with Coke, Jimmy Carter was elected president of the United States. The arrival of this southern president, who had spent long years in Atlanta, Coke's home town, gave Coke a friend in the White House. In 1977, the company gained sales in both Egypt and Israel when Carter brokered the Camp David peace accord between them. Coke moved into China shortly after the US established formal diplomatic relations with China in the wake of Mao's and Nixon's ping-pong diplomacy. Interestingly, two years after Coke did its deal with FIFA, it was banned from India after it refused to disclose its supposedly secret formula. Coke had been close to Mrs Gandhi and her election defeat in 1977 did not help. It was another decade before it returned, but that was more a reflection of India opening its economy.

Coke made the most of Havelange's relentless expansion plans. Under him, and his anointed successor Blatter, the number of FIFA tournaments grew exponentially, from two in 1974 to eleven, and Coke was all too happy to be the drink of the world's most popular sport, cutting across political and cultural divides.

But even as Havelange went round the world opening new tournaments, he knew that the World Cup he had inherited was the only product that would make money for FIFA. In 2008, the FIFA World Cup made $550 million from broadcasting rights, other FIFA events a mere $6 million. In 2009, FIFA World Cup's broadcast revenue was $623 million; only $27 million came from other events, and in 2010, the year of the World Cup in South Africa, FIFA made $2.4 billion from broadcasters, while other events contributed $40 million. In 2010, for the first time, FIFA gave a breakdown of what it made from marketing rights and the picture was even more revealing. The South African World Cup generated $1.07 billion; the marketing income from the other ten events was just $25 million.

Nobody understood the potential of this World Cup cash cow better than Dassler and, almost as soon as he had helped Havelange win the top job in football, Dassler had fashioned a remarkable company to make the most of the riches this competition offered. This involved teaming up with WestNally, a London-based company set up by Patrick Nally, an advertising man, and Peter West, a former BBC commentator. The pair had succeeded in persuading companies like Gillette and Benson & Hedges to sponsor cricket and snooker tournaments. It was Nally who had helped land Coke, and with Havelange in charge, Dassler knew he could now market football and also make a lot of money for himself. But he needed a vehicle and in February 1977, SMPI was set up. Forty-five per cent was owned by WestNally and 55 per cent by Horst Dassler, with many of the transactions routed through offshore accounts.

Today we take the marketing of sport for granted. But back in the 1970s that sport, any sport, could be treated as a marketing tool was a revolutionary idea. Until well into the 1970s clubs paid for their own kit, some clubs, like Arsenal, did not even carry advertisements in their programmes, as they felt this was against the spirt of the game. Football was about spectators paying at the gate and a ground carried little or no advertising. In that sense the actual organization of a sporting event had not changed much since Coubertin had revived the Olympics. World Cups and Olympic Games relied on the money they received from the spectators. The matches were televised but this brought in little income. Dassler set out to change all that. He was determined to make the World Cup more like a trade fair with the marketing of products built round the events on the playing field. And, with Havelange about to organize his first World Cup in Argentina in 1978, Dassler had the ideal opportunity to launch himself as the marketer of football.

With SMPI up and running, Dassler's first big deal was the 1978 Argentina World Cup. Promising the organizers 12 million Swiss francs, this sum being effectively underwritten by Coca-Cola, the company had acquired the rights to sell advertising boards round the ground. It knew it could make money and nearly doubled its outlay, securing 22 million Swiss francs by persuading many other companies to book space.

If all this was setting new landmarks in sports business, it could not satisfy Dassler. He had his sights on the biggest sports market of all – the Olympics – and even before he had helped Havelange get world football power, he had already started cultivating the man who wanted to head the Olympic movement. Like so many of Dassler's moves, he used a social setting to snare his man.

In June 1973, Avery Brundage, then president of the IOC, married Mariann Princess Reuss. He invited Juan Antonio Samaranch to the wedding. He had already seen him as a future president and made him a member of the IOC in 1966. In doing so, Brundage was breaking an IOC rule. This stated that a country that had never hosted the Games could have only one member. Spain, which had then not hosted an Olympics, already had a representative on the IOC.

Samaranch had been a Franco loyalist and owed much to the regime, which was still ruling Spain. In the fifties, when Franco's Spain was still something of a pariah, he organized an international roller hockey sports meet and then a Mediterranean sports festival. As a successful textile businessman, he also became friendly with Carmen, the dictator's daughter. In December 1966 he was made minister of sport in Franco's government. He was also elected a member of the Cortes from Barcelona, although this was election to a parliament under a fascist dictatorship, far removed from a proper democratic vote. Samaranch's friends have always defended him by saying too much should not be made of his Franco associations. Then you were either with Franco, or a Communist and in jail – Samaranch, no Communist, clearly chose the path of least resistance.

Also present at the Brundage wedding was Christian Jannette, the Dassler man whose job it was to cultivate contacts, particularly in the Soviet Union. He approached Samaranch and asked him whether he would like to meet Horst. In September 1973, Samaranch invited Dassler to Barcelona, where he was shown round Nou Camp, FC Barcelona's famous home. He was also taken to a nautical show and a black-tie dinner with Samaranch and his wife. Dassler knew Spain. As a young boy he had lived with a pro-Franco Spanish family. Early in his career, not long after Horst had moved to France to set up the Adidas operations there, he had had balls stitched by men and women in prison in Franco's Spain. Inside each of the balls there was a paper bearing a handwritten name and a cell number. This was meant to ensure that quality control could be checked.

Dassler had chosen his man with care. Samaranch was, by now, well established in the exclusive sports club of the IOC, having skilfully made his way up the ladder. This included holding the post of chief of protocol, a very significant position, which opened many doors. Samaranch knew what he wanted, how to get there and worked tirelessly in pursuit of his goals. Not long after he met Dassler, Samaranch set his sights on becoming his country's ambassador in Moscow.

Franco's Spain had always had a very frosty relationship with the Soviet Union – hardly surprising, given how Franco had used Hitler and Mussolini to defeat the Soviet-backed Republicans in a bloody civil war. By the time of Franco's death in 1975, Spain did not have an ambassador in Moscow. Soon afterwards, however, Samaranch persuaded the Spanish government to appoint him as ambassador, well aware he was going exactly at the right time for his Olympic ambitions. It was now November 1975 and Moscow would host the 1980 Olympics. That year would also see the IOC elect a new president. Lord Killanin, who had succeeded Brundage, had made it clear he would not seek a second term. Samaranch was now in an ideal position to gain supreme power in the Olympic movement.

In Moscow, Samaranch made sure that he looked after Dassler and his men. When Christian Jannette had a hernia operation in the Soviet capital, Samaranch's wife Bibis visited him every day, with fresh fruit and Spanish dishes. He also made sure he looked after every Olympic visitor to Moscow. Such bonhomie was combined with skills that showed Samaranch as the equal of Havelange in playing the sport political game.

In 1979, Samaranch was re-elected to the IOC Executive Board, essential for any chance of becoming president. Later that year he was in Puerto Rico to see Mario Vázquez Raña, a rich Mexican with a large media empire, become the president of the Association of National Olympic Committees. Raña's election, like that of Havelange, was an indication that power was moving from the Anglo-Saxon to the Latin world. Samaranch quickly sensed the importance of the Association and saw Raña (who speaks only Spanish) as an important ally. So did Dassler.

Yet, as the battered Olympic movement gathered in Moscow in the summer of 1980, with half the world, led by the United States, boycotting the Games, it was no means certain Samaranch would win the presidential election. The IOC then, even more than now, had a strong European majority and, without European support, no candidate could succeed. Initially the job looked likely to go to the German Willi Daume. As organizer of the 1972 Munich Games he carried a certain authority in the Olympic movement and Adidas's main office in Herzogenaurach rooted for the German. However, West Germany's boycott of the Moscow Olympics did not help his cause and he faced another European rival in the Swiss member, Marc Holder, who made a strong late run, with Jim Worrall of Canada also taking some of the Scandinavian votes.

The fifth candidate, Sir Lance Cross from New Zealand, withdrew in favour of Samaranch.

With the European vote split, Dassler knew his man could win if he made sure the rest of the non-European vote was solid for Samaranch. Dassler did his job and Samaranch duly won on the first round. On the evening of 16 July 1980, Samaranch celebrated his victory at the Moskva hotel, where the IOC was based during the Olympics. Among the most joyous people there were Horst Dassler and Christian Jannette.

Dick Pound, who the night before was told by Killanin that Samaranch would make a better president than many people thought, would later wonder how a candidate without much European support had won in both FIFA and the IOC. 'Rumours abound as to the possible role of money to assist the winning candidates on both occasions and the role of Dassler in such activities. To my knowledge no evidence has ever surfaced to support such rumours.'

The Moscow Olympics was to see another clever piece of politicking by Dassler, who helped his friend, the Italian Primo Nebiolo, take over the International Amateur Athletics Federation. Although the most important sport in the Olympics, it made little money and had been run by men who had been athletes of note rather than businessmen. Its first president, the Swede Sigfrid Edström, had combined studying for engineering with setting a Swedish 150 metres record. He had helped organize the 1912 Olympics and the inaugural Congress in July of that year, which led to the formation of the International Association of Athletics Federations (IAAF).

The man who put the stamp on the organization was the British politician Lord Burghley. Born David Cecil, he had won the gold medal in the 400m hurdles in the 1928 Games in an Olympic record time of 53.4 seconds. In 1932, he took time off from being a Conservative MP to compete in Los Angeles. Then, having served as governor of Bermuda during the war, he helped organize the 1948 Games. After Edström became president of the

IOC, Burghley took over the IAAF, moving the headquarters to London from Sweden. Lord Burghley, who became Marquess of Exeter in 1956, made no secret of his loathing for commercialization. He sounded off against wearing sponsored shoes as he left office at the end of the Montreal Olympics. But his lordly ways also bred resentment from the countries outside Europe, who felt that he neglected them. This was to be exploited to the full by Nebiolo with the help of Dassler.

But first he had to get rid of Burghley's successor, the Dutchman Adriaan Paulen. A resistance fighter during the war, he had a distinguished athletic record – Dutch champion at 400m and 800m and a competitor at three Olympic Games. Also a motor sports fanatic, he competed eight times in the Monte Carlo Rally. Paulen recognized that times were changing and in 1973 he organized the first IAAF World Cup and set in motion events that led to the first IAAF World Championships in 1983. But while he was a friend of Dassler, and enjoyed his Landersheim hospitality, he could not be easily manipulated.

Nebiolo, with the help of Dassler, ensured the IAAF elections due in Moscow in 1980 were postponed for a year and held in Rome at the time of the third athletics World Cup. The intervening year was used to persuade Paulen he could not beat Nebiolo, given the support the Italian had in Asia and Africa. Dassler's plan worked, and just before the elections, at a meeting in Paris at one of the places Dassler used to entertain guests, Paulen agreed to withdraw, after securing guarantees that he would have a role in the movement. Within four years he was dead and Nebiolo was riding high.

Nebiolo's sporting achievements as a long jumper were modest, but he knew which way to jump in sports politics, to which he brought the same sort of skills as Havelange and Samaranch. A lawyer by profession, who made his money in the construction business, Nebiolo had come into sports administration by organizing the 1959 World Student Games in Turin. From the beginning, like Havelange, he was keen to reshape the sport, introducing events such as the IAAF World Junior Championships, moving the showpiece IAAF World Championships to a two-yearly cycle and changing the voting structure of Congress. The IAAF, as the Asians and Africans had been campaigning for a long time, moved to 'one member, one vote', removing the biased vote advantage given to the founding European members. By the time this change came in 1987, Nebiolo had also moved the head-quarters from London to Monaco. As he opened the new headquarters on 10 June 1994 in the presence of Samaranch, Carl Lewis and Prince Albert of Monaco, he grandly declared, 'After eighty-two years, the IAAF has finally found its true home. Monaco has welcomed us with open arms and I hope that this city will become the city of athletics for the whole international sport-ing community.' It said much about Nebiolo that he saw the place where the rich went to play as the true home of a sport that had never generated much money and, probably, requires the least amount of expenditure to organize. Long before this, much to Dassler's joy, the IAAF had begun looking to increase its revenues via commercial sponsorship and television income.

Nineteen eighty-one was a busy year for Dassler. In addition to helping Nebiolo get into his position, it was also the year he began to groom the third man in that funeral photograph, Sepp Blatter. His rise within FIFA demonstrated how the shoemaker operated in the corridors of power – it involved getting rid of FIFA's long-term secretary, Helmut Kaiser. Kaiser threatened Dassler's business interests. He was part of an other-worldly pre-Havelange FIFA, working in a little office in Zurich where he even kept two sleepy dogs under his desk. He did not like Havelange and his friends, and whether this was the motivation or not Kaiser suddenly granted very attractive marketing rights for 12 years for the FIFA emblem and mascots, neither of which had existed before, to a German called Rolf Deyhle. In fact, Deyhle, an enterprising German, who also owned a London cartoon studio, had the bright idea of getting a Hungarian artist to design two characters, Sport Billy and Sport Suzy, who could be marketed as FIFA mascots. Deyhle devised the emblem himself: two overlapping globes shaped like footballs.

Dassler got Havelange to cancel the contract, but the Swiss court upheld the deal. This forced Dassler to work with a fellow German who could be as tricky as he was. A really nasty moment came just before the 1982 World Cup. On this occasion, Patrick Nally had again brought in Coca-Cola as sponsor, but then Deyhle sold the emblem rights to Pepsi, causing a near war and requiring hard work from Nally to stop the deal from falling apart.

In response, Dassler decided Kaiser had to go. He was to be replaced by the man Dassler had moulded. The way in which Dassler went about getting rid of Kaiser and installing his man showed the lengths to which he would go to get what he wanted. He first turned to Andre Guelfi, who ran Le Coq Sportif, of which Adidas France owned 49 per cent – although Horst secretly, unknown to the rest of his family, had another 2 per cent, and an option to buy the remaining 49 per cent whenever he wanted. Guelfi had been brought into the French company at the request of the French government, which was worried that the company was about to collapse. A flamboyant entrepreneur, Guelfi was a Corsican who grew up in Morocco and was a friend of General Oufkir, Morocco's interior minister. A French judge would later describe Guelfi as 'a business parasite', 'an old bandit', and 'a manufacturer of false bills by the kilometre'.

Given such a background, when Dassler asked the Corsican to put the frighteners on Kaiser Guelfi had few problems doing so and he did so in no uncertain way. At one stage Kaiser thought he was being stalked and realized it was best to go. As Guelfi later described it, 'I told him he'd better leave with his head held high and negotiate for his safety.' In May 1981, the FIFA executive committee parted company with Kaiser and by then Horst had his replacement already installed in FIFA.

The man had been recommended by Tommy Keller, who worked for Swiss Timing, a Swiss watch-making group, and was also head of the International Rowing Federation. The man Keller recommended was head of public relations at Longines, which was a leading brand in Swiss Timing: Sepp Blatter. He was brought over to Dassler's offices in Landersheim to prepare for his mission. Years later Blatter would tell Barbara Smit, 'From the beginning Horst and myself felt that we were kindred spirits. He taught me the finer points of sports politics – an excellent education for me.' Horst also taught him to smoke a good cigar. It helped that with birthdays two days apart, Blatter on 10 March 1936, Dassler on 12 March 1936, they could often have a joint birthday party every 11 March at Landersheim.

Christian Jannette told Smit, 'They held discussions in which Horst plainly issued instructions to Blatter. Horst openly talked of Blatter as a puppet – he introduced Blatter as one of us.' Guelfi went even further, telling Smit, 'He was an insignificant character entirely at Horst's command. When the three of us had lunch together Blatter looked up at Dassler as if he was God, knowing full well that he wouldn't stand a chance to get the FIFA job without Dassler.'

Blatter had always been a showman. As a child he liked nothing better than to be in the pantomime. He had first announced himself to the world when as a 35-year-old, back in 1971, he became president of the World Society of Friends of Suspenders, whose mission statement regretted 'women replacing suspenders with pantyhose'. Years later, after he became president of FIFA, he confessed to me that the only thing he did not like about his job as president was that he could no longer conduct the World Cup draws. That had been one of the highlights of his previous job as FIFA's general secretary. He recalled the excitement he felt drawing out the various coloured balls from the glass bowls in front of a live worldwide television audience.

But just as Dassler was cementing his control over FIFA, he was also about to cut his links with Nally. The two had just done what was then the biggest-ever football deal for the 1982 Spanish World Cup. More money had been required, because in keeping with Havelange's election promise, the World Cup would see 24 teams taking part. This meant SMPI securing 63 million Swiss francs in order to fund the deal. For this SMPI got not only the rights to the Spanish World Cup, Mundial as it was called, but also some rights from UEFA and two football federations.

Soon Horst had parted company with Nally. The split started in 1981 when Horst asked Nally to buy him out, but in the end it was Horst who bought out Nally. Indeed, at Orly airport an agreement was reached for Nally to buy out Dassler for 36 million Swiss francs. But then Dassler called off the deal. Nally could not work out why and in the end, as Mundial was coming to an end, it was Nally who was pushed out. There were more meetings at airports and at Brown's hotel in London. Nally got 3.6 million Swiss francs for giving up his stake in SMPI and left bemused, as Horst provided no explanation. He had just decided he did not want to work with Nally. Such sudden rejection by Dassler of a once close colleague was not unknown. Some years earlier Jannette, having served his usefulness in helping get Samaranch elected as IOC president, was also dismissed. He was told Dassler could not trust him anymore but not why.

Horst accused Nally of all sorts of things. For good measure he got two of Nally's executives, Steve Dixon and Peter Sporgis, to work for him in the new company that he was setting up. This was International Sport and Leisure (ISL), owned 50-50 by Horst Dassler and Dentsu, the Japanese advertising company. The move against Nally did have Japanese undertones. Dentsu was keen to get back into the sports sponsorship business where its great competitor Hackhudo had taken a big lead, helped by Nally.

The principle of ISL and SMPI was the same. They acted as brokers between FIFA (or any other world body) and companies wanting to use the FIFA brand to advertise their products. For the 1986 Mexico World Cup, ISL arranged deals worth 200 million Swiss francs from which it was said to have made a 30 per cent commission. Soon, with broadcasting rights included, its coffers swelled even more. What is more, many of these rights were given without any other bidder in the classic smoke-filled, closed-door room scenario. But with FIFA, Dassler had a product he could sell: the World Cup. The Olympic Games were an entirely different matter.

Outwardly the Olympics was the biggest sports event in the world controlled by the IOC. But this control did not translate into any real rights over the Games. On the field of play, the Olympics were a collage of world championships, with each sports federation responsible for organizing the event according to its own rules. Off the field, the money to be made from the Games was largely controlled by the city organizing the Olympics. Coubertin had ensured that the Greeks paid for the very first Olympics and, since then, the IOC had had a walk-on part in the financial aspects of the Games. In the early years, there was little money to be made. Indeed, the Olympics were associated with huge losses, and the 1976 Montreal Olympics were the most quoted example of why cities should not seek to host the Games. Curiously, the 1976 Games in the Canadian city made an operating profit of $223 million, its revenues of $430 million easily outstripping its operating expenses of $207 million. But this was before the capital cost of the games, such as stadiums and even a new airport, which meant that citizens of Montreal continued to pay for the Olympics until 2006, by which time their total cost had risen to $2 billion.

The leaders of the Olympic movement had a long history of shunning television and took longer than most sports organizations to understand its importance. During the 1960 Rome Olympics, Brundage, in words that would haunt his successors, declared that the Games had had no need of television for 60 years and he saw no need for it in the future. For the Rome Games, CBS had paid $400,000 for US rights, the worldwide sales bringing the total to $1.2 million. The income from television had kept growing and by the time of the 1984 Los Angeles Games, they were worth $287 million. But even then the IOC might not have realized the need to control television rights, but for the strong-arm tactics of Los Angeles, which treated the organization more like an interloper that should be grateful for what it was getting.

As with all Games in the United States, there was no government support. Worse still, 83 per cent of the citizens of Los Angeles had voted not to provide any funding. The Games were being staged by a collection of private individuals led by Peter Uberroth and their objective was to make sure they came out in the black. It led to much anger in the IOC and Sir Reginald Alexander of Kenya told Uberroth during the IOC session in Moscow, 'You, Mr Uberroth represent the ugly face of capitalism [. . .] and its attempt to take over the Olympic movement and commercialize the Olympic Games.'

Uberroth knew that he was in a position to dictate terms, as no one else wanted the Games. At one meeting with the IOC, Tom Bradley, mayor of Los Angeles, even gave the Games back to Killanin, saying the demands of the Olympic movement were too much. Killanin did look for an alternative host, but could not find one. Indeed, when Samaranch took over in Moscow, the feeling in the IOC was that even if the Los Angeles Games were held, no one would want to host subsequent games. At that stage only Nagoya, a Japanese industrial city, was bidding for the 1988 Games. By 1981, when the decision was made, Seoul did make it into a contest and won the chance to host the 1988 Games, but even that meant bending IOC rules. It had not answered the IOC questionnaire or submitted its bid by the deadline. South Korea was technically still at war with North Korea, prompting the ABC sportscaster Howard Cosell to say, 'You can't hold an Olympics in a war zone.' The South claimed to be a democracy, but it was a fragile one where the ruler, the former General Chun Doo Hwan, had come to power through a coup. Only 60 of the 160 countries due to take part in the Games even recognized South Korea.

Nevertheless, the Games had an appeal for television, particularly in the American domestic market. And, ironically, Uberroth's success in squeezing money from American television made the IOC realize it had an asset, one it should not allow the organizers to milk but claim as its own.

By the time the television rights for the Los Angeles Games

were being negotiated, the IOC had moved some way from Brundage's dismissal of television as a medium but was content to take a back seat to the host city. The host city negotiated the deal, giving the IOC a third of the rights fees. But the IOC paid so little attention to the deal that it did not make even sure that it had ownership of footage after the Games were over. Without an explicit agreement, the broadcasters assumed it was theirs, making it impossible for the IOC to keep a historical record of past games without paying heavy fees.

The IOC could veto deals, however. So Samaranch would not allow Uberroth to sell Italian rights to Silvio Berlusconi's pay television because he felt the Games should always be on free to air television. But it was rights for the US market that really mattered. For Los Angeles, US television paid $225 million. This was not only a huge increase on Moscow where the US rights had gone for $87 million but not much short of what the rest of the world paid: $287 million. Not surprisingly Los Angeles behaved as if it owned the Games.

Uberroth's committee decided more than half the money received from US television, $125 million, should be put against the cost of building the facilities. The IOC would get its third but a third not of $225 million but of $100 million: $33 million. This was more than the Olympics had ever had from television and Uberroth and his colleagues felt the IOC should be grateful to his committee. After all, what had the IOC done to deserve such a large sum? And if the IOC cut up rough, Uberroth could always say the Olympics did not even know how to make the most of the money it received. This was demonstrated when the IOC counsel, who had been given a cheque of $25 million as advance payment by Los Angeles, put it in his back pocket as he headed off for his holidays. It was not cashed for three weeks, costing the IOC some $100,000 in interest. There could have been no better proof if Uberroth needed evidence of how inept Lausanne was.

Samaranch was determined to put these matters right, more so because, like Havelange, he needed money, having taken over an organization which had just $200,000 in the bank and $2 million in assets. In his first letter to members, Samaranch wrote, 'The financing of the IOC is a matter of some urgency.' It was another three years before this need could be addressed and it came in the unlikely setting of Delhi in 1983 when the IOC, for the first time ever, had a session in the Indian capital, in a part of the world they rarely visited. Only three of the previous 85 sessions had been in Asia, in Tokyo and a 1967 session in Tehran when the Shah was laying grandiose plans for staging the Olympics. India then was a country more feared for giving visitors Delhi belly than valued for its call centres or its economy. In the Olympics, its hockey heyday was history and it was so much of an Olympic also-ran that it had not even won an individual Olympic gold – that momentous event did not arrive for another quarter of a century.

However, within weeks of the IOC session, the Indian cricket team unexpectedly won the World Cup, further boosting this sport and consigning the Olympics to the margins. But, like his friend Havelange, Samaranch saw taking such sessions to new places as keeping his constituents happy and, with the rest of the IOC not expecting much from Delhi, Samaranch used the occasion to put his commercial plans for the Olympics in place. These included taking charge of television and finding commercial partners who would pour money into the Olympics. Samaranch asked Dick Pound, who had just been elected to the executive board, to take charge of the television negotiations. As Pound recalls, Samaranch said, 'Deek, I want you to become chairman of the IOC television negotiations committee.' Host cities would no longer negotiate and send the IOC a cheque as Los Angeles had done. Now the IOC would be at the table and decide how much they received.

The first such negotiations in Lausanne in January 1984 have come to be known as the scorpion wars. ABC, the long-established US rights holder, bid $300m for the 1988 Calgary Winter Games, $217 million more than it bid for Sarajevo, a 337 per cent rise, but

NBC bid the same amount. With the hour late, Pound told the two broadcasters each bid would have to be raised by a million, every 15 minutes. To decide which station bid first Pound flipped a coin. However, the NBC man failed to call as the coin was tossed and Pound had to flip the coin again. In the end it took just one more round of bidding. NBC bid $304 million, ABC came back with $309 million and won. Upset by the new process, ABC's Roone Arledge refused to join in the celebrations in Lausanne Lake Place Hotel. Years later, Arledge explained to Pound that privately ABC had given him the codename Sterling and had expected 'Sterling' to stop the bidding once the auction went beyond $280 million. Arledge's belief was that $280 million would be the IOC's limit. ABC was hurt that it was forced to bid another $29 million to retain what it felt to be its historic property. Unfortunately for ABC, Pound did not know he was being nicknamed 'Sterling', let alone that he was expected to stop the bidding at a certain stage. As events would prove, ABC's hold over the Olympics was weakening and soon NBC would supplant it.

Samaranch's appointment of Pound as the Olympic television czar in Delhi may have set a rights battle going but the Delhi session should be remembered for what Horst Dassler did to change Coubertin's organization. Sale of television rights was not the only way the Olympics could make money. There was enormous potential to market the Olympic rings and attract sponsors. Samaranch had given Dassler a platform in Delhi to outline his commercial plans With the help of a short video presentation Dassler had a simple, very blunt message. 'You, the International Olympic Committee, own the most valuable and sought-after property in the world. Yet the Olympic rings are the most unexploited trademarks in the world. No major corporation in the world would tolerate such a situation.' Nobody had ever before proposed such a shotgun wedding between the sport that valued its amateur principles and Mammon. The Dassler plan meant that this once Corinthian body was launched on the road to commercialism.

Dassler's idea was for all the marketing rights belonging to the IOC, for both Summer and Winter Games, to be bundled together with those held by some 170 Olympic committees and sold as one single package to sponsors. It would be presented as a one-stop marketing exercise. However, the simplicity of the idea could not conceal the difficulty of implementing it and it would be another two years before the IOC could start. This involved Samaranch getting rid of Monique Berlioux, the IOC's longstanding director, for whom Samaranch did not care and who, in turn, distrusted Dassler.

The main problem for the Dassler proposal was that it had never been done before. In selling the Olympics collectively the IOC was taking rights which until then had belonged to individual Olympic committees. Some of these were not enamoured of the idea. It also meant finding sponsors who would be interested in such a collective package. Dassler had said the marketing programme could generate $300 million – an eye-watering sum given that the rights had previously fetched no more than $95 million. But Michael Payne, who worked with Dassler on the project, has revealed that Dassler did not say when this figure would be reached and at the time there was not 'a long queue of companies wanting to exploit the potential of a global Olympic association'.

The programme was meant to start at Seoul in 1988, but by 1985, after three years of effort, there were only three sponsors. Dick Pound was not sure Dassler's ideas would work. In addition to his television brief he had been asked by Samaranch to take charge of the marketing project primarily to make sure he did not raise too many awkward questions. As the Dassler plan limped to the starting line, Pound told the media, 'This is a trial. If it works, great, if not we will go back to the old way.' Even Payne was sceptical, and while the project was called Top, this was just a codename that meant nothing. It only acquired meaning when it became a success. Then it became The Olympic Programme and later the even cosier The Olympic Partners, now a much sought-after world brand.

American Express, the long-standing sponsors of the Olympics, did not feel the idea would work and not even a personal appeal by Samaranch to its president could persuade the organization. Visa, which was then an association of over 20,000 member banks, was considered too diffuse an organization to benefit, but it was persuaded and years later would thank American Express for dropping the ball and providing it with a world platform during the Seoul Games. Such was Visa's success that in subsequent Olympics, AmEx would organize elaborate ambush plans, one of them being a medallion programme allegedly authorized by an organization with a name similar to the IOC. Pound was so upset he threatened to call a press conference and cut his AmEx card in half.

The doubts of American Express and others had centred round the fact that for this to work, Dassler and the IOC would have to persuade the 170-odd national Olympic committees to give up their rights. It seemed a herculean task, even though many of these Olympic bodies had done little with the rights. But those that had feared that such global packaging would make money at their expense. Others, which were government funded, did not want too much commercial revenue. Their government money had given them an edge over privately funded Olympic committees. If these committees now got more money as a result of the joint marketing effort, the public-sector funded Olympic bodies would have to go back to their government to maintain their edge.

The United States Olympic Committee (USOC) posed the trickiest problem for the Dassler plan to make money from the rings. It controlled access to the biggest market, generated the most money and, under a special act of Congress, it could exploit the rings and Olympic trademarks. It refused to sign unless it received special privileges, and in the end these had to be guaranteed. In theory all Olympic committees were equal but the share-out of the Dassler marketing plan made the US more equal than others. The original IOC formula for distributing the marketing money was that half should go to the city hosting the Games. The other half was meant to be split: 80 per cent to the national Olympic committees and 20 per cent for the IOC. The USOC insisted it could not be treated like other national Olympic committees and secured half the amount intended for all the world's Olympic committees put together.

This concession to the US bred great resentment, especially because over the years non-US sponsors came in and other markets grew. Although the ongoing dispute is still unresolved, a new principle had been established in the share-out: the Olympic movement had, for the first time, started to behave like a corporation. It was no longer a non-profit sporting organization running a sports festival every four years. As Pound explained, the Top marketing programme relationship with a country was based not on 'the importance of a country within the Olympic movement (in the form of the number of athletes who participated in the games or the number of medals won) but only on the desirability of access to the various markets by commercial sponsors'. Mammon was now very much part of the Games, although the Olympics official philosophy was still based on the principle of unpaid athletes competing only for medals.

The Top programme had also turned the Olympics into a franchise operation, very like that operated by McDonald's, one of the Games long-established sponsors. The IOC had all the rights, it brought in all the money and it dictated the privileges it granted the local Games organizers. Not all the franchise outlets cooperated with the IOC headquarters. While local organizing committees could, and had to, supplement their income by national deals they could not undercut a Top sponsor. However, in Sydney during the 2000 Games, the local organizing committee did a deal with TNT, an Australian company and a rival of United Parcel Service, a Top sponsor. When the IOC complained, Sydney, says Pound, used 'pretexts, such as being unable to get the [UPS] delivery envelopes ready in time, that were patently false as justification for its behaviour'. UPS withdrew from Top. This caused such problems that the IOC failed to replace it as a sponsor by the time Athens took place four years later.

Over the years, Pound, a tax lawyer in a Montreal firm, grew close to Dassler and even acted as his adviser when Adidas had problems in the US. He saw no conflict of interest in this and does not even mention it in his Olympic memoir. He is keen to talk about helping the IOC avoid the hazards of associating with Dassler, something that FIFA, in particular, failed to do. So he vetoed Dassler's idea of having Coke as a shareholder in ISL. Dassler was clearly trying to work the formula he had with football but Pound argued that, as ISL went to various countries buying up rights, having Coke as partner might depress the price. He told Coke it would not be wise to link its name with ISL.

He also told Dassler that Adidas could not be in any product category. Dassler, records Pound, was 'profoundly disappointed', but accepted this would be a conflict of interest. But Pound was immensely pleased by what he sees as his best move, persuading ISL to sack the IOC. This came eight years after Dassler's death. The Summer Games in Atlanta in 1996 were on the horizon, the marketing revenues had grown from $95 million in 1985 to $376 million. But Pound and Payne, who had since started working for the IOC, were worried by Dassler's successors running ISL. Payne believed that Christoph Malms, Dassler's brother-in-law, who had become managing director, knew nothing about the business. Pound was convinced that Malms had a 'completely unrealistic view of what was needed', and ISL had taken on 'a series of financial commitments that seemed to us to be wildly extravagant'.

Pound wanted to end the marriage, but to present it as a divorce instigated by ISL. The crucial meeting took place in Karuizawa in Japan, in late 1995, with Jean-Marie Weber, a long-time associate of Dassler. The Frenchman had first worked for the German as an accountant but became such a confidant that he was often seen carrying a large bag, which gave him the nickname of Dassler's bag man. The speculation was that it contained documents, possibly cash. Weber, now ISL chairman, was convinced by Pound that the IOC was no good for ISL. Continuing to be associated with the Olympics was making ISL look bad and it was best if ISL walked away. Pound promised to say the IOC would reluctantly accept this and declare how wonderful ISL had been. Weber agreed. 'By the time they figured out what had happened,' wrote Pound, 'it was too late.'

Samaranch was not happy with what Pound had done, but in the end, he too accepted the relationship had to end. Pound could not stop expressing his delight at the divorce. Pound wrote,

> It proved to have been an enlightened decision because only a few years later ISL's financial mismanagement caught up with it and it was forced into an acrimonious bankruptcy that was surrounded by allegations of fraud and other secret financial transactions. Several international federations, such as FIFA, had all their eggs in the ISL basket and were put in very difficult circumstances. ISL owed them millions, which they had little hope of collecting. The IOC was the only organization that had seen the signs of disintegration in time and had taken timely steps to dissociate itself from ISL.

Pound's self-congratulation may have been overdone, but given what happened to FIFA, he was right. FIFA's failure to have a Pound-like figure would prove costly, particularly when Dassler's successors began to display the hubris that can so often be fatal. Dassler had concentrated mostly on sports he knew, football and the Olympics, apart from going into athletics in 1983, two years after helping Nebiolo gain the presidency. But after his death, ISL started seeking out various other sports, including basketball, the Asian Games, swimming, auto racing, both the ATP and ITF in tennis and Latin American soccer. The years between 1996 and the end of the century would see feverish activity by the company. In July 1996, ISL bought exclusive television rights for the World Cups in 2002 and 2006, paying around $1.6 billion. By December 1997 it had won a FIFA marketing contract for 2002 and 2006. Six months later in July 1998, ISL sold a share of the World Cup television rights to the Brazilian TVGlobo at a price of $60 million, of which approximately $22 million was meant to be provided to FIFA. ISL's appetite for global domination seemed insatiable. In April 1999 it spent $1.2 billion securing what was described as a ground-breaking 10-year television and marketing contract with the ATP tennis tour, including among other events the nine yearly Masters tournaments. Such commercial expansion was not only reckless and landed the company in trouble but what was worse was that beneath this was a huge story of bribery and kickbacks, a story that a decade later has still not fully unravelled. And may never do.

In May 2001 ISL went into liquidation owing more than 450 million euros to creditors. ISL's collapse was the second biggest in Swiss history, after Swissair in 2001. The same month, FIFA lodged a criminal complaint against ISL executives for around 75 million euros due from TV Globo and Dentsu. FIFA had been chafing about this money for some time. Back in September 1998, FIFA, in a letter to Jean-Marie Weber, demanded ISL hand over FIFA's share of the TVGlobo television rights payment. Then, in May 2000, FIFA, which had not yet received its share of the TVGlobo money, made another request, but got nowhere. Now, as ISL hit the rocks, Blatter told a journalist, 'I am not bribable. Otherwise you can chop off both of my hands.'

What followed were two fascinating parallel courses of action. The ISL bankruptcy made such a huge dent in FIFA's finances that, with the first World Cup in Asia only a year away, there was concern about the financial stability of the world body. FIFA hurriedly had to follow the IOC model and set up its own market-ing company to sell the television and marketing rights for the 2002 and 2006 World Cups. Blatter publicly blamed ISL for break-ing trust but there were many who were convinced that Blatter had failed to properly oversee marketing deals.

This conviction soon spread to some within FIFA, creating intense pressure on Blatter from his fellow members of the execu-tive led by UEFA president Lennart Johansson. Blatter had beaten the Swede for the presidency in 1998 in controversial circum-stances, amid allegations of bribery which Blatter had loftily dismissed. However, in the years that followed, he had had to battle against his own executive where at times he was in a minority. Now, as they asked questions about ISL and FIFA's link with the failed company, Blatter complained that UEFA had tackled him 'from behind'. However, the problems created by the ISL collapse were serious, and it seemed that UEFA might have found the scapegoat they were looking for.

In July 2001, FIFA held an extraordinary Congress in Buenos Aires. Johansson and his UEFA colleagues were convinced they could nail Blatter and laid out a careful plan to question him in detail about FIFA's finances, with Mathieu Sprengers, the president of the Dutch Federation and treasurer of UEFA, detailed to make the speech. The night before Blatter tried to persuade UEFA not to bring what he felt was dirty washing into the public arena, but failed. He decided on a bold counterstroke, effectively taking over the Congress and turning on his tormentors.

FIFA's Congress requires a short welcome from the president, then a roll call. It is only after this that the Congress officially goes into session. Blatter turned his welcome speech into a major address, throwing out a mass of figures to show the finances were healthy and FIFA would recover all the money ISL had cost the organization. His supporters from round the world then started eulogizing him, starting with India. Haiti, Jamaica, Peru and Cuba joined in. Finally, Ivan Slavkov, president of the Bulgarian Football Association, who four years later would be expelled from the IOC following a BBC Panorama investigation, proposed a motion endorsing everything Blatter had said. Michel Zen-Ruffinen, the FIFA general secretary, protested that Congress was not in session and a vote could not be taken on the motion. But Blatter brushed it aside as if this was a detail. UEFA had been flattened even before it could make the charge. It was a performance that a seasoned politician would have envied.

Despite this victory, for another year Blatter remained under pressure and by the following summer appeared to face a tricky re-election as president against Issa Hayatou from Cameroon.

Hayatou headed the African Federation, was backed by Johansson and UEFA, and had promised to clean up FIFA. In May there followed a stormy FIFA executive meeting which saw Michel Zen-Ruffinen, together with Johansson and ten other members of the Executive Committee, start legal proceedings against Blatter. Nothing like this had ever happened in FIFA's history. Their case seemed substantial, based on a 300-page-long indictment alleging misuse of funds and negligent financial management.

The events as FIFA gathered in Seoul in June 2002 for its Congress were even more explosive. The day before the Congress was due to vote to choose between Blatter and Hayatou, tempers were so frayed that, on the dais, the two men seemed to come close to having a physical fight. Blatter was criticized by delegates including Adam Crozier, then chief executive of the FA, and other national associations. However, when the vote took place, Blatter easily beat Hayatou on the first ballot. Blatter accepted the congratulations as if he was a king being crowned. And so quickly did his re-election change everything, it demonstrated that the FIFA that Havelange had created, and Blatter sustained, worshipped power. The prosecution against him was withdrawn and soon Zen-Ruffinen was out of a job. The anti-Blatter momentum that Johansson had built up collapsed like a pricked balloon. This destroyed the already weakening hope that FIFA would investigate the collapse of its long-standing marketing partner. FIFA declared that it had restructured its finances and pretended that all this was a passing storm that had done it no permanent damage.

However, in the meantime, the Swiss authorities had not been inactive. Thomas Baur, ISL's liquidator, quickly found payments in the books which looked very odd, possibly bribes, of some 3.5 million Swiss francs. He began by demanding this amount be paid back so that creditors of ISL could in turn be paid. He wrote to some 20 high-ranking sports officials and succeeded in getting some money back in 2004. That was to create a saga of its own: the money came not in various sums from the different officials, but in one payment of around 2.5 million Swiss francs. Moreover, the man who organized the payment, the well-known Swiss lawyer Peter Nobel, who had also acted for Blatter, convinced the country's highest court that no names should be disclosed. The money was transferred by Nobel on behalf of his client Jean-Marie Weber. Although this was never stated, the implication was that Weber was the one who had paid almost all the bribes and the only person who knew the names of the bribed officials. He was not talking and in 2005 the Swiss Federal Court ruled that nobody need talk.

Baur, happy with getting the money back, withdrew the civil complaints against the officials. In June 2004, soon after the payment was made, FIFA also withdrew its criminal complaint against ISL directors for allegedly embezzling TV-Globo television money. However, this did not stop the wheels of Swiss justice.

In addition to Baur, the Zug investigating magistrate, Thomas Hildbrand, had also been busy. In November 2002, Weber and other ISL executives had been arrested for a few days and questioned. It was Hildbrand who had tried to get Nobel to disclose details of the payment he had made to Baur, and in November 2005 he launched a new ISL-related investigation and raided FIFA's Zurich headquarters seeking evidence.

In July 2008 the case against six former ISL executives, including Weber, came to a conclusion in Zug, the canton in Switzerland where ISL had been based. The court ruled that FIFA had failed to exercise proper oversight over marketing payments worth hundreds of millions of dollars.

The three-judge panel said that FIFA was aware of the financial difficulties of ISL months before it went bankrupt. FIFA was ordered to pay about 118,000 Swiss francs in costs for lodging the criminal complaint that sparked the fraud inquiry. The judges concluded that FIFA's claim that it was caught unawares by the sudden lack of funds was not credible. This was because FIFA had insight into the ISL account at all times.

During the hearing in Zug, it had emerged that for years sports officials had received large sums from ISL for arranging lucrative sponsorship and broadcast deals. The word used in court was

Schmiergeld, German for bribes. The money was part of a larger amount totalling 140 million Swiss francs that ISL funnelled through Liechtenstein and the British Virgin Islands accounts of high-ranking sports leaders over the course of more than a decade.

Among those explicitly named in court documents as receiving some of this money was the head of the South American Soccer Confederation (CONMEBOL), Nicolás Leoz, an 81-year-old lawyer from Paraguay, who has been president since 1986 and a member of the FIFA executive. He was sent two payments in 2000 totalling some 130,000 Swiss francs, the documents said. Leoz had not been accused of acting illegally and had previously denied any connection with the marketing company.

The judges could not treat such payments as bribes, a reflection of the legal situation in Switzerland when these transactions took place. At the time they were made such payments were not illegal in Switzerland. They did not become illegal until new anti-corruption legislation was passed in 2006, long after the collapse of ISL. According to the defendant ISL directors, these payments were therefore to be regarded as a normal and integral part of the daily sports business and a pre-condition if ISL wanted to sign contracts with their customers. 'I was told the company would not have existed if it had not made such payments,' said Christoph Malms, ISL's managing director. He was backed by the former director of finances, Hans-Jürg Schmid. 'It was like paying salaries. Otherwise they would have stopped working immediately,' he said about the sports officials.

Present in the Zug court was a former employee of ISL, Roland Buechel, who by then was a local councillor for the Swiss People's Party in the nearby city of St Gallen. He blamed the defendants for the company's collapse, but accepted the peculiarities of Swiss law which had in effect condoned such practices. 'The law allows for these payments, but I'm really disappointed that the Swiss taxpayer will end up with the bill.' As he told me, 'When I worked for ISL we knew certain things were going on but not on this scale. The court hearings in Zug in 2008 surprised me completely.'

The six men were cleared of most of the fraud charges resulting from ISL's collapse. The result of this extraordinary trial was the six defendants, having been cleared, were even awarded compensation ranging from 17,000 francs to 190,000 francs, less court costs. Such compensation payments – often paid by the government or another party making accusations – are frequently ordered in Switzerland when defendants are acquitted. While the lead prosecutor, Marc von Dach, spoke of appealing he also admitted, 'In complex business cases you always have to expect that innocent verdicts can be handed down.'

The judges in Zug did fine Jean-Marie Weber for embezelling cash and their comments about the man who ran ISL after Dassler's death make fascinating reading:

The 66-year-old accused Jean-Marie Weber today works as a consultant in the field of sport for Winleads AG which he owns . . . The accused lives in a rented apartment in well-ordered personal circumstances. He has a half-share in a family house in France and has no special maintenance obligations . . . The accused J.-M. Weber has a Swiss criminal record with a fine of 700.00 Swiss francs from 2004 due to serious violation of road traffic regulations . . .

In the opinion of the criminal court, the culpability of the accused Jean-Marie Weber is fairly serious. Nunca and Sunbow S.A. [Lichtenstein based companies] placed immense trust in him for the assets invested by the ISMM Group and he knew that no-one could monitor him in 'actual reality' after the death of Horst Dassler. He exploited this situation for egotistical reasons, by transferring an amount of 90,000 Swiss francs to his own account. To add to the seriousness of the case, he was very well remunerated for his activities for the ISMM Group and was not at all dependent on this 'additional transfer' . . . In mitigation, the fact that more than seven and a half years have passed since the crime and – apart from a contravention of road traffic regulations . . . as far as is known he has behaved well since then should be taken into account. His otherwise unblemished reputation should also be regarded as a positive factor.

... In summary, the accused Jean-Marie Weber is therefore sentenced to a fine of 240 daily rates at 350.00 Swiss francs, taking into account the period of eight days in custody suffered whilst awaiting trial and granting respite for a probationary period of two years ...

For the sake of completeness it should be noted that in the case of the accused Jean-Marie Weber, according to the principle that 'Crime should not pay' it would have been possible to add forfeiture of the embezzled sum of 90,000.00 Swiss francs ... Since the Public Prosecutors have not, however, made a corresponding application, the criminal court will refrain from doing so.

Weber's lawyer, Marc Engler, made it clear that his client was likely to appeal this conviction for embezzlement on procedural grounds. 'Our client doesn't have to prove his innocence by declaring the reason for the payment. He has to be assumed innocent,' Engler said.

The judges also found two other defendants, Hans-Jüeg Schmid and Hans-Peter Weber, unrelated to Jean-Marie Weber, guilty of deviously obtaining false documents in multiple cases.The two men had set up sham companies with the sole aim of diverting funds from the ailing ISMM mother company.

The ISL saga publicly came to a close two years later on 24 June 2010. Then the Zug prosecution authorities cleared Blatter of wrongdoing even as they confirmed that FIFA officials had taken bribes. The statement said, 'Foreign persons of FIFA-institutions have received provisions from the ISL/ISMM.' Blatter, being Swiss, was clearly not guilty. Note the use of the word 'provisions', as if these were supplies of some sort when most people in most countries would understand them as bribes.

The officials who received the bribes were not named as none of the defendants was facing bribery charges, bribery not being recognized as an offence at the time under Swiss law. The statement from the Prosecutor's Office said:

In the proceedings the accused have denied criminal responsibility, but not the receiving of the funds. They are, however,
willing to pay by the prosecution of redress available the qualified amount of 5.5 million Swiss francs (£3.3/$4.9 million). Part of
the restitution payment in the amount of 2.5 million Swiss francs
(£1.5 million/$2.2 million) is to non-profit organisations. The
defendants have also assumed the costs.

In effect an out of court settlement had been made and names of
those who had received or given the bribes would for ever remain
secret. The statement came in the middle of the World Cup, a
timing that may not have been entirely coincidental. The entire
FIFA hierarchy was in South Africa and no doubt happy for the
news to be buried. In a statement, the world body noted:

> FIFA is pleased that the prosecutor of Zug has finalised his inves-
> tigations which followed the 'ISL/ISMM case'. It is important to
> recall that the decision was made on matters which took place
> prior to the year 2000 and that there has been no court conviction
> against FIFA. In addition, the FIFA President has been cleared of
> any wrong-doing in this matter. As the investigation and the case
> are now definitely closed, FIFA will make no further comment.

Yet this was nothing that could be remotely described as
closure. Indeed since then further investigations by Swiss and
German media and two *Panaroma* specials on FIFA suggest the
full story is yet to emerge. Buechel, now a member of the Swiss
parliament, has also led a one-man campaign to get to the bottom
of what really happened and make FIFA more transparent. But
while the whole story may still unravel, for the moment, the
conclusions of this saga can only be very bleak for those who
believe sport has a higher morality.

The effect, in the picturesque words of Jens Sejer Andersen,
international director and founder of the organization Play the
Game, was like magic: 'A number of corruption scandals in the

highest ranks of sports leadership continue to vanish, even before we realize that they actually exist.' As Jens Weinrich, a journalist who has diligently pursued this case, declared, it left many questions unanswered: 'Who took which amount of bribery payments? Who made which decision after these payments? Who paid the so-called "compensation payment" to the prosecutor's office?'

When the administrators of the world's most popular sport refuse to answer any of these questions – or even attempt to find the answers – it becomes impossible to justify the pretensions of sport to build character and promote a higher morality. Their attitude tells us a great deal about how Dassler, and people like him, changed sport. They induced sport to join the cult of Mammon, to seek and accept huge sums of money, but not the responsibilities which come with them. When the shoemaker marched sport into the corporate world he may have had no intention of opening sport up to large-scale bribery. But he built a system in which his successors found it impossible to operate without bribes. He had left a legacy where sports organizations behaved as if the world was still governed by the ethics of nineteenth-century American capitalism. The modern corporate world had long recognized the need to embrace transparency and disclosure, but sport behaved as if it was above and beyond such considerations. Although football provided the most catastrophic failure to live up to its high ideals, there were other sports whose moral code could not cope with the modern corporate world of sport. They included the sport that had long asserted its superior moral values: cricket.

CHAPTER 13

THE RUPEE TAKEAWAY

In September 2007, the day before India played Pakistan in the first Twenty20 World Cup final in Johannesburg, a meeting took place in the city's plush Sandton Sun hotel. The meeting, called by the then chief executive of the ICC, Malcolm Speed, was with Sir Allen Stanford, a Texan then claiming to be worth around $18 billion.

Today Stanford languishes in a jail some 50 miles from Houston, facing charges of having defrauded investors to the tune of $7 billion. He has been beaten up in prison and is far from the uncrowned King of Antigua he was when he walked into the Sandton Sun on that southern hemisphere spring day in 2007. At that stage Stanford's position in the Caribbean could not be questioned; having settled in Antigua he gave the impression of owning it. Indeed he had been knighted by the Caribbean island and was hailed by many in the West Indies as the saviour of the game. Next to the airport he had built a new cricket stadium and the previous year he had organized a successful Twenty20 tournament in the Caribbean. His board of directors was literally a West Indian Hall of cricketing fame: Everton Weekes, Andy Roberts, Michael Holding, Vivian Richards, Wes Hall, Lance Gibbs, Joel Garner and Desmond Haynes. He was said to be paying each of his board members $8,000 a month.

Early in the spring of 2007, as the 50-over World Cup was being held in the West Indies, Ken Gordon, a Trinidad entrepreneur who had been given the task of reviving the financial fortunes of the West Indian game, had arranged a meeting between Speed, Percy Sonn, then ICC president, and the Texan.

At this meeting in Jamaica's Montego Bay, Stanford compared himself to Kerry Packer and outlined his proposal for a tournament where three teams would come to Antigua and play each other to decide which of them would then play his team, the Stanford Superstars, in a winner-take-all $20 million match. In the course of the meeting, Stanford gave the impression that he owned West Indian cricket. When Speed proposed that he sponsor the West Indies team, Stanford interjected that when they played they must play not as the West Indies but as the Stanford Superstars. The West Indies Cricket Board, far from objecting, was keen on the idea as this would bring it much-needed money.

Stanford's meeting with Speed and Sonn did not go well however, and for the ICC this brought up the old problem of official and unofficial matches. National sides played each other and these matches were recognized as international but if a national team played an unofficial team then it did not count towards the players' personal records or the records of the team. There was also the problem that the $20 million prize money would go straight to the players. This would place them at a huge advantage compared to those who did not play this form of cricket and distort the wage structure of the various cricket boards. However, with the West Indies desperate for money, the ICC agreed to carry on talking with Stanford.

The Sandton Sun meeting was to prove one of the most dramatic in recent cricket history. Although Speed had planned it as a small gathering, Stanford came with his entire board dressed up in red Stanford Superstars polo shirts. Stanford had also decided that he, not the ICC, would be in charge of the meeting, so he had changed the venue to a bigger room in the hotel in contrast to the smaller one Speed had chosen. Indeed, he summoned the ICC to that room. Two women, one of them Holding's wife Laurie-Ann, recorded the proceedings and Julian Hunte, who had just taken over as president of West Indian cricket, was also present.

Stanford had clearly planned to use the occasion to show-boat what he had done for West Indian cricket, with a few of his board of ex-cricketers adding their voices in a chorus of support. Stanford started by declaring that he had changed his proposal. He now wanted the winner of the next day's final between India and Pakistan to go to Antigua and play his team for $5 million in a winner-takes-all prize. He was sure it would attract an audience of a billion.

Speed, surprised by how the meeting was going, pointed out that India, which already earned $8 million in television rights for each 50-over match it played, was unlikely to travel to the Caribbean on the off-chance of getting $5 million. Speed also felt it was nonsense that such a match would attract a billion viewers and proposed a carefully worked out ICC alternative. Every season the higher ranked of the two Test teams that toured the West Indies would play the Stanford Superstars in an unofficial match. If the Test side won, its board, not the players, would get $10 million and the other $10 million would be shared by the other ICC members. The match would not count as part of the official records. Stanford indignantly rejected the proposal and the meeting went from bad to worse. Eventually Stanford, claiming Speed had insulted him, walked out. As he did so he knocked over a chair.

Speed, in his memoir *Sticky Wicket*, describes what happened next:

> Then there was a very loud outburst from Desmond Haynes directed at me. He claimed that I was solely responsible for the demise of West Indian cricket. I had introduced the future Tours programme (not true) that made it impossible for the West Indies to function profitably (not true), I was a racist (not true). I was a disgrace, and I and others had done this knowingly so that a black team would no longer dominate world cricket (not true). It was a disgrace, I had behaved disgracefully in the meeting and I was not fit to be chief executive of the ICC. He was ranting and

yelling and he was very angry. While he was doing this, Vivian Richards, who was sitting at the end of the table (I think he had been next to Stanford), started banging loudly on the table with both hands. The rest of the group (particularly Hall, Holding and Gibbs) seemed to be quite shell-shocked by the walkout and Haynes' ranting. He and Richards were strongly supporting their Chairman, as would be expected of two such aggressive cricketers. It was the most amazing incident in which I was involved in 11 years of cricket administration. The walkout was childish. Haynes and Richards were out of control. Morgan [David, ICC vice-president], Mali [Ray, who had taken over as ICC president following the death of his fellow South African Percy Sonn)], and I withdrew quietly and left Richards banging on the table and Haynes yelling.

The next day India beat Pakistan in a thrilling final and this meeting at the Sandton Sun formed a curious footnote to cricket history. The Indian victory led to dramatic consequences for world cricket, completely putting into shade Stanford's plans. His aim was to use West Indian cricket as a commercial power base for his own ends. Even if Stanford had not been accused of fraudulent behaviour, his basic premise was faulty. Stanford believed he could revive the West Indian domination of cricket which, starting in the 1970s, had peaked in the early 1990s. But this was cricket's version of luring passengers away from long-distance air travel back to passenger ships. It just could not work.

The West Indian domination of cricket had come when the game was based on bilateral tours. Then the Caribbean team was the best, although it probably did not get as much credit as it should have done. Despite this, the basic political grip of England and Australia on the world game, reflecting their pioneering position, had not changed. However, West Indian cricket could make money as it could command good fees for playing Test and other international cricket. This was how cricket had always been organized and it suited the Caribbean islands perfectly. The visits by their wonderfully gifted teams to other Test nations generated huge crowds and big revenues and other countries could come on a leisurely island-hopping tour of the Caribbean, which also made good money for them. Indeed in the late 1960s England, keen to attract crowds back to cricket, had radically changed its entire international calendar, instituting twin tours in an English summer so that the West Indies could tour England more often. But in the 1990s the marketing of the sport, in line with many other sports, fundamentally changed.

Television now provided the major source of income. Yet the West Indies were not a nation and their television market was not developed. The economic change coincided with a dramatic decline in West Indian cricket. This was horribly illustrated just months before the dramatic meeting with Stanford at the Sandton Sun. In 2007, for the first time, the West Indies hosted the 50-over World Cup. It was such a disaster that, in his book, Speed chose the chapter heading 'Cricket World Cup 2007 West Indies: The event from Hell'.

Although in popular cricketing memory the West Indies are seen as one entity, in reality they are 13 mainly small islands spread over a vast area, all of them fairly underdeveloped and each with their own government. The West Indies board, keen that the World Cup should take in as much of the Caribbean as possible, spread the tournament over eight islands and they were hopeful that this would bring in huge numbers of tourists. The omens were good as they succeeded in attracting foreign investment: the Chinese and the Indian governments, for their own political reasons, even funded new cricket stadiums. But this meant the World Cup was being staged in the equivalent of a country of 7 million, less than the population of London, or even that of most Indian cities, with teams required to travel the distance between London and Rome for some matches.

If the logistics were a nightmare, the nadir came with the final at Barbados providing one of the most ridiculous ever conclusions for a major international competition. With rain disrupting play the match finished in darkness as some of the best umpires in the world got the rules wrong. Having decided play would carry over to the next day, the umpires then reversed their decision and called the players back. Asked by journalists why players were going back to the middle in the dark, Speed said in exasperation, 'I have no fucking idea,' although to his relief his words were not reported. But that moment illustrated the failure to revive a once great centre of cricket. What was worse, the event, as Speed admits, will for ever be marked by the death of the Pakistan cricket coach Bob Woolmer in Kingston.

The Jamaican police immediately announced that they suspected murder and there was speculation that the death, coming after Pakistan had sensationally lost to Ireland, involved match fixing. The Pakistan team were, at one stage, considered likely suspects and Mark Shields, a former City of London police-man who was the deputy commissioner of the Jamaican Police, was convinced that Woolmer had been strangled. Interestingly Peter Rees, the former Scotland Yard man in charge of the ICC Anti-Corruption Unit, always had his doubts that it was murder. Rees was eventually proved right. But that was months after an almost farcical investigation and lurid speculation in the press. During the World Cup, a media circus developed, concentrating not on the cricket, but on the murder investigation and how Woolmer might have been the victim of criminal gangs trying to fix matches.

All this demonstrated that the West Indian islands were incap-able of providing a centre for world cricket that could rival India, let alone match its growing economic power. India was to demon-strate its own power less than a year after the West Indian World Cup debacle. Then seizing on its unexpected win in the Twenty20 World Cup final in Johannesburg, it unleashed the Indian Premier League, a Twenty20 tournament which combined cricket with Bollywood and money. It is hard to argue with historian Boria Majumdar that '18 April 2008 will go down in cricket history as the date when cricket changed for ever.'

The nature of the change cannot be overestimated. Ever since the game took its modern form, the English cricket season had been sacrosanct. All other countries stopped playing as soon as the season started in England, as if England was still the mother country of the game. Over the years, cricket in other countries has slowly intruded: today, Test matches in the West Indies go on till early July and Sri Lanka play some Test cricket during an English summer. But such overseas cricket is seen at best as a starter or a side dish while the main cricket course during the northern hemisphere summer has always been in England. The game, of course, had also developed into an odd team game where domestic cricket, even in England, just did not pay. It attracted few spectators, brought in little money and the domestic game was only possible because of the heavy subsidy it received from the international game. This is in marked contrast to most other team games like football or rugby where international matches are the cream on top of a thriving domestic structure.

Now the Indians used Twenty20 to prove that cricket did not need national contests to attract television and crowds. A domestic tournament, rightly targeted, could bring in huge sums of money, and could attract players from all over the world. It even changed the television viewing habits of India. The sheer money it generated was staggering enough: the television rights for a 10-year period went for $1 billion and Sony, who acquired the rights, was happy to pay such sums as it sold 12,700 advertisement slots for the 59 games being played in the six-week period between mid-April and early June. The players earned millions and Indian families abandoned soaps to watch cricket. The Indians had not just found a domestic model that worked; the new format was about to challenge the historic English domination of the game.

With the matches being played until well into May, the Indian tournament encroached on the English season, providing a more lucrative source of income for the top cricketers of the world. Until the IPL emerged, the start of the northern hemisphere summer would see many of the game's leading cricketers leave their countries to journey to England to play county cricket, the only source of lucrative employment for many overseas cricketers. Indeed since the late 1960s, after English cricket liberalized the qualifying rules for overseas players, a whole generation had used county cricket almost as a finishing school. This included some of the greatest names in cricket: players like Viv Richards, Malcolm Marshall, Imran Khan, Javed Miandad and Greg Chappell. Interestingly, even then not many Indians, with the odd exception of Bishen Singh Bedi, had taken to county cricket.

Now the IPL offered riches that had previously been the preserve of footballers. In 2009 Freddie Flintoff and Kevin Pietersen were offered $1.55 million each for little more than six weeks of Twenty20 cricket. For many cricketers such money was so tempting that they did not worry about missing the start of the English season to play in India – that mattered little. And, since the launch of IPL in 2008, it has become common for teams touring England to arrive without their leading stars as they are too busy completing their IPL contracts. Once the world had stopped and all eyes turned to England as the first ball of the season was bowled at Lord's. Now English cricket waited until the end of the IPL to get its full complement of players. Within two years of the launch of IPL, the first ball of the English season, in the shape of the match between the MCC and the champion county, was not even being bowled at Lord's. The event had moved to the Middle East, a move dictated by money. It amounted to as great a revolution in the game as the legislation of round-arm bowling (which, for the first time, allowed the bowling arm to be raised above the shoulder) more than a century earlier. It confirmed that this very English game was now firmly in the hands of the Indians.

It was the first time that the overall control of a game had passed from the West to a non-white power. It also marked a major evolution of the game the English sailors had brought to India all those centuries ago. During this period Indians had gone from supplicants to owners. Nobody could have anticipated the form of the Indian takeover, not even the Indians, who celebrated their Twenty20 World Cup victory that evening in Johannesburg. For a start the Indians had always disdained this new form of the game. They were making huge amounts of money from the 50-over game and saw no need for a new, shorter, untested format. Back in 2006 when the format was first discussed Niranjan Shah, then the Indian board secretary, commented, 'Twenty20, why not ten-ten, or five-five or one-one?' Indeed the international cricket authorities had to use a number of stratagems, including suggesting the subcontinent might not get support to host the 50-over World Cup in 2011, even to get India to participate in the Twenty20 World Cup.

Nevertheless such was their lack of enthusiasm for this form of the game that they had come to the World Cup expecting nothing and all their major players, led by Sachin Tendulkar, had missed the tournament. For the Twenty20 World Cup they were under a rookie captain, Mahendra Singh Dhoni. Dhoni's team surprised itself as much as the world by winning and, as after the equally unexpected 1983 World Cup win, Indian cricket was to change dramatically. The difference from 1983 was that this change was coming against the background of India as a rising economic power. They now had the financial muscle to rock the cricket world. The surprise was not that the Indians had taken over cricket but the speed of the Indian takeover – the IPL was launched just eight months after India's Johannesburg victory.

The Indians had always paid due homage to the game's high moral purpose and many Indians echoed the words of Tom Brown to his friend Arthur and the master that cricket is 'more than a game, it's an institution'. Indeed the English expression 'it's not cricket', denoting moral censure, was used by Indians who did not even speak English. For many Indians it was often the only English expression they knew. However, from the moment the Indians had taken to this English game, they had also shaped cricket to suit their circumstances, combining glamour with money and politics in a manner that was foreign to the English. In

Indian eyes, for all the talk of the spirit of the game, there was the hard-edged realization that the game could be a great vehicle for material advancement. All this was very evident when India first burst on to cricket's world stage.

In many ways the man who became the first great Indian star of the game, indeed one of the game's most cherished players, can be seen as a forerunner of the IPL revolution. He became known as the great prince of cricket but he had no royal blood and used cricket to achieve his royal status. It was a wonderful illustration of how Indians could use sport. In the closing years of the nineteenth century Kumar Shri Ranjitsinhji lit up English cricket so brilliantly that he became a giant in the golden age of cricket. So much so that his cricketing style and deeds defined the era. *The Complete Who's Who of Test Cricketers* described him as the man who 'brought Eastern magic to the cricket fields of England, America and Australia'. Alan Ross, probably his most famous biographer, wrote that Ranji was one of only half a dozen in the history of the game who had added something new to it. He was, wrote Ross, 'The Indian Prince, in all his finery, abroad in an English summer'. Sir Edwin Arnold, indulging in the sort of sentimentality that came so naturally to Victorians, spoke of a 'star from the east bursting upon the cricketing world'. Ranji, said John Lord in *The Maharajas*, was 'the first Indian of any kind to become universally known and popular'. Although this was a rather Anglo-centric view, reflecting the idea that only an Indian who had made a reputation in England could be considered truly world famous, it nevertheless emphasized the position Ranji attained during the Victorian age.

The image of Ranji with his bat, mastering bowlers on the cricket fields of the country that occupied India, certainly played an important part in fostering Indian pride and self-respect. As Ross puts it, this 'contributed more than anything else to the Indian cricketer's realization of his own possibilities'. Even today schoolchildren in India read Neville Cardus' marvellous essay on Ranji with delight and wonder. Cardus narrates how every year

Yorkshire came down to Hove to play Sussex. The moist air was heavy and Yorkshire grabbed a couple of early wickets. Then Ranji and C. B. Fry got together and by the end of the day the score was 390 for 2.

It mattered little that Cardus may have made up the story – as he did with other cricket anecdotes – or that the story was told through Ted Wainwright, the Yorkshire player, whose dialect was incomprehensible to Indian schoolchildren. This essay was part of my school syllabus growing up in Bombay in the 1960s and, by the time we read the essay, the events described by Cardus were almost a century old. But the idea of an Indian dominating Yorkshire – one of the greatest of English cricket powers – had a great effect on us. It conjured up a strong romantic image of an Indian conquering the English on their own cricket fields.

That Ranji the cricketer had great natural gifts cannot be doubted. He combined those gifts with dedication and discipline, all of which helped him create a batting revolution, particularly his famous leg glance. In his public pronouncements Ranji always made sure that he was in tune with the prevailing views of cricket and its high moral purpose. In his classic *The Jubilee Book of Cricket*, he spoke like the true Victorian gentleman. Published in 1897 and dedicated to Queen Victoria 'by her gracious permission', as Ranji put it, he expressed sentiments that Victoria would have endorsed:

> Games do more than strengthen muscles and teach courage and endurance. They give those who play them an unconquerable joie de vivre – a buoyancy that refuses to be overwhelmed. It is this pleasure in life, these eternal good spirits, that, in addition to courage, endurance and physical powers, are the great benefits England has reaped and is still reaping for her love for games.

Ranji went on to quote approvingly a writer who had described cricket 'as a liberal education in itself, [which] demands temper, justice and perseverance'. As Ranji saw it 'it is the spirit of cricket – of the game itself – that glorifies everything connected with it

[. . .] cricket is a gem fair in itself, apart from the beauty of its setting – a gem quite worthy of a niche in Queen Victoria's crown.'

Ranji made it clear that he saw no purpose in cricket providing money for anybody.

> Men ought not to get incomes out of games. They ought to be so employed that their means of livelihood is also a benefit to their fellow-men and to society. They ought to be helping to supply some parts of the world's requirements. Cricket is not a waste of time as recreation and a physical training but as an occupation it is. Even if the life of a cricketer does no harm to the individual who follows it, what excuse is there for the existence in the community of a class that does nothing for the general welfare?

Thomas Hughes could not have put it better.

Yet Ranji used his great cricketing gifts to secure the throne he coveted. He may have been a great Victorian sporting star but he proved to be a cool, calculating star who knew what he wanted from cricket and how best to make use of his gifts for his personal enrichment. Ranji, in that sense, was a unique story of a very special kind of immigrant. He did not set up business abroad or win prizes in science, medicine, arts or writing as the modern immigrant might. The glory he earned on the cricket fields of England proved invaluable as he sought the throne of Nawanagar, a small kingdom in western India. Ranji was not a prince; he was not even a direct descendant of the Nawanagar rulers. He was the grandson of an officer who had served the state and hailed from one of its small, unremarkable villages. He had been adopted by the ruler as his successor but then ignored and had no official status when he came to England in 1888. But once in the mother country all this was obscured by his cricketing deeds and a lifestyle that lived up to every occidental's idea of Indian princely behaviour.

Ranji had to overcome racial barriers, this being the age when the idea that the European races were superior to all others was almost an article of faith. Indeed he made his debut for England not at Lord's, the home of cricket, but at Old Trafford. No official reason for his rejection by Lord's was ever given. Lord Harris, the former governor of Bombay, was the president of the MCC and is said to have argued that Ranji, not being born in England, could not qualify. Harris himself had been born in Trinidad but he was manifestly of British stock. Lancashire ignored what Lord's had done and chose him both on the basis of his cricketing merit and that he was also a great draw. All this made Ranji keener to play the part of an Eastern potentate who brought a strange, magical light to the English game.

Living like a prince meant Ranji was often in debt. But he knew that by presenting himself as the princely cricketer he would open the door to social acceptability at the highest levels of English society. This proved particularly useful when he returned to India in November 1904 and found that, despite his fame as one of England's cricketing greats, his chances of becoming ruler were negligible. There was a ruler already on the Nawanagar throne and he was younger than Ranji. But he suddenly died of typhoid. That was when Ranji's cultivation of his fellow princes and, more particularly, of British officials with the power to decide on a successor proved very useful. On 10 March 1907 Ranji struck gold and became the ruler of Nawanagar.

Four years after he was proclaimed ruler, an Indian team toured England for the first time. The 1911 All India team (the term All India meant it combined British India and the Indian princely states) received support from the British rulers in India. Framji Patel, the Parsi who was a leading light of Bombay cricket, made no secret of the wider purpose of the tour:

> I am a firm believer in the educational and political advantages of such a tour, because cricket has an Imperial side to it [. . .] Cricket in the end will kill racial antagonism. Let us try our best to send the friendly cricketing mission to the old country, which is the chosen home of the King of games, and thus strengthen

at the present juncture the bonds of union that always ought to exist between England and India. There are many links that bind us together as citizens of the greatest Empire the world has ever seen, and among those the Imperial game of cricket is not the least.

These were sentiments Ranji would often publicly echo but he did nothing to help. He made it clear that he did not see himself as an Indian cricketer. The result was that the team, which Ranji could have captained, was selected by a committee presided over by Major John Glennie Greig, a Hampshire cricketer, and made up of Indians from various religious groups. In keeping with the times an Englishman had to preside over such a committee.

However, despite his disdain for his countrymen's efforts, Ranji never forgot how useful cricket could be for his own personal gain and to help him reach out to the people that mattered in Britain. So just after the First World War, he returned to England to play cricket. He was 48, had lost an eye in a shooting accident during the war – he was shooting grouse, not Germans – and there were no other cricket fields left for him to conquer. He was a rotund shadow of the pre-war elegant Ranji. He played thrice for Sussex – scoring 16, 9 and 13, and explained that he wanted to write a book on the art of batting with one eye. But he also let slip that the king wished him to play. Pleasing the king was more important than writing the book, a book in any case he never wrote. Ranji's object was to make his state a major princely power.

Cricket may have looked up to Ranji but in kingship the standards he set were hardly admirable. Contrary to the image fostered by his English hagiographers, Ranji proved less a far-sighted ruler, more an absentee landlord much given to squeezing money out of his subjects for his spendthrift ways. In that sense he was in the traditions of Nawanagar, a state not much blessed by either beneficial nature or good rulers. Plague alternated with famines, of which, in the 10 years after Ranji became ruler, there were four.

None of this mattered to the British Raj and it mattered even less after the First World War when the British found Ranji very useful, particularly after the creation of the League of Nations. India was one of its founding members and Indian revenues financed the organization. The British had no desire to give India freedom but it suited them to give India a seat at the League. Not only did it increase overall British Empire representation in the League but it helped convince the world that Indians were slowly being taught how to rule themselves. It was at this stage that British leaders like Lord Curzon estimated that it would take Indians 500 years to learn how to rule themselves.

Ranji was the most flamboyant member of the League in Geneva, arriving in 1920 as one of India's three representatives with two Englishmen: Colonel Berthon, who helped him run Nawanagar, and C. B. Fry. In Geneva Ranji lived up to the image of the money-no-object, eccentric Indian prince. When he got to the Hotel de la Paix and found the huge Japanese delegation had taken all the best rooms, and the city full of Rising Sun flags, he told the secretary of state for India that the Indian flag should be displayed as prominently as that of any other state. He was upset at a dinner when he did not have a higher position than some dominion representatives, claiming that this belittled his status as the only sovereign ruler present. He threatened to walk out of a banquet given by Sir Eric Drummond, the general secretary of the League, when the same seat was allocated in error to both Ranji and a delegate from Central America. Drummond drolly commented, 'The time has not yet arrived when an Indian Prince can share a seat at table with someone else.'

But what made Ranji most famous was his extravagant parties, to which some of the best-looking women in Geneva were invited and showered with gifts. He had arrived in Switzerland after a massive spending spree in Britain in the summer of 1920. He had bought paintings from the Royal Academy, large quantities of diamond-encrusted jewellery from Cartier and a number of expensive racehorses, including one (the Goodwood Cup winner,

Western Wave) that had cost him 9,000 guineas. In Geneva, as his hagiographer Roland Wild conceded, he 'brought a new technique of buying into Switzerland'. The technique was to sip coffee for hours in an antique shop, admire the *objets d'art*, and then 'suddenly stand up, finish the interview, and remark as he left: "I want that and that, and that and that [. . .]" The remark sometimes cost him £20,000.'

Ranji combined this extravagance with making speeches in the League, the speeches being written for him by Fry. Fry would later claim that one of the speeches helped reverse Mussolini's invasion of Corfu. There was also an apparent offer to Fry to become King of Albania, which came to nothing. But cricket could not overcome the idea that it was unacceptable for Indians and English to intermarry. So Ranji, aware of how any such liaison would scandalize the English, kept his love affairs with English women very secret. So secret that, almost a century later, researchers cannot be sure how many English women he was involved with.

Ranji's fellow Indian princes closely studied how Ranji had used cricket and they began to copy his methods. While there was princely involvement in cricket before the Great War, it really blossomed after the war. Then, fearing how the British might react to the Indian nationalists' demand for independence, the Indian princes took to the game hoping to curry favour with the British. There was an element of Indians mimicking the British class division between amateurs and professionals. In English cricket an amateur, whatever his playing merits, was always captain. In India it was felt that the captain of the cricket team must be a prince. So the 1932 Indian touring team, which saw India make its debut in Test cricket, was led by the Maharaja of Porbandar. But Porbandar was sensible enough to realize that, while socially he made a very acceptable captain, as a cricketer he was not up to much. He played in the first four matches in 1932 making 0, 2, 0, 2, 2, and averaging 0.66. It was said of him that he was the only first-class cricketer in England that season who had more Rolls-Royces than runs. So for the Test match at

Lord's, C. K. Nayudu, a commoner but India's greatest cricketer of that era, captained the side.

For all the colourful stories it produced, the princely interest in Indian cricket lasted a mere 20 years between the 1920s and 1940s. Then businessmen and bankers moved in. These businessmen, almost to a man, spoke of cricket in language that could have been borrowed from Thomas Hughes. They eulogized about the higher purpose of the game and many even said how important it was for a batsman to walk if he knew he was out, irrespective of whether the umpire gave him out. Yet, in taking to cricket, these businessmen were marrying the Indian game to Mammon much earlier than sport in most other countries, discovered money. But this was done in a very Indian way.

For almost 50 years from the 1940s to well into the 1990s, a company in India seeking to publicize itself acquired a cricket team. This desire to use cricket to enhance commercial status was to lead to perhaps the most remarkable tournament in any sport: a cricket tournament for office teams sponsored by the *Times* of India, Bombay's leading newspaper and now the largest English-language circulation newspaper in the world. At its height in the 1980s, this inter-office tournament had seven divisions with some 300 office teams participating. The early winners were utilities; the Bombay Electric Supply and Tramways Company, known popularly in the city as BEST, was the most successful of the pre-independence teams, winning the Shield six times between 1937 and 1944. It was one of the first companies to realize the need to recruit good cricketers. They were employed for their cricket and it was understood that they would get time off from work every day for net practice.

As India began to industrialize after independence these old utility companies fell away to be replaced by commercial firms such as Tatas and then the Associated Cement Corporation. In the 1950s and 1960s the Tatas–ACC matches in the *Times* of India Shield rivalled matches in the Ranji trophy, India's national championships, and at times attracted a bigger crowd. It was not uncommon for cricketers to move between companies in football-style transfers of players between clubs.

By the early 1960s other commercial teams had emerged, like Nirlon, specializing in synthetic textiles and part of the new industrial scene of India. The Nirlon team, led by Sunil Gavaskar, was a near Test side which included Ravi Shastri, then widely tipped as India's future captain, Sandip Patil, the then great heart-throb of Indian cricket, and the former opening bowler Karsan Ghavri. Its prominence in the *Times* of India tournament almost exactly mirrored Nirlon's economic expansion. It first won the Shield in 1969–70 and then established a virtual stranglehold, winning it continuously between 1971–2 and 1977–8.

The devotion to cricket of Virenchee Sagar, the managing direc-tor of Nirlon, could not be doubted. When he spoke of the game you felt he might have been at school with Tom Brown. But he also frankly acknowledged the reason for the cricket patronage. Sagar, who had great contempt for the Indian princes, made no secret that success in cricket brought the company free publicity and goodwill and cricket costs were a reallocation of his com-pany's annual advertising budget. Promoting a product, or a company, was not the only objective. Many of the Indian industri-alists talked of using cricket to develop a more professional and businesslike approach in their company. Discipline is something highly valued in India, but rarely found. Urban India, as Professor Galbraith, a former US ambassador to India, has said can be a functioning anarchy. Cricket with its intricate rules was seen as a game that could promote order in a society so fond of chaos.

For a time in the 1960s and 1970s it seemed as if the private sector's involvement in cricket would face a challenge from state institutions – particularly the State Bank of India. After Mrs Gandhi nationalized all the major Indian banks in 1971, the State Bank, as the largest, became the pivotal bank in the Indian econ-omy. Its heavy promotion of cricket in the mid-1960s and early 1970s was dramatic. Not only did it win the *Times* of India Shield four years running in the late 1960s but, at one stage, the State

Bank of India could probably have fielded an eleven that could have represented India in Test cricket. To match Nirlon's most prominent employee, Sunil Gavaskar, the State Bank team was captained by Ajit Wadekar. His rise also showed the decline of princely power as, in 1971, he displaced a prince, the Nawab of Pataudi, as captain of India. But his leadership made history as he led India to its first ever Test wins in the West Indies and England.

This rise of commerce in cricket came when India hardly counted as an economic power and the country seemed happy to be cut off from the world both economically and on the cricket field. India's isolation was vividly illustrated in 1977 when Kerry Packer threatened to revolutionize the cricket world, yet Packer did not recruit a single Indian cricketer. In contrast all the leading Pakistani cricketers were signed up. India was so dead set against Packer, proclaiming its eternal love for five-day Test cricket and distrust of the one-day instant variety, that Sunil Gavaskar lost his captaincy just for having contact with the Packer rebels. Packer's cricket had been driven by television. Well into the late 1970s India had barely entered the television age and, as Packer made his bid for world cricket, the country, whose population was already over 600 million, had just 676,615 sets. At that stage not a single ball of cricket had ever been televised in India.

It was during the England tour of 1981–2 that, for the first time, visiting cricketers began to appreciate and profit from the marriage of cricket and money in India. This was only the second time that a full-strength England team was touring India. As I arrived in Bombay in November 1981 to report the series, it seemed that nearly all the English cricketers had been recruited by Indian advertising agencies to promote some or other Indian product. Geoff Boycott, shown in his cover drive pose, advised Indians either to drink Seven Seas cod liver oil or fly Cathay Pacific jets, the advertisements taking up almost a quarter of the sports pages of most Indian papers. Ian Botham had linked up with Gavaskar to promote tea, and nearly every Indian newspaper or magazine seemed to have the syndicated thoughts of

Botham, Keith Fletcher and many other English cricketers. On the drive from the airport to the city centre, past some of the biggest and most wretched slums in India, there were numerous advertising hoardings using cricket to sell various products. One local butter manufacturer showed its mascot struggling to tie the laces of his cricket boots underneath a slogan reading: 'If you dilly-dally, butter will melt', a reference to the boot problems that Graham Dilley had on that tour.

In the years that followed the riches on offer to visiting cricketers were, if anything, to increase and cricketers as diverse as Vivian Richards, Hansie Cronje, Jonty Rhodes, Steve Waugh and Brett Lee all found how easy and profitable it was to become great marketing symbols in India. Far from their foreign origins making them remote from Indians, it enhanced their appeal. The subtext here was if these visiting sporting celebrities could be seen endorsing Indian products then these products must be all right for Indians to use. It reflected the old colonial feeling of foreign endorsement validating an Indian product.

The advertisements demonstrated how well the Indian companies realized the commercial power of cricket at an international level. It also explained both the nature of commercial sponsorship in Indian cricket and the existence of a plethora of prizes. So many that when Chris Tavare was made man of the match for his century in the third Test in Delhi during the 1981–2 series, he found himself not with a solitary prize, as in England, but with nearly half a dozen: a television set, a Thermos flask, an attaché case and even a scooter. Wisely, Tavare had already arranged to exchange his prizes for Indian rupees rather than lug them all back.

More than 20 years later the growth of televised cricket had brought much more money into the Indian game but this penchant for using cricket to publicize commercial products did not change. In November 2004, as India beat South Africa in Kolkata to win the series 1–0, both the man of the series and the man of the match, Virendra Sehwag and Harbhajan Singh, in addition to their cheques, received a large television set. Harbhajan got a 28-inch screen model; Sehwag received a plasma screen TV. As they posed against the sets as if they were teenagers getting their first grown-up toys, the marketing men totted up the sales such publicity generated.

By then Indian cricket had long broken out of its isolation and was well on the road to world domination, a road that had opened up quite unexpectedly on a lovely June evening in 1983 at Lord's. Then India, perhaps to its surprise, won the World Cup. This was the third edition of the competition, all three tournaments having been staged in England where the idea for the competition had been born in 1973. Then, after an England–West Indies one-day international at Headingley, some officials of the then Test and County Cricket Board met the marketing man from the Prudential. There, in the small bar below the main Leeds complex, they convinced the man from Pru to sponsor a cricket World Cup.

The idea for the competition was to fill a hole as 1975 had origin-ally been earmarked for a tour by South Africa, which was now ruled out by the sports boycott. Prudential, after some haggling, offered £100,000 to have its name on the Cup and the TCCB was confident that the competition would wash its face, even produce a small profit. But just to make sure the summer proved profit-able, the TCCB tagged on a four-Test Ashes series to follow the World Cup. This was seen as the major draw for the summer.

The World Cup proved a success and, for almost a decade, it remained a special English preserve. Not that this benefited the English team for, by the time the third World Cup came round in 1983, the West Indies were so invincible that they had not only won the previous two, beating Australia in 1975 and England in 1979, but they had won nine of the ten matches they had played. The full set could not be completed because one of the matches, against Sri Lanka, had been rained off.

India, in contrast, had lost five of its six World Cup matches. Its solitary victory had come over East Africa, a non-Test-playing nation. During that time India had lost to England, New Zealand, the West Indies and, in 1979, Sri Lanka – then also not a Test-playing nation. As far as the world at large was concerned, India and one-day cricket just did not go. It had played its first one-day international only on the 1981–2 visit of England. In 1982 when India toured England and lost the one-day matches, Raj Singh, the Indian manager and a leading cricket administrator, had dismissed one-day cricket as something Indians did not care for. All India cared for, he said, was five-day Test cricket. What had been little noticed was that the new captain, Kapil Dev, had brought entirely new thinking. And, on a tour of the West Indies just before the World Cup, the Indians had actually beaten the West Indies in a one-day match in Berbice, Guyana. There, amidst West Indians of Indian origin, Kapil Dev had found a winning formula.

In 1983 in England Kapil used what he had learned in Guyana to devastating effect. India did what no other country had done before to the West Indies in a World Cup. It beat them not once but twice, once in the opening match and, more sensationally, in the final at Lord's. It was after this that this supposedly slow country showed how quickly it could change. India had always been the land where its people loved to shout *juldi, juldi*, hurry, hurry. The only problem was the circumstances, such as poor infrastructure and wretched communication links, meant these cries of *juldi, juldi* never translated into urgent action and created the impression that the country was slow by choice. In fact it was a country that wanted to go fast but could not. In cricket India showed that *juldi, juldi* was not mere hot air; the country could move quickly.

For Indians the victory meant the nation had arrived. As Mrs Gandhi put it, it proved that India could do it. In addition, the world title victory had been televised live back to India and watched by millions in their own living rooms. For a whole generation of Indian cricketing greats, like Sachin Tendulkar and Rahul Dravid, this was the first time they saw cricket on television. As Dravid recalls,

It was one of the first matches I saw on TV at a very impressionable age and that made a huge impact on the cricketers of my generation. I think that World Cup triumph, if you ask any of the guys within our generation, Sachin, Anil [Kumble], they'll all tell you that some of their earliest memories are related to that 1983 triumph of India.

For a country that craved sporting success but had few to boast of, the World Cup victory was like a drug and India used its victory to demand the right to stage the next tournament in 1987. This forced a dramatic change to the format of the game. The first three World Cups, being held in England in high summer with play possible until 8 p.m. or even later, had been 60-over matches. With India getting dark by 5 p.m., or even earlier in winter, only 50 overs a side were possible. The format change of the 1987 World Cup was never reversed and, in one of the great ironies of the game, the last 60-over World Cup game was the one India had so unexpectedly won at Lord's in June 1983.

For Indian cricket to seize world power, however, would require major changes in India itself. All these came together in 1991, a momentous year for modern India. In July of that year, with the Indian economy teetering on the brink of collapse and India running out of foreign exchange, pressure from the World Bank forced the politicians to open up the economy and allow foreign investment into what had been one of the most protected markets in the world.

Two other events took place that year and had a profound impact on Indian cricket. The Gulf War, a war made for television, finally brought this medium to India on a major scale. Sales of television sets boomed, cable operators acquired dishes and just flung cable over treetops and verandas to provide this new service to the mushrooming high-rise homes in India's metropolitan cities. Television also began to reach India's villages for the first time. Village shopkeepers abandoned their normal businesses to become very profitable cable operators.

It was also the year when cricket finally became one family. South Africa, having shed sporting apartheid, played a non-white country for the first time, a one-day series in India. It was then, as a result of enquiries from South African television, that the Indian Cricket Board realized it had television rights it could sell. Before that Doordarshan, the state broadcaster, had televised domestic cricket and, far from paying anything, had often demanded fees from the Indian board to cover the cost of production. Now two South African television channels contacted the Indian board and asked to buy the rights for the one-day series.

Amrit Mathur, who worked for the then Indian board president Madhavrao Scindia, has a precise recollection of what happened. 'We had to first find out who owned the rights and then how much they were worth.' Mathur discovered that the rights belonged to the Indian board and then, alongside other board officials, discussed what they might ask from the South Africans, only to find that the South African broadcasters, who were used to paying for rights, offered 10 times as much. The Indians were staggered. So, in another of the great ironies of cricket, as South Africa at last discovered what it was to play against a non-white country, the Indians discovered that they were sitting on a gold mine which could bring in much more money than ticket sales ever could.

It would take the Indian board some time to work the mine. In 1992 Andrew Wildblood of sports management agency IMG did a deal with the Indian board for $200,000. This included paying $25,000 for three Tests and five one-day internationals; it was money that today, as he says, would barely get one over's coverage. In 1993, Sky, in its efforts to get access to live events for the first time, televised the England Test and one-day matches being played in India. This was new ground for the Indians and the Indian government asked Sky to have not only English commentary, but also a Hindi one. Sky, always prepared to come to terms with the powers that be, agreed. The result was that I suddenly got a call from Dave Hill, now the supremo of Fox in America, to ask whether I could be one of the Hindi commentators, a language I had not used much since my childhood. Intrigued by the idea, I agreed. It turned out that Sky viewers could push a switch to listen to a couple of others and me prattling away in Hindi. It was all good fun and it opened the Indian door for Sky.

The Indian board might never have begun to mine this gold but for another change in the wider world: the first-time migration of Indians to the United States. Removal of racist US immigration laws meant that, from the 1960s, educated Indians began to arrive in the US. They came with their love of cricket. One of the Indians was Mark Mascarenhas from Bangalore. Proud of his Indian roots, he kept close links with his family back in Bangalore, and went back very often. He was to die in a car crash in January 2002 while on a visit home. He found it easier to operate his business from Connecticut and was quick to realize the growing power of the Indian Diaspora. He found that Indians missed their cricket and were willing to pay top dollar for sports through pay-per-view television. For years, one of his major deals was televising the cricket in Sharjah, in the United Arab Emirates. This cricket in the desert had been created by an Arab who, after studying in Pakistan, became fascinated by the game. Sharjah provided a convenient venue for benefit matches for Indian and Pakistani cricketers who do not have the English-style benefit system. The Gulf had also seen a large migration of working-class Indians and Pakistanis and their appetite for the game matched that of the mostly middle-class Indians who had gone to the States. A century after migration from England had spread the game, migration from the subcontinent was now taking the game to new parts of the world.

Mascarenhas, who was later to become more famous as Sachin Tendulkar's agent, making him the highest-paid cricketer in the world, was convinced that cricket rights could fetch big money. He demonstrated this when he bought the rights for the 1996 World Cup held in the subcontinent. In a style that could have been copied from Dassler, he guaranteed PILCOM, the Pakistan India Sri Lanka Organizing Committee, $14 million. Seasoned British broadcasters thought Mascarenhas was crazy but not only did he make money, he delivered $30 million to PILCOM. Ehsan

Mani, the Pakistani who later became president of the ICC and was involved in organizing the event, believes that the 1996 World Cup was the 'turning point' for the sale of cricket's televised rights. The UK rights fetched $7.5 million, compared to $1 million for the 1992 World Cup staged in Australia.

In addition to television, the organizers ruthlessly commercialized the competition, with the tournament marketed on a scale never before seen in cricket. There was an official sponsor for every conceivable product, including the official World Cup chewing gum. Coca-Cola and Pepsi Cola both wanted to be the official drinks supplier. Coke won by paying $3.8 million, much more than Benson and Hedges had paid the Australians to be the main sponsor for the 1992 World Cup. The main sponsors, Wills, the Indian tobacco offshoot of British American Tobacco, paid four times as much: $12 million.

Such competition between sponsors inevitably led to ambush marketing, although in this case it was done with a touch of wit. Pepsi, eager to get back at Coke, decided to hire some of the game's best-known names including Sachin Tendulkar and umpire Dickie Bird, and filmed them with a bottle of Pepsi. Their pictures with the words 'Nothing official about it' were plastered on huge billboards outside Indian grounds. The Indians were much taken by the advertisements and Pepsi easily outsold Coke.

The subcontinental alliance's eagerness to exploit the competition was all the greater because they were able to keep all the profits, once they had met expenses. This meant paying £250,000 to each of the competing Test countries, an amount that did not even cover the expenses of some of the teams. It has been estimated that India and Pakistan pocketed a profit of almost $50 million each – the figures have never been officially released. There was so much money made that every major cricket ground in India was equipped with floodlights, further fuelling the expansion of the one-day game in the country. Contrast this subcontinental bonanza with the 1996 European Soccer Championship, held later that year in England, which saw a loss of £1.7 million.

By then there had been a huge growth in one-day matches. The Indians, having shunned one-day cricket before 1983, now did not miss a chance to play, almost acting like missionaries, taking cricket to the most unlikely places. Between June 1974, when India played its first one-day international at Leeds, and June 1983, when India won the World Cup at Lord's, the country had played only 48 such matches. By the time India took the field for the first match of the 1996 World Cup, it had played another 223 matches. As Justice Malik Mohammad Qayyum pointed out in his inquiry into match-fixing submitted to the Pakistan government in 1999, 'with the massive influx of money and sheer increase in the number of matches played, cricket has become a business'. But it was a business that was run like a private club.

Sharjah was not the only venue for what Indians call these *masala* or spice matches – *masala* meaning something made up and not quite real. Such *masala* one-day series between India and Pakistan were also played in Toronto, which provided a haven for the two teams when the political situation meant that they could not play in the subcontinent. The teams also travelled to Singapore and played in other tournaments, which provided commercial opportunities for those seeking to reach the new emerging Indian middle classes. Many of these mini-series were sponsored by firms such as Singer and Pepsi with extensive interests in south Asia; they saw the marketing advantages of being associated with Indian cricket.

The marketing opportunities had also been sensed by foreign television companies such as Rupert Murdoch's Star television and Disney's ESPN. With estimates that every second person watching cricket in the world was an Indian, it was a market worth cultivating and both Star and ESPN were keen to reach this important economic group. For a time in the late 1990s, the two giants fought each other over Indian cricket rights. But soon they formed a joint venture company, ESPN Star Sports (ESS), and decided not to bid against each other. While they continued to run their own separate sports channels, they divided up Indian cricket between them.

The money to be made from cricket had also produced the most extraordinary alliance, proof that sport could go where nothing else could. This was the bond that had developed between the cricket administrators of India and Pakistan. The countries could go to war, their politicians squabbled and their people found it difficult to visit each other. But their cricket administrators could come together. Just as India's victory in 1983 had brought the World Cup to the subcontinent, so the springboard for its return in 1996 was Pakistan winning the 1992 tournament held in Australia. The subcontinent now snatched the prize from England in the first demonstration to the old masters of how the game they had created was changing.

The English had come to the crucial meeting at Lord's in 1993 in the belief that there was a long-standing gentlemen's agreement that England would host the 1996 tournament. At the meeting, they were shocked to discover that not only did the subcontinentals refuse to accept that any such agreement existed, but treated the event like an American political convention. The English administrators were made so uncomfortable by these tactics that they later briefed the press that it was the most unpleasant meeting ever of the International Cricket Council. This might have served as a balm for their defeat, but the meeting marked the emergence of the new cricket order. What mattered now was not gentlemen's agreements but the use of money to get sporting power.

For a start India-Pakistan had roped in Sri Lanka, making it an all-subcontinental offer. This was despite the fact that the Sri Lankans, worrying that the competition might not make money, did not agree to underwrite the costs and therefore could not participate in the profits. But with a civil war raging in their country, they were keen to have matches played on their island to give the appearance of normality. Their consolation was that they eventually went on to win the competition.

The subcontinent came to Lord's fully prepared for any eventuality. They had wheeled in politicians, looked up the rules, even engaged lawyers to help when the exact meaning of a rule was disputed, and targeted the ICC's associate members. In the past these members had been shunned by cricket's Test-playing nations and treated as country cousins. Now they were promised £100,000 if they voted for the subcontinent, £40,000 more than England offered. England just did not know what had hit it.

The Indian money machine was driven by Jagmohan Dalmiya. Known to all as Jaggu, his official title for the 1996 World Cup was convener of PILCOM. Dalmiya hails from the Indian Marwari community, people whose business skills are both feared and respected. The joke in India goes: if you see a Marwari and a tiger in the jungle, shoot the Marwari first. Dalmiya's weapon of choice was his briefcase from which, for many years, he ran Indian and world cricket. At that stage he was not even the Indian board president. But he had made such a financial success of the World Cup that all doors were now open. Indeed the suggestion that he should go for the top job in cricket had come just before the start of the World Cup from Anna Puchi Hewa, president of Sri Lankan cricket.

Dalmiya ran his election as if it was an American presidential race, energetically wooing the associates. But, despite twice winning the vote of the ICC members, the old powers were reluctant to accept him. The result was a brown versus white (and black) battle with England, Australia, New Zealand and the West Indies against the subcontinent. It was so bitter that it created scars that have still not healed. The old powers felt that the new kids on the block were not following gentlemanly ways or doing anything about cricketing corruption, which had begun to rear its head. The Asians resented the fact that England and Australia would not accept them as equals. This war was to see many battles in many venues starting at Lord's, going on to Singapore and finally ending in Kuala Lumpur before Dalmiya was accepted. It showed how cricket was changing, but it also brought large sums to the ICC for the first time in its history.

Before Dalmiya arrived, the ICC's income was little more

than the subscriptions the members paid. Dalmiya began to harvest television income for the first time and started by launching the controversial ICC knockout tournaments – later renamed the Champions Trophy. In a way he was copying Coubertin's idea of encouraging international sporting competitions. But where Coubertin saw these tournaments as a way of improving international intercourse, Dalmiya wanted to make money. This mini-World Cup between Test nations brought the ICC £12 million, at the time the biggest deal it had transacted. And Dalmiya persuaded the then Bangladesh prime minister to host the competition in words that Coubertin would have applauded. He convinced Sheikh Hasina that the tournament would help boost the pride of her country. It would be the first time one of the poorest nations on earth would host such an international competition, visible proof it had arrived in the comity of nations.

But while the Indians were reinventing cricket, by 1996 the dark side of the game – match-fixing – which had been banished more than a century ago, re-emerged. The expansion of the game, particularly the one-day game, was a fertile field for some of the game's most notorious match-fixers. One man in particular had taken to the game some months after India's victory in the 1983 World Cup. One evening a Delhi bank clerk, Mukesh Kumar Gupta, was walking near his home in the grimy bylanes of old Delhi when he saw some people betting small amounts on a cricket match. This, as he would later tell the Central Bureau of Investigation, India's top investigators, fired his imagination. Having ascertained that the punters were neither well educated nor well informed about cricket, Gupta began to hone his cricket knowledge by listening to the BBC. And over the next decade he would travel the world following cricket, meeting many of the world's top cricketers and bribing them.

Gupta was well aware of the Indian love for betting, despite it being illegal. Over the years the activities of Gupta and other match-fixers had led to rumours and some investigation generally in the Indian media. But international cricket paid little attention. As Ali Bacher put it to me

> There was a power struggle going in international cricket. The Asian countries were resentful of England, the old colonial power. But the subcontinent did not help by being very defensive about match-fixing. We have known for years that match-fixing goes on, helped by the fact that betting is illegal and in the hands of criminals there. But, in the past, whenever the matter was raised they said, 'We are cricket administrators, not cops.' Then a clean-cut white South African, Hansie Cronje, was caught in the net, the game changed and everyone had to come clean.

Ironically it was a Delhi crime-branch detective, Ishwar Singh Redhu, who in April 2000 forced everyone to come clean. Asked to investigate complaints by Delhi businessmen of extortion with menace, he was listening to telephone taps on two suspects when the name of Hansie Cronje, then the South African cricket captain, cropped up in the context of fixing one-day matches in the series between India and South Africa. Cronje himself was heard discussing the fixing of matches with a London-based Indian businessman called Sanjeev (also known as Sanjav) Chavla.

By that time, five and a half years had passed since Shane Warne, Mark Waugh and Tim May had made allegations of match-fixing against the Pakistan captain Salim Malik. He was alleged to have offered $200,000 to the Australians to under-perform. The allegations did not surface until 1995, a year later. The Australians did not go to Pakistan to give evidence to the inquiry in person and, largely for this reason, the former Pakistani attorney general Fakruddin Ebrahim concluded that there was no proof. There were other allegations, inquiries in India and investigations in the Indian media. The Pakistanis had a second more extensive inquiry conducted by Justice Malik Mohammed Qayyum, a High Court judge. But by the time Cronje's match-fixing emerged his report had not been released.

There had also been a rather curious cover-up on the issue. The Australian board had imposed fines on Waugh and Warne for receiving $A6,000 and $A5,000 respectively from an Indian book-maker, known as John, in return for information. The payment had been made in 1994, the players had been fined in 1995, and the story did not emerge until the Australian press broke it in December 1998. The story shocked Australia and led the news, with John Howard, the Australian prime minister, critical of the board. The *Sydney Morning Herald* asked, 'Why the sorrow, why the sense of national loss? This is normally a mood associated with a state funeral or death of a national hero, the announcement of war or some national disaster.' It demonstrated how sport, particularly cricket, was still seen as providing a positive moral focus. The cover-up, even more than the alleged corruption, caused outrage that the spirit of sport had been defiled. Redhu's police work changed everything. It meant that match-fixing could no longer be shrugged off as an occasional isolated instance. His investigation revealed the modern history of cricket corruption, an intricate tale that extended to all cricket-playing countries.

The reaction to Cronje's fall said much about how the world saw India and cricket. Initially, there was disbelief that Cronje could be guilty. I was on a Radio Five Live programme soon after the news broke and Bob Woolmer, who had been coach to the South African team and close to Cronje, dismissed it as an inven-tion of the Indians. The Indians had just lost to South Africa at home and he saw this as revenge. It later emerged that Woolmer himself had known how, on the 1996 tour of India, the entire South Africa team had discussed throwing a one-day match. Some players were tempted by the $250,000 Gupta offered but, in the end, at a 3 a.m. meeting with Gupta, Cronje turned down the offer. Woolmer would eventually conclude that Cronje 'got too much power and felt invulnerable'.

Cronje later confessed he could not do without bookies; they were like a drug to him. The fact is that during his visits to India, Cronje found himself in a world where the cricketer was not only a star but was showered with offers of money. The money was from marketing men and it made this young South African very money conscious. It is interesting that when the story broke Indians burned posters of Cronje modelling a suit in India.

Cronje had been introduced to Gupta by the then Indian captain Mohammed Azharuddin. The Indian Muslim and the South African could not have come from more contrasting backgrounds, yet they formed one of the most amazing bonds two sportsmen have ever formed. Gupta's blandishments convinced Cronje money was there to be made, and it was just too difficult to resist. It is interesting to note how, even when all the damming facts had emerged, Cronje felt able to rationalize his actions by insisting that he never intended to lose a match, nor dishonour the name of his country. He clung to this even after the revelations of Marlon Aronstam, a South African gambler, who was responsible for the most remarkable Test match of all time. Until Cronje was exposed, it seemed that this Test result was like something out of fantasy land, enshrining all the best in the game, proof of the highest principles of sportsmanship in this material world. Then it emerged it was the result of a crooked bet which involved the gift of a leather jacket.

Aronstam contacted Cronje in January 2000 on the fourth evening of the fifth Test at Centurion between England and South Africa. The Test had seen no play for three days, the South African first innings was still not complete and there was no possibility of a result. Now Aronstam, keen to make money, rang Cronje on a mobile phone and so tempted Cronje with his idea that Cronje invited him to his hotel room at 10 p.m. that night. There Aronstam sketched out an offer which could make, as he put it, a match of it and money both for Aronstam and Cronje. Aronstam would later tell the South Africa King Commission, which investigated match-fixing, that he gave Cronje 53,000 rand and a leather jacket for his wife. He also agreed to give 200,000 rand to a charity of Cronje's choice. (Cronje remembered the figure as 500,000 rand.) The money for charity never materialized. And Aronstam, who had hoped to back both sides at long odds, never got round to placing his bets as it was too late by the time the final-day fix was set up.

The Cronje offer was that England forfeit their first innings, South Africa their second, leaving England to chase a target for victory. However, it did not seem that the fix would work. Nasser Hussain, the England captain, totally unaware of what Cronje had secretly agreed, initially turned Cronje down. He was worried how the wicket might play. But as South Africa, resuming their first innings on the fifth morning, scored freely he sought out Cronje and accepted his offer. England was given a target of 251 and won by two wickets with five balls to spare. While this sort of result was not unusual in county cricket, nothing like this had ever been seen in Test cricket, nor is it sanctioned by the laws of the game. Teams with national pride at stake just did not make a match of it in this fashion. Everyone hailed it as a great moment for cricket and the eternal spirit of the sport.

Cronje was showered with praise for bringing cricket back to its golden age when the game was played for thrill not money. After the match he spoke like a hero who was doing his best to revive Test cricket, which was under such threat from the one-day game. He said, 'Test cricket needs to do everything it can to advertise itself and be competitive in a sporting market. It hurts to lose – we lost a 14-match unbeaten run because of this – but it was a fabulous game in the end. And people deserve to be entertained.'

The Wisden match report, written after Cronje had been unmasked, concluded:

Yet the cricket was played as hard as both teams were able, and that is some consolation. Cronje's goal was to achieve a positive result and, while a captain without thought of personal gain might have opted for defence and the safety of a draw when the match was slipping away, South Africa did almost pull off a remarkable win.

Aronstam claimed that Cronje had implied that the only way to make money from cricket was by fixing matches, and gave the impression that he would be prepared to throw a one-day international, 'once South Africa has qualified for a final'. He also offered to throw the first one-day international against India in Kochi, when South Africa toured there after the triangular series between South Africa, England and Zimbabwe. Cronje would later try to qualify his offer but it remains extraordinary that he had such a discussion with a man he had only just met. Cronje, till the end, kept denying the match was fixed. The fact that he wanted money for charity shows what a curious match-fixer he was. This may or may not explain why many in South Africa refused to accept he had done anything wrong. While the initial reaction was, as the South African paper *Mercury* put it, 'Shame the man who brought the cricket and his country to its knees', soon many in South Africa felt differently. Three years later, not long after Cronje was dead, as South Africa staged the 2003 World Cup the players and many supporters wore wrist bands dedicating the World Cup to Cronje's memory.

It is interesting to compare what happened to Cronje with what happened to Azharuddin. Initially he faced the wrath of the Indian cricket followers and his effigy was burnt. He was banned from cricket and never fulfilled his dream of playing in 100 Tests, permanently stuck on 99. This was despite the efforts of Raj Singh, the former Indian prince who had appointed Azharuddin captain. Singh was extremely fond of him, did not believe it was possible for cricketers to fix matches and he was desperately keen that Azharuddin should be allowed to get to a century of Tests. But, while Raj Singh failed in this objective, almost a decade later Azharuddin was elected to the Indian parliament with a comfortable majority and struck up a wonderful rapport with his constituents. It also meant he could travel the world on a diplomatic passport.

Cronje's fall came as Dalmiya was coming to the end of his controversial three-year reign as ICC president. Dalmiya had long argued that he could do nothing about match-fixing unless he was given proof and resented the fact that his ability to make money for cricket was overshadowed by this crisis. To be fair to Dalmiya, while he was the most prominent figure in world cricket when the crisis broke, it was not all down to him. Many in Indian and world cricket, including some on his own board like Raj Singh, refused to believe match-fixing was possible.

The Cronje affair did force the ICC, at the initiative of Lord MacLaurin, then head of English cricket, to hold an emergency session at Lord's. Just before Dalmiya opened the session, MacLaurin passed round a statement on ECB notepaper which he asked all the ICC delegates to sign, declaring that they were honest men. Everyone duly complied but it revealed the curious state of an organization whose senior administrators had to declare they were clean before they could consider corruption among the players.

Friends of Dalmiya hinted darkly that this was some English plot. But by then questions had been raised in India about how Dalmiya had conducted the negotiations for the television rights for the 1998 ICC knockout tournament in Dhaka. Soon, an Indian inquiry conducted by the Central Bureau of Investigation would be set up to examine the deal and the links between Dalmiya and Mark Mascarenhas' media television company World-Tel. CBI officers visited Dalmiya's offices in Calcutta and there was also a raid by income tax officials. Dalmiya insisted he had done nothing wrong. The ICC, he said, had not lost out. And if Doordarshan paid over the odds that was their responsibility. As for the raids, he claimed, they had nothing to do with cricket and were common to all business houses in India.

In the end Dalmiya saw off the CBI inquiry and his remarks summed up the immense cultural divide that cricket corruption poses. In Pakistan, the cricket board is at the mercy of the government. The president of the country is the patron and appoints the head of the board. In India the cricket board is autonomous and has annual elections which are fiercely contested and are huge media events. But in both countries the game is administered against a background of much corruption in public life and police and tax inquiries into prominent persons are a fact of life.

Dalmiya may have left the ICC under a cloud, with international cricket bearing the scars of match-fixing, but the authorities responded to the allegations by setting up an anti-corruption unit headed by Lord Condon, the former head of the Metropolitan Police. Condon quickly realized the hub of modern match-fixing was India, worked closely with the CBI, whose work he always praised, and estimated that in any one match involving India and Pakistan some $500 million could be bet. The numbers and how the bets are made give some indication of the size of the problem. During the entire 2010 Australian Football season $200 million was bet, but this was through proper gambling companies. The $500 million bet on a single match is through illegal gamblers, unregulated, and untaxed, with no records kept. Indeed, each India match, even those not against Pakistan, can attract as much money as the entire Australian football season does. Malcolm Speed has regretted that, during his time in charge, the ICC never caught the big fish that swam in this filthy cricket lake.

Indeed Speed wrote that, for all the work of Condon and his successors, match-fixers had not been thrown out of the temple. Now they were back as spot-fixers, where a player deliberately bowls no-balls, in exchange for money, as Mohammad Amir and Mohammad Asif did during the Lord's Test of 2010 in cahoots with their captain Salman Butt; they were, as so often, exposed by the media. Speed, Condon and many others believed the return of the scourge was due to the Indian Premier League and its unregulated ways. Ironically that tournament might never have been created had Dalmiya still been in charge. Its rise was both a reflection of the rise of Indian cricket and the curious way the Indian game works.

In the decade since leaving the ICC, Dalmiya had had a rollercoaster cricket career. This saw him gain supreme power in Indian cricket, power he used to torment the ICC. Speed devotes a whole chapter of his book to Dalmiya. But, after years of plotting, in the middle of the new century his enemies in India, led by Sharad Pawar, also a prominent Indian politician, finally gathered enough strength to force him off the Board of Control for Cricket in India and from his regional power base in Bengal. He was to make a comeback in Bengal shortly before the 2011 World Cup, but not on the national stage. By then there had also been a series of law suits and counter suits between him and the Indian board. The curtain finally fell in September 2010 when the board withdrew its civil suit against Dalmiya and also the 2006 expulsion notice. Dalmiya praised board members for acting fairly.

In most other countries, certainly in the Western world, such power struggles in the governing body of a sport would do immense damage to a game. But in India they had no impact on the continuing rise of cricket. In retrospect, the Cronje affair was no more than a little hiccup in the now well-established Indian cricket love story. And, for all the battles in the Indian board, cricket remained a very lucrative product for the television companies. So much so that, as the new century dawned, companies that had shunned it in the past took to cricket. So Zee TV, which had been set up in 1992 and had shown no interest in cricket, preferring movies, Indian sitcoms and other standard general entertainment programmes, suddenly decided it would go for cricket.

In the summer of 2000, the ICC met in Paris to consider bids for the 2003 and 2007 World Cups and other ICC tournaments. That it was meeting in Paris showed how the money Dalmiya had brought had changed the game. The ICC had asked the British government for exempt tax status and been refused. The organization after detailed tax advice from PricewaterhouseCoopers had decided that, to reduce tax liability in the UK, it needed to split itself into two companies, one based in the UK, the other overseas. The overseas company received all the money the ICC made from television and other deals and was outside the jurisdiction of UK taxation. The UK-based company, which continued to operate from Lord's, did not make any money and therefore avoided paying tax. Eventually the ICC was to move from Lord's to Dubai because of the more attractive financial regime in the Middle East. At the Paris meeting, Zee TV tabled the biggest bid in the history of the game: $660 million, $110 million more than World Sports, the group backed by Rupert Murdoch. But with the Cronje scandal fresh in everyone's minds the ICC, unsure of the future, decided to play safe. They were impressed by Murdoch's backing for World Sports and accepted the lower bid. For most of the ICC, Zee was an unknown Indian company.

Three years later there was another surprising Indian intervention from a rival of Zee and ESPN Star. This was Sony, which, for some years, had been running a general entertainment channel with occasional forays into cricket. Sony bid nearly $230 million for the Indian rights to the 2003 and 2007 World Cups. Sony's then chief executive Kunal Dasgupta made it very clear what the logic of this huge bid was. 'Cricket is the only product in India which unites the whole country. It transcends class, religion, regional and language differences. You do not require words to explain Sachin Tendulkar or Rahul Dravid.' Sony used the World Cup to increase its share of the market by 24 per cent while Murdoch's Star lost 47 per cent of its viewers.

Indian advertisers had no doubts about cricket's drawing power. In February 2004, with an election on the horizon, the *Economic Times* reported that major companies preferred to spend more money buying advertisement spots when cricket rather than election news was on. Cricket excited the viewers in a way politics did not. Just as Murdoch had used Premier League football in England to drive the sales of satellite dishes and attract the young males advertisers find so difficult to reach, Sony was using World Cup cricket.

Later that year came final confirmation of how far Indian cricket had travelled since the days of Packer. Zee tried to return to cricket when it bid $308 million for four years of Indian cricket, starting with the 2004 season. The bid would later run into all sorts of problems and involve lawsuits in the Indian Supreme Court, but Zee's offer for a total of 108 days of international cricket was fascinating. The offer valued each day's cricket at $2.85 million: Zee was prepared to pay for one day's cricket very nearly what Kerry Packer offered to pay for all five years of Australian cricket back in 1977 ($3.25 million). Even allowing for inflation, this demonstrated how big the Indian cricket market was. Never in its history had cricket been so lucrative.

India, it seemed, had reversed the old cliché of the thin man trying to get out of a fat one. This was still a country of some 600 million who lived on less than two dollars a day. But it had some 400 million well-off Indians and these fat Indians were trying to shrug off the embrace of their more numerous emaciated country-men and women. Such was the hunger for televised cricket in India that audiences of over 200 million for a game were not unknown. World cricket had never before seen anything like it. And, in a remarkable illustration of how sport can change society, such economics were converting people who had previously shunned India.

In 1997 when Speed, a lawyer by profession, took over Australian cricket, he had never visited India and had no desire to. In the next decade he would make 40 trips there and, in his book, he devotes a whole chapter to explaining that India is cricket's unique selling point and why this is a great boon for the game. His reasoning is that, by 2050, India will have a population of 1.6 billion, 200 million more than China. Its population of working-age people will be 230 million more than China's and 500 million more than America's. India's population already easily outnumbers the rest of the cricket world many times over, and, as it grows further, Speed argues, more Indians keen on cricket with money to spare can only be good for the game. No other country can match India.

And in India, in contrast to other countries, cricket is expand-ing. While in England, and particularly in the West Indies, cricket is losing popularity to other sports making claims on leisure time, in India cricket is reaching out beyond the big metropolis to the smaller provincial cities and towns. So much so that Mahendra Singh Dhoni, the Indian captain, hails from Ranchi, a town that was until recently more famous for its mental asylums. All this means that an Indian visit is much prized by other cricket countries as they can be certain of selling their television rights to the expanding Indian market.

The very presence of the Indian team in England in the summer of 2004 testified to that. India had come to play not Tests but a series of one-day matches with England. These matches were shown live in India and the money this earned for the England and Wales Cricket Board was much needed to finance the English game. Next was the ICC Champions Trophy, where all the sponsors were either Indian companies or international companies operating in the Indian market. These matches were also televised and during the Champions Trophy final, despite the fact that it was between England and the West Indies, very often names of Indian companies such as Bharat Petroleum, complete with its Sanskrit logo, would flash up on the Oval scoreboard.

All this had made Indian players almost into a new cricketing caste, a fact that Nasser Hussain, the England captain, ruefully acknowledged during India's tour of England in 2002.

The tour was to be followed by the Champions Trophy in Sri Lanka. The ICC, like many other sports organizers, was vigilant about 'ambush marketing'. It wanted to make sure that the sponsors who had paid large sums did not lose out to rivals who may not have sponsored the event but wanted to use it to advertise their products. The ICC required all the world's cricketers taking part in the tournament to sign a declaration that for a period before, during and after the tournament they would not be involved in any advertising that was in competition with ICC sponsors. But India's leading cricketers had contracts with companies that were rivals of ICC's sponsors and they refused to sign. So while India faced up to England at Headingley, seeking a win to square the series, off the field the Indian players were locked in a grim battle with their own board.

When Hussain was asked about the controversy, he expressed sympathy but also confessed that England's cricketers did not have such problems because they did not enjoy such sponsorships. As it happens, India won a massive victory at Headingley with the cricketers saying the fight with their board had made them more determined. The dispute lingered on as India played England at the Oval and in the end a compromise was found. But six months later the dispute flared up again during the 2003 World Cup in South Africa, and this time the ICC held back money owed to India.

The Indian cricketers did not have contracts – it was some years before they did – and the Indian board was run as if cricket was still a weekend recreational activity, not a huge business on its own.

At this time cricket was not the only sport trying to make money – so was football. But here the power firmly resided with the Europeans. It is fascinating to contrast the changes in football with those in cricket. In 1992, almost as if football was in step with changes in cricket, both English and European football changed dramatically. UEFA was worried about the future of the European Cup, the competition started in 1955 for the champions of Europe. Lennart Johansson, then president of UEFA, recalls:

There was no money to be made from football. We had some 15 million Swiss francs in the bank. Two men from the marketing company, Team, Klaus Hempel and Jüegen Lens, who we knew, came to see me and Gerhard Aigner [UEFA general secretary]. They had worked with ISL (they both set out on their own sometime after Dassler's death). We could trust them. They said the European Cup is a dead duck. They brought the idea of the Champions League to be promoted with the help of television and sponsorship. Even then ticket sales for the European Cup were not bringing much money. Much of the income came from marketing and sponsorship. We were both taken by the idea. But football is very conservative. The UEFA executive was opposed, the national associations were opposed and even the players did not like the idea. We spoke to the Barcelona players, including the Bulgarian Hristo Stoichkov, and they all said no, do not change the European Cup. The proposal was only accepted by the UEFA executive a few days before the deadline, at about 12 o'clock at night, during a meeting in London. There were a number of other conflicting issues the UEFA executive were considering and by then the members were probably too tired. We came down to the lobby of the hotel and told Team.

But that was not the end of the problems, as Johansson found out.

We had to find 90 million Swiss francs to launch it and Deutsche Bank and ABN Amro rejected the idea. I also met Silvio Berlusconi. He came for a meeting and I could see he was very tired. He was not interested in the project. I asked him why. I told him, 'From a political point of view it will bring you support. The Italian people will like it. And it will be good for your club, A.C. Milan.' In the end he came round and thanked me for it. But to launch it was difficult and we had to work hard to get backers. However, if we were taking a chance with the Champions League, the bigger chance would have been carrying on with the old European Cup. It was dying. We could not save it.

The change worked so well that UEFA, in effect, succeeded in creating the sort of mid-week European league many of the leading clubs were clamouring for. Nineteen ninety-two had also seen the launch of the Premier League, a breakaway from the Football League, the oldest professional league in the world. Its creation was driven by the desire of the top English clubs to have a larger share of television money. However, in order to cloak this desire for money with high-sounding principles, much was made of the fact that the English Premier League would actually help the English national team. Later events were to show that this was just a cosmetic veneer to cover up the desire by big clubs to get what they felt was their rightful share of the television cake.

But both these changes in the world's most popular sport did not change the global structure of football. The economic power-house remained in Europe and, if anything, it was strengthened. So much so that other countries, even whole continents, had to pay homage to it. In effect these changes in football meant European money was now allied to the flair and style of South America. Here the parallel with cricket is interesting.

Just as South America had traditionally provided some of the best footballers and had won the World Cup more often than Europe, so had West Indian cricket dominated on the field of play. But, like the West Indian islands, South America had little or no money. As the Champions League took off, South America was forced to sell its best players to European clubs. And so was the rest of the world. The result was that, in a replay of what had happened in the closing years of the nineteenth century when Europe had grabbed land in Africa, as the twentieth century drew to a close Europe grabbed the world's best footballers. Every week both the Champions League and various national European leagues, led by the Premier League, provided a world stage for talent from South America, Africa and even from Asia. This forced many great South American countries including Brazil and Argentina to play some of their 'home' matches in Europe. With European football televised round the world, its power was instantly visible in the remotest towns and villages of the globe. Also endless repeats, both on screens in the under-ground in places like Kolkata and in many airports around the world, made a global display of European sporting power. So compelling has this football beamed from Europe proved that, in many countries, locals have turned away from their domestic football. Many in these lands see this as the return of a new form of European colonialism.

The new football relationship between Europe and South America, once equal partners, was vividly demonstrated in 1998, six years after the launch of the Champions and Premier Leagues. In May 1998 Peter Kenyon, then chief executive of Manchester

United, and Maurice Watkins, a director, were on a trip to São Paolo in Brazil. They had been invited by Pele, then the Brazilian sports minister, who was involved in restructuring Brazilian football. He was keen that Manchester United should take part in a conference in São Paolo to discuss the implications of what was called the Pele Law. Designed to restructure the game there, it was meant to address the problem of Brazilian football: there was plenty of raw talent but the infrastructure and organization was a complete nightmare. Pele wanted to look at role models within the Premier League, in particular Manchester United, and consider the opportunities for deriving additional revenues. He was also keen to explore the idea of Brazilian clubs listing on the stock exchange, following the example of Manchester United.

During the conference, as Kenyon and Watkins had a drink in the low-ceilinged bar of the São Paulo Intercontinental, they were presented with plans for a European Super League. The presentation was made by two Italians, Andrea Locatelli and Paolo Taveggia, and a Swede, Peter Ecelund. They were representing a company called Media Partners. Media Partners proposed a mid-week league of 24 or 32 teams whose membership would partly be determined by merit and partly by status, such as previous record in Europe and the size of the club. The most radical part of the plan was that there would be a group of founder members who would enjoy a permanent membership of the league because of their size and wealth. The new concept, promised Media Partners, would derive vastly more money than the clubs got from UEFA's Champions League.

Some months later, after the world learned of the plans for a European Super League, there would be intense speculation about who the Mr Big behind Media Partners was. Most of the management were virtually unknown and were soon dubbed by UEFA the boys from the Milan tennis club. Not all of them were from Milan but seven were Italians; their president Rodolfo Hecht Lucari was an A.C. Milan supporter and Locatelli had played for A.C. Milan. Lucari and Taveggia had also worked for Berlusconi.

The Italian prime minister was then out of office and all these connections convinced many that the Mr Big was Berlusconi.

Media Partners refuted this, saying they were nobody's puppets; many of their partners had worked for Berlusconi but they were the sole owners of their company, one which had a good track record in sports rights, having put together football's first pay-per-view television contract for Italian television. What they shared was the Berlusconi vision for European football: 'There will be a league formed outside UEFA with a team from each country sponsored by that country's biggest company [. . .] a super professional football league like American football, which will attract millions of viewers.' As Lucari put it, 'The way the Champions League is formatted today it is an underperforming asset. We believe we can do better. I think sport in Europe is ready to be privatized.'

Such an idea could hardly be acceptable to UEFA and, alarmed that it would be blown away, UEFA secretary Gerhard Aigner began a frantic football shuttle diplomacy to the various capitals of Europe. UEFA, which had always been aloof from the clubs, even began to court them and completely reshaped the Champions League. The top five European countries, including England, were given four places each, the UEFA Cup and Cup Winners Cup were merged into one competition and UEFA offered the clubs a much bigger share of television money. All this saw off Media Partners.

In some ways Lalit Modi, the brain behind the IPL, was like an Indian version of Media Partners with one important difference. The way Indians organized their cricket meant he could become part of the Indian Cricket Board and make revolutionary changes from within. He only became an outsider when the board turned against him. Modi likes to see himself as cricket's Bernie Ecclestone and his talk is of products, consumers, eyeballs and ratings. But, unlike Ecclestone, Modi has no passport, the Indian government having revoked it in March 2011. The previous October the Indian government had issued a 'look out circular' requiring security personnel at airports and other entry points to watch for him. He is being investigated for alleged violations of foreign exchange regulations in connection with the IPL and tax offences. The Board of Control for Cricket in India launched disciplinary proceedings, making serious allegations about his stewardship of the IPL, and the board secretary also filed a complaint with the police accusing him of false accounting. Modi, while denying he is a fugitive, is in exile in London because he claims his security staff have told him it would be unsafe to go back to India. This is backed up by the revelation of the Mumbai police that a gangster had sent two assassins to kill him. In that sense he is not so much the master chef of the IPL, as Ecclestone still is of Formula One, but more like a revolutionary devoured by his own revolution.

Like Mascarenhas and ironically the man who helped bring him down, the Indian politician Shashi Tharoor, Modi is part of that generation of Indians made by America. A member of a rich family, he acquired a US degree but was also convicted of cocaine possession and abduction. In 1985 he escaped jail by plea bargaining, agreeing to a five-year probation and 100 hours of community service. Once he had graduated, he persuaded a US court to let him return to India on health grounds. There have been suggestions that this required influence and perhaps liberal use of money from his wealthy family. This is an area of his past Modi is not keen to talk about.

After his return to India, Modi, while building up his television expertise bringing Disney and ESPN to the country, soon became involved in cricket administration. He quickly formed an alliance led by Sharad Pawar to oust Dalmiya. In 2005, when his group won, Modi became one of the vice-presidents of the BCCI. He had the job in cricket he wanted: to run the board's marketing department. He had long concluded he could beat even the money man Dalmiya when it came to selling cricket. As he would tell me later,

At that point in time the BCCI made 20 to 40 million dollars. I changed the marketing structure, changed the way we did business and the BCCI today is locked in contracts of six or seven billion dollars. India was a poor country; we never had money to build any infrastructure. Today we are a power house. I did that in my own time, at my own cost.

His major innovation came with the launching of the IPL in April 2008. Modi successfully married two of India's greatest passions: Bollywood and cricket. This was Indian *tamasha*, an Indian word that means spicy, mischievous, fun. Modi reduced a game of cricket to the length of a three-hour Bollywood movie played at about the same time as the late movie – from 8 p.m. to around 11 p.m., with Bollywood stars not only in attendance, but also owning many of the cricket franchises.

Long before adapting this English concept for the Indian market, Modi, whose US experience had made him aware of sporting franchises, had been working on an idea of a cricket competition built around city-based leagues. His original plan involved the 50-over game. Modi had always been intrigued that, while other sports had leagues, cricket was the only game in the world where there were no city-based leagues. Modi had studied the various leagues around the world such as the National Hockey League in America, the English Premier League and their use of television and was determined to outdo them. It was at Wimbledon in July 2007, as he had tea with Andrew Wildblood of IMG, that plans for a league based on the Twenty20 format began to be formed. India's victory in Johannesburg later that year gave just the impetus that the idea needed. The creation of such a league was also spurred on by Subash Chandra of Zee TV. Upset at being unable to get the rights for televised cricket, Chandra set up the Indian Cricket League. 'They denied us the cricket content,' said Himanshu Mody, business head of the new league and in charge of Zee Sports, 'so, we had to create our own content.' Its creation alarmed Modi's colleagues in the board and they quickly agreed to Modi launching the IPL. Modi's boast is that the IPL is unique.

There's no other league like that in the world. Every member, every constituent actually makes money. How many teams in the English Premier League make money? If you look at the balance sheet of practically every club, all of them are in debt. One of the fundamental core principles of our idea was that we build equal teams. We came up with a unique concept: a process where all players were put into an auction. All players could only be bought through that process. The idea was that all teams will be equal. For a broadcaster nothing could be better than to deliver equal rating. Then the advertiser is guaranteed viewership. That's what he's paying for at the end of the day. He's paying for eyeballs; eyeballs directly translate into ratings. Whether you like it or not, television pays for sports. I am extremely happy and proud of what I delivered. I have no regrets.

Such bombast is part of the Modi style. But he could point to the fact that, in 2008, its very first year, the IPL alone earned the Indian board Rs 350 crore ($78 million), compared to Rs 235 crore ($52 million) profit it had made for the previous non-IPL year from all its activities. In year one, franchise owners like the legendary Bollywood star Shahrukh Khan had already broken even. In 2009, while the rest of the world was coping with a downturn, Modi had renegotiated a nine-year television deal of $1.6 billion. In 2010 the third edition attracted 143 million viewers, an increase of 20 million on the previous year, with advertising revenues up by 60 per cent.

Modi makes no secret that his mission went beyond cricket and was meant to show to the world what this new, modern India could do.

My job out there was to deliver a world-class league that benefits everybody and can go out there and, with our heads high, show to the world that yes, we in modern India can do it. We hired the best people, the best companies, we had people like IMG who would not allow me to cut corners even when you pioneer an innovative product.

This new India was even exported. In 2009 the IPL took place in South Africa, a country where, before Mandela's rainbow nation emerged, Indians were derided as coolies, and where cricket struggles to get a toehold against the dominance of rugby among the whites. The move was forced on the IPL because Indian elections meant the Indian government could not provide the security needed for the tournament. For Modi, it was another advertisement for the new India. 'I showed the world that I could move a product in 21 days, move tens of thousands of people across continents for a product that people take years to build.' It is interesting to contrast this with Formula One, when the teams said they could not fit in the postponed Bahrain Grand Prix because of the logistics of the move. As we have seen, then there were other broader issues, but this highlights the differences between a well-established Western-run sport and a freewheeling Indian enterprise where one man was allowed to call the shots and did so with impunity.

In 2010, at the start of the third IPL, Modi had begun to dream of more worlds to conquer. In *The Times* on 14 March 2010, Rhys Blakely, interviewing Modi at Mumbai's Wankhede stadium – the headquarters of the Indian game – outlined Modi's vision of taking the game to China and the United States. 'I see the IPL', Modi boasted, 'becoming bigger than the NFL, NBA and the Premier League.' Yet even as he spoke the seeds of his own downfall had been laid.

Modi's plans began to unravel when, with every Indian city wanting an IPL franchise, Modi offered two more franchises for the 2010 season. The two franchises seemed to bear out the extraordinary product Modi had devised. They fetched $700 million, more than all the eight original franchises had fetched two years earlier. However, during the bidding process Modi fatally collided with Shashi Tharoor, minister of state for foreign affairs.

Like Modi, Tharoor had been educated in the US but acquired a much more distinguished record. He made history by completing a PhD from the Fletcher School of Law and Diplomacy at Tufts

University, Massachusetts, at 22 — still a Fletcher record. Then, after working for the United Nations for nearly 30 years, he missed out on becoming secretary general to the South Korean Ban Ki-moon. In 2009, despite strong opposition from the local Congress party, Tharoor was parachuted in to contest the safe Kerala seat of Thiruvananthapuram and made a minister. All this was largely on the insistence of Congress leader Sonia Gandhi, who saw him as the sort of man to help her son Rahul as she groomed him to take over as prime minister. The newly elected MP, Tharoor, was keen for Kochi, a Kerala coastal town, to have a franchise. The winning bid was not the favourite but it beat powerful rivals, including some headed by the big beasts of the Indian corporate jungle.

Then, in the sort of script that Bollywood might reject, Modi, who loves to use the social networking site Twitter, revealed that 25 per cent of the franchise was held by Rendezvous Sports World and among the stakeholders in RSW was a Dubai-based Indian lady, Sunanda Pushkar. Modi's tweet also revealed that Tharoor had asked for details of the franchise ownership not to be revealed, therefore implying that Tharoor had a financial interest in the franchise, which Tharoor denied. It emerged that Pushkar had 'sweat equity' in return for contributing event management expertise, that Tharoor was about to divorce his Canadian wife, and that he and Pushkar were an item (they have since married). So while Tharoor was not guilty of financial impropriety, questions about his judgement were raised. The political storm took place as the Indian prime minister Manmohan Singh was visiting President Obama in the White House.

The government could not have been more embarrassed and the Congress decided that Tharoor could not be saved. But in tweeting, Modi invited a backlash and it duly came. There were demands in the Indian parliament that the IPL be investigated and India's finance minister Pranab Mukherjee asked his officials, including those in the Economic Offences Wing, to investigate the IPL's alleged financial irregularities. Soon it was being alleged that

Modi had tried to bribe the Kochi franchise to back away in favour of a rival bid from Ahmedabad, capital of Gujarat. One investor in the Kochi franchise alleged that Modi had offered $50 million for the winning bid to be withdrawn. Modi denied offering a bribe, but he had been courting Gujarat's powerful chief minister Narendra Modi, who wanted IPL cricket for his state and was in a position to do Modi favours.

There followed other allegations. That Modi's family and friends held stakes in three franchises, that there were many undisclosed owners in other franchises, that the television deal was murky, leading to a payment of $85 million by Sony to get the deal from World Sports Group. There were even wilder allegations, for which no proof has emerged, that some of the IPL franchises were vehicles for illegal money laundered into the country.

In April 2010, immediately after the conclusion of the third tournament, Modi was suspended as chairman and commissioner of the IPL. This was followed by the board issuing a 34-page letter stating 22 charges of impropriety, which was served on Modi via email. The burden of the charges was that Modi had created the IPL to benefit himself and his family. Modi, even before he left India, protested his innocence and his defence since then provides a revealing picture of how the IPL was created and how cricket's most powerful board works.

Modi does not deny that the IPL made money for his friends and relatives.

> Of course it made money for my relations. When I conceived the IPL, everybody thought it was a harebrained scheme. The business model was not known. None of the traditional sport financiers wanted to be part of it. We had no buyers, no advertisers and no broadcasters. Nobody believed in domestic cricket. People didn't understand my concept. In a country where people only watch the national team, we were trying to build city-based loyalties around a Twenty20 tournament. There were no bidders for the teams. If friends and family had not bid, we wouldn't

have had the IPL in the first place. For eight teams we had eleven bids! The bidding was totally transparent. Everybody concerned, from the governing council to the BCCI members, was very much present in the room. And in fact everybody was just happy at that point in time that we got any bids!

Nor does he deny his extravagance, of which much was made in the Indian media after his fall, including his plane with its golden toilet fittings. The BCCI charge sheet encouraged the idea that the IPL was designed not to benefit cricket but enrich Modi. For Modi nothing could be more grotesque.

> I have not pocketed any money from the IPL. I created something out of nothing; the benefit, 100 per cent, accrues to the BCCI. The BCCI will benefit in the next ten years in excess of $2 billion. That was never in their projections. I've been able to create something that is of tremendous value, has world recognition and has put India on the map.

One of the most fascinating points in the BCCI charge sheet against Modi is that he behaved like a modern British Raj official. During the time of the Raj, officials would tour far flung districts carrying all their papers with them and write letters and memos headed 'camp so and so' from wherever they were based. Modi based himself in Mumbai's Four Seasons hotel and often wrote letters and memos in a similar style, saying 'Camp at Four Seasons'. He also kept all the papers and documentation of the IPL there. In other words, he did not follow anything like a proper office routine.

Modi's defence is that the Indian cricket board does not have what the world would recognize as an office. It may have been in existence for nearly 100 years, it may be the richest, but it still operates like a weekend club. 'The BCCI is run by individual, ordinary people like me and they run it out of their offices or homes wherever they are. And it has traditionally been the case for the last 100 years! The IPL was actually the first organization, or division of the BCCI, which started to professionalize and hire people.'

This may seem odd in a sports world where governing bodies such as FIFA, the IOC and even the Football Association boast of their headquarters. But in India it is not surprising. When Malcolm Speed first met Dalmiya he had to go to Dalmiya's offices in Kolkata, not Mumbai where the India board is meant to have its headquarters. 'Dalmiya ran the BCCI from his office in Kolkata. He had a large business that focused on industrial property development. He had two persons employed by his private company who did most of the work for the BCCI. He ran the BCCI as though it formed part of his personal business empire.'

Perhaps, because the IPL is not run like a conventional business, Modi can even claim to be an old-fashioned Corinthian sports administrator, a throwback to the days of the former IOC president, the American millionaire Brundage. Far from drawing any money from the IOC, Brundage paid the IOC a fee to be a member. Modi says, 'I fly at my cost, stay in hotels at my own cost; I ran the IPL on my own time. I have people working in the IPL that are my personal staff which I pay for. I was born into a very wealthy family. We are not dependent on anything to do with cricket.'

This must be one of the great ironies of modern sport. FIFA never stops talking about the good of the game in lofty tones that might have been written by Thomas Hughes or Pierre Coubertin. One slogan says: 'for the game, for the world'. Yet it pays its president and executive members handsomely. Even the IOC president, while a volunteer who is not paid, admits he and his members could not do their work if their travelling and board and lodging expenses were not reimbursed. Yet it is Modi, who appears unacquainted with *Tom Brown's Schooldays* or Coubertin's ideas, who presents himself as an administrator in the mould of which these founders of modern sport would have approved.

If this gives some idea of the almost Alice in Wonderland world of Indian cricket, then the great advantage for Modi was that its structure, or lack of it, meant he could do as he wished. Not that he needed much invitation. While he denies that instructions were given to the cameras to focus on him at every IPL match – the camera was dubbed 'Modicam' – he admits,

> You've gotta understand the IPL was something that I conceived. I conceived every element of it, put every element of it together. At the end of the day, IPL is a product closely identified with me, similar to what you would see in Formula One. It was Bernie Ecclestone and his work, the way he put it together, that made it literally a global phenomenon. Everything that he does is picked up by the media. Similarly, when we look at the IPL it wasn't just another cricket match, it's just not another entertainment property, it's the mixture of many, many things and all of these things were being done on the run. We ran it as a one-man show and I was the one that was running it. What we did was cricket with entertainment and with glamour which has resulted in the IPL today. To do that you are going to change rules, need to think outside the box and, of course, it upsets some people.

That Modi did not care whom he upset is best illustrated by the fact that a feature of the IPL is American-style blonde pom-pom girls gyrating on special platforms at the edge of the boundary every time a four or six is hit. That the land which gave the world Kama Sutra should seek sensation from American blondes said much about Modi's methods of projecting modern India. He could claim that was what Indians wanted. After Modi's fall, the organizers tried to Indianize this phenomenon and the Pune Warriors team had cheerleaders in saris, but this found little favour with the fans. As the *Hindustan Times* put it, 'The sari is not sexy enough.'

The irony for Modi is that, having created a sports product which fits in neatly with shiny new India, a country courted at the World Economic Forum at Davos and the creator of Nano, the world's cheapest car, his fall has led to talk of the old India of sleaze, possible tax evasion, money laundering, bogus companies and sweetheart deals with little or no governance. Since his fall, many Indians have also begun to ask why the Indian Cricket Board, a not-for-profit body which receives many tax and other concessions from both the central and state governments, has been allowed to set up a money machine like the IPL.

And, for all Modi's talk of having created a unique product, as we have seen, he is not the only sports pioneer. The founders of the English Premier League and the Champions League and those who run the NFL and the NBA can also claim to be pioneers. But they are not in exile from their homelands, let alone facing serious allegations of wrongdoing. Much as Modi dislikes the comparison, it is hard for him to escape the charge that in creating the IPL he behaved like a nineteenth-century American buccaneer keen to cut corners and take liberties. When I suggested that to him, he reacted as if he might lose his cool, saying,

I don't believe a word you're saying is right. It's nice to put it like that and make it sound superior. You may call it buccaneering or nineteenth century but we thought outside the box. Please do not compare me to the English Premier League or to any other league. We are unique. What is it that I have done apart from creating the world's hottest league? Yes, my style is different, but styles of different entrepreneurs are different, whether it's a Bernie Ecclestone, a Rupert Murdoch or a Donald Trump. They may upset people but they are judged by the results. Similarly I should be judged by my results. I am extremely happy and proud of what I delivered. I have no regrets at all. What I face are not charges, they're allegations. Anybody can allege anything. Nobody has charged me with anything. Nothing has been proven. I sleep very well at night. I have no problems. I go out, I have time to spend with my family. That's one good thing about it. When I was running the IPL, I had no time to be with my family. And I know how it's gonna end, by me getting a clean slate.

Modi may or may not be proved right. Investigations in India can take a long time. Since they were launched, the government has been mired in much bigger corruption scandals, and it is unlikely these Modi investigations will go anywhere soon. The Indian Cricket Board has also suffered significant defeats. Two franchises, Rajasthan Royals and King XI Punjab, which were expelled from the IPL, were reinstated by court orders and took part in the 2011 IPL.

This, the first IPL since Modi had been ousted, was just as appealing to the Indian public. The players' auctions were watched live by 20 million and fetched $62 million. The Pathan brothers, Yusuf and Irfan, who struggle to get into the Indian national teams, were awarded contracts jointly worth $4 million. Not bad for six weeks of cricket. The success of the auction and the tournament that followed emphasized how Modi, the ultimate sports businessman, had bequeathed to his successors the most successful domestic tournament in the history of the game. In the process, he had converted a recreational sport into one of the most marketable products in the world.

But such success also meant that the Indian cricket authorities had allowed a rich caste of cricketers to develop whose primary loyalty is to Mammon rather than to the national cause. So Virender Sehwag, one of India's best batsmen, delayed his shoulder surgery in order to play in the 2011 IPL. The result: he missed the first two Tests of the series against England in the summer of 2011 and when he did play, he looked far from his old self, suggesting he was not match fit for such a gruelling series.

The Indians had come to England as the top Test-playing nation, a position they had occupied since 2009 and four months after winning the 50-over World Cup. They knew the series would decide whether they retained their top dog status in Test cricket with England providing a formidable challenge. But they came so badly prepared that England dethroned and humiliated India, winning all four Test matches, two of them by innings. Not even the most optimistic of English fans could have hoped for such a result. Bookmakers, who always have a shrewd idea about such things, were so convinced this was unlikely that, at the beginning of the series, they were offering odds of 25-1 against such an outcome. Indians did put up a fight in the one-day series that followed but failed to win a single international match in the summer, which recalled the dark days of Indian cricket back in the 1950s.

Throughout the tour much was made of India being the moneybags of the game. Large crowds were attracted to the matches, with many Indian supporters eager to see their heroes. The money allure of the Indians even extended to what were essentially practice matches, as the experience of Northants showed. The Midlands county staged a two-day match for the Indians. It did not even count as a first-class match. Yet the county made a profit of £100,000, far in excess of anything they had ever made for such matches, and much more than most of their bread and butter county cricket matches which lose money. In 2010 the county had made an overall loss of £27,000, one of many counties to lose money.

The English trick in humbling the richer Indians was to realize how best to maximize what resources it has. County cricket may lose money but it has been converted into a marvellous finishing school, producing players of high quality to represent the national team. Once they are deemed good enough to play for England, they are given central contracts and, after that, they rarely ever play for their county side. They concentrate on England and make sure they showcase their country to the best possible advantage to an international audience as the team did so brilliantly in the summer of 2011. It is as if a company were to take one of its old plants, once profitable but now no longer so, and convert it into a research and development operation producing products that can be successfully marketed. In contrast Indian cricket had swung so far in the money direction that the talk was always about the eyeballs its product attracts on television not on how the money could be best used to further the game.

The result was India, the rich man of cricket, had proved that money on its own is not enough to win sporting success. It needs to be used properly and methodically, otherwise a less wealthy competitor like England will triumph. In the retail trade, the superstore may always overwhelm the corner shop. But a smartly run sports corner shop, which knows exactly what it is doing, can beat a badly organized sports superstore.

It also emphasized that, for all the talk of modern sport being a business, sport can never be just a product due to the high moral ground it claims, upholding the Corinthian spirit of the game. So, where does this leave the values of the game today? This question was to become even more insistent in the summer of 2011 when the governance problems surrounding FIFA dominated the media. FIFA's limp-wristed response raised the question of whether it was not time for sport finally to abandon the lofty ideals of Thomas Hughes and Pierre de Coubertin. It had become a business and all talk of the spirit of sport was just marketing froth.

CHAPTER 14

WHAT SHALL WE DO WITH SPORT?

What is wrong with sport? The excesses of sportsmen and women and the wretched governance of sport may make many feel that *Tom Brown's Schooldays* created an impossible ideal. The temptation is to echo another schoolboy, Gordon Caruthers, when he concluded, 'We can see games as they really are without any false mist of sentiment, and we can see that for years we have been worshipping something utterly wrong.' Or even Ferrers, the radical schoolmaster of Fernhurst, who asked, 'How much longer are we going to waste our time, our energy, our force on kicking a football? We have no strength for anything else. And all the time, while Germany has been plotting against us, piling up armaments, we have been cheering on Chelsea and West Ham United.'

Like Tom Brown, both Caruthers and Ferrers were fictional characters in Alec Waugh's novel *The Loom of Youth*. Waugh, the older brother of Evelyn, wrote the book when he was only 17, preparing for a commission as a junior officer in the First World War. Like Hughes he had been to a public school. In the novel his school, Sherborne, became Fernhurst, where sporting success gives boys a licence to behave like 'bloods': slackers, cheats, bullies, drinkers and gamblers. They humiliate weak masters and prefects. They make sexual advances to younger boys and have open relationships with them. They are cynical about Christianity and despise any display or advocacy of effort or virtue, even in sport. The 'bloods' are admired and no one expects them to behave morally.

Caruthers, arriving at the school aged 13, immediately sets his heart on becoming a 'blood'. He is good at sport, socially adept, and achieves his ambitions ahead of time owing to the war. Caruthers and other boys regularly flaunt the values of their school. Here is Jeffries, a sporting hero facing expulsion over an affair with a smaller boy.

> Who made me what I am but Fernhurst? Two years ago I came here as innocent as Caruthers there; never knew anything. Fernhurst taught me everything; Fernhurst made me worship games and think that they alone mattered, and everything else could go to the deuce. I heard men say about bloods whose lives were an open scandal, 'Oh, it's all right, they can play football.'

By the end of the novel Caruthers comes to realize that his triumphs were hollow and that the school's fixation on sport was destructive and useless. In compensation, Caruthers has discovered the possibilities of poetry and literature and the qualities of boys and masters who are not sportsmen. Caruthers is not alone in rejecting the ethos of the school and the debating society carries overwhelmingly a motion against athletics. It is the perfect fictional end to the novel. But even in 1917, when the novel was published, Waugh must have known sport was sufficiently established not to be so easily overthrown. Like *Tom Brown's Schooldays*, the novel was a bestseller, but its impact was not on sport – rather that it openly discussed homosexual relations, leading to Waugh being expelled from the Sherborne old boys' society.

Since then sport has become such a colossal force in global society that if Gordon Caruthers were around, he would argue that the 'bloods' of modern sport have created Thomas Arnold's unintended monster. The economic figures are revealing enough, measured not just in terms of direct payments to take part in sport, view sporting events, or purchase sporting goods, but in the value of all the non-sporting goods and services promoted by sport. In 2004 the value of the US sports industry was double that of its automotive industry. A recent study of the global sports market by the consultancy A. T. Kearney placed its annual value at between US $480 billion and $620 billion. This aggregated spending on sports events, stadium management and construction, rights management, live events and content. The figure is roughly equivalent to the GDP of Switzerland or one quarter the GDP of the United Kingdom.

This economic behemoth reflects the fact that sport has become so much bigger than itself – more than a means of passing time or gaining exercise or having a pretext for a wager. No other single phenomenon exercises such a force in global society. As we have seen, this owes a lot to the two men who made modern sport: Thomas Hughes, who first took up the baton of sport in the name of an unsuspecting Thomas Arnold, and Pierre de Coubertin, who seized the baton. In the century and a half since Hughes started this particular race, the two ideas these men spawned have truly become global concepts.

Hughes' big idea was in the private realm, that sport develops character and playing sport makes you not only fitter but a different, better person. This lies behind every commercial attempt to use sport and athletes to sell goods and services. It underpins the personal relationship of all participants and all spectators with their chosen sports. Coubertin's big idea was in the public realm, that sport could transmit values within and between nations through regular international competition. This lies behind every political attempt to use sport and athletes as a mark of national or local identity, to promote public policy and advance the careers of individual politicians.

The problem is the way modern sport operates.

There is often an unbridgeable gap between the two ideas, more so in an age where sport is business and watching or playing it is also very popular with billions of people across the world. The result is that Coubertin's big idea often threatens to undermine the lofty principles of Hughes' idea, a process worsened by the fact that Coubertin's idea not only took off long after Hughes' definition of sport was universally accepted but also, in recent years, it has been ruthlessly exploited by people who would never have anything in common with Hughes, let alone Thomas Arnold.

To judge how Coubertin's idea has grown, consider that back in 1968 the writer Hunter S. Thompson, riding in the limo of Richard Nixon during the New Hampshire primary, was surprised to find how well informed Nixon was about American football. He later wrote 'whatever else might be said about Nixon – and there is still serious doubt in my mind that he could pass for Human – he is a goddamn stone fanatic on every facet of pro football'. He noted with admiration his encyclopaedic recollection of an obscure Oakland receiver's background. Since then the modern politicians' interest in sport has grown so much that it is almost obligatory to display it.

The result is that politicians routinely use participation, or at least interest, in sport as evidence that they are likeable people, or at least normal. So in the spring of 2011 Barack Obama, making his first state visit to London, played table tennis with the British prime minister, David Cameron, in public against schoolboys. British papers, particularly the serious ones, made much of this sporting moment and analysed their ability and playing styles as indicators of their performance in office. Cameron also played lawn tennis with Andrew Castle, a former top British tennis player, who described him as 'a good player, he's tenacious, he chases every ball and he never lets the ball bounce twice'. A *Guardian* writer commented, 'It seems the prime minister could learn a lesson from tennis in his political career.'

Even in Thomas Arnold's days, which marked the arrival of popular democracy, politicians seeking to identify themselves with their electors were not unknown. But to do so through sport would have been unimaginable. (Thomas Arnold would, of course, also have had to get over the shock of seeing the British prime minister as the junior partner in a relationship with America.)

The appeal of sport to modern politicians is, at least in part, that sports events attract large crowds, particularly on television. Sports organizers never fail to remind the world of this appeal. The 1996 Olympic Games in Atlanta were seen by an estimated 3.2 billion viewers out of a possible 3.5 billion worldwide. FIFA claimed that the 2010 World Cup final was watched live by around 700 million people – nearly one in ten of the world's population. This compares with the combined population of the two countries playing the final, the Netherlands and Spain, of under 60 million.

It is interesting to reflect that, when Waugh was writing his critique on sport, not only was there no television but the idea that sports should be treated as part of public policy was not accepted by many governments, certainly not by the country whose empire made it the foremost nation on earth. Three years after Waugh's novel was published, there were serious doubts as to whether Britain could send a team to the 1920 Antwerp Olympics. Something between £10,000 and £20,000 was needed and Winston Churchill, secretary of state for war, made an appeal for money in a speech at the Criterion Restaurant in London. The Games had been given to Belgium in compensation for the horrors the country had suffered during the war. The Foreign Office had accepted the invitation and the king was keen the team should go. Failure to attend might have been politically awkward.

Churchill's speech was directed at the north of England, which was contributing half the athletes and was richer than the south but had not done much to help. However, Churchill refused any government help. As the *Guardian* noted, 'An outside observer might think it up to our Government to help the scheme without fear of criticism, but Mr Churchill held out no hopes of that kind in his speech.' Roll forward nearly a century and you see Churchill's successors spending millions to procure success in international competitions and billions to get the right to stage them, the government budget for London 2012 being £9.3 billion. Indeed hosting an Olympics is seen as a mark of a nation's status. This was certainly the view taken by Tessa Jowell, then secretary of state for Culture, Media and Sport when London bid for 2012.

There was much scepticism about London making the bid. The decision was made against a background where bidding for the Olympics was like waiting for a British winner at Wimbledon. In the decade leading up to the success in Singapore in 2005, two bids by Manchester and one by Birmingham had failed. Then, having secured the 2005 World Athletics Championships, the British behaved almost like a Third World country and gave the championships back. The reason given was that Britain could not afford to build the required facilities. There was also the on-going saga about Wembley Stadium and the bailout by the government of the 2002 Manchester Commonwealth Games. It also required convincing a sceptical Treasury and, in particular, Chancellor Gordon Brown, who had set his heart on getting the World Cup back to this country.

It was against this background that Jowell persuaded Tony Blair to back the Olympics by telling him that it would be a great shame if the fourth largest economy [as the UK then was] could not even bid for the greatest show on earth. Jowell was so successful in her mission that her good friend Cherie Blair wanted to head the London bid. Indeed she was so keen that I was asked to brief her as to what would be involved.

I was working at the *Daily Telegraph*, whose then sports editor, David Welch, had launched the campaign for London's bid. As the paper's chief sports reporter, I was leading the campaign. Cherie Blair and I met for tea at the Reform Club, where she had been brought by Michael Beloff, the QC who shares her barristers' chambers. As it happens both Beloff and I are members of the club and we met in the room where the committee of the club normally holds its meeting. I explained to her that bidding meant hanging around the hotel lobbies of the world cosying up to fairly old, invariably male, members of the International Olympic Committee. This did not seem to daunt Cherie Blair and we had not had many sips of tea when it became clear that she was keen to do the job. Our meeting ended with her words: 'Of course he will have to be consulted.' She did not have to specify who he was.

In the summer of 2011 Tony Blair was making his first visit to the Olympic stadium in the east end of London. He recalled to me how he was persuaded to back the bid:

Looking round this stadium now, it is incredible to think that it began as a conversation between Tessa [Jowell] and myself. It was the summer of 2003, because we were outside in the Downing Street garden. Tessa was saying that we should bid and I was saying, 'Well look, Tessa, it's all very well but it's going to be such a lot of work. What happens if we lose, we're going to get slaughtered. I don't want to be humiliated by the French.' She said – and she knew exactly how to put this to me, 'You know this is not the Tony Blair I know, cautious and timid.' So I said, 'Oh all right, let's give it a go then.'

And whatever doubts he had were finally removed by Cherie:

She was very passionate about the Olympic bid. When I discussed it with her before we agreed to go for the bid, she was wildly enthusiastic. She said, 'Go for it, it's the greatest sporting event in the world, why on earth not? If the people in London and the athletics people are prepared to get behind it, why should we not do it?' I was frankly worried it was going to take up a lot of time and we'd fail. But she rightly said, 'Well you don't succeed unless you're prepared to fail, so give it a go.'

521

For Blair hosting the Olympics was a win-win situation for a country:

> Of course it costs money, but think of the amount of money that's going to come in. I mean they were telling me the merchandising is going to be a billion pounds alone. Economically once you add in the invisibles as well as the visibles, it's got to be a good thing. The reason why people compete so hard for the events like the Olympics, and to a lesser extent the World Cup, is because you've got the eyes of the world on you. It is a vast showcase for the country, a great way of projecting the country. Just so many people watch it. It's a huge event. For three weeks billions of people will spend a part of their day thinking and watching the Olympics. What could be better than that for a country like us?

The idea of sport having such an impact would be unthinkable in Arnold's days. Then leaders used exhibitions to advertise national glory, as Prince Albert did in organizing the Great Exhibition. Now 'Expos' pass unnoticed, while hosting Olympics and World Cups proclaims a nation's first-class status. Modern political leaders do not seem to mind that to get their country into this new premier league they need to charm a club whose elections are more like those of a local golf club. And while the members of such clubs, self-elected in the case of the Olympics, range from royalty to associates of former dictators, all of them see their club as exclusive and the events they promote almost as their personal property, of which they are fiercely protective.

Some politicians understand this better than others: Tony and Cherie Blair certainly did. They cosied up so effectively to IOC members in Singapore in 2005 that it helped London beat the favourite, Paris. Leading up to Singapore Cherie Blair had also done a lot of canvassing for London. As Blair puts it:

> She worked out that in the Olympic Committee, there are obviously the great and the good and the princes and princesses and all

that, but there are also – I don't know quite how to put it – the less well-known and less high-profile people. But they all have one vote and so she made friends with all those people. She would go out to their countries and see them and talk to them. She just kept up the contacts with them. So, when we got to Singapore, she was bumping into old friends. That was the reason why, when I was in Singapore, I thought, hey maybe we've got a chance of winning this.

Blair squeezed in his visit to Singapore in June 2005 despite the fact that the vote there was on the eve of the G8 summit in Gleneagles. Blair, as host, was due to preside over arguably the most important summit of world leaders. He could not get out of that commitment so he and his advisers, led by London bid leaders Seb Coe and Keith Mills, decided on a clever wheeze: go to Singapore for a few days before the vote, meet IOC members individually and then leave just before the vote, pleading high matters of state.

It worked like a dream. The 40-odd members he met were charmed, while the rest appreciated he had gone all that way to court them. And at Gleneagles, with four of the top countries, Britain, the US, Russia and France, having their capitals or most important city (New York for the Americans) bidding, Blair could also score some brownie points. Two years later Vladmir Putin, aware Moscow had finished last in Singapore and determined to win, consulted people who had worked on the 2012 bid and closely studied Blair's campaign. The result was that Sochi, a rank outsider with few winter facilities, won the right to stage the 2014 Winter Games, beating the picture-postcard winter city Salzburg.

Curiously, the archetypal politician of our time, Barack Obama, while convinced of the importance of such events, did not understand how the system worked. He flew into Copenhagen in September 2009, confident that his home town of Chicago could win the 2016 Olympics. Not long before President Obama addressed the International Olympic Committee, a gridlock created by his presence in Copenhagen held up for an hour and a half a bus carrying IOC members to the hall where they were going to vote. The members arrived less than pleased with this particular Obama effect. The result was one of the most sensational recent Olympic decisions: not only did Rio win 2016 but Chicago was dumped out in the first round of voting.

Nobody knows how many of them in that bus were responsible for the tremendous snub they delivered to the US president but the IOC member who told me the story had a real edge in his voice as he added,

> He may be the leader of the free world but that does not mean he can behave like God. Because of his five-hour presence in this town, traffic was snarled up, flights in and out of Copenhagen were delayed. All he told us was: give me the Olympics because I live just down the road from where it will be staged. He did not even stay for the vote or mix with the members; that was very disrespectful.

Now this may be an extreme view but many others echoed it and compared the performance of the most important leader of the world very unfavourably with that of President Lula of Brazil. Lula hobnobbed with IOC members before the vote, then shed copious tears as Rio was chosen to become the first South American city to host the Games. Lula's tears showed how much hosting the Olympics meant as Brazil seeks to join the top table of world powers. For IOC members, this mattered.

Politicians waking up to the power of global sporting events is a fairly recent phenomenon and, ironically, it was the Colombians in 1973 who can be said to have invented modern football World Cup bidding. Seeking the 1986 World Cup, they entertained a visiting FIFA delegation lavishly and at a reception the president, Dr Borrero, made it clear that hosting the competition would prove Colombia had arrived as a nation. 'It is in everyone's mutual interest to demonstrate to the world that a country such as ours is perfectly competent to put this challenge to its sports administration, thus conveying to all other nations just how capable it is of organizing an event of this magnitude in 1986.' The Colombians then made declarations that have become so familiar over the years. 'If it is necessary to construct new stadia, we shall do so with the people's backing in the knowledge of the Colombians' love of football.'

Colombia in the end failed to meet its commitments and the 1986 World Cup was given to Mexico. That decision was arrived at most curiously. Mexico was up against a USA bid which had the support of Warner Communications, backers of the North American Soccer League, and was led by Henry Kissinger. When the FIFA executive met in Stockholm, Kissinger made an hour-long presentation providing the sort of details Americans thought would convince the executive members. In contrast, Mexico made an eight-minute presentation. But it was soon evident that the presentation was just a show. Even as Kissinger was speaking, the Mexicans were preparing to party in a Stockholm hotel in anticipation of victory, FIFA president João Havelange having gained the executive approval for Mexico at a breakfast that morning.

By the time the contest for the 1998 World Cup took place, bidding nations had begun to treat the FIFA president as if he was a head of state who had to be courted and humoured. Switzerland was so keen to host the competition that the president of the Swiss Football Association nominated Havelange for the Nobel Peace Prize. Havelange, in return, waxed eloquent about the Swiss bid. Switzerland's chances blossomed as their main rival, France, initially fell out with Havelange. The then French prime minister Jacques Chirac accused Havelange of bias against the French Olympic bid for Paris to stage the 1992 Games. So upset was Chirac that he even threatened to use French influence in Africa to stop him getting re-elected. However, the French soon realized Havelange had to be wooed. By September 1991 the French Football Federation was ready to spend up to 7 million francs targeting FIFA committee members. And then came the French masterstroke: in a ceremony at the presidential palace François Mitterrand inducted Havelange into France's Légion d'Honneur, describing him as 'one of the great figures of today's sporting world'. Morocco, another nation in the race, got Havelange to visit Rabat to be received by King Hassan II. However, the unpredictable monarch, who had kept Queen Elizabeth waiting, also made Havelange wait, to the great fury of the Brazilian. In July 1992 France won the right to host the 1998 World Cup.

In many ways the most revealing political wooing was that by Nelson Mandela to secure South Africa the 2010 World Cup. South Africa had used Mandela for their failed 2006 bid and, with only African nations allowed to bid for the 2010 competition, South Africa was determined to have it. I was made vividly aware of all this on 14 May 2004, 24 hours before the FIFA executive met to vote on the bid. I was just outside a third-floor suite of Zurich's Grand Dolder Hotel, which is in the hills above the headquarters of FIFA. Mandela and many of the top brass of FIFA were staying there. As I waited I saw Nelson Mandela and Thabo Mbeki, then president of South Africa, emerge from their suite in the company of Jack Warner, then a FIFA vice-president and a key player. Warner, having for so long been warm to South Africa, had turned hostile. A few weeks before, I had met him in London and he was scathing about the South Africans and very warm to Morocco. Now he was so hostile to South Africa he was even refusing to return calls from the South African bid team. Everyone knew how crucial Warner was. He controlled three votes on the 24-man executive and could swing the election.

South Africa had sent Bishop Desmond Tutu to Warner's country, Trinidad, to hold a special mass to humour him. But even that had not quite done the trick. With a day to go the trump card had to be played and Mandela and Mbeki flew into Zurich to meet Warner. What these men discussed has never been revealed, but I caught up with Warner in the corridor immediately after the meeting. When I asked him who was going to win, Morocco or South Africa, he said, 'Who knows, anything can happen.' Then he gave a big smile, suggesting that the Mandela trump card had worked.

Until that moment the Moroccans were very sure that they had secured Warner's votes. They had spent millions on their campaign, employing so many experts from all over the world that theirs was almost an 'outsourced' bid. It was difficult to find a Moroccan in the bid team. The Moroccan bid prediction was that they would beat South Africa by 14 votes to 10. But, the next day, it was South Africa that won 14–10. It was very clear for whom Warner and his colleagues had voted. That afternoon, as the South Africans held a celebratory lunch at the Grand Dolder, Mandela duly raised a glass to his new friends. For Mandela, the man who is nearest to a modern-day Gandhi, to be forced to 'schmooze' Warner shows that, when your country wants the World Cup, you have to take any road you can. The trick here is to pretend you are travelling on a high road talking of how well-equipped you are to hold the World Cup and all the good it will do both for the country and the world. But the real journey is along the low road, making deals with FIFA executive members, however dubious they may be.

This was certainly what David Cameron was also prepared to do when England was bidding for the 2018 World Cup. Then the British prime minister treated Sepp Blatter as if he was a head of a state. At a reception for him at Downing Street this is what Cameron said:

> One of the first things I did when I became prime minister was to call you to reconfirm the new government's full support for England 2018 and since then we have been involved on a daily basis strengthening it wherever possible. The government may have changed, but our commitment to hosting the World Cup has not changed. Mr President, you have done a huge amount for football during your whole life. The decisions you have made have been instrumental in taking the game to new heights, breaking boundaries and reaching new people, culminating in what we were just discussing together – bringing that hugely successful World Cup to Africa just a few months ago. It was an inspirational thing to see. It will have had a transformational effect, not just in South Africa but right across that continent, country after country. In 50 days' time, you and the FIFA executive will make

another crucial decision, deciding who hosts the 2018 World Cup. I hope you see that England has got what it takes to host the greatest tournament on earth. I hope you can see how much our country wants this.

Yet even as he spoke, members of the England bid team were well aware that FIFA executive members had asked for favours in exchange for votes. Indeed Lord Triesman, the Football Association chairman, had to resign when a private conversation in which he had alleged that there might be corruption involved in the bidding process was leaked. Long after the bid was history Triesman testified to a House of Commons committee about the various favours FIFA members wanted. It also emerged that the bid's chief executive Andy Anson, in a private briefing with journalists, had said votes could be bought. But with England still hopeful of winning the bid it was clearly felt all this could not be disclosed. Indeed when there was unfavourable media publicity about FIFA the bid criticized it as unhelpful to England's chances. For the bid this was war, albeit without weapons, and the British press was expected to line up behind the bid, not create trouble.

Politicians have also become adept at using major events to further the political agenda, as was demonstrated when the Indian subcontinent staged the 50-over cricket World Cup in the spring of 2011. The competition was fraught with problems: security, or lack of it, meant no matches were held in Pakistan. Relations between India and Pakistan have never been good: since 1947 the two neighbours have fought three wars and they are yet to recover from the 2008 terrorist attack on Mumbai by Pakistani-based terror groups. Pakistani players are not allowed to play in the Indian Premier League. But when India played its semi-final against Pakistan in India, cricket provided a link that nothing else could. Pakistani fans came to watch, the match was a success and the Pakistan prime minister was a guest of the Indians. The Indian prime minister held a dinner for his Pakistani counterpart, thanking him for 'watching this beautiful game of cricket' and hoped this would be the start of reconciliation between the two countries. It was a wonderful illustration of politicians seeking to use a game of cricket to open doors that nothing else could.

This power of modern sporting events is further reinforced by the fact that, by bringing diverse elements together at an Olympics or World Cup, nations get a chance not merely to prove athletic prowess on the field of play. They can also generate business. So, although British athletes returned from Vancouver in 2010 holding up the bottom of the Winter Games medals table, along with Estonia and Kazakhstan, away from the ski slopes and ice venues, British officials were hailing the Games as a triumph. In Vancouver the British were determined to prove that when it comes to wining, dining and holding breakfast meetings to promote trade it will always be near the top of the medals table.

Nothing illustrated this better than the event held at Vancouver's BC Place not long after Amy Williams had won Britain's solitary gold in the skeleton competition. Inside this venue, advertised as Vancouver's great business place, the British paraded what they saw as their unique trade skills. A film called *Love and Money* was screened, a sort of business version of *Love Actually*. Meant to celebrate 50 years of Britain's creative genius, it featured everything from the Mini and mini skirt to Wallace & Gromit, C. S. Lewis, Damien Hirst, Hockney, Dyson, Helen Mirren, Kate Winslet, Mary Quant, Roald Dahl and the Rolling Stones. Drinks and canapés were on offer, Sir Steve Redgrave, Princess Anne and Tessa Jowell were in attendance and the event was billed as British Olympians helping British businesses to go for gold. Its significance lay in the fact that the UK is the second-largest destination for Canadian investment outside the US, while Canada is the UK's third largest export market outside Europe. The British were very proud of how they had exploited London hosting 2012. Through Host2Host agreements, they had targeted other places staging major sporting events and the government estimated that Britain had won £2 billion of business at the Beijing Olympics. The British were not the only ones in search of lucre. Vancouver promoted itself as a convention centre, hoping to share in the lucrative market that more often heads for American cities like Seattle and San Francisco.

Such is the modern link between sport and politics that, just as politicians enlist sport to promote health and education, deter crime or racism and encourage volunteering, so sports officials use almost the same language to extol the virtues of their sport. Organizations like FIFA never miss a chance to push this message. During the 2010 World Cup famous footballers regularly held media conferences to publicize efforts being made to eradicate disease in Africa. At the FIFA Congress in Zurich in June 2011, delegates were given a document entitled *Football for Hope.* Given the corruption charges faced by the organization, every page of this had the feel of the sort of unwitting parody of the FIFA crisis of which the creators of Monty Python would have been proud. But it could also be read as a sports political manifesto by FIFA.

So the first page had a picture of Sepp Blatter with Kofi Annan, the former secretary-general of the United Nations, with Annan saying football improves 'health and education for the world's children and prevents HIV Aids'. Sepp Blatter declared that football has 'unique appeal and core values that reach across generations' and 'football is and needs to remain a school for life'. On the inside pages FIFA described the good it brings to the world, which included bringing together Palestinian and Israeli children between the ages of six and fourteen. FIFA's great role in the other trouble spots of the world, like Bosnia-Herzegovina, Rwanda and Sierra Leone, were also highlighted. There was even mention of the United Kingdom's Street League built, said FIFA, 'on the principles of inclusiveness, sustainability and diversity, with the aim of promoting healthy lifestyles, social integration, crime reduction, non-formal education and long-term employment'. All this was capped by FIFA's partners, Adidas, Coke, Emirates, Hyundai, Sony and Visa declaring how 'Football for

Hope is a movement that uses the power of the game for social development. It is led by FIFA and streetfootballworld.'

The power of modern sport was to be, perhaps, most vividly demonstrated in the winter of 2010. It came in the very contrasting reactions to elections to decide the members of the United Nations Security Council and the hosts for the 2018 and 2022 World Cups. The October 2010 UN vote was to select five of the ten elected members of the Security Council. The ten elected members do not have the power of the five permanent members – the United States, China, Russia, France and Britain – all of whom have the right of veto. But it is still a hugely prestigious slot at the top table of a world body charged with maintaining peace round the globe.

Canada was very keen to be elected, having served six terms on the Security Council, every decade since its inception. During the election Canada had portrayed itself as a model global citizen and, up against Portugal, was confident of success. Just before the delegates of the 192 countries marked their choice on paper ballots, the countries seeking election put a small gift on their desks, Canada's gift being a vial of maple syrup. But this did not sweeten the voters and, after two rounds of voting with Portugal ahead, Canada withdrew from the race. The defeat was a huge shock for the Canadians. The *Globe and Mail* commented,

> Such campaigns are not won on international reputation alone
> [. . .] Nations have been known to promise their support to one
> candidate only to switch allegiance in the final vote. A former
> Australian ambassador to the UN called it the 'rotten lying
> bastards' phenomenon after his country lost a bid for a seat on
> the Security Council.

But for all the political anguish in Canada the story generated no wider interest and even in Canada it was soon overtaken by other political events.

In contrast the story the *Sunday Times* broke that very weekend caused such a tidal wave that it spawned many others and is resonating even as I write. That story concerned not seats on a council that can decide between war and peace, but vote-buying in FIFA by countries seeking to host the 2018 and 2022 World Cups. England, like Canada, was very confident it could win the right to stage the 2018 World Cup. But when the members of the FIFA executive committee gathered in Zurich in December 2010 England got only two votes, one of them from the Englishman on the committee. This was followed by Qatar, quite sensationally, winning the right to stage the 2022 World Cup.

Both results, but particularly England's defeat, caused outrage in the country. Soon the bid leaders, echoing the Australian ambassador, were telling the English press how FIFA executive members had 'lied' to them about their voting intentions. The *Sunday Times* followed up its story with more revelations, other media sources did as well and six months later a Commons select committee heard evidence from Lord Triesman that FIFA members asked for favours in return for votes. By then the bid corruption story was rumbling on with such fury that the *Financial Times*, not a paper noted for its sports coverage, was leading with stories on its front page about FIFA in chaos. There were calls by British politicians that FIFA be destroyed and a new FIFA set up. David Cameron, having lauded Blatter only months earlier, now called for the FIFA presidential elections to be postponed. Other politicians in many parts of the world, while not going quite as far as the British, urged FIFA to reform. Sepp Blatter was not completely isolated in the political world. Vladimir Putin, the Russian prime minister, whose country had beaten England in the race to stage the 2018 World Cup, dismissed as 'rubbish' claims that Blatter was corrupt. His intervention merely highlighted the interest shown in the FIFA elections, a non-governmental body involved in providing a leisure activity, when the elections to a body supposed to preserve world peace hardly generated much attention.

Such interest would have astonished Thomas Arnold, Hughes or even Coubertin. It underlined how both sport and the world had changed since their days and highlighted the problems faced by those seeking to make sports organizations suitable for the stringent requirements of the twenty-first century. It is worth dwelling on the *Sunday Times* investigation to appreciate the enormity of what has happened.

Jonathan Calvert and Claire Newell, of the paper's Insight team, had just carried out an investigation into buying votes on the International Whaling Commission, an intergovernmental organization of about 100 nations. The story was about how Japan subverts the whole process by buying the votes of other countries so it can carry on whaling. One of their sources, who had read the article, said they should look at football. At the same time John Witherow, the editor, had been told that the FIFA bidding process for the World Cup needed to be looked at. Calvert had done some sports investigation and is interested in sport, being a Leeds United supporter. Newell had neither investigated sport, nor has any great interest in it. Newell also has a rather charmingly eccentric habit of carrying her own bread to meals.

They were both aware how secretive football was and that this had to be an undercover operation. They pretended to be representing a company that was trying to help secure the United States the World Cup. Calvert explains, 'The reason we decided not to have an English company is that by being American you are one step removed. We thought it was easier for there to be confusion about who we were. Whereas if we were going to be based in London and be part of the England bid, it was quite easy to check out what was going on.'

One of their most productive contacts was Michel Zen-Ruffinen. As we have seen, he fought Blatter in the name of a clean FIFA back in 2002. Now Calvert and Newell met him for lunch in Geneva and secretly filmed him. Newell said that they were surprised how easy it was to get FIFA people to open up and admit that votes could be bought. 'You talk to the former deputy head of the whole organization who is now offering himself as a consultant and when it comes to strategy for winning bids it wasn't about having the best stadiums and things like that. It was all about paying for it or politics. We couldn't believe how straightforwardly open it all was.'

Their most interesting meeting was in London with Ismail Bhamjee from Botswana, who had been a FIFA executive member until 2006 when he had had to resign after it emerged he had sold some World Cup tickets. Bhamjee, recalls Newell, took them to a

> very nice fish restaurant, delicious food. He wouldn't let us pay. That was a real embarrassment to us because obviously we felt we should pay. But he was so keen to take the work. And just like Zen-Ruffinen, he instantly launched into 'Well what you have got to do is pay these people.' He then gave us examples of how they had got paid before.

The pair videoed Bhamjee providing details of how FIFA executive members had been bribed by previous World Cup bidders. 'He told us', recalls Calvert,

> a great story actually about how he was in the car and he got a call from a fellow FIFA executive member because apparently Bhamjee's telephone number at the time was very similar to someone from one of the bids. And apparently this FIFA member said, 'Where is my money? Where is my bloody money?' And he started shouting. Bhamjee had to say, 'Oh this isn't the bid, this is me, Bhamjee.' And then the FIFA executive member said, 'Oh, OK,' and just put the phone down.

Bhamjee also revealed details of the current World Cup bids. But for legal reasons the reporters could not report this in the detail Bhamjee provided.

The Insight pair struck gold when they met Amos Adamu, then the FIFA member from Nigeria, in the Hilton at the top of Edgware Road. 'Adamu', recalls Newell,

kept us waiting for thirty minutes in the lobby. He was so important. And then eventually he emerged with his wife and children.
I seem to remember his wife went shopping. We then had a meeting in a sort of bar. It was incredibly noisy, there was really loud
music and people laughing and we couldn't really hear what he
was saying. We thought this is going to be an absolute nightmare
to record him so I said, 'Oh, Jonathan can't hear very well; why
don't we move into that room and we can talk a bit better.' We
went to a quieter room.

Adamu did not waste time making it clear what he wanted.
Calvert recalls,

He said he wants his two projects and we asked, 'Do you want
the money to be paid to your football federation or to you?' And
he said he wanted the money. The problem was he initially said
come to Nigeria, and there is absolutely no way we were going to
do covert recording in Nigeria. We then agreed to meet in Cairo
in a couple of weeks, because he was going to be there for the
African football confederation (CAF) meeting.

In Cairo, Zen-Ruffinen took the reporters to meet Issa Hayatou at the
CAF headquarters, around 30 miles outside the city. Calvert says,

It was a rather strange day. Hayatou wasn't ready for us so we
were waiting around and eventually we were called and asked if
we would like to have lunch with Hayatou. Lunch with Hayatou
was in this tiny room which was the CAF canteen! It was actually
very awkward. On the table there was lots of foil-wrapped cold
fish. We had already eaten but we thought we should eat to be
polite. It was a very small group; there were about eight of us
along with Jean-Marie Weber, the former ISL man. Nobody knew
what to talk about. And there sat opposite us was Adamu. We
just nodded our heads to him. The night before he had agreed to
sell his vote to us in the hotel.

535

That final meeting with Adamu, says Calvert,

> was rather weird. He had this friend who presumably worked
> in football as well, who sat on the table opposite us and watched
> what we were doing. Adamu made us sit in the darkest corner
> of the hotel, which was a nightmare for undercover filming. The
> sound is perfect on the filming but the video is just terrible. The
> camera is just black.

Calvert had to make the long trip to New Zealand to meet a
second FIFA executive member, Tahitian Reynald Temarii,
Oceania president. The meeting took some organizing and was in
the offices of the Oceania Federation. 'Temarii', says Calvert, 'was
genuinely asking for money for his federation and not himself.
But that has got to be wrong. You don't vote because someone
pays your federation. And he was saying that others had offered
him $10 million dollars or something for the vote.'

FIFA treated the *Sunday Times* stories as if family secrets had
been revealed. Adamu and Temarii were suspended from the
executive and were unable to vote when the decisions for the 2018
and 2022 World Cup bids were made. Four others named by the
paper were also suspended. But the paper was also criticized and
accused of misrepresentation, even making things up. This
considerably angered the two journalists. They felt they had gone
out of their way to help FIFA with the material and instead of
being thanked they were being abused.

The *Sunday Times*, for legal reasons, could not publish all the
material they had. They got an opportunity when a British
parliamentary select committee, which was examining the governance of football, decided to extend its remit to the World Cup bid.
The *Sunday Times* made a submission to the committee and the
material it could not previously publish now came into the public
domain, protected by parliamentary privilege. In this submission
the reporters said:

Last December we spoke to a whistleblower who had worked with the Qatar bid. The whistleblower claimed Qatar had paid $1.5 million to two FIFA ExCo members – Hayatou and Jacques Anouma of the Ivory Coast – to secure their votes. It was alleged that a similar deal had been struck with Amos Adamu, although he was prevented from voting because he was suspended following our original article. The whistleblower said the cash was going to the three members' football federations but that there would be no questions asked about how the money was used: 'It was said in such a way that "we are giving it to you". It was going to their federation. If they took it we don't give a jack,' the whistleblower told us.

Qatar in response made a submission to the committee and vigorously denied the allegations, describing them as 'unsubstantiated and false'. Blatter claimed there was no evidence from the *Sunday Times* or the whistleblower regarding the 2022 World Cup bid and no need to re-examine the Qatar bid. The *Sunday Times* disputed this, saying that the whistleblower's lawyers wanted certain assurances, to which FIFA's head of security initially agreed, but that agreement was vetoed by its director of legal affairs. FIFA argued the whistleblower had made impossible demands. The whistleblower could give 'no warranty for the accuracy and correctness of the information' provided, wanted the right to destroy the information at any time and that the information not be made public. FIFA was also asked to 'cover the costs to indemnify the whistleblower for any breaches of contract . . . for any liabilities and for any potential criminal proceedings related to the agreement, as well as for an unlimited witness protection program'.

Qatari officials had suggested that the whistleblower was 'an embittered ex-employee' and that is exactly how it turned out some weeks later. Phaedra Almajid, who worked as an international media specialist in Qatar's bid team for just under a year, confessed that she had made up the bribe story. She had been hurt by the bid saying she was not competent and was 'acting irrationally' and wanted to 'hurt' the bid. Her motive for lying was to demonstrate, 'I could control the international media.' Her statement, posted on a website designed for this purpose, said, 'The decision to make this admission is entirely my own. I have not been subject to any form of pressure or been offered any financial inducement.'

In the middle of all this a FIFA insider turned whistleblower, which had a dramatic impact on FIFA. Chuck Blazer, an executive member and secretary of the Confederation of North, Central American and Caribbean Association Federation (CONCACAF), whose president was Jack Warner, was given damning evidence about corruption in FIFA. This concerned a meeting at the waterfront Hyatt Regency hotel in Port of Spain in Trinidad on 10 May 2011 where 25 members of the Caribbean Football Union had gathered to hear Mohammed Bin Hammam make his pitch against Sepp Blatter for the FIFA presidency. The evidence was that the delegates then went to a room in the luxury hotel and picked up envelopes addressed to them filled with dollars, some of them containing as much as $40,000. Warner had organized the meeting and what is more Warner had told Blatter of this attempted vote buying.

Both Warner and Bin Hammam were suspended and Bin Hammam also withdrew from the contest. Blatter admitted he was made aware the vote buying was taking place. But, since this constituted intention and not an actual deal, FIFA's Ethics Committee decided that Blatter had breached no rules and had no case to answer. Within days he was re-elected FIFA president unopposed. A month after the elections Warner resigned from FIFA, with the organization giving the impression it was bidding goodbye to a great figure in world football. The statement put out by FIFA on its website was something of which totalitarian countries, trying to massage a change of personnel, would have been proud:

FIFA regrets the turn of events that have led to Mr Warner's decision [. . .] Mr Warner is leaving FIFA by his own volition after
nearly thirty years of service [. . .] The FIFA Executive Committee,
the FIFA President and the FIFA management thank Mr Warner
for his services to Caribbean, CONCACAF and international
football over his many years devoted to football at both regional
and international level, and wish him well for the future. As a
consequence of Mr Warner's self-determined resignation, all
Ethics Committee procedures against him have been closed and
the presumption of innocence is maintained.

Yet within two days a report of the Ethics Committee was leaked
to the British Press Association. The report described Warner's
evidence as 'mere self-serving declarations' and that he 'failed
to provide the FIFA Ethics Committee with a plausible
explanation'.

The report stated:

The FIFA Ethics Committee is of the primary opinion that the
accused [Warner] had knowledge of the respective payments and
condoned them. It seems quite likely that the accused [Warner]
contributed himself to the relevant actions, thereby acting as an
accessory to corruption. The Committee is also of the opinion that
the respective money gifts can probably only be explained if they
are associated with the FIFA Presidential elections of 1 June 2011.
Therefore it appears rather compelling to consider the actions
of Mr Bin Hammam constitute prima facie an act of bribery,
or at least an attempt to commit bribery. It appears prima facie
impossible, in the opinion of the FIFA Ethics Committee, that the
accused [Warner] could have considered the money distributed
[. . .] as legally or ethically proper and without any connection
to the upcoming FIFA Presidential election. Consequently, the
accused would at least be considered as an accessory to the afore-
mentioned violations.

The Ethics Committee report went on to conclude 'that Mr Bin Hammam appears to have intended to influence the voting behaviour of the CFU member associations on the occasion of the FIFA Presidential elections in his favour.' Within weeks the Ethics Committee had imposed a lifetime ban on Bin Hamman even as he continued to protest his innocence.

As for Warner it was hard to resist the conclusion that the Trinidadian had resigned to avoid further damage, well aware that his departure meant the investigation would stop and there was nothing FIFA could now do to him. He was not able to avoid some political damage as the Trinidad prime minister, under immense pressure in the country to sack him, was forced to downgrade his ministerial status. The transport part of his Works and Transport portfolio was taken away and he was left with works. This, as one paper commented, meant he would continue to be responsible for the country's drains.

FIFA's performance led to the British select committee for Culture, Media and Sport issuing a report in which MPs said they were 'appalled' by the way FIFA had swept aside 'allegations of corruption' against members of its executive, treating those making the allegations with 'contempt'.

The select committee chairman John Whittingdale accepted that England could be seen as bad losers:

> There is a danger that having got a derisory two votes, one of them English, we will be accused of sour grapes. But it is not. The evidence of corruption is overwhelming now. We have some criticism about the England bid. But there was substantial corruption in the process and that was an additional hurdle and put a huge question mark over the entire bid.

Whittingdale, who held several posts in Tory shadow cabinets before taking over as chairman of the select committee five years ago, had no doubts that FIFA's system of deciding World Cup hosts 'is deeply flawed. A relatively small number of individuals decide which countries should host the competitions. This provides an extremely lucrative opportunity for them. Therefore a great deal of money is at stake. And, given the process is also shrouded in mystery, it is immensely susceptible to corruption.'

And worse still, the MPs on the select committee had little confidence that FIFA could reform. Whittingdale said,

> FIFA does not inspire confidence that the recognition of the need for change has got through. We were astonished at the way FIFA appeared to dismiss the allegations Lord Triesman made to us regarding four members of the executive. We wrote to Sepp Blatter asking him to appear before the committee. He declined but said FIFA was investigating. The FA then sent him a report on the Triesman allegations. This essentially said, 'We have not been able to talk to the key individuals – the accused executive members – and we cannot prove either way.' FIFA used the report to suggest they saw no grounds for further investigation. That is absolutely not true. The FA report did not clear the individuals concerned. We cannot allow this to be swept to one side.

The MPs were even more appalled at the way FIFA had treated its own Ethics Committee report on Warner.

> The Ethics Committee report we understand has serious questions to answer on the part of Jack Warner. He then resigns and FIFA says we don't need to do anything and will drop the investigation. That is extraordinary. FIFA needs to publish the Ethics Committee report. It is in desperate need of fundamental reform and pressure for change is substantial.

Whittingdale took some comfort from the fact that, led by the British, governments were putting pressure on FIFA. But he realized that if Sepp Blatter did not deliver on reform as he promised, the Football Association might have to consider leaving the world body. That, as he put it, would be very much 'the FA's nuclear option'.

Whittingdale did concede that Triesman could be criticized for not making the corruption allegations while he was running the England bid.

> He told us that, if he had said this while he was bid leader, it would have made absolutely certain that any chance England had of winning would have gone out of the window. I am not sure that is a wholly convincing reason for suppressing very serious allegations of corruption. And it does not explain why he did not reveal this as soon as the result was known. That would have been the time to say, 'Yes we lost but the whole process is riddled with corruption.' He told us that he felt he would not have an opportunity to set out his allegations in such detail except to a select committee. A select committee does carry Parliamentary privilege. We are able to protect witnesses and that process was not abused by David Triesman.

Had Thomas Arnold been alive today, he might have looked at the report, in the traditional green for such parliamentary select committee reports, and concluded that FIFA was a new kind of church, one with its own very special rules of worship. Indeed it would be tempting to say that this crisis has again demonstrated that FIFA struts around the world as if it is the Vatican of Sport, a nation state which does not have territory or an army but, through football, can reach places no one else can. Sepp Blatter always makes much of the fact that FIFA has more members than the United Nations and that its yearly Congress brings together a worldwide assembly, the like of which cannot be matched by any other body. But, while even the Church of Rome accepts that it must take into account what the wider public says, FIFA, as the bribery allegations show, continues to insist that it is so unique that it is answerable only to its own members, or football family, to use Blatter's favourite phrase. And, like the sort of joint family that has long gone out of fashion even on the Indian subcontinent, FIFA bristles at the very thought that non-family members may have any right to pry into its affairs, let alone tell it how to behave. And, to bolster all this, FIFA also claims to be beyond the law.

Article 64 (sections 2 and 3) of the FIFA statutes, titled Obligation, spells this out very clearly:

> 2 Recourse to ordinary courts of law is prohibited unless specifically provided for in the FIFA regulations.
>
> 3 The Associations shall insert a clause in their statutes or regulations, stipulating that it is prohibited to take disputes in the Association or disputes affecting Leagues, members of Leagues, clubs, members of clubs, Players, Officials and other Association Officials to ordinary courts of law, unless the FIFA regulations or binding legal provisions specifically provide for or stipulate recourse to ordinary courts of law. Instead of recourse to ordinary courts of law, provision shall be made for arbitration. Such disputes shall be taken to an independent and duly constituted arbitration tribunal recognised under the rules of the Association or Confederation or to CAS [Court of Arbitration for Sport]. The Associations shall also ensure that this stipulation is implemented in the Association, if necessary by imposing a binding obligation on its members. The Associations shall impose sanctions on any party that fails to respect this obligation and ensure that any appeal against such sanctions shall likewise be strictly submitted to arbitration, and not to ordinary courts of law.

And when the law intervenes, as the highest court in Europe did in the Jean-Marc Bosman transfer case, FIFA can be loftily dismissive. The Bosman ruling, based on the Treaty of Rome provisions of the free movement of labour, caused a revolution in European football. For years FIFA fought against its effect and, while in the end it had to concede defeat, it clung to its belief that it is beyond government and law.

To reinforce its image as the Vatican of Sport, FIFA is also adept at using a specialized sports language which makes it sound like a religious sect. So, while FIFA is a fair-sized company with post-tax profit in 2010 of US $202 million, nowhere in its 116-page accounts is the word 'profit' used. Like a Victorian maiden reacting to the word 'sex', it calls profit 'result', as if it were a football score. But then secrecy in accounting is something of a FIFA speciality. It accounts in detail the millions it makes from the World Cup. But that is the only FIFA event that makes money. All its other events do not and there are very sparse details of how much they lose. There is also very little clarity about what its officials and executives earn. The message FIFA gives is that it likes making money but not the burden that goes with it, the need for transparent corporate governance.

FIFA could argue that it is only following the example of its older Olympic brother, the IOC. The IOC may be vastly more transparent, but it is almost a master of such sports religious language with all its talk of 'Olympic family'. In reality modern Olympics, like modern World Cups, are tightly controlled McDonald's-style franchises with the host country having to adhere to very tight rules. So the Olympics specify the height of the buildings in the Athletes Village. FIFA, following in the footsteps of the Olympics, has gone even further. The World Cup in South Africa provided many examples of this. Television stations were under orders always to refer to the 2010 World Cup as the FIFA World Cup, lest anyone got the impression there was an imposter World Cup going on elsewhere. Blatter always addressed his correspondence to the South African president and got upset when he did not reply personally. FIFA even made the South African government change its laws so that football-related offences were brought to court within weeks of the alleged offence being committed. This in a country where it can take years for a normal case to come to court. FIFA secured generous tax concessions from the government – it demands this of all host countries – and so extensive were the powers given to FIFA that some South

Africans felt their country had been occupied by another country called FIFA during the World Cup.

Commercial enterprises promising to bring jobs are known to extract similar concessions but they do not pretend that their purpose is anything other than to make money. However, sports administrators, organizing modern sports events as businesses, want the money and behave like a car manufacturer seeking a new factory, but shy away from using the sort of language that the car manufacturer would have no problems with.

This problem is particularly acute for the Olympics, which prides itself on being the last bastion of Corinthianism in sport: athletes competing for honour, not money, and living communally in a specially constructed village. So much so that once the 2012 Games start, President Jacques Rogge will leave his Park Lane Hotel and live in the Olympic Village, as he always does. And the Olympic 'Corinthian spirit' dictates athletes cannot display sponsors' names on their clothes like sportsmen in their events nor are any advertisements allowed at the Olympic venues. And this can mean, as I discovered during the 2010 Vancouver Winter Games, that, in an Olympic city, you have to abandon the bottled water you brought with you.

Picture the scene. I am interviewing an Olympic official at the Westin Bayshore, the hotel along the city's glistening waterfront where the top bosses of the Olympics, including Rogge and Princess Anne, are staying. I have just ordered a bottle of Perrier when the waitress turns to me with a rueful smile and says, 'Two weeks ago I could have served a Perrier. But not now. I can, however, give you a Dasani.' Dasani was Coke's answer to Perrier and, being one of the sponsors of the Olympics, its products must be served at all Olympic venues. During the London Olympics Coke's bottled water, Abbey Well, will be on offer

This is one of the conditions laid down by the International Olympic Committee for all hotels who serve the Olympic family: no hotel can have products that rival that of an Olympic sponsor, and this forced all sorts of changes at the Westin Bayshore. They had to cover up the kiosk of Starbucks coffee and also change several other drinks, including the apple juice they traditionally serve.

This power extends far beyond hotels to Olympic venues and indeed the whole of an Olympic city. So at the Vancouver Olympics, one of the volunteers, Urvasi Naidoo, whose day job in Manchester is to run the International Netball Federation, went to venues carrying masking tape in her bag. She explained to me, 'What I was looking for was a group of people all wearing T-shirts advertising a rival product. I would try and get them to wear the T-shirts inside out. If that did not work then I would use masking tape to cover up the advertisement. The point was to make sure it was not visible on television. Sponsors pay a lot of money for the Olympics and they are entitled to protect their investment.'

But what makes the IOC's control of a city's business special is its insistence that a 'clean city' is delivered for the Games. This means that it must ensure billboard advertising products that rival those of Olympic sponsors be removed. This caused Vancouver a major headache when the Squamish (who were once known as Canada's Indians and are now described as one of the first nations of Canada) suddenly erected giant billboards on their land. Being sovereign Indian land, the Vancouver organizers could do nothing and hurriedly had to pay the Indians a couple of million dollars to buy up space on their billboards to ensure they did not carry advertisements for products that rivalled Olympic sponsors.

The IOC does the same for every Olympics. But talk to Craig Reedie, the Briton who serves on the IOC's executive board, and he feels it is necessary to spell out the greater good that the prevention of ambush marketing brings about. 'Take Athens for instance. Before the Olympics the city was disfigured with billboards. We got them to take them down and several were found to be illegal. The result was the entire look of the city was transformed. What we did was not just to protect our commercial sponsors but also to improve the city.'

The problem for modern sports is that the world sees events

like the Olympics as the commercial enterprise they are. Not surprisingly they are confused and angered that there are special Olympic lanes in cities hosting the games and that the Olympic family turns out to include all sorts of undesirable people like the son of Muammar Gaddafi, the now deposed Libyan dictator. This contributed to a public relations disaster for London 2012 after the first-round sale of Olympic tickets. It emerged that Gaddafi's son Muhammad al-Gaddafi, whose country was then subject to NATO bombing, had been allocated 1,000 tickets as head of Libya's Olympic committee. He was part of the Olympic family and remained in good standing as he had done nothing against the Olympics, whatever his father and family might have done against the Libyan people. The tickets were withdrawn but it provoked commentator Allison Pearson, unhappy with her own ticket allocation, to suggest that in future rounds tickets would go to 'Robert Mugabe, 'Sepp Blatter and 500 squeaky clean FIFA offi-cials, Sharon Shoesmith and Haringey child protection department, Lord Lucan, the creditors of the Duchess of York, President Assad and the crack Syrian Shotgun squad. And not forgetting the girl-friends of Ryan Giggs.'

One of the problems is that the model used for most sports organ-izations is still the nineteenth-century one provided by Britain: one body covers the sport at all levels from the grass roots to the highest professional clubs. So, in England, both Manchester United and the team on Hackney Marshes belong to the Football Association. This creates a complex social and political agenda, particularly in many Third World countries. There are many different pathways into sports administration, including out-and-out patronage. There is no need to display commercial or any other sort of competence. Once on the inside track in sports administration, the men concerned (it is almost invariably men) are generally unaccount-able to anyone outside their particular sectional interest.

This makes reform of such organizations all the more difficult. However, despite the IOC's use of language such as 'Olympic family', making it sound as much of a sporting religious body as

FIFA, on the broader question of corruption the IOC has shown the way. In the closing years of the last century, it had its FIFA-style corruption scandal and came out of it a better organization. The IOC may not admit that it is a corporate body but, in the way it runs its business, it behaves like one. So much so that the IOC is now seen as a beacon for the football body, or for that matter any other sport organization accused of corruption. It is worth dwelling on how Coubertin's organization dealt with a crisis that was just as serious, if not more so, than the one faced by FIFA.

Back in 1998 it was widely believed that cities could bribe their way to host the Olympics – indeed many were alleged to have done so. But these allegations remained whispers and nothing concrete had emerged. This was until an unexpected explosion on a quiet December Saturday afternoon in 1998 in the very centre of the IOC headquarters in Lausanne. The explosion came from the 80-year-old Swiss head of a Swiss law firm, who had held almost every senior IOC post since he joined in 1963, and had nearly become president of the movement.

A few weeks earlier KTVX-TV, a television station in Salt Lake City, which had won the right to host the 2002 Winter Games, had revealed that a scholarship had been provided to Sonia Essomba, the daughter of Cameroon IOC member Rene Essomba, to attend university in Washington. When it first emerged, it seemed no more than a local story. Winter Games do not attract too much attention and Salt Lake, a Mormon city, was expected to attract even less. The IOC had formed an ad hoc commission to investigate the Salt Lake City scholarship, with Dick Pound in charge. However, it was not seen as a big story and, in the run up to this final executive meeting of 1998, the IOC itself was more concerned about setting up its proposed World Anti-Doping Agency. Very few journalists were covering the meeting, so routine was it expected to be. I personally was there because I happened to be in Lausanne for what was then the much bigger story of UEFA, threatened by a breakaway European league, being forced to completely reshape its Champions League.

Then, as the morning session of the executive was ending on Saturday, 12 December 1998, Marc Hodler created a totally unexpected storm. He suddenly came down to the lobby where we journalists were chatting and in a series of unscripted, impromptu briefings began telling us how deeply the Olympics were mired in corruption. In an organization that controlled the flow of information, nothing like this had ever been seen. As bemused journalists moved round the conference hall, Hodler huddled with them, tearing away the pretence, so studiously maintained up to that moment, that there was no corruption in the Olympic movement.

Hodler alleged among other things that the successful bids by Atlanta for the 1996 Olympic Games, Sydney for the 2000 Games, Nagano for the 1998 Winter Games and Salt Lake City for the 2002 Winter Games were not clean. Not only could IOC members' votes be bought but there were agents specializing in such deals; one agent was himself an IOC member. He described the scholarship Salt Lake had given as a bribe. Hodler had been a great champion of Salt Lake. He felt upset that they were being singled out and his point was that everyone was doing it. What is more, he felt that the IOC was to blame. 'The cities are the victim, not the villain,' he announced.

For such a senior IOC member, one who had unsuccessfully stood against Juan Antonio Samaranch for the IOC presidency, to say this was sensational. We had the feeling that we were hearing hidden secrets which were never meant to be recorded. Hodler gave the appearance of a man who had carried this dreadful secret of Olympic corruption for too long and wanted to unburden himself.

The IOC tried hard to stifle these astonishing allegations. Eventually the Swiss was led away from the journalists by Françoise Zweifel, then IOC secretary general, as if he was an old uncle who had lost his way. The drama reached its climax on the Sunday afternoon when Hodler failed to take his place on the podium for a press conference about Salt Lake City and the 2002

Winter Games. As chairman of the coordinating commission for the Games, he should have been there. It later emerged that Hodler had been ordered by Samaranch himself not to be present. Hodler confirmed this when he emerged for lunch. Asked if he had been silenced, he made a motion across his lips like a zip being closed and said, 'Exactly. I have been muzzled [using the German word *Maulkorb*, the muzzle put on guard-dogs].' Then he added, 'Apparently I said too much.' However, what he had said could not be unsaid and his intervention meant IOC corruption, long suspected, could no longer be pushed under the carpet. Soon others were testifying to corruption.

Atlanta, Sydney and Nagano all vigorously denied any wrong-doing during their successful bids. Sydney confirmed they had received an offer from an unnamed agent to buy African votes, but said they had turned it down. Pound, commenting on Hodler's allegations, said: 'We are aware that there are agents; we are aware of the identity of some of them. What seems to be developing is a professional class of Olympic agents offering services for bidding committees.' Pound also confirmed that, even before the Hodler explosion, the IOC, concerned about agents, had warned cities bidding for the Winter Games in 2006 to tread very carefully.

The biggest repercussions from the Olympic corruption story were felt in Salt Lake City where the Salt Lake Board of Ethics investigated, producing a report that ran to more than 300 pages. It was a devastating indictment of the corruption in the Olympics movement. It showed how sport can be corrupted in the name of altruism, and how those who have made themselves leaders of sports can use them to make money in a way that the commercial world would never tolerate.

Jacques Rogge, then a member of the executive board, recalls the shock he felt that day in Lausanne.

We were in the middle of an executive board meeting. What we heard was Françoise Zweifel whispering something at the ear of Samaranch. I don't know the exact wording but that there was a press conference going on. Samaranch then said, 'My dear colleagues, there seems to be a press conference downstairs and we will suspend the meeting and will resume later on.' And I remember the moment very well. We were on the floor named after Pierre Coubertin and went to the balcony and saw the media listening to Marc. I was surprised and I had big concerns. But I did not know the extent of the damage caused.

Soon the IOC was aware of the damage, a crisis as great if not greater than the one posed by the boycott of the 1980 Moscow Olympics. Critics were convinced that the IOC was so corrupt it could not be reformed. As with FIFA now, many including some government ministers demanded that the IOC be scrapped and a new body formed to run the Olympics. However that did not happen and Rogge is convinced it was because of how Juan Antonio Samaranch reacted to the crisis.

When we came back, Samaranch immediately said we have to cut to the bone; 'I make a commission and you must make proposals.' At the same time he said, 'We have to look at the long-term issues.' He did not speak at that time of the long-term changes to the IOC because he wanted to know exactly what had happened. We gave him pretty quickly an overview of the whole situation. We had a meeting on the same day in Lausanne in the office of François Carrard [then the IOC director general]. A couple of days later we were called to go to New York because we had the evidence of the Salt Lake City bidding committee that was repatriated to the law office there. Then we had a couple of further meetings in Lausanne and we gave a report to Samaranch saying these are the recommendations that we need to implement. And Samaranch called an extraordinary session of the IOC.

By this time the Dick Pound commission had found enough evidence to enable the IOC to expel ten IOC members. Interestingly, none of this came from Hodler. Pound, in his memoirs, *Inside the*

Olympics, has described how, when Hodler came before his commission, he could provide no proof.

> To our astonishment he had no facts whatsoever and he had been speaking solely from hearsay. Furthermore, much of the corruption that he was ranting about turned out to relate to the ski federation of which he had been president during the entire period that the impugned conduct had apparently occurred. The wrongdoing he railed about had not involved IOC members at all.

Indeed the Hodler drama was to have a strange sequel. Many of Hodler's stories concerned wrongdoing by the Agnelli family, with Ferraris being given away so Italy could host World Ski Championships. Reporting the Hodler outburst, one of the doyens of Olympic journalism, the Italian Gianni Merlo, speculated that Hodler's aim was to damage Turin's bid for the 2006 Winter Games and help the rival bid of the Swiss city of Sion. The next day, in the IOC lobby, Hodler confronted him and called him names. Merlo successfully sued and collected damages from Hodler.

What enabled the IOC to act, says Rogge was, 'first of all admitting that there was an issue. We were not in denial. We had enough hard evidence not to be in denial. We had evidence because we had the accounts of the Salt Lake City bidding committee and we had evidence that sums had been paid to various persons.' The documented proof provided by Salt Lake City meant the guilty IOC members could not contest the evidence.

But just as important, argues Rogge,

> is that Samaranch understood that it was not enough just to take care of the corruption but he had the vision to see that we had to review the whole functioning of the IOC in a far broader sense. That has led to a number of issues, like the setting up of the Athletes Commission. I gave a presentation to the International Federations and the National Olympic Committees within the IOC. It led to the

Ethics Commission. It led to the Code of Conduct of the members, the rules of conflict of interest. It led to the new rules on candidate cities. We banned visits to the bidding city itself and considered a whole range of other issues. It led to the fact that candidate cities cannot play with incentives such as coaching camps or scholarships or building of infrastructure for the countries and the members. So all of that was something that Samaranch took a view on. We also decided to have total visibility on our finances. We have an external audit, we have an internal audit, and we have a compliance officer. Samaranch understood that we had to move from a sports club to an international organization.

One factor pushing Samaranch into action was that he knew the IOC had to act to protect its business, worried that sponsors might walk away. Following the Hodler bombshell, Michael Payne, then IOC marketing director, flew to Atlanta to talk to Coke, a sponsor since the 1928 Amsterdam Games, to make sure they stayed. There was much worry about John Hancock, an American insurance company. Its chief executive David D'Alessandro had said, 'If they fail to investigate, the rings will not be tarnished, they will be broken. A failure to do so will cost the IOC its golden aura and the Olympics will become a mere mortal like the NBA and NFL.'

If this suggests that the Olympics are a rather special event, then what also helped the IOC reform was that the organization Coubertin created remains the very antithesis of democracy, composed as it is of 113 self-elected members. Most of the members are from Europe, some like Britain have four members, while India and China, whose combined population is many times that of the UK, have three: China: two, India: one. And many countries do not have any IOC members. Also, from its inception, the IOC, while promoting sporting nationalism, has tried to distance itself from being a collection of national representatives. As Rogge puts it, 'IOC's structure on purpose, the whole theory of Pierre de Coubertin was that you have an IOC member in your country but not of your country.'

In contrast FIFA, strange as it may seem, is actually a democratic body. Every country with a football association has a vote and all football associations are equal. This does give the FIFA Congress the feel of a parliament, although the way it operates underlines the curiously dysfunctional nature of the organization. So the Congress has little effective power, apart from electing a president. And for all Blatter's pose as a head of state, he cannot even select his own cabinet. The members of FIFA's executive, his cabinet, are selected not by him, nor are they even elected by the Congress but by the confederations. Some of the elections are curious to say the least, with some votes more equal than others. So, as we have seen, the British home nations have four seats on FIFA and elect their own FIFA vice-president to the executive. To balance this privilege the four British home nations are not allowed to vote in the UEFA election which chooses the other seven European FIFA executive members.

The central organization in Zurich obscures the fact that FIFA is a series of confederations. Some, like UEFA, are far richer and more powerful than others but each of the confederations has its own method of working. In that sense FIFA is more like the Mughal empire of India in the eighteenth century, or China under the warlords in the nineteenth century. The empires of these ancient lands had one thing in common. While the emperor in Delhi or Beijing was meant to be the supreme ruler, and treated as such, with the visible display of his power suggesting he could get many things done, the reality was that he could only do as much as his regional barons allowed. So, for all the glory of the central ruler, his ability to influence events in the far-flung corners of his empire was often extremely limited, particularly if the regional war lords were themselves powerful. FIFA is the modern-day equivalent.

FIFA's executive has in-built power blocks which owe their allegiance, not to the president or the Congress, but to their own confederation. It is this that has made FIFA the most curious of organizations, with two concentric circles of sport politicians constantly trying to please their constituents. It has meant that many of the leaders of confederations are more like war lords. In some ways the alleged vote-buying between bin Hammam and Warner was like a meeting of war lords.

Mohammed bin Hammam, smarting from his life-ban, accused FIFA of racism alleging that, had he been a European, FIFA officials would not have dared 'lay a finger' on him. Race, of course, is always a very emotive issue and it is not uncommon for people who feel victimized, as bin Hammam clearly does, to raise race issues. And, because the accused is one race and the accuser another, it does not mean the whole thing is motivated by race. However, bin Hammam's reference to race threw a huge spotlight on a very interesting aspect of FIFA's corruption scandal. This was that none of the four members forced to leave the FIFA executive was European: Reynald Temarii (Tahiti), Amos Adamu (Nigeria), Mohammed bin Hammam (Qatar) and Jack Warner (Trinidad).

This begged an explosive question: is an organization shaped and influenced by Europe less susceptible to corruption? Does it, because of its cultural roots, have higher standards? While the European members of the FIFA executive would not put it quite that way, one member, Michel D'Hooghe, the Belgian who has been on the FIFA executive since 1988, was prepared to discuss what he called cultural differences in the world body.

D'Hooghe himself was drawn into the FIFA corruption scandal when the *Sunday Times* revealed that, just before he and his fellow executive members chose Russia for the 2018 World Cup, he had received a painting from the Russians. However, he insisted that this was a present from a Russian who was old family friend with whom he had served on the FIFA executive. The painting had no value and there had been no question of him voting for the Russians. Belgium was bidding and he supported his country in the two rounds of voting before Russia emerged as the winner.

This is when D'Hooghe discussed FIFA's cultural problems:

Let's compare for a moment UEFA to FIFA. I know people in both. I am sitting in both assemblies (D'Hooghe, like all European FIFA executive members, can attend UEFA executive meetings). In UEFA, they nearly all have the same mentality even if you come from Cyprus or from Iceland. Well, of course there are individual differences but the global vision is the same. In FIFA, there are people sitting around the same table about whom I don't know. If you asked me something about the member of French Polynesia or the member of Sri Lanka, I know him, but don't ask me who he is. Don't ask me, 'what is his mentality?' Don't ask me what his moral values are. I don't know that. I can only speak for myself and for my European colleagues. You must understand that there is a difference of culture throughout these things and this makes it sometimes more difficult.

D'Hooghe's use of the word culture should not be seen as a code word for race. After all, people of different races can share a culture and those of the same race can have different cultures. And UEFA includes Turkey, a people not only of a different race but a different religion from most of Europe. But the way D'Hooghe saw the issue did raise the larger question of whether FIFA can formulate an acceptable code of governance that unites the different cultures of its much trumpeted family.

The structure of FIFA also means that there is less chance of another factor that aided IOC reform coming into play – the involvement of governments around the world. The Hodler bombshell came just as the Olympics needed urgent government help. At that moment the IOC, having for years ignored drugs in the Olympics, was forced to take action by the French government in the summer of 1998. The investigations by the French police uncovered massive drug-taking in the Tour de France. That saga of drug-taking, in what is a national institution in France, still rolls on but it could not have been exposed without the judicial powers of the government.

This made the IOC recognize that, for all its vaunted

independence from government, there are certain areas of sport it cannot reach without government help. The Olympics' response was to enlist government help to form an international body to combat drugs in sport. The result was the creation of the World Anti Doping Agency, a partnership between sport and government. It was not easy to convince governments, and even more so after the Hodler revelations. The IOC had to demonstrate that it was prepared to reform, prepared for the necessary surgery in light of the Salt Lake City evidence, before a sport – government partnership could be formed. The IOC could not afford to stay still. Even then the partnership took years to build.

A similar partnership is now being constructed to combat illegal betting and match-fixing. Jacques Rogge sees match-fixing as a worse manipulator of sports than drug-taking. 'Imagine', he says 'a team sport with one player being doped – that one player will not make the difference to the result. But if you have match-rigging with the goalkeeper being paid off and jumping over the ball, it's the whole match that is lost. So the scale is far more important in terms of match manipulation.'

Even more than the Olympics, match-fixing is a huge problem in football and all the sports organizations know they need the cooperation of governments to tackle the scourge. It could result in a betting agency similar to WADA. So, just as the formation of WADA aided reform, could an international agency to tackle match-fixing provide a chance for a similar reform at FIFA? But, unlike drugs, where all governments can agree on the evils of drug-taking, there is no uniform policy on betting. And no sign of one developing.

Gamblers being involved in sport is hardly a new story. The early history of sport is full of gamblers, and indeed without their influence many sports may never have got started. However, when some of them tried to corrupt the cricketers, they were dealt with firmly. The Nottinghamshire cricketer William Lambert was found guilty of throwing a match in 1818 and the Reverend James Pycroft in his 1851 history, *The Cricket Field*, included a section entitled 'A dark chapter in the history of cricket' which detailed more examples. But, with sport still a recreation, the authorities dealt with it and banned bookmakers from Lord's. Now the gambling problem is international and multi-layered.

Gambling, once frowned upon, has been legalized in much of the developed world and sports administrators have established links with gambling companies to ensure that, should there be any hint of match-fixing, it is quickly dealt with. The problem arises in countries that are discovering sports and which treat betting like the Americans tried to deal with drinking between the wars, by pretending it does not exist. These are countries in Eastern Europe, where match-fixing in football is a huge problem. Or the Indian subcontinent, where match-fixing in cricket is a similar problem. Then there are the Islamic countries, keen to get into sport, but where any form of gambling is illegal by Islamic law. How can these countries be brought into a system which ensures that, while there is betting in sport, it is legal and monitored?

The recent conference between sport and governments organized by the IOC to discuss match-fixing has illustrated the divide on this issue. The government delegates were from the developed world; missing were the Indian subcontinent and Eastern Europe, where much illegal gambling takes place. Rogge admits that to bring them in will take time, maybe years. If these countries are not even interested in discussing how to combat illegal gambling, the idea that they might want to help reform institutions like FIFA, aware of its power to grant such prestigious events as World Cups, seems remote.

One avenue for reform could be if the sports institutions of the old world were to learn from the new world how to run modern, commercial sport.

The world's only superpower may not play most of the sports other countries do but it can claim to have the most focused and successful sports administrations. American sports administration has one crucial advantage over almost everywhere else in the world. At the highest level, all of its major spectator sports – baseball, American football, basketball and ice hockey – are run by commercial organizations. They exist to maximize the franchise owners' income. They are uncluttered by wider responsibilities, such as international competition, grassroots development, or the role of their particular sport in American or world society. In short, they have no political or social agenda.

They meet no demands from government, and they demand nothing from government, except, crucially, the right to continue to operate as an anti-competitive cartel in a nation with a long and fierce history of anti-trust legislation. America's major sports have secured several important legal exemptions from the laws of the land and, in return, the American central government has no responsibility for sport of any kind. So much so that, as we have seen, when America hosts the Olympics, it is a private affair. Unlike the rest of the world, the US government does not get involved in funding Olympic Games; neither at the presidential nor the state level do the Americans have a sports policy. In contrast, in Europe, politicians like dabbling in sport but often do not seem to know how to handle it. The result is that sport comes under a variety of departments from culture, education, youth, health, social solidarity, agriculture, the family and in Greece, religion.

What the Americans do is recognize sport as special and, at the highest level, they practise a form of sporting socialism that is unique and would be unthinkable in Europe. Consider that this is a country where even modest health reform can be seen as the worst form of socialist control and a president like Obama, who would be seen as centre-right in Europe, is viewed by many as a dangerous leftist. Yet, at the highest level of sport, Americans do believe in sharing equally. So, in the NFL, all income is shared equally and the famous draft system means that the team that has come bottom of the league gets the pick of the best of next year's college players. Even allowing for the special nature of American sport, with no promotion and relegation and the unique college system for breeding players, Europe just could not attempt such socialism. Recall that when Coubertin was fighting the Americans to get Thomas Arnold's ideas accepted, he was critical of the American college system. Yet its existence allows American sport at its top level to have a system of corporate governance and a truly socialist system of sharing that would be beyond FIFA or any other European sports organization.

This American sporting socialism is combined with a very business-like approach to running sport, an open acceptance that modern sport is big business. So, at the highest level, major American sports are run by high-powered business people, with clear commercial objectives, and clear commercial disciplines and accountabilities. Essentially, no one assumes any responsibility anywhere in any major American sport without business and administrative competence. Not for American sport the European talk of family and sport for all. When the NFL comes to London for what is now its regular season game, the NFL Commissioner happily talks of the new markets the sport is seeking. It is a commercial exercise and this is acknowledged. If it were FIFA or even the IOC, any such venture would come with talk of family values and the greater good, as if money and the search for new markets were not driving the change.

American sports administrators also understand the nature and usefulness of transparency and communicating to the modern media. The bidding for the Superbowls is so transparent that the actual voting is televised, something that would horrify FIFA, and no scandal has ever been reported. The actual event, which in America has a status higher than the World Cup Final, sees every-one connected with the two teams – players, administrators, owners – made freely available to the media. And after matches the media, including women reporters, are allowed into the dress-ing rooms. Again that would be unthinkable in Europe. Europe tolerates rather than welcomes the media and this is exemplified in a strange phenomenon called 'the mixed zone'. This is a corri-dor, generally in the bowels of the stadium. Athletes come by on their way from the dressing rooms to the team bus and, as they do, reporters, penned in behind a barrier, shout questions. They hold out microphones in front of them much like hawkers in an Eastern bazaar holding out goodies for sale. The 'sale' the reporters are hoping for is a few choice words that could help them write a story.

Not that the American sporting system means that there are no scandals in American sport. But they are, generally, of personal nature – athletes like Marion Jones cheating with drugs, or men like Tiger Woods proving to be fallible human beings. They raise questions not so much of sporting governance but why modern society has made sports stars into idols. The rise of sports stars as role models, like using sporting events to validate a nation, is a fairly recent phenomenon. It has come at a time when there is more emphasis on the individual rather than society. David Brooks, the American social commentator and author of *The Social Animal*, points out that Americans of the present generation talk more about themselves than did previous generations. 'In 1950, the Gallup organization asked high school students, "Are you a very important person?" and 12 per cent said yes. They asked the same question in 2006, and the proportion was 80 per cent.' What is true of America may well be true of most of the developed world. It is easy to see why identification with sporting stars becomes important in a society where individuals are more inclined to talk about themselves, what they are doing and why they are important.

This has coincided with the wider society losing its traditional role models such as politicians, church leaders, men of science or letters. In his memoirs, written in the 1960s, Harold Macmillan, the British prime minister, could talk of economists and archbishops being role models and why economic competence created an aura round Stafford Cripps, the austere British Labour politician. Such an idea would be risible today. The result is sports stars have filled the vacuum. That they should fill the gap left behind by the disappearance of great church men is all the more curious as this has also been an era where sport is seen as a secular religion. Religious language is certainly becoming a cliché in sports writing: athletes are routinely described as immortal or godlike; stadiums regularly become cathedrals of sport.

Sport can indeed supply some of the ingredients associated with religious observance: theatre, ritual, beauty, belonging, a source of hope and belief and a space to express extreme feelings, a sense of right and wrong, even a glimpse of another kind of existence. A visit with fellow supporters to an important fixture away from home, especially overseas, has some of the character of a medieval pilgrimage. In certain respects, belief in a team or an athlete is a 'safer' investment than belief in a religious faith.

You may not take your feelings quite as far as religious fervour but supporting a team or player gives you many ways to put some meaning into your life and to express your identity. We have seen how sport creates such personal space in totalitarian countries. Your favourite player can be an imaginary family member, companion or lover. Your chosen team can put you into a community which is as big or as small as you choose. Thanks to the internet, that community no longer has to be based locally. You can regard your sporting identity as an integral part of you or as an add-on – a club which you drop in to, rather than the home where you live. Unlike religion, sporting results cannot be disputed. Sport has become a rare source of trusted news in a sceptical world where more and more information arrives either in the form of hearsay, rumour or planted propaganda. There is no room to argue over the facts recorded on the sports pages, and, on those pages, there is always a clear distinction between fact and opinion. A sporting fact may not be palatable but you are not required to go to a higher authority with special knowledge to make sense of it, as you do in religion. In sport, you can nearly always find experts to back you up, but you are quite free to ignore them. And, in doing so, you are not likely to be accused of blasphemy. It is a lot easier to sack an incompetent football manager than an incompetent bishop.

The certainty of sporting achievement has made it easier to acclaim sportsmen and women as the best of their times. This would be unthinkable in the case of other 'opinion formers' such as politicians and judges. So, when Muhammad Ali claimed that he was the greatest of all time, he could point to his victories over distinguished rivals like Joe Frazier and George Foreman. If a politician claimed to be the greatest of all time, people would laugh, even if he could produce statistics showing the best economic performance or the fastest fall in crime. Many people today would assume that the statistics had been manipulated and even those who believed them would not give credit to the politician.

All this has helped to make top athletes the most sought-after role models, eagerly courted by marketers to endorse their goods and services. But, in endorsing a product, the athlete is presented as a person who has higher moral values. A great shot in tennis from a seemingly impossible position becomes a demonstration of courage. What should be a matter of superior sporting skill is seen as conveying that the athlete is a better human being than the rest of us. And this is where the problem is created.

One of Ryan Giggs' many sponsors, a Swiss watchmaker, explained why they use the Manchester United player: 'Ryan Giggs provides the perfect match for CYMA watches, with his role model attitude towards loyalty. And fair play and discipline, as well as excellent match play. He showcases CYMA's brand values built upon a passion for impeccable craftsmanship and dedication to Swiss watchmaking tradition.' As it emerged that Giggs had been a serial adulterer and had an eight-year affair with his brother's wife, there was much talk of hypocrisy by the advertisers. But it could be argued that the Swiss watchmakers were referring not to his personal character but his exemplary record with Manchester United: always with one club, hard working, a good player and not an offender on the field.

More curious was the long and expensive relationship between Accenture and Tiger Woods. Accenture is a management consultancy which does not operate in the mass market. It sells expensive, specialist services to supposedly hard-headed business leaders and government officials. Accenture assessed that even these people would be influenced by its association with a golfer who was a winner and was seen as having strong family values. The result was utter confusion when Tiger Woods failed, not on the golf course, but in his private life. Having built him up as a man he could not be, he had to be quickly abandoned.

But the blame for this cannot be laid at sport's door. It reflects a consumer society seeking role models and burdening sportsmen and women with a weight they cannot possibly carry. It is easy to understand why the makers of products have taken to sport. Sport is simultaneously a global language and a creator of personal and local identity. A contest in a popular sport is one of the few experiences that can be understood by, and excite passion in, people all over the world regardless of language, culture or intellect. You do not have to know Portuguese or indeed know anything about Brazil to appreciate Brazilian football. It also helps that people who play a popular sport follow the same rules. Some do it with more skill than others and with better equipment, facilities and rewards, but they still share a common experience. Sportspeople can meet with nothing in common except the means to play their chosen sport and they can begin a contest immediately.

And while sport can generate ill-will and has even led to war amongst nations, it also has the capacity to rise above petty nationalism. Nothing demonstrated this better than the 2011 summer cricket series. English cricket, fresh from its triumphs in Australia, loved to thrash the Indians, the rich boys of cricket. Yet throughout the summer many English cricket fans wanted Sachin Tendulkar, who had arrived having scored 99 international 100s, to reach this never before achieved landmark on English soil. Every time he walked out to bat, the crowd cheered as if they expected to see Tendulkar return with a 100 to his name. Indeed, at the Oval when he was given out leg before wicket for 91, having tried hard to save his country from defeat, some felt the English bowlers should not have appealed. That would have gone too far but it chimed in with the immortal sentiments Neville Cardus had felt, back in the summer of 1902, when as boy he went to watch his Australian hero Victor Trumper. For England to win, which young Neville wanted dearly, Trumper needed to be out first ball but that thought was also unbearable. It led to Cardus devising a very special prayer: 'Please God let Victor Trumper score a century today for Australia against England – out of a total of 137 all out.'

That, more than a century later, in a world which could not be more different, many English fans could still have similar feelings about another great batsman shows the unique power of sport. Sport can nourish nationalism and yet make you feel you are a good, caring, human being.

Sport is often compared to an art form, but unlike other arts, it generates objective facts in the form of results and statistics, which in turn create accepted rankings of individual performers and teams. The only objective facts for other forms of the arts are sales and the earnings of artists. But no one is obliged to accept these as indicators of artistic merit. Indeed, the prevailing artistic myth is that true genius is unrecognized in its lifetime. Almost as strong is the myth that commercial success is synonymous with selling out.

It has been argued that music is just as global a phenomenon as sport. Musicians, or at least some of them, have a global following, but there is no common set of rules, conventions and implements which make any particular kind of music a global activity. Quite the opposite: music has very different conventions across the world, in terms of fundamental structure, tempo, melody, harmony, tone, colour and much more. Western music, especially at a popular level, may be the most pervasive and the most commercially successful but that is largely a product of technology and conquest. It has been assimilated by other cultures (and influenced by them), but it does not form part of a global experience in the same way as global sport.

Western musical conventions are not shared by most of the world's musical population, including that of India, China,

Japan or the Arab world and, even within the Western world, there are strong musical cultures which use different systems. Sport, in contrast, has a tendency to codify – to invent rules and conditions to create a common experience. It also makes sport fans intensely conservative and the world's most popular sport, football, is the most conservative. Many sports have accepted modern technology and television replays to help make decisions, but it has been a long struggle to convince sceptics to accept change. When FIFA introduced the 'no back pass' rule, prohibiting goalkeepers from using their hands to collect balls passed back by their own players, many reacted as if the game would end. It did not. A similar conservative streak has made it impossible for football to accept modern goal-line technology.

Music is the exact opposite – it constantly invents new forms and styles; established genres of music readily split into different strands, and elements from one style are commonly fused into another. If you give 20 footballers a football each, most of them will instantly do the same things with it. If you give 20 pianists a piano, each will play it in a different way – some classical, some jazz, some rock, some completely improvisational. Assume that the 20 pianists are of equal technical ability and are each directed to perform the same piece of music – each one will interpret it differently. That points to another important difference between sport and music. In any sport, even the most indifferent player occasionally matches the performance of the greatest. The park footballer produces a dribble like Lionel Messi; the park cricketer uncorks a shot to match Sachin Tendulkar. For the great ones, such performance is routine; for the park player it happens once in a lifetime, but the emotional impact can be permanent and life-changing. It is an aspect of sport that forms the theme of Richard Heller's short story, *An Excellent Moment*. Such an experience never comes to amateur pianists. If they are honest with themselves, they have to admit that they never play anything as well as Yehudi Menuhin, or Art Tatum – or even Liberace.

The net result is that for all the grandeur and complexity of modern sport and its frequent descents into folly and scandal, the spirit of Thomas Hughes is still alive. Consider the case of the world's best footballer, Lionel Messi. I once heard him described as 'playing the kind of football you would want your son to play'. He is phenomenally skilful but also brave, unselfish and honest. Although only 24, he still looks like an eager teenager. An internet search reveals no hint of scandal about his personal life. Remembering his own childhood illness, whose treatment was paid for by a soccer-loving patron, he has set up his own charity for sick children. For all the horrors of modern sport, such examples, and they are not unique, sustain the belief in the essential spirit of sport.

And there are many people administering sport who still believe that Thomas Hughes' values of sport have practical relevance today. So, with a year to go for the London Olympics, Sir Clive Woodward, the British Olympic Association's director of sport, set out the 15 'bare minimum standards' the 550-strong Team GB athletes had to satisfy. Reflecting on the behaviour of the British team in Beijing, Woodward had been impressed that cycling and some other sports had higher standards of behaviour not reflected in the entire squad. 'We weren't one team in the cultures, the standards and how we operated. So we have come up with five key words: performance, responsibility, unity, pride and respect.' Respect he defined as not using bad language in public, not making too much noise and being 'responsible' in using social media. For Woodward responsibility also involved keeping the accommodation at the Olympic Village neat and tidy.

For all that has changed since Thomas Hughes wrote his novel, Woodward could well have had *Tom Brown's Schooldays* open at the page describing the speech Brooke made after School-house beat School. As we have seen, that was all about good behaviour leading to victory on the sporting field. That 150 years later such sentiments are seen as the springboard of sporting success demonstrates the longevity of traditional sporting values.

What is even more astonishing is, for all the battering it has taken, how much the spirit of sport can still inspire and reach out to a man who, on the face of it, has nothing in common with Brooke or Tom Brown and comes from a very alien world thousands of miles away from Rugby. But, in his 2011 MCC Spirit of Cricket Cowdrey Lecture at Lord's, Kumar Sangakkara, the former Sri Lankan captain, could well have been the modern day Brooke. Sangakkara, speaking against a background of immense problems in Sri Lankan cricket, beset with government interference, began with a warning: 'I strongly believe that we have reached a critical juncture in the game's history and that unless we better sustain Test cricket, embrace technology enthusiastically, protect the game's global governance from narrow self-interest, and more aggressively root out corruption then cricket will face an uncertain future.' Then he went on to talk about his homeland and how the spirit of sport and cricket had sustained it through many dark years:

> Cricket in Sri Lanka is no longer just a sport: it is a shared passion that is a source of fun and a force for unity. It is a treasured sport that occupies a celebrated place in our society. It is remarkable that in a very short period an alien game has become our national obsession, played and followed with almost fanatical passion and love. A game that brings the nation to a standstill; a sport so powerful it is capable of transcending war and politics [. . .] the history of my country extends over 2,500 years. A beautiful island situated in an advantageously strategic position in the Indian Ocean has long attracted the attentions of the world at times to both our disadvantage and at times to our advantage [. . .] Over 400 years of colonization by the Portuguese, the Dutch and the British has failed to crush or temper our indomitable spirit [. . .]
>
> Sri Lankans for centuries have fiercely resisted the Westernization of our society, at times summarily dismissing Western tradition and influence as evil and detrimental. Yet cricket, somehow, managed to slip through the crack in our anti-Western defences and has now become the most precious

heirloom of our British Colonial inheritance [. . .] Our cricket embodied everything in our lives, our laughter and tears, our hospitality, our generosity, our music, our food and drink. It was normality, a hope and inspiration in a war-ravaged island. In it was our culture and heritage, enriched by our myriad ethnicities and religions. In it we were untouched, at least for a while, by petty politics and division. It is indeed a pity that life is not cricket. If it were, we would not have seen the festering wounds of an ignorant war. The emergence of cricket and the new role of cricket within Sri Lankan society also meant that cricketers had bigger responsibilities than merely playing on the field. We needed to live positive lifestyles off the field and we need to also give back. The same people that applaud us every game need us to contribute back positively to their lives. We needed to inspire not just on the field but also off it.

His most telling point about the spirit of sport came when he described what happened when the Sri Lankan team returned home after their coach was attacked by terrorists in the middle of the Lahore Test match in 2009:

A week after our arrival in Colombo from Pakistan I was driving about town and was stopped at a checkpoint. A soldier politely inquired as to my health after the attack. I said I was fine and added that what they as soldiers experience every day we only experienced for a few minutes, but managed to grab all the news headlines. That soldier looked me in the eye and replied: 'It is OK if I die because it is my job and I am ready for it. But you are a hero and if you were to die it would be a great loss for our country.' I was taken aback. How can this man value his life less than mine? His sincerity was overwhelming. I felt humbled [. . .] My loyalty will be to the ordinary Sri Lankan fan, their 20 million hearts beating collectively as one to our island rhythm and filled with an undying and ever-loyal love for this our game. Fans of different races, castes, ethnicities and religions who together celebrate their diversity by uniting for a common national cause. They are my foundation, they are my family. I will play my cricket for them. Their spirit is the true spirit of cricket. With me are all my people. I am Tamil, Sinhalese, Muslim and Burgher. I am a Buddhist, a Hindu, a follower of Islam and Christianity. I am today, and always, proudly Sri Lankan.

Brooke could not have put it better.

That the spirit of sport can mean so much to a modern professional cricketer is testimony to the enduring values created by Thomas Hughes and Pierre de Coubertin. But those two men could not have anticipated how successful they would be, let alone that sport would become so central to our lives or how much it would be targeted by money men and politicians. The successors of Hughes and Coubertin who administer sport have been wretchedly slow in rising to the challenges these changes have brought. They have got into bed with Mammon and courted politicians, but not accepted the obligations such relationships impose. To do that, those involved – performers and administrators alike – must accept that modern sport is quite unique and that, like Caesar's wife, they must be above suspicion. That cannot be easy.

Sport is simultaneously a global phenomenon and a local and personal one. It is simultaneously a gigantic commercial business and a gigantic voluntary enterprise. It is both dependent on government and a major influence on public policy. It offers simultaneously role models and bad examples, conformists and free spirits. It can serve to promote good citizenship and be a vehicle for crime. It combines entertainment and authority: it can serve millions of people as a diversion from ordinary life and give millions of others a meaning to their lives. Sport fulfils all of these conflicting roles in global society through a multi-layered and mutually dependent relationship with the media and other commercial interests. There is no simple definition of what modern sport stands for and therefore no simple solution to its many problems.

If those who are involved in sport cannot work out the solution, then the tragedy will be that in the years to come Sangakkara's beautiful evocation of the spirit of sport will seem like a cry in the wilderness. And, while occasionally sport may make us agree with J. M. Barrie's lyrical description of cricket as a gift of the gods, it will be just another commercial product, more successful, more widely sought after, but neither enriching our lives nor providing the one enduring and unifying force in the modern world.

BIBLIOGRAPHY

This bibliography is not exhaustive, but is a selection of the sources I found most useful.

Interviews

Kareem Abdul-Jabbar
Zayed Alzayani
Chris Aston
Adel Taarabt
Franz Beckenbauer
Amit Bhatia
Tony Blair
Sepp Blatter
Steve Borthwick
Schalk Brits
Keith Bradshaw
Roland Buchel
Michael Carrick
Pat Cash
Greg Clarke
Jonathan Calvert and Claire Newell
Lord Coe
Nic Coward
David Davies

Dan Doctoroff
Rahul Dravid
Roger Draper
Shaun Edwards
Paul Elliott
Clive Everton
Andy Farrell
Tony Fernandez
Tony Flood
Andy Flower
Will Greenwood
David Haye
John Higgins
Barry Hearn
Nicky Henderson
Kate Hoey
Roy Hodgson
Michel D'Hooghe
Gerard Houllier
Chris Hughton
Lennart Johansson
Michael Johnson
Martin Johnson
Danny Jordaan
Tim Lamb
Mike Lee
Clive Lloyd
Haroon Lorgat
Amrit Mathur
Nigel Mansell
Lord March
Sir Terence Matthews
Lord Brian Mawhinney
Alex McLeish
Sir Keith Mills

Lakshmi Mittal
Lalit Modi
Peter Moores
David Morgan
Max Mosley
Lord Moynihan
Urvasi Naidoo
Martina Navratilova
Paul Nicholls
Rick Parry
Chris Powell
Rob Purdham
Sir Craig Reedie
Uwe Rosler
Hugh Robertson
Jacques Rogge
Michael Slater
Alexis Sorokin
Malcolm Speed
Lord John Stevens
Andrew Strauss
Lord Alan Sugar
David Sullivan
Gordon Taylor
Phil Taylor
Jonathan Trott
Brendan Venter
Neil Warnock
Frank Warren
John Warren
Lee Westwood
John Whittingdale

Official Sources

Central Council for Physical Recreation (CCPR), Sport and the Community: The Report of the Wolfenden Committee on Sport 1960 (2009 web edition), Recommendations.

Foreign Office report in September 1955 on Sport Behind The Iron Curtain. Reference FO 975/82, section II.

House of Commons Culture, Media and Sport Committee (2011) 2018 World Cup Bid: Sixth Report of Session 2010–12

Scottish Executive (2001) Working Together for Scotland: A Programme For Government, 2.14.

Judgement in the ISL case given in the Criminal Court, Zug on 26 June 2008

Archives/Libraries

UK National Archives, Kew
British Library
London Library
MCC Library, Lord's

Books

This is a selection of the books I found most useful.

Agassi, A., *Open*, London: Harper Collins, 2009.
Ali, M., *The Soul of a Butterfly*, New York: Bantam Books, 2004.
Arantes do Nascimento, E., *Pelé*, London: Simon & Schuster, 2006.
Aris, S., *Sportsbiz*, London: Hutchinson, 1990.
Assael, S., *Steroid Nation*, New York: ESPN Books, 2007.
Atyeo, D., *Blood & Guts, Violence in Sports*, London: Paddington Press, 1979.

Bale, J. (Ed.) & Maguire, J. (Ed.), *The Global Sports Arena*, London: Frank Cass, 1994.
Ball, P., *White Storm*, Edinburgh: Mainstream, 2002.
Bamford, T. W., *Thomas Arnold*, London: The Cresset Press, 1960.

Barend, F. & Van Dorp, H., *Ajaz, Barcelona, Cruyff*, London: Bloomsbury, 1998.

Bellos, A., *Futebol*, London: Bloomsbury, 2002.

Birley, D., *A Social History of English Cricket*, London: Arum Press, 1999.

——, *Playing the Game*, Manchester: Manchester University Press, 1996.

Bloomfield, S., *Africa United*, Edinburgh: Canongate Books, 2010.

Booth, D., *The Race Game*, London: Frank Cass, 1998.

Bower, T., *No Angel*, London: Faber and Faber, 2011.

Brolin C., *Overdrive*, Vatersay Books, 2010.

Brownell, S., *Beijing's Games*, Lanham: Rowman & Littlefield, 2008.

Brady, F., *Profile of a Prodigy*, London: Nicholas Kaye, 1965.

Budd, A. & others, *Culture, Sport, Society*, volume IV, No. 1, Spring 2001.

Burns, J., *Barça*, London: Bloomsbury, 1999.

Butler, B., *The Official History of the Football Association*, London: Queen Anne Press, 1991.

Cagan, J. & de Mause, N., *Field of Schemes*, Monroe: Common Courage Press, 1998.

Calder, A., *The People's War*, London: Jonathan Cape, 1969.

Cardus, N., *Cardus on Cricket*, London: Souvenier Press, 1977.

Carlin, J., *Playing the Enemy*, London: Atlantic Books, 2008.

Castro, R., *Garrincha*, (translated by A. Downie), London: Yellow Jersey, 2005.

Chase, S., 'Play', in C. A. Beard, *Whither Mankind: A Panorama of Modern Civilization*, Westport: Greenwood Press, 1973.

Chauduri, N. C., *The Autobiography of an Unknown in India*, Bombay: Jaico Books, 1976.

Chauduri, N. C., *Thy Hand, Great Anarch! India 1921–1952*, London: Chatto & Windus, 1987.

Clay, C., *Trautman's Journey*, London: Yellow Jersey, 2010.

Cohen, R., *By the Sword*, New York: Random House, 2002.

Collins, T., *A Social History of English Rugby Union*, Abingdon: Routledge, 2009.

Conn, D., *The Football Business*, Edinburgh: Mainstream, 1997.

Cooke, A., *Fun & Games with Alistair Cooke*, New York: Arcade, 1994.

de Courbertin, P., *Olympic Memoirs*, Lausanne: International Olympic Committee, 1997.

—, *Une Campagne de 21 ans*, Paris: Librairie de l'Éducation Physique, 1908

—, *L'Éducation en Angleterre*, Paris: Hachette, 1888.

Cox, G. (Ed.), *The Dictionary of Sport*, London: Carlton Books, 1999.

Crolley, L. (Ed.) & Hand, D. (Ed.), *Football, Europe and the Press*, London: Frank Cass, 2002.

Crouch, T., *The World Cup*, London: Aurum Press, 2006.

Danielson, M. N., *Home Team*, Princeton: Princeton University Press, 1997.

Darby, P., *Africa, Football and FIFA*, London: Frank Cass, 2002.

Davies, D., *FA Confidential*, London: Simon & Schuster, 2008.

Deighton, L., *Blood, Tears and Folly*, London: Pimlico, 1995.

Dempsey, P. & Reilly, K., *Big Money, Beautiful Game*, London: Nicholas Brealey, 1998.

Dimeo, P., *A History of Drug Use in Sport 1876–1976*, Abingdon: Routledge, 2007.

Dundee, A., *My View From the Corner*, New York: McGraw-Hill, 2008.

Dunstan, K., *Sports*, Melbourne: Cassell Australia, 1973.

Eliot, E., *Portrait of a Sport*, London: Longmans, Green & Co., 1957.

Entine, J., *Taboo*, New York: Public Affairs, 2000.

Everton, C., *Black Farce and Cue Ball Wizards*, Edinburgh: Mainstream, 2007.

Faber, D., *Munich*, Simon & Schuster, 2008.

Fainaru-Wada, M. & Williams, L., *Game of Shadows*, New York: Gotham Books, 2006.

Fetter, H. D., *Taking on the Yankees*, New York: W.W. Norton, 2003.

Finn, G. P. T. (Ed.) & Giulianotti, R., *Football Culture*, London: Frank Cass, 2000.

Foer, F., *How Soccer Explains the World*, New York: HarperCollins, 2004.

Foot, J., *Calcio*, London: Fourth Estate, 2006.

Freeman, S. and Boyes, R., *Sport Behind the Iron Curtain*, London: Proteus, 1980.

Frith, D., *Bodyline Autopsy*, London: Aurum, 2002.

Fynn, A. & Guest, L., *For Love or Money*, London: Boxtree, 1998.

Gallivan, J., *Oi, Ref! A Novel About Love, Hate & Football*, London: Hodder & Stoughton, 1997.

Gandhi, M. K,. *An Autobiography or The Story of my Experiments with Truth*, Harmondsworth: Penguin Books, 1982.

Gardner, P., *The Simplest Game*, New York: Macmillan, 1996.

—, *Nice Guys Finish Last*, London: Allen Lane, 1974.

Glanville, B., *Football Memories*, London: Virgin, 1999.

Goldblatt, D., *The Ball is Round*, London: Viking, 2006.

Gould, S. J., *Triumph and Tragedy in Mudville*, London: Jonathan Cape, 2004.

Graves, R. and Hodge, A., *The Long Weekend*, London: Abacus, 1985.

Green, T., *The Dark Side of the Game*, New York: Warner Books, 1996.

Greenberg, S., *Whitaker's Olympic Almanac*, London: The Stationery Office, 2000.

Griffiths, R., *Racing in the Dock*, Newbury: Highdown, 2002.

Guha, R., *A Corner of a Foreign Field*, London: Picador, 2002.

Gumbrecht, H. U., *In Praise of Athletic Beauty*, Cambridge: The Belknap Press of Harvard University Press, 2006.

Guttmann, A., *The Olympics*, University of Illinois Press, 1992.

Haddon, C., *The First Ever English Olimpick Games*, London: Hodder & Stoughton, 2004.

Halberstam, D., *Playing for Keeps*, New York: Random House, 1999.

Halberstam, D. (Ed.) & Stout, G. (Ed.), *The Best American Sports Writing of the Century*, Boston: Houghton Mifflin Company, 1999.

Haldeman, H. R., *The Haldeman Diaries*, New York: G. P. Putnam's Sons, 1994

Hamilton, D., *Harold Larwood*, London: Quercus, 2010.

Hamilton, M., *Frank Williams*, London: Macmillan, 1998.

Hampton, J., *The Austerity Olympics*, London: Aurum, 2008.

Harding, J., *Behind the Glory*, Derby: Breedon Books, 2009.

Harris, T., *Sport*, London: Yellow Jersey, 2007.

Hauser, T., *Muhammad Ali*, London: Robson Books, 1991.

Hawkey, I., *Feet of the Chameleon*, London: Portico Books, 2009.

Heller, R., *A Tale Of Ten Wickets*, London: Oval Books, 2006.

Helyar, J., *Lords of the Realm*, New York: Ballantine Books, 1994.

Henderson, J., *The Last Champion*, London: Yellow Jersey, 2009.

Henderson, M., *50 People Who Fouled Up Football*, London: Constable, 2009.

Hennessy, P., *Having it so Good*, London: Penguin Books, 2006

Hill, J., *Sport, Leisure & Culture in Twentieth Century Britain*, Basingstoke: Palgrave Macmillan, 2002.

Hilton, C., *Hitler's Olympics*, Stroud Sutton Publishing, 2006.

Horsman, M., *Sky High*, London: Orion Business Books, 1997.

Houlihan, B., *Dying to Win*, Strasbourg: Council of Europe, 1999.

Howard, P., *Sex, Lies and Handlebar Tape*, Edinburgh: Mainstream, 2008.

Huggins, M., *Flat Racing and British Society 1790–1914. A Social and Economic History*, London: Frank Cass, 2000.

—, *Horseracing and the British 1919–39*, Manchester University Press, 2003.

—, *The Victorians and Sport*, London: Hambledon and London, 2004.

Huggins, M. and Williams, J., *Sport and the English 1918–1939*, Abingdon Routledge, 2006.

Hughes, M., *Lewis Hamilton*, Cambridge: Icon Books, 2007.

Hughes, T., *Tom Brown's Schooldays*, London: Harper & Brothers, 1911.

Humphries, N., *Match Fixer*, Singapore: Marshall Cavendish Editions, 2010.

Inglis, S., *The Official Centenary History of the Football League 1888–1988*, London: Willow Books, 1988.

James, C. L. R., *Beyond a Boundary*, London: Stanley Paul, 1986.

Jenkins, S., *The Real All Americans*, New York: Broadway Books, 2007.

Jennings, A., *Foul! The Secret World of FIFA*, London: HarperSport, 2006.

Jennings, A. & Sambrook, C., *The Great Olympic Swindle*, London: Simon & Schuster, 2000.

Johnson, D., *White King and Red Queen*, London: Atlantic, 2007, pp. 10-11.

Johnson, P., *A History of the American People*, Weidenfeld & Nicolson, 1997.

Kahn, R., *The Boys of Summer*, New York: Harper & Row, 1972.

Killanin, M. M., *My Olympic Years*, London: Secker and Warburg, 1983.

Killanin, M. M. & Rodda, J. (Ed.), *The Olympic Game, 1980*, New York: Collier, 1980.

—, *The Olympic Games, 1984*, New York: M. Joseph, 1983

King, J., *The Football Factory*, London: Jonathan Cape, 1996.

Kissinger, H., *Diplomacy*, New York: Simon & Schuster, 1994.

Kissinger, H. *White House Years*, Boston: Little, Brown, 1979.

Kluger, R., *Ashes to Ashes*, New York: Vintage Books, 1997.

Korr, C. P., *The End of Baseball As We Knew It*, Illinois: University of Illinois, 2002.

Kuper, S. & Szymanski, S., *Why England Lose & Other Curious Football Phenomena Explained*, London: Harper Collins, 2009.

Kuper, S., *Ajax, The Dutch, The War*, London: Orion Books, 2003.

Kynaston, D., *Austerity Britain*, London: Bloomsbury, 2006.

—, *Family Britain*, London: Bloomsbury, 2007.

Lacy, J., *God is Brazilian*, Stroud: Tempus, 2005.

Lee, M., *The Race for the 2012 Olympics*, London: Virgin Books, 2006.

Levinson, D. (Ed.) and Christiansen, K. (Ed.), *Enclycopedia of World Sport*, Santa Barbara: ABC-Clio, 1996.

Lewis, M., *Moneyball*, New York: W.W. Norton, 2003.

—, *The Blind Side*, New York: W.W. Norton, 2006.

Liang, L., *He Zhenliang and China's Olympic Dream*, Beijing: Foreign Languages Press, 2007.

Llewellyn Smith, M., *Olympics in Athens 1896*, London: Profile Books, 2004.

Lois, G. (Ed.), *Ali Rap*, New York: ESPN Books/Taschen, 2006.

Longmore, A. & Morton, N., *The Olympic Games*, London: Dakini Media, 2008.

Lonsdale, Earl of (Ed.) & Parker, E. (Ed.), *Flat Racing*, The Lonsdale Library, volume XXVIII, London: Seeley Service & Co, 1940.

MacAloon, J. J., *This Great Symbol*, Chicago: University of Chicago Press, 1981.

MacCambridge, M., *America's Game*, New York: Anchor Books, 2004.

Mack, E. C. & Armytage, W. H. G., *Thomas Hughes*, London: Ernest Benn, 1952.

MacMillan, M., *Peacemakers*, London: John Murray, 2001.

Major, J., *More Than a Game*, London: Harper, 2007.

Majumdar, B. & Bandyopadhyay, K., *A Social History of Indian Football*, Abingdon: Routledge, 2006.

Majumdar, B. & Mehta, N., *Sellotape Legacy*, New Delhi: HarperCollins Publishers India, 2010.

—, *Olympics*, New Delhi: HarperCollins India, 2008.

Mangan, J. A. (Ed.), *Pleasure, Profit, Proselytism, 1700–1914*, London: Frank Cass, 1988.

—, *The Cultural Bond*, London: Frank Cass, 1992.

Mangan, J. A. (Ed.) & Hong, F. (Ed.), *Sports in Asian Society*, London: Frank Cass, 2003.

Maradona, D., *El Diego*, London: Yellow Jersey, 2005.

Maraniss, D., *When Pride Still Mattered*, New York: Touchstone, 2000.

Margolick, D., *Beyond Glory*, London: Bloomsbury, 2005.

Marqusee, M. *Redemption son*, London: Verso, 1999.

Martin, S., *Football and Fascism*, Berg, 2004.

Mayer, P. Y., *Jews and the Olympic Games*, London: Vallentine Mitchell, 2004.

Mbaye, K., *The International Olympic Committee and South Africa*, Le Mont-sur-Lausanne: International Olympic Committee, 1995.

McCrum, M., *Thomas Arnold, Headmaster*, Oxford: Oxford University Press, 1989.

McNamee, M., *Sports, Virtues and Vices*, Abingdon: Routledge, 2008.

McRae, D., *In Black & White*, London: Simon & Schuster, 2002.

—, *Dark Trade*, Edinburgh: Mainstream, 1996.

Miller, D., *Athens to Athens, 1894–2004*, Edinburgh: Mainstream, 2003.

—, *Olympic Revolution*, London: Pavilion Books, 1992.

Miller, S. L., *Why Teams Win*, Mississauga: Jossey-Bass, 2009.

Mong-Joon, C., *This I Say to Japan*, Seoul: Gimm-Young Publishers, 2002.

Morrow, S., *The People's Game? Football, Finance and Society*, Basingstoke: Palgrave Macmillan, 2003.

Mowat, C. L., *Britain Between the Wars*, London: Methuen, 1955.

Munting, R., *Hedges and Hurdles*, London: J. A. Allen, 1987.

Murray, A., *Race to the Finish*, London: Robson Books, 2003.

Nasaw, D., *The Chief*, London: Gibson Square Books, 2003.

Nevill, R., *The Sport of Kings*, London: Methuen, 1926.

Norridge, J., *Can We Have Our Balls Back, Please?*, London: Allen Lane, 2008.

Novak, M., *The Joy of Sports*, Lanham: Madison Books, 1994.

Oborne, P., *Basil D'Oliveira: Cricket and Conspiracy*, London: Little, Brown, 2004.

O'Connor, I., *Arnie & Jack*, London: Yellow Jersey, 2008.

Orwell, S. & Angus, I., *The Collected Essays, Journalism and Letters of George Orwell*, volume IV, London: Penguin, 1970.

Parisotto, R., *Blood Sports*, Victoria: Hardie Grant Books, 2006.

Payne, M., *Olympic Turnaround*, London Business Press, 2006.

Pelser, H., *Henk's War*, London: Portell, 2006.

Polley, M., *The British Olympics*, Swindon: English Heritage, 2011.

Pendergrast, M., *For God, Country and Coca-Cola*, London: Phoenix, 1994.

Pope, S. W. (Ed.) & Nauright, J. R. (Ed.), *Routledge Companion to Sports History*, Abingdon: Routledge, 2010.

Porter, B., *The Absent-Minded Imperialists*, Oxford: Oxford University Press, 2004.

Potter, D., *The Victor's Crown*, London: Quercus, 2011.

Pound, R. W., *Inside the Olympics*, John Wiley & Sons Canada, 2004.

Pound, R. W., *Five Rings over Korea*, Boston: Little, Brown, 1994.

Radice, G., *The Tortoise and the Hares*, London: Politico, 2008.

Radomski, K., *Bases Loaded*, New York: Hudson Street Press, 2009.

Rambali, P., *Barefoot Runner*, London: Serpent's Tail, 2006.

Ranjitsinhji, K. S., *The Jubilee Book of Cricket*, London: William Blackwood and Sons, 1897.

Remnick, D., *King of the World*, London: Picador, 1999.

Roberts, R., *Joe Louis*, New Haven: Yale University Press, 2010.

Rogosin, D., *Invisible Men*, New York: Kodansha America, 1995.

Rother, R. (Ed.), *Historic Site*, Berlin: Jovis Verlag, 2006.

Rubython, T., *The Life of Senna*, London: BusinessF1 Books, 2004.

Ryan, B., *The Best of Sport*, Toronto: Sport Media, 2003.

Sebag Montefiore, S., *Stalin*, London: Phoenix, 2004.

Sharpe, G., *Gambling on Goals*, Edinburgh: Mainstream, 1997.

Simons, R., *Bamboo Goalposts*, London: Macmillan, 2008.

Simson, V. & Jennings, A., *The Lord of the Rings*, London: Simon & Schuster, 1992.

Smit, B., *Pitch Invasion*, London: Allen Lane, 2006.

Smith, A. & Westerbeek, H., *The Sport Business Future*, New York: Palgrave Macmillan, 2004.

Speed, M., *Sticky Wicket*, Sydney: HarperSports, 2011.

Srivinas, A. & Vivek, T. R., *IPL an Inside Story*, New Delhi: Roli Books, 2009.

St John, A., *The Billion Dollar Game*, New York: Doubleday, 2009.

Stanley, A. P., *The Life and Correspondence of Thomas Arnold*, volumes 1 & 2, London: B. Fellowes, 1845.

Staudohar, P. D. (Ed.), *More Sports Best Short Stories*, Chicago: Chicago Review Press, 2004.

Stoddart, B. and Sandiford, K., *The Imperial Game*, Manchester: Manchester University Press, 1998.

Sugden, J. & Tomlinson, A., *FIFA and the Contest for World Football. Who Rules the Peoples' Game?*, Cambridge: Polity Press, 1998.

—, *Great Balls of Fire*, Edinburgh: Mainstream, 1999.

Sun, H., *The Man Who Brought the Olympics to China*, Beijing: New World Press, 2008

Supovitz, F., *The Sports Event Management and Marketing Playbook*, Chichester: John Wiley & Sons, 2005.

Suyin, H., *The Morning Deluge*, London: Jonathan Cape, 1972.

Szymanski, S. & Kuypers, T., *Winners and Losers*, London: Viking, 1999.

Taine, H., *Notes on England*, London: Caliban Books, 1995.

Tattersall, E. J., *Europe At Play*, London: William Heinemann, 1938.

Taylor, C., *The Beautiful Game*, London: Victor Gollancz, 1998.

Telfer, K., *Peter Pan's First XI: The Extraordinary Story of J. M. Barries's Cricket Team*, London: Sceptre, 2010.

Thompson, W. N., *Gambling in America*, Santa Barbara: ABC-Clio, 2001.

Tibballs, G., *The Olympics' Strangest Moments*, London: Robson Books, 2004.

Tomlinson, A., *A Dictionary of Sports Studies*, Oxford: Oxford University Press, 2010.

Tosches, N., *Night Train*, London: Hamish Hamilton, 2000.

Troup, Major W., *Sporting Memories*, London: Hutchinson, 1924.

Tygiel, J., *Baseball's Great Experiment*, New York: Oxford University Press, 1983.

Tyson, F., *A Typhoon Called Tyson*, London: Sportsman's Book Club, 1962.

Vamplew, W., *The Turf*, London: Penguin Books, 1976.

Van den Heuvel, C. (Ed.) & Tamura, N. (Ed.), *Baseball Haiku*, New York: W.W. Norton, 2007.

Vaughan, J. & Murray, C., *Fighting Talk*, London: Hodder & Stoughton, 2008.

Véliz, C., *The New World of the Gothic Fox*, Berkeley: University of California Press, 1994.

BIBLIOGRAPHY

Walters, G., *Berlin Games*, London: John Murray, 2006.

Walvin, J., *Leisure and Society 1830– 1950*, London: Longman Group, 1978.

— , *The People's Game*, London: Mainstream, 1994.

Ward, G. C., *Unforgivable Blackness*, London: Pimlico, 2005.

White, G. E., *Creating the National Pastime*, Princeton: Princeton University Press, 1996.

White, J., *Manchester United*, London: Sphere, 2008.

White, P. (Ed.), *Chambers Sport Factfinder*, Edinburgh: Chambers, 2005.

Wilde, S., *Ranji: A Genius Rich and Strange*, London: The Kingswood Press, 1990.

Williams, C., *Bradman*, Abacus, 1997.

Williams, R., *Football's Dreamers, Schemers, Playmakers and Playboys*, London: Faber and Faber, 2006.

Wilson, M., *The Sports Business*, London: Judy Piatkus, 1988.

Wilson, W. (Ed.) & Derse, E. (Ed.), *Doping in Elite Sport*, Champaign: Human Kinetics , 2001.

Wilton, I., *C. B. Fry*, London: Metro , 2002.

Witzig, R., *The Global Art of Soccer* New Orleans: CusiBoy, 2006.

Xu, G., *Olympic Dreams*, Cambridge: Harvard University Press, 2008.

Zimbalist, A. S., *Baseball and Billions*, New York: Basic Books, 1992.

585

Newspapers/Magazines

The Times
Daily Telegraph
New York Times
Wall Street Journal
Sports Illustrated
Evening Standard
Guardian
Sun
Daily Mirror
Daily Mail
Mail on Sunday
Sunday Mirror
News of the World
Observer
Independent
Washington Post
Der Spiegel
Sports Pro
The Sports Market
Financial Times
Times of India
Hindustan Times
eStatesman
The New Statesman
The Spectator
World Soccer
Champions
Sport and Pastime
Time
Newsweek
Economist
Los Angeles Times
The New Yorker
The New York Review of Books
Le Qui
Gazetta Delo Sport

Media sources

BBC Panorama programme 'FIFA: Football's Shame?' Broadcast on BBC 1 on Monday 23 May 2011 at 20:30

BBC Panorama programme 'FIFA's Dirty Secrets' Broadcast on BBC 1 on Monday 29 Nov 2010 at 20:30

Online sources

www.playthegame.org

www.jensweirich.de

www.insidethegames.biz

www.insideworldfootball.biz

Botvinnik's obituary: http://www.independent.co.uk/news/people/obituary--mikhail-botvinnik-1618645.html

J. A. Hobson on Imperialism, cited in http://files.libertyfund.org/pll/quotes/262.html

Venu Palaparthi, 'The 1859 Cricket Tour': http://www.dreamcricket.com/dreamcricket/news.hspl?nid=6801&ntid=3

J. Riordan, 'The Rise And Fall Of Soviet Olympic Champions', Olympika 1993: http://www.la84foundation.org/SportsLibrary/Olympika/Olympika_1993/olympika0201c.pdf

http://bleacherreport.com/articles/11611-charles-miller-scotlands-gift-to-brazil

Bill Wall, 'Alexander Alekhine and the Nazis': http://www.chess.com/article/view/alexander-alekhine-and-the-nazis

US Bureau of Labor Statistics, 'Employment status of the civilian non-institutional population, 1940 to date': http://www.bls.gov/cps/cpsaat1.pdf

http://www.boxrec.com/media/index.php/Primo_Carnera

Allan May, 'History of the Race Wire Service': http://www.crimemagazine.com/history-race-wire-service-part-ii

United States Holocaust Memorial Museum Holocaust Encyclopedia: Indoctrinating Youth: http://www.ushmm.org/wlc/en/article.php?ModuleId=10007820

Jerry Martin in http://www.ultimatecapper.com/history-of-sports-betting.htm

INDEX